(4-3-64 39-31244)

SAMUEL JONES TILDEN

A STUDY IN POLITICAL SAGACITY

SAMUEL J. TILDEN

SAMUEL JONES TILDEN

A Study in Political Sagacity

By

ALEXANDER CLARENCE FLICK

Assisted by

GUSTAV S. LOBRANO

ILLUSTRATED

KENNIKAT PRESS, INC./PORT WASHINGTON, N. Y.

INTRODUCTION

SAMUEL JONES TILDEN's life covered about three-fourths of the formative nineteenth century. His prominence, if not pre-eminence, in the economic and political evolution of the nation was notable. His contribution to industrial development occurred mostly prior to 1870 and his political leadership principally after that date although he was interested in politics for the long span from Jackson to Cleveland. The three peaks in his career as a constructive statesman were: the overthrow of the Tweed Ring; the disruption of the upstate Canal Ring; and his candidacy as a reform President.

Three lives of Tilden have appeared—those by Cook and Cornell as uncritical campaign biographies—and Bigelow's two-volume work written in 1895 not as an impartial historian but as an intimate and sympathetic friend to defend his reputation against his political foes If Bigelow's nearness and devotion gave bias to his perspective as apologist and warped his judgments, yet his *Writings, Life* and *L* of Tilden, based on personal relations of more than half a cent tive participation in events, and access to all of Tilden's une papers, are the most valuable printed sources for a moder tion.

More than half a century has passed since Tilden's years since Bigelow wrote the life of his hero. Tod dispassionately the man and the reform move augurated. Moreover many new sources of th and unprinted, are now available. The gr Papers has been deposited in the New York to investigators. Hence with these unuse seems opportune for a new interpreta of the man who, it is now concede United States in 1876 but excluded

This biography was begun nin the spare time of an active pr thor has been supplemented who helped in the arduou

narrative. Dorothy Jean Lobrano corrected, condensed and retyped large portions of the original manuscript, and has read the proofs with a watchful eye. Dr. Victor Hugo Paltsits, of the New York Public Library, courteously made available to the author the mass of unorganized and uncatalogued Tilden Papers. Mrs. George W. Smith, who as the wife of Tilden's personal secretary knew Tilden intimately for many years and was the surviving executor of his estate, has turned over to the author her manuscript Notes on Tilden and materials supplementing the Tilden Papers. She has graciously granted the author interviews and out of her vast fund of knowledge helped to settle many difficult problems. John J. Cahill, the only surviving clerk of Tilden, has supplied information orally and by letter and loaned valuable papers. Members of the Tilden family have kindly answered

about their eminent kinsman. The late James Franklin

Manuscripts Division of the Library of Congress,

materials in various collections under his

tracted notes from manuscripts

S. Bixby of Plattsburgh

's disposition. Col. and

with recollections of

reminiscences of his

help given by the

supplied Tilden

critical reading

subtractions,

volume will

politician

statesmen

FLICK

CONTENTS

CONTENTS

ILLUSTRATIONS

SAMUEL JONES TILDEN

A STUDY IN POLITICAL SAGACITY

HAD Lebanon Mountain been Olympus, then February 9, 1814, had been a day of portents—of mighty upheavals, of thunder on the left.

On that day in the snow-covered village of New Lebanon, New York, was born a sickly infant destined to develop into the man whose fortunes were closely identified with those of his country. His family name was Tilden; he was christened Samuel Jones; [1] and he has been called, not without justification, the Nineteenth President of the United States.

Here was a man who perhaps faltered in the greatest crisis of his life but whose commanding dignity and equable philosophy deprived even frustration of ignominy. He was an ardent disciple of Jeffersonian principles, the greatest political strategist of his time, and the holder at his death of one of the largest private fortunes in the nation. Despite a weak physical constitution and a cold, forbidding presence, he dominated his party by the force of his intellect, the shrewdness of his political judgment, and the boldness of his political vision. He had abundant reason to believe himself the victim of political intrigue and persecution, but his concern for the governed was unfaltering, and he retained to the end of his life an abiding faith in democratic institutions, in the ultimate soundness of popular judgment and in the unquestionable validity of popular verdict. He is one of the most arresting figures of American political history and his memory has suffered an undeserved neglect.

Samuel J. Tilden's life spanned a turbulent period. At his death, in 1886, the country still suffered from the sectional hatred, financial distress and corruption which followed the Civil War. At his birth, the memory of the sacrifices of the Revolution was still fresh, and the hardships of the French and Indian wars were unforgotten. During his boyhood, tradition was a part of environment. The stirring events of the past took actuality from the experiences of friends and relatives who had played a part in them. His maternal grandfather, Samuel Jones,

---

[1] After Samuel Jones, his maternal grandfather. The family genealogy, however, reveals many Samuel Tildens. The history of the English branch of the Tildens has been compiled by H. E. Rudkin of Compton, Guilford, England; and the American branch by Mrs. G. W. Smith of Harrison, N. Y., and John W. Linzee of Boston, Mass.

served as an officer in the New York militia during the Revolution.[2] His great-uncle, John Patterson, died as a result of confinement in the Jersey prison ship.[3] Dr. Moses Younglove, husband of young Samuel's beloved Great-aunt Polly, was a surgeon on the staff of General Herkimer, and was captured by the Indians at Oriskany. His paternal grandfather, John Tilden, took part in the capture of Louisburg; and the smoothbore French musket, with its flaring muzzle and flintlock, which he brought home, was stowed with care in the lumbering family oxcart, when, in 1790, he trekked with his family through the wilderness to settle in Columbia County, New York.[4]

The dominant pioneer spirit of New England, with its urge to subject the wilderness to the hearth, was a strong factor in Samuel J. Tilden's ancestral background. From the time that his immigrant ancestor, Nathaniel Tilden—with his wife, seven children and seven servants—left his comfortable home in Kent, in 1630, to seek freedom in the New World, the Tilden family in America had moved on to settle new lands. Established first in Scituate, Massachusetts, they had for four generations moved westward. Adventurous, industrious, and thrifty, they enjoyed the esteem of their contemporaries and took a prominent part in the communities which they helped to form.

Because Samuel J. Tilden felt that "a heredity in mental and moral as well as in physical capacities and qualities" existed at least "as a tendency," and believed that a "knowledge of one's descent from a line of virtuous, honorable and reputable ancestors who performed their part worthily in their day and generation" was "an incentive to emulate their example," [5] he took an honest pride in his heritage. In middle life he formed a habit of "throwing into a drawer" notes and memoranda relating to his family. These data were supplemented from time to time by investigations of experts.

It is, however, an amusing commentary on his fundamental democracy that, when he had traced his lineage back a hundred years in England and the trail became obscure, Tilden preferred to trace his descent not from "the ruffian and robber chivalry of Normandy" but from the "yeomanry of Saxon Kent" who maintained their equality of inheritance, and in every conflict were "on the side of the largest liberties" and

[2] Bigelow, John, *Life of Samuel J. Tilden*, I, Appendix, 356. Hereafter reference to this indispensable work will be merely *Life*.
[3] *Ib.*, 357, 361.   [4] *Ib.*, 333.   [5] *Ib.*, I, Appendix, 317–318.

free institutions.[6] At the age of sixty-three, Tilden revisited Europe. He was a sick man—his frail body worn out by a strenuous life, his step faltering, his voice weak, and his heart and stomach in an alarming condition, but his mind as keen as ever. One purpose of this trip was to extend his study of the Tilden family in the ancestral home. His letters, written with a palsied hand, show how much pleasure he derived from visits to distant relatives, stopping at old Tilden manor houses, peering into churches which his ancestors attended, and absorbing local atmosphere and color.

During the last week of his life Tilden finished his "Notes on the Origin of the Tilden Name and Family." [7] For the greater part of the previous year this compilation had been his happy diversion. Although it is to be wished that he had devoted his last hours to interpreting the age in which he lived or recording his own accomplishments, it is a peaceful picture—that of this fine old gentleman on the porch of Graystone overlooking the Hudson, happily finishing the last task he had set himself.

Elam, Samuel's father, was nine years old when John Tilden left Lebanon, Connecticut, and moved with his family to the hilly portion of Columbia County, New York, where some Connecticut families had settled as early as 1750. Influenced by that nostalgic impulse which so often moved the pioneers, the community was called New Lebanon. Elam readily adapted himself to the new environment and grew up as a farmer's boy. Such elementary education as the region offered—little enough in a backwoods settlement—he eagerly absorbed. The open book of nature had much to teach. He profited from the high intelligence of the community and entered with zest into the conversation of his elders on all sorts of topics. Books and newspapers, while not plentiful, were at least sufficient to satisfy his hunger for knowledge. He also listened to the grave converse of the elders of the village—men in whom the fervor of the Revolution burned, in whom the convictions of the Fathers were alive—and thus he grew up in the atmosphere of the new democracy.

Elam had scarcely attained his majority when, on February 8, 1802,[8] he married Polly Younglove Jones, adopted daughter of Dr. Moses Younglove, long a friend of the Tilden family. Polly, a young woman of good education and gentility, became a faithful wife and devoted

[6] *Life*, I, 4.   [7] *Ib.*, I, Appendix, 314–363.   [8] *Ib.*, I, 7–8.

mother, who always had the confidence of her children. She was sweet-tempered and considerate, and, although she seldom displayed much initiative, she revealed poise and sense in many a domestic crisis when Elam lost his nerve or was prostrated with illness. Numerous were the trials she had to endure—sickness, hard times, bad crops, poor business and the death of five children, two in their infancy and three in their youth.

Polly was frugal; Elam, thrifty and industrious. With careful management, and some assistance from their families, they became the owners of a good farm. Elam was a progressive farmer. His letters to the local newspapers reveal an interest in improved fruit culture and in the raising of sheep. When Chancellor Robert R. Livingston imported merino sheep, Elam applied to him in 1810 for four or five pounds of wool to make a coat.[9] Obviously the canny Elam intended to test the quality of the wool before stocking his own farm with this breed of sheep.

The Tilden farm included the rich bottom land south of the main road through New Lebanon. The house in which Samuel was born was a large two-storied frame building on a corner formed by the main east and west road and another road running southward from it.[10] With its capacious veranda it fronted on this branch road. It was surrounded by a wooden fence which enclosed attractive shrubbery and trees. As the most conspicuous house in the village, it advertised the material prosperity and social prestige of the family.

To a man of Elam's natural fondness for society, the long days of solitary field labor seemed wasted opportunities, and eventually he put in execution his project of opening a general store. As village storekeeper he was in a more favorable position to keep abreast of current events, both local and national, and to increase his prestige as the political oracle of the community. His new position also gave scope for his interest in novel devices. He soon became agent for a local firm which manufactured thermometers and barometers, while he acted as a distributing agent for seeds and herbs, particularly those of a medicinal nature, for the nearby Shaker settlement. The Shaker records

---

[9] Bigelow, John, *Letters and Literary Memorials of Samuel J. Tilden*, I, 1–2. This important collection will be referred to hereafter as *Letters*.
[10] Burned Mar. 29, 1914. *Pittsfield Journal*, Mar. 30, 1914.

state that on March 10, 1807: "Nathan Rindall Delivered to Elam Tilden One Box of Garden Seed which amt. as pr. Bil, to twenty dollars and ninety cents. To be Sold Commissions of fifteen pr. Cent." [11] The modest business in herbs started by Elam grew to a rather extensive manufacture of medicines and chemicals, and was later developed into a profitable industry by Elam's sons Henry and Moses. In 1811 Governor Tompkins in a message to the legislature referred to the purchase of niter which was turned over to Messrs. Tilden, Patterson & Co., who had a contract for the manufacture of gunpowder for the State. The following year the Governor referred to "Dr. Tilden" as a "Republican friend of Canaan" which suggests that, because of his dabbling in drugs and medicines, Elam was dubbed "Doc" by his acquaintances.[12]

Samuel J. Tilden missed the best experiences of childhood. Those golden hours with their spontaneous laughter, their joyous and winning irresponsibility, their romantic dreaming and robustious gusto were, unhappily, never a part of his life. His importunate mind leaped the span of childhood, and in so doing deprived his character of those qualities which would have mellowed and completed it; and there perished in those days the capacity for friendship, the experience of shared adventure which is the basis of trust, and—most tragic of all—the free spirit of fun which would have made his character more responsive and his personality more likable. A few men, such as John L. O'Sullivan and Francis P. Blair, romanticized Tilden and, under the influence of their romanticism, yielded him a sentimental, almost maudlin, regard; but apparently there were no contemporaries, John Bigelow perhaps excepted, capable of according him that affectionate understanding, or, where understanding fails, that generous sympathy which is the essence of a personal friendship. His personality was elusive, and even those men who hated him, such as John Kelly and William Tweed, did so rather as the embodiment of principles than as a personality.

Tilden was an undersized, sickly child, the object of constant solicitude on the part of his mother. At the age of three a severe illness caused him such agony that he "clawed the inside of his mouth till it bled," and could be soothed only by being carried in the arms of his wearied mother. The family doctor, summoned in haste by Elam, was baffled by the

[11] Andrews, E. D., *New York Shakers and Their Industries*, 68.
[12] *Military Papers of Daniel D. Tompkins*, II, 259, 539.

child's ailment. With the hope of relieving the exhausted mother,[13] he administered a generous quantity of laudanum. Overdoses of this potent and at that time little understood drug may have left Samuel, as is alleged, "with a weakened stomach and impaired digestive apparatus" for life. John Bigelow even declared that it deprived the United States of one of its greatest Presidents.[14]

Samuel grew up into an abnormally delicate youth. He was zealously guarded against exposure of all kinds, padded with heavy clothing, warned against wet feet, and confined a great deal of the time within the house. As the family sat around the fireside in the evenings Elam was wont to give a mournful account of his own ills and to conclude, with a morbid satisfaction and pride, that Sammy had "the same constitution." Thus coddled and impressed with his own frailty, it would have been surprising if the lad had not conceived an exaggerated impression of the gravity of his ailments. His early life seems to have been a succession of colds, fevers, and stomach troubles, and his earliest notes are crammed with recipes for remedies, long accounts of afflictions of his throat, lungs, teeth and stomach, and detailed descriptions of treatments to relieve pain. He tried taking opium to induce sleep after a raging toothache, experimented with innumerable varieties of pills and patent medicines, resorted to massage of the stomach (according to a system recommended by a bookseller!), subjected himself to rigid dieting, and followed a system of calisthenics. This tendency toward hypochondriasis lessened after he passed the age of thirty-five and became absorbed in his profession, but to the end of his life he never escaped it. In his last years, although he never had much faith in the medical profession, Tilden resorted to the advice of specialists and paid them large fees.[15]

The region in which Samuel grew to manhood was delightful and healthful. The sports and amusements included fishing, hunting, climbing, riding and neighborhood frolics, but so completely did his parents protect him that, although his boyish fancies turned toward these diversions, his indulgence therein was sternly restricted. While other boys of the neighborhood were playing ball or casting trout lines in shaded pools, young Tilden remained at home absorbed in political

[13] Samuel was the fifth of nine children. Mrs. G. W. Smith, Ms. Genealogy of the Tilden Family.
[14] Dodd, W. E., "Samuel J. Tilden—a Prophet Unheeded," *Times,* Apr. 17, 1927.
[15] *Life,* I, 18.

philosophy or in swapping symptoms with his father. Such a mode of living made him introspective, oversensitive and grave beyond his years. When he indulged in outdoor sport, he was awkward and self-conscious. "I always shrank," he said, "from killing harmless birds and animals for sport," and toward the close of his life he recorded his last, perhaps his only, hunting expedition. At fourteen he took the old smoothbore musket which his grandfather had brought home from the French and Indian War. The doctor had suggested hunting as a beneficial exercise, and one wonders if Samuel would have undertaken this one expedition if it had not been presented as a sort of cure. He set out doggedly, taking his small brother Henry with him to save himself the exertion of carrying cartridges and such game as might be bagged. The expedition was not wholly successful:

"It was nearly as dangerous to be behind the gun as in front of it. . . . My first fire was at a small flock of pigeons perched on a tree. . . . I did not get a good rest against my shoulder; and on the discharge the old musket swept so violently across my face that I dropped the gun on the ground to hold my face between my hands. On the next fire I missed my aim. The net result of eight discharges was sixteen pigeons. I stood on my honors as a sportsman, and never made another trial." [16]

The one outdoor exercise in which young Tilden took genuine pleasure was riding. In common with most of the village boys, he learned to ride at an early age. Elam gave his sanction to this recreation as healthful, and Samuel wrote, when a student at Yale, that he thought it might benefit him.[17] He missed this indulgence during his early residence in New York City and often mentioned his desire to return home to do some riding. From his admission to the bar until death he owned horses and was very fond of them. As a boy he liked to explore on horseback the beloved hills and dales around New Lebanon. A keen student of nature, he pursued with intense interest the bird and plant life of the region.

In Tilden's boyhood New Lebanon had advanced considerably beyond the stage of a frontier community, though social and economic conditions were still primitive. The village, for some time known as "Tilden's," [18] consisted of perhaps a dozen houses strung along the

16 *Life*, I, 7, 333.
17 Tilden Papers, S. J. Tilden to Elam Tilden. This title, Tilden Papers, will be used to designate the large uncatalogued (1937) collection of letters, writings, pamphlets and newspaper clippings in the New York Public Library.   18 French, *Gazetteer* (1860), 248.

wide highway called the Pittsfield-Albany turnpike, and several of these attractive early homes are still occupied. The only church was the Presbyterian, just across the side road in front of the Tilden home. The villagers were served by a single store, a tavern and, later, an academy. The population did not exceed one hundred. This quiet, self-sufficient village was connected with the outside world by stagecoaches, running eastward into New England and westward to Hudson, the county seat, and to Albany, twenty-five miles distant. The newspapers of Albany, Kinderhook, Hudson and New York City were in most of the homes, and by the time Tilden was a young man the railroad and telegraph had brought the village still closer to the large centers.

On Lebanon Mountain, just above New Lebanon, was the Shaker Settlement, one of the first societies of its kind organized in America. The growth of this colony, in view of the Shakers' cardinal principle of celibacy, is a striking tribute to the evangelical ardor of the founders. By 1842 the six hundred members owned six thousand acres of land, thirty workshops and a number of seed and herb gardens.[19] Samuel Tilden as a youth made frequent visits to the colony and was on intimate terms with its leaders in whose social-religious experiment he was deeply interested.[20] Moreover, not only did Elam Tilden become a commission merchant for Shaker products, but in 1849 his son, Moses, was one of the trustees of the society. When Moses died in 1876, among the mourners were many Shakers, including the venerable Edward Fowler.[21]

Tilden found his chief boyhood pleasure and recreation in books, periodicals, and the society of his elders. Bigelow writes that until he was eight or nine years old the confinement of a school was out of the question. Perhaps this statement is too sweeping, but, whether by attendance at school or by private tutoring at home, Tilden at an early age acquired the elements of a common school education. His knowledge was amplified rapidly by his studious habits. Before he was fifteen he had read Jonathan Edward's *Freedom of the Will* and *Original Sin*, and never thereafter manifested any interest in theology. The unnatural gravity of his youthful intellect is nowhere more strikingly illustrated

[19] Evans, F. W., *Ann Lee* (1858).

[20] Bigelow, John, *The Writings and Speeches of Samuel J. Tilden*, I, 89. Reference to this essential collection hereafter will be *Writings*.

[21] Hudson *Register and Gazette*, Sept. 10, 1876.

than by his spending a gold piece to purchase a copy of Adam Smith's *Wealth of Nations*.[22]

These were the beginnings of the development of that crystalline mind which made Tilden the master political strategist of his time, but which interposed an impenetrable barrier between the man and normal passions. His concern was to be with logic, principle, and dogma, rather than with personality and emotion. This, perhaps, is the best answer to those critics who blame Tilden overmuch for sitting at home "dreaming of a lawsuit," when vigorous action might have altered history in the disputed election of 1876. It is inconceivable that he would have gone to Washington to be sworn in as President of the United States by a group of his political friends with dubious qualifications for administering the oath. The trend of his entire life and thought was opposed to such action. The occasion called for vigorous expression of personality inspired by strong emotional conviction. Tilden was incapable of feeling, much less of being governed by, such an impulse.

From their remote vantage ground, Elam, the "Oracle of New Lebanon," and Samuel, with his old head on youthful shoulders, studied the happenings of Columbia County, Albany, Washington, and Europe, and had a remarkably clear perspective on transpiring events. All about them lived men and women who had helped to create the Union and liked to boast of their accomplishments. When Samuel was born, the War of 1812 was in its final year, and everyone was excited over the battles of Chippewa and Lundy's Lane, and the naval victory at Plattsburg. The Capitol was burned, and early in 1815 came the stirring news of Jackson's triumph at New Orleans. The entire nation, with the exception of New England, was so solidly behind President Madison in his prosecution of the war that the conservative Federalist Party was almost destroyed. A new epoch in American history had opened. The "Robustious Democracy," still looking to the venerable Jefferson for inspiration, had a group of new leaders—Clay, Monroe, Jackson, De-Witt Clinton and Martin Van Buren. As a boy of fourteen Tilden saw his hero, General Jackson, elected President, and the family friend and neighbor, Martin Van Buren, appointed Secretary of State. He had just passed his majority when this same friend was elevated to the highest office in the nation.

[22] *Life*, I, 19–20.

For a country hamlet New Lebanon saw much more of the outside world than might be supposed. It was on the main highway from New England to the Hudson Valley and the West. The summer stagecoaches carried passengers thrice daily (except Sunday) and many travelers stopped off for health or recreation at the famous warm sulphur spring, a mile and a half up the valley from New Lebanon. The Tildens must have met many of them. After the War of 1812 a new tide of emigrants set in from New England to the West. Tilden remembered them passing by his home "in a large wagon drawn by horses or oxen," the wagon, "covered with a high canvas top stretched over a frame made of hoop-poles," containing personal effects and provisions. It was an "endless procession" of straggling humanity by day and many camp fires by night.[23] Other travelers in sprightlier outfits spent the night at the "Connecticut Coffee House" or the tavern kept by Aaron Betts. The mail came daily. Here were abundant opportunities for personal contacts which Samuel was quick to improve.

It was an era of spread-eagle oratory, of big ambitions and wholesome reforms. The old aristocratic era was passing. In New York in 1821 the property qualifications for voting gave way to universal white manhood suffrage. Presidential electors were chosen by popular vote; and, in 1817, an act was passed providing for the complete abolition of slavery in New York within ten years.[24] Turnpikes, followed by canals and railroads, facilitated travel and transportation. Steamboats plied the Hudson and across some of the inland lakes. Numerous inventions were fostering the industrial revolution. Modern machinery was beginning to lighten labor on the farm, in the home and shop. Temperance became a political issue. The youthful Tilden stood alert, expectant, and thrilled amid these surroundings.

Samuel was receiving political instruction from his father constantly, but perhaps his most influential early guidance was derived from avid reading of the newly published set of Thomas Jefferson's letters and papers. This set was purchased by his great-aunt, Mrs. Moses Young-love, who bound the precious volumes in "tea-colored muslin," and loaned them to her young relatives. Samuel "read them over and over again, and thus became thoroughly imbued with Jeffersonian political ideas." [25] Aunt Polly was a remarkable woman. She had no children

[23] Tilden Papers.   [24] *Laws of New York*, 1817. Chap. 137; Lincoln, *Messages*, II, 880.
[25] *Life*, Supplement, I, 363.

and so devoted herself to her nephews and nieces, especially to Samuel. From her well-stocked mind he learned of the French and Indian War and of the Revolution, in which her husband had fought. She told him dramatic stories of the formation of the Federal Government and of the organization of the Federalists and Democrats; she discussed with him current political issues. With her brilliant gifts and her passionate admiration of Jefferson, she exerted a great influence over Samuel.

His brain thus teeming with Jeffersonian ideas, the boy was a rapt listener to the political discussions between his father and visiting leaders of the Democracy. Elam was conspicuous in New Lebanon as a man of business ability, but his real fame rested upon his clear thinking and encyclopedic mind. Looked to as the spokesman of the community on political issues, he was a sort of local party leader, watching political trends with a discerning eye. His circle of political friends widened to Albany and even Washington, and his political advice was sought by those in high authority. Van Buren consulted him; Silas Wright wrote to him from Washington regarding appointments, and his home at New Lebanon was the scene of many political conferences. Among the eminent politicians who visited him at one time or another were the Van Nesses, Peter Van Schaick, Edward Livingston, Robert R. Livingston, General William J. Worth, Ambrose Spencer, Benjamin F. Butler, Amos Eaton, John W. Edmunds, Jacob R. Van Rensselaer, the Tallmadges, John C. Hogeboom, the Vanderpoels, Peter Sylvester, William L. Marcy, Azariah C. Flagg, Edwin Croswell, and Silas Wright —a notable galaxy of political leaders. Among these men, Van Buren, Wright, Marcy, Croswell and Butler were the dominating members of the Albany Regency, that small group which, beginning with the election of Van Buren as Governor in 1828, ruled the State until 1839.[26] They have been denounced for their arbitrary favoritism, and for the "spoils system," but their bitterest foe and critic, Thurlow Weed, acknowledged that he "had never known a body of men who possessed so much power and used it so well." [27] Elam was a confidant of the Regency, and when the group met at his house Samuel was privileged to overhear their conferences. We can easily imagine how his eyes sparkled as he listened to the conversations of these prominent leaders. Van Buren and Wright, because of their continued and more intimate relationship

[26] *Life*, I, 19.
[27] Weed, Harriet A., ed., *Autobiography of Thurlow Weed*, I, 103.

with Elam, no doubt exerted a deep and lasting influence upon him.

Elam, pleased by his son's aptitude for politics, discussed with him freely and without condescension the affairs of the day. In time Elam came to defer to Samuel's opinions as wiser and sounder than his own on public questions, and to the time of his death, in 1842, Elam seldom wrote a letter to Sam or received one from him which did not contain some reference to politics. William Cullen Bryant was fond of telling about a visit of the two Tildens to his office when the son was still in a short jacket. Bryant was editor of the *New York Evening Post* and a personal friend of Elam. The conversation shifted, as was inevitable, to politics, and with "comical deference" Elam turned to Samuel for his opinion after every statement. After grave deliberation the judgment would be given in stilted but exact phrases, and so the conversation proceeded, to the delighted amusement of the poet-editor.

In appearance Samuel Tilden resembled his mother, and from her he inherited his mild manners and soft voice, his self-confident poise, his good sense and his aloofness. Her influence on his intellectual development is not so apparent. It was more subtle, more intimate and familiar, relating to lighter literature, religion, personal and social habits and manners, but she was doubtless the most normal influence in his early life. He wrote few letters to her as compared with those to Elam, but his frequent visits home were made largely for the purpose of seeing her. To the end of his life he showed her a deference and courteous kindness quite unusual. In writing to his father, Samuel was wont to add in parentheses, "Ma will understand." [28] Polly understood his foibles and peculiarities because in thought and temperament he was so like his father. He absorbed not only his father's political convictions but also his methods and modes of expression. From Elam he derived his mental keenness, his extraordinary interest in politics, finance and economics, his feeble constitution and alarm over minor ailments, his philosophical mind, his studious nature and love of argument, his clever expression of convictions, and his love of learning and fondness of books. From sources beyond his parents must have come his legal mind, his indignation at existing evils and his boldness in combating them, his wisdom as an administrator, his capacity for leadership, and his unchanging belief in the principles of democracy.

[28] Tilden Papers.

In the spring of 1830 Samuel was driven to Williamstown, Massachusetts, by Elam, and entered in the preparatory academy associated with Williams College. It was a rather wistful boy of sixteen who, accustomed to the constant ministrations of his family, waved good-bye to his father and settled down to the study of Latin, French, algebra and English, in preparation for college. Although such a course was clearly appropriate, it had not been decided without discussion. No matter, however trivial, was decided in the Tilden household without serious consideration in the family forum. Gathered in conclave, the several members would advance arguments pro and con, examining each at length. The decision that Samuel, described by Martin Van Buren as a boy who always "had a plan," [1] should be destined for the law, was almost inevitable. His frail health unfitted him for an occupation demanding physical labor. His alertness of mind gave clear indication of his fitness for academic training. And Elam's pride in his son's precocious political judgment suggested that he might attain eminence in the Jeffersonian party. Then as now, the law was the usual entrance to politics.

Although Samuel's ambition was fixed, his first venture from home was not conspicuously successful. Until he settled down to the practice of law in New York City, his progress was marked by frequent abrupt retreats to New Lebanon. He was never to adapt himself quickly to changed conditions.

At sixteen, despite his wide reading, he had only the rudiments of an education. Low as college requirements were at that time, he had much to make up. There is no record why the academy at Williamstown was chosen for his preparatory work, but Samuel almost immediately reported: "I can't say that I am as pleased with the academy as I had anticipated, but I get my lessons and recite them." He found his teacher a pleasant man, but had not yet had time to "judge" him. Characteristically, he put himself on a schedule, rising every morning between four-thirty and five, and retiring between nine and ten in the evening.

[1] *Life*, I, 21.

With Yankee thrift he was able to "procure" six hourly recitations in French per week for 42 cents. Some solutions of problems in elementary algebra and some English compositions, in boyish hand, are preserved among his papers. That he found the pace rather swift is suggested by his writing home for "two or three compositions which may be found in my bureau." A commission, evidence of Elam's regard for his judgment, to select a teacher for the "classical school" at New Lebanon,[2] was the occasion of much grave correspondence. Homesickness tinged all of his activities and he asked hungrily for the "news" and the local papers. He finished the term of three months but did not return as a student, contenting himself for the next two years with such instruction as could be secured in New Lebanon.

Soon Tilden was busily involved in the local debating society, probably acting as secretary, for the minutes are among his papers. This course in neighborhood forensics was no poor substitute for what he was missing in regular academic studies. Oratory was in accord with the temper of the times, and the subjects discussed are illustrative of current trends of thought. They included "Lying," "Novel Reading," "Spontaneous Production of the Earth," "Washington and Columbus," "Public Opinion," and "Party Obligation." Among Samuel's notes on these debates are found the germs of many ideas which he championed later.[3]

In the spring of 1832, at eighteen, Samuel was sent to New York to continue his studies. At the same time it was thought that his health might be improved by the opportunity to consult physicians in the metropolis. There were family friends and relatives in the city and it was arranged for the boy to board with his mother's sister, Mrs. D. A. Barnes, and room with his uncle, the Reverend Henry Dana Ward. Aunt Polly Barnes, despite an impractical nature, was attempting to run a fashionable boarding house, with Elam as her financial guarantor. She was gentle and kindly, but had no conception of business. Her youthful nephew took her affairs in hand and attempted to keep her accounts balanced. She was usually in difficulty, however, and proved a thorn in the side of Elam and Samuel for many years. Henry Dana Ward was a Harvard graduate, a lecturer, and a man of some prominence in literary circles. He took a deep interest in his nephew, gave him good advice, wrote delightful letters to him, and enjoyed twitting

[2] *Life*, I, 21–23.   [3] Tilden Papers.

him about his political convictions.

Samuel and his father exchanged letters with frequency, sometimes three times a week, a practice which they continued until Elam's death. The earliest known letter from Elam, dated March 5, 1832, fixes the date of Samuel's removal with approximate accuracy. Though Elam told of an illness due to a fall from a horse, he found space to discuss local, State, and national politics, as he did in nearly all subsequent letters, often with the added admonition, "tell your Uncle Ward about conditions." When Aaron Vanderpoel wrote a congratulatory letter to Elam in connection with the latter's victory in a local poll, it was duly forwarded for Sam's perusal. A letter from Alfred A. Smith regretted that Sam "had the Dyspepsie—he is a terrible acquaintance," and urged him to run away for a sea voyage. This idea Sam cherished for many years. The boy had the family fondness for letter writing, and the stream of his correspondence, later to become voluminous, started its prodigal flow. C. H. Bronhall wrote to him about politics; Dr. Stephen D. Hand was interested in his intellectual progress; and of course, his brothers and sisters reported the neighborhood gossip in detail.[4]

Life in the great seaport was an adventure for a country boy, and particularly for one of Samuel's keen observation and varying interests. His letters are full of happenings in the metropolis but precisely what arrangements he made to continue college preparatory studies in New York is not clear from the sources. For some months he apparently did little in the way of methodical study under tutors. Somehow, perhaps because of enthusiasm aroused in the New Lebanon Debating Society and by the orations of Clay and Webster, he became interested in elocution and decided that the systematic development of his declamatory talent would be a fair substitute for a college course. When the matter was broached from New York to Elam and Polly, however, they objected on the ground that elocution would injure Sam's throat and lungs, which, they apprehended, were already threatened with tuberculosis.[5] The matter was stubbornly argued, and on May 23, 1832, Samuel put his concluding brief in the mails. Marshaling his arguments he stated his belief that these lessons would benefit his health. Long experience had convinced him that a "regular occupation" was not "less neces-

[4] Tilden Papers, various dates.
[5] *Ib.*, various letters, particularly May 26, 1832.

sary than regularity of diet or exercise." Without some stimulating
activity he feared that "a lassitude and indisposition to exertion" unfavorable to health would creep "through the frame." He felt that
"vacuity of mind, too, is as prejudicial to health as an exciting, stimulating ardor and activity are beneficial to it." [6] Elam, possibly because
of his pleasure in the force and expression of Samuel's plea, gave way,
and Samuel soon afterward was taking three lessons daily.

He soon found, however, that recitations were a poor substitute for
the excitement of debate, and he lost his belief in elocution as a remedy
for his ills or as a substitute for a college education. He became preoccupied with a novel cure for his chronic dyspepsia. Yielding to the
advice of a friendly bookseller, a Mr. Halstead, he made an earnest
trial of a system of crude massage and the use of senna, without, however, abandoning entirely Mead's pills or the use of soda. Bigelow states
that "a gambling sort of faith in drugs . . . had already become so
confirmed in him that it was not shaken by more than fifty years' subsequent experience of their ravages upon his constitution." [7]

He returned home from New York in June, 1832. The months spent
there had been neither particularly pleasant nor profitable. Elocution
had proved a delusion, the Barnes accounts a source of annoyance, and
the experiments in remedies abortive. In addition to these things Sam
had had thrust upon him by Elam the task of peddling the thermometers
and barometers of the Kendall firm for which Elam had a distributing
agency. Sam was being pressed constantly to find orders in New York
City. All of these things he left willingly enough. There was, however,
one bright spot in these months of annoyances and dawdling, a circumstance which may have strengthened his decision to study law. On one
of his visits to Halstead's book shop Sam was, thanks to the benign
proprietor, introduced to the great Chancellor James Kent. The Chancellor unbent and talked with the eager boy for about half an hour, even
reading to him the latest preface to the famous *Commentaries*.[8] All in
all, however, no definite progress had been made.

The summer of 1832 in New Lebanon was a busy and happy one.
Sam's health was improved by his removal from New York. He spent
many pleasant hours on horseback or tramping across the hills and
valleys. He devoted himself with more seriousness to college preparatory
studies, and made considerable progress. His instructor, C. B. Sherman,

<hr/>

[6] *Life*, I, 24.   [7] *Ib.*, 25.   [8] *Ib.*, 26.

praised his essays for their style and ideas, and among his papers are found some of Cicero's *Orations* which he translated into English about this time.[9]

It was with difficulty that he concentrated on classical subjects during this period, however, for the political situation was exciting and it was not easy to translate a passage from Cicero when the air was ringing with political discussion. His hero, President Jackson, was up for re-election and Martin Van Buren, true friend of his father and himself, was candidate for the Vice-Presidency. At the same time William L. Marcy was running for Governor as a Democrat in opposition to both the National Republicans and Antimasons. Toward fall the campaign waxed hot, and Sam, in a fever of excitement, pitched his geometry and Cicero into a corner and turned to politics.

After the Democratic-Republicans of New York State ratified the national ticket, on September 10, and nominated Marcy for Governor, county conventions were held to endorse this action. Sam and his brother Moses were sent as delegates to the county convention at Hudson. Following the ratification, Samuel moved the creation of a county committee of correspondence. The motion was carried and Moses appointed chairman.[10]

The secretary of the New Lebanon Debating Society was all aflame with political zeal, and even the recollection of eloquence in such controversies as "The Duty to Belong to a Temperance Society" paled. Soon came a glowing opportunity to speak for his embattled and beloved party and the cause of his friends, and he began the preparation of a speech to be delivered at "Johnson's" on September 14 before a hundred and fifty young men of New Lebanon. In "a spirited and eloquent manner" he assailed the United States Bank for debauching the press, for influencing Congress through favoritism, for attempting to force a renewal of its charter through financial coercion, for trying to establish "a modern dynasty of associated wealth," and for refusing to submit to congressional investigation. Give the Bank a new charter, he declared, and it will "exist forever" as the "stronghold of the money power" dominating this "free and happy people." Did Americans want to be ruled like the English by "a heartless, soulless moneyed power? Are not monopolies and corporations springing up like hydras in every part of the nation?" Had not the Bank won the rich class to its support?

[9] Tilden Papers.   [10] *Life*, I, 38–39.

Did it not seek "to rob the mechanicks and working classes of the right of suffrage" by taking their jobs from them unless their votes could be dictated? If Jackson could not check this peril, he asked, who could? [11]

The National Republicans, later to become Whigs, and the Antimasons were presenting a united front against the Democrats. It was feared that this alliance meant defeat. Samuel's uncle, probably Henry Dana Ward, who was visiting in New Lebanon, suggested a method of successfully meeting the crisis and regretted that he could not give publicity to it.[12] Samuel was deeply impressed by the proposal and devoted several days to its elaboration on paper. When it was completed he asked his father to listen to the interpretation of the strategy which he had written. Elam was delighted but, distrusting his own judgment, proposed that they take it to Martin Van Buren who was resting at Lebanon Springs.[13] Van Buren thought so well of it that he proposed to have it endorsed by the signatures of prominent Democrats and then printed in the Albany *Argus*.[14] He may have polished it up here and there before turning it over to Edwin Croswell for publication in his Democratic paper.

It appeared first as a broadside on September 14, under the title "To Republican Antimason Electors of the County of Columbia" and was signed by seven Democrats, no Tilden being among them. Croswell printed a part of it on September 18 and the whole of it on October 6,[15] with the editorial comment that it was an "able and conclusive address" and that, "Whoever the author of the appeal is, he holds an able pen." The Albany *Evening Journal* naturally attributed it to Van Buren [16]— a fine compliment to the young author. The *Argus*, "on the authority of Mr. Van Buren," denied his authorship.

This address, written when Tilden was eighteen, was a masterpiece of campaign literature because, like all of his political essays, it made people think. He reviewed the history of the coalition between the National Republicans and the Antimasons and then pointed out its insincerity and folly. Since some of the Tildens were Masons, he knew what arguments might appeal to Masons generally. He showed how politicians had not scrupled to use both Masons and Antimasons to oppose Jackson. He revealed how the two conventions had joined in

[11] *Life*, I, 39–40.
[12] *Ib.*, 27; Cook, T. F., *The Biography and Public Services of Hon. Samuel J. Tilden*, 7.
[13] *Life*, I, 27.   [14] Albany *Argus*, Aug. 3, 1832.   [15] *Ib.*, Oct. 6, 1832.
[16] *Life*, I, 27.

presenting a joint State ticket and called attention to their lack of a constructive platform. If the New York coalition benefited Clay as the Presidential nominee of the National Republicans, it would injure Wirt, the national candidate of the Antimasons. Were the Antimasons ready to do that? If it helped Wirt, it would hurt Clay. Were the National Republicans willing to sacrifice their idol in such a plot? Thus point by point the situation was discussed with vigor, logic and telling effect.

Van Buren had, of course, known "Sammy" Tilden for some years, but this incident brought about an intimacy that endured throughout Van Buren's life. Bigelow, perhaps too sweepingly, asserts that from this time on Van Buren rarely "made an important communication to the public which he did not submit to Mr. Tilden for his criticism or took any step of political importance about which he did not seek his advice."

The Antimasons and National Republicans in New York became distrustful of each other, and the campaign culminated with Jackson and Van Buren winning the national election and Marcy carrying the Democratic banner to victory in the State.[17] The New York Democrats were jubilant; the country was secure for another four years, and young Sam, feeling that he had a share in the triumph, was free to devote himself once more to his studies. Even amid the political excitement of September he had found time to write to C. B. Sherman, his educational adviser, about schools and tutoring in New York.

By November 19, 1832, young Tilden was back in New York, where, with the exception of a brief period at the Kinderhook Academy, and three short visits to New Lebanon, he remained until the spring of 1834. He continued to board with his Aunt Polly Barnes and room with Uncle Ward. A brief diary on the first page of a small memorandum book, crudely homemade, with cover and leaves pinned together, fixes the dates of the winter and spring of 1832–33. An inventory of his "goods," "clothes" and "furniture" on the second page and "Memo of Expenses" on the following pages give a vivid picture of his domestic economy, recreations, medical treatments and activities. He acquired a stove, tin basin (for 8 cents), shovel, tongs and lamp for his room, and furnished his own bedding. He bought his own wood, and the cost, $8 for two loads—with carting, sawing, and splitting—was an item of some importance in a young student's budget. On one occasion while taking a

17 Cook, T. F., *Hon Samuel J. Tilden,* 8.

heavy stick from the top of the pile Samuel dropped it on his toe. This incident brought a tart admonition from his father that he should learn to pile wood so that it could be removed without personal injury, and the practical suggestion that he wrap flannel about his foot and wear a large shoe in order not to miss his recitations. Moses wrote, "Ma says to 'put cotton wool soaked in rum around it.' " [18]

Samuel was by training and necessity frugal. Such articles as shoe brush, strop and razor, knife, flatiron, door key, and watch and chain were listed with care, for they could not be lightly replaced. Such significant items as 37½ cents for candles, $1 for three bath tickets, 25 cents for three stage door tickets, Dr. Pleasant's bill for $10, $18.50 "for Rubbing," 25 cents for "Adam and Eve," 50 cents for Pope's Homer, 50 cents for Greek exercises, 94 cents for Mead's pills and wafers, and, with great honesty, 50 cents "for contingencies of which I have no recollections" appear among his expenditures.[19] Of course he was well supplied with drugs and medicines. Dignity was the keynote of a young gentleman's wardrobe in the early nineteenth century. Young Tilden at eighteen possessed: a camelot cloak, brown surtout, three broadcloth coats, three pairs of pantaloons, four vests—black cloth, "sattin," figured, and buff—ten shirts, ten bosoms, and two stocks. Dressed in his mulberry frock coat, mulberry pantaloons, buff waistcoat, wearing a silk hat and cotton gloves, and carrying his silk umbrella, he no doubt made an adequately dignified impression, despite his lack of stature and avoirdupois.

Modest as Samuel's expenses appear today, it was with difficulty that Elam was able to meet them. The anxious refrain, "Do you need money?" appears in many of his letters, and at least once, in a moment of strain, he wrote, "I don't know what you'll do for funds without you go out and keep school awhile." [20] The family drug business was expanding but ready money was scarce. Although somewhat "ashamed" of the rôle of a patent medicine vendor, Elam had, in 1833, contracted for a half interest in the sale and manufacture of West's "Patent Chlorine Cosmetic and Pills," a "most valuable remedy," guaranteed to cure "the most obstinate cases of ringworm, salt rheum, scald head and in general all eruptions of the skin." Without too much difficulty, Elam allowed himself to become convinced of its genuine curative qualities and pushed the sales with Yankee shrewdness. Samuel, already harassed

[18] Tilden Papers, Dec. 17, 1832.   [19] Ib.   [20] Ib., Mar. 25, 1833.

with the task of selling the Kendall thermometers and barometers, was now importuned to secure testimonials and arrange for the distribution of "C. C. & Pills" in New York City. Prodded by Elam, he bartered barometers for books, collected bills and tried to discharge the other obligations put upon him, but his interests were elsewhere, and he was neither by nature nor inclination fitted to be a salesman. Elam was often impatient. Samuel's carelessness about details irritated him. "Your letter of I don't know when," he wrote, testily, "came Saturday. Like the man whose child went without a name till it was four years old for lack of time to give it one, I suppose you had no time to date it." [21] "Write plainer," he grumbled, "I am not a Greek scholar and it costs me too much time to *spell out the writing*. Neither am I a stenographer." Elam's wit was heavy but it was pointed.

Samuel's interests were elsewhere, and so to a large extent, despite his carping, were Elam's, for the political cauldron was boiling. In November the legislature of South Carolina declared that the Tariff Acts of 1828 and 1832 were "null, void, and no law" and that any attempt to enforce them in that State would be just cause for secession from the Union. Jackson replied with his famous Nullification Proclamation on December 10, 1832. Elam wrote enthusiastically from New Lebanon, "General Jackson becomes greater than ever." And Samuel declared to his friend David Webb in Hudson that it was a "remarkable paper . . . a little ultra on some points, which has set the whole pack of Federalists hallooing in full chorus after it." With enthusiasm he continued, "This is an age of wonders—messages, reports, addresses, and manifestoes come one after another, and proclamations follow like Thunderbolts." [22] Jackson in a long message to Congress on January 16, 1833, asserted that South Carolina's attempt to "annul a law of the United States" would destroy the Union [23] and wrote privately that he would send 40,000 men to enforce the law.

This period marks an important advance in Samuel's development as a publicist. He had gone through the exciting campaign of 1832 with his eyes and ears open, discussing the issues with his father and friends orally and by letter, and, as the opportunities offered, making his contributions. Now he was prepared to arrange his convictions on paper. While Van Buren was helping Jackson with his message, young Tilden

21 Tilden Papers, Dec. 17, 1832.   22 *Ib.*, Dec. 22, 1832.
23 Richardson, *Messages,* III, 1203.

prepared to set forth his views on the tariff crisis. His letter printed in
the *Columbia Centinel* January 17, 1832, favored a protective system,
if it were not prohibitory, but declared that if it drove the South to
disunion "it must go." "Let the protective system be made a peace offering on the altar of union." "Mutual conciliation and compromise" were
advocated. He suggested that the tariff be reduced so gradually that it
would become "incidental," thus not ruining the manufacturers, and
yet appeasing the South.[24] His position, based on the doctrines of Adam
Smith, was in accord with that of Senator Silas Wright who favored
a tariff for revenue only. In the meantime Clay's compromise tariff
was passed and South Carolina rescinded her ordinance of nullification.

The country seethed with controversy. The opposition papers accused
Jackson of enforcing Federal laws in South Carolina and permitting
them to be repudiated in Georgia. Colonel William L. Stone, the learned
editor of the New York *Commercial Advertiser,* declared that the em-
broilment in South Carolina was a personal quarrel between Jackson
and Calhoun and saw no reason for "the friends of the Constitution to
interfere." The young crusader from New Lebanon unsheathed his pen
with joy and plunged into the fray. His article "Nullification and the
Opposition" was printed in March in the *Kinderhook Centinel.* These
"false and slanderous" charges, he maintained, were made to counteract
Jackson's message, which arrayed "moral force" and public opinion
"in support of government." The "reckless editor" of the *Commercial
Advertiser,* who opposed Jackson for enforcing the law, would oppose
him for nonenforcement. Colonel Stone and the other "friends of the
Constitution" were willing to "sever the bonds of the Union" and
"strengthen disaffection" if they could only embroil the President.

A few weeks later he attacked Clay in an article on "The Clay Compromise of 1833 and Nullification," printed April 11 in the *Columbia
Centinel.* Clay's former position as champion of the "American system"
of protection left him open to attack on the ground of consistency.
Friends of the administration who had advocated reduction of the tariff
had been accused of bartering away the national welfare to win southern
support for Van Buren for the Presidency. Tilden at nineteen was far
too partisan to credit Clay with sincerity in the rôle of peacemaker.
"Whence this change in the course of Mr. Clay?" he demanded. "Has

[24] *Life,* I, 34.

the Union become more valuable now that it is no longer to Mr. Clay's interest to pursue a course that had well-nigh ruined it? Is the tariff less essential to the interests of the country now that his boisterous support of it cannot longer be made the means of elevating him to power and place?" He decried Clay and Calhoun as saviors of the Union and asked: "Saved the Union from what? From themselves!"—from the warring systems they championed, which endangered it. "Their modesty is equaled only by that of the assassin" who, when he cannot strike your heart, "claims eternal gratitude for having preserved your life." At the late election, he declared, it was Jackson and Van Buren who wished to "reconcile conflicting interests and restore peace to the country," while Clay, in contrast, sought to "avail himself of sectional prejudices at the expense of the country." [25] An invective a bit too strong and historically unfair.

Little mention is made in his correspondence of the progress of his work during the winter of 1832–33. He was two months behind in his classes when he started work in November, but apparently worked hard, made fair progress and declared himself "tolerably well satisfied." [26] As spring came, the Berkshire Hills exerted their appeal, and on April 26 Sam returned to New Lebanon with the thought of possibly continuing his studies at the Kinderhook Academy. This project was not carried through, however, and Sam's sojourn at home was short. By May 17 he had recommenced his recitations in New York, but in June he grew impatient and somewhat alarmed about his desultory and sporadic preparation and looked forward with apprehension to spending the bloom of his youth in the classroom. In rueful vein he wrote to his father, "I am growing old; to take four years and three for a profession (if I should have one) would send me upon the world at 26 or 27, a time when a man ought to have *accomplished* something." He thought it "dishonorable and criminal to be content with mere equality in anything worthy of pursuit." Shaking himself out of his lassitude he suggested that he drop his tutoring in New York immediately and go either to Kinderhook Academy or Yale College to tutor for entrance examinations, where "teachers are fixed and studies and vacations determined."

He felt that immediate, decisive action was necessary to avoid "spending yet another year in preparatory studies." In fact he became so agitated by his own analysis of his situation and so exasperated by the sudden realization of his aimless drifting that he stuck this letter in his pocket and, without waiting to weigh the merits of such a course with his family, set out forthwith for New Haven on a hasty reconnoitering expedition. He discovered that he would have to double up on Latin and Greek, that private tuition would cost about the same as in New York, and that room and board would cost from $16 to $20 a month. He found New Haven "very beautiful" and his determination to begin work at once was strengthened. He wrote Elam, "if I have to leave this city (New York) for any place, I should like to do it very soon," and asked for an immediate reply.[27] The submission of the question to the family council was fatal to its expeditious settlement.

Elam was not favorable toward Yale where his own brother had had an unfortunate experience. There were too many students, with the consequence of "insubordination and riots." He "always had a preference for either Amherst or Union," colleges nearer home and less expensive.[28] The question of Samuel's health again became paramount, and it was finally decided that he should wait another year before entering college. Nine months later, when the subject was revived, Elam still urged the selection of Union "on the ground of expense and ease of getting home." "I am willing to help," he wrote, "but I am past earning much more." [29]

In the meantime after a short trial of the Kinderhook Academy from August to October, Samuel returned to New York. While in Kinderhook he found occasion to wield his pen in defense of his friend and patron, Martin Van Buren, who, because of his prominence as the leading contender for the Democratic nomination in 1836, had been bitterly attacked. "Drinking in political truth at the great Spring in Kinderhook," [30] he rushed to Van Buren's defense in a loyal if extravagant article on "Van Buren and the Nullifiers." He drew a chimerical picture of Van Buren as given in the opposition press—a "wily politician, too versatile and too cunning to express an opinion," an intriguing partisan, a fomenter of strife between Jackson and Calhoun and a shirker of responsibility. These charges were swept away and his friend was portrayed as a man of principle, a thinker whose convictions were so well

[27] *Life,* I, 30.   [28] Tilden Papers, June 15, 1833.   [29] *Ib.,* Mar. 28, 1834.
[30] *Ib.,* Henry Dana Ward to S. J. Tilden.

reasoned that he "rarely if ever had taken ground which it afterward became necessary to abandon," a man of such "public and private virtue" that, after a lifetime of politics, "no perfidious friend or malignant enemy" could fix upon him "one act of dishonor." [31] Returning to the city in the autumn, he said little about Latin and Greek but much about Jackson's quarrel with the Bank.

Tilden's article, "Is the Treasury an Executive Department?"—a "model state paper," reviewing the case historically and constitutionally, defended the right of the President to remove the Secretary of the Treasury.[32] While his son was absorbed in writing such essays, Elam, waiting impatiently for political news, asked, "Have you forgot that you live in the United States?" Sam soon wrote about the panic and predicted that it would be over in three months. He reported that "Old Nick" Biddle was using his "screws" to break the *Standard*. The hostility of the middle class and the lower classes to the Bank would be the decisive factor in the approaching city election.[33] He predicted that Cornelius W. Lawrence, the Democratic nominee for Mayor, a negative sort of candidate, would win by a majority of 2,000 to 4,000 votes.[34] Samuel was a little too optimistic, for Lawrence was elected by a scant 181 votes.[35]

A few weeks later Samuel underwent an experience which would have shaken the nerves of most men. Mr. Huntington, a young merchant who roomed at the Wards', was taken ill. The doctor diagnosed the case as "a fever resulting from a cold." He was delirious for several days and on April 28 died of smallpox. Following his death two servants in the house contracted and died of the same disease. Roomers and servants fled, and young Sam was the only person who slept in the house the night following Huntington's death. It is difficult to reconcile his insouciance in this instance with the unremitting care which he usually accorded his own health. He wrote to his father, giving a detailed account of the tragedy but expressing no personal alarm. It is possible that this direful event just casually pierced his preoccupation with the exciting political events of the time. At the end of his letter he dropped consideration of the late Huntington to remark, "Things look rather

[31] *Writings*, I, 20; *Columbia Centinel*, Sept. 12, 1833.
[32] *Writings*, I, 27; New York *Standard and Statesman*, Feb. 14, 1834.
[33] *Life*, I, 41, Mar. 22, 1834.   [34] *Ib.*, 41.
[35] Hone, *Diary*, I, 124.

squally in Virginia!" [36] Elam ignored the squalls in Virginia. Upon hearing of the "melancholy death of Mr. Huntington," he wrote, "You may escape, but if attacked you will be better off here," and, in a panic, ordered Sam to leave his bedding and hurry home.[37]

[36] *Life*, I, 44, letter, Apr. 29, 1834.   [37] Tilden Papers, May 2, 1834.

Chapter III   *Tilden Experiments with a College Education*

EARLY in June, 1834, Samuel was matriculated in the third term of the freshman year at Yale College. Father and son, the former just recovering from a sore eye, arrived at New Haven by steam packet from New York. With characteristic deliberation they called on the dean and several professors and inspected a number of rooming houses. It was decided that Sam should not live in the College buildings, and the Tontine was established as his mailing address.

Tilden's Yale was conservative—steeped in the tradition of Puritan New England. The classics were the backbone of the curriculum. Daily attendance at prayers was required. Compulsory attendance for meals at the College Commons gave some semblance to a boarding school. About four hundred students were enrolled as candidates for a degree. A dozen buildings, dormitories and recitation halls, were grouped around the elm-shaded College Square. The faculty were men of scholarly attainment. Sam was to study Latin under James L. Kingsley, the learned professor of Latin, and Greek under Dwight Woolsey, a scholar of distinction, who twelve years later succeeded to the presidency of Yale.[1]

Sam, now in his twentieth year, was determined to give some aspect of consistency to the disjointed tutoring and academy work that had so far characterized his efforts to secure an education. His haphazard training, however, made it difficult for him to accommodate himself to classroom routine and the confinement irked him. Lessons "came thick and fast." "Every moment of my time," he wrote his father, "and every energy of my mind has been unavoidably expended in fulfilling my class requisitions." [2] It is doubtful, too, whether the subjects in the curriculum of the third term of the freshman year were the most congenial to the young political enthusiast. These were: Horace (begun); *Graeca Majora,* Vol. II (begun); and five books of Playfair's Euclid [3]—a concentrated dose of classics and mathematics.

Neither the atmosphere nor the food at the noisy Commons pleased him. The articles of diet that Samuel considered necessary to "sustain"

[1] *Yale Catalogue,* 1834.   [2] Tilden Papers.   [3] *Catalogue,* 1834.

27

him in a program of heavy study were not forthcoming.[4] Of pie, which his mother had declared he could not "do without," there was none.[5] He was unable to satisfy his preference for "well-done and stale bread." "Boiled shad and potatoes," he wrote irritably to his father, are "enough for those who could eat such things. . . . I could sometimes eat them, but I could not do so constantly."[6] Elam agreed; Polly emphatically seconded him, and permission was sought from the college authorities to leave the Commons. At a cost of $2.50 a week board was secured from a Mrs. Fletcher, and "by preference" Samuel arranged to "eat alone." The landladies of New Haven—such as the "barefoot woman who hesitated about showing the chamber because it was in disorder"—next monopolized the correspondence between father and son until Samuel was satisfactorily settled with the Goodmans, who were "Yankees" and might do.[7]

A compiler of "Eminent Yale Men," up to 1910, includes Tilden's name in a list of seventy-nine, and places him at the head of Yale men from New York who have influenced the nation.[8] But the aristocratic atmosphere of the college, stiff with precedents and customs of a century's growth, was not altogether congenial to the young follower of Jackson. Early in July he wrote ruefully to his father, "I have entirely foresworn politics."[9] Although he attended the public sessions of the Linonian Society, and on one occasion enjoyed an oration on "The Decline of Empire,"[10] apparently he was not a member of either of the two great debating societies.

Among his classmates were Aaron L. Chapin, who became president of Beloit College; William M. Evarts, later Secretary of State and Senator; Benjamin N. Martin, who was afterward a professor in New York University; Edward S. Pierrepont, who was to be Minister to England; and Morrison R. Waite, a future Chief Justice of the Supreme Court.[11] Later Samuel came to know Pierrepont and Evarts well, but at New Haven he made few acquaintances. The sharpness of his intellect and habit of rather dogmatic assertion, which induced flattering attention from Elam's friends, did not attract young men of his own age. Nor did he meet with much sympathy for his ill health and morbid

[4] *Life*, I, 47.
[5] Tilden Papers, Sept. 15, 1833 (while at the Kinderhook Academy).
[6] *Life*, I, 47.   [7] Tilden Papers.
[8] Stokes, A. P., *Memorials of Eminent Yale Men*, II, 402.
[9] Tilden Papers, July 3, 1834.   [10] *Ib.*, July 11, 1834, "Order of Exercises."
[11] Stokes, A. P., *op. cit.*

absorption with remedies. "The embarrassments of broken health in the situation in which I am, are indescribable," [12] he wrote to his father. Naturally aloof, he was lonely.

Toward the middle of the term he had settled into the routine of freshman life, but was still unhappy. "Seven weeks will be quickly gone," he wrote home, "and I say (what I am not at all apt to do) the sooner the better." [13] In his homesickness he relished every scrap of news from New Lebanon, even such dispiriting items as that George had "a pain in his bust," that Mary was sick in New York, and that Elam, recovering from the worst "decline" in years, could not even "write politics." [14] As at Williamstown he insisted that Elam send the local papers.[15]

Sam had neither the inclination nor money for social display. The Tilden budget had been stretched to allow attendance at Yale, and economy was necessary. Unfortunately, he found that it was "easier to tell the direction in which my money flows than to stop the current." He bought his books in New York, or tried to exchange thermometers for them, and declared that, although his hat was eight months old, he did not need a new one. A few horseback rides, ostensibly to improve his health, were his one extravagance and one of his few recreations.

He left New Haven in the latter part of August, having passed in Latin, Greek and algebra with a general average of 6.25 on a scale of 9, or about 70%.[16] Certainly, this was not a brilliant record, but in view of the distractions from which he suffered, real and imaginary, it is surprising that he even finished the term. Its completion represented his most persistent effort toward a formal education up to that time. Since it was assumed that he would return, some of his more unwieldy belongings were left behind.[17] Elam, however, had become genuinely alarmed about Sam's physical condition. His letters toward the end of the term had expressed the fear that his son could not "endure the fatigue of . . . labor in college," and contained frequent warnings against "empty honors" won at the expense of health.[18] Other members of the family shared Elam's anxiety. On his return to New Lebanon, young Tilden tried horseback riding, but without any decided advan-

---

[12] *Life*, I, 48.   [13] *Ib.*   [14] Tilden Papers, July 8, 1834.
[15] *Ib.*, June 11, 1834.
[16] Letter of Yale Registrar, A. K. Merritt, May 24, 1930.
[17] Tilden Papers.
[18] *Ib.*, Aug. 4, 1834; various other letters.

tage. After ten days Elam was shocked to discover that Sam had lost ten pounds, and shortly afterward it was decided that he should not return to New Haven. His emaciation was apparently the occasion of some good-humored badinage, for some months later he wrote to his father from New York, "Our Hudson tailors took the doctor's (Young-love) directions to make my pantaloons on his broomsticks quite liter-ally, so that I shall send them back to be let out." [19]

The campaign of 1834 for the Governorship was getting under way, with Governor Marcy a candidate for re-election. Sam was an ardent supporter and worked with the county committee to book speakers and get out the campaign literature. His friend Elias Pitts, a printer of Kinderhook, was belabored with political correspondence and wailed that Sam filled his head so full of politics that he was left dazed.[20] Pitts was a young man of intelligence, but he had not the genius for politics that characterized Sam Tilden. He enjoyed dabbling in politics, but found himself out of his depth in the discussion of abstract political theories. In October he cried out in distress, "Politics, politics, and nothing but politics, are the themes on which I am compelled to think and converse from morning till night." Sam could not comprehend such an attitude. Political treatises streamed from his pen, and when he was not writing for the newspapers he set himself to other forms of electioneering, even preparing an address in October on "Nullification, Indians, and Opposition." He was beginning to be valued by the party, and some of his political writings were distributed in pamphlet form.[21]

The decision that Sam should not resume his studies at Yale keenly disappointed C. B. Sherman in New York. He had envisioned a brilliant career for his young friend, and urged him to hold out for another term or two. He seems to have understood the Tilden tendency to exaggerate physical ailments, and attempted to combat it in a mild way, but with only indirect effect. "If you are giving up college," he asked, "what is your substitute?" [22] Elam had eliminated further study at Yale from Sam's educational program without any regret, but Sherman's pointed question set him thinking. After due reflection, he sent for a catalogue of New York University. Both father and son were pleased with this liberal university, recently opened "to the poor and the rich without distinction of sect or party" as a protest against the aristocratic older

[19] *Life*, I, 49.   [20] Tilden Papers, Sept. 6, 1834.
[21] *Ib.*, Oct. 6, 1834.   [22] *Ib.*, Sept. 2, 1834.

institutions.[23] The tuition was $10 less per annum than at Columbia, and the democratic purposes set forth in the catalogue made a powerful appeal. So it was settled that Samuel should return to New York and matriculate at New York University. Sherman suggested that they share a "joint room," [24] but it was finally determined, for financial and other reasons, that he should board again with Aunt Polly Barnes and room with his benign Uncle Henry Dana Ward. Home and family remedies would be easily accessible, and his mother would always be ready to come to the city should serious illness threaten. Sam gave desultory attention to his college texts in preparation for entrance in the January term, but his activities continued to be preponderantly political. It was not until the campaign closed with the re-election of Marcy [25] that his thoughts turned to the resumption of his college work, and on November 11 he wrote to his aunt that he would arrive in New York within a fortnight.[26] On December 1, 1834, Sam took up his residence again with his Uncle Ward in the city that was to be his home for nearly half a century. Before his death he was to see the straggling seaport emerge into a modern metropolis, whose commercial and financial supremacy was uncontested. A cold sense of civic fraternity would bind the busy corporation lawyer to the noisy populace.

The bustling, lively atmosphere of the growing city suited young Tilden. The varied opportunities stimulated his interest, and even his responsibilities were not too displeasing. During the month before the opening of the January term, he discharged innumerable business commissions for friends and relatives. He attended the theater and was particularly charmed by a performance of the *Chinese Lady*, a handbill of which has been preserved among his papers.[27] He went to see Mr. West's picture of "Death on the Pale Horse." His position as major domo in Mrs. Barnes' boarding house, requiring some tact and patience, was resumed. With his gift for expression Tilden might well have gained distinction in the literary world. The eccentricities of Aunt Polly's boarders furnished ample material for his descriptive talents. One of his letters home contains a vivid account of a disturbance caused by the premature removal of a platter of pancakes from the range of a Mrs. Whittlesey, a violently articulate boarder, whom Sam characterized as

---

[23] *Catalogue* of New York University, 1834.
[24] Tilden Papers, Sept. 16, 1834, and later.
[25] Alexander, D. S., *Political History of New York,* I, 404.
[26] Tilden Papers.   [27] *Ib.,* Dec. 18, 1834.

a "female Daniel Lambert." [28]

But the die of politics had been cast too strongly and Sam was to develop his literary abilities only in political writings and private correspondence. He even felt competent to advise men at the head of the Democratic Party and of the nation, and asked Elam to write to Van Buren "urging him to impress as much as he can on the President the necessity of avoiding everything that may seem violent and high-handed." He believed that Jackson should respect the Senate's rejection of his appointments and make others, because "Moderation on his part will put them in wrong before the nation." He felt that, by a stubborn rejection of all Jackson's appointments and suggested appropriations, the opposition would seal its own doom. [29]

Sam entered New York University in the January term, 1835, as a special student. Indeed, his preparation for college had been so whimsical that he could not be definitely classified. At his suggestion Elam wrote to Yale for a certificate of dismissal, and had the following reply from the president:

Dear Sir: In compliance with your request I enclose a dismission for your son. I regret that his health is so delicate as to lay him under the necessity of intermitting his studies. I hope that by skillful attention he may still [be] invigorated so as to be able to gratify his laudable desire of attaining a thorough education. Remember me kindly to him.

With respectful regard

J. Day [30]

This ended Samuel's connection with Yale until, in 1875, he was awarded an honorary degree and enrolled with his class.

The faculty minutes of New York University record that in 1835-36 Sam attended for the winter terms, and in 1837 was present for two consecutive terms from January to July. In 1835 he was reported as a member of the sophomore class in Latin under Professor John Proudfit. [31] Though he appears to have given only casual attention to his college work, there were occasions when his interest was alert. In February, 1835, he wrote home that he "went to the University in a snow storm." This to a normal boy, would, of course, have meant nothing, but with Tilden it amounted to temerity. One of the traditions about his work

[28] Tilden Papers, Dec. 18, 1834.   [29] Life, I, 49.   [30] Tilden Papers, Feb. 13, 1835.
[31] Report of Registrar of New York University, T. F. Jones, May 26, 1930.

relates to a recitation in Juvenal. Professor Tappan called on him to recite the first four lines: "so finished in style, and yet so fully did he give the meaning of the author, that the Professor had him proceed with the translation of the whole lesson. He did so to the delight of all." [32] Human nature among sophomores being fairly constant, the delight of his classmates in seeing him carry the entire burden of a recitation is quite understandable. But there were too many pitfalls against which the leaders of the Democratic Party must be warned to permit Sam to concentrate too steadily on Latin declensions. More than once he was reported absent from examinations. In 1835 he had returned to New Lebanon to "recruit himself." On other occasions he was possibly too busy with an election pamphlet or penning advice to the President of the United States.

On February 9, 1835, he reached his majority. This momentous event was taken with seriousness by both father and son. It meant that Sam, who had for years worked for his party's welfare, could now vote and hold office. Unfortunately, some disquieting gossip had reached New Lebanon. Polly was fearful lest Sam marry before he was prepared for such an obligation, and Elam apparently apprehended something worse. He wrote to his son expressing his alarm and demanded an explanation of the rumors. He urged Sam to take the occasion of his coming of age to review his past and his prospects, and to weigh his values in life. In something of a boastful spirit Sam replied: "I have the pleasure to inform you that the apprehensions you express are entirely unfounded. . . . The preponderant feeling, at the eventful moment you allude to, was one of gratulation that I had arrived at it free from all the entanglement and consequences of youthful folly." [33]

Samuel's supposed indiscretion is of significance because up to the age of twenty-one he had taken no interest in girls of his own age. He seems to have suffered from a habitual inability to be at perfect ease with them and a complete incapacity to master the technique of gallantry. Coupled with this inability was a rather pathetic yearning for feminine sympathy. He was deeply attached to his mother and sisters, and prized his contacts with older female relatives. There is little evidence that he sought female friends outside of his own family, although he was more at ease with older women than with girls. A letter, formal

[32] McElroy and McBride, *Government Officers*, 7.
[33] Tilden Papers, Feb. 20, 1835.

in content and stilted in style, written to a Miss Prescott, is one of the few of its kind known to exist. The recipient may have been the dressmaker of whom Aunt Polly Barnes wrote to Sam's mother: "Miss Prescott is visiting a friend uptown but will help make dresses." [34]

Early in May Sam returned to New Lebanon "much better than he was when he came home from New Haven last summer." He remained there all summer, and in fact did not return to New York until November. The summer, saddened by the death of his younger brother, George Frederick,[35] was spent in the usual pursuits of riding and tramping over the beautiful Berkshire Hills, and in correspondence with friends and relatives. On the whole he seems to have been rather healthy during this interim, although he did write to Elam that his voice was hoarse and his cough persistent. Elam replied at length. They relished these indispositions, both father and son, and discovered infinite variety in them, like travelers in a strange and wonderful land. The sharing of morbid experiences bound them closely together in an unwholesome sympathy.

While still in New Lebanon in the early fall of 1835, Sam broached the subject of foreign travel. "I am ready to go to England," he wrote his father, "if the circumstances are favorable." Although Elam gave him no encouragement, he continued to press the benefits of a trip abroad with characteristic persistence during the ensuing year. Elias Pitts, who was quite as much concerned about Samuel's health as any member of the family, bluntly told him, "You must relinquish hard study." But neither from Pitts nor anyone else was he ready to accept such a decision as final, for late November saw him again in the metropolis ready to resume his college work. On December 2, 1835, Elam wrote that he was pleased to know that Sam was well settled in his quarters for the winter.[36] Sam sent his father a vivid account of the great fire the loss of which he estimated at $20,000,000, and boasted with boyish pride, "I have business acquaintance with a great number of the sufferers." [37] The voluminous correspondence between father and son during the winter of 1835–36, Elam writing every other day, had to do with the usual three themes—health, the sale of pills and thermometers, and politics. There are but feeble references to Sam's college work. When

[34] Tilden Papers, Jan. 31, 1836.   [35] Ib., Elam to Polly Barnes, fall of 1835.
[36] Ib., autumn and early winter, 1835.
[37] Letters, I, 2, Dec. 17, 1833. An error in date which should be 1835. See Hone, Diary, I, 135.

he reported the loss of one of his front teeth, Elam consoled him with the statement, "I lost one of my front teeth when I was 20." [38]

By the middle of April, 1836, Elam was urging Sam to return home and suggesting that it might be more convenient for his son to attend Union College. "You may rely upon it," he added, "that it is vain to look to any remedy with much confidence while you *continue the same habits,* and if by an effort you get better, returning to study would in all probability bring them back." He suggested the possibility of an active business career and proposed that they talk it over when Samuel came home. [39]

For once the approach of spring did not lure Samuel back to New Lebanon. He had discontinued his attendance at New York University, with the exception of an examination when the winter term ended on April 16, and seemed to be uncertain as to his future activities. In this preoccupied and indecisive mood he informed his father in April, "I wrote a day or two ago but could not find my letter to put into the office yesterday—whether I had already done so, or lost it, I can not tell." [40] Business commissions from home he found more than usually burdensome. Aunt Polly Barnes understood better than anyone else what was bothering her moping nephew. She informed Elam that a Mr. Ellison was going to Liverpool in May and had invited Sam to go with him. Believing that the excitement and stimulus of travel would be beneficial to Sam, she urged her brother-in-law to let him go, because "his constitution needs renovation" to prepare him for the rigors of another winter. [41]

To appease the restless young man, Elam proposed an inexpensive sea trip to Nantucket as a substitute for a journey to Europe. This suggestion brought the sarcastic query from Sam as to whether a voyage to Nantucket would not "disturb the functions of the system without producing a permanent change?" He also rejected any plans to visit relatives, asserting that he "preferred to be among strangers or at home." Then Moses suggested a trip to Washington to call on Van Buren and other friends. This idea found an assent and Sam appealed to his father to accompany him to the national capital, to Madison's home, then west to Pittsburgh and back home. "I want something constant, active, exciting and presenting a rapid succession of objects which is wholly inde-

[38] Tilden Papers, Apr. 14, 18, 1836.   [39] *Ib.,* Apr. 14, 18, 1836.
[40] *Life,* I, 52.   [41] Tilden Papers, Apr. 10, 1836.

pendent of my will," he declared. This impulse for far horizons during the late spring of his twenty-second year doubtless represented a violent reaction against a life circumscribed by family pressures. He was even strongly inclined to give up his studies altogether. None of these travel plans materialized, however, and he lingered in New York until June, helping Mrs. Barnes to move to a new location, and undergoing an "operation" on his teeth which brought him great relief, although he lost "most of the double teeth." Shortly afterward, against his inclination for the first time, he returned to New Lebanon.[42]

In November, 1836, however, occurred an event, which made Sam forget his urge to travel and stirred the entire Tilden family, namely, the election of "Friend Van Buren" as President of the United States. It is to be regretted keenly that Tilden's letters and public papers covering this important period are not fully preserved. There is ample evidence, however, that Sam thrilled to the prospect of Van Buren's nomination and election. Three months prior to the election he presented to his father a rough sketch of the strategical plan which he believed would insure Democratic success. The Antimasons, whose stronghold was New York State, were obviously a factor in the campaign. The matter of their treatment was rather delicate, in view of the hot prejudices which might be fanned to fanatical proportions by inept handling, and it was Sam's suggestion that this troublesome element should be conciliated by a campaign of indirection which would avoid open allegiance and obligation. He suggested that the spokesmen for Van Buren should not state definitely the stand of their champion but rather should report "in conversation" that Van Buren deprecated secret societies in general. He cautioned against committing anything to writing, and felt that by following this plan the regular Masons would not be offended and the Antimasons would not be openly "courted." It was, in effect, a whispering campaign which he suggested. Sam feared an open coalition with the Antimasons, but worked for their "informal support." He felt that Van Buren could best advance his own interests by making himself "unobjectionable" to the Antimasons and believed that such an attitude would "increase accession from their ranks." If it became necessary to give a written opinion, Sam advised that this should take the form of a reply to the Antimasonic circular sent to the Presidential candidates, since this would remove "all appearance of collusion." [43]

[42] Tilden Papers, June 4, 1836, and other dates.   [43] *Life,* I, 50, Feb. 14, 1835.

Van Buren followed precisely the plan outlined by his youthful admirer. He opposed the Abolitionists to win support in the South, assailed the Bank to conciliate the working classes, and adroitly side-stepped the Masonic issue so as to hold the support of both the Antimasons and their opponents. In the Electoral College he received 170 votes to General Harrison's 73. It is impossible to say whether Van Buren was influenced in his course by Sam's suggestions; but, even if the young enthusiast did not see further and more clearly than the leaders of his party, he at least saw as far and as clearly, and we have impressive evidence of the early maturity of his political instinct. Sam wrote gleefully to Elam that, "Considering the game that was played against him, the combination of discordant and powerful factions, the multiplicity of candidates, enlisting in their favor local and sectional interests, artfully calculated to divide and to prevent an election by the people, I must regard such a majority over the whole of them as a more triumphant victory than receiving two-thirds or three-quarters of all the votes against a single candidate." He reported that Senator Tracy had said of Van Buren, "Let the little devil once get in and you will never get him out," but he was sure of Van Buren's triumph despite the "bluster" and organization of the opposition.[44] Elam's reply refers complacently to Van Buren's "splendid triumph." [45]

Reinvigorated by Van Buren's victory, Sam returned to college in November, 1836.[46] This should have been his senior year had he pursued his studies with due regularity. For the first time he attended the university for two consecutive terms from January to July, 1837. The faculty minutes for February 25 show that he was a member of the senior class in Latin and Greek, in which he passed. He also took junior Greek but was "absent from examination." On April 16 he wrote, "I have suspended my studies." [47] The next term he took junior courses in Latin, Greek and natural philosophy but absented himself from all three examinations. Resorting to cathartics, morphine and creosote for his aching teeth, he came through this period tolerably well. When Elam expressed alarm at the use of creosote, Sam reassured him, "I do not drink it." His voluminous correspondence only occasionally refers to "the lectures" at the university but reveals a deep interest in the projected railroad through New Lebanon—a forecast of his vast railroad interests.

44 Tilden Papers, Dec. 12, 1836.   45 *Ib.*, Dec. 16, 1836.   46 *Ib.*
47 Report of Registrar of New York University, T. F. Jones, May 26, 1930.

He advised his father to speculate in land along the new roadway, sent him a report on his property in New York City, and interpreted the money panic for his benefit. For the first time he expressed a willingness to assist Elam in selling thermometers and pills. His letters of this year reveal a pronounced maturity.[48]

Van Buren's Inaugural Address on March 4, 1837,[49] announced that he would veto any bill to abolish slavery in the District of Columbia. When William Leggett, editor of the New York *Plaindealer,* took this occasion to make a violent attack on the President, comparing him unfavorably with Jackson and denouncing his first message to Congress, young Tilden sprang to the defense of his friend. Leggett had paraded as a Jackson Democrat and the reversal of form evidenced in his attack surprised Van Buren's and his own friends. Without waiting for a more experienced man to reply to Leggett, Tilden, "on a sudden impulse," prepared a castigation in the form of three letters to the *New York Times* written over the *nom de plume* of "Jacksonis Amicus." [50]

In the first letter Tilden declared the "animadversions" on Van Buren to be "singularly unjust." He refuted the charge of "vagueness" in Van Buren's as compared with Jefferson's Inaugural Address. He urged that Van Buren was seeking to pacify the nation and to preserve the Union. And in the light of this interpretation Tilden professed to be unable to see how Leggett could charge the President with a "gross breach of political decorum . . . and a cringing spirit."

In the second letter Tilden accused the *Plaindealer* of garbling quotations from Van Buren's message and scouted the expression of fears that the President "means to act contrary to his whole public life . . . and to his solemn pledges." He accused Leggett of an imperfect knowledge of the two original political parties and of outrageous treachery and hypocritical professions of friendship. He then launched into a caustic description of the "I-always-speak-my-mind" nuisance, "who seems to think it a virtue to violate the comities of social intercourse, and always to sacrifice the feelings of others to their own caprice or ill nature." This type of person, Tilden declared, "fancies that, as a universal Aristarchus, he rules and rights the world; while he serves it, if at all, as a public flagellator." He concluded, "I have drawn a picture—I leave it to the public to say if it be a portrait."

When the *Plaindealer* sought to ward off these blows by publishing

[48] Tilden Papers.   [49] Richardson, *Messages,* IV, 1590.   [50] *Writings,* I, 38

Tilden's letters in its own columns with a reply, he wrote a third letter in which he reiterated the previous charges of garbled passages and incorrect party history.[51]

No sooner were these letters out of his hands than this political Sir Galahad took up a defense of Van Buren's attitude toward the United States Bank. Tilden studied the approach of the panic of 1837 with deep concern. He reported to his father that sixty-five mercantile houses had failed and that few of the "land jobbers" could meet their liabilities. "There is scarcely a house that does not tremble to its foundations," he wrote and added the opinion that, should foreign exchange rise, "specie payment will be inevitably suspended by every bank in the city, and probably the country ones will follow." He was sorry to note that the usury bill had passed at Albany because it would "merely increase the embarrassments of the borrower." [52] A little over a month after Tilden's prediction, the banks of New York suspended specie payment and the country banks followed suit. New York State legalized the suspension, an action regretted by Sam who thought the banks should resume specie payments "at the earliest moment possible." He feared that the act would encourage banks to "continue a state of things profitable to themselves but ruinous to the public" and that they would not resume specie payments until forced to do so. He was apprehensive, too, lest a "delusive appearance of prosperity" should sway the support of public opinion to further issues of paper money, and felt that "a permanent currency of irredeemable paper is a more intolerable curse than war, pestilence or famine" and should be resisted by the people.[53] Thus at the age of twenty-three he took a positive stand for the gold standard.

In July Sam wrote to his father, "Yesterday was Commencement and I attended." [54] This attendance, probably as a spectator, marked the close of an epoch in his life. Some of his biographers state that he graduated from New York University but there is no evidence to sustain this claim.

The late summer and fall of 1837 were spent again in New Lebanon, and no doubt Sam and Elam used most of the time in making excuses for "friend Van Buren" and damning his foes. The financial panic induced Van Buren to call a special session of Congress in September, 1837, and to advise the divorce of the Government from the banks and the estab-

51 *Life*, I, 56, gives Tilden's letter of Mar. 25, 1837, to his father, explaining how he came to write these articles.
52 *Ib.*, 61, Apr. 5, 1837.   53 *Ib.*, Letter, May 13, 1837.   54 Tilden Papers.

lishment of an Independent Treasury. An uproar of debate, violent and vituperative, spread across the land. In a reply to a series of letters to the Albany *Argus* by "Marshall," opposing the President's recommendations, Tilden under the name of "Crino" replied. At first the *Argus* refused to print any of Sam's articles until after election. Elam informed Van Buren: "We have been betrayed and sold . . . by the influence of the Bank monopoly." [55] But two letters did appear. In the first,[56] Sam defended Van Buren's recommendation of the disuse of bank notes by the Government. "A very small share of common sense," he wrote, "or a very slight acquaintance with the subject of currency, are, either of them, sufficient to show that paper, convertible into coin, cannot depreciate as compared with coin; and with this radical fallacy falls the whole superstructure of mischiefs" which "Marshall" reared upon it. In Tilden's opinion the establishment of the Independent Treasury would have a highly salutary effect upon business. The second letter,[57] defending the President's message, charged: "You assume that the disuse of bills . . . will destroy the banks" and render specie insufficient. "You establish your first proposition by your second, then your second by the first, and offer no other evidence in support of either!"

These juvenile polemics made quite a stir in Columbia County. They reveal a clear understanding of the party issues in the thirties and show a familiarity with the stock arguments of the day. In a young man of twenty-three they indicate an extraordinary grasp of political science, economics, finance and current problems. It is no surprise to find that they were ascribed to Judge Esek Cowen, an able Supreme Court Justice, who, in smiling silence, did not open his mouth to repudiate the accusation. His acquiescence in this misconception was relished as a joke which Edwin Croswell, editor of the *Argus*, was fond of relating.[58]

Although Tilden received no diploma at the end of his college career, because of frequent interruptions on account of illness, still he did acquire, even with these handicaps, what was substantially a college course. He was acquainted with the atmosphere of three colleges and enjoyed the association with teachers and fellow students. The reading he did, particularly in newspapers and current periodicals, was prodigious and must have been a substitute for what he lost in the drudgery of the classroom. His letter writing and political essays gave him training

[55] Van Buren Papers, Elam Tilden to Van Buren, Nov. 23, 1837.
[56] *Writings*, I, 57, Sept. 28, 1837. [57] *Ib.*, I, 64, Oct. 20, 1837. [58] *Life*, I, 68.

in expression, in logical thinking and in problems of the day which no college courses of that time afforded. When his college days closed he was a well-educated young man, master of his own faculties, and confident of his own judgment.

IN corporation law, public finance, constitutional law, and administrative reform Samuel J. Tilden stands the peer of any American lawyer during the third quarter of the nineteenth century. The stages by which he attained this pre-eminence are worthy of study.

If heredity was a factor in his brilliant career as a lawyer, one can point to a long line of ancestors who were country squires, magistrates, barristers, mayors and governors. His absorption as a youth in law and politics seems to indicate that he was born with a predilection for those subjects. This bent was accentuated by the intelligent enthusiasm of his father for local, State and national politics—an enthusiasm by which Tilden profited from childhood. His Aunt Polly Younglove, an intense admirer of Jeffersonian principles, loved the serious lad as her own son, and discussed current problems with him as an equal. Adult friends of the family, like John W. Edmunds, Martin Van Buren, Benjamin F. Butler and Aaron Vanderpoel, who gave the intellectually matured boy friendly approval, strengthened convictions already forming. His brothers, Moses and Henry, almost as deeply interested in politics as he, encouraged his aspirations for a legal career.

Moreover, the period in which Tilden grew to manhood was one of intense party activity and strong political convictions. Newspapers were filled with crude, vehement, and ofttimes vindictive discussions of men and issues. Social friendships were based on party loyalties; business was determined by partisanship; the legal profession was considered essential for entry into politics; and even the talk of schoolboys reflected the breach between Democrats and Federalists. Such conditions affected a youth as sensitive as Tilden. These influences explain why from boyhood his mind turned toward law as a profession, and why his keenest pleasure came from reports of party activities, books on finance and economics, and discussions of political issues with his elders.

From these sources rather than the classics he derived an education which made him one of the ablest lawyers of his age. Although always an intense partisan, he had an extraordinarily judicial temperament. He studied all sides of a question and understood his adversary's position as well as his own. This made him a convincing debater and his arguments almost invulnerable. He was exact in expression, even-tempered in controversy, cautious to an irritating degree, and uniformly courteous to a foe. If his pen was sarcastic, it was only to stress a point and never to make a venomous attack. His triumphs were due to a mastery of facts, to convincing logic, and to skill in annihilating his opponent's arguments. From youth he formed the habit of setting forth all sides of every question—health, domestic problems, business matters and political issues. This mental attitude won confidence, made him a trusted party leader, and brought him important cases in law. He would have made an excellent judge, and at one time was suggested for the Supreme Court of New York,[1] but had no ambitions in that direction.

Years before he was old enough to vote, he identified himself with the machinery of the Democratic Party in Columbia County as an active party worker. He sat on committees, helped organize public meetings, drew up resolutions, wrote campaign documents, attended local caucuses and conventions, and thus made himself a valuable party worker. It was early taken for granted by his relatives and friends that he would become a lawyer. After long discussions with his father, his profession was settled when it was decided that he should go to college. Consequently his reading, party activities and school work were all regarded as preparatory to a legal career. Wherever his future is mentioned in his own or his father's letters, the inference is that, after finishing a liberal arts course, he would take up legal training. When he was preparing for college in 1833 his brother Moses asked, "Are you aware that if you study law it will be necessary to obtain a certificate from each teacher of the length of time you took the work, which must be put on file by the attorney with whom you study?"

When Tilden left New York University in 1837 he entered John W. Edmunds' office as law clerk. It was during this clerkship that John Bigelow, while boarding with Mrs. Barnes at the corner of Eighth Street and Fifth Avenue, met Tilden. Bigelow was impressed with the fact that "his mind was already wholly engrossed in practical politics." From this mutual interest there developed a lifelong friendship.[2] Edmunds took a keen interest in Sam and was not exacting in the matter of his attendance at the office. He spent hours in discussion of party politics

[1] Tilden Papers.
[2] Bigelow, John, *Retrospections of an Active Life*, I, 55. Hereafter reference to this work will be merely *Retrospections*.

with his precocious clerk and later on furthered his legal career. In turn, Tilden had the pleasure of assisting Edmunds to obtain a judgeship in the Supreme Court of the State.[3]

About the time that he entered Edmunds' office Tilden registered in the first class organized in the new Law School at New York University —the first one in New York State. He was influenced in this by Benjamin F. Butler, a lifelong friend of Elam Tilden, and a former law partner of Van Buren. Butler, while Attorney General under Jackson, in 1835, sketched out a plan for a law college at New York University.[4] Under this plan the course of study was for three years, with a professor for each year, and the sessions were held in the afternoons and evenings in order to permit students to discharge their duties as clerks in city offices during the forenoons. Butler was at first too busy to accept the principalship, and so the opening was postponed until 1838, when he felt able to undertake the position. For the first year he had David Graham, Jr., associated with him as instructor, and the following year, with the addition of William Kent and Anthony L. Robertson to the faculty, the Law School was under full headway. Butler was professor of general law and real property, Kent taught the law of personal property, and Graham held classes in pleading and practice. The three classes received in common a course by Butler on general law. The work consisted of lectures and discussions, as Tilden explained, "with examinations three times a week on what we read." [5]

Sam wrote to his father in August, 1838, that the law faculty "are going to assign us subjects to write upon at the opening of next term, to be read to the bar and the public generally after the college fashion." [6] He saw "the utility of the school in a stronger light" than he had anticipated and now considered a clerkship in a law office of "doubtful advantage" during the first year or two of a law course.[7] It seems probable that Tilden took the full course of three years and graduated with the first class, but the records are indefinite.[8]

Tilden's work in the Law School also laid the ground for his extensive and accurate knowledge of American history. In the course which Benjamin F. Butler outlined in his syllabus were lectures on the "Politi-

[3] Edmunds wrote a book on spiritualism and claimed power to speak with the dead, but Tilden was not afflicted with these vagaries. *Dict. Am. Biog.*, VI, 23.
[4] Jones, T. F., *New York University 1832–1932*, 239.
[5] Tilden Papers.   [6] *Life*, I, 79.   [7] Tilden Papers.
[8] Letter of Registrar of New York University.

cal and Civil History of the United States Prior to the Confederation in 1781"; "The Decline and Fall of the Confederation and the Formation of the Constitution of 1787"; "General View of the Constitution," the Power of Congress, the Executive Power, the Judicial Power, and kindred subjects.[9]

Among Tilden's papers of this period is a somewhat enlarged list of his personal belongings. Most noticeable is the increase in his stock of books—nine texts of Latin classics and nine of Greek, five volumes on mathematics, a dozen on English and elocution, Webster's Dictionary, the *New York Red Book*,[10] the Bible, a few works on nature study and poetry, the *Debates on the Federal Constitution*, political pamphlets, including his own articles and speeches, notes on law lectures and collateral reading, and diverse leaflets about Yale and New York University. Here one may detect tokens of a book collector.[11]

Meanwhile Tilden kept a political eye on the panic of 1837 which had thrown the city into an uproar. The charter of the United States Bank had expired; the Democrats refused to renew it, and proposed to establish an independent department to handle Federal money, but Van Buren's Independent Treasury Bill was defeated in the House. The success of his administration was at stake. Business men, disposed to bear known evils rather than risk a radical remedy, were inclined to believe that the earlier prosperity was due to the "regulating" influence of the Bank and that Van Buren was inviting disaster. The wage-earners, however, who were not borrowers, were disposed to side with the President. The Democratic-Republican mechanics and workingmen met at Tammany Hall on February 6, 1838, and adopted resolutions, written by Tilden, expressing hostility to the Bank.[12]

These resolutions urged the increase of "small bills" to accommodate the people, assailed a "monarchy and a privileged nobility to regulate our affairs," declared that the national banking laws levied "an indirect tax upon the unprivileged masses for the benefit of the few," and urged the divorce of the banks from the Government. Tilden urged the people not to be frightened by cries of "agrarian" and "Leveler," and insisted that institutions are founded not on "property but upon humanity." [13] Elam Tilden proudly informed Van Buren that his son had formulated

[9] Copy of Syllabus in Tilden Papers.
[10] A manual giving activities of the State government.
[11] Tilden Papers.   [12] *Writings*, I, 87. Widely copied in the party press.
[13] *Evening Post*, Feb. 7, 1838.

the resolutions.[14] This enthusiastic assembly voted to send an address to the Democrats of the country, and a committee of fifteen, charged with its preparation asked Tilden to write it.[15] He declined at first, pleading ill health and the pressure of affairs, but finally consented after having been "very urgently solicited." At a meeting on February 26, he climbed to the speaker's rostrum and read it.[16] This was his first appearance on the platform of a New York City political meeting. He had passed his twenty-fourth birthday scarcely two weeks before.

In this "Address to the Farmers, Mechanics and Workingmen," Tilden professed sympathy for the industrial classes and a desire to harmonize the factions in the Democratic Party. The people themselves, he explained, were called upon to decide the question of the separation of the "financial affairs of the Government from those of private individuals and corporations." Could the Federal Government safely manage its own finances? Could it command the efficiency and experience which characterized private enterprises? A review of the management of the United States Mint for fifty years was the answer. Competition of powerful moneyed institutions for "exclusive favor" enlarged "executive influence." To relieve local banks from "unequal competition" would react favorably on all business. The Bank party sought to give government "an aristocratic bias"; the Democratic Party was the champion of equality.

When Elam read this address he criticized it severely,[17] and Sam replied that he had never before felt such a "deep disgust" for any task and was content to "get out of the scrape in any way that avoided positive disgrace." Still he thought it was "a useful exercise;" and some gentlemen were so pleased with it that they asked him to take charge of a morning Democratic paper.[18]

The year 1839 was an uneventful period. Tilden quietly fell into the beaten path of his law studies and the duties of his clerkship. When Congress adjourned he was glad "the agitators must go home." He predicted that the Democrats would carry the charter election in New York City by from 2,000 to 2,500,[19] but the actual majority was only 1,200. The arrival of the steam packet *Great Western* on April 15 [20] and the lazy

[14] Van Buren Papers, Feb. 22, 1838.
[15] Tilden Papers, Committee of Fifteen to Tilden, Feb. 20, 1838.
[16] *Writings*, I, 79; *Evening Post*, Mar. 5, Feb. 7, 1838; *Life*, I, 71; the *Post*, Mar. 5, 1838, said that Thomas N. Carr read it.
[17] Tilden Papers, Mar. 18, 1838.   [18] *Life*, I, 72, Mar. 24, 1838.
[19] Tilden Papers.   [20] Hone, *Diary*, I, 388.

days of spring revived the dream of a voyage to Europe. Once more Aunt Polly Barnes attempted to break down Elam's obduracy, and sisters Hetty and Mary as well as Ma Tilden dropped hopeful hints in his ear.[21] Elam was deaf to the suggestion, however, and Sam bore his disappointment in silence. One bright event stood out in this dull year. President Van Buren visited New York City on July 2 and was greeted with a grand military parade. Since Edmunds delivered the address of welcome, which Tilden may have helped to prepare, no doubt he had an opportunity for a satisfactory neighborly political conference with his great friend.[22]

"Bad health" continued to pester the young law student, and mention of it might be curtailed were it not a predominant factor in his development. This formative year was one of physical torment and constant experimentation with specifics for colds, neuralgia, swellings, lameness, chills and fever, and rheumatism. He employed such remedies as bleeding, ice packs, poultices, morphine, mustard plasters, exercises, and dieting. Physicians and dentists profited by his ailments. Doubtless his sufferings were genuine, but aggravated by fears and mental exaggerations. "I feel better when I forget about it," he confessed. This lugubrious catalogue of ills was continued four years longer before he reported, "I am on the whole better than for several winters." [23] His letters then ceased being monologues on diseases, and it was no longer necessary to spend six months at home recuperating.

During this period Sam had a tilt with Senator Nathaniel P. Tallmadge, who bolted the Democratic Party on the Bank issue and then spoke at a political meeting to win adherents for the anti-Van Buren movement. Getting wind of the gathering, Tilden rallied all the old-line, staunch Democrats to attend. In his address the Senator attempted to justify his action by asserting that the Democratic Party's principles had changed while those of himself and friends had remained constant. At the close of his speech a Whig leader moved that the Democrats be permitted to reply. Young members from the rear of the hall called for Sam Tilden as spokesman. Mounting the platform, he contested the charge of inconsistency, defended his party, and then cleverly built up the hypothesis that if Senator Tallmadge's principles had remained unchanged, the Whigs must have altered their traditional beliefs in order to find the Senator congenial political company. Finally he turned with courteous reference to Mr. Gilbert, a man of eighty, chairman of the meeting, and said, "Since Senator Tallmadge remains unchanged, I assume it is you, sir, who have changed your views." The venerable farmer gave his "No" in a loud, determined voice which aroused laughter, and marked the turning point of the meeting. Playing on this unguarded confession of his old neighbor, the young debater proceeded to demolish the plausible structure which the preceding speaker had erected. Elam, delighted at Sam's performance, sent a full account of the affair to Silas Wright, who thanked Sam for "rebuking a traitor in the midst of his assembled friends" and commended this method of dealing with the "lying spirits throughout the State." [24] The youthful speaker was invited to make other addresses in the county.

Proof that Tilden's influence extended to Albany is shown by a pamphlet of his opposing the Shakers' request to the legislature for a special exemption from the law of trusts.[25] Knowing them well, he felt that they were amply protected by the law covering religious corporations and that a special law would affect the descent of property and be "inconsistent with the fundamental principles of our institutions." He gave Bryant a copy of the brochure and the next day was gratified to see the *Evening Post* support his arguments. The bill was defeated.[26]

No longer an irresponsible youth, Sam began to assume an attitude of authority toward affairs at home. His eighteen-year-old sister, Hetty, had fallen in love with a man whom she had come to distrust. Sam, as the sober elder brother, was given her confidence, and from New York wrote her a long treatise on love, courtship and marriage, so complete that one might conclude that he himself had the fullest experience of such matters.[27]

There is something pathetic in the spectacle of the grave brother attempting through the chill medium of logic, stilted in expression, to comfort his sister. He commended her decision to end the affair, and after drawing a gloomy description of a marriage made unhappy by jealousy and distrust, proceeded to portray the "life infinitely worse than death" which might be expected to result from an unfortunate union. There followed explicit stage directions for the jilting: "Treat him, then, politely, but indifferently; in your manners be circumspect, slightly reserved and distant, yet not markedly so. . . . Say that you

---

[24] *Life*, I, 76.   [25] *Writings*, I, 89.   [26] *Life*, I, 79.
[27] Tilden Papers, June 5, 1839.

have recently become *convinced that his habits are such that you could not be happy with him.* . . . Should he be offended . . . and demand to know your evidence, you must reply that *a lady can never know with certainty the truth of such things . . . that your opinion is fully made up, and upon evidence as satisfactory as you could hope to obtain."* [28] This disquisition seems to have been comforting to the distracted girl.

Turning detective, Sam reported a few weeks later that the man was vicious and "foremost among the dissolute." [29] Still later he admonished her that true affection should be "approved by the judgment" and that love was "an illusion of the fancy" found in poetry and novels. To console her, he sent her a fine ring. But lovelorn Hetty fell seriously ill, and before the end of the year she died of "congestion of the brain." Elam bore the shock with Calvinistic fortitude.[30]

This wretched experience tapped a reservoir of sentiment in Sam of which he was scarcely conscious, and bound him more closely to his family, if that were possible. When an officious relative reminded him that his parents were aged and decrepit, and that his father particularly was in a bad way, Sam in a burst of affection, wrote Elam: "You could do nothing, my dear father, so valuable in every sense to us all, as to preserve yourself for us as long as possible. For our sakes, then, let that object control everything that is inconsistent with it." For once he forgot about home-used drugs and besought his father to seek the best possible medical advice, to avoid overexertion, and "to submit to the inevitable" limitations of old age. It is apparent that Sam was maturing emotionally as well as mentally; and he even admitted now and then that he was homesick.[31]

In this softer mood he began to feel troubled about his cousin Julia Barnes, for whom he had an affectionate regard. He dreaded to see her grow up in "the social slavery" of a boarding house life "opposed to every good habit and in favor of every bad habit." He was deeply distressed over "a disease so full of terror" which he suspected was fastening itself on Julia. That he saw no remedy for the situation was gall to his soul.[32] This incident is evidence of a growing sense of social responsibility.

The immediate goal of Sam's labors—admission to the bar—was now in sight, but there was a matter of infinitely more importance to claim

---

[28] *Letters,* I, 5; *Life,* I, 80.　　　　[29] Tilden Papers; *Life,* I, 84.
[30] *Ib.,* July 21, 1839.　　　　[31] *Ib.,* June 17, 1839; *Life,* I, 84.
[32] *Letters,* I, 6, to Hetty, July 15, 1839.

his attention. His friend, President Martin Van Buren, on May 4, 1840, was renominated. From that day until the election six months later Sam threw himself body and soul into the contest for his hero's vindication. Except for a few weeks in October, and an occasional visit, he did not go home, but remained on the firing line in the city. So busy was he that only short notes were sent to New Lebanon. The time between letters lengthened until Elam wrote, "Your letter of the 6th, altered to the 18th, came yesterday, the 29th," and filled several sheets with political questions. The time had come, Sam felt, when he must assert his independence even of his father, so he announced that he would write ordinarily once a fortnight. Even that promise was not kept, for Elam soon complained, "No word of you for a month." Here is unmistakable evidence that Sam Tilden had grown to manhood and felt competent to manage his own affairs. One of his tasks was the preparation of a biographical sketch of Van Buren for the approaching campaign.[33]

The Whigs selected William Henry Harrison and charged the blame for financial disorder and low wages against the Subtreasury Bill which Silas Wright had sponsored and which Van Buren signed July 4, 1840. It was apparent to Sam that a tremendous effort would be made by the Whigs to win the farmers and laboring classes. His opening gun was an article on "Plans for the Election of 1840."

At New Lebanon on October 3, 1840, Sam delivered an address on "Prices, Currency, and Wages," to refute the extravagantly alarming Whig statements concerning the national situation.[34] Later this speech was amplified and distributed by the Albany Democratic Committee as a campaign pamphlet. It was a sound study of finance and economics in both Europe and America, and presaged the able messages which Governor Tilden sent to the legislature thirty-five years later. But it is questionable whether it exerted any considerable influence on the voters who, in 1840 as today, cared more for fireworks than figures. It did increase Sam's prestige, however, for Condy Raguet, the prominent Philadelphia economist, called it a "most masterly production" and sent a copy to a friend in England.[35] William M. Gouge, who had written a "Whiggish" book on banking, requested copies to send to Henry Lee of Boston and to other "gentlemen who know how to appreciate the worth of sound doctrine sent forth in clear and intelligible language." [36]

[33] Tilden Papers.   [34] *Writings*, I, 103.   [35] *Life*, I, 93, Dec. 31, 1840.
[36] *Ib.* Lee was candidate of the Nullifiers for Vice President.

Senator John M. Niles of Connecticut said it was worth more than all the speeches Webster made on the currency question.[37]

Van Buren's defeat by 60 electoral votes to Harrison's 234 was due to the Subtreasury system and the hard times. The Whigs caught the popular fancy with the log cabin, hard cider and raccoon. Van Buren's dinners, with cut glass and fancy china, and his social levees were set forth as undemocratic; the popular tide against him could not be stemmed, and by November discerning Democrats saw certain defeat. All the Tildens felt the result of the election grievously. Sam wrote "How the Political Results of 1840 Were Effected," and also replied in the *Columbian Republican* to a newspaper article by a Berkshire manufacturer.[38] When the ex-President, on his way to Lindenwald, stopped in New York on March 23, 1841, Sam had the satisfaction of talking over with him the causes of defeat.[39]

Although Sam had let his studies languish while he participated in a political contest, yet he completed his law course. He expected to take his bar examination in the fall, but postponed it until the January, 1841, term of court. Elam was displeased with this procrastination, and "Uncle John," to save legal fees, deferred a contemplated lawsuit. The January term passed and still Sam delayed. These delays increased his nervousness about the ordeal and he was "disturbed by gloomy forebodings" of a lack of ability to succeed in his profession. As a shorter road to a competent income he seriously considered taking a position in business. To his father he wrote, "I have often been disheartened as to the prospect of being able to *depend* upon my profession for support," because in law "personal effort is literally everything; and health, which might not very materially disable in other vocations, might almost incapacitate from its practice." Robust health would be "a large capital" for him, and to possess it he "would be willing to start in life naked." He had no intention of abandoning his profession "without an experiment," but thought that he might find some other work so that meanwhile he would not feel so uneasy about "an absolute dependence" on success at law. And once during this anxious period he declared in despair that he cared little about his future and thought he ought to have some outdoor calling.[40]

These moods faded, however, and at the May term of the Supreme

[37] *Letters*, I, 6, Dec. 12, 1840. [38] Tilden Papers. Copy preserved.
[39] Hone, *Diary*, II, 533. [40] *Life*, I, 95, Feb. 23, 1841.

Court in New York he passed the examination and was admitted to the bar along with William M. Evarts, his Yale classmate. He squared his thin shoulders, rented a part of Edmunds' office, hung out his shingle, and was ready for a new chapter in his life. His business card read:

SAMUEL J. TILDEN
ATTORNEY AND SOLICITOR
No. 13 PINE STREET
NEW YORK

To the day of his death Tilden preserved the parchment certificate of his admission to the bar. In his own hand he wrote on the back, characteristically, the fees for license to practice in the various courts, as one of the 2,390 lawyers in New York.[41] In 1845 he was authorized to practice in the Superior Court of the State and the following year Chancellor Carroll admitted him to conduct legal business in the Court of Chancery. Then followed the certificate that, on motion of Henry D. Gilpin, he was "duly admitted and qualified as an Attorney . . . of the Supreme Court of the United States." Thus six years after he hung out his shingle, he was eligible to practice in the highest court of the land.[42]

While still a student, Sam had begun collecting a legal library, together with works on economics and finance. He bought in 1839 the last edition of the *New Statutes,* for $8—"worth $12"—and some volumes from David Graham's library.[43] In 1840 he heard of a sale of English law books which he wanted to buy "if cheap." The next year at an auction he purchased *Digests* for $20.[44] He secured in 1842, "at a very low price," 61 volumes of *New York State Reports,* and spoke of spending $200. When he asked Elam to "spare him" $100 to pay for legal works, the latter objected to such extravagance.[45] The young lawyer had the acquisitive instinct of the collector, which developed until at his death he had accumulated one of the largest private libraries in America, and which induced him to leave his vast fortune for the establishment of a great public library. Not only did he subscribe for newspapers and periodicals,[46] but he was also a paying member of the New York Society Library, the Mercantile Library Association, and several other such institutions. In 1842 he was elected to the New York Law Institute

[41] Tilden Papers. [42] *Ib.,* Feb. 12, 1847. [43] *Ib.,* Dec. 9, 1839.
[44] *Ib.,* Jan. 5, 1841. [45] *Life,* I, 99.
[46] *Lady's Book; United States Magazine; Democratic Review,* etc.

and paid his fee of $20 for the privilege of using its books and attending its lectures.[47] Here is evidence of an intellectual interest much wider than the field of law.

Now that Tilden was a regular attorney, his father continually urged him to collect delinquent bills and notes and to handle family lawsuits. When Elam discovered that a tenant had cut off some of the timber, he asked Sam to bring suit for $500 damages. Sam boasted that he was getting Uncle Ward out of a debt of $1,500. His *Law Register* contained the following items for 1841: "Nov. tried one case non-suit $5. Dec. 1 Brownings v. D. P. Gilbert $8. Dec. Hill v. Hall $10. Henry Dana Ward v. W. Makepiece $12.50." [48] In 1842 half a dozen cases were recorded, one involving $17,000, and $1 was received for drawing a will. Martin Van Buren used him for all sorts of commissions in the metropolis, and when Sam displayed absent-mindedness, Van Buren wrote, "I trouble you again by way of revenge." [49]

The young attorney had hardly time to hang his shingle before he felt impelled to ride full tilt against the victorious Whigs who were agitating the recharter of the United States Bank and the presentation to that institution of a charter which Congress would be powerless to revoke. Sam, who perhaps should have been scurrying for clients, dropped all other matters for the preparation of an article entitled, "Is the United States Bank Charter Repealable?" This essay was published in the *Democratic Review* of Washington in August, 1841.[50] It was a sound legal brief. Congress refused to grant the Bank a new charter. The Whigs made one last effort, which took the form of a modified proposal for the establishment of a "Fiscal Bank," but this effort was frustrated by President Tyler's vetoes. Sam, who wrote a criticism of Ewing's Bank Bill, praised Tyler for these vetoes, but otherwise refused to support him, unless the Whigs should seek "to intimidate him to a surrender of his constitutional authorities." He never "regarded Tyler as a man of high capacity." [51]

Sam spoke at a public meeting held in New York to oppose a coercive bankrupt law,[52] and published in the *Evening Post* an exposure of the illegal voting in the recent Presidential election, which was charged to Edward Curtis, Collector of the Port. These articles, written in collabo-

[47] Tilden Papers, Jan. 5, 1841.   [48] *Ib.* This *Register* ran from May 17, 1841 to 1859.
[49] *Letters,* I, 12; Tilden Papers, Oct. 29, 1842.
[50] *Writings,* I, 165; *Life,* I, 97—this number was sold out immediately; Tilden Papers.
[51] Tilden Papers, June 25, 1841.   [52] *Life,* I, 98.

ration with Bryant, "made a great sensation" and annoyed the Whigs "amazingly." The frauds were executed by James B. Glentworth, an "adventurer," and the letters when printed were called the "Glentworth Pamphlet." [53] This controversy is worthy of note because it marks Tilden's first venture in the correction of political evils. Sam told Silas Wright all about it when the latter stopped in New York.[54]

These public appearances in person and in print were winning Sam a certain amount of prominence, but his shrewd Yankee father was impatient for the time when this prestige would be converted into substantial earnings. He felt that Sam should be devoting himself to a paying clientele, and expressed fear that he was meddling in politics to the neglect of his law business.[55] The young man replied brazenly, "I have nothing to do with politics and meddle no more than is compatible with, if not conducive to, professional success." Elam was not convinced. He knew too well the family failing for hiding cold facts beneath elaborate phraseology, and asked point-blank whether Sam was "getting any business." Sam replied, on February 7, 1842, "I expect $15 or $20 this week from my professional earnings, though I have to advance for costs and have expenses to pay incident to commencing in business." Shortly afterward he announced that he was moving to a new office and "might need a little more help, but will do with as little as I can." [56] More prosperous days were ahead. His sister Mary, who was in New York, soon informed her mother that Samuel was so busy with his law work that she seldom saw him.[57]

The five-year period of Tilden's life covered in this chapter was formative in character, habits, and outlook. The attainment of a professional goal, a source of self-satisfaction in itself, pointed toward economic independence. Widened social contacts were bringing their rewards. As a judge of essays at the Albany Female Academy, he was asked to present the prizes.[58] He was invited to meet the Governor and a few friends.[59] Young law students sought his advice,[60] and earlier friends were eager to continue their acquaintance with him. However, the keenest gratification came from increased opportunities for party service. It was a great asset to have such prominent political friends as Martin Van Buren and Silas Wright; to be associated with men like Flagg, Corning, Dix, Cagger and Van Dyck, members of the State Democratic

53 *Life*, I, 98.　　54 *Letters*, I, 9.　　55 Tilden Papers, Feb. 7, 1842.
56 *Life*, I, 101.　　57 Tilden Papers.　　58 *Ib.*, letter of A. Crittendon.
59 *Ib.*, J. W. Edwards, July 5, 1841.　　60 *Ib.*, P. M. Hitchcock, Jan. 1, 1841.

Committee, and to help prepare party literature.[61] To serve as secretary of the "Repeal Committee" was valuable experience. In the campaign for the election of Bouck for Governor, he was chairman of the Democratic-Republican Young Men's General Committee in New York City, which met at Tammany Hall, arranged mass meetings, and sent out publicity to denounce "Whig ascendancy" and to win support for Democratic policies and candidates.[62] The landslide that sent Bouck to the Executive Mansion and gave him a sympathetic legislature brought Tilden intense satisfaction and the feeling that he, too, might look for some party reward.

But just as Sam's course was directed steadily toward a future of bright promises, he suffered the greatest sorrow of his life—the death of his father on April 10, 1842, at the age of sixty-one.[63] Elam had been afflicted with real and imaginary ills all his life, but in the latter years these assumed a more sinister aspect. "I'm purty nearly worked out," he wrote Sam, and later remarked, "I feel as if I had done about enough for one life." [64] His obstinate allegiance to freak cures probably shortened his life. Only three letters of condolence have survived. Edmunds was "inexpressively shocked" at the news [65] and Sam's friend Sherman, who loved Elam as a father, knew that his death would be "a stunning blow to you." [66] Not a line revealing the effect of this tragedy on Sam has been preserved—it was one time in his life when he was incapable of producing any studied composition, when language must have seemed futile and hollow.

Elam had been the close friend and confidant of his son in all the details of his life. Their letters were long exchanged two and three times a week, and the father's thoughts help to explain the son's intellectual growth. Elam was a man with a modern mind—open, frank and honest. In religion and politics he was fearless and progressive. Gifted with wisdom and good sense, he had an intelligent grasp of local and national politics, yet never sought office higher than that of postmaster. He was a typical Yankee, shrewd, adventurous where there was a prospect of making an honest dollar, and with a dry humor. On one occasion Elam wrote Sam that he put St. Croix rum on a sore finger to see whether it was a temperance or anti-temperance sore and dryly remarked, "It was

[61] Tilden Papers, circular of Oct. 1, 1841.
[62] Ib., circular letter with Tilden's name among others.
[63] Life, I, 101.   [64] Tilden Papers, Dec. 14, 1839; Feb. 24, 1842.
[65] Ib., Apr. 17, 1842.   [66] Ib., Aug. 12, 1842.

the latter." When Aaron Gilbert, an employee, falsified the books, Elam complained that he was a "notorious liar" and reminded him of an incident in the Revolution. In a hospital camp the men who passed through the camp calling for the dead to be brought out were dubbed "The Black Cat." Upon one occasion "The Black Cat" was told that a victim might be found in a certain tent. Going in to get the corpse, "The Black Cat" soon came out saying, "Why, that soldier says he isn't dead." "Well," replied the informer, "that man lies so damned much that I didn't know whether to believe him or not."

Elam was the father of his son in the fullest sense of that relationship. He encouraged Sam's predisposition to politics; indeed it might be said that he created it. Revering the traditions of the Old Democracy, he imparted them to his son in their pristine virility. His sturdy honesty recommended him to the leaders of the Democracy and enabled him to bring his son to the notice of those of his party in power. He led Sam to the threshold of his career well prepared to meet its exigencies. The threshold of that career opened on a vista of the New Democracy.

TILDEN'S more and more frequent public appearances at Democratic functions, serving for instance as vice president at a Tammany meeting,[1] were outward manifestations of his increasing prestige in the inner circle of the party. A letter to his brother Moses reveals the trusted party worker engaged in the delicate task of distributing patronage. The number of applicants for party jobs was "without any parallel because of the large number of places vacant." The business depression swelled the ranks of the unemployed and many saw in political jobs their only hope of a living wage. The desperate pleas of this class did anything but lighten the task of the young attorney.[2] His position was a tribute to his finesse.

Tilden was himself a candidate for public office in the spring of 1843, with the strong backing of party leaders. In seeking the office of Corporation Counsel of New York City he did not, however, depend upon past laurels to carry him into office. He became extraordinarily industrious in his own interest and prepared his way to preferment with the same painstaking thoroughness that later characterized the preparation of his important legal briefs. Quite apart from immediate financial return and political prominence, he saw in the office a short cut to establishment in his private practice.

Since the appointment was to be made by the Common Council, Sam's plan was to arm himself with weighty references and carry the City Fathers by assault. His first resource was to old family friends, men of substance in the New York Democracy. His legal instructor, Edmunds, responded grandly and wrote a letter characterizing him as a well-educated lawyer and a young man of "talent, discretion, and judgment." Judge Aaron Vanderpoel, another Columbia County neighbor, had known Tilden "from boyhood" and thought him exceptionally well qualified for the post.[3] Sam had also the enthusiastic backing of the General Committee of Democratic-Republican Young Men of the City and County of New York, of which body he was president. The fact that the rules governing this organization were adopted only in April

[1] Tilden Papers, Apr. 6, 1834.   [2] *Ib.*, Jan. 3, 1843.   [3] *Ib.*, Apr. 27, 1843.

lends color to the suspicion that Sam's object in organizing it may not have been entirely unselfish. A printed letter signed by eight prominent Democrats urged his appointment, while a petition was signed by eighteen members of the bar saying that his qualifications "are such that his appointment would give the highest satisfaction to the Democratic Party, the legal profession, and the public generally." Among names appended were John R. Livingston, Jr., James J. Roosevelt, Thos. R. Lee, and Lathrop S. Eddy.[4] Finally, forty-eight prominent citizens petitioned the Common Council to appoint Tilden because "his services to the Democratic Cause entitle him to the appointment." Mayor Robert H. Morris also assumed a benevolent attitude. On May 9 Sam reported to Moses that he had won the nomination by 20 out of 26 votes.[5] At the age of twenty-seven he was an official of the great city which had so stirred his imagination as he listened to the conversation of the big-wigs in the rambling old house at New Lebanon.

The "Corporation Attorney's Office Portfolio,"[6] in which Tilden preserved his letters and official papers, throws considerable light on his duties and activities. At the beginning he was besieged by seekers after subordinate positions in his department. As might be expected, too, he found his duties arduous. The office involved the handling of many complex legal problems of the great metropolis. It was an undertaking which might have taxed a seasoned lawyer, and Tilden suffered from the combined effect of inexperience and conscientiousness. After three months of service he reported that he had heard many cases against the municipality which had been dropped, acted on 500 complaints, sent out 400 notices of violations of ordinances, issued 300 processes, and interviewed innumerable persons on a bewildering variety of subjects. He tried 20 or 30 cases a week, and his office was open from nine in the morning until six in the evening and often later.[7] The *Complaint Book 1843–44* which he faithfully kept indicates that his cases were concerned with encumbrances on sidewalks, Sunday cabs, selling without license, selling liquor on Sunday, overhanging signs, "keeping more hogs than allowed by law," selling decayed oranges, driving at more than five miles an hour, casting coal ashes into the street, letting stages stand in front of private houses, using false weights, and shaking carpets in the streets.[8]

[4] *Letters,* I, 13.   [5] Tilden Papers.   [6] *Ib.*
[7] *Ib.,* Aug. 7, 1843.   [8] *Ib.*

Tilden's compensation was $2,500 per year and costs of suits in courts of record, and he estimated that after paying all expenses he still made something over $2,000 clear. But he complained that his duties were very exacting and did not enable him to "get away a day for the country."[9] As time passed he became more familiar with the routine, and reported to Moses on December 7 that "the business is not now as laborious as when you were here." He was imbued with a new confidence and Mayor Morris consulted him frequently. The youthful Corporation Counsel opened a checking account and, as a man of importance, was asked to meet President Tyler at the City Hall.[10] He was president of the Democratic-Republican Young Men, was chosen as a delegate to the Democratic National Convention at Baltimore, and took time to write a paper on "The Right of Democratic Legislators to Express their Views." His *Legal Diary* shows that he had six cases for June, was busy during the following months and appeared before the Supreme Court. His *Lawyer's Daily Journal* was blank except for a few items from January to April.[11]

In making a report to the Grand Jury, Tilden let it be known that he was a friend of the common people: "There is a class of whom the public hears little but of whom I have occasion to know something; and that is those who suffer injury and inconveniences from violations of the law and seek its protection at my hands." In all such instances he saw that justice was done.[12] Monthly reports showed receipts and expenditures of his office. His tenure in the only appointive office he ever held was short. In April, 1844, James Harper was elected Mayor by the Native Americans and the Whigs, and began promptly to make a clean sweep of all unsympathetic officeholders. Tilden's exit under these circumstances was inevitable, but he chose the more graceful form and sent his resignation to the president of the Common Council on May 25, 1844, to take effect on the day after its joint meeting.[13] He was removed from office, however, on May 31, while at the Baltimore Convention,[14] yet for several weeks he assisted his successor to familiarize himself with the office routine.

Tilden's labors as Corporation Counsel were by no means wasted, because there was crowded into that one year experience that would have come only with several years of private practice. His legal knowl-

9 Tilden Papers.   10 *Ib.*, June 12, 1843.   11 *Ib.*, Oct. 20, 1843.
12 *Ib.*, Feb. 23, 1844.   13 *Letters*, I, 16.   14 *Letters*, I, 16.

edge was increased in practical ways, he became more familiar with the procedure of the New York courts, he dealt with many of the city lawyers, and he acquired a higher standing in his profession. Not only was his promotion to office a tangible token of party recognition but his contacts with the inner workings of party machinery were multiplied. Since his duties compelled him to meet a wide variety of men, he gained more polish and poise, and the timidity of the country boy was erased. A widened acquaintance and official prominence increased his law practice —an advantage which he had anticipated. One year was sufficient, too, to bring substantial prestige, and a longer term might have been a detriment both to his legal work and to his importance in the party organization. One now finds him attending Tammany meetings, addressing party gatherings [15] and otherwise active in politics. When J. W. Edmunds wished to be appointed Surrogate of New York County, Tilden repaid his preceptor's kindness by having "nearly the whole general committee" sign a petition in his behalf. When Edmunds failed to receive this position Tilden was instrumental in having him given a better place on the Supreme Court.[16]

As the national campaign of 1844 approached, the Whigs at Baltimore nominated Henry Clay. Waiting until the Whigs had selected their standard bearer, the Democrats convened in the same city. Martin Van Buren, their outstanding candidate, and his friends were confident of his nomination. Failure to select him, Silas Wright said, would disrupt the party.[17] True enough, his letter of April 20 opposing the annexation of Texas offended the South and raised threats of another candidate, but the manifesto had been written, craftily, subsequent to the election of several Southern delegates who had been instructed to vote for him.[18]

Tilden communicated with his civic mentor about the political situation and pronounced the Texas letter a strong, wise document which would justify the confidence of the people in its author. He reported, on the word of O'Sullivan, that Bancroft had refused to acknowledge that he had shared in the authorship, and thought that a mistake. To cheer Van Buren he promised that the Southern gloom would soon "clear away." The Southerners wanted the Northerners "to carry their knapsacks" and were disappointed when they refused. "If there is danger in the South, the only thing to do is to make the better battle in the North

---

[15] Tilden Papers, invitation from the 17th ward, Mar. 8, 1844.   [16] *Ib.*
[17] Butler Papers, Wright to Butler, May 25, 1844.   [18] Donovan, *Barnburners,* 54.

—especially in New York, Pennsylvania, Ohio and Michigan." [19] Now
for the nomination! A fortnight later Tilden was confident that things
were improving; he thought the convention was safe, but it was hard to
tell "who is honest"; and there were strange rumors about the New York
delegates. "The only safe rule is to count all the chances as adverse, and
act adequately to the worst contingency." Once the nomination was
made, the situation would improve rapidly.[20]

Sam Tilden, wrote a stirring public letter to "Democrats of the
Union" [21] justifying a second term for Van Buren, and went down to
Baltimore enthusiastically certain that the powerful friend of his father
and himself would triumph. His correspondence overflowed with praise
for his political mentor. Van Buren wrote B. F. Butler that he would
"stand and let others dissolve the party if they chose. . . . Thank Mr.
Tilden for his letter and say to him that Mr. Bancroft will with pleasure
do what he suggests." [22]

Sam wrote to Moses from Baltimore that there was "excitement and
great uncertainty." North Carolina, Virginia, Georgia, Mississippi,
Louisiana, and probably Maryland and Indiana are "against us," but
New York, Ohio, New Hampshire, Vermont, Rhode Island, and Pennsylvania are "reliable." We have "a small fixed majority," [23] which was
the hope of Van Buren's friends—a hope that was dashed when the convention, controlled by the strategy of Van Buren's opponents, voted the
adoption of the two-thirds rule.

On the first ballot Van Buren received a full majority of the votes
but lacked the necessary two-thirds for the nomination. His trusted
associate, Benjamin F. Butler, who led the opposition to the two-thirds
rule, made a valiant effort; but when, after seven ballots, it became
evident that Van Buren could make no further gains, Butler, with Van
Buren's "perfect concurrence," [24] withdrew his name. On the eighth
ballot Polk was proposed as a compromise and chosen unanimously.
Silas Wright, Jr., senatorial friend of Van Buren, was nominated for
Vice President, but declined to run, saying that he did not choose "to
ride behind the black pony." Had he been asked what he thought of
Polk, Tilden might have exclaimed with Governor Letcher of Kentucky,
"Polk! Great God, what a nomination!" [25] But disappointed as he was

[19] Van Buren Papers, Tilden to Van Buren, May 4, 1844.
[20] *Ib.*, May 17, 1844.
[21] Tilden Papers.   [22] Butler Papers, May 20, 1844.   [23] *Letters*, I, 14, May 27, 1844.
[24] Butler Papers, Van Buren to Butler, Feb. 4, 1845.   [25] Alexander, II, 73.

at Van Buren's defeat, he put party loyalty above personal feelings.

New York was the battle ground of the campaign. The Democrats needed the State to win the national election and victory was jeopardized by the split into Radicals and Conservatives. Senator Silas Wright, Jr., seemed to be the only man who could unite the two factions, and he was reluctant to run for Governor.[26] Yielding finally to the importunities of Van Buren, Tilden chiefly, and other close friends, he was nominated, and carried the State by a plurality of 10,033 against Fillmore.[27] With his help Polk led Clay by a little over 5,000 votes. "What a shameful election!" was Van Buren's comment.[28] But the Democrats retained control of New York State, and had saved Polk as well.

Tilden had nothing to do with Polk's nomination but he helped to persuade Wright to save the day [29] and his efforts were unremitting for a Democratic triumph. Long before any nominations were made, he had sagaciously conceived the idea of establishing a newspaper as a Democratic publicity organ. In New York there was not a single Democratic newspaper of "influence or repute." The Albany *Argus* had lost its leadership, and Bryant's *Evening Post* "had never been looked to for party lead." Keenly feeling this serious deficiency, he consulted leading Democrats. In April, 1844, he went to Washington to discuss the project with Senator Wright, and found a sympathetic ear.[30]

Both Tilden and Wright expected to use the paper to elect Van Buren, for on April 11 Wright wrote Tilden that he was convinced of the "importance of such a paper for our cause" and suggested that publication begin "with the nominations." Western friends were ready to help. He advised Tilden to take Van Buren's counsel "about the whole matter" and wrote to the ex-President at once,[31] "Mr. Tilden will visit you in a few days to consult about establishing a cheap paper in New York." [32] That conference soon followed, and Tilden reported on April 25 that Van Buren "was anxious to have it undertaken" and tendered some aid.[33] Five days later Wright cautioned Tilden not to become pecuniarily involved in the venture and complimented his plan for a "minute organization."

The establishment of this party news organ was Tilden's first opportunity to test his capacity as an organizer and promoter. Character-

[26] *Life*, I, 102, Wright to Elam Tilden, July 3, 1840.
[27] *Ib.*, 109.   [28] Butler Papers, Nov. 17, 1844.   [29] *Writings*, I, 16.
[30] *Ib.*, 20.   [31] *Ib.*, 21, Apr. 11, 1844.   [32] Van Buren Papers.
[33] Tilden Papers; *Writings*, I, 19.

istically the details were worked out in his own mind before he submitted them for approval to Wright and Van Buren. His plan was to raise $5,000 by selling subscription shares to prominent and well-to-do Democrats.[34] An edition of 25,000 copies was to be distributed to the subscribers, presumably according to the shares held, to be sold at or below cost in every part of the land. With a working capital of $5,000 Tilden thought it possible to publish an edition as high as 125,000 copies.[35]

The next practical step was to arrange for editors and a capable business manager. Tilden assumed the rôle of editor in chief and associated with himself his long-time party friend, John L. O'Sullivan. John Bigelow was to edit reviews, the drama and the opera.[36] On the staff were H. G. Langley, N. J. Waterbury, Clement Guion and O'Sullivan's brother. In May, Tilden, confident of an early start, asked Senator Wright whether he could send Government franks to New York for mailing out the paper. Unable to do that, Wright agreed to take charge of the distribution from Washington.[37] Wright's recent speech was to go into the first issue, and other articles were contributed later.

Van Buren's defeat at Baltimore chilled Tilden's ardor for a Democratic publicity organ for a few months. Probably confident that Wright would run for Governor and knowing that Van Buren was supporting Polk, Tilden went ahead with the project. A contract was drawn up with O'Sullivan, by which he was to be an equal partner with Tilden, each drawing out of profits $30 a week for editorial work.[38] If either wished to withdraw, the other might purchase his interest. In case of failure or both wishing to give up the enterprise, the assets were to be vested in trust for the Democratic Party. It appears that a capital of $7,000 was on hand for the venture.[39]

Tilden and O'Sullivan were not ill-mated for the task to which they had set themselves. Sam had been a political writer almost since childhood. He had written a great deal for newspapers, was one of the best informed men of the day on political matters, and had assisted Bryant in editing the *Evening Post* for several months in 1843. Besides his editorial equipment, Sam's standing in the party and his close association with the leaders were calculated to lend a note of authority to his utterances. Despite his high editorial talent it was doubtless his identifica-

---

[34] Letters, I, 20, Apr. 11, 1844.   [35] *Ib.*, 19, Apr. 25, 1844.   [36] *Retrospections*, I, 65.
[37] *Letters*, I, 15, May 10, 1844.   [38] *Ib.*, 17, July 13, 1844.   [39] Tilden Papers.

tion with the controlling element of the party that was his most valuable contribution to the *Daily New York Morning News*. His close association with the sheet was equivalent to the slogan "Democratic papers please copy."

O'Sullivan, the perfect foil to Tilden, supplied the qualifications which Tilden lacked to win friends and popularity for the new paper. He was an accomplished scholar, a witty writer, and an extremely sociable man. He was something of a visionary and matched the industry of his colleague with a laziness which, while it detracted little from the attractiveness of his personality, handicapped him effectively as a man of practical affairs. He had had experience in editing the *Democratic Review* at Washington and in New York, 1837–46, and so brought to the new enterprise an experience of technicalities. It appears that Tilden, O'Sullivan, and H. G. Langley supplied some of the capital to start the paper,[40] but the proportion of their contributions is unknown.

The first issue appeared on August 21, 1844. It was conducted with "so much vigor and enterprise" that the success of the Democratic ticket in New York was commonly attributed to its publicity. Tilden's objectives in founding the paper were realized; the Democrats were sufficiently united to elect Silas Wright Governor and, by carrying New York State, to elect Polk President. Polk was deeply indebted to the New York Democrats. It was an obligation which he could not fail to recognize, and it was not until later that the deluded New Yorkers were to discover that the recognition was to be given only a specious acknowledgment.

It was characteristic of Tilden that, having accomplished a set objective, he lost interest in it and turned to fresher considerations. So it was in this instance. He had no intention of becoming an editor and, when the *News* had served its purpose in the campaign, he presented his interest to O'Sullivan and Langley and withdrew.[41] It is not improbable that he was shrewd enough to realize that, however useful the *News* might be politically, it could not be a financial success. By the end of its first year, it had absorbed $15,000 and was weakening. N. J. Waterbury, who had joined the venture in the beginning, told Tilden that the paper must have city advertising to survive. He wrote to Governor Wright that "Tilden, a young lawyer, indissolubly wedded to a public life . . . was . . . obstinately blind to the truth which all his

[40] Tilden Papers.　　　　　[41] *Letters,* I, 47.

friends could not but realize. With certain powers calculated to make him one of the most successful in legal *argument*, other attributes are wanting to make those powers practically effective. It was . . . an experiment to push off from the law on an uncertain voyage as an editor. Yet when he decided on it, he should have taken the helm boldly; but, instead, he kept watching the prospect from the cabin-door, and in a few months withdrew; he did either himself or the paper very little good." [42] Clement Guion, business manager, wrote Tilden on September 8, 1846, "The long agony is over—the *Morning News* is dead—dead!" [43]

After the retirement of Van Buren, the election of Silas Wright, Jr., as Governor, made him the head of the Democratic Party in New York, and, in the eyes of his friends, the logical successor to President Polk in 1848. But his hostility to the extension of slave territory by the annexation of Texas arrayed the Southern Democrats against him and widened the breach between the party factions in his own State. By all standards of common courtesy, Wright was the logical man to be consulted about the distribution of New York patronage, but Polk, safely ensconced in the Presidential chair and liking the feel of it, was guided in his policy of appointments by political expediency.

He started in the right direction by asking Van Buren to suggest a New Yorker for his Cabinet. Van Buren, after consulting with Wright, suggested that Benjamin F. Butler, as Secretary of State, or Azariah C. Flagg, as Secretary of the Treasury, would be acceptable. [44] Meanwhile Polk, lending his ear to schemers, repented his impetuous honesty and squirmed uncomfortably in the predicament in which he had placed himself. At this juncture he was succored by the veteran Edwin Croswell, publisher of the Albany *Argus* and scarred centurion of the New York Democracy, who pointed out the tortuous means of escape. Following the advice of the wily Croswell, Polk offered the Treasury Department to Silas Wright, [45] who had declared repeatedly during his campaign that if elected Governor he would not take a place in the Cabinet; hence he declined the appointment. The plot continued its oily course with the offer of the War Department to Butler [46] who, having been Attorney General under Jackson and Van Buren, refused to take a secondary place among Polk's advisers.

[42] Tilden Papers, Aug. 30, 1846.   [43] *Letters*, I, 46.   [44] Donovan, *Barnburners*, 62.
[45] Gillet, *Life and Times of Silas Wright*, I, 1630.   [46] Feb. 25, 1845.

Instead of writing to Polk, Butler sent Tilden to Washington with written instructions. He had a frank conference with Polk for more than an hour and wrote a full account of it to Butler. He reported that Polk wanted a strong Cabinet free from Presidential candidates and was sorry Butler refused the position tendered. Much as he wanted Butler, Tilden did not believe he would recast his Cabinet to get him. A substitute for Butler was impliedly left to Wright and Van Buren. Tilden found in the Capital "strong resistance if not denunciation" to the New York Softs and feared these opponents might select a man to take Butler's place; hence he urged Butler to hurry to Washington to have the right man selected.[47] Tilden remained over for a second conference with Polk about New York patronage. Acting as the spokesman of a group of New Yorkers who accompanied him, he made it clear to Polk that appointments must have the endorsement of Wright and Van Buren. The President, "convinced" that his early appointments were a mistake, said they were due to bad counsel and assured the Softs that they need have no fear of the influence of their opponents. But Tilden had "more fears than hopes," because Polk, though honest, was "weak as dishwater." [48] The only staunch friend the Softs had was George Bancroft, but how could he "stand up against all the others?" [49] Nothing demonstrates better than this mission the trusted place Tilden had won at the age of thirty in that wing of the party to which he adhered.

Finding himself with a free hand, Polk tendered the War portfolio to William L. Marcy,[50] a leader of the New York Conservatives who controlled the legislature and, with Marcy's help, the Federal patronage. This was a stunning blow to the Radicals with whom Wright was more closely identified. Thus there emerged in the Empire State two Democratic leaders—Governor Wright in Albany and Marcy with Polk back of him at Washington; two Democratic parties—the "Hardshells" or "Hunkers" under Marcy's banner, and the "Softshells" or "Barnburners" who followed Wright; and two attitudes toward slavery—one favoring and the other opposing the expansion of slavery into territories where hitherto it had not existed. Thus Albany was arrayed against Washington, and the logic of leadership forced Wright to succeed himself in 1846 and to reach the White House in 1848; and Marcy either to defeat Wright or face political annihilation. Marcy and Polk sought

---

47 Butler Papers, Mar. 1, 1845.
49 *Ib.*, 24, 26.
48 *Letters*, I, 28, Mar. 8, 1845.
50 Polk to Van Buren, Mar. 1, 1845.

to seduce Tilden from his loyalty to Wright by offering him the naval office in New York with emoluments of $20,000 a year—a post scarcely an impediment to a struggling young attorney. He refused the tempting bait, however, because upon his admission to the bar he resolved to accept no office merely for its income—it must be either a post of honor or connected with his profession.[51]

Although Sam had an abundance of legal matters to occupy his time, he supported his colleagues who were seeking to influence Polk and Marcy in their distribution of minor patronage. He wrote a letter, intended for Marcy, protesting the appointment of Cornelius P. Van Ness as Collector of the Port of New York and stigmatizing him as a man untrue to President Polk, "an intriguing little politician in control of a small faction of Tyler Democrats, and in no sense the representatives of 19/20ths of the party." [52] Marcy's attitude was uncertain, however, and Tilden felt that the administration was "captured by the quasi-Van Buren men who went with us before Baltimore but deserted us there." [53] Polk, alas, was a slender reed, sorely buffeted and bent by the cross winds of the New York tempest. He sensed keenly the indignity of being the successful "dark horse," the first of the species to occupy the White House, and could not of course derive any moral support by foreseeing the long and dismal list of successors who were destined to share his hue.

In May, 1845, Sam was again in Washington attending the President's levee, for the matter of the New York collectorship was not yet settled.[54] He wrote to O'Sullivan that he had an appointment to see the President the following day.[55] His task was one of extreme delicacy, for Polk's sensitiveness about his position had not been at all assuaged. He had all of the vain weak man's dread of an exhibition of his weakness and he was quick to resent advice in which a suggestion of his own inadequacy was implicit. Tilden's object in the interview was to press for the removal of Van Ness and the appointment of Jonathan I. Coddington in his place. Sam, who had ventured while still a sophomore in college to send advice to President Jackson, undertook his delicate task with unshaken aplomb. He felt sure that he knew his man well enough to avoid serious mistakes in tactics. His opinion of Polk is well summed up in the following amusing account:

[51] *Life*, I, 110.   [52] *Letters*, I, 24.   [53] *Ib.*, Tilden to Havemeyer, Mar. 4, 1845.
[54] Tilden Papers.   [55] *Letters*, I, 33, May 31, 1845.

"He complained bitterly of the attempts to intimidate and coerce him—talking magnificently about being himself President and the *locum tenens* for nobody; said that in his own time . . . Van Ness should be removed, but swore with that terrible oath, 'if the heavens and earth come together' . . . he would not appoint Coddington. He should select a man, he said, who would be received with applause throughout the State. . . . Probably the question may now be deemed settled; for you remember he employed the same planetary concussion to illustrate the fixed irrevocable fate by which Marcy was to represent New York in the Cabinet. His solemn form of fiat . . . is undoubtedly of an improved quality of imaginary thunder. Still it did not shake my nerves as a lady's displeasure might." [56]

When Tilden's own name was mentioned "in highly respectable quarters" for the collectorship of New York, he announced that he did not consider himself an applicant, but would "seek advice." [57] It seems that his friend O'Sullivan, with the best intentions, embarrassed Tilden by urging his appointment.

After his father's death Tilden's relations with his family were not so intimate as earlier and his trips home infrequent. Like a dutiful unmarried son he wrote short letters to his mother at irregular intervals to prevent her from "keeping awake" with worry. Her replies were full of maternal solicitude about his health and his wardrobe. His sister, Mary B. Pelton, when not with him in New York, sent affectionate letters inquiring about his comfort, his activities and his shirts; and even "Little Willie," her son, childishly printed a letter to "My Dear Uncle." [58] Moses and Henry penned notes about home affairs and business matters.

So greatly had Tilden's physical condition improved that there are few references in his letters to ailments and these of an insignificant character. The period of running errands for Mrs. Barnes and of selling thermometers had passed. He had become a lawyer of some prominence, a man of affairs, and a shrewd, useful party leader. His correspondence had attained such a volume that several stenographers, had they been available, could have been kept busy. But he was not even blessed with a fountain pen to lighten his labors.

[56] *Letters*, 35.   [57] *Ib.*, 29, Mar. 29, 1845.   [58] Tilden Papers, Apr. 8, 1844.

SILAS WRIGHT was inaugurated Governor on January 1, 1845. His election had been a personal triumph and had saved the Presidency for the Democrats. He brought to the unsought Governorship a reputation for native ability and able statesmanship. The Assembly had a Democratic cast. But actually Wright's position was far from enviable, and despite his victory he was a disappointed man. He had asked nothing better than to be sustained in his senatorial seat. His was an open nature, with enough ambition to make him seek eminence but governed by a sensitive modesty which shrank from pre-eminence. He resigned himself to the rôle for which his partisans cast him and derived only a wistful satisfaction from his success at the polls, which he seems to have accepted as a foretaste of the doom awaiting him. His fundamental kindliness unfitted him for the place, and this unfitness, so obvious today, must have been recognized by his colleagues. It is possible that they saw his inevitable political ruin and still failed to realize that in ruining the politician they were breaking the man.

The Hards and Softs came to grips over the election of a Speaker. The Softs supported William C. Crain against the adroit and polished Horatio Seymour, who won by a vote of 35 to 30.[1] Wright, favoring Crain, was humiliated by the defeat of his friends. In the election of United States Senators, the Softs favored John A. Dix and Michael Hoffman while Daniel S. Dickinson and Henry A. Foster were candidates of the Hards.[2] The situation was critical, for it was apparent that President Polk would present the laurel of Cabinet preferment to the victors. The Softs' strategy was successful; Dix was selected to fill Wright's unexpired four years and Dickinson was named to Tallmadge's remaining month. When the Softs then clamored for adjournment, their demand was blocked; and, under the lashing of Edwin Croswell and the beguilement of Seymour, the Hards secured for Dickinson the new senatorial term of six years. Following this defeat, the sorely tried Softs were still further bruised by Polk's duplicity, which culminated in his naming Marcy to the Cabinet.[3]

[1] Alexander, *Pol. Hist.*, II, 92.   [2] *Ib.*, 93.
[3] *Letters,* I, 37, to Charles P. Brown, Oct. 13, 1845.

In the fall of 1845 Tilden learned that his name was to be presented to the Democratic Convention for election to the Assembly. He thought that he had made his "strong repugnance to any nomination this fall so clear that there could be no misapprehension" as to his position. If the situation were one of "peculiar or unusual importance" to the party, he would render any service within his power. But, as it was a period of "political calm," he felt that he should devote his attention to his "professional and private business"; therefore he tried to decline the nomination. But Silas Wright at Albany, finding the Governor's seat only slightly more comfortable than a griddle, was in no position to discern that "political calm" of which Sam wrote so glibly. Feeling his career as a statesman in jeopardy, he must have loyal men; hence at his instance Tilden entered the fray, certain of election but expecting some of the foes of Van Buren and Wright—"the Tyler rowdies"—to scratch his name. On the list of thirteen Assemblymen certified in New York County, his name was third.[4] Thirty years later Tilden said, "In 1846 I went to the Assembly for a special object—to help Mr. Wright in a crisis of his administration."

Before going to Albany he made a business arrangement with Andrew H. Green, a young attorney with whom he had been intimate since 1842, who now moved into Tilden's office to look after legal affairs.[5] The two were destined to become lifelong friends. Of New England stock and yeoman origin, both became permanent residents of New York City. Absorbed in politics but caring little for office, both fought to improve local government and to elevate the moral standard of the Democratic Party. Both were successful business men and accumulated wealth as partners in various enterprises. Both were unmarried and bequeathed their accumulations for worthy projects in the metropolis. Green outlived Tilden and was one of the executors of his will. Another friend of these days was John Bigelow.

Even at this early date Tilden was not a favorite in Tammany Hall. Andrew H. Green, on October 31, 1845, recorded in his journal that at a "rowdy meeting of Tammany Hall last night . . . it was moved that my friend Tilden be stricken from the Assembly ticket. This was an operation of a loafer crew." Green set to work to counteract this effort of "the spawn of Tammany" and was gratified to find that, while Tilden ran 250

---

[4] *Letters*, I, 38, Nov. 4, 1845.
[5] Foord, *Green*, 28, Dec. 30, 1845.

votes behind the highest in his district, he was high above others on the ticket "in spite of misrepresentation and malignity." [6]

Tilden's experience as a legislator at Albany opened a new chapter in his political life. He went to the State Capital without misgivings, was glad to be in the close confidence of Silas Wright and not far from the home of the past master of civic tactics at Kinderhook. The Governor regarded him as his closest, most discreet and most effective friend. He was always a welcome guest at Wright's home. On one of these calls he introduced John Bigelow to the Governor. Then, as was his wont, Tilden hitched his chair up beside the Governor's, leaned forward and talked in a low voice in Wright's ear. Three different times Bigelow, embarrassed, tried to excuse himself and depart. Each time Tilden said, "Don't go—I'll be through in a few minutes." But the muffled dialogue lasted over two hours. Tilden also took Bigelow, together with W. A. Butler and T. B. Meyers, to call on Van Buren at Lindenwald, where they dined, talked politics and had a jolly time.[7]

John Bigelow wrote, "I hope you enjoy your new relations as well as you expected—nay—better." A Brooklyn friend advised him to stay at the Governor Clinton Hotel where he could safeguard his "health and comfort," but he preferred the Congress Hotel. Judge Vanderpoel cautioned him to look out for tricksters and to lock up all his papers. He was mentioned as a passive candidate for Speaker,[8] but Tilden would not have welcomed the honor had it been proffered. His colleagues, quickly discovering his ability, trusted his judgment, admired his shrewdness and of course loaded him down with work. He served on important committees such as canals, finance, and antirent troubles.[9]

As a conspicuous Soft, he helped to engineer the election of John A. Dix as United States Senator. Representing with Dix the antislavery Democrats of New York, Tilden believed that Congress should not interfere with slavery where it existed but should absolutely prohibit it in the territories where it did not exist. Through Dix, Tilden kept in close touch with Washington affairs and particularly with the manipulations of patronage in the Empire State.[10] Tilden's proneness to circumlocution is illustrated by a letter which he wrote to N. P. Tallmadge, whose brother had asked for a consulship in a mild climate. Convinced that he did not merit such a reward, Tilden took about five hundred words to

[6] Foord, *Green*, 30. [7] *Retrospections*, I, 65. [8] Tilden Papers, Jan., 1846.
[9] *Assembly Journal*. [10] *Letters*, I, 39, Dec. 19, 1845 and later.

say that he would not advise the President to make the appointment. One sentence consisted of 130 words.[11]

In one difficult problem before the legislature Tilden effected a notable adjustment. In counties along the Upper Hudson, land titles carried from colonial days certain manorial rights which the Revolution had not abolished. Proprietors let the land on perpetual leases, with an annual rent payable in produce, poultry and personal services. Although the leased farms, with cultivation and the erection of buildings, increased in value, yet the landlords and not the tenants benefited from the improvement. The largest parcel of leased land was owned by Stephen Van Rensselaer, who on his death in 1839 still held 1,152 square miles on both sides of the Hudson at Albany. His tenants resisted payment of these feudal dues until their arrears amounted to $400,000. Sheriffs sent out to collect the rents were fired upon and forced to flee. A series of disturbances of this sort was termed the Antirent War.[12]

Governor Wright asked for a solution of this problem [13] and the Assembly appointed a committee to make recommendations.[14] Tilden, who was born in one of the manorial counties, was chairman. Hearings were held at which both landlords and tenants stated their cases. Tenants asked that the landlords' interest in the long-term leases be taxed, that back rents be abolished, and that they be given free titles to their farms.

Tilden's report on March 28 gave a fair report of the situation. In his canvass for a seat in the Assembly he had discussed this land problem and held that large tracts in a few hands retarded prosperity, and that the monopoly of tenures was unfavorable to the "happiness of individuals." His report was the most scholarly study of the subject made up to that time. It included a complete history of the manors of Rensselaerswyck, Livingston, Scott, Duane, Corry, Stamford, Kortwright, Hardenburg, Lewis, Verplank, Desbrosses, Hunter, Overings, Banyar, and others in eleven counties. The evils complained of by the tenants were reviewed and shown to be unfavorable to agricultural prosperity and social order. The legal aspects of the question were discussed, with many citations of law. Tilden argued that the legislature could produce a rapid extinction of the leasehold tenures without injustice to any person.[15]

[11] *Letters*, Dec. 25, 1845.
[12] Cheney, "The Antirent Movement," in Flick, *Hist. of the State of New York*, VI, 285.
[13] Lincoln, *Messages*, IV, 87.   [14] *Assembly Journal*, 1846.
[15] *Assembly Documents*, 1846, No. 156; *Writings*, I, 188.

The committee drafted two bills which were enacted into law. The first one provided for taxation, in the locality where the land lay, of the rents reserved upon perpetual and other leases. The second one prohibited future leases of agricultural land for a period of more than ten years. To take care of the rights of the landlords, Tilden proposed that they be converted "into mortgages payable at once or in reasonable instalments." [16] The report declared that the reservation of quarter and other proportional sales were invalid, and some years later the courts decided in favor of this interpretation. Thus through Tilden's efforts an old controversy was compromised if not entirely settled, and the antirent troubles largely subsided.

The settlement of this vexatious problem was a master achievement, and particularly so since it appealed to the reason of all parties concerned. The Antirent Party was enthusiastic over Tilden's report and their representatives in the legislature gave him their earnest support and helped him to frame the laws. The press of the State generally commended his treatment of the baffling puzzle; and the poor tenants, who made so much of their grievances, applauded Tilden and talked of him for a higher office. The attitude of the landlords is shown in a letter of Andrew H. Green who reported that he had seen "one of the Van Rensselaers and he feels secure about his property." Tilden's cautious friend, Judge Aaron Vanderpoel, always asking him to be sure to burn his letters, praised his "admirable speech on antirent," as did the Tilden household. J. I. Roosevelt lauded his "able report on antirent" and asked for a copy.[17] Although the aggravating remnants of feudal land tenure in New York were greatly curtailed, they were not wholly obliterated, and some of them remained as annoyances for many years.

During the consideration of this problem Tilden received many letters of commendation, of criticism and of censure. To him were even sent claims for compensation for service in the Antirent War with the thought that he could have them paid. The publicity gave him a prominence in his own party and among the citizens of the State generally which he had not enjoyed hitherto.

As an Assemblyman from the metropolis it was natural that appeals for assistance of all sorts should be made to him. He had a certain amount of petty patronage at his disposal and influence with men who had greater favors to bestow. Naturally he was importuned by various

[16] *Life*, I, 112.   [17] Tilden Papers, Jan. 26, 1846, and later dates.

office seekers and not a few of them were assisted. Governor Wright expected him to make "sound and judicious" appointments. He was asked to name trustees for the Seaman's Board and the Seaman's Retreat; to help the New York Typographical Society; to incorporate the Philharmonic Society; to safeguard the interests of the East River Insurance Company, the Atlantic Steam Navigation Company and the Ocean Steam Navigation Company; to interest himself in the troubles of Trinity Church; to help found the American Institute; to incorporate the Colored Orphans' Asylum; to promote the National Fine Arts Association; to send information about the Agricultural Association; to aid life insurance companies; and to promote the New York Pilots' Association.[18]

These miscellaneous appeals were endless. One person was raising money, "confidentially" of course, for a portrait and biography of Silas Wright. Mayor Havemeyer asked that the Police Bill be changed. The defects of the quarantine regulations were cited. It was suggested that grants to the universities should go to the public schools; and amendments to the School Law were agitated. Parke Godwin, Bryant's son-in-law, was anxious to become secretary to the Legation at Berlin. Party "Bolters" were reported. Dr. Patterson wanted a bill creating a Medical University. Uriah Edwards solicited aid for the American and Foreign Bible Society. S. C. Jones wished a charter for a cotton factory in Rochester. There were requests for assistance in connection with docks around New York City and canals upstate. Military organizations sought help; county clerks urged an increase in their fees; seamen sought immunity from taxation; Judge Vanderpoel of the Supreme Court hoped the fee system would not be abolished; and J. W. Edmunds asked "Dear Tilden" to act as his agent. Such was the medley of requests that went to Assemblyman Tilden, and all petitioners were patiently and tactfully answered. More pleasant than these importunities was the invitation to a Washington birthday dinner at Troy.[19]

Prophetically significant was the number of railroads that appealed to Tilden at this time for relief or for privileges. This seems to have been the beginning of his legal connection with railroads which grew until some years later he was the foremost railroad lawyer in the nation. The Hudson River, New Haven and Hartford, New York Central, and Long Island Railroads all asked favors. Interesting communications came

[18] Tilden Papers.   [19] *Ib.*

from Jacob Gould of Rochester who fussed over railroads like an old hen over her brood. He remonstrated against permitting the Common Council to "increase our taxes," hoped the Railroad Bill would reduce fares "according to cost and receipts, or net profits of all the roads, and not put the Auburn and Rochester at the same fare as the Schenectady and Utica Railroad because the latter has double the traffic ours has." Owners of railroads, he thought, should be permitted to pay for their roads and make some profits. He alluded to "the magnetic telegraph" and predicted that it would "destroy the large city newspapers and ruin the Post Office service"—a prophecy that missed fire.[20]

In view of the trend of his activity, Tilden came to be looked upon in the Assembly as a moderate reformer; and, having shown a leaning toward reform, he was sought by some who urged him to militancy. He opposed creating smaller electoral districts because they would encourage fraud.[21] He was pressed particularly about desirable changes in the City Charter, a matter which was to engage his serious attention later when he strove to free the city from the strangling toils of Boss Tweed and his associates. Waterbury of the *News* was the most urgent of those who would make him a reformer first and a statesman second. "The people want most thorough reform," he wrote. "Don't forget this above all." He wished Tilden to convince the city electorate of his reform leanings and felt that he was wasting opportunity in devoting his attention to such matters as the Antirent settlement.[22] To Governor Wright he complained, "When we sent Mr. Tilden to the Assembly, we flattered ourselves that we should have sound and judicious appointments. We were awakened from the delusion by the appointment of Judge Scott as Recorder. . . . The truth of the matter is my friend Tilden (who is the soundest and truest politician I have ever known and who is no less personally than politically my friend) has had too much on his hands; and his unfortunate constitutional nervousness has agitated his mind so completely with a few matters of great importance that he has given no thought to others of lesser concern, but of the most essential consequence as affecting his relation with constituents and the Democracy of this city. . . . Antirentism has swallowed up City Reform." [23] This was a remarkably accurate description of Tilden's single-track mind.

---

20 Tilden Papers, various dates.
22 *Ib.*, Mar. 4, 1846.
21 *Ib.*, Apr. 20, 1846.
23 *Ib.*, Mar. 31, 1846.

The forward-looking Albany editor, William Cassidy, was convinced that Tilden should be the "headman in . . . Charter Reform." Let your opponents *"see* you prominent in it and they will think you a much better Democrat than before." "You have started well," said H. Butler. "Pursue your way asking wisdom from above." We look to you as *"a light on a hill"*—keep it shining in this "sliding age." People ascribed the same "political infallibility to Wright, Tilden and B. F. Butler that Catholics do to the Pope." He should remember that he had a "State, a nation, to look after." "Albany outrivals Washington," which was stupid by comparison.[24]

Another reform that received Tilden's attention was the abolition of the office of State Printer and abuses connected with it. This lucrative office went as a political reward to the Albany printer whose party was in power. At this time the Hards and Softs both had papers in the capital city. The mouthpiece of the Hunkers was the *Argus* under Croswell, while the friends of Van Buren and Wright controlled the *Atlas* under the editorship of Van Dyke and Cassidy. Efforts to unite the two papers in the interest of Democratic solidarity led to a clash between Croswell and Tilden who suspected the former's insincerity.[25] This factional rivalry lay behind Tilden's support of the Assembly bill which eliminated the State Printer in the interest of economy. In a long speech in which Tilden made public honesty the keynote, he denounced the sale of offices, and took a shot at pseudo-reformers who wished to auction off public printing regardless of quality of work. "Men who favored no reforms are now for reforms." He urged the abolition of the publication of legal notices. Why should the public treasury support a journal? It was not "sound political morals" to do so. The Democrats should have a paper in Albany which would represent not Governor Wright but the whole party. In concluding his speech he said of his political foes, "I am as proud of their enmity as any gentleman can be of their friendship."[26] Waterbury's comment, "I fear you are whipped on the printer," was correct; but before the public Tilden had taken a firm stand for honest government. Brother Henry returned home from Albany with the report that there was talk of making Samuel State Printer at a salary of $5,000.[27]

So satisfactory to his party friends and constituents was Tilden's

[24] Tilden Papers, Mar. 6, 10, 1846.
[26] *Assembly Journal*, 1846.

[25] *Letters*, I, 41, 42.
[27] Tilden Papers, Moses to Samuel.

work in the Assembly that he was favored as a delegate to the Constitutional Convention of 1846, at Albany, which was called by the legislature to revise the Constitution of 1821. When he hesitated Judge Vanderpoel urged, "You should go." [28] The nominating committee meeting in Tammany Hall named Tilden on the first ballot as a "man of the Wright stamp." He was elected on April 14, third in a group of sixteen delegates from the metropolis.[29] There followed the inevitable applications for positions as clerks and pages.

The convention met on June 1, 1846, and sat till October 9. Tilden's associates were men who would control political affairs for the next generation or two—Charles O'Conor, Michael Hoffman, Churchill C. Cambreling, Samuel Nelson, William C. Bouck and Ambrose L. Jordan. Adam P. Park thought "the truest and most talented Democrats" were in the convention and hoped a constitution "based upon the dearest Democratic principles" would be drawn up.[30] Tilden took an active part in the organization of the convention. In a lengthy argument he favored letting the Committee of the Whole decide the order of business as the most democratic procedure, but by a vote of 91 to 30 this work was turned over to a committee of seventeen. He participated in the division of the convention into committees to study specific problems. He expressed a preference for assignment to the Judiciary Committee but at the request of Governor Wright and A. C. Flagg was placed second on the committee dealing with finance and canals, of which Michael Hoffman was chairman. But it was he who assembled the materials for a constructive report recommending that the State should not compromise with debtors, or sell its canals and salt mines, or loan its credit, but should create sinking funds.[31] These measures were all incorporated in the Constitution.

Tilden defeated an effort to require the legislature to limit the aggregate amount of bank notes in the State, because the "laws of trade" and not the Government should determine the quantity. Forty years later he wrote George Bancroft that in 1846 he had "recognized the disability of any government . . . State or Federal, to make a legal tender of anything but gold or silver." [32]

Acting on Tilden's report to the Assembly, the first article of the Constitution of 1846 abolished "feudal tenures of every description"

[28] Tilden Papers, Jan. 17, 1846.   [29] *Ib.*, J. D. Kellogg to Tilden, Apr. 23, 1846.
[30] *Ib.*   [31] *Constitutional Convention of 1846*, 41.
[32] *Life*, I, 115, Feb. 12, 1886.

and limited leases on agricultural lands to twelve years. As chairman of a special committee on corporations he reported the provision for their creation under a general law rather than by special acts and the right of the legislature to change or repeal charters. He participated in the debate on the reduction of the Governor's powers, the limitation of Senators' terms to two years, and the election of members of the legislature from single districts instead of by counties. His vote was cast against the extension of the right to vote to all male colored citizens but he favored granting it to those who owned freeholds valued at $250. The sections relating to the management of the canals were largely shaped by him.[33] And he heartily endorsed the creation of an elective judiciary, the decentralization of political responsibility, free public education, the elimination of aristocratic practices and the institution of a more ideal democracy.

Although among the youngest men in the convention, he was regarded as one of the best informed, and his brief comments and few lengthy speeches were given strict attention. Attendance was quite irregular, as the polls of votes show, but his voting on all measures was intelligent and independent. Well might he and his friends take pride in giving the State a constitution which with few amendments is still the fundamental law, and which the people endorsed by a vote of 221,528 to 92,436.[34]

Knowing that the convention had produced, as a result of careful study and serious debate, a basic guide for the Commonwealth that would worthily meet the needs of a growing people, Tilden was greatly amused at the comments of some of his acquaintances. For instance Eugene Cassidy flippantly wrote that "A Constitution which settles the inalienable rights of man in one section, and in the next the salary of the Governor's private secretary, strikes me as the pink of two and six penny law-making. I am afraid that our Mountain will hardly bring forth a mouse-trap . . . not even a mouse." There are too many "small potato reforms." [35]

The burdens of a conscientious legislator, Tilden discovered, robbed his frail body of vitality and kept his pocketbook flat. Instead of being time lost, however, his Albany experience was reflected in more clients than if he had remained at his lawyer's desk; it brought contacts with railroads, canals and business concerns which increased legal fees.

[33] *Journal of the Convention, 1846*, 113.   [34] *Civil List* (1888), 130.
[35] Tilden Papers, June 10, 1846.

Forced to meet men as colleagues and constituents, he overcame much of his timidity and aloofness and gained a better comprehension of State politics and party machinery. His academic knowledge of the governmental affairs of the Empire State was substituted for reality. The experience of 1846 was the greatest revelation of his own ability that had yet come to him and henceforth stood out as a landmark of his career.

Tilden's activities in the Assembly and the Constitutional Convention accentuated his standing as one of the recognized leaders of the Democratic Party in the State. As a result, before the adjournment of the convention, his city friends were openly working for his nomination to Congress. If he preferred either the Assembly or the State Senate, Waterbury told him, that could easily be arranged.[36] Vanderpoel also informed him of the plan to send him to Washington. His inclination was not in the direction of a political career, however, and he resolutely refused to heed the importunities of his friends but centered his attention on his business connections and legal profession. Little did he suspect, at that period of his life, that his resolution would be shattered by circumstances compelling him to serve the public.

This decision to refuse public office marked the opening of a career which was to establish him eventually as one of the foremost corporation lawyers of his time and to bring him opportunities to become a millionaire. It was the farewell gesture, too, to the humble status of the country boy imbued with the democratic principles of the pioneer, his spirit afire with the fervor of pure patriotism. Looking backward from this turn in the road, the old white farmhouse at New Lebanon was lost to view, but in the dim distance ahead loomed the towers of Graystone on the Hudson.

[36] Tilden Papers.

THE Democrats unanimously renominated Governor Wright, whose most formidable opponent was John Young, nominee of the Whigs and Antirenters. "With all the devotion which love inspires," Tilden threw himself into the campaign, making speeches and using his personal influence. Had Wright been re-elected, he would have been the logical Democratic candidate for President in 1848; and, with him as President, Tilden would have entered the Cabinet. Wright, however, was doomed. His path was thorny enough, what with the unhealed schism in his own party, his forthright refusal to barter pardons for Antirent votes, and the shrewd campaigning of his opponent; but the crushing blow came in the midst of the desperate canvass when William C. Bouck, an arch-Hunker, was appointed Subtreasurer in New York City. President Polk seemed destined, however unwittingly, to play the part of public executioner of Wright, and this cruelly timed appointment, which indicated the President's opposition to Wright's re-election, was a fitting climax to a course of ruthless ingratitude. To Tilden, Wright's defeat was a deep grief. Sick of politics, he explained that "the disastrous defeat" was the work of the Hunkers.[1]

As Wright was making the dreary retreat to Canton, Tilden was resuming the practice of law which absence for part of a year had seriously disrupted. For the time being, the defeat of his party closed all doors for public advancement. Now that he was no longer a State official, his correspondence declined, doubtless to his relief, but he kept in close touch with party leaders. To Tilden had been committed the task of completing "Mr. Wright's Memoir." We learn from Theodore Sedgwick that he had soon finished the biographical sketch, "all but a few dates." [2] For the remainder of his life Tilden never lost an opportunity to express his indebtedness to Silas Wright's lofty political vision.

Of various issues the radical Democrats or Barnburners gave prominence to free-soil. The Wilmot Proviso presented a practical test of every man's attitude upon the extension of slavery into territories. This was the "cloud no bigger than a man's hand" which was to grow into a hurricane

[1] *Writings*, I, 234.

[2] Tilden Papers, Jan. 20, 1848.

before most people realized the danger and to split the Democratic Party. In Congress Preston King was declaring that "the time has come when the Republic should declare by law that it will not" extend slavery. All New York Democratic Congressmen but one voted to enforce the spirit of the Wilmot Proviso.[3]

The legislature by resolution approved Preston King's attitude, and New York Democrats generally, including Tilden, favored the Wilmot Proviso, particularly after Van Buren came out openly for it. Since he had definitely declared "I am not a candidate," and was busy with fine stock and fancy apples, no one could accuse him of playing politics. Young Democrats like Tilden looked at him through a magnifying glass and so numerous were his followers that they felt themselves the Democratic Party in the State. But in the Democratic State Convention at Syracuse, September 29, 1847, the Hunkers, with 73 delegates to the Barnburners' 63, quickly demonstrated who controlled the party.[4] When David Dudley Field offered a resolution endorsing the Wilmot Proviso as sound Democratic doctrine, he was peremptorily ruled out of order, an uproar ensuing. The radicals were charged with a wish to burn down the barn to get rid of the rats—hence the name Barnburners; while the conservatives were dubbed the "rule or ruin" party or the "Albany clique." Reporting the convention, the Albany *Atlas* laconically commented: "Split on resolutions. . . . Disgraceful conduct. . . . Excitement."[5] A few days later J. W. Hoffman sardonically asked Tilden to pay his subscription to the new Tammany Hall.[6] The Hunkers in control named a State ticket and reorganized the State Committee.[7]

The inflamed Barnburners, against the advice of Van Buren and Flagg, held their own convention at Herkimer, October 26—their first official gathering and one of significance for the future. Attendance was estimated as high as 3,000. Cambreling presided and John Van Buren justified the assembly.[8] Field's Wilmot Proviso resolution was passed with a shout of defiance; and each congressional district was permitted to send a delegate to the next Democratic National Convention. Another Democratic State ticket was nominated, thus insuring a Whig triumph in the ensuing election.[9] Each faction claimed to be the true Democratic Party in New York; each had its State Committee and each sent dele-

[3] Donovan, *Barnburners*, 85–86.
[4] *Ib.*, 93; Alexander, II, 127, gives the wrong date, Sept. 7.
[5] Sept. 30, 1847. [6] Tilden Papers, Oct. 2, 1847. [7] Donovan, 94.
[8] Gardiner, O. C., *The Great Issue*, 50. [9] Alexander, II, 127.

gates to the National Convention at Baltimore on May 22, 1848.

The breach between the "conservative Hunkers" and the "radical Barnburners" was now irreconcilable. Marcy accepted the leadership of the former while Van Buren, Butler, and Tilden directed the policy of the latter. The Hunkers sympathized with Southern Democrats in the annexation of Texas and the extension of Slavery, and were joined by a few pro-slavery Whigs. On the other hand the Barnburners veered toward the free-soil views of the Whigs. As a result, the campaign of 1848 was a hodgepodge of cliques and candidates.

Tilden was an earnest champion of the exclusion of slavery from every part of the territory acquired from Mexico. Consequently he took a keen interest in both the State and national elections of 1848. In New York City the Barnburners elected a Mayor, and Tilden was congratulated on the victory.[10] Barnburners in the legislature defended their attitude in a masterful state paper written by Van Buren, with the assistance of his son John and Tilden. Spending the winter of 1847–48 in the metropolis, Van Buren saw much of Tilden. One day he handed the young man a manuscript with the comment: "If you wish to be immortal, take this home with you, revise it . . . and give it to the public." Tilden agreed with John to revamp the report. Presenting it to the ex-President, who asked, "Well, what have you done with Niagara Falls?" Tilden replied, "We struck that out," and Van Buren laughed. The three collaborators gave it to friends in the legislature, who issued it as a Barnburner address.[11]

This manifesto of forty pages has been called the "cornerstone of the Free-Soil Party" and the "first gun for Free-Soil." John Van Buren wrote four introductory pages; Martin Van Buren contributed the next twenty-two pages; Tilden then inserted several pages of his own; and the remainder was from the pen of the former President. But Tilden's hand may be seen on every page. The introduction reviewed the process by which 36 delegates, of whom Tilden was one, had been selected to attend the Democratic National Convention at Baltimore in May, 1848, and recited the history of the Democratic Party in New York after 1841, with caustic remarks upon the Hunkers. The second part asserted that the ceded Mexican territory should be free and that New York's delegates to the National Convention were instructed to so vote. Southern

[10] Tilden Papers, R. R. Shekell to Tilden, Apr. 16, 1848.
[11] *Life*, I, 118; *Writings*, II, 534.

delegates, on the contrary, were instructed to oppose the power of Congress or territorial legislatures in excluding slavery from such territory. The South was accused of ignoring the Constitution and of threatening war to support slavery.

Tilden's specific contribution to the address was a summary of the New York Democrats' attitude. The South, he declared, was calling upon Northern Democrats to deny the power of Congress to prevent slavery in Federal territory or of the people of such territory to prohibit slavery, while insisting that they had the constitutional right to take their slaves into such regions and that "wherever the flag goes, it carries slavery with it" and overthrows the local institutions of personal freedom. This doctrine, wrote Tilden, was contrary to the spirit of the Constitution and abhorrent to the principles of its framers. The Democracy of New York refused to believe that the Democrats of the South could hold such views. The extension of slavery "to territories now free from it can never be made acceptable to the freemen of the North." For sixty years Congress had "by solemn acts" excluded slavery from its territories. If the slaveholders wished to take their slaves to new territory, they should go where slavery was permitted, or else sell their slaves and employ free labor. Thousands had done the latter and were happy in the experiment. Tilden was willing to protect the Southerners in their slave property but unalterably opposed to extending slavery to new territory.

Before the National Democratic Convention met in Baltimore, the 36 Barnburner delegates met in Tilden's office to agree upon some plan of action.[12] In Baltimore they found the Hunker delegation claiming to represent New York. The convention, after much wrangling, admitted both delegations, which neutralized the Barnburners' vote; and it was said that the Barnburners "might occupy half a seat apiece provided each of them would let a Hunker sit on his lap." [13] The Free-Soil delegates vehemently protested that if they should "consent to divide with them [the Hunkers] our seats and our votes, we should betray the principles and forfeit the confidence of the pure and fearless party whose commission we bear." In an angry mood, they declined to take their seats and left for their homes, "outlawed by their party." [14] The National Convention then proceeded to nominate Lewis Cass for President.

[12] Tilden Papers, May 16, 1848; Donovan, 98.
[13] Stanton, *Rand. Recol.*, 161.   [14] Tilden Papers.

The Whigs seized upon General Zachary Taylor as the most available candidate, with Millard Fillmore as a running mate.

Immediately upon returning to New York City, where an enthusiastic reception was given them in City Hall Park,[15] Tilden and other Free-Soil Democrats called a State convention at Utica, June 22, 1848. Representatives from several other States also appeared. A report from the rejected delegates, prepared by Tilden and signed by the whole delegation, was read to the indignant gathering.[16] It recounted how the delegation had been excluded from the Baltimore Convention, and continued that "under these circumstances we had no hesitation as to our duty" to withdraw. "We could not have stood there, as men falsely claiming to be your representatives did, to argue down the honest repugnance of fair men to do what they thought would degrade us and betray you who had clothed us with our high trust." Sent to "confer with our political brethren of other States" about "our common country," we could enter the convention only "on terms of equality and reciprocity and no others." The convention at Utica then adopted a platform, a third of which dealt with the Wilmot Proviso, and created a national sensation by proposing Van Buren for President.[17] Men like B. F. Angel of Geneseo thought his nomination "unfortunate." [18]

The result of the slap in the face which the New York Free-Soil Democrats had received at Baltimore was that they supported a National Convention of Free-Soilers—Barnburners, Whigs and Abolitionists—in Buffalo on August 9, 1848.[19] Ohioans joined New Yorkers in preparing for this gathering. S. P. Chase wrote to ask John Van Buren what the New York Democrats would do about the convention, and suggested that either Martin Van Buren or John himself should be the Presidential nominee. Tilden, at Bryant's suggestion, assumed authority to reply. "With perfect candor" he informed Chase that the Barnburners would be informally represented at Buffalo. They would stand for Martin Van Buren and no other for President; and they commanded "more than 50 presses . . . and . . . an organization penetrating every county & town . . . and . . . not less than 150,000 voters." [20] Tilden thought that New York would favor the nomination of Judge McLean for Vice President. Meantime with characteristic coyness Van Buren was writing

[15] Donovan, 103. [16] *Writings*, I, 234. [17] Donovan, 104.
[18] Tilden Papers, June 25, 1848. [19] Alexander, II, 132.
[20] *Letters*, I, 50, June 19, 1848, 54. More complete letter in Chase, *Diary and Corresp.*, *Ann. Rep. Am. Hist. Assn.* 1902, II, 468.

to his friend B. F. Butler: "I never want to be a candidate for President again or any other office." [21]

The most extreme stand taken by Tilden on the slavery issue was in connection with this Free-Soil movement in 1848. The Free-Soil League of the 15th ward of New York City sent him as a delegate to the Buffalo Convention. Items among his papers indicate that he served on the Committee on Resolutions. One paper, seemingly in his hand, covered the duty of the Federal Government to maintain freedom in the territory acquired from Mexico, stating that slavery had "sprung from force or fraud" and had "grown up without the original authority of law." The attempt of Congress "to authorize it by express enactment" was the first instance in which "so monstrous and revolting a proposition had ever been made." For enlightened America to extend "its blighting presence" to a region from which even semibarbarous Mexico had excluded it, "would be the greatest opprobrium of our age," would retard the progress of free institutions, and would "cover with shame those who are struggling to establish them throughout the world." [22] These statements expressed Tilden's extreme views at the age of thirty-four. Later, as slavery threatened war and as the support of his party came more and more from the South, Tilden sought to explain these views away as juvenile utterances.

With men like Richmond, Church, Bryant, Field, King, Wadsworth, Dix and Fenton, Tilden attended the Buffalo Convention to secure "free soil for a free people." After much discussion it was decided to follow the lead of the Utica Convention, so Martin Van Buren and Charles Francis Adams were nominated—"the codfish and cabbage" ticket. Webster ridiculed "the leader of the Free-Spoil Party becoming the leader of the Free-Soil Party," while Sumner said he was supporting the reformed Van Buren. [23]

Tilden took an active part in the spirited campaign and used his gifted pen to write an effective pamphlet on "The Position of the Radical Democracy in New York." His old friend Pitts invited him to speak at New Windsor and Newburgh. [24] His services were placed freely at the command of Van Buren and many were the errands he performed. For example, when Thomas Van Rensselaer, a colored editor of the *Ram's Horn,* asked Van Buren for funds, the latter passed the letter on to

---

[21] Butler Papers, Aug. 2, 1848.   [22] Tilden Papers.   [23] Alexander, II, 132.
[24] Tilden Papers, July 8, Oct. 31, 1848.

Tilden with a request that he see the editor and explain the situation.[25]

In New York the Presidential election complicated the gubernatorial contest. The Barnburners Convention at Utica, on September 14, 1848, nominated Senator John A. Dix for Governor and Seth Gates for Lieutenant Governor, against the Hunkers' ticket, Walworth and O'Conor, and the hopeful Whigs' candidates, Fish and Patterson. After a short campaign of almost unprecedented blackguardism, Taylor received 218,603 votes in New York, Van Buren 120,510, and Cass 114,318. The national poll was: Taylor 1,360,000; Cass 1,220,000; and Van Buren 291,263, or 10% of the total.[26] Had the Democrats as a unit supported Cass, he would have been elected. New York's 36 electoral votes for Taylor elected him. In the State canvass Fish and the entire Whig ticket were successful.

That Tilden was far from displeased by the defeat of Cass is clear. Although now free once more to turn his attention to his profession, he could not keep his mind off the important issues of the day. This is shown by a series of political letters which he wrote for the *Evening Post*.

An aftermath of the three-cornered campaign of 1848 was a newspaper discussion with Congressman Horace Greeley,[27] who had voted for Taylor and was supporting the Douglas Bill. Thinking free-soil "the question of questions," Tilden denounced Greeley for inconsistently turning his back on all former professions about slavery and for supporting the dangerous Greeley-Douglas "juggle," which would let newly formed State legislatures settle the issue. Cass's plan to let territorial legislatures decide was franker and more honest because they would be subject to the Federal Government. Tilden himself believed that Congress, not a few thousand settlers, should forbid slavery in the territories.[28] His attitude may be summarized in the notation he made on his manuscript letter: "Mr. Tilden opposed the claim of the slaveholders of the constitutional right to take slaves into all territories; opposed the Missouri Compromise; and believed that a Union party could save the Union." [29]

Within a few years the cleavage between the two Democratic factions in New York reached a logical conclusion. The leading Barnburners, joining the Free-Soil Whigs, formed a new party, the Republican, which Senator Hoar later declared to have originated in the Buffalo Conven-

[25] *Letters,* Oct. 16, 18, 1848.   [26] Stanwood, *A Hist. of the Presidency,* 176.
[27] Greeley's letter in *Tribune,* Dec. 16, 1848.
[28] *Evening Post,* Dec. 23, 1848, gives Tilden's letter.   [29] Tilden Papers.

tion.[30] To Tilden, O'Conor, Seymour and others, the issue of slavery did not loom so large; they accepted the Compromise of 1850 as a reasonable solution and remained within the Democratic fold.

Tilden, somewhat fatigued by the hurly-burly, was disposed to accept the invitation of his wise friend and counselor, William Cullen Bryant, to accompany him to Europe. The passport [31] which he obtained describes him as 35 years old, 5 feet 9 inches in height, with a high forehead, blue eyes, large nose, medium mouth, prominent chin, light complexion and an oval face. Letters of introduction to prominent Europeans were obtained. But this tour abroad was abandoned, and Tilden returned to a law practice which, after eight years, was now well established. His letter files show a noticeable increase in legal business, and a few items help to picture his activities. He obtained judgment of $662.63 against Edward McLean for W. W. Pineo and Tilden & Company. A divorce case brought a fee of $28. For services to the Pequa Railroad Company he received $145. He sent a bill for $205 for merging the Washington Coal Company with the Pennsylvania Coal Company. For settling the E. A. Smith land controversy he charged $225.[32] To amend the charter of the Susquehannah Coal Company he was paid $150,[33] and for reorganizing the Chestnut Iron Company, $550. For uniting the Dauphin & Susquehannah Coal Company with the Pequa Railroad & Improvement Company he collected $175.[34] His work for the Pennsylvania Coal Company was valued at $1,780.[35] These instances, from many cases covering several years, indicate that Tilden was becoming a corporation lawyer of prominence; his low fees may explain why such business was coming to his office, which, in 1850, he moved to No. 1 Jauncy Court. His landlord was Alexander Hamilton, Jr., and the annual rental $425. Cautious always, in this lease for two rooms on the third floor, he stipulated that no rent would be paid in case of fire until repairs were made.[36]

Among his clients were men who appreciated his trustworthiness, business ability, and good judgment. Van Buren wanted advice about investing $5,000 in Erie bonds, thanked him for collecting his dividends [37] and sent $5,000 to be invested in "good coal stock." Other commissions followed, and so far as the records show no bill was ever sent to his

[30] Hoar, *Autobiography*.   [31] Tilden Papers. Dated June 11, 1849.   [32] *Ib.*
[33] *Letters*, I, 65.   [34] Tilden Papers.   [35] *Letters*, I, 66.
[36] *Ib.*, 63. After three years the rent was raised to $550.
[37] *Ib.*, 76, 81.

old friend for professional service. Tilden discounted notes and acted as a loan agent, letting Eugene Cassidy have $250, W. A. Butler, $2,000, I. V. Tonten $1,000, and Parke Godwin $236. Debts were collected, of course—in one instance $10,000 for J. A. W. Menie.[38] Tilden & Company at New Lebanon naturally expected him to handle all their legal business. In the drafting of incorporation papers O'Conor's legal erudition was employed. To Mrs. Franklin Chase, an old friend whose husband was consul at Tampico, he sent information about the organization of a line of steamers to Vera Cruz and conservative advice concerning investments: U.S. sixes and New York stocks to be placed first, and preference given to 7% real estate mortgages. Stocks of private companies earning up to 10%, he cautioned, were affected by depressions. In confidence he mentioned the D. & H. Canal Company, which paid 16%, and a "similar concern" in which he himself had invested. He recommended diversified holdings for safety and thought it best for her to keep her money in the bank until she could consult him in New York.[39]

Tilden's income by 1851 was gratifying but not affluent. He was saving money and making investments. He lived at 11 Fifth Avenue and paid a tax of $23.66 on personal property valued at $2,000. Perhaps for a client, he paid President Eliphalet Nott of Union College $420 interest on a $12,000 mortgage which had been assigned to him. With O'Sullivan, Waterbury, and Secor, he invested in the first Balance Dry Dock in New York Harbor and served for a time as president. This venture brought Tilden more trouble than financial reward, and for some years he had to defend the company's rights in the courts. When Judge Roosevelt ruled that the wharves of East River could not be used as a dry dock, Tilden, representing two-thirds of the stockholders, sought to have the legislature legalize such use.[40]

One might think that, since he was so successful, he was exceedingly methodical, but this was not the fact. Ordinarily he was neither industrious nor busy, he boasted.[41] Attacks of illness so prostrated him that he dropped all work for days at a time. He enjoyed being swept along "incessantly" by some "current of affairs" to which he could give his undivided attention, and it was this concentrated devotion to a problem that made him so masterful.

The cascade of business details did not drown his interest in national

[38] Tilden Papers.   [39] *Letters*, I, 72.   [40] *Ib.*, 67.
[41] *Ib.*, 72, to Mrs. Ann Chase.

affairs, and from a matter of percentages he turned to deeper issues when in 1850 he wrote: "I do not share, to any considerable extent, the apprehension entertained or professed by many as to a dissolution of our federative union." Danger would call forth better men than the "holiday patriots" to save the nation. American nationality was a stabilizing force. He felt that Providence was preparing the country for a grander rôle in a great plan "to be wrought out, not by an indolent repose on what our ancestors have ordained for us, but by . . . earnest efforts to solve the great social and civic questions" of the nation. Union was an essential condition for such a destiny, and he believed it was strong enough "to endure the conflict of social and political forces . . . going on in its bosom. It will survive them all." [42] In these prophetic words one sees the optimistic democrat, the unionist, and the reformer. Tilden never deviated from these early convictions.

So deeply enmeshed in politics was he that he could not escape demands from aspirants for office and for all sorts of service. When the "Canal Counties" in 1851 introduced a bill to increase the State debt $9,000,000 to expand the Erie Canal, D. Burwell appealed to him to defeat it.[43] Alarmed by this effort to violate the Constitution of 1846, he sent William Cassidy, editor of the Albany *Atlas,* a letter of 10,000 words [44] denouncing the scheme. Although "having neither leisure nor inclination for politics" and being "more oppressed" with professional engagements than ever in his life, yet he felt that he owed it to the memory of Michael Hoffman and Silas Wright to thwart the effort to violate the fundamental law of the State. He denied both the need and the constitutionality of the measure. Enlargements might be made by raising the locks, thus deepening the water for larger boats. In conclusion he held that the canal funds had been spent inefficiently, and that it would be a calamitous "social dishonor" to ignore the financial safeguards of the Constitution. "It is pleasant to borrow money. It is easy to spend. It is hard to repay." The proposal was "folly and madness" and should be voted down. "I rely upon the people—their wisdom, honor and morality." [45]

Again national politics intruded and Gideon Welles asked about the Democratic attitude toward the next President. He favored Benton [46] and Tilden sent him the news. Governor Marcy, eager to unite the party

---

[42] *Letters,* I, 68, to Mrs. Franklin Chase, Nov. 29, 1850.   [43] *Ib.,* 76, Mar. 30, 1851.
[44] *Writings,* I, 249, Apr. 7, 1851.   [45] *Ib.,* 248.   [46] *Letters,* I, 78.

to further his candidacy for the Presidency, reported prospects improved and asked Tilden to meet him in Albany a few days before the delegates met.[47] Tilden obeyed the summons. Van Buren longed for "an old-fashioned chat." [48] Tilden took no part in the National Convention at Baltimore, which nominated Pierce for President. To Pierce he was a stranger who called with a letter of introduction, but he labored hard for his election, and collected funds for the campaign.[49] The election proved to be a Democratic landslide.

Never had Tilden manifested any timidity in giving advice to Democratic Presidents from Andrew Jackson onward. Now that Franklin Pierce was President-elect he drafted a long letter which expressed the sort of a Chief Executive he hoped Pierce would be—a hope which was not long cherished. In the first place Tilden, who at this time held a high office in the organization, sent the "cordial congratulations of The Council of Sachems of the Tammany Society," which was "coeval with the government itself." He hoped Pierce's election meant "a salutary jealousy of the encroachments of power upon the liberties of the individual and the rights of the States." "Professional statesmen of the most distinguished ability" were often distrusted by the people for their "intrigue and selfishness." Their highest confidence and strongest affection were reserved for persons of "opposite characters." It was his "honesty and courage," not his mental endowments or military fame that "commanded their support." Disinterestedness of mind made Silas Wright a model republican statesman, trusted and loved.[50]

Nothing better illustrates Tilden's ability to pass accurate judgment on public men than his advice to Pierce about the make-up of his Cabinet. The selections must insure a united party. All aspirants for the Presidency must be excluded; otherwise he would be like the old man who announced his death and asked the boys to scramble for his inheritance. "Polk tried that" and the "inheritance went to strangers." If Pierce decided not to take a New Yorker, Tilden would not "personally complain," but he thought New York should not be overlooked. Who, then, should it be—O'Conor, Dickinson, Marcy or Dix? Tilden set forth the good and bad qualifications of O'Conor as a man of legal learning and acute reasoning, who was vehement and sarcastic, able rather than wise, inexperienced and not co-operative; yet he thought

[47] Tilden Papers, Aug., 1850.   [48] *Letters,* I, 80, Apr. 2, 1852.
[49] Nichols, *The Democratic Machine 1850-54,* 161–162.   [50] Tilden Papers.

he might make an excellent Attorney General. Dickinson was inferior to O'Conor in ability, not strong in his State, not a far-sighted politician, and apt to be on the wrong side. Marcy and Dix were both "capable of fulfilling the duties . . . with signal . . . distinction," but between the two he recommended Dix who was acceptable to both New York and Southern Democrats. Southern objections to Dix should be ignored. To have a strong Cabinet he must avoid "combining negatives." He should bury dissensions, pursue a "decisive course," and remember that "Boldness is the highest prudence." Several "States Rights Democrats" should be taken into the Cabinet. Protect the people from plunder under the forms of legislation and also from administrative abuses.[51]

It seems evident from Tilden's papers that his relations with Pierce were closer than is commonly known. When Pierce passed through New York on his way to Washington, Tilden met him and again discussed Cabinet possibilities. On February 23 he wrote Pierce from Harrisburg, Pennsylvania, that he had seen Governor Bigler who felt that Campbell, a Catholic, should not be made Postmaster General because he would have to pass on local Catholic postmasters, which would arouse some feeling. Tilden's engagements prevented his presence at Pierce's Inauguration, but he hoped to see him "soon after." Although Marcy, not Dix, was selected as Secretary of State, and James Campbell Postmaster General, against Tilden's advice, yet he continued on terms of intimacy with the President. He offered suggestions on appointments to New York offices and sought to have high-grade Democrats, not the "most vulgar sort," named. To Pierce he wrote: "You should rest your administration on the . . . moral power of the community, by an appointment which should appeal to them. . . . Do this and you will rise above the altitude of mere politicians." [52] He again urged, but in vain,[53] that Dix, as a representative of the Barnburner Democrats, be given the collectorship or a foreign mission.[54] When Pierce in 1854 sent him his message to Congress, Tilden replied that in substance and style it was the best the President had yet written.

Marcy, now on friendly terms with Tilden, consulted him about New York appointments.[55] Reminding him of an acquaintance of twenty years, Tilden wrote him frankly concerning the mistakes made by the

[51] *Letters,* I, 81, Tilden to Gen. C. H. Peaslee, Jan. 15, 1853. Attributed by Bigelow to G. W. Newell. Letter covers 13 printed pages.
[52] Tilden Papers.   [53] Dix, *Memoirs,* I, 271.   [54] Tilden Papers.
[55] *Letters,* I, 101, Apr. 4, 1853.

administration in New York patronage.[56] Marcy showed the letter to
Pierce and warned Tilden about the peremptory actions of John Van
Buren.[57] But friendly as these relations seemed on the surface, neither
Tilden nor Marcy could wholly forget the scars of earlier battles. Even
if his recommendations were largely unheeded, it expanded Tilden's
egotism to be consulted by a President and his Secretary of State.

Among liberal Democrats Tilden had a wide circle of acquaintances
but few close friends. When his Uncle Henry Dana Ward went to Richmond, Virginia, Tilden was able to give him letters of introduction to
a number of prominent men.[58] Bryant continued to be a companion who
enjoyed having Tilden as his house guest. The Van Burens were never
out of touch, and Tilden was bound to them by numerous sentimental
bonds. Horatio Seymour, who had been a mild political foe and was to
be intimately associated with Tilden for years, began to appear in Tilden's correspondence, chiefly as a legal client. From Wisconsin he wrote
that he heard Tilden had been organizing a railroad and wished he had
seen him. He asked Tilden to relieve him from an unfortunate endorsement of a note; [59] also to help him raise $15,000 for "the Fox & W. Co."
What a relief it must have been to have his Hibernian friend O'Sullivan
call him "Old fellow" and say "God bless you—adieu." [60]

More and more during Pierce's administration, Tilden withdrew from
political activities and devoted himself to legal matters. In August of
1854 he was at Newport, Rhode Island, "for a few days' relaxation and
sea bathing"—an unusual experience. Reflecting on his primary concerns at that time, he wrote, "The moment I return to the routine of my
home life there are, at present, so many business obligations and responsibilities claiming my thoughts and exhausting my activity that I
could not, if disposed to do so, give much habitual attention to politics."
He did not favor a new fusion party to restore the Missouri Compromise. If the Kansas-Nebraska question could be settled right, there would
be no need for such a party. Doubting that the free-soil enthusiasm of
1848 could be revived among the Democrats, he was rather pessimistic
about the outlook for 1856. Benton was not his choice for a Presidential
candidate, but in characteristic fashion he failed to state who was.
Washington was viewed with "disgust, indifference and . . . opposition." Some expected the Democratic Party to be "broken down for

[56] *Letters*, 106, Oct. 12, 1853.   [57] *Ib.*, 110, Oct. 16, 1853.   [58] Tilden Papers.
[59] *Letters*, I, 110, Aug. 8, 1854.
[60] Tilden Papers, July 20, 1854. O'Sullivan had been appointed Minister to Portugal.

the time"; others believed that the folly of the Democratic leaders would benefit the Whigs; and still others were either indifferent or framing a new ticket. He knew none who would join the Whigs permanently; most disgruntled Democrats wanted to see the party rise again purified.[61]

As the Convention of Barnburners approached, he wrote to a friend that in the chaotic state of things all he hoped for was "the harmony of the radical democracy—a confederacy of men that has done some public service and is worth preserving." The convention split on the Wilmot Proviso; and King, followed by a hundred delegates, marched out of the hall. Those remaining nominated Seymour for Governor amid gloomy faces. The Hunkers selected Greene C. Bronson; the Whigs, Myron H. Clark; and the Know-Nothings, Daniel Ullman. The campaign turned upon the Nebraska Act and prohibition,[62] and Clark won by a narrow margin.[63] Tilden's opinion of the election is not on record, but with all his acumen he did see clearly that the old parties were breaking up and that forces were giving birth to a Republican Party which would replace the Whigs. He hoped that out of the many shifts his beloved "radical democracy" would emerge triumphant.

[61] Tilden Papers, letter of Aug. 12, 1854, to ——; *Letters*, I, 111, Tilden to ——, Aug. 26, 1854.
[62] Alexander, II, 203.   [63] *Civil List* (1887), 166.

IN the prime of life, with a lucrative law practice, Tilden was inclined
to regard politics as a mere collateral interest and gave no thought to
public office. Doubtless he was flattered to be consulted by leaders of
his party, and he found time to write long letters setting forth in involved phraseology his political ideas. The issues of the day did not
baffle him, nor was his confidence in his earlier principles shaken. Indeed he saw party machinations with a more practiced eye, and he
estimated men and measures with a greater assurance. But there was
a subsidence of his earlier ardor for accomplishing great things for society through political programs. He was no longer the "stripling knight
astride a dream" but a seasoned campaigner.

Tilden's papers show that he was wholly absorbed in his profession.[1]
Important cases required his closest attention and he derived enjoyment from their successful issue. Railroads, canals, coal and mining companies, and other businesses were eager to employ his legal
talent, and kept him busy traveling to various parts of the country.
Then, too, there were frequent trips to New Lebanon to visit his family
and to straighten out the business tangles of his inept brothers. He was
a busy man of affairs.

The muddle over slavery and the party factions in New York also
contributed to Tilden's loss of his earlier enthusiasm for politics. To his
logical mind the sensible thing to do was to thrash out these misunder-
standings before the people as judges. Instead, he saw prejudice, personal ambition, and ignorance conspiring to make matters worse. Although normally optimistic, yet he saw the futility of sacrificing himself
without accomplishing any substantial good. Hence he was disposed to
let matters drift until an enlightened public opinion developed.

Meanwhile party wrangles went on with all the confusion of the period. The Hards met at Syracuse on August 25, 1855, declining to invite
the Softs, approved the Kansas-Nebraska Act, rebuked the efforts to
restore the Missouri Compromise, and denounced the State Prohibition
Law as unconstitutional. The Softs met at the same place four days later

[1] Tilden Papers

and in a stormy session disapproved of prohibition, praised Pierce's administration, and straddled the slavery issue.[2] In making up the State tickets Tilden's name was mentioned for Comptroller or Secretary of State, but he begged his "old friends" to prevent his nomination for either, because legal obligations made it "incompatible" to accept.[3] At the same time he may have let it be known that he would consider the Attorney-Generalship.

He was nominated for the office of Attorney General, and notified officially of the unanimous action of the convention. His closest political friends urged him to accept and argued that the duties of the office were so light as to constitute no serious interference with his regular law practice. Still Tilden hesitated. It was never easy for him to reach a decision quickly, and he probably felt a real reluctance to enter the fray when the probabilities were strongly opposed to success. He argued with himself and his friends that he was worn out from overwork, and that he had more cases on hand than he could handle in "the next six months." He asserted that he was not afraid of defeat for himself if he could help his friends on the ticket, but that he dreaded the "special annoyances" of a campaign and feared that more would be expected of him in the canvass than he could perform. "I therefore greatly desire," he wrote Dean Richmond, "that you should make up the ticket so as to let me off." [4] His better judgment was broken down by the importunities of party associates, and on September 14 he informed the Committee on Notification that he accepted the nomination "conferred by a convention in which was assembled so much of remarkable and varied ability, of political virtue and personal worth, and enhanced with a ticket" which, if elected, would bring about the *"re-establishment of good government within this State."* [5] Thus Tilden endeavored to accept the inevitable graciously. Supplementing the State tickets of the Hards and Softs were six others to add variety to the campaign. The Whigs and Republicans nominated a joint ticket; the Native Americans made their own selections; and the Free Democrats and Liberty Party were in the field, the latter with Frederick Douglass, the young colored orator, among its candidates.[6] Not since the days of De Witt Clinton had the State been in such a political muddle.

The Hard candidate for Attorney General, J. S. Sutherland, to force

[2] Alexander, II, 209, 210.   [3] *Letters*, I, 116, Aug. 26, 1855.
[4] *Ib.*, 117, Sept. 9, 1855.   [5] *Ib.*, 117, Sept. 14, 1855.
[6] Alexander, II, 211, 215, 216.

Tilden to take a stand against the Pierce administration, offered to withdraw provided Tilden would affirm his belief that the people of a State should decide the question of slavery, that the Kansas-Nebraska Bill was satisfactory, that Congress had no right to decide the slavery issue in a territory, and that he was opposed to the "Black Republican" ticket headed by Preston King.[7] Tilden replied that not he but his party should act on the proposal for a union of the two factions; and that "no delicacy" toward him need restrain his friends from acting.[8]

Prohibition was regarded by Tilden not only as a local issue that might turn the election, but also as one involving a fundamental principle. When the Prohibitionists offered Tilden their endorsement in exchange for support of their program, he refused; and when they sent a note to all candidates for the Attorney-Generalship demanding an opinion on the Maine Liquor Law, he prepared a reply based on "the principles of political economy" and "convictions as to the proper sphere of government." His arguments against "coercive temperance," used over eighty years ago, were urged but recently by the opponents of the Eighteenth Amendment. The common law did not warrant the control of the personal habits of 3,500,000 people by "special criminal procedure." The Liquor Law confiscated personal property contrary to constitutional guarantees and hence was void. It left no room for "individual reason and conscience." It violated a cardinal principle of the Democratic Party, which opposed governmental interference [9] even for the best purposes. It was a step backward toward the "barbarian age" of paternalism. This argument was characteristic of Tilden. He had positive convictions and at the right time he uttered them fearlessly. If he swathed his ideas in a mass of verbiage it was for exactness, not obscurity. He himself enjoyed a glass of wine or a whiskey and soda but was temperate throughout his life.

On immigration and religious freedom Tilden had convictions which it required high moral courage to defend at a time when many people of the Empire State were obsessed with prejudice against foreigners and Roman Catholics—a resentment crystallizing in the Native American Party. The population of New York County was half foreign-born. These newly arrived Americans were easily naturalized, and their votes, predominantly Democratic, were sufficient to carry elections. No

---

[7] *Life*, I, 128, Oct. 12, 1855.
[9] *Writings*, I, 279, Oct. 3, 1855.

[8] *Ib.*, I, 130, Oct. 18, 1855.

doubt Tilden's ideas were colored by this consideration, but he was sincerely interested in the immigrants entirely apart from politics. We find him inviting a group of friends to confer about "the critical state of affairs" in Ireland, and at the same time consulting with upstate New Yorkers about sending out literature in German to win the German vote. His pamphlet on prohibition was translated into German and widely distributed. Since most of these foreign-born citizens were Roman Catholics, the question of religious toleration was injected into the campaign, which became vindictive. Thousands of Democrats and Whigs deserted their parties to vote with the Native Americans. Even Moses Tilden had to have his equilibrium restored by the earnest arguments of the family friend, Van Buren, who said it would be a "crying shame" to break the Democratic continuity which ran "from Dr. and Mrs. Younglove to Sammy." Moses, on "sober second thought," voted for the Softs' candidates.[10]

The feeling against foreigners and Roman Catholics was so great in 1855 that Whigs and Democrats alike, Tilden among them, went down to defeat, and the Know-Nothings elected their ticket. Had the two wings of the Democratic Party been consolidated, Tilden might have won. Instead of being disappointed, he was elated to have sacrificed himself for free-soil, freedom from compulsory temperance, and freedom of religion.

A law case resulting from the election of 1855 brought Tilden more public notice than all his campaigning for the Attorney-Generalship. In New York City Azariah C. Flagg was a candidate for re-election as Comptroller. Flagg was a lifelong friend of Tilden and an honest official. His record justified his continuance in office. The candidate of the Know-Nothing Party was one Giles, vehemently supported by petty grafters and malcontents. The election returns showed that Flagg had received only 179 more votes than Giles. The result was shocking to the friends of Giles who had expected an easy victory, and to lose by so narrow a margin "was more than humiliating—it was exasperating." A cry of fraud was raised, and the election was carried into court to test by *quo warranto* proceedings Flagg's title to the office.[11]

The case attracted widespread attention. Tilden volunteered his services in behalf of his long-time friend, and was associated with Charles O'Conor and William M. Evarts. The Know-Nothings retained James

[10] *Letters,* I, 117, Sept. 14, 1855.   [11] Alexander, II, 219.

T. Brady and Judge John W. Edmunds, Tilden's tutor in law.[12] The case was tried before Judge James Emott of the Supreme Court, in 1856. The certified return of the first election district in the nineteenth ward gave Flagg 316 votes and Giles 186 votes. Giles's attorneys claimed that by a clerical error these figures had been accidentally transposed. To prove their case they presented as witness an inspector of elections who swore positively that the mistake had been made, and another inspector who corroborated this testimony in part. Other witnesses testified that the third inspector was drunk at the time the returns were made out. A clerk of the poll substantiated these alleged facts. Still other witnesses testified to being present when the results of the election were announced and to having written the figures in notebooks. The prosecution thus had a case as strong as the testimony of witnesses could make it.

Tilden and his colleagues had no witnesses of their own, and could gain little by cross-examination. They demanded the tally of the regular votes, but it had disappeared. They then attempted to reconstruct the missing tally by the recollection of witnesses and the use of collateral tallies, but the split tallies, comprising three foolscap sheets, transfers, and summaries, served only to substantiate the testimony of the witnesses for Giles. Flagg and his friends felt that the case was lost and waited despondently for Tilden's acknowledgment of surrender.

Meanwhile Tilden had devoted two nights to a careful study of the transfers and summaries from the missing tallies. As a result, he discovered a method of reconstructing these lost tallies. He knew the total number of votes, and that there were twelve candidates. He saw that whenever a candidate on a regular tally received a vote, eleven other candidates on that tally must necessarily have received the same vote. This was used as the basis for a series of complex mathematical calculations based upon a fixed relationship between the split tallies and the regular tallies. Following out this method, it became perfectly obvious that the ballots had been tampered with and it was possible even to prove with mathematical exactness the actual vote received by each candidate. There is some doubt whether this ingenious idea of a possible mathematical solution to the problem originated with Charles O'Conor or with Tilden, but it is certain that the method and solution were worked out by Henry J. Anderson of Columbia College.

[12] *Life*, I, 131.

The fact that a mathematical solution had been discovered was kept secret until Tilden was called to open the case for the defense. He began with the following words, which must almost immediately have shattered the smug composure of his adversaries:

"If, by a violent blow, I should break out the corner of this table, split a piece off, the fractured and abraded fibers of the wood would be left in forms so peculiar that, though all human ingenuity might be employed to fashion a piece that would fit in the place . . . it could not be done. These things are the work of God. . . . So in interpreting this sort of evidence . . . where you have a fabricated testimony, what you have to do is to study all the other facts, so you can spread out a full map of the fabricated testimony in equal detail. If, after all this has been done patiently and thoroughly, if the lie escape the ordeal I shall believe that the God of justice and truth has not well constructed the work of his hands . . .

"So it is with truth. It is consistent with itself. There is no one true fact which is not consistent with every other true fact in the universe. But a lie . . . does not fit in anywhere with truth. If you can only get at a sufficient amount of detail of the real state of the facts, aside from this particular one in controversy, to enable you to judge from them what this one must be, it will seldom happen . . . that you will fail of finding the exact fragment of truth which has been torn out of the mass that remains, or at least of discovering the falsehood that is attempted to be fitted and joined in its place." [13]

Following his introductory remarks, Tilden gave the judge and each juror a printed form which was an exact replica of the missing regular tallies, except that no figures appeared beside the names of the candidates. He then proceeded, according to the method of Professor Anderson, to reconstruct the missing tallies, and at the conclusion of his address the judge and each juror held in his hand a document which had been proved beyond the suggestion of doubt to be an exact copy of the missing regular tallies. Giles and his friends stood unveiled as clumsy perjurers, and the jury returned a verdict for Flagg within fifteen minutes after receiving the case. The verdict was a victory for a competent official, and a triumph for fair elections and good government. The newspapers gave considerable publicity to the trial and Tilden's snatching of victory from the jaws of defeat won him a professional prominence which he had not hitherto attained.[14]

The year after the triumph in the Flagg case, Tilden gained more renown in the famous Burdell murder case. Dr. Harvey Burdell was a New York dentist whom Tilden had known personally and profession-

[13] Tilden Papers; *Life*, I, 130.   [14] *Life*, I, 131–135.

ally since 1849 when he paid him a bill of $30—$25 for inserting upper teeth and $5 for "an under tooth." [15] Dr. Burdell had rented a part of his dwelling to a Mrs. Cunningham. After the dentist's death in his home on January 31, 1857, this widow was suspected of having murdered him, tried, and found "not guilty." Shortly thereafter she asserted that she had been married to Dr. Burdell privately and applied to the Surrogate for letters of administration and her share of the estate. At this point Tilden was employed by the heirs to contest the alleged marriage.[16]

In the trial Mrs. Cunningham's lawyer produced the marriage certificate, the clergyman who under oath asserted that he had solemnized the marriage, the testimony of a daughter who witnessed the ceremony and swore that her mother slept in a room adjoining that of her husband, and the two maids who had witnessed the marriage certificate. Although Tilden was convinced that Dr. Burdell had been murdered and that there had been no marriage, he did not have a single witness who from personal knowledge could substantiate his surmises.[17]

Tilden now resorted to the principle that had guided him in the Flagg case, namely, that the truth of each particular fact must harmonize with all other facts while a falsehood could be harmonized with only a limited number of facts. Consequently the 150 witnesses were cross-examined not on the main facts but on collateral facts, in order to preclude the introduction of new witnesses to alter the original statements on record. Then the few main witnesses were hammered until they contradicted some of the preliminary testimony. In this manner he showed that the minister had innocently married another man and not Dr. Burdell; that the widow, instead of sleeping in an adjoining room, had slept on an upper floor; that Dr. Burdell was in Brooklyn at eight o'clock in the evening when he was alleged to have been married at seven. Tilden's keen, logical handling of the case did not leave a shred of proof of the alleged marriage, and the Surrogate refused to confer on Mrs. Cunningham letters of administration. Tilden also proved that Dr. Burdell had been killed by a left-handed man such as Mrs. Cunningham's brother, a butcher. Seldom has such a marvelous employment of psychological powers been witnessed in a court room. The public was convinced that she had participated in the murder, but,

[15] Tilden Papers.   [16] *Life*, I, 135; Wilson, *Mem. Hist.*, III, 454.
[17] *Life*, I, 136.

since she had been acquitted already, she could not be tried a second time. The newspapers carried a full account of the case and greatly added to the professional prestige of the eminent lawyer.[18]

Another case of this period revealed the wide range of resources on which Tilden could draw for legal victories—legal knowledge, economics, political science, finance, logic and psychology. The Pennsylvania Coal Company employed Tilden to defend their rights against the Delaware & Hudson Canal Company. A contract had been entered into by these concerns in which it was agreed that in case the canal was enlarged the coal company should pay an extra toll equal to such proportion of one-half the reduction in the expense of transportation as might result from such enlargement. When the extra toll was demanded, the coal company denied that the enlargement had reduced the cost of shipment. The canal company instituted suit, and the case came before Judge Hogeboom as referee. Seventy odd days were consumed in the hearing. Tilden's defense was a complete surprise which rendered the testimony of the plaintiff worthless.

Tilden persuaded his clients to go to the expense of tabulating all the trips of their boats for a period of four years on the old canal and four years on the enlarged canal, and then deduced the average time of a single trip. The results were presented to the court in a summary that could be read in five minutes. The tables compiled proved to a mathematical certainty that the round trip on the enlarged canal took 40% more time than the small boats on the original canal and increased the cost of transportation correspondingly. There was no escape from a verdict for his clients, who were saved the payment of a claim of about a million dollars. There seems to be no record of Tilden's fee in this particular case.[19]

In presenting his irrefutable array of statistics to the judge, Tilden cited the remark of John Randolph when told by an admiring friend that his speech in the House of Representatives had not been answered. "Answered, sir!" said he. "It was not made to be answered." "And so, sir, these tables were not made to be confuted. They are made according to the best process of scientific analysis; proved, step by step, from the records of the plaintiffs themselves, and are introduced here in strict-

[18] *New York Evening Post*, Sept. 17, 1887. See Bradford's *Reports* for a full report of the trial. Tilden preserved among his papers the bogus marriage certificate, dated Oct. 28, 1856.
[19] *Life*, I, 138–143.

conformity to the rules of evidence. They will establish and do establish the proposition they were intended to determine."

Another famous case in which Tilden figured as the chief legal personage was the suit brought in 1858, on the ground of fraud and misrepresentation, by the Cumberland Coal & Iron Company against two of its directors who had bought a large tract of the company's lands. An injunction was asked from the Supreme Court against the transfer of the lands and an effort to dissolve the injunction was opposed by Tilden and C. A. Rapallo. In this instance Tilden argued that the recognized principle that trustees should not become the purchasers of property entrusted to them should also be applied to corporations. This was a new idea but the validity of it was recognized by the court then and is generally accepted now.[20]

With legal triumphs like these to his credit, it is not surprising that Tilden became the most sought-for corporation lawyer in America. His power lay not so much in his legal acumen as in the thorough and original way in which he used it. He took no chances, but made the fullest preparation possible, insured his case against every contingency, anticipated every move of his adversary, and spared no time or labor to make his stand impregnable.

[20] *Life*, I, 141, 143.

A FRIEND declared Tilden's success to be a result of "the happy combination . . . of qualities. . . . He is a political economist . . . a logician . . . a politician; he is a man of the world. He is, besides, a great lawyer." [1] This flattering summation was made after he had passed forty, when he had acquired the poise and suavity which justified his designation as "a man of the world." Prior to that time he was retiring, without boon companions and living quietly with his books.

Poor health, real or imaginary, had a pronounced psychological effect on Tilden's social outlook. It created a shyness that gave impetus to his natural bent for written expression. A more normal boy would not have produced the masterly civic essays which came from this studious recluse. Although never physically robust, yet after thirty he was less absorbed with his ailments and the earlier graphic descriptions of symptoms and remedies disappear. Immersed in law and civic affairs, he was too busy to think of ills and almost forgot them. He took on weight, appeared more fit, and along with this change came a marked social transformation.

This altered attitude is first noticeable in Tilden's dealings with men. Conscious of intellectual superiority when measured with others and flattered with leadership, he squared his round shoulders and held his head higher in a world of men. He was never a roisterer of the back-slapping, stale-joke type, and it would be as fantastic to think of Tilden duplicating Grover Cleveland in besting a bully in a saloon brawl or in sitting up all night to play poker as it would be to think of Thomas DeWitt Talmage in that rôle. Nor was he a rough and ready man of the Jackson type, given to violent speech. Too resourceful to resort to that frontier style of emphasis, he let his brother Henry monopolize profanity in the family. Nor was he a club man, although he paid dues in many such organizations.

Always Tilden was the thinker, the coiner of apt expressions and the prophet of a better day. When men sought him out, as they did with increasing frequency, it was for business or political reasons rather

---

[1] Watterson, *Marse Henry*, I, 273. "He was truly a man of the world among men of letters and a man of letters among men of the world."

than friendship. The same motives prompted his calls on other men. There is no evidence that he feared men or was abashed in their presence. Indeed, if thrown into a group, he was certain to attract attention and to dominate the gathering, but he did not seek out males for entertainment. While the society of intellectual people was more congenial to him, yet most of his professional work and public life was of necessity with practical, combative types of men. There was something fine-grained in his make-up—a delicacy of feeling and a modesty of behavior—which set him apart as a man of "cultivated literary and artistic tastes." From no man did he derive more satisfactory comradeship than O'Conor with all his moods; O'Sullivan's Irish stories convulsed him with laughter—this man who seldom laughed; and witty John Van Buren on one occasion wrote, "The Widow thinks it will be such a proud day for our basement" when you come to dine.

The range of Tilden's tastes may be gleaned from some of his relations with cultural institutions. He regarded himself a Presbyterian and supported the charities of that denomination but attended church only occasionally. He believed in education but gave no special assistance to any college. After organizing an association "to diffuse knowledge" about government, he brought to the metropolis men like Channing, Bancroft and Buchanan to deliver lectures. He supported a course of public debates at the Broadway Tabernacle and endorsed the lyceum work of the Clinton Hall Association. He was an honorary member of the American Board of Foreign Missions, the New York Historical Society, and a Fellow in Perpetuity of the Metropolitan Museum of Art. He served as vice president of the Bar Association.[2] These examples reveal Tilden's prominence in his city wholly apart from political interests.

Tilden's easy social contacts with women developed later than with men. He was so inordinately shy of the gentler sex that one might think his world made up entirely of males. Somehow sexual inhibitions lay behind this defensive attitude. Letters of an aging mother and a fond sister constitute a chronicle of fussy solicitude about his wardrobe and well-being. They could not realize that the Honorable Samuel J. Tilden was not still a thoughtless lad who needed a clean handkerchief and buttons sewed on his shirts. And indeed he had but recently emerged from that state of tutelage. With the physical change there appeared

[2] Tilden Papers.

a noticeable yearning for the companionship of women, which produced a pronounced transformation.

Significantly enough, one of the results of Tilden's plunge into a woman's world was the appearance of maidens and matrons among his law clients. Women's names appear frequently in his correspondence. Julia M. Sands, a sister of the poet Robert C. Sands, asked favors and invited him to meet "Miss Nellie" at dinner. Letters on his monogrammed stationery display an extravagant gallantry which was deemed pure elegance in that day. For example, to an inquiry about his recovery from an injury, he wrote, "I should be very ungrateful if I did not resume my pen for the first time to thank you for your benevolent enquiries about me," and added that the numerous calls "made Medicus shake his ambrosial locks." To another fair one's invitation, he replied: "Just as I was offering on the morning altar the sacrifice of a reeking buckwheat cake, four-cornered Mercury stood before me with a message from the queenly Juno. Her command is law." His answer to Susan O'Sullivan, who threatened to put his "closet in order" if he did not make her either postmistress or chargé at Geneva, is not recorded. Such effusions reveal a side of Tilden not suspected by those who know him only in the courts and party conventions.[3]

The first woman to awaken Tilden's profound admiration was Mrs. Franklin Chase, Irish-born and Tilden's elder by five years, who played a heroic rôle in the Mexican War. He must have known her intimately for many years and in 1850 wrote her the longest letter he ever sent to any woman, a letter, he said, which was like a politician's speech—not intended to be answered. But it resulted in a revealing exchange of letters and an invitation to visit the Chases in Tampico. To her as to none other he confided his higher purposes:

"My life has vibrated between a leisure in which I amuse myself with books, and the greatest activity in public and private affairs. . . . My disposition is not to permit merely private business to engross me; nor to be in any of an unprofessional nature. . . . I have never been accustomed to surrender to it my inner life. . . . But I desire to reserve something to better purpose—something to friends and to myself, and possibly, if hereafter I can recall the enthusiasm of . . . early years, something to consecrate life by a sense that it has not been wholly given to objects so selfishly egotistical as are most of those which we pursue." [4]

[3] Tilden Papers, various dates.
[4] *Letters*, I, 72.

He was "waiting patiently" to hear that she would return to New York, which she did the following year. He had the satisfaction of putting her finances in good order, if nothing else; and she in turn tried to interest her "Esteemed Friend" in a Miss Hedges, who showered him with invitations to call and "would be happy to see him at any time," but without touching his heart. Mrs. Chase took Tilden a client, Mrs. General Gains, thanked him for his "kind care . . . at all times" and said, "Although I cannot reciprocate your kindness, I live in hope that I may be able to do so." [5] The sequel to this beautiful friendship is not known.

From 1850 onward Tilden was something of a social lion. He had a dignified presence, was a witty, well-informed conversationalist, prominent in political circles, and a bachelor with a growing income and influential friends. Hence frequent invitations came to him to dine, to attend parties of various sorts and to make calls. The preservation of these invitations indicates that he set some value on such social engagements. Matrons with eligible daughters were anxious to have him grace their tables. Mrs. B. F. Butler, a long-time friend, who had several attractive daughters, was Tilden's first patroness. She invited him to her home repeatedly, both alone and in company, for teas, dinners and other social events. Her notes to him are full of wit and motherly chidings. Had he "made off with himself"—gone to Texas or New Lebanon—or hid himself among his books in his neglected room? If he dropped in to see some ladies he would find "food for his philosophic mind." He often escorted the Misses Butler to theaters and art galleries and,[6] it is said, repeatedly proposed to Miss Harriet.[7]

Another patroness responsible for introducing Tilden to New York Society was Mrs. William Cullen Bryant who not only had him at her own home but also assumed responsibility for having him invited to gatherings of literary people.[8] Mrs. Edward Cooper likewise took him in tow socially. Many ladies asked him to call or to attend some function. "Kitty" wrote "Dear Samuel" that she would visit him Saturday night if it was satisfactory and attend church on Sunday. Miss E. Easul asked him to bring Mr. O'Sullivan—"We will treat you munificently as we did the other night. . . . Take your own time between 6 and 12"—and "we hope you will be in your talking mood." One young lady

[5] *Letters*, I, 72; Tilden Papers.   [6] Tilden Papers.
[7] Statement of a niece, Miss Harriet Butler, Yonkers, N. Y.   [8] Tilden Papers.

who offered to provide the carriage asked him "to accompany two un-protected women" to see the S. F. B. Morse statue unveiled. This partial list of invitations is sufficient evidence that Tilden's monastic days had ended. He discovered a new aspect of life; something suppressed within him sprang into being; and Christmas presents and valentines —one of the latter inscribed the "Bank of True Love" cherished till his death—took the place of a catalogue of bodily ailments.

It was probably in the year 1852 that Tilden, in a prospective mood, wrote on a slip of paper a list of his chief feminine interests which runs:

> Miss Butler (17 Washington Place)
> Miss Hedges (212 Cherry Street)
> The lady you met on the boat
> Miss Butterman
> Miss Skinner
> Miss Hess
> Miss McKern
> Miss Smith
> Miss Wainwright
> The lady who makes your heart thump
> The lady with *eyes* [9]

The foregoing list would indicate that Tilden became absorbed in his adventures in polite society even to the extent of savoring of mooning over his experiences in retrospect. That he was capable of such romantic anonymity as "The lady who makes your heart thump" is a significant indication of his temper during this period.

It was perhaps inevitable that this social spree should result in some sort of emotional crisis. For several years he ran the gauntlet of eligible young ladies. The first intimation that his immunity had been pierced was a letter from his aged friend, Martin Van Buren,—in his day an excellent judge of an attractive woman—who wrote to him:

My dear Tilden:

I regretted not to see you during my short stay at New York, but was happy to hear that you are about to do what you ought to have done long ago, and if the young lady I had the pleasure to see at Rome is the happy fair one, you have my ready and hearty consent.[10]

Some months later, exercising the prerogative of a political daddy, Van Buren commented: "I see that, in addition to giving up matrimony,

---

[9] Tilden Papers.   [10] *Ib.*, Aug. 3, 1855.

you have also abandoned politics. What is to become of you?" His devoted matronly adviser, Mrs. B. F. Butler, held up her hands in despair and pronounced him hopeless. The young lady on whom the venerable Sage of Kinderhook bestowed a premature benediction is unknown. Tilden's secretiveness was so well developed that, if he thought any injury would come to her, he would not leave a shred of testimony to assist a puzzled biographer who can only guess that she might have been "the lady with *eyes*" or the lass who sent Tilden a valentine in color, depicting a pair of scales with a heart pierced by Cupid's arrow in one balance and the phrase "Settlement for pin money and $2,500 per annum" in the other.[11]

In 1856 Tilden, attracted by Miss Eloise E. Payne, engaged in a sprightly correspondence with her along with personal calls. When he confessed that he had "been asleep," she seemed pleased that he had awakened. She gave up a trip to Boston to see him at Jamaica Pond. He sent her Christmas presents and took her to the theater; but when she wrote him a note, excusing its brevity because there was "company in the parlor," he took the hint and the curtain dropped.[12] Tilden's bachelor days were to continue many a year before there was another rumor of his marriage. He found a fairly satisfactory substitute for a sweetheart and children in his absorbing law work.

While Tilden was no adornment for a five o'clock tea, still women of the intellectual type with a flair for politics enjoyed his society. He was at his best at a small dinner party of friends, where his comments on books, persons, politics and current events were listened to with something of awe. He also had a fund of captivating satire and dry wit. He was past the age of forty-two and perhaps past the period of ardent attachment. If Sam Tilden was not a man's man, neither was he a woman's man. To him there were objectives more worthwhile than matrimony. Moved to act by calm reason, he was not demonstrative—even to his mother he never showed any warm affection. In all his letters to women there is scarcely one phrase of tenderness. His deepest feelings were reserved for a great cause—a reform, a burning party issue or a sacred principle. To him love was merely sexual foolishness.

At this period Tilden was of medium height, slender rather than thin, with a quick nervous walk and gesture, erect and self-important and

[11] Tilden Papers, Dec. 19, 1856.   [12] *Ib.*

with a face that would arrest attention in a crowd. His round, well-formed countenance reflected intelligence, mental alertness and contentment. His brow was high and wide, indicating the student, his light-blue eyes were large, wide apart, slow-moving, and penetrating. His chin was square and showed stubbornness. His mouth was the least attractive part of his round face and its character was due to the early loss of teeth. Later his teeth were all removed and replaced by artificial ones which changed his facial expression considerably. His head, covered with an abundant crop of chestnut-colored hair, was well-formed and rather out of proportion to his frail body. His complexion was light, with a suffusion of color when excited or tired. There was a gentility about his dress suggesting the professional gentleman. He was fond of appearing in a Prince Albert coat because it accentuated his height and weight, and a high stiff collar with a long black bow tie. His shoes were small and nicely polished. All in all his appearance was that of a man of importance, and yet for some reason his clothes never seemed to fit him quite right.

Tilden gave the impression of being indolent, but such was not the case. If he missed examinations and postponed his legal tests for admission to the bar, it was because he was engrossed in something more important or on account of illness. As a matter of fact he was tremendously industrious, although he lacked pertinacity in following the thing he had to do to its conclusion. He would begin a letter and then carry it around in his pocket or portfolio a week before finishing it. His mind jumped from one thing to another, and his major interest always had his undivided attention. He would begin a book and then read two or three others suggested by it before he came back to finish it. He would start out to make a call and en route meet an acquaintance or two with whom he would talk politics the whole morning, and return to his office with his call uncompleted. His time sense was not well co-ordinated. Van Buren sent him money to be invested and after ten days wrote to ask whether he had received it. His father was everlastingly asking him to reply to questions which had been asked in previous letters. No wonder he was accused of forgetfulness and absent-mindedness. His invariable reply, that he was "too busy," was the real explanation of what seemed like reprehensible carelessness—minor matters were subordinated to major. He never observed his office hours and no one could tell when he would be found in. Bryant wrote him curtly:

I have called at your office twice today on some business of my own. Will you oblige me by letting me know when you are in your office? [13]

He made engagements and did not keep them. His sense of honor was that of the "old school"—his promise, although extremely difficult to obtain, once given was sacred. Nothing brought greater disgust than dishonesty, whether in private or public affairs. Some great men are not so much immoral as unmoral—their standards and not those commonly accepted by society are right. Tilden accepted the time-honored canons of honesty and insisted upon applying them to all his human relations. In this respect he was a literalist and did not hesitate to reject retainers for questionable cases. But, once he had taken on a client, he worked staunchly for his rights within the law. He looked farther and deeper than most people, and this made him impatient with the superficial assertions he heard on all sides.

As a rule people did not like Tilden at a first meeting. He seemed cold, self-centered, vain, too cocksure, and too omniscient. To those who knew him well his personal vanity was not objectionable because they understood its source. But he had a habit of saying "I told you so" in a way that humiliated his listener and made him appear an ignoramus. He readily discussed the pros and cons of a question, but refused to give an immediate, positive answer. This annoying hesitation occasioned much jocular criticism. Such a trait looked like indecision, but it was merely a suspension of judgment until all the facts were weighed. It was said that Tilden invented the phrase, "See you later," which was a polite hint that he wished time for further reflection. He employed subordinates, but found it difficult to delegate authority to them, preferring to make all decisions himself. Hence he never took a law partner, although it was proposed repeatedly. "I have not been very fortunate in deputizing such business as I have generally had," he said. "I am exacting as to the mode in which my clients are served."

It is not true that Tilden had no friends, for the Van Burens, Butler, Wright, Bigelow, O'Sullivan, Seymour, Havemeyer, O'Conor and others regarded him highly. But he was not intimate with his best friends because he neglected them and at times was censorious and almost vindictive. Strangers spoke of him as queer, but he was only unusual

[13] Tilden Papers, 1854.

and extraordinary. He did not run true to the common type; hence he was abormal, and that was the evidence of his greatness. Lacking personal magnetism, animation and a strong voice, he made a poor public address unless moved by intense feeling. In the court room Judge Hogeboom said he "spoke as if in a trance," yet held judge and jury by the logic of his arguments expressed in clear English.

Van Buren's alarm lest this "man of the world" had "abandoned politics" was quite needless. Tilden's frequent declarations that he was "out of politics" merely meant that he did not wish to be a candidate for public office or embroiled in conventions and campaigns. To break off relations with his party associates and to ignore public issues was farthest from his thought. So highly prized was his political judgment that his retirement was regretted by party leaders seeking advice. With a Presidential campaign in the offing in 1856, he attended scouting parties to discuss candidates and was the only member to oppose the selection of Frémont, whom the Republicans later nominated.[14] He predicted that the Democratic National Convention would favor, first, the renomination of Pierce, then Buchanan and last Douglas.[15]

Dean Richmond informed Tilden that he must attend the State Democratic Convention to select Soft delegates,[16] but he found himself too busy to do so. The Softs supported the renomination of Pierce while the Hards voted for Buchanan, who became the standard bearer. Tilden was absent from the Cincinnati Convention but professed to be pleased with Buchanan's triumph. Nor did he participate in the nomination of Amasa J. Parker for Governor against John A. King, the Republican nominee. But during the last two weeks of the campaign he addressed meetings almost nightly in New York City, on Long Island and up the Hudson.[17] The outcome of the election could not have pleased him, for King defeated Parker by over 65,000 votes and Frémont received in New York 80,000 more votes than Buchanan. The latter was elected President but did not receive a majority of the popular vote.[18]

After Buchanan's inauguration, Tilden's relations with him were relatively insignificant. In July he visited the President about New York patronage, but the result was not satisfactory.[19] Needy Democrats, believing that Tilden had considerable influence at Washington, importuned him to obtain offices for them; but the Hards had the President's

14 Smith, *The Blair Family*, I, 342; Nevins, *Frémont*, II, 479.
15 Van Buren Papers, May 15, 1856.   16 Tilden Papers, Jan. 4, 1856.
17 Tilden Papers.   18 Alexander, II, 242.   19 Tilden Papers.

ear and controlled all appointments. Perhaps Tilden was "out of politics" a little too much for his own peace of mind. Although a member of the State Democratic Committee who paid his assessments regularly, yet Tilden's party activities were at a low ebb. When requested by Cagger to see President Buchanan in 1858 about appointments, however, he dropped everything and hurried down to Washington. One finds him serving as a vice president of a Tammany mass meeting and attending a reception to Douglas.[20] With little influence at Washington and at Albany, it is difficult to see what advantage a more active course could have brought either to his party or to himself.

"Out of politics" brought no lessened prestige with his party in New York City. In Tammany Hall his influence was as great as ever. The committee to prepare a program for the "Festival of Tammany" met in his office.[21] He was a member of the committee to arrange for the observance of the 43rd anniversary of the Battle of New Orleans; and had invitations to all the balls. He was elected a sachem of Tammany as early as 1856 and was prominent in the counsels of the society.[22] Men like W. F. Havemeyer consulted him about the mayoralty election in 1859; [23] and he was informed that Tammany had nominated him for Corporation Counsel.[24] Publicity cards announcing his candidacy appeared; he joined the "Vigilance Committee" and the Taxpayers Association. With Fernando Wood as the opposition candidate for Mayor, Tilden evinced his earlier interest in politics and acted like a war horse sniffing the smoke of battle. The Havemeyer-Tilden ticket presented as its program a thorough reformation of city government. In a hot and furious campaign Tilden wrote, "I have been in an ice-pack of engagements which accumulated around me in a ten-days' career as a politician." [25]

The reform ticket was badly beaten, and Tilden was far more piqued by this defeat than by his previous loss of the office of Attorney General. Feeling that he had lost "prestige," he was "overworn," "morbid," and disgusted with Wood's triumph. Consoling himself with the confession that it might have been impossible anyhow to reconstruct the city government, he was glad to be relieved of the "burden" and had no regret for having done his duty. To Van Buren he wrote that he was "just ill enough" over the election to decline "all dinners," criticized Tam-

[20] Tilden Papers.   [21] Ib., Jan. 8, 1857.
[22] Ib., May 5, 1857; Myers, Tammany, 184.   [23] Tilden Papers, May 6, 1859.
[24] Ib., May 5, 1859.   [25] Ib., to Cassidy, Jan. 6, 1860.

many for abolishing ward committees and charged the defeat to the ignorant Irish, "many special interests" and the "jobbing Republicans," who made a bargain with Wood. He predicted that the gigantic scheme to plunder the city would "presently appear"—a prophecy that was to be fulfilled not many years later.[26]

Tilden may have been "out of politics" but he did not separate himself from his closest party associates. When they sought his advice or co-operation, as was mostly the case now, his response was friendly and helpful. The beautiful friendship between the New York lawyer and the aged Sage of Lindenwald continued. Sam as a lad idolized Van Buren and as he grew older each developed a mutual confidence in the other's integrity. In berating Tilden's shortcomings, the ex-President exercised the affectionate prerogatives of a father. Disappointed in not seeing Tilden, who had promised to come but was taken ill, the fussy old man wrote, "It is a pity that a man who is so wise as you is not sensible enough to appreciate the importance of health." Fearing that his jokes had offended Tilden, he commented: "If so . . . it must have been owing to the state of . . . your nerves. Forgive me." [27]

Tilden preserved many short, witty notes from "Little Van" about business, politics, a position for his nephew; [28] purchase of a family Bible, a newspaper or a book. Since Tilden had a library "but no time to read and never will have," Van Buren asked for the loan of books. Thanking Tilden for the Cicero he dryly remarked that he had to cut the leaves.[29] For twenty years Tilden was his investment agent, items running as high as $10,000. If legal advice was needed, Tilden gave it; and it was he who drew up Van Buren's will. On one occasion when Tilden failed to keep an engagement Van Buren remarked, sarcastically, "I waited for you till nine o'clock and then retired. . . . When I am gone, I trust you will, as my confidential representative, be more punctual." [30] More than to any other, Tilden gave his full confidence to this experienced statesman; and if he did not always act on the advice given, it was not for lack of trust but because he believed his own judgment better. Moses Y. Tilden once suggested that Van Buren should complete his autobiography, but Van Buren replied, "There is another man in this State who could do it far more justice than I could hope for, and that is your brother Samuel." [31] There is no evidence, however, that

[26] Tilden Papers. [27] *Ib.*, Aug. 22, 1859. [28] *Ib.*, Dec. 22, 1856.
[29] *Letters*, I, 125. [30] Tilden Papers, June 16, 1858. [31] *Letters*, I, 160, May 31, 1861.

Samuel ever gave any thought to the suggestion.

"Prince John" Van Buren, Tilden's senior by four years, took no notice of him until both had passed their thirtieth year. With the emergence of the Barnburners, he came to know Tilden as a lawyer and party organizer. Both were for a time Free-Soilers and both returned to be Softs in the Democratic Party. When John threatened to denounce President Pierce publicly in 1853, Tilden's level head quieted him. Like his father, John turned to Tilden for financial service.[32] For some time John was anxious to become a law partner of Tilden and his father finally proposed such an arrangement,[33] but Tilden, after waiting six weeks, told him that it would not be "a desirable combination."[34]

After the death of Marcy in 1857, the most important Democratic leader in New York was Horatio Seymour. He and Tilden respected but did not quite trust each other; and it was always Seymour who sought a better understanding. Like the Van Burens, Seymour turned to Tilden for financial assistance, and received it. During Seymour's first term as Governor few communications passed between him and Tilden.[35] When Seymour went to Wisconsin he asked Tilden for more than a year to get him out of a financial "scrape."[36] Later he addressed Tilden as his "Conscience Keeper." Not until the Civil War did the reserve between these two men disappear.

Dean Richmond, the Nestor of the Democrats in New York, was in constant communication with Tilden for a decade preceding the Civil War. Not cultured, ungrammatical in his almost illegible letters, given to habitual swearing, but energetic, friendly and honest, he had a profound admiration for Tilden's political shrewdness and rare business ability. An original Barnburner and a pronounced Soft, he was Chairman of the State Committee for sixteen years; and his letters to Tilden bulk larger than those of any other party acquaintance.

William Cassidy, son of an Albany Irish Catholic butcher, a graduate of Union College and a law student under John Van Buren, like Tilden wrote able political essays at an early age. He was Tilden's source of political gossip and his broadcaster. In 1856 he combined the *Atlas* and the *Argus* to support Pierce and Buchanan and two years later purchased the paper. Tilden not only subscribed for the support of this party organ but raised $3,000 in New York City.[37] Deluded as Tilden

[32] Tilden Papers.   [33] *Letters*, I, 130.   [34] *Ib.*, Mar. 28, 1860.
[35] Tilden Papers.   [36] *Letters*, I, 110; Tilden Papers, Mar. 26, 1860.
[37] Tilden Papers, Feb. 15, 1856, Jan. 14, 1858.

was by the thought that he was "out of politics," contacts with the men who were managing the affairs of the party demonstrate quite clearly how much they relied on his counsel.

By far the major portion of Tilden's time was devoted to railroads and investments. He was wont to speak of his law practice as private, yet his office at 43 Wall Street was besieged with callers and was the scene of business and legal conferences. He employed a clerk, Paterson I. M. Todd, but refused to take a law partner. Tilden & Company at New Lebanon, under the management of Moses and Henry, who were not able business men, caused Samuel an immense amount of annoyance. Henry, a large, aggressive man, pompous, given to profanity, was the head of the concern; while Moses, a short, fat, good-natured person, played a minor rôle. The brothers were pitifully dependent on Samuel's legal help, and yet seldom acted on his suggestions. Moses became involved with the Lebanon Railroad and appealed to his lawyer-brother for assistance; but try as hard as he might, Sam could not induce his brothers to supply him with facts sufficiently reliable to enable him to help them as much as they thought he should. Despite solemn promises that they would stay out of debt, they were continually in financial trouble. Now and then, too, they were soundly denounced for interfering in politics. When Tilden's letters were published, Randolph advised the omission of those of Moses because he was only "a boil on Samuel's body," and Henry's because they might mortify his children.[38]

Tilden's law work, restricted almost wholly to corporations, is vividly pictured in the following record for one day in his *Legal Diary:*

Feb. 25. Drawing amendment to charter of Chestnut Hill Iron Co. Interview with Mason about North Bend. Consulted about Cumberland. Interview with Litchfield about Terre Haute & Alton. Long examination of statistics and conference about Penn. Coal Co. Evening long talk with Gen. McEwen on Penn. suit. Chicago, St. Paul & Fond du Lac consultation about consolidation.

And so the *Diary* runs day after day except for such records as:

Aug. 26. Left for Lebanon
Sunday to Tuesday at Rockaway
May 27-June 24 Absent in West on R.R. business
April 22 Mr. Gould about his affairs [39]

[38] Tilden Papers.
[39] *Ib.*

Business called him so frequently to Albany, Washington and other parts of the country that Havemeyer insisted upon knowing when he was coming home to confer about the Pennsylvania Loan Mortgage.[40]

The *Memo Book* of this period contains Tilden's notes on various railroads and the operators with whom he had confidential relations.[41] The man with whom he was chiefly associated was William B. Ogden, a New Yorker by birth, ten years Tilden's senior, who as an Assemblyman had championed the building of the Erie Railroad. Going to Chicago, he became the first Mayor in 1837 on the Democratic ticket. He and others in 1846 began to build the Galena & Chicago Union Railroad, incorporated ten years before with a stock of $100,000, and Ogden became president. The charter was revised and in 1847 $250,000 worth of stock sold. The capital stock was increased to $5,000,000 in 1854 and the following year the Mississippi & Rock River Junction Railroad was absorbed. Ogden next became interested in the Chicago, St. Paul & Fond du Lac Railroad and was made its president in 1855. This road ran into financial difficulty and Tilden was consulted about its condition.[42] But bankruptcy ensued and in 1859 Tilden purchased it at auction for $10,849,938 in stocks and bonds of the new organization called the Chicago & Northwestern Railroad. Five years later the Galena & Chicago was absorbed by the Northwestern, which became the "leading railroad of the West." This was Tilden's earliest triumph in successfully rehabilitating a crippled railroad. His pay, taken in securities, was the basis for his fortune.

Another railroad with which Tilden was connected as a financial physician was the Pittsburgh, Fort Wayne & Chicago. Ogden was its president in 1853 and when it became insolvent in the panic of 1857, he served as receiver. Tilden studied every phase of the problem and then drew a plan for reorganization by merging it with the Pennsylvania Railroad, incorporated in 1847. N. H. Swayne wrote him that the directors and many of the stockholders were satisfied with his reorganization, "especially since you propose to do it with such an air of innocent unconsciousness." [43] Since it was an inter-State line passing through Pennsylvania, Ohio, Indiana and Illinois, Tilden proposed to have a parent incorporation act passed by the Pennsylvania legislature and permissive acts or general laws enacted in the other States. Influential

40 *Ib.*, Aug. 17, 1859.   41 Tilden Papers.   42 *Ib.*, Oct. 28, 1857.
43 *Ib.; Letters*, I, 129, 141.

men like N. H. Swayne, Hunter, Thomson, Thurman, Sherman and Stansbury co-operated in having the right laws passed.[44] The new charter was obtained and this railroad became one of the most profitable in the nation.

These two successful rescues of crippled railroads brought Tilden a reputation which for the next fifteen years made him a corporation lawyer with scarcely a peer. Requests poured in for him to reorganize other railroads—like the Terre Haute, Alton & St. Louis; the St. Louis Railroad Company; the Greenville & Miami, and the Belleville & Illinoistown; [45] to incorporate concerns like the Atlantic Telegraph Company; to put shaky corporations like the Ogden, Fleetwood Company on their feet; to defend the legal rights of coal and iron companies and canals; and to sell land such as the 4,446 acres in Herkimer County for P. M. Hitchcock.[46]

In these years Tilden also acted as an investment broker for his political friends and others. He weathered the panic of 1857 without any serious disaster, selecting stocks and bonds with unusual sagacity. Collections of debts, interest and dividends were made for his clients, and mortgages were handled. Notes were discounted and judicious loans were made. One finds him negotiating with Knox and Morgan for 1,000 tons of rails "besides 2,470 bars"—probably for railroad purposes.[47] On one occasion, losing his customary caution, he endorsed a bank loan for a friend, which proved to be a "legacy of trouble" for more than a year.[48]

Altogether this was an exceedingly busy period in Tilden's life, and he was continually complaining about "the *rush* of things in which I live." He made engagements and broke them without notification; he promised calls and did not make them; he spent a month at a time looking after Western railroads; and yet he found time to attend the sessions of his party's State Committee, to be present at the anniversary of the storming of Stony Point, to listen to appeals from the colored people for help, to serve as a trustee of the New York Medical College, and to give wise advice to ambitious young law students. "Overworked by a momentary press of business and . . . unwell," no great disquisitions on political science, economics or finance came from his pen as earlier and later. In fact he was too immersed in practical affairs to give much thought to the fact that a fratricidal war was just a step away —ample proof that he actually was "out of politics." [49]

[44] *Letters*, I, 141.   [45] *American Almanac*, 1856, 222.
[46] Tilden Papers.   [47] *Ib.*   [48] *Letters*, I, 114.   [49] Tilden Papers.

ALTHOUGH absorbed in reorganizing railroads, in extricating industries from legal difficulties, in incorporating iron ore concerns, and in investigating oil fields in Pennsylvania, yet Tilden was not too busy to be concerned over the rising tide of sectional passion. Realizing that a terrible civil conflict might follow the election in 1860, he was solicitous that a Democrat of sound principles should succeed Buchanan.[1] To the Charleston Convention, April 23, the Softs sent 35 delegates, with Dean Richmond in command. Tilden may have been an alternate, for Watterson first met him there. Fernando Wood's group of delegates, with pro-Southern leanings, demanded equality with the regulars but were not seated. The Softs were pledged to Douglas as first choice and to James Guthrie, a rich Kentucky railroad promoter, as second. Although true to Douglas, Richmond really hoped that in the shuffle Seymour would win. The Douglasites were distrustful of the New Yorkers, however, and D. S. Dickinson with a few New York supporters had unbounded confidence in Southern backing. That New York had a controlling voice in the convention was generally admitted.[2]

Disagreement over the slavery planks resulted in the secession of seven Southern States with 51 delegates. The remaining 253 delegates, unable to make a nomination after 57 ballots, adjourned to meet in Baltimore on June 15.[3] During the recess Tilden consulted with party leaders and believed that Guthrie, as a practical business man, would be most likely to win the election by harmonizing discordant factions.[4]

Meanwhile, the Constitutional Union Party met in Baltimore on May 9 and complicated the situation by nominating John Bell of Tennessee.[5] A week later the Republicans at Chicago astonished the East by choosing Lincoln instead of Seward on a platform radical as to slavery.[6] Guthrie informed Tilden, "The Republicans nominated their best man—far better than Seward, Chase or Banks"; denounced Douglas for his rule or ruin attitude; and cheered Tilden by saying, "I will

---

[1] *Life*, I, 152.   [2] Alexander, II, 270–279.   [3] *Ib.*, 279.
[4] Tilden Papers; Nevins, *Hewitt*, 191.
[5] Alexander, II, 275; *Dict. of Am. Biog.*, II, 158.
[6] Stanwood, *Hist. of Pres.*, 291–294.

not withdraw my name." [7] Supporters of Guthrie wrote Tilden from Washington, "Come on here and see about it." [8] The Southern bolters on June 11 met at Richmond, but not until the 23rd did they nominate John C. Breckenridge.

As the time approached for the adjourned Democratic Convention at Baltimore, Tilden was substituted for a delegate who had withdrawn. It was reported that Buchanan would accept either Seymour or Dickinson, but not Douglas.[9] "Our people can win if they select their candidate," said a Breckenridge supporter, "but if they remain tied fast to Douglas, they will be beaten and Lincoln elected." [10] That seemed to be Tilden's own opinion, yet in holding the New York delegates in line for Douglas, he seemed to co-operate with Dean Richmond who wrote [11] him, "I can spare you $27,000"—possibly for use in the convention.

Tilden was present at the Baltimore Convention on June 18, made several speeches and apparently introduced the following friendly resolution, "Resolved that the Delegations which withdrew at the Charleston Convention be readmitted to their seats and in case any shall again withdraw, contesting delegates shall be admitted to their places." [12] The wrangle over the admission of the bolters resulted in a second secession. With New York no longer insisting on the unit rule, Douglas was nominated on the second ballot. There is reason to believe that Tilden, conforming to the strategy worked out by Dean Richmond, reluctantly gave his vote to Douglas, although his acquaintance with him was slight and his personal preference was Guthrie.[13] The seceders at Richmond had some hope that Tilden would support their candidate, for they asked him to co-operate in drawing up the platform for Breckenridge, but he remained loyal to Douglas.[14]

Tilden had met Lincoln several times "before he was thought of for the Presidency" and again when he delivered his Cooper Institute address. He also knew much of him "from his friends and neighbors," and never treated him "so uncharitable" as did members of the Republican Party. Yet Lincoln's nomination "filled Mr. Tilden's mind with the gravest apprehension," because he could not receive an electoral vote

[7] Tilden Papers, Guthrie to Tilden, May 13, 1860.
[8] *Ib.*, G. W. Newell to Tilden, May 17, 1860.
[9] Auchampaugh, *R. Tyler*, 301, 365 note 40.
[10] Tilden Papers, S. L. M. Barlow, June, 1860.   [11] *Ib.* May 14, 1860.
[12] Tilden Papers.
[13] A photograph of Douglas is the only souvenir of Douglas in the Tilden Papers.
[14] Tilden Papers, G. Hine to Tilden, July 2, 1860.

in the South and, if elected, would be a President with "no affiliations in the Slave States." Hence "unimaginable disasters" would result. It would be better, therefore, to elect any one of his opponents—Douglas, Breckenridge or Bell—because he would have supporters in the South.[15]

The factions among the New York Democrats reflected the split-up of the party nationally, and seemed to guarantee defeat at the polls. The Hards, in resentment against Richmond, held a Breckenridge convention at Syracuse on August 8, under the guidance of O'Conor, Bronson and Dix, nominated James T. Brady, for Governor, chose an electoral ticket, and appointed a new State Committee.[16] Before the Hards had adjourned, the Softs, hoping for a unified Democratic ticket, or at least a fusion electoral ticket through a State-wide committee, called a meeting at Belmont's home on August 10. Belmont urged Tilden to attend this gathering "to save New York from the Republicans and to save the Federal Union from the calamities of the election of Lincoln." The meeting would be private and among the thirty-one persons invited were: Seymour, the two Kellys, Corning, Richmond, the Astors, Havemeyer, Potter, Cagger and West. Belmont was chairman and John Handy secretary. The steps taken for harmonious action were wise and moderate, and based on Tilden's advice. Meanwhile Tilden had sent his brother Henry to scout among the prominent Softs to ascertain who might be an acceptable candidate for Governor; and also to lodge in their minds the name of William Kelly, a philanthropic Free-Soiler and a family friend of the Tildens. Evidently Henry did his job well because he reported that Richmond, Cagger, Comstock and others confirmed Sam Tilden's judgment, and that Kelly was willing to be drafted.[17]

After this satisfactory conference, the Softs met in convention on August 15, indorsed Douglas and his doctrines, for the sake of unity admitted Wood's New York City delegates on an equality with Tammany's, and enthusiastically nominated William Kelly of Hudson. Kelly immediately asked Tilden to induce Brady to withdraw before the Hard delegates got back to the metropolis. A week later, on August 22, the Republicans with remarkable unanimity renominated Governor Morgan and approved of Lincoln and the Chicago platform. In their anti-slavery stand, they swept into their party such thoughtful men as W. C. Bryant, the radical Democrat, and J. O. Putnam, the Clay Whig. The

15 *Writings*, I, 284, 338.   16 Alexander, II, 324–325.   17 Tilden Papers.

trend of popular sentiment was in their direction.[18]

A Union Mass Meeting was held at Cooper Institute on September 17 to unite all Democratic factions on a single electoral ticket. Tilden encouraged the project and agreed to read the resolutions.[19] Dix was chairman and J. W. Gerard and Charles O'Conor the orators. Tilden offered the resolutions and "made a short speech." The *Evening Post* poked fun at the gathering, said that Tilden "retired with his speech as good as new," and offered to print it so he could explain "by what process so clever a man has reasoned himself into such bad company." [20]

Tilden denied that he had prepared a written address for the meeting but promised the *Post* that if he could prepare one on "the present state of the country" between the "intervals of exhausting daily engagements" he would do so.[21] Knowing that "Mr. Tilden never writes or speaks without having something worth hearing," the *Post* agreed to wait for it. Bigelow urged him to send the manuscript at once because he wished to place him in the position of "a most capable champion and defender" of his party. "Write as a statesman," Bigelow advised, "and not as a partisan . . . and perhaps we Republicans . . . may profit by your teachings." [22] Cassidy, hearing of Tilden's answer, was eager to see it so he could prepare an editorial in the *Atlas and Argus*.[23] Richmond consulted Tilden about the article and may have given him some pertinent ideas. Peter B. Sweeny wanted a copy of the resolutions and the address for publication. Havemeyer asked impatiently: "How about that letter to the *Post?* Hurry up or the election will be over!" [24] But most New Yorkers were less interested in Sam Tilden's answer to the *Post* than the visit of the Prince of Wales. So it was not until October 26 that the *Kent Letter* was signed and sent to the *Post* which gave it to the public four days later. It was at once reprinted as the famous pamphlet, "The Union, Its Dangers and How They Can Be Averted."

This communication, the most significant document of the campaign, issued just before the election, addressed to an old friend, son of the illustrious Chancellor Kent, was a remarkable survey of the use of parties, the value of Federal self-government, an analysis of the Republican Party, education for "chronic sectionalism," organized agitation against slavery, danger of the "irrepressible conflict" doctrine, the territorial

[18] Alexander, II, 325–327.   [19] Tilden Papers; *Herald*, Sept. 20, 1860.
[20] *Letters*, I, 135.   [21] *Ib.*, 132, Oct. 9, 1860.   [22] *Ib.*, 139, Oct. 10, 1860.
[23] *Ib.*, 137.   [24] Tilden Papers, Oct. 27, 1860.

question, Northern immigration's effect on the exclusion of slavery, and the possible forms of compromise. The conclusions were:

1. The Southern States, determined "to preserve the social supremacy of their race," would not accept the Republican creed about slavery.

2. The rule of a party with no affiliations in the South would provoke secession and dissolve the Union unless that party became national in its structure and adopted a policy of "absolute non-action" on slavery.

3. Lincoln's election by a third of the votes of the people would alarm the South because fatal to their "vital interest," whereas the triumph of a partisan Southern President would merely offend Northern ideas.

4. "If we are not wise enough to abstain from creating such a state of things, what right have we to suppose the South will accept it?" Lincoln's victory would result in the call of State conventions to deliberate on the continuance of the Union and bring consternation to patriotic Unionists in the South.

5. "What will Mr. Lincoln do?" Could he rise above "his own partisan policy?" If he failed to meet these "great exigencies," the inevitable result would follow. "If he should act in a spirit of large patriotism," as Jackson did, he would still lack a single local leader or newspaper to aid him. "The whole shock of the crisis would be thrown upon the mere intrinsic strength of our Federal Government."

"I for one cannot assent to the creation of such a state of things. I have faith in our popular system . . . but I dare not precipitate it upon such a trial. . . . Those who think it free from the most imminent peril display the courage of men who, having eyes, cannot see." Lincoln's election would result in a crisis. History was full of the "inadequate policy" which met civil convulsions with concessions made too late." "Elect Lincoln, and we invite those perils which we cannot measure. We attempt in vain to conquer the South to an impracticable and intolerable policy." The only hope was that he would abandon the principles and pledges on which he would have been elected. "Defeat Lincoln, and all our great interests and hopes are, unquestionably safe."

"It is too late! It is too late! We are upon the breakers. Whose eye quails now? Whose cheek blanches? It is not mine, who felt a 'provident fear,' and have done all I could. . . . Where are the thoughtless, reckless seamen who taunted me with cowardice when I vainly strove to warn them? I hear only the wailing cry of selfish terror . . . as I . . .

watch the rage of the sea. My mind is filled, my heart swells with the thought that yon wave which towers above us will engulf more of human happiness and human hopes than have perished in any one catastrophe since the world began." [25]

This lamentation of a modern political Jeremiah was read across the continent, and created a sensation. Newspapers north and south commented on it editorially and numerous letters appeared in their columns, both commending and denouncing it. Even Europeans took notice of it. Not only did it attract attention in 1860 but it was reprinted in 1863, when its dire prophecies seemed to be fulfilled.[26] Once more in 1876 it was put out by Tilden's foes as evidence of his treason to a holy cause. All in all it was probably one of the most influential of all his public writings. A penciled copy of the editorial in the *Post* of October 30, 1860, was preserved by Tilden until within a few months of his death, when with a significant smile he handed it to Bigelow, the editor, who had promised but never written a conclusive reply.[27]

The *Kent Letter* called forth a mass of communications, mostly congratulatory but some frankly critical. Edward Everett wrote, "Nothing which I have met with on the dreadful subject which now convulses the country has seemed to me more clearly or forcibly urged." [28] Senator J. M. Mason of Virginia thanked Tilden for his "great contribution to American thought," asked for twenty copies and hoped the North would read it widely, but feared it was "too late to arrest the catastrophe." [29] Seymour was eager to see it and to talk over its contents. E. C. Litchfield found it "well-reasoned, logical and conclusive" but thought it should have been printed sooner. J. S. Thrasher promised to mention it in the *Herald*. Preston King was glad to have it but felt that the election had answered it. Although G. S. Davis of Massachusetts pronounced it "the ablest on the subject," yet Lincoln's election was "necessary," [30] and G. S. Hillard of Boston said it was "sound, wise and patriotic. . . . Anybody who preaches moderation and . . . endeavors to calm the tempest . . . is called a skulking neutral. . . . The Union party alone can save the country." [31] In a more critical tone G. W. Palmer of Plattsburg wrote : "Candor compels me to say that I have no sympathy what-

[25] *Writings*, I, 289.　　[26] New York *World*, Feb. 21, 1863.
[27] *Life*, I, 155, Editorial reprinted.　　[28] *Letters*, I, 139, Nov. 6, 1860.
[29] *Ib.*, Nov. 12, 1860.　　[30] Tilden Papers, various dates.
[31] *Letters*, I, 140, Nov. 19, 1860.

ever with the letter or with the motive for publication. . . . I have more respect for . . . the patriotism of those *southern* men who maintain that the Union is not to be imperiled by . . . a Republican President . . . than I have for those *northern* men . . . like yourself, whom I had the honor to work with in 1848, who have undertaken a 'revolution backward' in the civilization of the age." [32]

The immediate result of the Union Mass Meeting on September 17 was the creation of the Committee of Fifteen representing the three Democratic factions to work out a fusion electoral ticket to defeat Lincoln. Tilden was an important member and with him were associated O'Conor, Croswell and Sweeny. Secretary Joshua J. Henry kept Tilden informed of the meetings of the committee to the end of October. Hostility to a fusion ticket came from both Hards and Softs. William Cassidy told Tilden plainly enough that the committee would do more harm than good. R. H. Gillet wanted a Breckenridge ticket whether Richmond, Cagger, Green and Tucker adopted it or not; he deprecated the old factional quarrels, and thought the situation would not be remedied until the leaders ceased to "bargain, buy and sell the votes of their followers. . . . Things must change or New York will be looked upon with contempt." Meanwhile Richmond's State Committee, of which Tilden was a member, tried to form its own fusion ticket. Tilden was the harmonizer, inducing Richmond to substitute six men proposed by the Committee of Fifteen.[33] Further negotiations resulted in an agreement by which of the 35 New York electors, 18 were assigned to Douglas, 10 to Bell and 7 to Breckenridge.[34]

The next problem before the Committee of Fifteen was to raise funds to insure victory for the fusion ticket. Cagger asked Tilden to persuade Belmont and ten others to give $2,500 each; and after Belmont was assured about the make-up of the ticket he gave it full support. The *Tribune* reported that four "nabobs" had pledged $25,000 each and that a million would be raised.[35] Southern newspapers declared that W. B. Astor had given that sum. Exaggerated as these rumors were, ample funds were available and Tilden acted as paymaster. Requests for cash came from various parts of the State—E. B. Sprague of Oswego; "Baker will spend $10,000 in Columbia County"; "I hear money was sent to

[32] Tilden Papers, Nov. 9, 1860.   [33] *Ib.*   [34] Alexander, II, 331.
[35] Tilden Papers, Oct. 5, 19, 1860.

Albany," "We need $1,000" for Long Island. Comstock urged Tilden to spend $700 in each county for organization and bringing out the vote. W. H. Ludlow of the State Committee wrote him "not as S.J.T. but as one of the Committee of 15" and asked for financial help. Tilden was also importuned to have this committee print the electoral and State tickets, and this was probably done.[36]

Meantime the campaign of 1860 was bitter and hard-fought, relieved by mass meetings and torchlight processions. Stocks fell and there was great uncertainty for the future. Seymour, always a pessimist, had early predicted defeat. "I may take a gloomy view of affairs," he wrote Tilden, "but I think we are beaten. . . . The town meetings have gone against us." Others were more hopeful, particularly after the fusion of the electoral ticket. The Empire State must "save the Union and keep the rail-splitter out of the White House," said the president of the Oswego Douglas Club. Theodore Miller of Hudson "never saw such large and enthusiastic audiences. . . . New York is the battle ground. We must not fail to beat Lincoln." Hiram Ketcham had a plan to capture "respectable Whigs" and Church said, "If you give us a majority of 40,000 in the city, we shall carry the State. Act accordingly."

Tilden's deep concern over the election may be seen from an incident narrated by Bigelow. A few days before the decision of ballots, Tilden popped into the office of the *Post* where some of his Republican friends began to chaff him about the political crisis. Listening with a stern, unsmiling face he broke out vehemently: "I would not have the responsibility of Bryant and Bigelow for all the wealth in the Subtreasury. If you have your way, civil war will divide this country and you will see blood running like water in the streets of this city." Then he hurled himself out of the office. To Andrew H. Green who called to find Tilden, Bigelow said: "He has just left. You had better look him up at once and get him home. He is very much excited and I fear for his sanity." [37]

After the election on November 7 the *Post* printed the "promised reply" to the *Kent Letter* in the form of election returns showing that Lincoln received 169 electoral votes, including New York's 35, while Breckenridge got 61, all Southern; Bell 57 from North and South; Douglas 9 from Missouri; and Oregon and California doubtful.[38] These figures were somewhat changed in the official report. Of the popular

[36] Tilden Papers, Oct. 10–26, 1860.   [37] *Life*, I, 153.   [38] *Letters*, I, 140.

vote Lincoln had 1,868,452 or nearly 40 %; Douglas 1,376,957; Breckenridge 849,781; and Bell 588,879.[39] A united Democracy would have defeated Lincoln. In New York Lincoln's majority was 50,138 and Morgan's plurality 63,460. William Kelly, the Softs' candidate for Governor, ran 27,689 behind the Democratic fusion electoral ticket. James T. Brady, the Hards' standard bearer, received only 19,841. The vote showed a pronounced trend toward the Republican platform.

Tilden now found solace in the companionship of old friends like O'Conor and Havemeyer with whom he dined frequently to discuss the situation in confidence. A great burden lay on the North, he felt, and wrote that it was the duty of the Union Committee "to recall our Northern people to the duty of justice and fraternity toward our Southern fellows. . . . We must save the political system." [40] To a Southern guest at the home of W. H. Aspinwall, he said that if the South seceded, they must not expect the Northern Democrats to hold the Federal Government while they were whipping it; that the breach had been inevitable; that peaceful separation was a delusion and even if attained would only bring troubles; and that the North would stand behind the President.[41] He attended private conferences to discuss the problem of secession—the "national crisis"—and his advice was always against hasty and ill-considered action.

Slavery, clearly, for millions, was now the moral, if not the political, issue. In the Free-Soil movement of 1848 Tilden was aroused to the point where he might have taken an emphatic stand on slavery as a moral issue. But his public utterances, even in that period of excitement, based his opposition to the extension of slavery on political and economic grounds rather than because of a violation of human rights or of social injustice. He left no expression of his reaction to the John Brown raid. A distant cousin was selected by Brown, however, to defend him.[42] Sam Tilden, like Elam his father, was intolerant of abolitionists but had no sympathy for slavery. His friend, George Hoadley, expressed sympathy for Brown but thought him a deluded fanatic,[43] an attitude which even Lincoln was disposed to take. So one may conclude that Tilden was somewhat horrified by Brown's disregard of law and the established order. Yet as far as records show, he never voiced an opinion on the

---

[39] Stanwood, *Hist. of Pres.*, 297.   [40] Tilden Papers, letter to Townsend Ward.
[41] *Life*, I, 167.
[42] Villard, *Brown*, 493; *Tribune*, Oct. 29, 1859.
[43] Villard, *Brown*, 587; Hoadley to Chase, Dec. 3, 1859, in Chase Papers.

moral aspects of slavery, and his sentiments in this direction may be predicated upon inference only; but there is sufficient evidence to spare such inference the implication of abortion.

The Tilden family held no slaves, but Samuel was not by this circumstance deprived of personal experience of the institution. There were slaveholders in Columbia County, even in the neighborhood of the little village of New Lebanon, where it pleased the vanity of the father of Aaron Gilbert, owner of the medical establishment to which Elam finally succeeded, to retain Negroes as household servants, and the Tildens were frequent visitors in the Gilbert home. In Tilden's youth his townsmen were not seriously concerned with the "irrepressible conflict." In the debating society to which he belonged slavery was not included as one of the topics of debate, as it would have been had it been one of the burning issues. The Tilden household's attitude may be seen from the fact that Elam asked Sam to stop the *New Echo* ōn account of its abolition gospel; and "Grandma wants you to discontinue the *Post* if the editor fills it with abolition news." [44]

Perhaps it was due to Tilden's precaution that Africans who were interested in a solution of the Negro Problem by other means than war turned to him as a sympathetic counselor. L. H. Putnam wrote him about a plan for emancipating the black man by sending him back to Africa where an "agricultural district" would be set aside for him and his kind.[45] Charles G. Halpin, editor of the New York *Leader*, reminded him that the Negro vote would be large in the coming election. "I'm anxious to put my oar in under your pilotage, in the next issue of our paper." [46] And other Negro leaders wrote him because they expected a sympathetic hearing.

Surely it was a malign fate that destined Tilden for party politics, and then cast him into the midst of political commotions whose violence has never been equaled in our history. He was strong enough to breast the set of a sinister tide in his native State, and, by saving himself, also to save his party; but in national politics he was engulfed finally by the backwash of passion, prejudice, and corruption which followed that ravaging flood of emotion whose culmination was the threat of disunion.

[44] Tilden Papers.   [45] *Ib.*, Aug. 10, 1860.
[46] *Ib.*, Sept. 10, 1860

AFTER the election of Lincoln, Tilden, realizing that there was "a crisis in the affairs of our country," used his influence to avert war. He believed that Lincoln, "a frank, genial, warm-hearted man," as President was bound to "take conservative views" and to have a strong, noble motive "to prevent his own name from closing, amid public sorrow and shame, the illustrious roll of American Presidents which began with Washington." Hence Tilden begged W. B. Ogden, who was no short-sighted partisan, to induce Lincoln to be "the Chief Magistrate of the whole country." This might give him "the power to save the country. . . . The reality of the *danger* of disunion, I think, cannot be doubted. The cotton States are far more unanimous for secession than our fathers were when they made our Revolution. . . . A statesmanlike policy would be to aid the formation of an effective minority . . . that may become a majority." He urged Ogden to make sure that Lincoln "comprehended the crisis. Nothing is so difficult . . . as to see both sides of a question." A man educated in "northern ideas" must be "almost more than a mortal . . . to take a perfectly candid and impartial view of the position of our adversaries. It is necessary to do more—to imagine ourselves in their positions, in order to form a policy adapted to their case." [1]

On the other hand he used his influence with those he knew in the South to allay their fears. At the "Pine Street Meeting" of December 15, 1860—probably in Tilden's office—over which O'Conor presided, Tilden helped to draft an appeal to Jefferson Davis and the Governors of South Carolina, Georgia and Alabama begging them not to act in haste.[2] Dickinson said, "If we remain a united people we must treat the Southern States . . . as political equals." [3] August Belmont wrote: "Last evening I was present at an informal meeting of about thirty gentlemen, comprising our leading men—Republicans, Union Men and Democrats—composed of such names as Astor, Aspinwall, Moses H. Grinnell, Hamilton Fish, R. M. Blatchford, etc. They were unanimous

---

[1] *Letters*, I, 147, Dec. 17, 1860.
[2] Wilson, *Mem. Hist.*, III, 479; Alexander, III, 4; Brummer, 101.
[3] Dickinson, *Life and Speeches*, I, 700.

in their voice that the first steps have to be taken in the North." [4]

Tilden was convinced that an "important reaction" in public opinion was taking place; that Lincoln's administration "must necessarily go utterly to pieces" in presenting "affirmative measures" or in distributing patronage; that the party disposed to do "the Southern States full justice" was growing larger and stronger. If Congress should prove inadequate to the task, then a Constitutional Convention should propose amendments for a satisfactory compromise patterned after Crittenden's propositions, which would be ratified by State conventions. He predicted that by the following summer the Republican Party would be "disintegrated," the "reaction perfected" and the Union saved. Believing that the people were "temporarily mislead," he was convinced that a vast majority were "conservative at the bottom" and only needed a little time to regain a sound attitude.[5]

While Governor Morgan in his address to the Republican legislature urged moderation and conciliation, the legislature itself on January 11 almost unanimously voted that, since South Carolina had "virtually declared war" on the United States by firing on the vessel sent to Fort Sumter, it would assist President Buchanan with men and money to preserve the Union.[6] Meantime the more moderate men in New York sent a widely signed petition to Congress praying that Southern States be assured that their property rights in slaves guaranteed by the Constitution would be respected either by legislation or a constitutional amendment. The New York Chamber of Commerce asked Congress to take steps for "mutual conciliation and compromise" because the "perpetuity of the Union" was more important than slavery. It approved the Border-States compromise and called for steps to put it into operation. A committee was appointed to secure signatures; more than 40,000 were obtained, and the memorial was delivered to Congress in February.[7]

A Union mass meeting was held in Cooper Institute on January 28, and three commissioners were sent to the Southern States to discuss measures for peace and unity. The Democratic State Central Committee called a convention at Albany on January 31 which demanded a

[4] *Letters of August Belmont*, Dec. 19, 1860; *Tribune*, Dec. 17, 1860.
[5] *Letters*, I, 150; Tilden to Wyndham Robertson, Jan. 13, 1861; Sanborn, *Reminiscences of Richard Lathers*, 91–112.
[6] Lincoln, *Messages*, V, 249–305, Jan. 2, 1861; *Assembly Journal*, 1861, 76–77; *Argus*, Jan. 12, 1861.
[7] *An. Cyc.* 1861, 520–521, Jan. 18, 1861.

"peaceful settlement. . . . Civil War will not restore the Union." The compromise suggested by the loyalists of the Border States was approved. Tilden declared that "he for one would resist, under any and all circumstances, the use of force to coerce the South into the Union." [8]

Several groups of Democrats assembled in this convention—those who were determined to save the Union by conciliation if possible but by war if necessary; those who were willing to go to almost any length for compromise; and those who were Southern in their sympathies. Sanford E. Church was temporary chairman and Amasa J. Parker permanent chairman. Chancellor Walworth and Seymour delivered powerful addresses in favor of peace by compromise.[9] Tilden wanted to placate the South and doubted the constitutional authority of the Federal Government to employ force to bring back the seceded States. On motion of Tilden a committee of correspondence similar to those used in the American Revolution was appointed to keep in touch with the Democrats in other States.

Meanwhile Governor Morgan informed the legislature that he had received an invitation from Virginia to send delegates to a convention at Washington, D.C., on February 4, 1861, to "adjust the unhappy controversies." [10] Dudley Burwell suggested that former Governors Throop, Hunt and Seymour, former President Fillmore, Brady, O'Conor, Tilden and Belmont be sent as delegates.[11] He urged that the Democrats should seek to realize Tilden's suggestion for a constitutional amendment. "Do not let the Democrats sink into an Opposition party"—they must be constructive.[12] The legislature chose 11 delegates—Tilden's name was not among them—to attend the Convention, representing fourteen States, which sat from February 4 to 26. Its recommendation for a thirteenth amendment was unsatisfactory to both North and South. The New York delegates were divided on nearly every vote.[13] Tilden watched the Washington gathering with profound concern and was kept informed of the proceedings by G. W. Newell, who thought that all Northerners who commanded the ears of Southern friends should hurry to the Capitol. He told Tilden that it was no use to talk to the bitter-enders in the South because they either had no ears or "very long ones and . . . other peculiarities of the animal

[8] *Argus,* Feb. 2, 1861; Brummer, 121; Greeley, *Am. Conflict,* I, 388.
[9] Alexander, II, 354; *Argus,* Feb. 1, 2, 1861; Brummer, 114–124.
[10] Lincoln, *Messages,* V, 309, Jan. 24, 1861.   [11] Brummer, 122, Jan. 29, 1861.
[12] *Letters,* I, 153, 154.   [13] *An. Cyc.,* 1861; 562; Alexander, II, 359.

whose head they adorn." The border men were open to reason. Tilden's *Kent Letter* gave him power "to influence these men; and it is a moment when you should make a sacrifice to exert it. . . . I think you should come at once." [14] There is no evidence that Tilden heeded the Macedonian call.

Meanwhile Tilden took time from his legal business to write a letter to the *World*,[15] to attend a caucus at Tammany Hall, to speak at the "private Union conference," to ask President Buchanan to appoint a judge recommended by the Bar Association,[16] and to read pungent letters from O'Sullivan in Paris. When O'Sullivan heard of the declaration of war, he exclaimed, "Gracious God, that we should ever live to see such things. . . . It drew from me convulsions of tears. . . . Do write me your views. . . . I shall . . . do my best . . . for *peaceful* separation if reunion has become impossible. . . . I suppose the North will be too hot to hold *me* hereafter." Later he reported that he was trying to buy rifles and artillery, presumably for the South, although he expected the North to win. He sent Tilden a manuscript copy of his pamphlet "Union, Disunion and Reunion." Tilden, not sympathizing with O'Sullivan's extreme views, did not answer his letters and advised against the publication of his diatribe. But it was printed in London.[17]

South Carolina seceded from the Union on December 20, 1860, and before the end of January 1861, six more States had followed its example. On the very day the Peace Conference convened in Washington, the seceding States formed a new Confederacy. Fort Sumter was surrendered on April 15, 1861, and at once President Lincoln called for 75,000 soldiers for three months to suppress the armed rebellion.[18] New York's quota was 13,000, but the legislature at once authorized the enrollment of 30,000 men for two years and appropriated $3,000,-000.[19] By November 6, 1861, the New York troops had been increased to 120,000, and arms were purchased in Europe.

In New York City, the financial center of the nation, every possible effort had been made to avert the chaos of war. After the call of Lincoln for troops, it was planned to hold a monster Union meeting at Union

---

[14] *Letters,* I, 155.   [15] Tilden Papers, Jan. 30, 1861.
[16] Tilden Papers, Jan. 18, 1861. Notice sent by P. B. Sweeny, Feb. 22, 1861. This may have been an adjourned session of the "Pine Street Meeting."
[17] *Ib.,* Mar. 31, May 6, May 26, June 25, July 22, Aug. 1, 1861.
[18] Richardson, J. D., *Messages,* VI, 13.   [19] Assembly *Journal,* 1861, 76–77.

Square on April 20, 1861.[20] While in court one day Tilden was called to the door by Samuel Sloan, president of the D. L. & W. Railroad, and asked to sign a call for the meeting. He said that he would first like to see the resolutions to be presented. "Very well, but you are with us, are you not?" asked his acquaintance. He replied, "I will do everything to sustain President Lincoln in the civil war, if it occurs, that I would do to sustain Andrew Jackson, if he were President." [21] He received a formal invitation to "serve as a vice president," [22] but his name does not appear in the printed list of 87 vice presidents. He called on the promoters to ascertain the character of the resolutions which were to be presented, gave them his endorsement and consented to act as an official. At the meeting of 100,000 citizens over which General Dix presided, Tilden sat on the platform, applauded the patriotic addresses, and voted for the resolutions pledging loyal support to the Government.[23] Although men like Daniel S. Dickinson, Fernando Wood, and John Cochrane turned political handsprings to show their support of the Union, and Tilden gave the impression of his loyalty to the Federal authorities, yet it was quickly noted that such intimates of Tilden as Dean Richmond, Peter Cagger, W. B. Ludlow, S. E. Church and Horatio Seymour from upstate had not participated in the gathering.

Earnestly hoping that some pacific settlement might be made, Tilden wrote to the aged Martin Van Buren that "a just compromise" was the only way to settle "the political complication." He suggested that the questions at issue be submitted to the former President, and while the people might not be ready to make concessions they soon would be. There must be either separation or compromise, and he requested Van Buren to prepare a series of articles covering the whole case. Tilden believed that the nation would listen to the Sage of Lindenwald and follow his advice.[24]

No man in America at that time had a keener understanding of American history than Tilden. His study of current problems ran back to the days of Andrew Jackson whose prompt suppression of nullification in South Carolina Tilden had applauded. From that time onward he had believed that the Constitution "is, by its own terms, declared to be perpetual." No State "in any contingency" can suspend or obstruct

---

[20] *An. Cyc.*, 1861, 531.   [21] *Cong. Record*, 1876, IV, 5653.   [22] Tilden Papers.
[23] Wilson, *Mem. Hist.*, III, 487; Alexander, III, 5–7; Brummer, 145; Tilden Papers, W. W. Gordon to Gen. E. F. Jones, Oct. 7, 1874.
[24] Van Buren Papers. Tilden to Van Buren, May 5, 1861.

it. "Any pretended act of nullification or secession . . . is absolutely void." The national Government could not exclude any single State from the Union for the offenses of individuals. It may be stated emphatically that Tilden had no sympathy with either slavery or with secession, and after 1854 he had few relations with slaveholding States. He reserved to himself during the course of the war the right to do and to say what he thought best for the country.[25]

Tilden saw the dangers confronting the nation more clearly than most men. In 1860 he believed civil war to be unnecessary if hasty action could be delayed. He had a horror of loss of life and property to obtain results which time and patience would have brought about in peaceful ways. His prophetic warnings were laughed at, yet he labored earnestly to avert the bloody strife. When war came, he never hesitated as to his course. The Constitution must be preserved. The Union must be saved. The Government must be sustained. After the fall of Fort Sumter, at a meeting in the home of General Dix, he declared that the war would be long and terrible; that the President should have called for 500,000 men instead of 75,000—250,000 for immediate use and 250,000 to be put in training camps. The struggle would require tremendous sacrifices and gigantic preparations. To Secretary of War Stanton who, upon accepting office in January, 1862, sought his advice, Tilden said that, since there was no great military genius available, he would have to rely upon "overwhelming numbers wisely concentrated." The North had three times the population and nine times the industrial resources of the South. It also had a great advantage in railways and supplies, and ample reserves. Thus it would be possible to concentrate forces on critical points and with the surplus man and money power win the war. Although Stanton agreed with these suggestions, the Government did not heed them. Eighteen months later, in Washington, Stanton said to Tilden, "I beg you to remember, my dear sir, I always agreed with you." [26]

To finance the war Tilden believed that the people should be taxed to meet a large share of the cost and was confident that they would make the sacrifice. Taxation should be supplemented by loans. He urged the restriction of the issue of treasury notes. Thus, he thought, the war could be carried on without the depreciation of government

---

[25] Tilden Papers, W. W. Gordon to Gen. E. F. Jones, Oct. 7, 1874.
[26] Cook, *Tilden*, 82.

bonds or the overinflation of prices. In 1875 he declared that if the
Government had paid out treasury notes, and had redeemed them with
the proceeds of taxes and loans, meanwhile borrowing money on bonds
secured by a sinking fund and taxes, the war would have cost less than
half what it did.[27] What influence he had was used to counteract the
financial errors of Lincoln's administration, but little heed was given
to his advice.

Further evidence of his constructive war activities is shown in the
stirring patriotic appeal made when he presented a stand of colors to
the 37th Regiment, N.Y.V.[28] He also contributed to the purchase of a
banner for the Jackson Regiment. Other contributions included $100
to the Finance Committee of the Bar in defense of the Union; $10 for
the Tammany Regiment; $25 for the 27th Regiment; $100 for the
Irish Brigade Band; $200 for the Sanitary Commission; and $1,000
as a testimonial to General Grant at the conclusion of the war. No
doubt there were other gifts.[29] Hewitt who saw Tilden almost daily
said: "I know that no more loyal . . . heart beat for the United
States. . . . No man in New York . . . was more frequently called
into counsel in Washington. . . . I know that twice he was called for
by President Lincoln . . . and held careful consultation with him.
. . . At no time was there ever a doubt expressed . . . as to the . . .
patriotism of Samuel J. Tilden." [30] When a member of Lincoln's Cabinet
consulted him about the Mason-Slidell affair, he advised, "We cannot
afford to have two wars at the same time" and promised that if the
Democrats criticized the administration, he would take the stump to
offset it. Twice he secured passes to visit sick soldiers in Virginia. He
aided Seymour to plan another convention at Albany to deal with the
crisis, and helped business concerns to conduct their enterprises under
war conditions.

Now that war had begun, Lincoln supporters proposed to combine
Republicans and Democrats into one powerful Union party to prosecute it to a successful conclusion. The Republican State Committee suggested to the Democratic State Committee in August, 1861, that a
single ticket be nominated on a common platform. After consulting
Tilden, Dean Richmond replied that the Democrats opposed the dissolution of the Union, repudiated the right of secession and called on

[27] *Life*, I, 170.   [28] Cook, 85; John T. Agnew in *Tribune*, Nov. 3, 1874.
[29] Tilden Papers, *Passim;* cf. July 3, 1861.   [30] Cook, 86; Nevins, *Hewitt*, 193.

all citizens to uphold the Constitution and to demand an honest State and Federal Government. A Union Committee representing both parties, of which Tilden was a member, was named.[31] The Democratic State Convention held at Syracuse on September 4, 1861, unwisely nominated a full ticket of minor State officers.[32] To catch such Democrats as favored a Union ticket, a People's Convention was held a week later at the same place, where the Republican Convention was also meeting. These two bodies named a joint ticket of four Democrats, four Republicans and one American.[33] As a result the Union ticket won a smashing victory.

As the gubernatorial campaign of 1862 approached, the Democratic Party in New York, chastened by defeat, found itself more unified than it had been for a generation. The leaders sought a standard bearer who would give enthusiastic support to the Union and the Constitution, and conservative assistance to Lincoln. Tilden went to Washington to consult Cameron and Preston King about the New York situation. He helped bring George Bancroft to New York City on February 22 to express the views of a staunch Northern Democrat who supported the President. He accepted the invitation of the Young Men's Democratic Union Club to address a mass meeting favoring nationalism but opposing "further agitation of the Negro question." This point of view expressed his attitude precisely.[34]

With this preliminary work, Tilden was ready by late summer to propose Dix as his candidate for Governor. When Dix was approached "confidentially," [35] he replied that he could not relinquish his "position in the field" to conduct a campaign run by the "old and everlasting office seekers." [36] At this juncture the Constitutional-Union Party, representing the old-time Whigs and now opposed to emancipation, met in Troy on September 9 and nominated Seymour. Tilden then switched his support to Seymour, who hurried to Buffalo to persuade Richmond to pass the honor to some other man, such as S. E. Church. Richmond bluntly told him that Church could not be elected and that he must serve the party when it called him.[37]

Evidently the Troy convention had been used as a stalking horse for the regular Democratic Convention on September 10 at Albany. Here

[31] Tilden Papers, Sept. 12, 1861.
[32] Alexander, III, 16, 21; *Herald*, Sept. 5, 1861; *Argus*, Sept. 5, 1861.
[33] Alexander, III, 21, 23.   [34] Tilden Papers.   [35] *Ib.*, Aug. 28, 1862.
[36] *Letters*, I, 167, Sept. 7, 1832.   [37] Alexander, III, 37–39.

Seymour was nominated on a platform which called for the preservation of the Union, deplored the civil war which had been precipitated by the disunionists, and opposed the unconstitutional arrest of citizens and the violation of their inherent rights.[38] Democrats generally were eager to rally about a leader whose life had been so closely identified with the party. Not since the sway of Martin Van Buren had the party witnessed such unchallenged leadership.

In their frantic search to find a candidate to offset the prestige of Seymour, Republican leaders resorted to Tilden's choice, General John A. Dix, whom the *Herald* strongly supported.[39] Governor Morgan proposed General Wadsworth, a popular officer like Dix, and both names were presented to the Republican Union Convention at Syracuse on September 25. On the first ballot Wadsworth was nominated by a large majority. The platform demanded the speeding up of the war, applauded emancipation, and denounced the Southern sympathizers in the North.[40]

The campaign was bitter and vindictive. The *Tribune* denounced Seymour as a demagogue whose friend was Vallandigham and whose supporters would recognize the independence of the South. Raymond asserted that a vote for him was one for treason. The *Herald* supported Seymour and called Wadsworth a "malignant abolition disorganizer." Seymour wanted to save the Union; Wadsworth would merely destroy slavery.[41] Mass meetings and parades covered the State. Tilden as a member of the State Committee, without taking the stump, aided the campaign in every possible way, particularly by generous contributions and by serving on the Finance Committee. One finds him conferring with Richmond and Cagger repeatedly about funds. For once in his life Seymour was an optimist and reported to Tilden, "All looks well," and, "The current is with us." [42] John Kelly asked Tilden for a personal subscription of $100 to help carry New York City. John Van Buren took an active part in the campaign, and like Tilden, he first supported Dix and later Seymour. After Lincoln on September 24 ordered all disloyalists arrested without benefit of *habeas corpus,* Van Buren wired the committee at Rome that he would "arrive at 2 o'clock —if not in Fort Lafayette."

As the campaign neared its end, party leaders consulted Tilden about

[38] *An. Cyc.,* 1862, 655.   [39] N.Y. *Herald,* Sept. 16, Oct. 15, 1862.
[40] Alexander, III, 43–45.   [41] N.Y. *Herald,* Sept. 26, Oct. 1, 9, 24, 1862.
[42] Tilden Papers, various dates.

an address Seymour was to deliver in Brooklyn on October 22. Tilden was anxious to have the Democratic attitude toward the war stated in an authoritative manner, and wrote the peroration to Seymour's address:

"If my voice could reach the Southern people . . . I would say . . . that in no event can the triumph . . . of New York . . . mean consent to disunion. . . . Its true import is restoration, North and South, of that Constitution which had secured every right . . . until you madly fled from its protection. It was your act which began this calamitous civil war. . . . Loyally as we maintained your rights, will we maintain the rights of the Government. We will not strike down its arm as long as yours is lifted against it. That noblest . . . work of our wise ancestors is not destined to perish. . . . If the old flag waves in the nerveless grasp of a fanatic and feeble faction to whom you and not we abandoned it, we . . . will . . . bear it onward . . . until it is again planted upon the towers of the Constitution. . . . Within the Union we will give you the Constitution you profess to revere, renewed with fresh guarantees of equal rights and equal safety; . . . but to dissolve the Federal bond between these States, to dismember our country, whoever else consents, we will not. No; never, never, never!" [43]

The political contest of 1862 was fairly even and before election both parties were predicting victory, but Seymour defeated Wadsworth by 10,752 votes. The Democrats elected their ticket and 17 out of 31 Congressmen.[44] At this distance the explanation of Seymour's triumph is simple enough. The Republicans were divided on emancipation, and those who opposed it voted for the Democratic candidate. Other Republicans opposed arbitrary arrests and the usurpation of powers by the President, while failures on the battlefields and the mounting debt made many more apprehensive. Even Seward gave Wadsworth no active support.[45] The Democrats, on the other hand, presented a united front, and Dix and his friends supported Seymour who, while criticizing administration policies, spoke respectfully of the President and staunchly upheld the Constitution and the Union.[46] Wadsworth was simply the victim of general reaction against the war.

Governor-elect Seymour wrote to Tilden: "Now that you and others have got me into this scrape, I wish you would tell me what to do. Give me some suggestions." [47] He wanted advice about his message as soon as convenient. After his inauguration he asked for assistance in mak-

[43] Letters, I, 167; Life, I, 173.   [44] An. Cyc., 1862, 656.
[45] Stanton, Rand. Recol., 216.   [46] Cook, 83; Knox, Seymour, 45–58.
[47] Letters, I, 168, Nov. 10, 1862.

ing appointments and during succeeding months leaned heavily on Tilden for help. He was continually asking him to run up to Albany or to meet him elsewhere. And when the opportunity came to toss Tilden an honor, Seymour did it gladly—as when he was appointed to represent the State at a convention in Chicago to discuss measures for opening navigation between the Great Lakes and the Mississippi. Because his letters were opened by Federal secret service men, Seymour had Tilden write him under the name "Ellen Comstock." [48]

The Inaugural Address which Tilden assisted Seymour to prepare declared that "under no circumstances can the division of the Union be conceded," and every effort must be made to induce the Southern States to return to their allegiance. But martial law was opposed as subversive of the rights of the States, and arbitrary arrests were assailed. The abolition of slavery to restore the Union would create a military despotism. Lincoln told Seymour that he had the opportunity to use his party to crush the rebellion and thus become his successor. Seymour replied that he was willing "to make any sacrifice" to save the Union but took no steps to bring about a better understanding. [49]

Although at variance with certain policies of the administration, Tilden placed his services unreservedly at the command of the President and his advisers. He did not abandon his right to criticize freely, but his attitude was always constructive, not negative. He held his party loyally for the Union and in later years had no regrets for the part he played. Perhaps his attitude toward the Civil War was never better summarized than by J. D. Caten, a Chief Justice of Illinois and a bosom friend of Lincoln: "If I had not known Mr. Tilden as long as I did Mr. Lincoln, I think I certainly know his sentiments on the subject of the late war, and there would be as much propriety in saying that Mr. Lincoln was an anti-war Republican as Samuel J. Tilden was an anti-war Democrat." [50]

The war afforded Tilden an extraordinary occasion for the expression of his theories of political science. His exposition of the purpose of civil government was in perfect consonance with his theories of the rights of business. Governmental agencies were established to protect and to aid industry under general laws but not to control it unduly. Although business was free to manage its own affairs, yet there was an intimate

[48] Tilden Papers, May 13, 1863.   [49] Nicolay-Hay, *Abraham Lincoln*, II, 428; VII, 11.
[50] Cook, 86, letter to A. S. Hewitt.

relation between business and politics which made it advantageous for promoters of great economic enterprises to seat friendly legislators, judges and administrative officials. The more enlightened and humane social view of a later day had not yet penetrated the thinking of men like Tilden. If war politics created unusual opportunities for money-making they saw no objections to taking advantage of them.

AUGUST BELMONT asked Tilden in 1863: "Don't you think it is high time for the conservative men to . . . make a powerful demonstration in our city and State in order to compel the administration to a change of men and measures? If nothing is done, I see but ruin and national bankruptcy before us." He then suggested that Governor Seymour send a strong message to the legislature calling a convention to discuss the situation.[1] Tilden was sympathetic, no doubt, but too cautious to approve hasty action.

To offset the influence of the Copperheads, a term which appeared first in the *Tribune* on January 12, 1863, Union League Clubs were organized to arrange for loyal addresses and distribute reading matter. Democrats like John Van Buren and James T. Brady joined the movement. The Loyal Publication Society was actively spreading publications. To set forth the constructive ideas of the war Democrats, Tilden's *Kent Letter* of 1860 was reprinted in the *World* [2] and then reissued as a pamphlet. Quite as much commendation was elicited as when it first appeared. "It is full of wisdom and accurate prophecy," wrote R. H. Gillet from Washington.[3] "Your predictions . . . have since been fulfilled," declared G. A. Thurston of Maryland,[4] who thanked Tilden for his "superior political sagacity." O'Conor asked him to send a copy to the editor of the *Metropolitan Record*.[5]

Tilden was instrumental in reviving the Society for the Diffusion of Political Information, with the thought that it might counteract the effects of the Union League Clubs and the Loyal Publication Society. Addresses were to be printed and distributed over the country. Branches were to be opened in all large cities. The society's motto was "Read—Discuss and Diffuse," and its purposes were to disseminate the principles of constitutional liberty, to explain the powers of the States and the rights of the people, to prevent usurpations, and to preserve the Union.[6] The society was given a new lease of life when, on February 6, 1863, a group of war Democrats met at Delmonico's to

[1] *Letters*, I, 169, Jan. 27, 1863.   [2] N. Y. *World*, Feb. 22, 1863.
[3] *Letters*, I, 169, Feb. 22, 1863.   [4] *Ib.*, 171, Feb. 23, 1863.
[5] Tilden Papers.   [6] Lynch, *Tweed*, 244.

consult on its reorganization.[7] George T. Curtis made the opening address and a committee was appointed to draft a new constitution. A week later the constitution was adopted and S. F. B. Morse was elected president. Regular meetings were held and more than twenty addresses by such men as Curtis, Seymour, Morse, Tilden, Marble, Hunt, Parker, Comstock, Brooks and Kettle were published.[8]

At the second meeting Curtis announced that "the writ of *habeas corpus* is suspended" and asked Tilden to confirm the fact and to analyze its significance. Tilden declared that "the whole thing should have been defined by legislative action." He thought that not only the Union but constitutional government, liberty, and personal rights were endangered by the violent modes of action proposed in every quarter. He traced the proper limits of a patriotic opposition in time of war. He believed that the constitutional powers of the Government were perfectly adequate to meet the crisis without resort to revolutionary action. The purpose of the society should be to defend constitutional liberty in every possible way.[9]

A brief, incorrect report of Tilden's speech appeared in the *Evening Post,* which interpreted his words as almost traitorous to President Lincoln.[10] Tilden immediately replied in a long letter to the *Post* headed "The Perils of the Union—The Limits of a Constitutional Opposition," which was reprinted in pamphlet form under the caption "Defense of Liberty—A Reply to the Evening Post." He repudiated the endeavor to characterize the meeting as "a revolutionary intrigue" and his speech as an advocacy of "revolutionary means" to effect a change in the policy of the administration. He denounced the newspapers for invoking violence "against dissentients from their opinions," and feared that mobs might replace political discussion. He had never failed to lift his voice against "any tendency of this kind," and pointed out that he had counseled "patience with errors" at the meeting, in which only "moderate, patriotic and constitutional" suggestions were offered. "No allusion to peace was made."

What could the War Democrats and the Republicans who thought the administration's course unwise and inadequate do to effect a remedy?—to guide a "ship with a false compass?" Sometimes minorities must be suppressed in time of public danger, but the dissemination of

[7] *Writings,* I, 331.
[8] Copies of most of these pamphlets are in the New York Public Library.
[9] Tilden Papers; *Writings,* I, 331.   [10] Lynch, *Tweed,* 243.

"documents teaching the fundamental ideas of civil liberty and constitutional government" might help to preserve free institutions. Experience and history showed the wisdom of developing the ability "to limit theory by practice, and to enlighten practice by theory." The present generation was guided in conduct by neither experience nor traditions, and statesmen did not take "inherited wisdom" as the lamp to direct their feet.

Lincoln's experience in "the lobby of Springfield" and in a single term of Congress hardly qualified him to "deal with the greatest questions and most complicated forces of modern history." But for two years longer Lincoln's administration must be used "as the instrument of national salvation." Tilden was a master of argument by understatement. When he intimated that a country lawyer, lobbyist and one-term Congressman was not equal to the national emergency, he may have understood the magnitude of the problems confronting the country, but he failed to see the real greatness of the man chosen to solve them. Tilden fully realized the difficulty of a constitutional opposition in time of war; yet it was the only means of both preserving civil liberty and obtaining peace. Since 1848, to save the nation as a whole had been his dominant motive. He was "ready to accept with candor any new light," but he still stood on the convictions uttered in the *Kent Letter*.[11]

The year 1863 was an exceedingly trying one for Governor Seymour, who continued to advise with Tilden about political questions. A typical note was, "I do not like to ask you to come to Albany too frequently but I am anxious to talk over public matters with you." [12] In the meantime Manton Marble was making the *World* a party publicity organ and looked for financial help to Tilden who collected $2,500 each from Griswold, Kelly, and Corning, and $5,000 from Richmond, probably contributing the same sum himself. With the approval of Corning and Davidson, Tilden prepared bonds to finance the paper, and Griswold was still selling them to good Democrats as late as February, 1864.[13]

When Vallandigham was first imprisoned and then ironically banished to the South for denouncing conscription, his treatment became a symbol of military tyranny to Peace Democrats, who held protest meetings from Long Island to Buffalo. Kalbfleisch organized such a gathering in Brooklyn, and Tilden entirely concurred in such opposition to Federal

---

[11] *Writings*, I, 333–340, Feb. 7, 1863; *Life*, I, 171.   [12] Tilden Papers, May 27, 1863.
[13] *Ib.*, Nov. 5, 1863, and later.

destruction of free speech and a free press.[14] His letter was loudly applauded by the Assembly. The Draft Act awakened stubborn resistance in New York City, and citizens of the eighteenth ward appealed to Tilden to help save a "number of good and useful men" from being taken from their families by conscription and to send his contribution to the cause.[15]

Tilden co-operated with Tammany in holding a mass meeting in the Brooklyn Academy of Music to observe July 4, 1863, at which Governor Seymour assailed the arbitrary measures of the administration.[16] Comparing Lincoln to Charles I, he condemned the Draft Act as unconstitutional. "Remember this," he said, "the bloody, treasonable doctrine of public necessity can be proclaimed by a mob as well as by a government." No paper but the *Daily News* printed the whole speech. Having delivered this philippic, Seymour went to New Brunswick, New Jersey, for a rest. Of course his political foes did not hesitate to say later that the draft riots resulted from his extravagant language.

Just a week after Seymour's impassioned oration, the draft commenced in the metropolis and occasioned a terrific upheaval, with loss of life and destruction of property. In response to a telegram of the Mayor, the Governor hurried back to New York, and after consultation with Hall, Tweed, and Opdyke issued a proclamation calling upon the rioters to be quiet and to appeal to the courts for redress, and asking all citizens to enroll for the preservation of order.[17] Before the day ended a second proclamation declared the city in a state of insurrection and threatened punishment for the instigators of the outbreak.[18] At the same time Seymour asked President Lincoln to suspend the draft until the courts could pass on its validity.[19]

On the frightful riots Tilden's papers are strangely silent. He disapproved of the draft as an invasion of the rights of the citizens, but it is inconceivable that he sanctioned the riots. Only one letter of those fearful days has survived. S. L. M. Barlow wrote, "I am sure the Governor ought today, *this morning,* send for Green's regiment, and no one but yourself can influence him to do this." [20] Not until July 28 have we a word from his pen in explanation. He had been out of the city, and

14 Tilden Papers, June 11, 1863.   15 *Letters*, I, 197 (probably erroneously dated).
16 *Ib.*, 184, Sept. 4, 1863; Seymour, *Public Record*, 118.
17 *An. Cyc.*, 1863, 814; Lincoln, *Messages*, V, 546.
18 *An. Cyc.*, 1863, 814; *Tribune*, July 15, 1863.
19 *An. Cyc.*, 1863, 816; *Herald*, Aug. 10, 1863.   20 Tilden Papers, July 15, 1863.

then wholly disabled for a week by illness from which he recovered after the commencement of the riots. Then followed "attention and counsel amid ten days of excitement and bustle."

Tilden wished to fight conscription in the courts. In March, in anticipation of the Draft Act, he had G. T. Curtis send Seymour an opinion on its constitutionality. Curtis suggested that application be made for a "writ of prohibition," and said that the case might be carried to the Federal court for revision, on which point Tilden should consult Judge Samuel Nelson. This information was immediately passed on to the Governor. Meanwhile, party friends in Pennsylvania were urging Tilden to obtain a speedy decision in the New York courts so as to make their own course easier.[21] Fearing that Governor Seymour was "in danger at any moment of secret arrest," Tilden hurried down to Washington to see what could be done. Welles recorded in his diary on July 23: "I had a call on Monday from Senator Morgan and Samuel J. Tilden of New York in relation to the draft; [they] seem to believe a draft cannot be enforced in New York." [22] Meanwhile Seymour, as a record, asked the President "for a test of the constitutionality of the measure." [23] In the end the matter was adjusted without serious trouble. Lou Payne of Columbia County later boasted that as United States marshal during the war he carried in his pocket an order for Tilden's arrest.[24]

After the trying days of the draft riots Tilden went to New Lebanon for a rest. To his friend Judge Henry Hogeboom he revealed his feelings about the state of affairs: [25]

"How swiftly events move and how greatly they change! . . . How deeply a few weeks ago I was involved in solicitude for the results of the military operations then reaching their crisis! At no time since the war commenced have I been so disturbed as before the battle of Gettysburg. . . . Since that, New York has been on the verge of a social peril, at that time wholly unexpected. . . . All my views of the future . . . may be colored by the peculiar uncertainties which now enshroud our horizon. . . . Who can compute the consequences of the loss of Washington, Baltimore and, perhaps, Philadelphia? Nor can I be insensible to the social disorders to which great cities are exposed during such civil convulsions . . . or to the military, political and financial vicissitudes to which all business in the city of New York is exposed."

[21] *Letters*, I, 176, 179, 180.   [22] Welles, *Diary*, I, 380.   [23] *Letters*, I, 183, Aug. 6, 1863.
[24] Statement of Major Albert H. Callan of Chatham, N. Y.
[25] *Letters*, I, 172, June 18, 1863.

Amid these uncertainties he advised the Judge, who had suggested a law partnership, to stick to his job—at least until the war ended. He doubted the advantage of a legal alliance. Without a regular clientele, he took up a new case only after finishing an old one, and felt it was too late to build up a regular law practice. Some years earlier "several intimate friends" had suggested organizing a law firm, but he shrank from such an obligation because his health was uncertain and a partnership, however pleasant, would rob him of his independence. "My habit . . . is to make no plans . . . except such as are inevitable . . . and to keep myself as prepared as possible to act, free from engagements and even from predeterminations of my own mind, according to the changing phases of affairs." [26] This revelation of Tilden's habits and intellectual traits is amply borne out by his papers. During this crucial epoch he played a triple rôle as a corporation lawyer, a prominent leader of his party, and a man engulfed in the chaos of a war he detested. Primarily he was a man of affairs occupied with transportation lines, mines, and investments which required exacting investigations, conferences, and extensive travel. Business was so intertwined with politics that he could not keep the two apart, even if he had wished to do so. Callers like Frémont, W. T. Sherman, Reverdy Johnson, and A. G. Thurman might wish to discuss either one or both. He continued to perform his duties as a member of the Democratic State Committee. By loaning money to the *Argus,* the *World* and the *National Intelligencer* he promoted party publicity. Congressmen consulted him about the introduction of bills and importuned him to write more political essays. Tammany continued to regard him as a loyal son and had his complete co-operation. He was elected to honorary membership in the Workingmen's Democratic-Republican Association and made a member of the Executive Committee of the National Democratic Association. James C. Van Dyke and nine other Democrats asked him to meet with them to arrange a preparatory program for the next Democratic National Convention. [27]

Flattering as these attentions were, Tilden could not forget the war. When an organization was formed to look after the returning sick and wounded soldiers, and to protect them from "robbery . . . and vice," he took a place on the Advisory Committee. [28] Men raising $10,000 to bury the Confederate dead at Gettysburg asked him for a donation.

[26] Tilden Papers, July 28, 1863. [27] *Ib.* [28] *Letters,* I, 174.

When the new Conscription Bill appeared in Congress, he was solicited for advice as to how it might be defeated. Amasa J. Parker, confident that the time was ripe to win the radical Republicans because Chase and others were "disgusted" with the frauds and violations of the rights of citizens, begged Tilden to consult with Bryant as to what might be done.[29] The crew of the Russian Squadron were given a Grand Ball, and he not only contributed to the expense but served on the committee of arrangements. Thus one task after another consumed his time and taxed his frail body.

In the midst of all these happenings Tilden purchased a home of his own at 15 Gramercy Park. His wealth was now sufficient to meet every desire and he decided to rebuild the old house. This enterprise gave him the keenest pleasure and consumed time which he did not begrudge. Tilden's home became a mecca for industrial magnates and Democratic leaders for the next generation. Among them was a young Bostonian, W. C. Whitney, a Yale graduate, who brought a letter of introduction asking for "a few words of friendly advice." This youth was destined to be Tilden's far-sighted business associate, party disciple, and staunch defender in an hour of need.[30]

By midsummer of 1864 four Southern representatives had made their way to the Canadian side of Niagara Falls to sound out the North as to terms of peace. They were soon in conference with leading Democrats and with peace Republicans such as Horace Greeley. On July 1 "P" wrote to Tilden from Buffalo that on Monday he had called on these "Representative Men of the South" at the Clifton House. He had a "full and frank" talk with Senator Clement C. Clay of Alabama and Senator Jacob Thompson of Mississippi—both trusted friends of Jeff Davis. Clay said that the defeat of Lincoln alone would save the nation and he thought that the Democrats if in power might restore the Union. "P" reported that "Sagacious and influential Democrats of Western New York will confer with these gentlemen. . . . I wish you could see them at an early date." George N. Sanders of Kentucky, a friend of J. L. O'Sullivan, wrote Tilden on July 5, asking for a copy of his *Kent Letter* of 1860. He explained why he had joined Clay and Thompson, and expressed the hope of seeing Tilden. "All the great difficulties," he urged, "resulting from this terrible war can be adjusted with honor to both sections." [31]

[29] Tilden Papers.   [30] *Letters,* I, 192, Sept. 27, 1864.   [31] Tilden Papers.

It was probably through Tilden that Sanders got the ear of Greeley and made it clear that the Southern delegation wished to visit Washington for a conference under a safe conduct. Greeley presented the request to Lincoln [32] who supplied the safe conduct, and on July 17 Greeley was delegated to go to Niagara Falls, to get in touch with Clay and Thompson and to bring them to Washington.[33] The President's peace conditions—"the integrity of the whole Union and the abandonment of slavery"—proved unacceptable to the Southerners, however, and there the matter dropped. No Tilden letters covering this episode have been found. It does not appear that he went to Niagara Falls. J. S. Black returned home from a visit to the Southern commissioners feeling that the South would not give up slavery and would insist upon a loose Union. From this time dates a long intimacy between Tilden and Black.[34]

On June 8 Lincoln was unanimously renominated despite Greeley's opposition. N. H. Swayne informed Tilden that "honest and glorious Old Abe" would certainly be re-elected as a "self-denying and most magnanimous man"; but Lincoln himself wrote, "it seems exceedingly probable that this administration will not be re-elected." [35]

The Democrats regarded Governor Seymour's message of January, 1864, which Tilden helped him prepare, as their guide for the Presidential campaign. His appeal pointed to the violation of the constitutional rights of the people and the States, to the usurpation of the functions of the courts, to the attack on popular rule and to the threatened national bankruptcy. The two paramount questions were: how to restore the Union and the Constitution; and how to return the revolted States without military despotism. The Democratic State Convention at Albany on February 24 selected delegates to the Chicago National Convention with Richmond and Tilden at their head, but excluded Fernando Wood and his brother, who withdrew and held a pacifist convention at Syracuse on August 18 to choose delegates. Tammany had also withdrawn in a huff. The unit rule was imposed on the regular delegates.[36]

Meanwhile there was much speculation as to Democratic candidates. Seymour announced through the *Argus* that he would not run,[37] but ex-

[32] Nicolay-Hay, IX, 185.
[33] *Official Records,* Ser. III, Vol. IV, 486, Lincoln to Greeley, July 9, 1864.
[34] Kirkland, *Peacemakers of 1864,* 84, 118.   [35] Nicolay-Hay, *Lincoln,* IX, 251.
[36] Alexander, III, 101; Brummer, 371.   [37] Aug. 19, 1864.

pressed no preference for anyone else. Richmond came out for Mc-Clellan, but was unable to commit Seymour, who was given an ovation on his way to Chicago.[38] There is no statement extant showing Tilden's choice, but the presumption is that he agreed with Richmond. Tilden, Seymour, Church, Fairchild and a few others accepted Richmond's invitation to ride with him on one of his boats from Buffalo to Detroit. In the discussion en route some favored peace by compromise, but Tilden and Seymour insisted upon a vigorous prosecution of the war with a liberal reconstruction policy following a Northern victory. "I remember the earnest talk of Tilden on this subject with those on the boat and with delegates after we got to Chicago. . . . His views did not prevail with the convention . . . they did affect the influence of the Democratic Party for years after." [39] Tilden slipped unobserved into Chicago, realizing that a breach between Peace and War Democrats would re-elect Lincoln and that the North desired peace and order.[40] The day before the convention opened, the New Yorkers by a vote of 38 to 23 refused to take a poll for President. There was some wild talk about Nelson, O'Conor, and Guthrie, which Tilden stopped by a long speech ending with an announcement that he would vote for McClellan.[41]

When the convention assembled on August 28 it was apparent that the conservative Democrats had control of the machinery. August Belmont, as Chairman of the National Committee, opened the session with an appeal for "devotion to the Union and the Constitution." Governor Seymour was made permanent chairman. His keynote address, delivered in an easy and convincing manner, was a bit antiquated and expressed in terms of 1860 rather than 1864. Then came the real contest of the convention—in the Committee of Resolutions behind closed doors. Vallandigham was determined to force the issue of peace. New Yorkers, with Tilden as their brainiest leader, vigorously opposed him, and made Guthrie chairman by a vote of 13 to 11.[42] Tilden was opposed to any declaration in favor of an armistice, because he believed that the President alone could determine when such a moment had come. The time for compromise had passed and the seceding States must be forced to return to the Union before there could be permanent peace.[43] He used all his influence to prevent a resolution to discourage

[38] Alexander, III, 107.   [39] Fairchild, *Memorial Address*, Feb. 10, 1914.
[40] Tilden Papers, Aug. 16, 25, 1864.   [41] Manton Marble, *World*, Aug. 29, 1864.
[42] Alexander, III, 110.
[43] *World*, Sept. 5, 1864.

the prosecution of the war.[44] The platform, after pledging "unswerving fidelity to the Union," declared that after four years of war the Union had not been restored; hence hostilities should cease, and a convention of the States be called to restore the Federal Union.[45] Vallandigham had won after all. The convention roared its approval. The peace party seemed to triumph.

In the face of taunts General George B. McClellan was nominated on the first ballot—Vallandigham's motion making it unanimous. The New York delegation, headed by Horatio Seymour and Tilden, voted for Governor Thomas H. Seymour of Connecticut, candidate of the peace men.[46] Pendleton, a pacifist, was named for Vice President. McClellan's letter of acceptance of September 8 declared that the sole object of the war was to save the Union; hence Union was the only condition of peace. Any State willing to return to the Union should be received with full rights. The people would hail peace "without the effusion of another drop of blood," but it must come on the basis of Union. There was not a word about slavery.[47]

Tilden had advised McClellan to ignore the peace plank, but he made the mistake of straddling and thus displeased both wings of the party and supplied a target for his political adversaries. When Tilden ran for the Presidency in 1876 the Republicans accused him of having acquiesced in the adoption of this objectionable plank, but Manton Marble spiked that gun by asserting that he himself had carried Tilden's message to McClellan.[48] Throughout the Presidential campaign of 1864, McClellan was wise enough to keep in close touch with influential New York Democrats. While Tilden did not take the stump, he supported the General in every other way, contributing liberally to the expenses.[49]

Following the nomination of McClellan, Democratic leaders in New York turned their attention to the selection of a candidate for Governor who would both help the national ticket and retain the Empire State. To ascertain how the sentiments of the leaders were crystallizing, Tilden sent his brother Henry to interview Seymour and others

---

[44] Cook, 88.   [45] New York *News,* Oct. 22, 1864.

[46] *Proceedings of the Democratic National Convention,* 1864, 43–44. New York changed its vote to McClellan and it was so recorded.

[47] *An. Cyc.,* 1864, 794.

[48] *Cong. Record* 1876, IV, 5655; Manton Marble to A. S. Hewitt, Aug. 15, 1876; A. C. Baldwin to Don M. Dickinson, Aug. 4, 1876.

[49] Myers, *Gen. George B. McClellan,* 459.

about the situation. A few days before the State Convention Henry reported: "Carroll wants you to head the ticket. . . . I know you don't want the place but can't say so. Telegraph me at Albany what to do." [50] Brother Henry was right—Sam Tilden was so overwhelmed with business commitments that he could not heed a party call to office; besides, the time was not propitious. A week after the Republicans nominated Reuben E. Fenton at Syracuse on September 7, the Democrats at Albany by acclamation selected Seymour for another term.[51] In the campaign their enthusiasm evaporated, and the Peace Democrats bolted the ticket. Tilden helped to supply funds and addressed a mass meeting in Brooklyn. To a group of Wall Street bankers he declared, "I am no more a friend of slavery . . . than Lincoln." [52]

The War Democrats held their final meeting on November 2 in Cooper Institute. Dix was the principal speaker, and Tilden was on the platform. The same day Governor Seymour issued a proclamation calling upon "all men of all political parties" to help preserve order at the polls; [53] and the Federal Government took precautions to prevent any outbreak. Lincoln electors were chosen in New York by a majority of only 6,749 votes, while Fenton defeated Seymour by 8,293. In the nation Lincoln was re-elected by a popular majority of 500,000.[54] Although the outcome revealed a widespread opposition to the continuance of the war, the victory was interpreted as meaning that the struggle would go on until the South was defeated. In New York the Republicans also controlled the legislature, and among the successful Congressmen was Roscoe Conkling, who had been defeated by Kernan in 1862.

It was apparent early in 1865 that the war would end shortly with the complete defeat of the South. A great celebration was planned in Union Square on March 4 to commemorate the "recent national victories." Invited to make an address, Tilden replied, "I am confined by illness, and expect to be, at the time of the meeting, totally disabled from speaking." None the less he rendered "the most grateful homage to the achievements of our gallant soldiers and sailors . . . toward preserving the unity of our Federal Republic. . . . These sentiments have never been weakened, even when . . . this great object . . . was

[50] Tilden Papers, Sept. 11, 1864.   [51] Alexander, III, 115–119.
[52] Tilden Papers, Nov. 1, 1864.
[53] An. Cyc., 1864, 583. Proclamation not given in Lincoln, Messages.
[54] An. Cyc., 1864, 798; Alexander, III, 125.

imperiled . . . by errors of civil policy or of military or financial administration. Nor . . . have I ever lost faith that . . . they would completely reestablish . . . constitutional government . . . individual liberty and personal rights." [55]

With the accession of Andrew Johnson to the Presidency, Democrats of the Tilden type changed their attitude toward the administration and pledged to support his reconstruction policy. Tilden was one of forty who presented him with a coach and horses, but he declined the gift. When he granted amnesty to the Southern States, a mass meeting at Cooper Institute endorsed his action.[56] Tilden was urged to obtain from Johnson definite assurance about civil rights and military power,[57] but his cautious nature prevented his rushing headlong to Washington to find out. Instead he followed a course of watchful waiting, and meanwhile did some intelligent scouting at the Capital and elsewhere. It took some months to assemble the information he desired, but when he was convinced that Johnson was determined to follow an enlightened course which War Democrats might endorse, Tilden took steps for a personal interview.

The State Conventions nominating minor officers in 1865 revealed an interesting shift of feeling toward President Johnson. The Democrats at Albany on September 6 promised him cordial support in restoring the Southern States to the Union, opposed forcing the South to adopt Negro suffrage, and named two former Republicans on the State ticket.[58] Tilden refused the use of his name for Attorney General and passed the honor to John Van Buren.[59] The Union Republicans at Syracuse on September 20 approved the President's program, but insisted that the Southern States, before readmission to the Union, must give full civil rights to all citizens and meet other conditions. Men of distinction in the war were given places on the State tickets.

In the campaign the Democrats disconcerted the Republicans by praising President Johnson's policies. Seymour made two speeches in which he discussed national issues. Tilden took little part in the campaign except to make a small contribution. He also united with others to organize the Manhattan Club, to counteract the influence of the Union League Club. One of the original managers, he gave $5,000 of the $55,000 raised to buy a house. President Andrew Johnson was

[55] *Letters,* I, 196, Mar. 3, 1865.   [56] Tilden Papers, May 17, May 19, June 7, 1865.
[57] *Letters,* I, 197, S. L. M. Barlow, Aug. 31, 1865.
[58] *Herald,* Sept. 9, 1865.   [59] Stebbins, 49.

elected to membership, but Tweed's name does not appear among the 120 members. The public organ of the Club was the *World*, which it was jokingly said Tilden, Barlow and Belmont edited with a little assistance from Marble. Tilden remained a member the rest of his life and entertained friends and distinguished visitors there.[60]

At the election on November 7, 1865, the Republicans elected their entire ticket and seated 116 Assemblymen against 44 Democrats. It was a crushing defeat in which such old party war horses as Richmond, Seymour and Tilden must have detected a popular distrust of their leadership as an aftermath of the war. They were put on the defensive, and forced to explain their conduct during the war.

No one, not even Tilden himself, has given a better brief summary of his attitude toward the Civil War and his actions throughout it than Manton Marble in these words: "He foresaw it and so long as there was any hope of averting it, labored to save the country from its evils. When it came, he was for carrying it on with the advantages and with the preparations commensurate with the magnitude of the struggle he had foreseen; by means which accord with the best military science and with sound finance, and involve the least peril to civil liberty. He was for giving the most liberal support to the administration, even when some of its measures were unsound and mischievous." [61]

The war undoubtedly afforded Tilden exceptional opportunities to increase his economic interests in railroads, iron mines and metal industries. Likewise his mastery of the principles of finance and an uncanny ability to detect trends enabled him to make money out of investments in stocks and bonds. How much wealth he accumulated through manipulations and war profits is not known, but he was a much richer man at the conclusion than at the beginning of the war. His support of the Union, his advocacy of peace, and his recommendation of liberal terms to the defeated South, however, were based not on expectation of personal gain but on fundamental convictions about an enlightened public policy.

[60] Watterson, *History of the Manhattan Club,* 49, 143. Organized Oct. 1, 1865.
[61] Marble Papers, Library of Congress.

THE period following the Civil War was full of perplexing problems—
Southern reconstruction, finance, unemployment, revival of business,
political readjustments, pensions, and public morality. Tilden, alive to
these issues, sought in a statesmanlike manner to help solve them. Experience had taught him that the most effective machinery was the
political party, which must be oiled with adequate funds and run by
reliable and trained men.

Tammany inspired in Tilden a reverence for its historic past; and,
while its current activities did not always meet his approval, he regarded himself as a member in good standing, contributing to meet its
bills. When John Kelly was confronted by a deficit of $1,500, he asked
Tilden to help wipe it out.[1] Tilden paid an assessment of $30 for the
liquor at the "Festival" [2] and served on committees, but was not active
otherwise except when campaigns were under way. Invited to help
dedicate Tammany's gaudily decorated new building, he declined because too busy. But he was not too occupied to address a political
homily to the sachems felicitating the "venerable society . . . upon its
political retrospect" and reviewing the doctrines of the fathers of the
Democratic Party. He rang the changes on the "danger of centralism
and despotism rampant," which violated the sacred rights of localities
and individuals, and denounced Congressmen, a rule unto themselves,
who were putting new manacles on trade and industry.

With the accession of President Johnson, Tilden believed the people
would reconstruct their political institutions in accord with the ideas
of Jefferson and Jackson. "Last year, at your Fourth-of-July celebration, I promised" President Johnson in your name hearty co-
operation; and "afterward repeated the assurance in person." The time
had come when all men who favored his "plan of pacification" must
take a stand in the next election. If in turn he co-operated with the
Democratic Party, he would be "triumphantly sustained." [3]

Does this letter indicate Tilden's belief that Johnson should be the
Democratic candidate in 1868? It certainly has the ring of a manifesto

---

[1] Tilden Papers, John Van Buren, Feb. 1, 1866.   [2] *Ib.*, Feb. 19, 1866.
[3] *Letters*, I, 237; *Life*, I, 212.

in his behalf, and explains Tilden's interest in the movement to unite
Democrats and Republicans, who were Johnson supporters, in the
National Union Convention in Philadelphia on August 14, 1866. Weed
and Richmond collaborated to make the preliminary State Convention
at Saratoga, August 9, a success. Democrats like Tilden, Kernan and
Church joined Republicans like Dix, Fish and Blatchford in support
of the movement. Four delegates at large were sent to Philadelphia—
Tilden, chairman, Church, Raymond and Dix.[4]

Gideon Welles, a prime mover in this effort to obtain a nationwide
endorsement of the Johnson administration,[5] consulted with Tilden.
The convention was composed of representatives from Northern and
Southern States who favored an immediate restoration of the Union
and the approbation of President Johnson's policies. In this notable
gathering Unionists and Confederates marched arm in arm into the
hall as the bands played The Star Spangled Banner and Dixie.[6] Randall called the meeting to order; Dix was temporary chairman; and
Senator J. R. Doolittle presided. The only note of discord was the exclusion of Vallandigham and Fernando Wood, notorious Copperheads,
from the convention. Tilden had helped to prepare the "Address to
the People" which after adoption was telegraphed to all parts of the
country.[7] He accompanied the Committee of One Hundred to Washington to carry greetings and promise support to the President.

Upon hearing of the Union meeting, Eugene Casserly, Democratic
leader of California, wrote Tilden: "I was glad to see that you were
a prominent member. . . . The Address . . . is a capital paper. . . .
I thought I recognized your hand. . . . *No Democrat should be appointed to any office* by the administration." [8] This letter was typical
of confidential letters to Tilden from various parts of the North, but
nothing came from the South. When shortly afterward, in his "swing
around the circle," Johnson visited New York, he was given a reception and a dinner at Delmonico's. Tilden met the President on this
occasion and helped to raise the $20,643 which the dinner cost.

The sudden death of Dean Richmond at Tilden's home in August,
1866, was a stunning blow. For years he and Tilden had been associated in party activities and business, and each had a high regard for

[4] Alexander, III, 144.   [5] Stryker, *Andrew Johnson*, 320.   [6] *An. Cyc.*, 1866, 757.
[7] Stryker, 321.   [8] Tilden Papers, Sept. 9, 1866.

the other. Richmond's death occurred when he was consulting Tilden about the approaching election of a Governor, and the removal of this dominant personality shifted leadership to the shoulders of Tilden. John Van Buren retailed to Tilden all the gossip about gubernatorial candidates; [9] Schell called Dix a "wet blanket" and thought "straight and honest" John Ganson the best prospect, while Robert Pruyn would be swallowed "very chokingly." [10] We find Tilden asking Tweed, who was still a pawn in his game of politics, to confer with him in Philadelphia and to give a job to a party worker.[11] As later Tilden asserted that he had never asked Tweed for more than three appointments, this must have been one of them.

Tilden hoped that a Union Party of Johnson supporters might be organized in New York. Following the Philadelphia meeting, plans were set on foot to place before the people a ticket with a Democrat as candidate for Governor and a Republican for Lieutenant Governor. Tilden expected that Dix would be the Democratic standard bearer, but this hope failed.[12] The Republican Convention met at Syracuse on September 5, 1866, renominated Governor Fenton, and adopted a platform that was regarded as anti-Johnson.[13] When the Democrats convened at Albany on September 11, a few conservative Republicans like Thurlow Weed were in attendance. After pronouncing a eulogy on Dean Richmond, Tilden surveyed national problems. "Will we restore the system of the Fathers or a Poland?" he asked. "Will we let the Civil War end in despotism? Thank God for the triumph of national unity—for Grant, Sherman, Sheridan and Slocum. We are threatened by the peril of anarchy. . . . Let no man say to me that Andrew Johnson sometimes makes passionate and angry remarks, and is guilty of indiscretions. I see him rebuilding constitutional liberty." [14]

Tilden and Weed sought to nominate Dix for Governor, but Seymour and Tammany, with $30,000 to spend, carried the convention by storm for Mayor John T. Hoffman. To placate the Dix supporters Robert H. Pruyn was named for Lieutenant Governor. The platform reaffirmed the principles of the Philadelphia Convention and denounced the recent legislation of the Republicans at Albany. Raymond and the *Times* had favored Dix but now gave approval to Fenton. Bennett's

[9] *Herald,* Aug. 28, 1866.　　[10] Tilden Papers.　　[11] *Ib.,* Aug. 12, 1866, for Samuel Allen.
[12] *Letters,* I, 203.　　[13] Stebbins, 91–98.　　[14] *Herald,* Sept. 13, 1866.

Herald also deserted the Democratic Party, while the *World* worked for the election of Hoffman, and Weed announced publicly that he would vote for him.[15]

A mass meeting was held in New York City on September 17 to ratify the Democratic State ticket and to endorse President Johnson's reconstruction policy. Chairman Dix introduced Tilden as the man who led the New York delegation at Philadelphia and asked him to make a report. Saying that the press had already informed the people of what happened there, Tilden inquired, "Why should we not stand by Andrew Johnson in the great contest for the Constitution and civil liberty?" Lauding him as the "restorer of the Republic," Tilden continued: "Now I hear it complained that . . . this heroic man . . . expresses something of indignation toward his assailants. . . . I thank God that Andrew Johnson is what he is, and not what his assailants wish him to be. Do any . . . pretend that he is not a sincere, earnest, truthful, honest man? Does anybody doubt his patriotism? . . . I say the doctrine on which he acted in 1861 . . . that the ten States . . . are still in the Union . . . is true constitutional doctrine." On the issue between him and the Republicans rested "the cause of free institutions and representative government all the world over." [16] This address was printed in pamphlet form under the title "Restoration and Peace."

John Van Buren had informed Tilden, "You must take Richmond's place as State Chairman—no one else can fill it." [17] From upstate S. E. Church wrote, "I hope the committee will make you chairman, and I have said so to everybody I have seen." Some Democrats objected to this promotion because Tilden was a New York City man. Church informed Tilden that it would be necessary to raise a large sum of money, so that $500 could go to each county to hire men to make a thorough canvass, and a second $500 be sent the week before election to get voters to the polls. A series of meetings should be held in each county and the "utmost care must be taken to have the money expended properly." [18]

Without much persuasion Tilden consented to accept the State Chairmanship which he held for nearly ten years. In that position he managed the campaign and raised the funds for it. In addition to his

[15] Stebbins, 100–109; *Times,* Oct. 5, 9, 1866; *Herald,* Sept. 15, 20, 1866.
[16] *Writings,* I, 342.   [17] Tilden Papers, Aug. 31, 1866.   [18] *Letters,* I, 204, Sept. 17, 1866.

own contribution he received from Hoffman $1,700, John Kelly $1,000, H. A. Smyth $2,000, and smaller sums from others. Requests for financial assistance came from all over the State; for example Judge Anderson asked for aid in running for Congress; Flower of Watertown wanted $500; Parker and Seymour needed funds as speakers; and W. C. Rowley requested assistance for a German paper in Rochester.[19] As the campaign closed, Tilden sent funds to the county and town organizations in a lithographed letter over his own signature to defray expenses for organization and providing ways "to bring the voters to the polls."

Hoffman, busy as Mayor, gave his time rather sparingly to speaking tours, and on a long journey to Elmira told Tilden, "I'll not go out again unless I can return within three days." Seymour's heart was not in the campaign, and he hesitated to speak in New York because "A Copperhead will harm the party more there than in the country." John Kelly co-operated with Tilden in every possible way, and in turn wanted help in naturalizing immigrants whose votes would be useful. Kernan, Dix and Schell sent in useful reports. As always patronage was a thorny problem. Meanwhile Tilden communicated with Democratic leaders in other States and at Washington.[20]

The campaign, waged on national rather than State issues, was colorful, with picturesque characters such as Henry Ward Beecher, Horace Greeley and Petroleum V. Nasby participating. Much was heard of the "Tammany Ring," Fenians and Antirenters. The out-State early fall elections were so overwhelmingly Republican that shrewd political observers had little doubt as to the outcome in New York in November. "We're beaten," wrote Hoffman to Tilden, and asked whether he might not take for expenses the $400 which had come in. "I'll take it like a philosopher," he added.[21] The outcome was decisive. Fenton received 13,789 more votes than Hoffman and carried the ticket with him, and the legislature remained Republican.[22] Hoffman was beaten, Dix informed Johnson, by the "utter selfishness of the Democratic managers," but he surely did not include Tilden among them.[23] As usual, Tilden discreetly refrained from expressing his opinion of the defeat, although he knew the causes better than any other.

One of the satisfactions that came to Tilden during this period was

[19] Tilden Papers, various dates.
[21] *Ib.*, Nov. 7, 1866.   [22] Stebbins, 133.

[20] Tilden Papers, Sept. and Oct., 1866.
[23] Tilden Papers.

the confidence reposed in him by President Johnson. Their relations were so intimate as to encourage Tilden to write the President frankly about patronage in the Empire State. Several hundred officials, he said, were "in fear of dismissal if they vote our ticket, to which they are inclined." He also asked the President to release the arms taken from the Fenians. In return, Johnson asked Tilden for "suggestions . . . in relation to public welfare, which would be of service to the country." It is a bit surprising to find Tilden's congratulations on the defeat of the efforts to impeach Johnson given merely as a postscript to a letter about political jobs.[24]

The intimacy of Tilden with Johnson awakened some apprehension among his Democratic friends. S. L. M. Barlow, understanding that Tilden was to assume control of Johnson's affairs "on his promise to surrender everything to the Democrats," and that he would take a portfolio in the Cabinet, thought he would run "a very serious risk of damaging his own record." Such action would hasten impeachment and defeat the Democrats in the Presidential race. He urged Tilden not to "countenance the plan in any form." [25]

The assistance of Secretary of the Treasury Hugh McCulloch was solicited in the matter of New York appointments. Since these places involved "the policy of President Johnson," Tilden asked that he and his friends be permitted to submit "their views" about them. To hand them out as "mere personal benefactions" of the President was both suicidal and "a betrayal of the supporters of his cause." A little later Tilden promised to see McCulloch personally about the matter. When Magone and Pierce wished to have a new revenue collector appointed for the St. Lawrence district, Tilden gave them a letter of introduction to McCulloch who reported that Johnson would make no such assignments until after the election. This is an illustration of how New York Democrats generally presented their applications for positions to the President through Tilden.[26]

Gideon Welles, with whom Tilden was intimate because of "friendship of other days," wrote him that public affairs were in a sad state. He felt that the Radicals would be defeated and was interested in results in New York. "The country yearns to have the Union reestablished," he confided, and expressed mortification at the course of

[24] *Letters*, I, 211; letter of George F. Milton, March 27, 1931.
[25] *Letters*, I, 149, wrongly dated.   [26] *Ib.*, 203, 206.

the *Evening Post*.[27] In his diary he recorded: "Sam J. Tilden and DeWolf of Oswego spent the evening with me. Tilden has good sense, intelligence, honesty, but is a strong party man. Sees everything with partisan eyes, yet understandingly." Welles went on: "During the war he did not side with the Rebels, but he disliked . . . the administration." Now he supported the President "but as a Democrat rather than a patriot," trying to identify Johnson with the Democratic Party. Welles regretted Tilden's attitude because he feared it would defeat the administration. "Tilden speaks of success which I am confident he cannot feel," because the Northern people were not ready to place the Government in Copperhead hands or even in Democratic hands.[28]

In the spring of 1867 there came the rumor that "The House would appoint Grant dictator of the South. Ask our friends," Barlow pleaded, "to get a resolution through the legislature . . . protesting against . . . such a bill and offering to support the President." [29] When Johnson vetoed Thaddeus Stevens' reconstruction bill, S. E. Church urged Tilden to have the State Democratic Committee circulate the veto widely. "If we cannot do anything else, let us howl," he advised. Criticizing Johnson, he said, "He should have forced Congress to let the South in at the start, but he failed, and it is now too late." Trembling for fear of impeachment, he will "give the radicals all the offices" to placate them. "They know that he is cowardly and will not fight, and they will for that reason go to the extreme. I know you are averse to a row ´. . . but I tell you there is no other way. . . . These devils are bent on destruction, and the sooner the crisis comes the better for us. . . . He ought to . . . let the fight commence now." Church begged Tilden to write him his views on the situation.[30]

Other correspondents directed Tilden's attention to different matters. Pleasanter reading must have been the notification from Chancellor Isaac Ferris of the University of the City of New York on May 17, 1867, that by the unanimous vote of the faculty the honorary degree of Doctor of Laws would be conferred on him at the following commencement. This honor suggests Tilden's standing at this time in the business world. With John A. Dix, Minister to France, he kept up a fruitful correspondence. Dix wrote him about conditions in Europe and incidentally reminded him of the balance due on a horse which he had sold

[27] Tilden Papers, Sept. 14, 1866.   [28] Welles, *Diary*, III, 223, 229.
[29] Tilden Papers, Jan. 11, 1867, S. L. M. Barlow.   [30] *Letters*, I, 207.

to Tilden for $300.[31] On September 6, 1867, came a letter from Montgomery Blair, who discovered from a talk with Johnson that he was hoping for "a general sweep" of his Cabinet. "Who can curb Seward?" Blair asked. "Pray sound out your sachems. I would appoint you, if I had my say." [32]

The Constitution of 1846 provided that in 1866 the people should vote whether a convention should be held to revise it. After an affirmative vote, the legislature ordered the election of 160 members to the new constituent body. Tilden was chosen a delegate from New York City and sat in the convention with S. E. Church, G. F. Comstock, G. W. Curtis, W. M. Evarts, Horace Greeley, Francis Kernan, Augustus Schell, Edward Pierrepont, Erastus Corning, A. J. Parker, G. W. Clinton and others.[33] His seat was number 22 in the front row at the chairman's left and near him sat Smith M. Weed and William Cassidy. The questions for discussion were: Negro suffrage, female suffrage, minority representation, taxation, finance, appointive judges, bribery, education, intemperance, canals, and home rule for cities—on all of which Tilden had decided convictions. He was a member of the Finance Committee, of which Church was chairman; of the committee on the best mode for revising the constitution; and of a committee on the "suppression of official corruption." The convention sat from June 4, 1867, to February 28, 1868.

Tilden's irregular attendance during the first part of the sessions caused Cassidy to write: "Your long absence gives anxiety to your friends here. We miss you in counsel and on the floor. You must come up soon, for we will have to meet the financial question and want you. You have lost nothing thus far."

The bitter antagonisms of the war cropped out frequently in the debates. The extension of Negro suffrage in New York was a topic of intense discussion. Tilden argued that this question should be presented separately to the people and was deeply disappointed when that was not done.[34]

The proposal for a costly enlargement of the Erie Canal was opposed by Tilden in a long speech on "The Canal Enlargement Fallacy," which was printed in a pamphlet with the title, "New York State Finances and Canals." [35] This was one of the most important addresses

[31] *Letters*, I, 207, 208, 209, 225.   [32] Tilden Papers, Aug. 10 and Sept. 4, 1867.
[33] *Convention Manual*, I, VII.   [34] *Life*, I, 178.
[35] *Writings*, I, 348.

made in the convention and was widely commented on by members of both parties. In beginning he apologized for "a hoarseness which, for the first time in my life, somewhat troubles me in the customary use of my voice." This affliction was to grow on him as the years passed. Some of his colleagues regarded him as a "railroad man" and he took pride in the fact that for the past fifteen years more than half of the railroads between the Hudson and the Mississippi north of the Ohio had been his clients. But he was now speaking for the people of New York and not the railroads. He had no prejudice against the Erie Canal. In principle he did not believe the State should "manage any kind of business," but he made an exception of the Erie Canal. In 1854 he had predicted, in opening the Rock Island Railroad, "that we would wrench the Father of Waters from its bed and make it pour its affluence of traffic into the harbor of New York." The Erie Canal was "a public water." The growth of railroads had been so surprising that "a prudent caution" should be exercised, but it should not be assumed that the Erie Canal was to be superseded. Indeed the State should protect and improve it. The canal should be considered as a trust and not as a means of revenue, and he thought that the railroads should be put in the same class. If properly cleaned and operated, the Canal would both handle all the business and greatly reduce expenses.[36] His comprehensive knowledge of the subject surprised everybody.

The Constitution of 1867 was submitted to the people on November 2, 1869. The judiciary article was approved as an amendment to the Constitution of 1846, but the remainder of the Constitution was rejected by a vote of 290,456 to 223,935. The Democrats were openly hostile to the proposed fundamental law, which they regarded as largely the work of Republicans, who controlled the convention. Independent Republicans like Horace Greeley also criticized it; and the Tweed Ring was a solid unit in opposition to a document which seemed inimical to its rule in the metropolis.[37]

Party activities and the framing of a constitution must not be permitted to conceal Tilden the corporation lawyer and business man. The war and the years immediately following not only increased his work in salvaging crippled industries but also supplied unusual opportunities for investment. The work kept him away from political conventions, and forced him to absent himself from his office for long periods of

[36] *Writings*, I, 348.   [37] Flick, *Hist. N. Y.*, VII, 206.

time. For instance, when Caleb B. Smith of Lincoln's Cabinet made him a commissioner to aid in the construction of a railroad and telegraph line to the Pacific, he spent more than a month in Chicago looking after the enterprise.[38] P. W. Hitchcock of Omaha offered him inducements to form a partnership for the purchase and sale of land warrants along that route, but he could not be tempted. When greenbacks were issued, he counseled his clients and friends to buy stocks and real estate which would rise in value or long term bonds which would weather the inflation—a practice which greatly augmented his own wealth. Abram S. Hewitt interested him in the Trenton Iron Company, in which he bought shares for $3,750.25, and consulted him frequently as a director. This commercial intimacy in turn created the closest political ties.[39] War demands caused his Michigan iron ore mines to flourish. When Secretary Stanton requisitioned the Peninsular Railroad, Tilden turned it over to the Government without a question. Governor Bigler tried to interest him in an oil well in Pennsylvania—300,000 shares at $10 each—but he preferred less speculative investments.[40] With Hewitt and others he owned the Phoenix Park Coal Company and the Franklin Coal Company near White Haven, Pennsylvania.[41]

His brokerage business in stocks and bonds during this period was large, but he conducted it more as a favor for friends like Millard Fillmore, Russell Sage and John Van Buren than for profit. In like manner he taxed his temper in fruitless efforts to ward off the chronic threat of bankruptcy confronting the chemical factory at New Lebanon. "Everybody but my own family seems glad to get my advice," he complained. Had his brother Henry not been so hot-tempered, the war might have afforded financial relief for the embarrassed company. A "coffee extract" paste had been discovered, which combined with milk and sugar made a fine drink. Stanton placed a large order and it was quite popular with the Army. Wager Swayne praised it as a fine "preparation for Army use." [42] After several carloads had been delivered, a shipload of quinine which Henry was smuggling into New Orleans was captured. As a result the Government canceled the order for "coffee extract." So angered was Henry that when Stanton later renewed the order he tore up the letter, saying to the agent, "Tell Stanton to go to

[38] Tilden Papers, Sept. 1–Oct. 6, 1862.   [39] Nevins, *Hewitt*, 265.
[40] Tilden Papers, Dec., 1864.   [41] Nevins, *Hewitt*, 252.   [42] Tilden Papers, Sept. 7, 1861.

hell," and thus all profits went glimmering.[43] In contrast to Henry's inept dealings was Samuel's sale of 6,000 tons of gun-barrel metal and wrought-iron machines to the Government at cost price.[44]

In 1864 Tilden consolidated the Peninsular Railroad, which he had built to certain ore beds, with the Chicago & Northwestern Railroad.[45] In a letter to the owners of the latter road he outlined the merger as a "conservative" arrangement. If they did not combine, competition would affect the price of ore at least 25 cents a ton, which on 300,000 tons would mean the loss of the interest on a million dollars. A merger would also improve their chances of getting favorable concessions from Congress. Both groups would benefit from the amalgamation. He had just reorganized the Fort Wayne Railroad and as a result the stock rose 40%. When told that only the price stood in the way of completing the deal, Tilden analyzed the "elements of difference" and worked out a proposition. He warned against the "evils of delay" and stressed the fact that this link would connect the ore fields with the leading roads of the nation. The Northwestern would build that link for which it would be easy to obtain the money. The two roads were amalgamated and the bonds were floated on the market at the rate of $82,500 a mile. It was said that Tilden made a million and a quarter out of the transaction and that he got rich while others were impoverished.[46]

Meanwhile the Iron Cliffs Company, from which Randolph said Tilden made some money but not "a very considerable portion of his fortune," was developed. Friends who had confidence in his business ability were invited to invest in the venture. Among these were William Kelly of Rhinebeck who sent $3,000 for shares in 1864 and later increased his holdings,[47] and George Bancroft who added to his investment, saying: "I shall obey your bidding." The Iron Cliffs Mine received Tilden's close supervision and he directed Curtis to write reports thrice weekly. S. C. Baldwin, who, with Wetmore, was a director, was delegated to act temporarily for the company in all important decisions. Baldwin was directed to let Tilden know whether a "mining head" should be employed for all operations and what was necessary

---

[43] Statement of Harry Cox of New Lebanon, manager of Tilden & Co., who said the formula had been lost.
[44] Peter H. Watson, in *Sun*, Sept. 29, 1876.
[45] *Letters*, I, 185, Mar. 24, Apr. 8, 1864; 189.
[46] Buckman, *Tilden Unmasked*, 4–13.   [47] Tilden Papers, Oct. 24, Nov. 2, 17, 1864.

for the sale and transportation of ore. Tilden frequently sought information about the Peninsular Railroad and a hundred other matters. The
New York Iron Mining Company, also in Michigan, described in Chapter XXXIX, was a successful investment.

Tilden continued to give his legal services to G. W. Cass and Thomas
A. Scott of the Pittsburg, Fort Wayne and Chicago Railroad in per-
fecting consolidations and issuing bonds, meanwhile using Cass's private car for travel over the system.[48] John Sherman praised his circular
to the bondholders of that line as clear and nothing "to be ashamed
of." [49] Jay Gould made contacts with Tilden in 1864 about railroad
matters and later repeatedly tried to obtain his services in connection
with the Erie Railroad. He kept calling at Tilden's home and finally
persuaded him to give legal advice, as was shown by the following note:
"My dear Mr. Tilden: Enclosed I hand you check as per agreement.
Please sign and enclose the attached vouchers. Yours, Jay Gould."
Eight months later he asked Tilden to meet the directors of the Cleveland & Pittsburg Railroad. Tilden also served the interests of James Fisk,
Jr., and Oakes Ames, and George Wakeman and W. C. Whitney communicated with him concerning railroads. The latter invited him to
become a trustee for the Dayton & Union Road.[50] He was interested in
the Pacific Mail Steamship Company and the steamboat *Oregon* was
sold through him, as broker, for $500,000.[51]

Carefully preserved by Tilden were some twenty passes over at least
eight railroads and their subsidiaries. Some were granted as legal adviser, trustee or director, and others were purely complimentary. These
passes give a realistic picture of his connection with these great common carriers from the New York Central in the East to the St. Louis,
Alton & Chicago Railroad in the Middle West. John Sherman and
Tilden had been associated for years in the affairs of Western railroads
and exchanged letters. One note reminded Tilden of a suggestion on a
train that Mr. Ogden would supply passes to Sherman and some
friends. "Our trip is quasi-public," wrote Sherman. "Send the passes to
me and I will distribute them." [52]

In the fall of 1866 James Parton published an anti-monopoly pamphlet entitled "Manual for the Instruction of 'Rings,' Railroad and
Political," in which he gave a detailed account of the Chicago & North-

[48] Tilden Papers.   [49] *Letters,* I, 254, Oct. 20, 1869.
[50] Tilden Papers, 1869, 1870, 1871.   [51] *Letters,* I, 248.
[52] Tilden Papers, Aug. 2, 1866.

western Railroad ring. Parton explained how Tilden and Ogden "by placing an over-issue of twenty millions, with a margin of three millions in three years," built up a great monopoly in the West and fleeced stockholders. An order was secured in the courts to have the entire edition suppressed, and Tilden supplied funds to have the copies in New York City and elsewhere purchased and destroyed. A few copies survived, however, and in the Hayes-Tilden contest the Illinois Republican State Committee had it reprinted for campaign purposes.[53]

In the decade following 1855 Tilden acquired his fortune through shrewd manipulations of business concerns and judicious investments. He made money easily because he seemed to know values intuitively—when to acquire and when to sell. He also had the wisdom to profit by the depreciation in government bonds. How much he made out of the reorganization of crippled railroads will never be known, but it was a large sum. His sagacity was also revealed in the amalgamation of independent lines into larger systems, with increased facilities for serving the public and hence better chances of earning dividends. Tilden's earnings from iron ore companies were considerable. His fortune grew so rapidly that he was accused of unscrupulous methods. This charge was made by party rivals as political innuendo, by some persons who were disappointed with their investments in enterprises which he reorganized, and by a few radical publicists with fancied grievances. Business men generally praised Tilden's extraordinary legal and financial ability, and commended his integrity. Measured by the standards of his day his acts were hardly censurable.

[53] Tilden Papers.

As the Presidential election of 1868 approached, the eyes of political leaders turned inquiringly toward the Chairman of the Democratic Committee of New York State. Samuel J. Tilden had been clothed with the mantle of Dean Richmond, a commanding figure in business and politics, and in addition to that prestige he had the advantage of a continuous political experience running back to the administration of Andrew Jackson. Since the ascendancy of the Sage of Kinderhook he had known intimately all the party leaders in the State and many outside. In close touch with most of the leaders of big business in the nation, he held a place of authority in the national councils of the Democratic Party.

During the skirmishing days of 1867 Gideon Welles was in touch with Tilden about candidates but did not wholly trust him. A friend who took a letter from Welles to Tilden on October 4 found that Tilden "talked well," but showed a tendency to maintain a New York party organization and to keep clear of Johnson as a candidate. Welles commented: "It is a party, not a patriotic scheme, and will fail. Tilden's partyism is weakness and does not surprise me." [1] With Seymour and Tilden, party was "paramount to country." They did not oppose Johnson openly, but they declined to be recognized as his supporters. They approved of his principles, yet had not voted for them. Welles was unalterably convinced that all the noise about Chase was merely a smoke screen for Seymour, and from first to last believed that Tilden was shaping his plans for Seymour's nomination.[2]

But there was nothing in Seymour's relations to Tilden that pointed in such a direction. Indeed, Seymour informed Tilden that he had taken his name "off the list of candidates" because he could not afford to run. A little later from a cozy fireside he sent Tilden a penetrating analysis of the past seven years and of current conditions. He thought that a small group—men like Tweed, Sweeny, and Hoffman—should meet in Albany to canvass the outlook. "Let us keep our power by holding ourselves free. . . . I wish you would let me know your views." Tilden attended this conference, and one in Washington of the

[1] Welles, *Diary*, III, 223.   [2] *Ib.*, 379, 381, 385, 390, 396.

chairmen of the Democratic committees of the Northern and Border States.[3] Meanwhile he kept his ear to the ground to detect all the indication of party sentiment upon candidates. Allen G. Thurman wrote Tilden that he regarded the national prospect as "gloomy" but added, "Let us all go into the fight with hope as well as energy and courage." [4]

By February, 1868, after a survey of the field, Tilden had tentatively selected a candidate and had revealed his name confidentially to Charles O'Conor, whom he asked to see James Gordon Bennett, Sr., about support in the *Herald*. O'Conor reported that he had conferred with "the Great Mogul," who cared more for the "cause" than the man. He rather likes "your man" and promised to let nothing "to his personal disadvantage" appear in the *Herald*. His advice is: "Train all your men; keep all their friends in hope till it's too late to back out; and then try to nominate with a sole view to victory." [5] Who was the "man" for whom Tilden was angling at this early date? While no name is mentioned, later developments point to Salmon P. Chase. When Governor Bigler of Pennsylvania insisted upon knowing whether New York wanted Seymour, Tilden asked him to prevent the instruction of his delegates for Seymour or any other candidate, and he promised to do so.[6]

At the Washington conference early in February, Tilden mentioned a number of possible candidates. After reflection on the names suggested, R. C. Root urged Tilden himself to come out for the nomination. "I know of not one more able, or who would nearer meet all the requirements. . . . No one doubts your ability or integrity; *you,* I think, could cut loose from old associations; . . . *you* have *not* been worn out on antiquated platforms. . . . I think you could be elected against Grant . . . if the party won't force on you a platform that *says* too much." [7] W. F. Allen, J. D. Van Buren, Jr., and John A. Dix also proposed his name.[8] And the Democrats of New York City, under Tilden's guidance, sent out an address on "The Path of Conservative Triumph," calling for "new measures and new men"—a noncommittal Tilden battle cry. Friends of other candidates, such as Pendleton and Hancock, began to toss their hats into the ring. Seymour wrote, "I think Hendricks will be as good a candidate for the Presidency as we can get. . . . I do not see how we could do better." And

3 *Letters*, I, 211, 214, 215, 221.　　4 Tilden Papers.　　5 *Ib.*, Feb. 10, 1868.
6 *Letters*, I, 216, 219, 221, 223.　　7 *Ib.*, 218, Feb. 10, 1868.
8 Tilden Papers.

Tilden dined with President and Mrs. Johnson to talk over Johnson's prospects as a Democratic standard bearer.[9]

By March, 1868, there was an abundance of candidates but none standing out in high relief like Grant. The State Convention on the 11th at Albany was expected to clear the political atmosphere.[10] Of Francis Kernan, known to favor Seymour for President, Tilden asked about Seymour's health and whether he would attend the convention, which would have to decide whether or not to present his name to the country. Kernan was urged to be at Albany on the 10th for a consultation. If they got their candidate on July 4, Tilden said, "with the blessings of God, we will stir up the youngsters all over the State." [11] Kernan replied that Seymour was physically fit for a Presidential candidate and should not be allowed to be a delegate to the National Convention. "This would be regarded as evidence that he was not to be our Presidential candidate in any contingency. . . . In reference to the candidate for President, I think we should select as delegates our wisest and most patriotic men. . . . Believing myself that Gov. Seymour is our best man for the times and the strongest man for the canvass, I hope the delegation will be composed of men friendly to his nomination. . . . The State Convention should . . . give expression to the . . . preference for Governor Seymour as the Presidential nominee." [12]

The State Convention met at Albany on March 11, 1868, to select delegates to the National Convention. Tilden called it to order and completed the organization without a contest. Marshall B. Champlain of Allegany was made president; and Tweed nominated the vice presidents. In Tweed's room at the Delavan House the program had been prearranged by Seymour, Tilden, Kernan, Tweed and others the previous evening.[13] In pursuance of this agreement, Seymour made a speech arguing that no candidate for President should be endorsed and that the delegates should go to the National Convention uninstructed.

Following Seymour, Tilden read a paper which was the chief event of the gathering. He had just returned from Washington and was primed to sound the keynote of the party. Congressman Fernando Wood, at Tilden's request, sent him reports on the War Department which he incorporated in his address.[14] Hoffman also offered suggestions. This speech, later printed as a pamphlet under the title "The

[9] Tilden Papers; *Letters,* I, 221, Mar. 4, 1868.   [10] Tilden Papers, Feb. 4, 1868.
[11] Kernan Papers, Mar. 5, 1868.   [12] *Letters,* I, 222.   [13] *Herald,* Mar. 12, 1868.
[14] Tilden Papers.

Republican Party Irritating" is worthy of attention because, with the Union Square address on "Restoring Representation in Congress to the Southern States," it outlines Tilden's views on reconstruction.

Down to 1860, he said, "the master-wisdom of governing little and leaving as much as possible to localities and to individuals, prevailed; and we . . . enlarged the domain of individual conscience and judgment." Then came the Civil War through which "the Northern systems of society and industry" prevailed. "I hoped that we might speedily restore the people of the revolted States to their true relations to the Union; and . . . begin to deal with administrative questions." But that fungus-growth, centralism, had rendered the Republican Party incapable of "any large, wise or firm statesmanship." It failed to "heal the bleeding wounds," and to revive the languishing industries. Instead, it inflicted anew on an exhausted people "the burdens of war" after war ended, established Negro supremacy, and sought to seat black representatives as allies in Congress to perpetuate Republican power. It would give 3,000,000 blacks twice the representation in the Senate which New York, Pennsylvania, Ohio, Indiana and Illinois had with 13,500,000 people. This policy meant government by the sword in the South, which added an annual burden of $186,000,000 to the war loss of 750,000 youths and $3,000,000,000. On the other hand, the restoration of their rights to the Southern States would save the nation $125,-000,000 yearly, reduce taxes and liberate industry.

Everything of value in the Constitution was jeopardized. The white people were forced into political partnership with an inferior race. Coordinate departments of the Government had been broken down in "an elective despotism." Congress had stripped the President of authority over his subordinates and threatened to remove him from office. The independence of the judiciary was menaced. These revolutionary changes, if continued, would end in imperialism. The claim that Congress could alter suffrage in Northern as well as Southern States must be defeated or government by the people would be at an end. White immigration would have solved the slavery question in time. The race problem should be considered wisely and humanely, and no man would rejoice more than he to see the Negroes advance in the scale of civilization. But he denied their right to rule the whites. Would the North accept the dominion of the "Negro power?" Democracy must take its stand for constitutional government and civil liberty. Change could come only by changing the men who administered the government.

An extract from this address was later printed by Tilden under the heading "With Whom Shall We Share Self-Government?"—with Mexicans? Chinese? Indians? Africans? In reply to the question Tilden asserted that European emigrants would probably form a "higher type of mankind." They helped to overthrow slavery in the North, and gave success to the North in the Civil War. The regeneration of the South, he hinted, must come from the same source. The admission of inferior races everywhere had been a failure. Would it prove to be so in the United States? [15] Seymour praised Tilden's speech as "original . . . philosophical . . . and suggestive. It not only gives views and facts, but sets men upon trains of thought. . . . Beyond anything I have read in a long time your words . . . have . . . given me new ideas." [16]

The delegates at large were: Tilden, Seymour, Church and H. C. Murphy. Each congressional district had its delegate, among them being Tilden's brother Henry A. of Columbia; Tweed, Morissy, Cardozo, Schell, Hall and Ottendorfer of New York; Cassidy of Albany; Beach of Jefferson; Kernan of Oneida; W. F. Allen of Oswego; and H. A. Richmond of Genesee.[17] The platform stressed the harmony in the party and denounced the Republican Congress for its waste, high tariffs, violated pledges and attempts to depose President Johnson. On reconstruction policies little was said, that being left to the National Convention.[18] Significantly there was no endorsement of any candidate for President. The Democratic National Convention was summoned by August Belmont to meet in New York City on July 4, 1868, a little less than four months away.

Thus far Tilden's strategy had worked without a hitch. The State Convention had selected delegates but had made no commitments to any candidate. The game was one of watchful waiting without arousing any hostility from any quarter. From the time Frank Blair on April 12 informed Tilden that he had pledged the Kansas delegates to his candidacy until June there was no dearth of candidates—Johnson, Chase, Seymour, Hancock, Pendleton, Hendricks, and McClellan. To this day no one can pick out of this list a name that had Tilden's unqualified endorsement, and possibly he kept his mind open to select the man who had the best chance of nomination and election.

---

[15] *Writings*, I, 394, 411.   [16] *Letters*, I, 224, Mar. 24, 1868.   [17] Stebbins, 323.
[18] *World* and *Herald*, Mar. 12, 1868.

In the choice of a standard bearer, he was tremendously interested and carried on a correspondence that must have taxed his strength. As his confidential agent he chose John Dash Van Buren, Jr., a young engineer eager to serve his party and whole-heartedly devoted to his political paragon. In April he was in Washington picking up information about candidates and sending it by code to Tilden who especially requested him to interview Hendricks. When Tilden sent him $200 to pay his dues in a New York City Club, he returned the check saying that he would not accept pay for his work for the State Committee; and to show his independence he forwarded $250 for the campaign fund.[19]

May was a hectic month and Tilden was simply deluged with rumors, advice, and demands from all over the nation. That Seymour regarded himself as a potential candidate is shown by the fact that he suggested Hancock as a running mate. Miller in Nebraska and Casserly in California were working for him. Leaders like Loomis of Little Falls expressed a preference for Seymour over Pendleton, and Hendricks for Vice President, and commented to Tilden, "Your position is potential in influence." But John Dash Van Buren, Jr., reported that other New Yorkers, Allen, Cagger and Champlain, were anti-Seymour men.[20] Gideon Welles was positive that support of Chase was merely a disguise for Seymour and was told by R. H. Pruyn that the nominee would be either Seymour or Chase.[21] Van Buren intimated to Seymour that some kind of a secret deal was afoot; but Seymour kept saying that he was not a candidate.

In the previous year Tilden had intimated repeatedly that he thought the Democrats should nominate Johnson. Then, as threats of impeachment arose, Tilden's support waned. With the failure of the trial, there was a revival of the Johnson boom among rejoicing Democrats and a rumor that Belmont, the National Chairman, was secretly for him. William S. Hawley told Tilden that the Johnson supporters would be glad to confer with him and his friends in New York at any time and added, "Johnson will help the Democrats." [22] Tilden sent William Cassidy to Washington to convey secret information to Johnson,[23] but just what does not appear.

Frank P. Blair persistently promoted his own candidacy and in-

[19] Tilden Papers; *Letters*, I, 212.   [20] Tilden Papers.   [21] Welles, *Diary*, III, 390.
[22] *Letters*, I, 228.   [23] Tilden Papers.

formed the "Dear Judge," as he called Tilden, that he had Missouri and was organizing Jackson Clubs throughout the country. Montgomery Blair was confident that the "Chase fever" would die out; anyhow Frank could carry ten Republican votes to Chase's one.[24] Days before the National Convention met he went to New York City to build the political fences his brother needed.[25] There is little evidence for thinking that Tilden regarded Frank P. Blair as a Presidential possibility at this time; but as a candidate for Vice President—that was a different matter.

On a trip to Washington Tilden consulted R. J. Walker about the best candidate, and the latter wrote out six well-argued reasons why Hancock should be taken.[26] Other men urged that since Hancock alone could carry Pennsylvania, he was the only Democrat who could be elected. Randall thought of him as a good nominee but preferred Chase, and Seymour regarded him highly. Pendleton and Hendricks had their champions in New York State and elsewhere, but Casserly told Tilden that Pendleton could not carry the Pacific States. "Pendleton stands next to Seymour; take Hendricks for Vice President" advised one New Yorker. Robert M. McLane wrote, "Mr. Tilden cannot accept as readily as myself the candidacy of Mr. Pendleton." [27] Not much was said about McClellan.

The one name that runs like a thread throughout all the correspondence of these pre-convention days is Chase. Bryant whose long experience enabled him to read the political trends was convinced weeks before the convention met that Chase would be nominated.[28] Indeed the tide was running so strongly for Chase that competent observers quite generally were convinced that, despite the many candidates in the field, he would win. That Chase was the choice of the leading New York Democrats is plainly written in the record. By March Cassidy in an *Argus* editorial proposed Chase's name, a suggestion that was taken up by the *Atlas, Sun* and other papers. The *World* expressed a doubt, however, whether he would accept a nomination. Then, after O'Conor visited Bennett, the *Herald* came out for him. By April he had agreed to permit the use of his name. The spokesman of his supporters was Tilden's confidant, Colonel John Dash Van Buren, Jr., who wrote

[24] *Letters*, I, 232.   [25] Smith, *Blair Family*, II, 405.   [26] *Letters*, I, 235.
[27] Tilden Papers.
[28] Chase, *Diary and Corresp.; Ann. Rept. Am. Hist. Assn.*, 1902, II, 519, June 23, 1868.

Chase [29] that he was the Moses to lead the Democrats out of the wilderness and virtually acted as his campaign manager. Belmont informed him on May 29 that with other party leaders he was for him "with all my heart," a statement he would not have made had he not known the inclination of Tilden and others.[30] Blaine was also confident that the New York Democrats wanted Chase.[31]

There is much to substantiate the belief that Tilden for several months had inclined toward Chase, but he was too adroit to show his hand, particularly when he saw that New York was far from acting as a unit. The man who swallowed Greeley in 1872 would not strain at Chase in 1868. Tilden had known Chase more or less intimately since 1848, and discerning men such as Bigelow and D. B. Hill said under their own signatures that at heart Tilden was for Chase. Other Democrats declared, "Chase's record is not a good one," and he "would be the weakest man we could have." Even Tweed was a Chase advocate.[32] Randall "asserted positively that Chase would accept a nomination from the Democrats," would bring an abundance of "material aid" to the campaign, and "with Chase and Hancock we could sweep the country." [33] Montgomery Blair warned that Chase was the "sheet anchor" of the reconstruction measures we propose to pull down. Robert McLane informed Tilden personally that the New York delegation ought to present Chase's name, but got no definite promise.[34] Barlow said "see Chase because he can win." [35] A. A. Aiken reported that the State Committee had favored him for a month.

Judge W. F. Allen in a humorous mood, knowing by experience how nominations were made, wanted to know how to vote on July 4 and said he had been "kept in ignorance long enough. I would like to know now who I am expected to hurrah for then, so that I can make affidavit that he is the spontaneous choice of the people." Select someone to head off Pendleton—someone acceptable to the *Evening Post*. "I think Bryant would be satisfied with yourself, or someone else that you could name." [36]

While Tilden and his party associates were discussing a suitable man

[29] Seymour Papers, New York Historical Society, May 1, 1868.
[30] Coleman, *Election of 1868*, 117, 119.   [31] Twenty Years, II, 393.
[32] *Times*, May 5, 1895; Phelps, *Kate Chase*, 44; Coleman, 132.
[33] *Letters*, I, 228.   [34] Tilden Papers.   [35] *Letters*, I, 231.
[36] *Ib.*, 231, May 25, 1868.

to lead them to victory, the Republican National Convention met in Chicago on May 20, 1868. On all sides the leadership was conceded to General Grant and he was nominated with acclaim. Chase was almost ignored. But four days before, the Republicans' attempt to impeach President Johnson had failed.

When some New York delegates urged a meeting to agree upon a plan of action, Tilden wired Smith M. Weed and Dan Manning, "after consultation with Church, Cassidy and others, I think advisable to defer meeting . . . until further notice."[37] Evidently he was not yet ready to take a stand openly. Sam Ward of Washington wanted some definite information, when Craig and other delegates declared that Chase would win, and cautioned, "Remember that Pendleton goes in with 149 votes and comes . . . with a following of 1,500." Tilden telegraphed Seymour, "I am extremely anxious to see you as soon as possible," so there could be no misunderstanding with his long-time friend.[38] The agreement to make Seymour chairman of the convention seemed to satisfy his ambition, and caused him once more to assert that he was not a candidate. While the *Sun, Times, Post, Herald* and *Independent* favored Chase, the *World* was lukewarm, Thurlow Weed denounced his nomination by any party, and Greeley veered to Seymour. Democratic papers generally disapproved of Chase, the West was for Pendleton and after the Chase boom subsided the East favored Seymour. In an address in New York City on June 25, Seymour asserted that the Democrats could win only with Chase and denounced Pendleton's money ideas. Both the *Herald* and *Tribune* accused Seymour of refusing the crown to make certain of getting it, and the *World* praised the speech but counseled caution. A reporter remarked that Seymour gave excellent reasons why he should not be selected and still better reasons why nobody else should be nominated.[39] Dr. Pierce told Chase, however, that in June he visited Tilden, Seymour and Church and found them ready to support Hendricks.[40] Such was the confusion and uncertainty prevailing in the Empire State.

By the end of June Tilden was openly hostile to Pendleton, secretly opposed to Hendricks but discreet in his commitments, friendly to Blair as a possibility—perhaps for Vice President, lukewarm toward Johnson and McClellan, open-minded as to Hancock, cool toward

---

[37] Tilden Papers, June 12, 1868.   [38] *Ib.,* June 22, 1868.   [39] *Post,* July 6, 1868.
[40] Warden, *Chase,* 709, July 14, 1868.

Chase, and uncertain about Seymour.[41] There can be little doubt that prior to July his first choice had been Chase, but, with his customary reticence, he kept his preference to himself—if he had one. To revive his interest in Chase, Barlow arranged a personal conference between the two men during the last week of June,[42] but it failed. With Seymour "declining peremptorily," Tilden was told that the field was open for Hendricks. "A great amount of private information" was brought him by men who wished to remain incognito.[43] Since money was to be a prime factor in the campaign, M. D. Landon of the Treasury Department thought Chase could obtain it and, moreover, since his face was "on all the dollar greenbacks" he "would carry every darky vote in the South." [44] Meanwhile, confident of the outcome, Chase and Van Buren drew up a platform of fifteen planks which seems to have had the approval of Tilden, Seymour, and others.[45]

The New York delegates assembled by Tilden on July 1 decided to vote for S. E. Church to conceal their intent until they could determine the outcome of the convention.[46] Van Buren had won over for Chase Sweeney who was "the real man in New York, and worth more than Belmont, Tilden . . . and twenty more such." All New York City delegates were for him. "Tilden is setting back against you." But Van Buren was still positive that Seymour would not be the candidate.[47] The Democratic National Convention opened in the Tammany Wigwam on July 4, 1868. Under Tweed a new building had been erected on East 14th Street, and Tilden helped to pay for it. Tammany, headed by Mayor Hoffman, Tweed's candidate for Governor, dedicated the Hall an hour before the convention opened, with the singing of America and the reading of the Declaration of Independence by Judge Albert Cardozo.[48] The weather was "too hot for the warm work on hand here," wrote Chase's daughter Kate,[49] now the wife of the calico manufacturer, Senator William Sprague. All hotels were full of delegates, clubs, and bands. Kate Chase Sprague's residence at 94 Fifth Avenue was the private headquarters of her father's supporters, where she met Tilden and Seymour in long interviews and had their

[41] Seymour Papers, N. Y. Hist. Soc.   [42] Tilden Papers; Schuckers, *Chase*, 563.
[43] Tilden Papers.
[44] Coleman, 125, 139; Chase Papers, Hist. Soc. of Penn.
[45] Tilden Papers.   [46] *World*, July 2, 3, 1868.
[47] Chase Papers, Hist. Soc. of Penn., July 2, 1868; J. V. L. Pruyn, *Journal*, July 2, 1868.
[48] Breen, *Thirty Years in New York Politics*, 167.
[49] Chase Papers, Hist. Soc. of Penn.

promise to support her worthy sire.[50] Seymour significantly stayed at the home of John Dash Van Buren.[51] Mrs. Sprague had charge of the Chase public headquarters at the Clarendon Hotel and reported daily to her father, but Van Buren, sensing the decline of the Chase boom, kept away from the politically minded daughter and thus awakened in her mind suspicions of his loyalty.[52]

At noon on July 4 August Belmont called the convention to order and urged the Democrats to rally around the "Union, the Constitution and the Laws." The Wigwam was jammed and women sat on the platform. Tilden's plan for organization was accepted without a hitch, making Seymour permanent chairman, Tweed one of the vice presidents, and adopting the two-thirds rule. Seymour's address was full of commonplaces and patriotic appeals for party unity and loyalty.[53] Every phrase uttered by Belmont and Seymour was greeted by applause. Three days later the platform which Tilden helped to write was adopted with unanimous enthusiasm. It arraigned the Republicans for foisting military despotism and Negro supremacy on the nation, demanded the restoration of the Southern States to the Union, and assailed the attempt to strip the President of his constitutional powers. The Reconstruction Acts of Congress were denounced as revolutionary, and Chase and Johnson were thanked for their resistance to usurpation of authority.[54]

On the first ballot Pendleton led with 105 votes while Johnson had 65, Hancock 33½, Church New York's 33, and 79½ were scattered.[55] The vote for Church which Tilden had arranged was thought by Welles to be a subterfuge for Seymour or Hendricks.[56] With New York's vote at his command, Tilden's strategy is not clear. A Chase supporter in Tilden's confidence said, "It is awkward to put a candidate in nomination who gets no vote out of his own State, and in leaving him to go for one who has but half of his own State" [Hendricks].[57] To kill off Pendleton, Tilden was switching to Hendricks against Barlow's judgment. On July 9 Clarkson N. Potter asked Tilden: "At this juncture is it not wise for the New York delegation to ask the Pendleton men whom they will support? If they answer Seymour, he *must not* decline.

[50] *Herald*, July 7, 1868.
[51] Seymour Papers. New York Hist. Soc., Seymour to G. L. Miller, June 10, 1868.
[52] Phelps, *Kate Chase*, 205–209.   [53] *World*, July 7, 1868; *Official Proceedings*, 24–27.
[54] *An. Cyc.*, 1868, 747.   [55] Stanwood, *Hist. of Pres.*, II, 325.
[56] *Diary*, III, 396.   [57] Tilden Papers, S. L. M. Barlow, July 8, 1868.

But I am confident it won't do to take up Governor Chase until the Pendleton men have been consulted." [58] This would indicate that Tilden's New York colleagues still believed that he was for Chase but would not be averse to Seymour if he could be persuaded to accept the nomination.

Balloting continued as Pendleton and Johnson lost and Hendricks and Hancock gained—neither one wholly acceptable to Tilden, who on the eighth ballot had New York drop Church and vote for Hendricks to cripple Pendleton.[59] It was significant that on July 10 in a test vote of the New York delegates Chase had 37 to 24 votes, his support coming from New York City and vicinity.[60] He might have been nominated had not the convention been stampeded. Seymour was openly for him,[61] although Tilden for some inexplicable reason seems to have grown lukewarm if not hostile. Of the Ohio delegation 11 favored him for second choice. The *Herald* was an outspoken advocate and the *World* was now not unfriendly. It seems evident that Chase was held back as a dark horse until the right moment. But on the 21st ballot General McCook of Ohio, in a stirring speech, perhaps with some thought of revenge on New York, stampeded the convention for Seymour—to the manifest surprise of Tilden. In vain Seymour protested, "Gentlemen, I thank you . . . but your candidate I cannot be." The shout of the delegates silenced his protest, and Kernan and Vallandigham declared his name must stand.[62] He attempted to propose the name of Chase but friends stopped him and forced him off the platform. When Tilden found him in one of the anterooms, Seymour waving his hands asked, "My God, Tilden, what shall I do?" "Your party has called you, and you will accept," calmly replied Tilden. Seymour was hurried away to the Manhattan Club—an abduction arranged, it was said, by Tilden.[63]

Welles explained Tilden's noncommittal attitude in these words:

"Blair tells me that Samuel Tilden wanted to be the candidate of the Democrats for President. It is hardly credible, and yet in that way, better than any other, can his conduct and that of the New York Democratic politicians be accounted for." [64] An additional ray of light is thrown on Tilden's conduct by A. S. Hewitt who said that the night

[58] *Letters*, I, 216.   [59] Coleman, 210.
[60] Chase Papers, J. D. Van Buren to Chase, July 24, 1868; Elliott, *Uncle Sam Ward*, 490.
[61] *An. Cyc.*, 1868, 751.
[62] Warden, 707; Alexander, III, 203; Rhodes, VI, 166.
[63] *World*, July 10, 1868.   [64] *Diary*, III, 446.

before Seymour was nominated, "Mr. Tilden, John Kelly, Governor Seymour, and myself dined together at the Manhattan Club, and there was a unanimous agreement that Chief Justice Chase was to receive the nomination next day." [65] But Seymour was named despite all efforts to stop it and "his reluctance was slowly overcome." Vallandigham later explained to Chase that he tried to persuade Tilden to vote for Chase or at least not to support Hendricks, but he refused to do either. Then he begged Seymour to accept the nomination only to meet the reply, "I cannot consent." [66] Colonel A. K. McClure also asserted that it was Tilden who defeated Chase in 1868.[67] Alexander Long declared that "artful Tilden" knew all about the "Ohio plan" when the New York delegates on the 21st ballot decided to swing to Chase. There is nothing in the Tilden Papers to substantiate the assertion that Tilden disliked Chase and hence refused to allow the New York delegate to vote for him before the stampede for Seymour.[68] Chase's explanation of his defeat was that a portion of Ohio and New York delegates planned the nomination of Seymour,[69] and it was commonly believed that Tilden was one of the schemers.[70]

By acclamation the second place on the ticket went to Frank P. Blair, Jr., and Tilden presided over the notification meeting on July 10, and also the ratification meeting in Tammany Hall. Seymour's formal letter of acceptance was postponed until August 4. Meanwhile the Union Soldiers National Convention met in New York and endorsed the Democratic platform and candidates.[71]

Nobody seemed pleased with the results of the convention. Seymour was forced to take an honor he did not want. After his demise twenty years later a reporter of the Utica *Herald* who professed to have his confidence said that he did not wish the nomination in 1868. Like Tilden, he was for Chase, and yielded to Tilden's strategy; and thought that with the right management Chase could have been named. But "Tilden withheld the vote from Chase in the hope of getting the nomination for himself." This ambition was thwarted by the enthusiastic stampede which forced Seymour to yield against his better judgment.[72] He had "sense enough to disbelieve in the possibility of his election," but

[65] Nevins, *Hewitt*, 265.   [66] Warden, *Chase*, 707.   [67] *Recollections*, 396.
[68] Coleman, *Election of 1868*, 227; Smith, II, 411.
[69] Chase Papers, Library of Congress, Chase to Smith, July 24, 1868.
[70] Alexander, III, 203.   [71] *Letters*, I, 228; *An. Cyc.*, 1868, 747.
[72] Feb. 13, 1886.

was overwhelmed by flattery.[73] In later years he asserted that his acceptance was "the great mistake of his life." [74]

Tilden got what he did not want—a candidate who could not win. He made the best of a bad situation, professed publicly that he was pleased at his old friend's triumph, but hurried to a retreat to hide his chagrin and to ruminate on what might have been. Doolittle was disgusted with the outcome and McCulloch thought no selection could have been worse. The *Tribune* represented Seymour and Blair on an ass, each in an end of the bag of wheat to balance his war record. Welles declared that the people could not be reconciled to such candidates.[75] Barlow said, "Our ticket creates almost universal execration." [76]

Chase's disappointment was assuaged by the cheering words of his friends. Shocked at first at Seymour's apparent deceit, he quickly recovered his poise and magnanimously said, "I do not hold Governor Seymour at all responsible. . . . I believe he was sincere throughout. He yielded where almost any man would have yielded." [77] He was further reconciled in this feeling toward Seymour when Van Buren reported that at midnight of July 8 Tilden in irritation asked, "What the devil does the Governor mean?" "What about?" asked Van Buren. "Why," said Tilden, "he has been around all the evening buttonholing the New York delegation one by one, electioneering with them to go for Chase in the morning." [78] The hopes of Kate Chase Sprague were blasted by the stampede to Seymour and she laid the defeat of her father to the betrayal of Tilden and Seymour, and the treason of Van Buren, "their tool." She added, sarcastically, "I fear that when the South seceded the brains of the party went with it." [79]

Johnson, perhaps, was the most peeved of all. His strong hopes were dashed to pieces by "duplicity, deceit, cunning management and sharp scheming." He was dissatisfied with the nominees and in an ill humor. J. D. Hoover urged Tilden to see the President, but instead of going himself Tilden, with Seymour and Schell, sent J. D. Van Buren, who reported to Seymour, "I found him not only cross but implacable—he thinks you are unfriendly to him personally. Everybody is 'crabbed' in Washington—Johnson men, Chase men, Hancock men—all except Hendricks." [80] Within a month, however, in a more amiable frame of

---

[73] Chase, *Diary and Cor.*, II, 520.   [74] Tilden Papers.   [75] *Diary*, III, 405, 411.
[76] Tilden Papers, July 10, 1868.   [77] Chase Papers.   [78] Coleman, 227.
[79] Hudson, 18–20.
[80] J. D. Van Buren to Seymour, July 20, 1868.

mind, President Johnson sent J. F. Coyle to convey his respects to Seymour and Tilden, and Coyle reported them friendly.

The only participants in the convention not in an ugly frame of mind, were the Southern delegates who, according to John Livingston, had defeated Chase.[81] Southerners like A. H. Stephens professed to be well-pleased with the nominations [82] and B. B. Chapman thought Seymour the best candidate that could have been selected.[83]

Tilden refused absolutely to accept responsibility for Seymour's nomination [84] although after it occurred so unexpectedly he professed to be pleased at the honor shown his friend and did everything within his power to bring about his election. Because of his experience in party conventions, his contacts with leading Democrats, and his native political shrewdness, Tilden must have known what manipulations and trades were being fathered. As the spokesman for New York he may have expected to play the rôle of Warwick. But proof is lacking for the assertion that he deliberately plotted for Seymour's nomination. That charge grew out of the proneness of wiseacres to explain the unexpected by a mysterious miracle wrought by a leader of Tilden's power. "I did not believe the event possible," he asserted, "unless Ohio demanded it." [85] The charge that Seymour was a party to Tilden's plot also falls to the ground for lack of evidence. Before and during the convention he declared again and again that he was not a candidate. After the nomination he continued to assert, "The nomination was unsought and unexpected." [86] His conduct during the campaign seems to bear out the truthfulness of that statement.[87]

[81] Coleman, 287, July 15, 1868.
[82] To J. B. Cohen, July 17, 1868.
[83] To A. H. Stephens, July, 1868.
[84] *Life*, I, 211. Yet Sam Ward wrote, "Instead of taking Chase, with whom we might have won, that arch wire-puller, Mrs. Tilden, persuaded Seymour to accept." Elliott, *Uncle Sam Ward*, 490.
[85] *World*, July 10, 1868.
[86] *Public Record*, 343.
[87] See Foord, *A. H. Green*, 84, for another post mortem explanation.

Chapter XV   Tilden Manages Seymour's Campaign in 1868

AFTER his nomination, Seymour hurried back to his farm at Deerfield to think over what had happened and to prepare his letter of acceptance. Letters came to him from friend and foe alike suggesting the wisdom of an emphatic declination. These communications, together with his own disinclination to run, kept him in a state of uncertainty for several weeks; and because of his silence close friends like Kernan were alarmed at the possible outcome. ·

To Kernan Tilden denied in July that he was responsible for forcing the nomination on Seymour. "I had no agency in getting Gov. Seymour in his present scrape," he wrote, "though I would have been glad of his nomination if his consent could have been freely given. I yielded to his wishes out of tender regard for him." As for the suggestion that Seymour should withdraw, he said: "I feel that I am the last man who can with delicacy bring a pressure to bear upon him; but my judgment is that acceptance, under present circumstances, would not compromise his reputation for sincerity. . . . I think a decision is necessary; for it is not possible to go thro' the canvass with a candidate declining." [1] At the same time he informed a Washington ratification meeting that an experience of thirty years led him to see "omens of victory" for the man who was the choice of the "harmonious judgment" of the convention. [2]

Tilden and the National Committee at once took up the important problem of publicity. R. W. Latham of Washington informed Tilden that the thirty reporters of that city could be secured for about $3,500 a month. They could influence "every important newspaper in the country" and were "worth more than all the stump orators in the field." He urged Tilden to come to the Capital "to attend to this matter" or send some reliable man. Governor F. P. Stanton might be willing to disburse the money and to take charge of the publicity bureau. [3]

Frank P. Blair, Sr., explained to Tilden how the *Herald* might be secured and himself offered to do considerable "scribbling." He was pleased with the ticket and the platform, although Seymour had been named

[1] *Letters*, I, 239.   [2] *Life*, I, 216.   [3] *Letters*, I, 240, July 13, 1868.

"by accident." [4] Later he praised Tilden for his Milwaukee speech and hoped his son Frank would measure up to Tilden's predictions of him as the heir of Old Hickory. The Blairs—father and sons Frank P., Jr., and Montgomery—kept closely in touch with Tilden throughout the whole campaign. When Frank's Brodhead letter about carpet bag government aroused so much hostility, Tilden had it reprinted in the *World* with explanations.[5] Montgomery informed Tilden, "Welles is very earnestly with us now," and suggested that Bennett be promised a foreign mission to get the use of the *Herald*.[6]

Seymour's letter of acceptance was delayed until August 4.[7] When he finally lined up for the race, definite plans for the campaign began. To supply funds, Tilden, Belmont, the two Schells, Magee, McCormick, O'Conor and Durant each agreed to give $10,000—a total of $80,000.[8] H. T. Helmbold, a patent medicine advertiser, contributed $40,000; [9] and Tweed and Sweeney paid $5,000 each. Seymour told Tilden that Corcoran, the Washington banker, would help to finance the campaign, that Mitchell of Milwaukee was friendly, and that J. B. Sevin of Binghamton would call. "I sent you Williams' check" he reported. G. S. Curtis could not give any money but volunteered to serve as a stump speaker. John T. Hoffman did not send in D. S. Lamont's contribution until November 4. Altogether the Democratic National Committee seems to have had something over $150,000 to offset the money bags of Jay Cooke.[10]

Tilden's duty as campaign manager was to assume a general oversight. Single items here and there in his correspondence offer but a slight conception of the multitudinous outlays for literature, publicity, speakers and other services. A few of these expenditures will suffice to show the wide variety. Since Pennsylvania was a pivotal State, W. A. Wallace asked for $25,000 immediately and Peter B. Sweeny sent $1,500 to the Laborer's Union and asked for a receipt. Sweeny complained that Tilden had no right to send bills to him for payment, but did send a check for $100 to pay German speakers. A bill for $530 for the entertainment of the Pendleton Escort during the National Convention was sent to Tilden for payment. A veritable flood of bills for

[4] *Letters,* I, 241, July 15, 1868.
[5] Tilden Papers, July 13, Aug. 10, 1868. See *An. Cyc.,* 1868, 746, letter dated June 30, 1868.
[6] *Letters,* I, 245, Aug. 19, 1868.   [7] *An. Cyc.,* 1868, 751.   [8] *Letters,* I, 245.
[9] Springfield *Republican,* Oct. 15; *Tribune,* Oct. 20, 1868; Mitchell, *Seymour,* 463.
[10] Tilden Papers.

printing, advertising, and office expenses was sent to National Headquarters for payment. As the campaign progressed Montgomery Blair
wanted $50,000 to finance the *National Intelligencer*—which was in-
debted to Jay Cooke and others, who were demanding their loans—but
failed to get it from Tilden. N. E. Paine asked for at least $25,000 for
use in Indiana because a Hendricks victory would carry Seymour
through, and Seymour thought both Indiana and Iowa should be helped.
By the end of September Pennsylvania and Indiana were begging
frantically for more money to win "an even fight." [11]

Seymour informed Tilden that he had "given much thought to the
subject of organization. . . . We must take a new course . . . organize our young men." He expected little help from the National
Committee; thought the secret Jackson clubs of New Jersey and
Connecticut good models; and asked Tilden to see Spencer of New
York and Palmer of Wisconsin who had a simple and economic plan.[12]
As a result of preliminary conferences, there was organized the Order of
the Union Democracy. Tilden was made "Chief," Schell "Vice Chief"
and J. C. Spencer national secretary. There were a National Union
and State Unions. The headquarters was at 18 Union Square in New
York City, where an executive committee, of which Cyrus H. McCormick was chairman, transacted business.[13] Evidently the Order made
an effort to organize the Democrats all over the nation. To what extent
its purposes were realized does not appear in the records.

In laying plans for the campaign, Tilden exercised his usual caution.
To Cyrus H. McCormick, from whom he expected financial co-operation, he wrote, "The situation in which the immediate friends of Governor
Seymour find themselves placed, render them extremely cautious to
whom they make the appeal which Mr. Spencer will submit to you." This
appeal had to do with the funds needed to launch the Democratic
secret society throughout the country. McCormick was told that the
news from Pennsylvania, Ohio and Indiana was of the "most encouraging and gratifying character." If the Democrats carried any two of them,
they would win. Hence more than ordinary efforts must be made through
organization and speakers.[14] Pennsylvania was clamoring for General
Hancock as a speaker and both Tilden and Seymour exerted their influence to induce him to take the platform, but he pleaded illness from

[11] Tilden Papers, Sept. and Oct., 1868. [12] *Letters*, I, 242, July 20, 1868.
[13] McCormick Papers. [14] *Ib.*, Sept. 19, 1868.

an old wound and the urgency of a court of inquiry. Besides he thought that his activity in a political campaign would set a bad example to the younger army officers.[15] In the organization of the new National Democratic Committee after Seymour's nomination, Belmont, a strong Chase man, was replaced as chairman by Augustus Schell. But only the urgent insistence of Tilden held him at the helm.[16]

While the Democrats were nominating Seymour for President, the Republicans at Syracuse on July 8 nominated John A. Griswold for Governor to strengthen the Grant ticket.[17] Tilden begged Kernan, because of his "skill and tact," to act as permanent chairman of the Democratic State Convention at Albany on September 2; [18] but, after Tilden called that body to order and made an optimistic speech, that honor went to Robert Earl. Grover Cleveland was a delegate and Tweed led the forces supporting, for Governor, John T. Hoffman who was nominated by acclamation.[19] After Judge Morris made a vehement attack on Tweed and Tammany Hall, A. C. Beach was selected for Lieutenant Governor.[20] Seymour was endorsed, and Tilden was retained as Chairman of the Democratic State Committee.[21] A compilation of expenses of the Federal Government since the close of the war was pounced upon with glee by Tilden who exclaimed, "At present nobody can advocate economy without thrusting a sword into the vitals of the Republican policy." [22]

Perhaps no campaign in American history has started under greater handicaps but Tilden scanned the political field and plotted his line of offense. He meant to carry the labor vote and generously supplied funds for speakers and publicity to win it. In the second place, he intended to reach the Irish and Germans through their own newspapers and orators. When the Republicans bought the *Irish Republic*, he considered establishing a Democratic Irish paper. In the third place, he planned to have the State leaders keep in close touch with their county leaders; and sent out telegrams asking for information as a sort of barometer of the political atmosphere. Cheering reports came as a response: "The Pacific States are sure. The President promises to carry Tennessee." Letters from the West were "confident in tone"; "The news

---

15 *Letters*, I, 249.   16 *Ib.*, 251.
17 Grant was nominated May 20, 1868.
18 Kernan Papers, Tilden to Kernan, Aug. 26, 1868.
19 Stebbins, 362.   20 *Times, World* and *Tribune*, Sept. 3, 1868.
21 *An. Cyc.*, 1868.   22 *World*, Oct. 2, 1868.

from Maine is hard" but a Republican New England would be offset by a Democratic West. Prospects in Pennsylvania were bright but McClellan must be sent there.[23] Blair was sent from New Jersey to the West.[24] And so the story went—on the whole encouraging in August and September. Seymour, placing the greatest confidence in Tilden's judgment, met him frequently until the campaign ended.

Tilden worked hard for Seymour's election. Not only did he manage finances and publicity, but he contributed a large sum himself and wrote letters for the press. He also took the stump, delivering addresses in the West as well as in the East, which were printed as campaign literature.[25] His ablest speech was made to his old neighbors at Chatham, on taxation, economy and reform in behalf of "the toiling millions." "In this great contest we shall wage no war of defense. We will carry our arms into Africa." [26] When his friend Isaac Butts of Rochester asked where he might find an accurate account of the national finances, Tilden prepared a statement on "The Waste of War." It was a masterful survey of the waste of capital, homes, food, farm equipment and other necessities brought about by the war and by burdensome taxation resulting from it. The pamphlet arraigned the "ruinous policy of the Radical majority of Congress" and the oppressive centralism for the heavy taxes inflicted on the nation.[27]

Ten weeks after his nomination, Seymour was complaining of his isolation. With the exception of his "consultations" with Tilden and "two or three others" he had seen no one. While there were "many advantages" in such a course, obviously "it should not be held too long." He proposed, therefore, to form a little secret kitchen council of ten or twelve persons with whom he could "talk matters over" during the canvass.[28] Tilden acquiesced in this arrangement, but so far as there was a manager of his campaign Seymour looked to Tilden. At times Seymour took matters in his own hands, as when he urged Tilden to send military men, such as Slocum, McClellan, Hancock and Franklin, into Pennsylvania to counteract the effects of the soldiers' meeting.[29] Earlier he had written Tilden: "I am anxious to have you get things in your hands as much as may be. It is a great thing to have unity of purpose and concentrated action. You and Schell will make your action count." [30]

[23] Tilden Papers, Aug. and Sept., 1868. [24] Smith, *Blair Family*, II, 416.
[25] *World*, Aug. 8, Sept. 15, 1868. [26] *Writings*, I, 422, Sept. 24, 1868.
[27] *Ib.*, I, 453; *World*, Oct. 12, 1868. [28] *Letters*, I, 247, Sept. 28, 1868.
[29] *Ib.*, 248, Oct. 1, 1868. [30] Tilden Papers.

At the outset of the campaign Seymour took the attitude that those who were responsible for his nomination should bear the brunt of the campaign. When at last, by October, Tilden persuaded him to begin a speaking tour of the middle West, he made a tremendous hit. President Johnson told Seymour on October 22 that he was glad to learn that he was going to take the stump and predicted victory.[31]

Godkin's assertion that the Democrats had no sooner nominated Seymour than they perceived their mistake and Marble's demand that Blair withdraw because of his letter on reconstruction may have been the natural results of a bitter contest, but it was soon apparent that a wave of discontent was spreading across the Democratic landscape. No one was more keenly aware of this than Tilden, but he felt that if Seymour played up to his obligations as head of the party, the rising storm might subside. To men like J. S. Black, who wrote "I cannot understand your candidate," he sent conciliatory explanations.[32] Gradually he seemed to be winning the support of the disappointed friends of the disappointed candidates. Then during September and October nine States went Republican in local elections. A blind man could see the meaning of that drift. Seymour, who had excellent political eyes, commented: "Well, sir, the Democracy cannot hold me responsible. I persistently and repeatedly declined the nomination." [33] To his nephew he remarked, "We shall save the State of New York and that is about all."

By mid-October the discontent with the Democratic ticket had become an uproar of disapproval. "There is positive dislike for Seymour," wrote Welles in his *Diary*. "It was not a time to nominate a Copperhead." [34] Something akin to a panic prevailed within the party—particularly among supporters of Chase and Johnson. Alexander Long attempted to induce Vallandigham and other "discreet friends" to have Seymour withdraw for Chase, if Pennsylvania, Ohio and Indiana went Republican, but Chase thought a "change of front" undesirable. Certain of defeat, Barlow begged Tilden to persuade Seymour to withdraw. "Call your committee together," wired Randall. "Withdraw Seymour and nominate Johnson or Chase. Act and win." To replace Seymour, the Indiana State Committee suggested first Hendricks, second Chase and third Hancock.[35] After the *World* accused Blair of dragging the party down to defeat and called upon Seymour to take the lead in saving

[31] *An. Cyc.*, 1868, 752.   [32] Tilden Papers, Aug. 15, 1868.   [33] *Times*, Oct. 18, 1868.
[34] *Diary*, III, 398.   [35] Tilden Papers, Oct. 15–17, 1868.

it, Blair publicly announced at St. Louis that he was ready to withdraw if his friends thought it best [36] and his venerable father hurried over to New York to see Tilden.[37] Yet just two weeks before Blair had boasted, "We will elect our President." [38]

Tilden was placed in one of the most embarrassing situations of his life. Could he betray an old friend to appease his critics? Could he in some tactful way persuade him to withdraw? And if he did, would it save the day? With Schell, Tilden hurried up to Utica on October 16 for a conference with Kernan and Seymour. Without the need of persuasion, Seymour announced that it would be a relief to withdraw. After a discussion of all angles of the situation, it was decided, to prevent injury to the party, to make no change.[39] To reach such a conclusion and to stand by it took courage and certain risks. As a setting for the announcement of this decision, a "Monster Mass Meeting" at Tammany Hall and in Union Square was called for October 27, to "repudiate the idea of any faltering" concerning the nominees. "Continue on the Ramparts" was to be the watchword. Tilden had arrived at a decision before he consulted Seymour, because on the day previous to his trip to Utica he wired J. D. Hoover: "No authority or possibility to change front. . . . We in New York are not panic stricken," and to W. F. Story: "The suggestion made to change ticket was wholly unauthorized and unknown to . . . Executive Committee. . . . The proposition is . . . absurd, and is received by our masses with astonishment . . . and indignation. . . . Resolved to renew contest under our chosen leaders . . . for rescue of constitutional government and civil liberty." He had Belmont issue an address to "Conservative Voters" extolling Seymour, stressing the need for party unity and boasting, "Our ranks are unbroken; and our courage is unabated." He also issued an appeal, "You have driven the Republicans to the baggage wagons. You have almost routed them. Fellow Democrats, is this a moment for doubt as to what you ought to do?" [40] To Blair, Tilden telegraphed, "Without contemplating any change . . . come here immediately." [41] Under Tilden's generalship following the mass meeting on October 27 all danger of revolt subsided.

By his heroic stand the Democratic Party was saved from a lament-

[36] *Times,* Oct. 18, 1868.   [37] *Letters,* I, 198, misdated 1865.
[38] Tilden Papers, Oct. 4, 1868.
[39] Tilden Papers; Utica *Observer,* Oct. 19, 1868.
[40] Tilden Papers, Oct. 15, 17, 1868; *Letters,* I, 250.   [41] *Letters,* I, 251, Oct. 21, 1868.

able fiasco. Everybody said that all chance of a Democratic national victory had vanished, but the State ticket might still be elected. The attitude of New York Democrats was expressed by Cassidy in a letter to Tilden, "We can save Hoffman, and under the circumstances that will be a victory." It may have been true that "The ranks are irritated at the leaders," but Tilden's prestige was enhanced by his rescue of the party from a bad muddle.[42]

A brave finish was made in a losing fight. Seymour received only 80 electoral votes to Grant's 214. In the popular vote, however, Grant's plurality was only a little over 300,000 out of a total of nearly 6,000,000. Stated differently, Grant received 53% and Seymour 47% of the ballots.[43] Seymour had the consolation of knowing that he carried New York by a majority of 10,000—and three other Northern States—but even that triumph was overshadowed by the fact that Hoffman was elected Governor by a majority of almost 28,000.[44]

The "landslide" for Grant never actually occurred, although historians have sometimes presented it in vivid colors. On the contrary, the gap in the popular vote between Grant and Seymour was surprisingly small. The vote was evidence of a strong popular current running in Seymour's favor. The situation was quite different among the leaders—no unity, almost utter indifference, a spirit of defeatism, and a flourishing crop of disappointed ambitions and jealousies. Had the leaders and party workers been as loyal to Seymour as the people were, and had they labored with as much zeal as they grumbled, he might have been elected. Had the South been able to poll its full Democratic strength as it did before the Civil War, and as it does today, the outcome of the election of 1868 would have been different. As it was, the South, with 650,000 Negro votes, was secure for the Republicans. Only Maryland, Georgia, Louisiana and Kentucky, with 34 electoral votes, went for Seymour, the remaining Southern States—Mississippi and Texas cast no votes—cast their 52 votes for Grant under Negro suffrage protected by Federal bayonets.[45] On Seymour's own head must fall full responsibility for his defeat, because in large measure he brought on the disorganization in the party.

Near the end of the campaign it was said that from the headquarters of the Democratic State Committee A. Oakey Hall, secretary, sent out a

---

[42] Tilden Papers.   [43] Smith, *Blair Family*, II, 429.
[44] *An. Cyc.*, 1868, 550; Mitchell, *Seymour*, 474.   [45] Stanwood, *Hist. of Pres.*, 269.

"strictly confidential" letter,[46] ostensibly signed by Tilden, to county leaders asking them to have some "reliable person" telegraph an estimate of the vote to William M. Tweed. The inference was that with this information he would round up enough votes to carry the election. The *Evening Post* on November 4 pronounced the letter a forgery and Tilden at once confirmed the assertion.[47] Other New York City papers charged that there had been fraudulent registration and voting; [48] only the *World* was silent. These frauds were connected chiefly with illegal naturalizations through the connivance of obliging judges. The Democrats admitted there were frauds, but asserted that as many such votes were Republican as Democratic.[49] In New York City in the charter election which followed on December 2, A. Oakey Hall, Democrat, won over Colonel F. A. Conkling, Republican, by a majority of over 54,000.[50]

Believing that Tilden was a passive accomplice in the election frauds, Greeley printed an open letter telling him that he could force his party to adhere to legal voting if he would and accusing him of being as "deeply implicated" as Hall or Tweed. "Now, Mr. Tilden," said Greeley, "I call on you to put a stop to this business. You have but to walk into the Sheriff's office . . . and say that there must be no more of it. . . . Will you do it? If we Republicans are swindled again . . . you and such as you will be responsible to God and man for the outrage." There is no record that Tilden answered this challenge but let it be forgotten as quickly as possible.[51] Indeed there is no evidence that at this time he was horrified at the political corruption in the metropolis and at Albany, although later when he was making open war on Tammany he asserted that as early as 1863 there developed "antagonisms" between those who formed the Ring and himself and that he kept the State Democratic organization "in absolute independence" of them.

The brief period between the campaign of 1868 and Tilden's assault on the Tweed Ring in 1870 was one of comparatively political quiet. As head of the party in the State he kept on friendly terms with Governor Hoffman, interested himself in patronage, and managed successfully the election of minor State officers in 1869.[52] He consulted O'Conor about

[46] Lynch, *Tweed*, 393, Oct. 27, 1868; Wingate, *North Am. Rev.*, Oct., 1874, 404.
[47] Wingate, *North Am. Rev.*, Oct., 1874, 405.
[48] *Sun, Tribune, Times, Post* and *Nation*, Nov. 4 to 10.
[49] Davenport, *Frauds in N. Y., 1860–70*, 107; Sen. Misc. Doc. No. 4, 3 sess. 40th Cong.; Report of Com. of H. R., 3 sess. 40th Cong., I, 148; II, No. 31; III, No. 4, 149.
[50] *Tribune Almanac*, 1869, 62.   [51] Lynch, *Tweed*, 294, Oct. 29, 1869; 295.
[52] Tilden Papers. See *Poll Book* of 1869 as an effective campaign device.

New York's repudiation of the Fourteenth Amendment. When the woman's Suffrage Association in convention at Saratoga asked his endorsement of their resolutions, he replied that he did not agree with them because nature had made the two sexes unequal. Entertaining "serious doubts as to the wisdom of . . . extending the elective franchise to the Negro," he was impressed with the "utter absurdity of rights of citizenship for women." He felt that, "The hardy frame of man makes him the natural defender and protector of the woman, whose frail physical organization combined with the duties of maternity . . . render her equality with man an utter impossibility.[53]

This hesitancy to impose new burdens on women did not deter Tilden from desiring their friendship. Not only did he entertain party and business associates, but their wives and daughters as well. Occasionally he gave a formal dinner to mixed groups, and there exists a table plan in his hand showing the seating arrangements for twenty-one guests. Once Curtis asked what kind of dress his wife should wear at Tilden's party. He particularly enjoyed an intellectual group with a feminine sparkle, and no doubt after the old Johannisberger was served it became a convivial group as well. This costly wine was sent out occasionally to old friends such as Gouverneur Kemble. With a rare human sympathy, Tilden wrote to Marble upon the death of his wife: "I share your sorrows for her who was so much more to you than to me. . . . An intellect so just and true, so independent and searching, always held by the polar attraction of a high, splendid nature . . . is not often given. I remember the life at 117 East 30th St. with a tender regret that it is passed."[54]

Thus the career of Samuel J. Tilden, the politician trained in the school of Jackson, Van Buren and Wright and the self-made business lawyer, entered a new phase. In politics, always the strongest type of a partisan, he had climbed upward to the headship of his party in the State, to the position of a Warwick in the nation, and had managed a Presidential campaign. His qualifications for directorship were widely recognized. As a lawyer he had reached the pinnacle of his profession. In business he had exhibited a remarkable capacity for arranging gigantic mergers. He had sat in halls of legislation and on boards of directors. The ablest men of the country were proud to be associated with him.

[53] Tilden Papers. Statement in the handwriting of Tilden's secretary.
[54] *Ib.*, Feb. 1, 1871.

With years of experience his provincialism was sloughed off and his intellectual and moral stature grew until he was respected for his sagacity, his superior judgment, and his qualities of leadership. Now he was to demonstrate that a good politician could become an able statesman.

To understand the rise of the Tweed Ring and Tilden's part in its over-throw, a brief survey of the history of local government in New York City is necessary. No person was better acquainted with this history than Tilden. He knew that under the Constitution of 1777 all local officers were designated by the Council of Appointment, and that this unwise system had resulted in an unseemly scramble for positions and much corruption. After the abolition of the council important local officials were elected, and minor officials were appointed by municipal authorities. The power of removing sheriffs and county clerks for cause was left in the hands of the Governor.[1]

The Charter of 1830 had placed the administration of the city in the hands of the Mayor and the Common Council.[2] This system was in operation when Tilden went to New York. As Corporation Counsel in 1843 he saw the government in practical operation, and as a lawyer he was familiar with the courts. He observed that repeatedly an aroused populace overthrew the administration in elections, and that the "exposure of publicity" made "plunder unsafe if not impossible." In 1846 the Governor's power of removal was extended to about five hundred offices in the County of New York. This change placed a check on dishonest officials.[3]

Tilden believed in a home rule which gave the people actual control over those who managed their political business, and thought that local elections should be divorced from State and national elections. The foundation of effective city rule was official accountability. "Public officers are the trustees of the people." When the legislature in 1857, under pretense of reform, created for the city an elective bipartisan board of supervisors and the next year increased their term to six years, a bipartisan ring resulted. Tilden protested because he saw the possibilities of graft. When William Marcy Tweed became a member of this board there began the Tweed Ring by which Republicans and Democrats entered into an unholy alliance for personal power and profit.

[1] Flick, H. M., *The Council of Appointment*, 1934; Tilden, "Municipal Reform Message," *Writings*, II, 125.
[2] *Writings*, II, 129; Myers, *Tammany Hall*, 92.   [3] *Writings*, II, 126, 129.

Since all real power was at Albany, the board went there for jobs and contracts. The system grew bolder, more corrupt; the Mayor and Common Council ceased to have much influence. There was no discussion, no publicity. The will of the people was impotent.

During the Civil War, with power concentrated at Washington and Albany, New York City was left in the hands of corrupt politicians. Through commissions named at Albany, dishonest men of both parties looted the city. Two sets of officials, city and county, made deals easier. The Governor and legislature too often shut their eyes to the evildoers or even abetted them. Good men not in the army were too absorbed in national issues or in business to heed conditions in the city. A flood of immigrants joined Democratic Tammany Hall. The demoralization of the war was carried over into civic life.[4]

At the conclusion of the war Tilden was conscious that municipal government in New York had undergone "injurious changes." Indeed, he believed that "the elective power of the people had been nugatory" for a generation and that in consequence civic training had decayed. With changes in the character of the population, there had come a voluntary withdrawal from participation in local government as well as "forced exclusion." Furthermore, the nonpolitical controversies resulted in "an almost total neglect" of local questions. Hence false theories of government arose, and the "spending officers" became exempt from regulation by legislative bodies and through their patronge secured control of the government. Thus elective control by the people became ineffectual; abuses and corruptions arose, and no regenerated public opinion cried out for adequate reforms from Albany.[5]

Prior to the war the Tweed Ring began to function in a small way. The first known act was in 1859, when Tweed and two Democratic supervisors bribed Supervisor Voorhees, a Republican colleague, for $2,500, to absent himself on the day when election inspectors were appointed.[6] The next step was to levy a percentage on all bills that this small clique permitted to be paid. Tweed soon succeeded Hoffman as Grand Sachem of Tammany and in 1863 was appointed Deputy Street Commissioner.[7] By this time he was designated as the "Boss" and about 10% was collected from contractors. In 1864 a fourth supervisor

[4] *Writings*, I, 127, 560; II, 130. [5] *Ib.*, II, 129.
[6] *Documents of the Board of Supervisors*, Part 2, No. 8, p. 15; New York *Sun*, Sept. 7, 1877, gives Tweed's confession.
[7] Myers, 255; *Commercial Advertiser*, Sept. 6, 1877.

was taken into the Ring; and others were added as expediency dictated. Their stealing was on a small scale, and neither clever nor particularly profitable.[8] By 1867 an understanding was reached with contractors who supplied the city with materials that their bills would be increased 35%. Of this sum Tweed kept 25% and paid 10% to Comptroller Connolly.[9]

The next step in the development of the Ring was to enlist powerful allies in the judiciary and at Albany. Meanwhile Boss Tweed as the powerful head of Tammany Hall added to the Ring Peter B. Sweeny, his influential supporter in Tammany and an experienced lawyer, who became the brains of the conspiracy. Richard D. Connolly, a naturalized Irish immigrant with a finger already in the profitable pie, was a clever local politician and officeholder, whose "smooth, oily and insinuating" personality made him a valuable tool in the hands of his bolder associates.[10]

How the Ring operated politically may be illustrated by the election of 1868 when Tweed was determined to seat Hoffman in the Governor's chair as the Ring's pliant representative. To make good A. Oakey Hall's promise of a majority of 90,000 in the metropolis for Hoffman,[11] the "friend of the poor" and of naturalized citizens, the Ring proceeded through accommodating judges such as McCunn to clothe with citizenship about 35,000 immigrants. Of these naturalized citizens 10,000 had not met the five years of residence required and 15,000 never bothered even to appear before the judge.[12] For electioneering purposes $1,000 was sent to each of the 327 election districts, and Tweed advised the usual practice of ballot-box stuffing, repeating, and trading votes. In the end not less than 25,000 fraudulent votes were cast. Later Tweed said that some of the 2,000 special inspectors reported election results without even counting the votes.[13] To prevent the Republicans from using the telegraph lines Tweed monopolized them with useless messages, even proposing if necessary to send the entire contents of the Bible. As a result he seated Hoffman as Governor—the vote exceeding by 8% the whole voting population, added to his own offices that of State Senator, and was ready to have laws passed to entrench himself further. It is no

[8] Wilson, *Mem. Hist.*, III, 541.   [9] Myers, 215.
[10] *Writings*, I, 562; Wingate, "An Episode in Municipal Government," *N. A. Rev.*, Oct., 1874.
[11] *Herald*, Sept. 3, 1868.   [12] *Nation*, Oct. 29, Nov. 12, 1868.
[13] Werner, *Tammany Hall*, 217; *Docs. of Board of Aldermen*, Pt. 2, No. 8, p. 225; Stebbins, *Pol. Hist.*, 394.

surprise to find that payments to the Ring from corrupt contractors such as Andrew J. Garvey, Ingersoll & Company and Keyser & Company increased in 1869 from 55% to 65%.[14]

Prior to 1870 Tilden may have been suspicious of Tweed and his associates, as he later declared, but he was not unfriendly to them. They were members of the same party and the insurance of victory in elections required some co-operation and at least outward manifestation of harmony. In Tilden's letter files there is ample proof of cordial co-operation. For example, Sweeny asked Tilden to get a "police job in Central Park" for a friend, recommended a stump speaker, introduced Colonel King as a friend, informed Tilden that Hugh Smith had given $2,500 to the Democratic Committee, announced that Hall would give his services until after election, and wrote: "A week ago I asked you for an advance. Why no reply?" Tweed was calling at Tilden's office "on important business," and writing that he would like to see him about party affairs in the first district. J. D. Van Buren, Jr., asked Tilden to get Tweed's signature to a public address because it was "wise and necessary," and Tilden informed Tweed that the National Democratic Committee would meet in Washington at the Metropolitan Hotel. Hall invited Tilden to meet with the local Democratic Committee. Hoffman informed Tilden that a friend wanted to buy $5,000 worth of bonds "at the price of mine," invited him to dine, sought his advice as "one of a few discreet friends," and sent him a check of $1,000 for the State Committee.[15] Tilden declared that while the Ring controlled Tammany he "had not set his foot" inside the Hall.[16] But there were many places outside of the Hall where he could and did meet members of the Ring. Nor was Tilden blind to the use of money in politics. Isaiah Blood, a rich Democratic leader of Balston Spa, told him that the canvass in his district was "horribly expensive," but with $30,000 he could win the race for State Senator. He asked Tilden to see Tweed and Sweeny and get $10,000. "I will put $20,000 to it," he added. "Bring it up in currency . . . in $5 and $10 bills, but mostly in $5's." [17]

For years Tilden had been identified with Tammany Hall and had served as a sachem. But as Tweed and Sweeny gained control, he became less and less active in its councils. Tweed became permanent chairman of the organization on January 1, 1863, and the new sachems

---

[14] *Documents of Board*, 226; Myers, *Tammany Hall*, 221.
[15] Tilden Papers, various dates.   [16] *Writings*, I, 574.
[17] Tilden Papers, Oct. 18, 1869.

elected at the same time were his henchmen. These leaders announced that the time had come when the old warriors should give up their seats at the council fires to younger braves. As Grand Sachem Tweed soon began to push his supporters into the key positions of the city and county.[18] Tilden did not actually withdraw from Tammany, because on October 17, 1867, Hoffman asked him to pay the balance of his subscription for the building of the "New Tammany Hall," and presumably he forwarded his check. By 1870 he had openly broken not with the organization but with Tweed and his lieutenants who were running it. After the downfall of Tweed, to anticipate a bit, under the Grand Sachemship of "Honest John" Kelly, Tilden, together with Seymour, Church, Belmont, Hewitt and Schell, again became active in Tammany Hall's political maneuvers.[19]

To insure safety in its looting projects, the Ring won over three judges—George G. Barnard, a Yale graduate; Albert Cardozo, of a prominent Jewish family; and John H. McCunn, an Irish lawyer. Barnard was insolent and unscrupulous. Cardozo, a Columbia graduate, was a learned legal gentleman who sold justice "as a grocer might have sold sugar." McCunn was ignorant of the law but as dishonest as his associates. With these judges, and possibly others, sharing in the thievery, the leaders of the Ring had little fear of being brought to justice for their crimes.

To mold public opinion in their favor, the gang planned to control the city press. Editors were cultivated; reporters were given lucrative jobs and tipped off about money-making possibilities in stocks and real estate. Advertising contracts were also used as bribes. In these ways some of the newspapers were persuaded to defend the manipulations of the Ring. Indeed the *Times*, the very paper that made the first successful exposure of the Ring, had $300,000 bid for it by the Ring after the death of the editor Henry J. Raymond, and Tweed meant to make A. Oakey Hall editor. But the friends of reform, by increasing the bid $50,000, secured control; [20] and George Jones, the new editor, emphatically denied the reported sale of the paper to the civic gangsters.

With their interests safeguarded by the "Ring Judges" and their reputations defended by a venal press, the Ring was ready to expand its

[18] Lynch, *Tweed*, 288; Werner, *Tammany*, 102.
[20] Wilson, *Mem. Hist.*, III, 543–544.   [19] Tilden Papers.

business. Perhaps the best illustration of its method of operation may be seen in the building of the New York County Court House, which was stipulated by law to be built for $250,000. In 1862, $1,000,000 was appropriated to begin the work, and in 1864, $800,000 to complete it; but year after year like sums were appropriated until, by 1872, not less than $6,000,000 was spent on the building. The stealings of the Ring brought its cost up to $14,000,000.[21] Then the Board of Supervisors in 1867 authorized Andrew H. Garvey to furnish the new building and this opened another field for peculation.

During this period from 1860 to 1868 John T. Hoffman was first Recorder and then Mayor. Apparently honest personally, he winked at financial irregularities and consequently was made Governor. Upon his resignation as Mayor, the reform party nominated John Kelly, but he was badly defeated by A. Oakey Hall, who at the time was District Attorney.[22] A versatile man and prominent in Tammany Hall, his connection with the Ring has never been made clear. It was Tilden's belief that he was the intellect of the gang. It seems probable that he was actuated more by ambitious vanity than greed, although Tweed had a contrary opinion, as will be seen. Whether personally guilty or not, Hall, like Hoffman, knew what was going on and closed his eyes to the looting of the city.[23]

The opening of 1869 saw the Tweed Ring in complete control of the metropolis under Mayor Hall.[24] A friendly Governor ruled in Albany. In the subservient legislature, the Democrats had a majority. Sweeny was City Chamberlain; Tweed, Street Commissioner; and Connolly, Comptroller. The three "Ring Judges" were in strategic positions. A large part of the press was either bribed or menaced to silence. Moreover, Tweed was sent to the State Senate to secure laws making New York City entirely independent of Albany. Although it was necessary to pay for the protective bills, the stolen funds were ample. Assured of noninterference at the Capital, the Ring began to pillage the city systematically. Garvey continued his mythical work on the Court House and sent in bills for acres of plastering amounting to nearly $3,500,000. A plumber named John H. Keyser was paid $1,508,410.89. Tweed's friend, James H. Ingersoll, sent in bills for carpets amounting to $4,-

[21] Wilson, *Mem. Hist.*, III, 544.   [22] Stebbins, *Pol. Hist.*, 404.

[23] *Dict. Am. Biog.*, VIII, 114.   [24] *Writings*, I, 562.

829,426.26—enough to have carpeted a large portion of the city. These moneys were paid into a special account and divided daily, as will be seen.[25]

Tweed now began to concern himself with railroads, through Jim Fisk and Jay Gould. While Tweed was looting the city, Fisk and Gould were looting the stockholders of the Erie Railroad, and it was not long before these birds of a feather were flocking together. To legalize the fraudulent stock of the Erie, at least $500,000 was paid, and Tweed was found to be a useful State official. At the suggestion of Fisk and Gould, he procured the passage of the Erie Classification Bill for which service they made him and Sweeny directors of the line. Tweed as a member of the Erie Ring was not only the holder of a large block of stock but became a member of the Executive Committee and greased the palms of judges who rendered favorable decisions. Tweed estimated his profits from the Erie for three months at $650,000.[26] Tweed and Fisk became close cronies and were much in each other's society, dining together with Josie Mansfield. Nor did they neglect to entertain pliant jurists like Judge Barnard.[27]

Tweed's investments now began to reach out to real estate, iron mines, gas companies and other corporations.[28] He and his fellow crooks owned their own newspapers, a printing shop, a stationer's store, and furniture factories, all of which were used as means for robbing the taxpayers.[29] These peculations could not be kept secret. By 1869 the Tweed Ring was assailed from two quarters—first by those greedy for a share in the spoils, and secondly by honest men who were disgusted with the flagrant corruption and hence wished to drive the thieves out of office and punish them. When the Ring supported the Roman Catholic schools, zealous Protestants raised a cry against it and called the Board of Education into the controversy.[30] The effective answer to that interference was the abolition of the board by the servile legislature. The Republican legislators who could be bribed, together with the Democrats, were dubbed the "Black Horse Cavalry." The Young Democracy, organized at the home of the pugilist, Congressman John Morrissey, sought to pass laws which would drive Tweed and his allies out of office but failed. In like manner the reformers who tried to expel Tweed from the Demo-

---

[25] Wilson, *Mem. Hist.*, III, 548; *Times*, Feb. 24, 1871.
[26] Myers, 266; Adams, *The New York Gold Conspiracy*, 328.
[27] Lynch, *Tweed*, 298.   [28] Myers, 268.
[29] *Times*, Aug. 10, 1871.   [30] *Writings*, I, 580; Wilson, *Mem. Hist.*, III, 548.

cratic State Committee were unsuccessful. The Ring was too strongly entrenched in Tammany Hall and in the State and City Governments to be dissolved without a tremendous blast of moral dynamite.[31]

With an inordinate cunning, the Ring had become adept at simulating reform measures. By political trickery one officer would be expelled and another just as bad substituted. The powers of one office would be abolished and then vested in another office or a commission. Consequently one abuse of power followed another. What had been done at first for good government was soon employed for the advantage of individuals and cliques. The government of New York City became the "traffic of lobbies" at Albany. Enacted to restore local self-government, Tweed's charter, good in principle, was the culmination of the Ring's "deceptive system." It abolished all control from Albany and professed to restore self-government to the people. But it stripped the two elective councils of all legislative power, which was transferred to the Mayor and to his appointees—the Commissioner of Public Works and the Commissioner of Parks—neither of whom could be removed by the Governor. The Comptroller and the Corporation Counsel were also named by the Mayor. Every device was adopted to make these officers totally irresponsible. The Mayor determined the salaries of all these officials. Thus in place of the elective power of the people there was set up an oligarchy with full authority over a million people. This Tweed charter became law on April 5, 1870, without an election, and turned the city over to the dishonest Ring. Then the County Board of Supervisors was abolished. All bills were audited by Hall, Connolly and Tweed, and soon $4,000,000 out of a pretended audit of $6,000,000 was divided by the Ring. The Mayor, Governor and legislature did not lift a finger in protest. Even reformers were disposed to say that the charter was an improvement over the old government. Tweed was shrewd enough to work hand in glove with the Republicans and even contributed to their party expenses. By bribery and intimidation the Ring enjoyed a "season of wicked prosperity" unparalleled in American municipal history. Public taxes increased from under $10,000,000 in 1860 to $23,000,000 in 1870 and the public debt was tripled.[32]

The day of reckoning was near at hand, however, much nearer than Tweed and his coadjutors dreamed. Although forced by party relations

[31] An. Cyc., 1869, 490; Doc. No. 8, 212.
[32] Myers, 271; Wilson, Mem. Hist., III, 550–552; Writings, II, 131.

to deal with them, Tilden had been at heart an inveterate foe of these ringsters because of "the incompatibility of their and my ideas of public duty. I distrusted them. They knew that they could not deceive or seduce me into any deviation from my principles." When he had the Broadway Railroad Bill killed, some of them were "deeply embittered." Seeing the "decay of civic morals" and knowing that corruption "had become almost universal," he accepted the State chairmanship to "save from degradation the great party whose principles and traditions were mine by inheritance and conviction" and to restore free government. "I never took a favor from these men or from any man I distrusted," he said during the fight on the Ring. He expected little help from the legislature, but he did hope to institute political reforms through the Democratic State Conventions to which the best men went as delegates.[33]

While Tilden knew of the frauds in a general way by 1869, he had no more knowledge of their extent than other citizens. Absorbed in national issues and overtaxed by his law practice, he made no effort to control local politics. Knowing he suspected them and was hostile, the ringsters feared him and sought to wrest from his control the State organization. At Albany Tweed asked, "What does old Sam Tilden want?" Answering his own question, he replied: "Sam Tilden wants to overthrow Tammany Hall. He wants to drive me out of politics. He wants to stop the pickings, starve out the boys, and run the city as if 'twas a damned little country store in New Lebanon. He wants to bring the hayloft and cheese-press down to the city, and crush out the machine. He wants to get a crowd of reformers in the legislature . . . who will cut down the tax levy below a living rate; and then, when he gets everything fixed to suit him, he wants to go to the United States Senate."[34]

The year 1869 was marked by the "saturnalia of injunctions and receiverships" in business, with all their complications in the courts. Jim Fisk tried to induce Tilden to handle his legal business by the promise of large retainers and by opportunities for making money. "We don't want anybody else; we want you," Fisk flatteringly said. But Tilden refused the lucrative offers because he was not in sympathy with Fisk's questionable methods. In April and May of that year, in the United States Circuit Court, Tilden denounced, as perversions of justice, the orders granted by the Ring tool, Judge Barnard, to Fisk, against the

[33] *Writings*, I, 563; *Life*, II, 184.   [34] Cook, 95.

Pacific Railroad. Tweed was a partner in this "freebooting specula-tion," and his son was Barnard's receiver. Tilden took the case because of his abhorrence of the "prostitution" of judicial power which touched the rights of every citizen and the honor of honest business men. He maintained successfully that the orders of Judge Barnard's court were "nullities." [35]

Tweed and his gang, angered by his upright course, then threatened to drive him out of State politics and to deprive him of leadership in the Democratic Party. In August of that same year Tilden accepted Tweed's challenge to his control of the State organization and was sustained in the State Convention, by 87% of the delegates, as Chair-man of the State Democratic Committee. This was regarded as a no-table triumph and was widely reported in the papers of the State.[36]

For four or five years following the close of the war, Tilden was im-mersed in a sea of legal business. At the same time, as a member of the Democratic State Committee, and its chairman from 1866, he knew all the political currents blowing both within the State and throughout the country. Because of his responsible relationship with the Democratic Party, he was forced either to play along with the corrupt leaders who controlled the metropolis and in 1869 were in control at Albany, or else denounce them and in consequence relinquish such leadership as he had with the better element in the party. There is no evidence in his letters of the period to show that he was outraged over graft and corruption in New York City or that the reform spirit in him was struggling for release. On the contrary he worked with might and main for party vic-tory. It may be said, however, that Tilden revealed no disposition to share in questionable party spoils or to associate with those who did. The evils against which he raised his voice in his public addresses and in private communications were those inflicted on the State and nation —social, economic, financial and administrative—as a result of the Civil War and the dominance of the Republican Party. These ills could be cured, he professed to believe, by placing the Democratic Party in power. If Tilden was the product of the higher moral level of his age, Tweed was just as truly created by the opportunities of the lower. The battle between them reflected the clash between New Lebanon and New York City.

[35] *Writings*, I, 564, "Rise and Fall of the Tweed Ring."   [36] *Ib.*, 563; *Life*, I, 184.

PUBLIC indignation is notoriously sluggish in expressing itself against corruption in government, due to the fact that public indignation, to be effectively articulate, must be focused in the person of a champion. No such champion had appeared by the end of 1869 to wage the people's battle against the Tweed Ring, but the first stirrings of public morality are discernible in the uneasiness among the members of the New York bar. These gentlemen, in daily contact with the judiciary of the State, could hardly fail to recognize the corruption in that system; and hence, to prevent its complete degeneracy, they decided to form a Bar Association.

It is significant of the attitude of the legal profession that Tilden was chosen to take a leading part in this movement, despite his known political affiliations. On December 1, 1869, he signed a call for a meeting to form the Bar Association, and at that meeting on February 1, 1870, he uttered his "unpremeditated thoughts," which breathed "a tone of defiant independence":

"If the bar is to become merely a mode of making money, making it in the most convenient way possible, but making it at all hazards, then the bar is degraded. If the bar is to be merely an institution that seeks to win causes, and win them by backdoor access to the judiciary, then it is not only degraded, but it is corrupt.

"The bar, if it is to continue to exist, if it would restore itself to the dignity and honor which it once possessed, must be bold in aggression. . . . It can have reformed constitutions; it can have a *reformed judiciary;* it can have the *administration of justice* made *pure* and *honorable;* and it can restore both the judiciary and *the bar,* until it shall be once more, as it formerly was, an *honorable and elevated* calling." [1]

Yet while Tilden was taking this lofty stand on professional ethics and a reformed judiciary, he wrote to Judge Albert Cardozo, asking that jurist to confine his sentence against Russell Sage to a fine and not to inflict the criminal penalty under the "barbarous" usury law of 1837. Sage was accused of "locking up greenbacks" in a scheme to make more than the 7% of legal interest on his money.[2]

[1] *Writings,* I, 565.   [2] *Letters,* I, 255.

Possibly it was Tilden's Bar Association address that inspired Jay Gould to the exercise of a malicious humor. In any case ten days after the delivery of that address Gould reminded Tilden that a year before he had accepted a retainer of $10,000 from the Erie Railroad Company and asked why he was now appearing against the Erie as counsel for the bondholders of the Atlantic & Great Western Railroad. Tilden replied that the retainer from the Erie was wholly distinct from the Atlantic & Great Western transaction. Gould retorted that he and his company regarded the retainer as one of a general character and that the only matters on which he had consulted Tilden had been on those relating to the Atlantic & Great Western.[3] This controversy dragged through several months, and Tilden, in explaining the "exact truth," declared that the fee was paid to him for "a year's service as counsel and arbiter in the executive committee of the Cleveland & Pittsburg Railroad Company," which in 1869 had been placed in receivership on the ground of fraud by the directors. G. W. Cass, who had made the arrangements for Tilden to act as arbiter, confirmed Tilden's version of the affair as "strictly correct." Tilden declared that he had repeatedly refused to take Erie cases, even though Fisk and Gould had suggested fees as high as $125,000.[4]

This troublesome incident was not so easily settled and was used by Gould and the powerful Erie interests for several years as a weapon in an attempt to discredit and plague Tilden. The way of Tilden, the reformer, was hard indeed. The prepotent enmity of such men as Gould and Fisk was no small consideration, and Tilden was particularly vulnerable to such embarrassments, real or fancied, as they might contrive because of his association with railroads and other large corporations. Yet it is possible to take this apparent enmity too seriously. At all events, in 1870 Tilden was on sufficiently familiar terms with James Fisk, Jr., to introduce attorney Henry Brodhead, who had charge of an accident case against the Erie, and to advise Fisk to make a "reasonable adjustment," because he could probably do better with Brodhead in conference than by a lawsuit.[5]

One of the chief concerns of Tilden in 1870 was the choice of honest men for the newly created Court of Appeals. To B. F. Angel of Geneseo, he expressed his fear that good Democrats might not realize the

[3] *Letters*, I, 258, 261.   [4] *Ib.*, 301, G. W. Cass to Tilden, Mar. 16, 1872.
[5] Tilden to Fisk, Apr. 15, 1870. Library of Congress.

importance of sending reliable delegates to the judicial convention. "Now that is not a safe conclusion, even as to nominations," he said, "and still less as to the measures and policy of the party," and its preservation from "those corrupt influences . . . extending through legislative and administrative trusts, and in some instances demoralizing judicial officers." Neither morally nor prudentially could the Democrats afford to be held responsible for these evils. How could the people call on the party for "reform" unless it kept pure and fit for such a mission? [6] Here was an early use of the word "reform" soon to be the slogan for action.

The previous year Cassidy had proposed Tilden's name for a judgeship because, he said in jest, it "would keep off a worse selection"; now he thought his name would help the ticket and tend to restore confidence in New York City. "Knowing Mr. S. J. T. to be an avaricious man, we have raised the salary to $7,000. Be a patriot and a man." [7] The feeling that Tilden should head the ticket was not restricted to Cassidy. To John R. Reid Tilden replied that the idea was contrary to his "settled preference . . . for freedom and relaxation." John Ganson was told, "I cannot reconcile myself to . . . being tied up for a series of years." To Comstock, Allen, Kernan and O'Conor he declared that "it was not within the plan" of his life. He wanted only to help make a "good selection," to devote all his energies to the election of the ticket, and then to have a "play spell." [8]

As an initial step in insuring a good ticket, Tilden on April 15 sent out his characteristic lithographed letter explaining that a chief justice and six associate judges would be nominated a fortnight later. With "a weakening of the trust of the people in the judiciary," he said, "it is more than ever important that we hold our standard of character and qualifications *high*. . . . A degradation of the administration of justice is the last calamity of a Republic." And he adjured the party leaders to send as delegates "wise, discreet and disinterested men" who could be relied upon to select the best candidates and thus win "the favorable opinion of the public and of the bar of the State." [9] So favorably was S. E. Church impressed with the letter that he thought it should be sent to every Democrat in the Commonwealth.[10] Without being conscious

[6] This letter was printed in 1876 as a campaign broadside.
[7] Tilden Papers, Mar. 10, 1870.   [8] *Letters,* I, 266, to John Ganson, Apr. 22, 1870.
[9] *Ib.,* 262.
[10] Tilden Papers.

of the significance of this fight for a clean Court of Appeals, Tilden in the spring of 1870 was qualifying for trusted leadership in the grapple with the corrupt judges of New York City and the harpies who benefited from their decisions.

As a figure of commanding influence in the party councils, he was besieged by potential candidates for judicial office—S. E. Church, Robert Earl, George F. Comstock, W. F. Allen and others. He adroitly held himself aloof from commitments. "As to candidates, I have carefully kept myself free; saying uniformly . . . that I intended to be perfectly and absolutely open . . . to do what might seem best." As a cynical benediction he added that he would not blame those who fix "strong affections on objects of an elevated ambition." But his hand was seen in the excellent ticket nominated: S. E. Church for Chief Judge, and W. F. Allen, M. Grover, R. W. Peckham, C. A. Rapallo and two Republicans, C. T. Folger and Charles Andrews, as associates. The next problem was to raise funds for the election. Successful candidates were expected to contribute $1,000 each, but a plea was made that Church, who was poor, should be let off "lightly." George F. Comstock, a defeated aspirant, sent a check for $500. In a second letter to Democratic leaders Tilden praised the men of "elevated purpose" who had been selected and said "WE MUST ELECT THIS TICKET." The full ticket was elected and Roswell P. Flower congratulated Tilden on his skill in organization and said that brains had won the election. "Three years ago you started with a Democratic mob; today you have an army." [11]

This spring triumph was followed by the fall campaign for Governor. Prior to the Democratic Convention at Rochester on September 21, it was rumored that Tweed would block Tilden's appointment as State Chairman. But with the help of loyal supporters Tilden retained the chairmanship.[12] He opened the convention and delivered an address on the general situation but made no attack on the Ring.[13] Tweed and his satellites rode high and renominated Hoffman and Beach by acclamation. During the turmoil Tilden's pocket was picked, to add to his discomfiture. The *Nation* commented, "We hope he has a realizing sense of the company he keeps, when he opens conventions for Mr. Tweed, Mr. Hall and Mr. Sweeny," but thought "Tilden's appearance ought to

---

[11] Tilden Papers, June 17, 1870.   [12] *Ib.*, Sept. 14, 30, 1870.
[13] *Writings*, I, 576; Wingate, "An Episode in Municipal Government," *N. A. Rev.*, Oct., 1874.

be the last exhibition the country is to witness of the alliance of decent men for any purpose with these wretched thieves and swindlers." Tilden made no addresses but seemed pleased when his party made a clean sweep in the State and city.

Tweed claimed the victory as a personal tribute and seemed to be securely entrenched. He moved from his modest home on Henry Street to a mansion on Fifth Avenue, rebuilt his stables at his summer home in Greenwich and gave his daughter a lavish marriage.[14] His followers, in an excess of admiration, proposed to erect a statue in his honor. Had subsequent events not dampened the ardor of his cronies, we might have had Tweed holding aloft the torch of civic virtue in New York Harbor.[15] No member of the Ring attempted to mollify Tilden, but men like Nathaniel Sands and Peter Cooper were sent to persuade him that "the Ring had become conservative," and that it might be perilous to turn them out. To these emissaries he said that he would "shelter no sham," that "the light and air of heaven must be let in upon the stagnant darkness of the city administration," and that he would support only officers elected by the people. The fires of reform were fanned by outraged citizens, by newspaper men, and by representatives of organizations like the Union League Club and Young Democracy who consulted Tilden about a program of action.[16]

More and more Tilden was looked to as one competent to indicate a way out of the grasp of the brigands in New York City. At Marble's suggestion, he attended several meetings of the Young Democracy who were drafting a city charter which provided for separate municipal elections yearly, the restoration of the Mayor's supervisory power over his government, and official responsibility. Reform groups like the Young Men's Municipal Reform Association and the Executive Committee of the Citizens and Taxpayers requested his advice and "moral support." [17] When this new charter was about ready to be submitted to the legislature, it was suddenly discovered that Tweed had proposed a charter of his own, drawn up by Sweeny with the assistance of Tilden's law mentor, J. W. Edmunds.[18]

Reform organizations and individuals immediately protested against the enactment of Tweed's charter; and Tilden, "convinced it would pass" with the purchase of Republican votes, appeared at Albany be-

[14] *Times*, May 21, 1871. [15] Breen, *Thirty Years*, 220.
[16] *Writings*, I, 566–567. [17] Tilden Papers. [18] *Letters*, I, 290, Dec. 12, 1871.

fore Tweed and his Senate committee. He pointed out that under this charter self-government would be in abeyance for eight years; that the Ring could perpetuate their own power; that the Mayor would be a mere figurehead; and that elections would be held concurrently with State and Federal elections. "I am not afraid of the sea of popular liberty. I still trust the people. . . . I still believe that in the . . . participation of the people in . . . government, you would have more purity and more safety. . . . It is through the stagnation of bureaus . . . that . . . abuses are generated." [19] Tweed, overconfident in the chair, treated Tilden contemptuously and sought in every way to humiliate him. Turning "ashy white" and revealing "suppressed rage," Tilden, upon concluding his remarks abruptly left the room. To Henry Richmond Tilden, still shaking with anger, vowed that Tweed would close his career in jail or in exile. Depew who was a witness of this scene and who knew Tilden well in railroad business, spoke of his analytic mind, tireless industry, ability to clarify difficulties, and genius for untangling impossible problems. He said that Tilden possessed some sort "of hypnotic power over people" [20] but apparently it did not work on Boss Tweed, for the burly ringster passed the "abominable charter" with only five votes in the Assembly and two in the Senate against it.[21] When he threatened to drive Tilden from the State leadership, Beach jeered, "You had better try it!" [22]

Despite brave words, Tilden knew that the battle for free government by the people had to be fought against desperate odds. The Ring was enthroned in the city with such a concentration of corrupt power as had never before been held by any set of men in a democratic country. Carried away by his bitter feeling, Tilden wrote the following satire on the legislature and Tweed's power as Commissioner of Public Works:

"We, the People of the State of New York, represented in Senate and Assembly, do, by our Supreme Legislative authority, hereby grant to William M. Tweed the office of Commissioner of Public Works and annex thereto, in addition to the powers heretofore held by the Street Commissioner, all the powers heretofore held by the various officers of the Groton Department, TO HAVE AND TO HOLD the same for four years, with the *privilege* of extending the term by surrounding any remnant thereof, and receiving a reappointment for a *further new term of four years;* which office shall be *free* and *dis-*

[19] *Writings,* I, 568. Part of address given.
[21] *Times,* Mar. 25, 1870; Myers, 272 (1901 ed.).
[20] Depew, *Memories,* 209.
[22] *Writings,* I, 569.

charged of the power of the Governor to remove for cause on charges, as in the case of sheriffs, and of all power of removal by the city government; and absolutely of *all accountability whatsoever,* unless Mayor Hall, or some successor, shall choose to prefer articles of impeachment to the Court of Common Pleas, and unless all the six judges shall attend to try such articles!"

It was the fight against this travesty on a municipal charter that awakened the first storm of opposition against the Ring. The fraudulent measure was immediately exposed by Tilden, Schultz, Bailey, Barnum, Greeley and others, by the Union League Club, and by the *World, Post, Sun, Tribune* and *Harper's Weekly.* "The air was full of rumors of corruption." [23] Reporters stumbled over each others' heels in hot-footing it after new clues of crookedness. Citizens rushed out for each new edition of the newspapers to obtain the latest gossip. [24]

Tweed later testified that he had paid about $600,000 to bribe the passage of the Charter of 1870—Tilden thought it cost a million. [25] Some of this was paid out of his own pocket; Fisk, Gould and the Erie Railroad paid a part; and the Ring contractors were forced to contribute from $25,000 to $50,000 each. He even bought his leading opponents, the Senators representing the Young Democracy. Six Republicans were purchased at $40,000 each. [26]

The *Times* hailed the charter as a reform, called Tweed a "reformer" and derided Green, the Union League and Tilden for their protests against it. Some reformers like Horace Greeley professed to see in the Tweed charter a step forward in local government but Tilden called the Ring "the most corrupt gang of political adventurers that ever ruled and robbed a helpless city." Thomas Nast's cartoons in *Harper's Weekly* created a sensation. At the time, however, it seemed impossible to prove these charges with facts and figures. [27] The Ring's newspapers answered the charges and Tweed and his fellows grew more powerful and more corrupt. Just before the election in the fall of 1870 six of the wealthiest and most respected citizens of New York—John Jacob Astor, Moses Taylor, Marshall O. Roberts, George S. Sistare, E. D. Brown, and Edward Schell—stated that they had personally examined the books of the city and found the accounts in excellent condition! [28]

Under the direction of George Jones in September, 1870, the *Times*

---

[23] *Writings*, I, 571.
[24] *Ib.*, 571.
[25] New York *Sun*, Sept. 7, 1877, gives Tweed's confession.
[26] *Writings*, I, 572; Werner, 272.
[27] *Times*, Sept. 20, 1870.
[28] Myers, 277; report dated Nov. 1, 1870.

began a campaign against the Ring which was pressed relentlessly and courageously until its overthrow. That this paper did not open its guns at an earlier date may be ascribed to the fact that J. B. Taylor, one of the three directors of the paper, was one of the four partners of Tweed in the New York Printing Company. Taylor's death freed Jones's pen. The *Times* called attention to Tweed's sudden wealth, asked for information concerning the city finances, and besought respectable Democrats to desert the Boss. The *Times* and *Harper's Weekly* continued their gallant fight in the face of the silence now noticeable in other journals which were profiting from city printing contracts.[29]

Throughout the year 1870 and during the early part of 1871 Tilden's position must have been one of acute discomfort. He felt a sincere contempt for thievery operating behind the mask of politics, and was revolted by the spectacle of Tweed's brazen plundering. On the other hand he was an intense partisan and a political rather than a moral reformer. He stood for clean politics, but still for politics, and had none of the sacrificial zeal which seeks reform regardless of incidental consequences. Tilden wanted reform but he was decidedly mindful of the consequences to the Democratic Party. He believed that reform should come from within the party to save the party from destruction. And so as a practical political reformer he bided his time until he could strike with devastating effect, until he could produce indisputable facts to prove his case and so avoid splitting his party asunder in a controversy based upon supposition. It was this attitude of watchful waiting which was misunderstood by the more forthright leaders of reform and which explains the seeming inconsistencies in Tilden's conduct prior to the actual launching of his campaign against the Ring. It explains his appearance on October 27, 1870, on the platform with Seymour, Governor Hoffman, Fisk and Tweed at a meeting to demonstrate the faith of the people in the Ring and its candidates. Tilden did not speak on this occasion and Seymour studiously evaded the issue by devoting his address to the canal.[30]

The *Times* seemed to be standing alone in its fight against the Ring and averred frequently that "such men as Tilden have no real influence." Tilden confessed that during the session of the legislature in 1871 he "did not set . . . foot in Albany . . . the legislative Sodom of the State." But he denied that he was "timid or selfishly reserved"

[29] Davis, *History of the New York Times,* 93–96.   [30] Myers, 275.

or that he "shrank from any responsibility." [31] Meanwhile the pillaging went recklessly forward in New York, and Tweed boasted that he was worth $20,000,000 and would soon be richer than Vanderbilt. But the reckoning was at hand.

Cupidity and envy now conspired to accomplish what the reformers could not. In the spring of 1871 Jimmy O'Brien, who as a Young Democracy leader frequently consulted Tilden,[32] completed a lucrative term as sheriff. His legitimate fees were very large, but seeing the Tweed regime rolling in wealth he too put in a bill for "extras" amounting to a quarter of a million dollars. Tweed's Board of Audit rejected the claim, together with another, presented by the stationers Edward Jones & Company, for nearly a million. O'Brien resorted to blackmail and threatened that unless his bill were paid he would publish the fraudulent bills which already had been paid by the Comptroller.[33] Fate played into O'Brien's hands. Because of the accidental death of City Auditor James Watson, O'Brien was able to place a confederate in Comptroller Connolly's office to do Watson's bookkeeping. This man, W. S. Copeland, quickly discovered the huge fraudulent bills, reported them to O'Brien and was induced to copy all such evidences of stealing as he could find. Once in possession of these records of peculation, O'Brien took them to the *Times* where they were received as a gift from the gods.[34] The publication of these records, from July, 1871, on through the summer, created a sensation. Here, for the first time, was substantial evidence to support the general charges which had been made for more than a year.

The records proving the frauds of Tweed and his group of municipal pirates, printed in the *Times*, were collected in a pamphlet and widely distributed. The Introduction stated that during 1869, 1870 and 1871 the legislature appropriated for the County Court House $1,400,000. For the decade prior to that $4,500,000 had been appropriated. And later in 1871 an additional $750,000 was appropriated, making a grand total of $6,650,000. Yet in the same years the Ring by its own confession spent on the Court House $8,223,979.89 and Tilden estimated the total cost at about $14,000,000. It should not have cost more than $3,000,000. The *Times* pointed out that the carpentry work should not have cost more than $30,000, yet bills were paid for $2,189,699.95.

[31] *Writings*, I, 578–579.   [32] Tilden Papers.
[33] Wilson, *Mem. Hist.*, III, 553; *Tribune*, Jan. 30, 1871.
[34] Wilson, *Mem. Hist.*, III, 556; Myers, 284.

The furniture bill of $1,575,782.96 was thought to be too high by $1,500,000. In the supplying of carpets, shades and curtains the city was swindled out of about $660,000. Plastering which should not have cost more than $30,000 was billed at over $500,000 and $873,525.15 was spent in repairing the plaster. The advertising, printing and stationery account for 1869 and 1870 totaled $5,259,353 for city and county, or eleven times that of 1859 and 1860, and most of that amount was paid to corporations owned by the Ring. The rents paid for armories and drill-rooms, many of these unused, for the quarter ending May 1, 1871, amounted to $269,600. Repairs costing $3,200,000 should not have exceeded $250,000 for two years.[35]

In 1872, a Joint Investigating Committee of Supervisors, Aldermen and Associated Citizens examined the public accounts and reported as follows on the County Court House:

Safes	Estimate value	$3,450	Cost	$482,500
Carpets	"	19,000	"	641,900
Furniture	"	309,000	"	1,849,400
Plumbing	"	74,000	"	914,000
Plastering	"	70,000	"	1,938,000
Carpentering	"	No estimate	"	1,022,000

All the vouchers and many of the warrants were missing. A large number of unnecessary persons were on the pay rolls. "Frauds and robberies of the most infamous character" had been perpetrated. All confidence in the city officials was destroyed. James Watson, City Auditor, connived with certain dishonest business men to certify fraudulent claims amounting to millions.[36] As an example of how the stealing was done, it was said that when Tweed was told that electric fire alarms would cost $60,000, he asked brazenly of a contractor, "If we get you a contract for $450,000 will you give us $225,000?" Upon receipt of an affirmative answer, the contract was awarded.[37]

When news of these scandals spread upstate and Tilden's leadership in combating them was recognized, valuable evidence against the Ring was sent to him. For example an anonymous note informed him that Lewis Greenleaf, lumber dealer and bank cashier of Watertown, and

[35] *How New York is Governed. Frauds of the Tammany Democrats.* Pub. by the *Times,* 1871.
[36] *Proceedings,* New York, 1872.
[37] Tilden Papers. Chesten's letter sent to Tilden by O'Conor.

T. R. Sweeney knew more about crooked deals than they would tell off the witness stand. Assurance came from H. A. Richmond that the best men had agreed "to stand by you through thick and thin." C. I. Lewis wanted good government established and the grafters exposed and punished, and begged to know the truth about Hall and Sweeny as sharers in the plunder. These are just a few specimens of a deluge of communications that came to Tilden from all parts of the State [38] and enabled him to realize that a great ground swell of reform was on the way.

Meanwhile the storm gathered. Shortly Tilden was to find himself breathless in the maelstrom of city politics. His life began to gather the terrific momentum which was to carry him through great triumphs over fraud and corruption to the heroic climax of his own tragic defeat in 1876. And the tireless and powerful ally of this crusade was Charles O'Conor, who had asserted that the trading politicians had discovered that New York City was the "Golconda of fraudulent cupidity." Tilden's own view of the situation was "that the system must be totally obliterated; . . . the city government must be changed; . . . the authors of the system . . . must be expelled. I have not doubted for a moment where the real issue is."

[38] Tilden Papers, Sept. 29, 1871, and other dates.

As the *Times* continued its merciless exposures, even the hardened Ring began to squirm. Connolly, driven to exasperation, offered editor Jones $5,000,000 to forget his figures.[1] Had not the gentle Tweed been restrained by consideration for his wife and children he would have killed Jones. Suddenly sensitive about Nast's cartoons, Tweed said: "I don't care what people write,. for my people can't read. But they have eyes and they can see as well as other folks." So a banker was sent to offer Nast $500,000 to take an unlimited tour of Europe.[2] Meanwhile the *Times* maddeningly challenged Hall and Connolly to bring suit for libel. Mayor Hall remarked in strained jest, "We are likely to have what befell Adam—an early Fall." [3]

The Ring, having weathered so many storms, thought it might even brazen through this one. When a *Times* reporter interviewed Tweed about the revelations, the Boss asked belligerently, "What are you going to do about it?" [4] And then the Ring members exposed their pettiness in a series of ineffectual reprisals. Harper Brothers' books were barred from the public schools. City officials were ordered to boycott the restaurant under the Times Building. It was announced that the city had refused to pay the *Times'* account for $13,764.36 because it was tainted with fraud, and sought to confiscate the Times Building because of an alleged defective title.[5]

Tilden was disposed to believe that the incredible figures in the *Times* were exaggerated, but he "soon became satisfied of the substantial truth of these statements" because of the "futility of the answers on behalf of the city officials." He realized then that "municipal frauds had been committed immeasurably transcending anything I had suspected." [6] Just going into the country, and being a "believer in the potency of facts," he took the revelations along with him to ponder over. Within a few days he had assimilated the salient facts and decided that the time had come at last to take decisive action against the

---

[1] Davis, *Hist. of the Times*, 103; Werner, 210; Paine, *Nast*, 181.
[2] Werner, 211; Paine, 179.
[3] *Times*, Aug. 29, 1871. Hall collected 14 vols. of clippings about himself which his daughter gave to the New York Public Library.
[4] Myers, 285; Werner, 217.   [5] Paine, 158.   [6] *Writings*, I, 587.

malefactors. If circumstances were not yet as propitious as he had hoped, the *Times* articles had precipitated a climax. They constituted a challenge, and further delay might result in leadership from without the Democratic Party, a contingency which Tilden wanted to avoid above all things.

Tilden came to the conclusion that, since Albany had created the evil system, only Albany could change it. His first step was to consult Francis Kernan, whom he met in Albany and accompanied to Utica to continue the conference.[7] Tilden's plan was to use the approaching Democratic Convention to beat the Tweed Ring and then to break their hold both in Albany and New York City. Kernan and Seymour both agreed to the wisdom of the plan. On the way home Tilden stopped at Saratoga, where he assured Jones, editor of the *Times*, that he would "appear in the field at the proper time." He returned to New York where Ottendorfer promised to support him. He hurried out to Washington Heights to confer with Charles O'Conor about the legal procedure against the Ring, then hastened up to Albany to inform Governor Hoffman of the arrangement with the Attorney General to have O'Conor institute suits.[8]

In the midst of Tilden's activities, the outraged citizens began to act. The Council for Political Reform held a mass meeting to consider "the alarming state of public affairs" and to find a remedy. Addresses by Henry Ward Beecher, Havemeyer, Evarts and others revealed the mounting cost of government from $36,000,000 in 1868 to $136,000,-000 in 1870. Wide publicity was given to the meeting.[9] Through the press a call was issued for "A meeting of taxpayers, irrespective of party, . . . opposed to the corrupt administration," at Cooper Institute on the evening of September 4, 1871. Ex-Mayor William F. Havemeyer presided and addresses were made by certain honorable gentlemen. Tilden was invited to speak about city finances.[10] The hall was overfilled and "thousands of citizens were obliged to return to their homes." Tilden had collaborated with Havemeyer, Joseph H. Choate and others in arranging for this meeting, but unaccountably his name does not appear in the long list of 227 vice presidents, or in the list of speakers, or as a member of the nonpartisan Committee of Seventy appointed at this meeting to investigate and to prosecute the Ring. It

[7] *Writings*, I, 588, Aug. 4, 1871.   [8] *Ib.*, I, 588–590.   [9] Myers, 282, Apr. 6, 1871.
[10] Tilden Papers, Aug. 22, 1871; *Times*, Sept. 5, 1871.

soon issued a ringing "Appeal to the People of the State of New York" for the complete overthrow of the Tweed Ring. Tilden did not become a member of the Committee of Seventy until a year later.[11]

The Committee of Seventy divided itself into sub-committees to gather evidence and to investigate the city accounts. The excitement was intensified when on September 11 the Comptroller's office in the City Hall was broken open and 3,500 incriminating vouchers were stolen, the charred remains of which were found in the attic.[12] The committee in October reported a number of instances of corruption, and asked Governor Hoffman for the co-operation of Attorney General Champlain in proceeding against the criminals. Champlain gave authority to Charles O'Conor to establish a Bureau of Municipal Correction in New York City as a branch of the Attorney General's office. O'Conor associated with himself as counsel William M. Evarts, William H. Peckham and Judge Emott.[13]

After the creation of this machinery, an injunction was obtained from Judge Barnard restraining the Comptroller from further payments of bills under the tax levy. This order was relaxed occasionally, however, to permit the partial payment of genuine bills against the city.[14] The Grand Jury of the Court of General Sessions, on the initiation of the Committee of Seventy, took the matter up and, after a long investigation, brought in indictments against officials and other persons implicated in the frauds. The November session of 1871 was prolonged from time to time to March, 1872, to allow the Grand Jury to complete its work.

Tilden, apprehensive lest the *Times'* exposures injure the Democratic Party, studied articles on the subject from papers in various parts of the country and sent forty such extracts to William Cassidy with the comment that they revealed a disposition to maintain that the "evils and abuses" in New York were "generally characteristic of the Democratic Party" and would occur in the Federal Government "if that party should come to power." Tilden believed that this falacious argument would commend itself to the "Republican mind" and so confuse the "Democratic mind" as to make it "ineffective and irresolute." He complained that the Republicans who controlled most of the newspapers were exploiting this "local cancer" and moaned, "We are out!"

---

[11] *Times,* Aug. 9, 1886. Statement by Simon Sterne.
[12] *Ib.,* Sept. 12, 1871; Myers, 287; Werner, 240.
[13] Myers, 288–290.   [14] Wilson, *Mem. Hist.,* III, 557.

Nevertheless he counseled firmness and aggressive action, and warned that if the party lost the "higher *morale*" and the "stronger ammunition" the battle was lost.[15]

Tilden was equally alarmed because the Democratic press was defending "the wrongs alleged," by implication "admitting responsibility for them," and thus conceding that Democrats were as corrupt as Republicans. "The idea should be kept *all the time* before the public mind that the Democratic Party is not responsible for these wrongs; that it will be the foremost in punishing the authors and in adopting all measures necessary to prevent their recurrence." He emphasized the necessity for making "the *first* impression" on the public mind and maintaining it by "persistent repetitions." [16]

Other leading Democrats were equally filled with alarm—Church, Seymour, Richmond, Dix, and Flower—and were encouraging Tilden: The "ventilation" of New York was hurting the party in the country; "We can lose nothing by stirring up questions of frauds"; "Every honest man must be sincerely desirous of a thorough investigation"; "Bully for you! Keep them on the run"; "The Country is for reform and honesty"; "A universal feeling of indignation here"; and "The Democratic Party must not be connected with the frauds." Thus Democratic leaders rang the changes of noble statesmanship, but assumed that he would shoulder the burden of the battle. Encouraging as these comments were, Tilden was not so sanguine as some of his political friends, and said: "I should be sorry to think the demoralization is so great that such things will not hurt us. We have to face the question whether we will fall with the wrongdoers or . . . separate . . . and take our chance of defeat now, with resurrection hereafter." [17]

Aware that the first combat would come in the State Convention, Tilden sent out his customary letter to 26,000 Democratic leaders asking them to begin the canvass for delegates at once. Times demanded "wisdom and courage, and devotion to principle and right." The twin evils were centralism and corruption. Conditions in New York City were what the Republican legislature made them. He clearly intimated his attitude in the coming convention, "Wherever the gangrene of corruption has reached the Democratic Party, we must take a knife and cut it out by the roots." [18] The manifesto struck fire over the State, and

[15] *Letters*, I, 272, Aug., 1871.
[16] Tilden Papers, Aug. 8, 1871.
[17] *Letters*, I, 275.
[18] *Ib.*, 276, Sept. 11, 1871.

the telegram from Comstock: "You are right. Stick!" was typical of the response. Full well Tilden knew that he must have enough upstate support to hold the balance against the Tweed Ring, but his immediate concern was to unite all anti-Tammany forces in the city. By the end of September he wired Kernan that the city delegation would be headed by O'Conor and Ottendorfer.[19] Meanwhile his upstate followers were busy choosing delegations that would give him loyal support in the contest; but he did not underestimate either the strength or the cunning of his adversaries.

While Tilden's letter was finding its way across the counties in the preliminary skirmish, forces within the Ring were working for its collapse. One of its important members watched with fear and a terrible fascination the accumulation of evidence and the acceleration of public indignation until finally, unable to endure the strain longer, he compromised. Comptroller Connolly sought out Tilden but was sternly told that he would not "be his counsel" and that the Ring's political careers were ended. Tilden persuaded him not to resign, as the Ring wished, but to appoint A. H. Green as his deputy, with custody of all documents, which he did. The Ring's attempt to replace Connolly was checkmated by O'Conor's assertion that he had acted in accordance with law.[20] Meanwhile John Foley, as a taypayer, secured an injunction against Connolly which prevented him from paying any further claims against the city. As a result business was deadlocked, and thousands of laborers, policemen, teachers, clerks and minor city employees went unpaid. Hard times resulted and many poor families suffered. An angry mob of 15,000 unpaid workingmen gathered about the City Hall threatening a riot. The city faced the future with an empty treasury, a dishonored government and the imminence of an uprising. But the Ring was still defiant, and working as busily as Tilden to control the coming Democratic State Convention.[21]

Two branches of the Democratic Party were each trying to control the political machinery of the State and the city. With Green in control of Comptroller Connolly's office, the reformers struck a telling blow beneath the Ring's armor. "While . . . Tilden and his friends are all smiles and think the country is saved," O'Conor had another story to tell. Many were sore not because Hall and his gang *stole the*

[19] Tilden Papers.
[20] *Writings*, I, 591–594; *Letters*, I, 278, 280; *Times*, Sept. 12, 1871.
[21] Werner, 222, 230.

money, but because they kept it all.[22] Havemeyer was convinced that it was impossible to "get any criminal charges against the Ring until they are thrown overboard. . . . Tweed & Company must go peaceably or forcibly." "You must command," he told Tilden. "Tammany must be confronted by a solid delegation . . . and be deprived of any representation on the ticket." [23]

Tilden had reason to be pleased with the preliminary skirmish over the city Comptroller's office, but he had no time to luxuriate over such a trivial matter. He now bent all his energies toward preparing for the Democratic State Convention set for October 4, 1871, at Rochester, to nominate minor officers. Convinced that the Ring, entrenched by legislation of its own manufacture at Albany, could be destroyed only from the Capital, he wanted Assemblymen and Senators inimical to Tweed. Hence at the instance of his friends, he agreed to stand for election to the Assembly. The pre-convention days were filled with hectic conferences, feverish interviews, and letters and telegrams from all parts of the State. Tilden had himself chosen as a delegate from Columbia County.[24] He was anxious to give force and drama to his attack on the Ring by having O'Conor and Green on hand to back him, but O'Conor deemed it imperative to press the Tweed investigations and inexpedient to send Green to Rochester "even for 24 hours." [25] O'Conor warned that compromise with Tammany would be "equivalent to ruin in State and nation." [26] Resolutions must be presented to the convention "to compel the robbers to disgorge." Would Slippery Dick Connolly stick to his promise in the face of hazards? "Strike while the iron is hot, get a resignation and the appointment of Handy Andy" before the "slow wits" of the Ring begin to call him. He had made up his mind for decisive action but had some scruples about those who were posing as anti-Ring representatives. Kernan agreed with O'Conor that compromise with Tammany would be "equivalent to ruin" and that action not words was expected by the masses. "We have no danger except in . . . half-hearted counsels." With such support Tilden was determined on "complete and decisive action." [27]

When the convention assembled at Rochester, Tilden as State Chairman called it to order and issued the battle cry for action: "Reverently

[22] Kernan Papers, Sept. 7, 19, 26, 1871.   [23] Tilden Papers, Sept. 26, 1871.
[24] *Life,* I, 190.   [25] Tilden Papers, Sept. 29, 1871.   [26] *Letters,* I, 281, 282.
[27] *Ib.,* 281, 282.

I thank God that when midnight darkness brooded over the Republic"
whose sacred traditions were created and upheld by the Democratic
fathers, and when true men "sat at their watch despondent," the cloud
showed its silver lining and Democracy advanced to "fight anew . . .
centralism and corruption." Disunion was dead, slavery crushed forever, and suffrage given irreversibly to the colored race, but a corrupt,
irresponsible centralism remained—"vulgar millionaires" were grasp-
ing "the highest seats of honor and power." Under Republican control,
legislative bodies became purchasable, and the office of United States
Senator was twice "knocked down to the highest bidder." [28] Corruptions in New York City were due to irresponsible power acting
through secret bureaus, the result of Republican legislation at Albany.
"A partnership of plunder between men of both parties" had been established; hence good men of both parties must cleanse "the leprous
spots." Let the people judge us by what we do to purify our parties
and to "elevate the standard of public morality." It is time to proclaim
that whoever "plunders the people, though he steal the livery of heaven
to serve the devil in, is no Democrat." [29]

With leers and squirmings the Tweed men listened to this castigation. So long as they were in control, however, and were reaping the
rewards of their nefarious peculations, such words put no fear of punishment in their hearts. They packed the convention with their "gangs
of New York thugs," [30] used money freely and nominated all their
candidates. In glee over his triumph, Tweed spoke of Tilden, Seymour
and Kernan as "three throublesome old fools." When Oswald Ottendorfer and W. E. Curtis threatened Tammany with exposure, Tweed
snapped his fingers in their faces.[31] He did wince when Tilden, believing that "the greatest audacity in the right" was the highest wisdom
and in the end the most consummate prudence, demanded that the
party cast out the local organization which controlled the patronage of
12,000 persons, annual disbursements of $30,000,000, the judiciary,
police and election officials.

The Ring-controlled delegates treated the city frauds as a local issue
and ruled out the reformers on the ground of party regularity. Tweed
did not sit in the convention but from nearby quarters directed the battle. Seymour went to Rochester to be chairman of the convention, but

[28] Senators not identified.   [29] *Writings,* I, 484.   [30] Werner, 230.
[31] Alexander, III, 272.

when he saw Lord in Tilden's room and knew "the switch had been changed," he hurriedly retreated to Utica.[32] But Tilden boldly led the reform delegates who succeeded in having adopted a platform which viewed "with indignation the corruption . . . in the management of municipal affairs of the city," denounced those responsible for it and demanded their punishment, called for a home rule charter, and attributed all the evils to the Republicans.[33] To have such a declaration given publicity was a triumph. Although determined, if possible, to prevent Tammany from driving the masses of the better Democrats out of the party, yet Tilden, following the Ring's hostile outburst, threatened: "I . . . avow before this convention that I shall not vote for any one of Mr. Tweed's members of the legislature. And if that is to be regarded as the regular ticket, I will resign my place as Chairman of the State Committee and help my people stem the tide of corruption. When I come to do my duty as an elector, I shall cast my vote for honest men." It took a brave man to utter such a defiance.

By this courageous stand Tilden inspired the best men in his party with a zeal for honest government and offered himself as the leader of the reform forces. "The Tammany Sachems are a banditti of conspirators against the people," wrote a New Yorker. "I am a member of the Society . . . but am willing to abolish it by law." [34] "A new party is made up," wrote Seymour to Tilden, "and we are outside of it. For this I am glad. . . . You would have been put off the State Committee . . . if they had thought it wise. . . . You must now count upon the hostility of old supporters and of all State officials. You are in the way. If you mean to fight . . . you must put yourself at the head of the reformers." [35] And so Tilden appeared cut adrift, supported only by a small group representing the militant decency in his party. But there was no ambiguity about his position now and, far from being discouraged, he set himself to deliver the deadly stroke which left the Ring damned and irretrievably exposed.

Indicative of the new strength Tilden was drawing to himself as a result of his challenge to Tammany was the letter of congratulation from young D. S. Lamont, destined to play a rôle in New York politics for some years, who applied for the secretaryship of the State Committee. Experienced Democrats like Cassidy, who wrote a searching "Exposi-

[32] *Times*, Oct. 9, 1871.
[34] Tilden Papers, F. W. Birdsall, Oct. 10, 1871.
[33] *An. Cyc.*, 1871, 556.
[35] *Letters*, I, 283, Oct. 8, 1871.

tion of the Convention," took the ground that Tammany had "cut adrift from the State organization" and must abdicate as the "city oligarchy." Francis Lynde Stetson rejoiced that he was working under one who "spared neither time nor attention in the public service, and the purity of whose motives I have from childhood been taught to respect." [36] Cheering words like these gave Tilden confidence in his leadership of a reformed party.

A few days after his return from Rochester, Tilden's wisdom in stationing A. H. Green in Connolly's office was confirmed. Detecting irregularity in the County Court House warrants, Green asked Tilden to examine the accounts in the National Broadway Bank. So startling was the revelation that Tilden, with two assistants, devoted ten days to the examination, and set forth the results in an affidavit entitled "Figures That Could Not Lie." [37] He proved that Tweed received 24% of all money collected from the city by the contractor Andrew J. Garvey and 42% of that by James H. Ingersoll, whose bills, totaling more than $6,312,000, were presented to the city and certified as valid by Hall, Conolly and Tweed.[38] To pay the claims the Comptroller then issued bonds which were sold to bona fide purchasers and deposited the money from the sale with the Broadway National Bank to the credit of the Chamberlain of the city as County Treasurer. Following these deposits, checks or warrants on the bank were issued to the claimants and paid. Then the contractors, through E. A. Woodward as a go-between, handed over to the Ring the percentage agreed upon.[39] So sure was Tweed of his immunity from discovery and prosecution that he allowed his split-ups to be deposited in the Broadway Bank as they accrued, thus making Tilden's discovery easier and his analysis more obvious and convincing.

After being prodded by Havemeyer,[40] Tilden on October 26 gave the findings to the newspapers for publication. The exposure created a tremendous stir and spurred to action vindictive or timid persons who had been withholding real or fancied evidence. As a result, there was placed in Tilden's hands information about Tweed's account in the Ocean Bank and the hint that the bank accounts of William Edelstein,

[36] Tilden Papers, Oct. 7, 9, Nov. 22, 1871.   [37] *Writings*, I, 505, Oct. 24, 1871.
[38] Foord, *Green*, 92. Wilson, *Mem. Hist.*, III, 558, states that the following percentages were received: Tweed 24, Connolly 20, Sweeny 10, Watson 5 and Woodward 5, making a total of 64.
[39] *Writings*, I, 514.   [40] Tilden Papers, Oct. 25, 1871.

his partner, should be investigated. He also learned of the accounts of Ingersoll, Smith and others in the Broadway National Bank, and the rumor that Ingersoll was selling his property. Commendation and encouragement poured in from all quarters, such as: "Push the scoundrels to the wall"; "Move on the enemy at once and trust to God Almighty for results"; "Whip the party back to right ground"; "Cut loose from Tammany Hall"; "There are no Sundays in revolutionary times. . . . Speed and vigor for God's sake and the Republic's." President T. A. Palmer of the Broadway National Bank, learning that Tilden was about to make public the results of his investigations of the Ring's accounts in that institution asked whether he might see what he intended "to say about us." [41] Unsolicited checks were sent to Tilden to carry on the fight,[42] in which both his heart and the future of his party were involved.

Tilden called the local convention at which the reform Democrats of the city organized and placed a strong union ticket in the field. Out of his own pocket he gave $10,000 to supply voting booths and ballots for the city election and helped the Committee of Seventy raise a like sum for campaign purposes. Without relinquishing his drive against the city grafters, he did his utmost to have a reform legislature elected. He tried to persuade O'Conor and Evarts to run for the Assembly, along with himself,[43] and hoped Seymour, Kernan and Minturn would do the same upstate.[44] An address was sent to the "Democratic masses" pointing out that the decision for or against good government depended upon their co-operation in electing the right kind of Assemblymen. An effort was made to win the county newspapers to support the reform program. The pre-election responses to his appeals were on the whole encouraging, but Whitelaw Reid complained about Tilden's "singularly unwise unfairness" in giving to the newspapers the documents exposing the manipulations of the conspirators who had robbed the city.[45]

Tilden carried out his intention, declared in the convention, to support only honest, anti-Tammany men, regardless of party. Indeed his independence was so militant as to alarm even the forthright O'Conor. Half an hour before Tilden started for a reform meeting held by the Committee of Seventy, O'Conor called and asked whether, in view of his State leadership, he might not be carrying his defiance of Tam-

[41] Tilden Papers, Richard Schell, Oct. 23 to Nov. 1, 1871.   [42] *Letters,* I, 287.
[43] *Writings,* I, 579.   [44] *Letters,* I, 286.   [45] Tilden Papers, Nov. 5, 1871.

many to an unreasonable extreme. Tilden replied that he would accept full responsibility for his position and that, if the party did not approve of his stand, he would resign the State chairmanship and take his place "as a private man with his plundered fellow citizens." That was a courageous attitude, but Tilden had reasoned it out with due care and was willing to abide by the consequences.[46]

The speech delivered by Tilden at Cooper Institute on the evening of November 2, 1871, was one of the most eloquent of his whole career:

"The million of people who compose our great metropolis have been the subject of a conspiracy the most audacious and most wicked ever known in our free and happy land. A cabal of corrupt men have seized upon all the powers of our local government and converted them, not only to the purposes of misgovernment, but also of personal plunder. It is . . . the foremost duty of every good citizen to join with his fellows in the effort to overthrow this corrupt and degrading tyranny; for that reason I stand before you tonight. If we found our dwelling wrapt in flames, we should not inquire whether . . . it was a Democrat or a Republican who lent us a hand to put out the fire. . . . Knowing nothing about the action of your Committee of Seventy except what I have heard, caring nothing who unites with us or with whom I unite . . . I come before you to advocate a union of all honest men against a combination of plunderers."

Then he gave a history of the Charter of 1870 as the product of a combination of corrupt Republicans and Democrats at Albany. "Under the pretense of giving back to the people . . . local self-government," they robbed the city of all power and vested it in the hands of half a dozen men for a period of from four to eight years. He was certain that Mr. Choate made a slip of the tongue when he said that the men in power were elected by the citizens. They "have been elected by no man's suffrage" but were put in power by the legislature "without consulting any of us." He declared that "the State has put these men on us, and the State must take them off." He continued:

"For ten years the Democratic Party had pledged itself to give back to the people of the city . . . the rights of self-government; and when it came into power it betrayed that pledge and violated that duty. Alone I went to Albany and recorded my protest against this outrage upon the city . . . a betrayal of the principles and doctrines and promises and professions of the Democratic Party. . . . And how was it accomplished? Why, by taking a million of dollars . . . and buying . . . the two houses of the legislature."

[46] *Writings*, I, 490.

The second act in the conspiracy was the innocent-looking County Tax Levy Bill which authorized Tweed, Hall and Connolly to audit all bills. Whose shrewdness contrived these measures? Sweeny and Hall. On Hall's motion all bills certified by Tweed and Young, president of the County Supervisors, should be paid. Then followed the collection and distribution of the money. Over $6,000,000 was stolen in 1869–70, of which 66% was turned over to Woodward who in turn paid 24% to Tweed. Then followed an explanation of how an examination of the accounts in the Broadway Bank revealed these facts. Tilden expressed his thanks to the New York *Times* for its "vigorous maintenance of the rights of the people against this corrupt and irresponsible cabal." During the past three months the Ring offered Tilden anything he might ask to give up the legislature but he "always declined," and said, "I know no duty paramount to that of standing by the people in this emergency." All persons interested in reforming the city should combine to send good men to the legislature. Such conditions could not last long because there was not money enough to stand "such a band of cormorants." He was willing to "stand or fall with those who have gathered around me." He had expected to pass the winter abroad resting after "twenty years of incessant labor in my profession," but under present conditions, he deemed it his duty:

". . . before I should finally withdraw from public affairs to make a campaign, to follow where any would dare to lead, to lead where any would dare to follow, in behalf of . . . American free government. . . . If you will not grow weary . . . I will stand by your side until not only civil government shall be reformed in the city . . . but until the State . . . shall once more have a pure . . . judiciary, and until the example of this great State shall be set up for imitation by all other States. When that is done, standing in the high noon of life, ready to begin its descent, I will take my place in the column that marches downward to the setting sun; and I shall at least hope to have the consolation that when at last, in advancing years, I come to be wrapped in the drapery of my couch, it will be done with the pleasant dream that the great country . . . established by Washington and Jefferson is destined to live forever, the pride of all lovers of liberty the world over." [47]

For independence of thought, logical arrayal of facts, appeal to the intellect and conscience, rounded phrases and moving sentiment, this address, consuming an hour and a half, and preserved only in an imperfect newspaper report, was without question Tilden's oratorical

[47] *Writings,* I, 491, "Combination against Conspiracy."

masterpiece. Another address on November 7 in Apollo Hall, on "Rule of the People," appealed for the support of the reform ticket against Tammany.[48] Civil action had already been instituted against the Ring. This suit, coupled with Tilden's exposure in his affidavit and addresses, had a decisive effect on the campaign.

In an exciting election on November 7 the reform candidates in New York City were swept into office by an overwhelming majority, but the Democrats were badly beaten in upstate districts. There was one significant exception to the reform victory in the metropolis, however; Boss Tweed was re-elected to his seat in the State Senate by fraud.[49] Yet the Tilden affidavit had dealt him a lethal blow. According to Charles O'Conor, "it produced upon Tweed a crushing effect." He never afterward dared to confront accusation, nor to take his seat in the Senate. That vacant seat awaited occupation for his whole term. His quondam associates in that body dared not pronounce it vacant. "Achilles was Achilles still." [50]

Hamilton Fish wrote Tilden on the day following the election:

"An old personal friend, whose views on political questions have generally differed from yours, thanks you from the bottom of his heart for your noble work—your manly, honest exposure of wrongs. On your election I do not congratulate you, but the public. There is light ahead!" [51]

With this cordial note Tilden was greatly pleased. Henry Adams of Harvard, assuming that the Ring was overthrown by the election, asked Tilden, who alone knew "the private history of the affair" and could ."estimate the actors at their proper value," to give him the facts for a nonpartisan historical account which he was writing for a magazine.[52]

The Committee of Seventy invited him to meet with it to discuss a reform program, and asked him to print and distribute 10,000 copies of Robert B. Roosevelt's speech on the Ring exposure. Senators T. F. Bayard and E. Casserly, who were investigating abuses in the New York Custom House, asked his advice. In a stronger position than ever to direct the fight against the Ring, he aided O'Conor to select a reliable legal staff to promote the suits against the corrupt officials, and consulted with men like Comstock about a legislative investigation of the Ring frauds.[53] He had to curb and if possible utilize ambitious men

[48] New York newspapers, Nov. 8, 1871.   [49] Myers, 292.
[50] Tilden Papers.   [51] *Letters*, I, 287.   [52] *Ib.*, 288.
[53] Tilden Papers, various dates.

in New York City who "would like to be leaders of the great reform movement," [54] and leaned heavily on Kernan, one of the most trusted Democrats in the State. Already there were intimations from Tilden that Kernan was the logical man for Governor in 1872.

After the election, O'Conor, Havemeyer and Green insisted that Tilden continue the investigations which had unearthed evidence of the frauds. In deference to their wishes, he gave all of his time for the next six weeks to bring to light evidences of corruption; [55] and for many months thereafter his time was donated generously to the prosecutions. Henry F. Taintor, an expert accountant, was employed December 1 to examine the bank accounts and in fact became Tilden's general utility man in overthrowing the Ring. Apparently living in Tilden's house, he reported his findings to him orally, when at home, and by letter when in Albany.[56] When Comptroller Green refused to pay Taintor and his five trusty workers, under the flimsy excuse that it would be difficult to "shake them off," Tilden paid them himself. For the next five years faithful Taintor was employed by Tilden.[57] A. E. Smith, a bank employee who lost his job for helping Taintor, was paid by Tilden for his work and also given a fine recommendation. O'Conor leaned heavily on Taintor for evidence and protected him against persecution by John Kelly. When Tilden was in the midst of the Presidential campaign of 1876, Taintor sent him a full account of the Tweed suits. Later his files were rifled and a number of papers abstracted, but afterward returned.[58]

The suits against the Ring which started in 1871 ran on aggravatingly year after year. Delays were caused by the difficulties of assembling evidence and witnesses; the Ring had powerful political friends and many persons feared their vengeance. Suits in the name of the people had to be directed by the Attorney General, although O'Conor was in immediate charge. Attorney General Francis C. Barlow had cooperated, but his successor, Daniel Pratt, was indifferent. Tilden and O'Conor had to press him for action and chafed considerably because of his indifference. "I observe with the new Attorney General," wrote O'Conor to Tilden, "a certain devil-may-care inattention to this business. . . . I will not appear in the court . . . until I have assurance that he will not treat it as impertinence. . . . Had you better not tele-

54 Kernan Papers, Dec. 16, 1871.   55 *Writings*, I, 598.
56 Tilden Papers, Jan. 6, 1872, and later.   57 *Letters*, I, 292.
58 Tilden Papers; *Letters*, I, 294.

graph him?" O'Conor, attracted by more lucrative legal business, could not at first give all his time to the Ring suits. When Green and others became "fidgety" at the procrastination, O'Conor assured Tilden that as soon as he had the Jumel case off his hands he would give all his time to the cause until "the corrupt gang of villains . . . shall have got their *quietus*." No private affairs would prevent his devotion to the prosecutions "in which you have so faithfully toiled . . . as the foremost champion." [59] And finally the Ring, with unlimited funds at their command, employed able attorneys who resorted to every legal subterfuge, technicality and political influence to block punishment of the criminals and to prevent restitution of the stolen money. [60]

During 1872–73 Tilden appeared again and again in court to give testimony, and to aid the attorneys prosecuting the suits. When the defendants appealed the overruling of a demurrer against bringing suits in the name of the people of the State, Tilden took part in the argument against an appeal and presented a long review of English cases in which the Crown had taken cognizance of municipal abuses. When the New York *Times* in the fall of 1872 made an attack on him, he issued a pamphlet, "The New York City Ring: Its Origin, Maturity and Fall," in which he defended his own connection with the reform movement. [61] It was widely read and helped to keep alive public interest in the suits. Tilden also drew the brief in the Ingersoll case and was complimented for its "strong points" by Robert B. Roosevelt. Elihu Root asked to have several copies of it. [62] During 1874 his was the directing force in the Ring prosecutions and O'Conor was in constant communication with him on all legal and political phases of the trials.

The decisive defeat at the city polls in 1871 had shattered what was left of the Ring morale. Sweeny accepted the verdict, resigned and, on the pretext of ill health, fled to Canada and later to Paris. From the latter safe haven he offered to repay the city $150,000 and give his note for $250,000 more in exchange for his freedom. Some years later he reappeared in New York City where he died. Jay Gould bought property from Sweeny and Hugh Smith to the value of $540,000 but no effort was made to recover it. Mayor A. Oakey Hall, proclaiming his innocence, clung to his office in the face of demands for his resigna-

[59] Tilden Papers.   [60] *Letters*, I, 624.   [61] *Writings*, I, 516, 553.
[62] Tilden Papers, Feb. 26, 1874.

tion. He was brought to trial in 1872 and Tilden was subpoenaed as a witness, but the jury rendered a verdict of not guilty. He appealed to Tilden's "large heart" to prevent Peckham, O'Conor's associate counsel, from procuring a duplicate charge against him for official neglect.[63] He continued to hold the office of Mayor until his term expired on January 1, 1873. Tweed in his confession under oath in 1877 asserted that Hall was guilty of taking money.

Connolly turned state's evidence and expected to escape prosecution. When his arrest followed on January 2, 1872, his lawyer, Samuel G. Courtney, in a "strictly private" communication to Tilden, stated that "our friends" were incensed and that Tilden and Havemeyer were denounced for deserting Connolly "in the hour of need." Connolly, in custody in the New York Hotel, could not obtain bail. "What's to be done?" Courtney meant to stand by Connolly whom he thought Tilden should call to see.[64] The District Attorney "managed to *nol. pros.* the indictments against Connolly and his relatives." Professing "friendship and esteem" for Tilden, he fled abroad with $6,000,000 and died there. Various lesser officials also ran away; others were sent to prison on the testimony of Garvey who turned state's evidence before departing for London where he lived under an assumed name.[65]

Tweed was indicted by the Grand Jury on 120 counts, among which were felony, forgery, grand larceny, false pretenses and conspiracy to defraud. He had been arrested on October 26, 1871, and was released on $1,000,000 bail, Jay Gould being one of the bondsmen.[66] He was arrested again on December 16, 1871, indicted for felony and committed to the Tombs without bail. Judge Barnard, against O'Conor's protest, reversed the decision and granted Tweed his liberty on $5,000 bail. He resigned as Commissioner of Public Works a fortnight later and Tammany deprived him of the office of Grand Sachem.[67] Trial was postponed for one reason or another until January 7, 1873. Tweed had a formidable array of attorneys, including young Elihu Root, David Dudley Field, John Graham, and five others. Without success he had offered Amasa J. Parker a large sum to defend him.[68] The trial was lengthy, bitterly contested and in the end the jury disagreed. Tilden

[63] Myers, 270.   [64] *Letters*, I, 270–271.
[65] Woodward fled to Montreal. *N.A. Review*, CXXIII, 373.
[66] Alexander, III, 246.   [67] Myers, 293.
[68] Tilden Papers, Parker to Manning, Dec. 17, 1874.

had been the star witness. Tweed fled to California but returned to New York and was arrested again. At a second trial on November 19, 1873, the jury rendered a verdict of guilty and Judge Noah Davis fined Tweed $12,500 and sentenced him to twelve years in prison.[69] After spending a year behind the bars, he was released on a technicality, but immediately rearrested on a civil charge and his bail fixed at $3,000,000, which he could not raise.

O'Conor was still convinced that there existed a "complete conspiracy" to protect Tweed. Hence Curtis and Porter, who had expressed doubts about the outcome of the trial, were replaced by Peckham and Wickham as his assistants. "All the scamps have fled except Tweed," O'Conor moaned. If Field gets a reversal, Tweed "will fly." "What are we to do?" he asked Tilden.[70]

On December 4, 1875, Tweed escaped from his custodians and fled first to Cuba and then to Spain where he was arrested, upon landing, as a kidnaper because of one of Nast's cartoons. Two years later he testified that this escape cost him $60,000.[71] While a refugee, a judgment was found against him for the sum of $6,000,000. Sheriff W. C. Conner on September 14, 1876, informed Tilden, then Governor of New York and Democratic nominee for the Presidency, and asked him to request the United States to obtain his extradition from Spain. Tilden made this request and was informed by the Secretary of State that his wish would be executed.[72]

Tweed was returned to New York City and put in Ludlow Street jail on November 23, 1876.[73] A year later he offered to testify against himself and his confederates and did so. His revelations are not comfortable reading. He paid out $400,000 in counsel fees from 1872 to 1875.[74] He died in prison on April 12, 1878, saying: "I guess Tilden and Fairchild have killed me at last. I hope they will be satisfied now." The newspapers were filled with moral editorials and his life was a theme for sermons in a thousand pulpits. Soft-hearted citizens thought the repentant sinner, after his confession, should have been released.

The total thefts of the Ring will never be known with certainty. Tilden does not seem to have left an opinion, but his chief investigator,

[69] Werner, 240.
[70] *Letters*, 1, 355, Jan. 7, 1875.
[71] Myers, 294; *Harper's Weekly*, Apr. 14, 1877; Werner, 246.
[72] *Tribune*, Oct. 18, 1877.
[73] *Letters*, II, 464, 469.
[74] Werner, 254; *Tribune*, Oct. 18, 1877.

Henry F. Taintor, estimated that from 1868 to 1871 approximately $50,000,000 was stolen.[75] The special aldermanic committee which reviewed the whole situation in 1877 placed the total stealings $10,000,-000 higher. Mathew J. O'Rourke, who studied the entire problem, increased the sum to $75,000,000 and asserted that from 1865 to 1871 the amount, including fraudulent bonds, reached $200,000,000. Yet the City of New York recovered only $876,000.[76]

Tilden's work was not finished with the exposures of the Ring's peculations. For the subsequent five years he patiently devoted time to litigation for the overthrow of the Ring. His persistence and patience resulted in the eventual punishment of Tweed and his associates and the recovery of a portion of the stolen money. No one knew better than he that the reform of the government of New York City could not be accomplished by a volcanic explosion of indignant citizens but would require heroic measures and unswerving devotion after the outbreak subsided. It was for that purpose that he went to Albany as an Assemblyman and became Governor. Great credit should be given Tilden for the overthrow of the Tweed Ring, but it should be remembered that to him the saving of his party from disintegration by the exposures was equally important. He retained the chairmanship of the State Committee and set himself the task of rebuilding the party from within after his own pattern—a pattern that chalked off the Tweed Ring as a localized infection repugnant to all good Democrats. The overthrow of the Tweed Ring to him was something more than a moral revolt—it was a demonstration of the triumph of democracy.

[75] Smith Papers with the Tilden Papers. Undated.

[76] Testimony, 1877. See *Sun,* Oct. 25, 1877. Document No. 8; Myers, 297. Wilson, *Mem. Hist.,* III, 562, states that the city recovered from Watson's estate $558,000, Sweeny $406,562, Woodward $151,779.

In 1872 Tilden was at the height of his fame as a corporation lawyer. A stranger passing down Wall Street would have noticed a tin sign with gilt letters announcing: "S. J. Tilden, Counsellor at Law." His office was up three flights, with no elevator, and consisted of three good-sized rooms and a small hall room. The walls were lined with his law library—over 4,000 volumes—many of them bought in the thirties when he was a student. Over an interior doorway stood a bust of Horatio Seymour. On the mantel of the first room was a framed picture of McClellan and above it an oil painting of the New York Balance Dock. The Seaman's Floating Church appeared in the picture. When a visitor asked whether it was a high church or a low church, Tilden answered with a chuckle, "Well, that depends upon the tide." On the mantel in the second room was a framed speech which Tilden had delivered at Union Square on September 17, 1860. In winter two of the rooms were heated with grate fires and the other two by a stove. Frequently Tilden could be seen on a cold day with his short-legged boots off, toasting his feet by the open fire.[1]

Throughout the business world Tilden's ability to salvage crippled industries and to add to the vigor of going concerns was recognized, and he was overwhelmed with importunities by captains of industry to handle their legal problems. Through legal fees and shrewd investments, he had amassed a fortune and was one of the richest lawyers in the United States. Socially he was accepted by the best families in the city. Commodore Vanderbilt wrote him familiarly, "I am sure the ladies would be pleased to see the light of your countenance once more."[2] At fifty-eight he had passed middle life and was looking forward to a period when he could travel, read his favorite authors, and have leisure to follow his tastes. But a life of ease was never to be his lot. Too many railroad presidents, factory and mine owners and politicians filled his office. His memory for facts and his choice of language were quite extraordinary. His legal training gave him an exceptional grasp of history and a keen sense of the value of sources, and he never

[1] John J. Cahill's address before the Tilden Memorial Association, Feb. 10, 1914.
[2] *Ib.*

allowed anything to be destroyed. Men found him companionable, "mild in manner, temperate in habits and indefatigable in work." Although careful of his wealth, he never knew how much money he carried and kept his bills and small change mixed up in one pocket. "Take care" was a habitual phrase used in speaking to his clerks and to bank presidents. At times he was humorous and witty but never coarse or vulgar. When a girl in his family married a butcher he commented with a smile, "Now she will get the choice cuts." [3]

Such was the man whose efforts to break up the Tweed Ring and to restore to the people a clean and free government had met with such gratifying results. Trustworthy friends like O'Conor, Green, Havemeyer, Cooper, Greeley and Evarts took off their coats and enlisted for the crusade against corruption. All the important papers lined up behind the movement. When Tweed, Sweeny, and Connolly were driven from office and confronting trial, the reform element thought the victory won. Not so Tilden. He knew that the triumph would not be decisive until the fundamental causes which gave rise to crooked politics were removed.

Repeatedly Tilden had declared publicly that the remedies of civic corruption must go deeper than merely driving scoundrels from office. Reform, to be thorough and lasting, must begin at Albany. Corrupt judges who had abetted the Tweed Ring must be impeached in the Capital. But it was discovered that no laws provided for the punishment of corruptionists, and it was largely for this purpose that Tilden went to the legislature to obtain remedial legislation. New laws must also be enacted to prevent the recurrence of the civic evils, if possible, or at least to make their reappearance more difficult. So confident was Tilden that this was the right solution of the problem that he urged O'Conor, Evarts and other trusted collaborators to join him in going to the legislature.

Tilden's willingness to run for Assemblyman in the eighteenth district of New York County was really a heroic act. He accepted this humble place because he believed it to be his duty to safeguard the good name of his city and of his State. There can be little doubt that he believed that his labors at Albany might also help to redeem his party from the bad name attached to it by the misdoings of a few disreputable members and to increase its prospects for a recovery of

[3] John J. Cahill's address before the Tilden Memorial Association, Feb. 10, 1914.

prestige and power. Tilden had an abiding faith in the Democratic Party and always acted as if it were his wife, his religion and his hope of Heaven.[4] With his experience of 1846 he harbored no delusions about the difficulties he would encounter, but he was not a man to be daunted.

The election of Tilden to the Assembly was of State-wide interest because he represented a great cause and not merely the eighteenth district of the metropolis. Congratulations spoke of a "victory against the Ring"; a "noble fight for the people"; and a "triumph of clean politics." [5] Newspapers commented on the significance of his election.

Three groups were especially interested in Tilden's work in the Assembly. Those who were conducting legal proceedings against the Ring expected the passage of laws that would facilitate their work. O'Conor outlined for Tilden a simple legislative reform program—a few brief bills and a new city charter. Realizing the party cast of the legislature, he thought Tilden might have to do some "fainting" to have his bills passed.[6] The second group consisted of reform Democrats who wished to see a purified and triumphant party emerge from defeat. John V. L. Pruyn felt that misgovernment in New York City was due to the neglect of the people.[7] General Franz Sigel commended his purpose and wished him success.[8]

A third group, made up of lawyers and judges who wished for a reformation of the judiciary, counted upon Tilden to lend his assistance in ousting corrupt judges. The Bar Association in New York City took the lead in this movement. Through Attorney General Francis C. Barlow it sought to have him appointed as chairman of the Assembly Judiciary Committee,[9] but Tilden declined. However, he co-operated with the association's committee in every possible way.[10]

About a week before the legislature convened, Seymour, out of his years of experience, sent Tilden a kindly letter of instructions. "What are you going to do at Albany?" he asked. "You will be in a minority, and more than "one-half of the members hate you." They expected to make money out of some ring. "You can scarcely put your finger upon a clean spot in Albany." They would praise your work against the rogues but "give you a fall if they can" by skillful combinations. "They

[4] D. B. Hill's *Speech at the Tilden Anniversary Dinner*. Brooklyn, Feb. 9, 1888.
[5] Tilden Papers, various dates in November, 1871.   [6] *Letters*, I, 291, Dec. 22, 1871.
[7] Tilden Papers, Jan. 4, 1871, from London.   [8] *Ib.*, Jan. 4, 1871.
[9] *Ib.*, Dec. 28, 1871.   [10] *Ib.*, Mar. 12, 1872.

can beat you in all these ways." Take my advice; "do not try to do too much." Take no more part than duty demands. Do not direct the City Charter, yet vote on it as you please. But "you must reform the judiciary." On judicial reform the ignorant legislators "will give up to you." The Ring was dead, but its friends, mortally hurt, were squirming. Men like Tweed and Fisk could do nothing without the help of the courts. You could clean out the foul judiciary of New York City in a big way and thus attract the attention of the State and nation. The entire legal profession would support you, and so would the business interests. This reform would lift you above the "squabbles and intrigues of the legislature." Investigate thoroughly through a good committee and impeach the guilty. "Make this your specialty, and give little attention to other matters." If you get tangled up in the new charter you will fail.[11] This advice, coinciding with his own judgment, was heeded by Tilden, and the records clearly show that he followed it to the letter. It makes clear why Tilden seemed to keep in the background and took such a small part in the proceedings.

The legislature convened on January 3, 1872, and adjourned on May 14.[12] In the Assembly were 97 Republicans and 31 Democrats; in the Senate 24 Republicans and 8 Democrats. In the preparation of his message Governor Hoffman called upon Tilden for counsel on State finance, taxation, canals, and reformation of government in New York City. The Governor recommended the improvement of the courts with particular emphasis.[13] This opening gun reflected the political morality Tilden had been preaching in his famous lithographed letters, and in his public addresses. Now that Governor Hoffman had broken with the Tweed gang and was posing as a converted reformer, Tilden was quite willing to co-operate with him, although he never seemed to be a very close confidant.

In the assignment of committees, by his own request, although Cook says through deliberate neglect,[14] he was not placed on any committee that meant either hard work or regular attendance, but was assigned to the Committee on Federal Relations, which had little to do. This left him free to give attention to the major objects that took him to Albany. Apparently he attended the sessions only when measures in which he

[11] *Life,* I, 194.
[13] Lincoln, *Messages,* VI, 348–404.
[12] *Assembly Journal,* 1872, I and II.
[14] Cook, *Tilden,* 137.

was deeply interested were up for consideration, because the *Journal* shows him present for a roll call on but twenty-six days. The Republican State Committee asserted that he voted only 98 times but failed to vote 1,555 times. Seymour explained that Tilden was absent because he was devoting his time to the Ring suits and the impeachment of corrupt judges.[15]

As a shrewd and experienced student of public opinion, Tilden knew that a spirit of reform was in the air. Party leaders were talking loudly and boldly by this time about "turning the rascals out," and he knew that under these circumstances political crooks would either keep in hiding without showing their hand or try to clothe themselves in garments of respectability. But there were staunch party men in both branches of the legislature on whose support he could count; and Governor Hoffman's office offset the Republican control of the legislature. All things considered, therefore, Tilden faced the situation with confidence.

There were brought before this Legislature four subjects in which Tilden took a deep interest—railroads, the reform of the courts, the impeachment of corrupt judges, and the reorganization of municipal government. In the opening days of the session he told D. B. Hill that his "principal mission to the legislature was to bring about the purification of the judiciary in the city of New York." [16]

The railroad bills, not particularly important, had to do mostly with the reorganization of the boards of directors of the Erie Railroad and the Atlantic & Great Western Railroad. Tilden was an intelligent friend of an improved administration of the roads, while young David B. Hill showed himself by his votes to be rather hostile, representing as he did the upstate rural point of view. With a view to a more expeditious trial of the members of the Tweed Ring, Tilden on March 15 introduced an "Act to provide for the holding of courts of oyer and terminer for the trial of certain cases by justices of the Supreme Court, to be assigned for that purpose" and an "Act to provide for more effective remedies in cases of fraudulent acquisition, payment, disposition or conversion of public money or property." Both acts were sent to the Judiciary Committee and were passed, but vetoed by Governor Hoffman because

[15] Seymour's printed speech on "Judicial Corruption," delivered in New York City, Oct. 27, 1874.
[16] *Speech at the Tilden Anniversary Dinner*, Brooklyn, Feb. 9, 1888.

the first was unconstitutional and Judge Church advised against the second.[17] Tilden took counsel with Judge Comstock and other eminent jurists about the Judiciary Bill.[18]

Ignoring Governor Hoffman's recommendation for an amended charter for New York, the legislature took up the charter prepared by the Committee of Seventy and passed it.[19] It was an excellent document but, while being praised for its good points, was objected to by Tilden because it cut off too summarily the terms of existing officers whose services were needed to bridge over the transition from the Tweed Charter to the new one. He praised in strong terms the provision for spring elections which would separate city from State and national elections and thus cure many evils. The creation of two houses in the Common Council was necessary as a security against hasty action and as a "check and balance of parliamentary government." The method of electing aldermen and assistant aldermen, as proposed by the Senate, was criticized as open to grave abuses. In an address in the Assembly on February 28, 1872, Tilden discussed the proposed charter with great candor, and in the end felt impelled to vote against its passage, together with 27 others.[20] It was carried by 89 votes, as a distinctly reform measure but was nevertheless vetoed by Governor Hoffman who sent a lengthy explanation of his action,[21] concluding, "So convinced am I that . . . disastrous evils . . . are likely to grow out of this charter, that if I knew every man in the city . . . was clamoring for it, I would not give it my approval." The argumentation, reflecting the mind of Tilden, so impressed the Assembly that an attempt to override the veto was lost by a vote of 79 to 28. Thus the Tweed charter continued in power until replaced in 1873 by one which contained most of the provisions recommended by Tilden.[22]

The third major problem which engaged Tilden's attention was the impeachment of the Tweed judges—George C. Barnard, John H. McCunn and Albert Cardozo. In preparation for this action, Tilden wrote an opinion on "What Are Impeachable Offenses?" which was quoted many years later in the impeachment of Governor Sulzer.[23] Tilden and his friends, on May 2, carried, by a vote of 93 to 16, the resolution presented by D. B. Hill's committee to impeach Judge Barnard "for mal

[17] Lincoln, *Messages*, VI, 429, 490.   [18] Tilden Papers.
[19] Argus, Feb. 28, 1872.   [20] *Life*, I, 196; *Assembly Journal*, 1872, I.
[21] Lincoln, *Messages*, VI, 453, Apr. 20, 1872.   [22] *Ib.*, VI, 453.
[23] *Writings*, I, 472.

and corrupt conduct in office." Nine managers were elected to present
the charges. Tilden's name was tenth on the list, with only 52 votes;
hence he did not obtain a place.[24] Kernan thought he was fortunate to
escape,[25] but the *Tribune* said that he should have been seated. Barnard was removed by the unanimous vote of the Senate and Court of
Appeals, on July 17, sitting as a Court of Impeachment at Saratoga,
and forever disqualified from public office. Tilden's address on "Judiciary Reforms" had much to do with this decisive vote. He watched
the trial, offered advice and after the decision gave a dinner to the
managers.[26] Judge McCunn was unanimously impeached by the Assembly on May 14; and the Senate, at the request of the Governor,
removed him as a justice of the Superior Court. He died a few days
later. A resolution was offered in the Assembly on May 7 to impeach
Judge Cardozo for corrupt and high crimes, but, since he had resigned,
the Judiciary Committee reported that the Assembly had no authority
to press the case.[27] There was a rumor that he might seek vindication
in a new election, but it was not attempted.[28] Speaking of these corrupt judges, O'Conor said: "That was all Tilden's work and no one's
else. . . . He went to the legislature and forced the impeachment
against every imaginable obstacle, open and covert, political and personal." [29] When Tammany proposed W. H. Peckham for the Supreme
Court, he informed Tilden at once that he had declined the honor from
their hands.[30]

In dealing with the corrupt judges Tilden used the same methods
of thoroughness in gathering evidence that he did in the suits against
the Tweed Ring. Taintor was employed to assemble all the charges
against Barnard, and begged Tilden to get legislation to widen the
examination. He had the Assembly Judiciary Committee on March 8
order certain New York City banks to report on the deposits of Judges
Barnard and Cardozo, or their wives, for the years 1868–72. Tilden's
papers show that many tips came in from anonymous sources. A
thorough study was made of previous cases and also of the laws that
might bear on the legal problems involved. Frank P. Blair announced
his readiness to appear as a witness against Barnard.[31] When Tilden
seemed to move too slowly, F. C. Barlow wrote: "For Heaven's saké

[24] *Assembly Journal*, 1872, II, 1629–1950.   [25] Tilden Papers, May 11, 1872.
[26] Hill Papers.   [27] Tilden Papers, F. C. Barlow to Tilden, May 3, 1872.
[28] *An. Cyc.*, 1872, 584.   [29] *Century*, Mar., 1885, 734.   [30] Tilden Papers.
[31] *Ib.*, Feb. 25, 1872.

don't be induced by Barnard's manifesto to leave the judicial investigation. Our great reliance is on you." [32]

Among other acts which Tilden favored were: one to "provide suitable testimonials for each officer and soldier who served during the War of the Rebellion"; permission to let the voters of any town, city or county prohibit the sale of liquor; and an act to legalize the work of the Grand Jury of New York City which had been trying the Tweed Ring. In the election of a Regent of the University of the State of New York on April 24, Tilden's name was presented for the honor, but among half a dozen candidates he received only one vote. Tilden cast his vote for Bishop William C. Doane.[33]

Tilden's success in the legislature fell short of his expectations. He had held the banner of reform high but he had not succeeded in taking many steps against the powerful enemy. The gratifying accomplishment was the impeachment of the judges who were tools of the nefarious Ring. Impatient folk criticized him for having accomplished so little, and some of his friends were much concerned about it. Seymour wrote him that he ought to send out a letter at once and follow it with a public address answering the charge "that you have done nothing at Albany." He should mention the Judiciary Act and other reformatory measures. "Model your letter after the one I send," but dress it up, and above all else do not "delay explaining." [34] No one knew better than the Sage of Deerfield Tilden's proneness to procrastination.

Acting on such advice Tilden accepted the invitation to preside at the City Bar Association on April 30, 1872, and to comment on the reform of the judiciary. "Substantial progress" had been made, he asserted, and the association's suggestions carried out. "Every judge against whom you made charges has been put on trial, except one who fled." The "managers" had ample proof of Judge Barnard's guilt and the people's counsel—Van Cott and Judge Comstock—would "faithfully prosecute the trial." Tilden had done everything possible to prepare the impeachment and felt that, if other reforms failed, the purification of the judiciary was "just cause for congratulation." He had predicted [35] that if the association did its duty, it could have the "administration of justice made . . . honorable." For that purpose and to obtain certain other measures to further reforms in the metropolis,

[32] Tilden Papers, Feb. 25, 1872.
[34] Tilden Papers, May 18, 1872.
[33] *Assembly Journal,* 1872, I–II.
[35] Feb. 1, 1870.

he had gone to the Assembly believing that it was necessary to concentrate on "a few measures to accomplish anything." But he was disappointed not to have the co-operation of O'Conor and Evarts in the legislature.

The "partnership of plunder" in the Capital under Tweed between men of both parties was reviewed and Tilden said:

"I never for a moment supposed that the knife and the cautery would be agreeable remedies, or that the silent partners of prosperous criminals would fall in love with those whose duty it is to detect and punish. I knew, therefore, that obstructions, under every pretext, were to be met at every step, and to be overcome. Let us thankfully accept what has been accomplished, and let us here, tonight, renew our faith that if the bar of this city and State will be united and persistent, every judicial reform in respect to men and . . . systems will be at last successfully achieved."

In conclusion he appealed to the young lawyers, for whose sake he had carried on the fight, to help make the profession of law a worthy one.[36]

In Tilden's life the year 1872 was crucial both for his own public career and for the future success of his party. No one saw this more clearly than he. At Albany he directed the remedial measures necessary to clean up the mess in New York City. As the head of the Democratic State Committee, he had to plan the gubernatorial election in New York—a task that was peculiarly difficult that year. And finally he was confronted by the Presidential campaign, which was perplexing and uncertain. To these problems Tilden devoted time, energy and his genius for political manipulation.

In a speech to the Assembly Tilden declared that while clean government was at stake he had not "selfishly secluded himself in any personal or private business. In the last five months I have not given five days to any professional or private business whatsoever. That time has been devoted to the service of that great community in which I have always lived. I have given it freely. I have contributed it ungrudgingly. I wish only that I could have multiplied myself by four, in order to perform the duties that pressed upon me." [37] This same sacrifice of his personal interests continued throughout the year 1872 which practically marked the end of his career as a corporation lawyer and a business man, and the resumption of the rôle of publicist and statesman. This does not mean that his law office was closed or that his

---

36 *Life*, I, 202.   37 *Ib.*, 202, Feb. 28, 1872.

business interests were dropped. He was involved in too many important professional commitments and business entanglements to withdraw so completely. He still sat on boards of railroads and mines, which necessitated a contribution of more or less legal advice.

But Tilden refrained from assuming new obligations and so far as possible turned his legal and financial affairs over to trusted bankers and subordinates in his office, giving them less and less personal oversight. His staff was not large but the members were devoted and competent under his training. George W. Smith had entered his office in 1866 as a law student and remained as his confidential secretary as long as Tilden lived. J. P. Sinnott entered his service later and was a useful employee. C. J. O'Brien had been taken into the office on the recommendation of Havemeyer. Charles F. McLean had a desk in Tilden's office and was assigned a certain amount of business to supplement his own. Smith took charge of the office and managed it with skill and success. Tilden placed great reliance in him and said repeatedly that he loved him like a son.[38] One finds these men writing Tilden's letters and keeping his books in long hand, the day of the stenographer and typist not having yet arrived. To him who alone knew the details, they carried knotty legal tangles and business snarls. Extensive travel was still necessary, and one finds William Vanderbilt and A. J. Cassatt supplying private cars and passes over their lines. Old friends insisted upon investment advice—Seymour for years was in debt to Tilden for sums as high as $5,000; [39] Mrs. William Cassidy had $10,000 in his hands; N. W. Parker gave him $5,775 for a safe investment. Tilden kept $50,000 in the banks so he could pick up bargains.[40]

Speaking of this period Tilden said later:

"The total surrender of my professional business . . . the nearly absolute withdrawal . . . from my private affairs and from all enterprises in which I am interested, have cost me a loss of actual income, which, with expenditures and contributions the contest has required, would be a respectable endowment of a public charity. I do not speak of these things to regret them. In my opinion, no instrumentality in human society is so potential in its influence on the well-being of mankind as the governmental machinery which administers justice and makes and executes the laws. No benefaction of private benevolence could be so fruitful in benefits as the rescue of this machinery from the

[38] Mrs. G. W. Smith, Ms. Notes.   [39] Tilden Papers.
[40] Letters, I, 316, 318.

perversion which has made it a means of conspiracy, fraud, and crime against the rights and the most sacred interests of a great community." [41]

This decision Tilden never regretted. Without foreseeing the political rewards that would come to him, he performed this service as a civic duty. Not only did he and O'Conor refuse all compensation for their laborious task, but Tilden advanced funds to carry on the legal work when public funds were not available. Tremaine, a Republican, and Peckham, a Democrat, charged the City of New York $75,000 in fees for their services—a charge which both Tilden and O'Conor believed to be just. [42] O'Conor declared repeatedly that Tilden "did more than anyone else" to overthrow and punish the Tweed Ring. Other individuals, organizations and newspapers, regardless of party affiliation, praised him for his devotion to civic righteousness. A Republican wrote:

"To you more directly than to any one else are we all indebted for the signal triumph of justice which has just been achieved . . . Your part in all this struggle and success is appreciated and borne in grateful remembrance by those who best know the qualities of head and heart which have enabled you to render the State such signal service." [43]

While endorsing Greeley's nomination for President by the Democrats in 1872, Tilden played the rôle of a spectator in the campaign. In contrast to this indifference, he labored with might and main for the nomination and election of Francis Kernan as Governor. The defeat of both the national and State Democratic tickets left Tilden free to realize a plan he had cherished for a quarter of a century for a trip to Europe. During the summer of 1873 he spent a month in England and then crossed to the Continent. From Geneva, Switzerland, he resigned the chairmanship of the Democratic State Committee. [44] Instead of heeding his wish, the Democrats re-elected him to that position during his absence, and he served in that capacity until he was nominated for Governor. [45] After four restful months abroad, he returned home in time to direct a successful campaign for minor State offices. [46]

[41] *Life*, I, 205.
[42] *Ib.*, 206; Louisville, Ky., *Jeffersonian Democrat*, O'Conor, March 30, 1874.
[43] *Life*, I, 207, William Allen Butler, Nov. 27, 1873.
[44] *Letters* I, 301, 304, 311, 320, 328.   [45] Cook, 137.
[46] *An. Cyc.*, 1873, 548–549.

TILDEN's supporters regarded him as the logical candidate for Governor long before he made up his mind to seek the honor. Indeed, for nearly ten years his name had been suggested for that office but no hint that he cared for it appeared in his papers. For months before the nominating convention met in 1874, he was importuned from various parts of the State to announce his candidacy. "No other name mentioned in Buffalo is so well known," it was declared, and there were 80 sure votes upstate; if he got New York City, he would be nominated. Beach urged him to head a strong ticket. "I am satisfied," wrote Kernan, "that if you will take the nomination . . . you will be strong in the country. Let your friends know before the convention." He was urged to attend the convention in person and told that he could not "fail to carry the State." While either C. N. Potter or John Ganson would make a "fair candidate," Magone declared, as in 1872, "my first and last choice is yourself." [1] The only objection urged against him was that he had attacked the Democratic Ring and would lose their votes. "I say away with such fears! If our party friends will not support brave, honest men because a Ring of plunderers . . . may be displeased, then let our opponents succeed!" [2]

Apparently this communication was the culmination of influences which helped Tilden make up his mind, because he said, "I did not come to entertain the idea of taking a nomination until the twenty-first of August." He wished to demonstrate that three years devoted to civic betterment was not a disqualification for public office, in order to encourage young men to participate in clean political life. [3] There is no evidence that he was ambitious to become Governor but much to prove that he did not shrink from his civic duty. As the test approached, his bandwagon became more and more crowded, and men like Daniel Manning brought encouraging surveys. Knowing Tilden's instinctive caution, Kernan advised, "You should say 'If nominated I will accept.' " [4] Although the Canal Ring defeated him as a delegate to the convention, yet Kernan kept reporting new recruits among the delegates. The Canal

---

[1] Tilden Papers, July 2, 22, Aug. 9, 1874.   [2] *Letters*, I, 333, Aug. 21.
[3] *Ib.*, 339.   [4] Tilden Papers, Aug. 30, 31, 1874.

Ring and the *Argus* were also doing everything possible to defeat Tilden in Albany County, but his supporters were checkmating every move.[5]

Knowing political life thoroughly, Tilden realized that to enter it more actively would bring criticism from a hostile press, and array every corruptionist in his party against him. Some of his best political friends were doubtful whether he could be nominated, and, if nominated, elected. Before the convention Seymour, well-intentioned but pessimistic, warned him that all the rings, some powerful interests, State officials, and the country press were determined to defeat him by keeping his supporters out of the convention. "Reformers are hated" and can win only when there is a "tempest of popular rage against corruption." You are "honest, able and fearless" but will have to take defeat from those who hate you. New Yorkers "want men in office who will not steal, but who will not interfere with those who do." Tilden was opposed by those whose schemes would prosper by his absence from Albany. But the gallant old farmer-warrior of many a bitter struggle who also enjoyed "the ill will of the Ring," upon reflection thought his views might be due to "the prejudices of an old man" and the "want of courage." In any event he promised to do all he could for Tilden.[6]

But Tilden knew the political map of New York more accurately than Seymour. In casting up accounts he was positive that the cause of reform would not be safe in the hands of any other leader. The next step was to make certain that other aspirants were eliminated either voluntarily or by circumstances. Then the cause of honest government, which had been endorsed in New York City, must be placed before the people, and, if sanctioned by them, instituted at Albany. Without committing himself up to the very day of the convention, he never worked so hard to strengthen his influence in every locality and to instill hope in the hearts of wavering party colleagues. And he knew the outcome when others doubted, but he kept his mouth shut and let his friends talk.

Powerful newspapers in some mysterious way became his champions. *Harper's Weekly* asserted that the nomination of Tilden—one of Democracy's "most reputable members"—would make the election one of principle, because, unlike Hoffman, he was the foe and not the tool of the Tweed Ring.[7] The *Tribune* declared that the personal qualities which made him the enemy of the disreputable faction of Democrats

---

[5] *Letters*, I, 334.
[6] *Life*, I, 221, Seymour to Tilden, Aug. 27, 1874; *Letters*, I, 335, Sept. 11, 1874.
[7] Sept. 10, 1874.

"commend him to the respect of all honest citizens." His nomination was "dictated in advance by the well-nigh unanimous sentiment of the people." [8] The *Times,* Grant's organ, asserted that he would make "a very good candidate," because he was "an able man, . . . of very high character." By running for Governor he would improve his party's "moral tone"—but Governor Dix would beat him.[9] To "straighten out" Bennett and the *Herald,* Tilden sent O'Conor to explain the situation, with satisfactory results.[10]

Early in 1874 Church, in an interview with Tilden, declined to be a candidate, but under pressure he abandoned his earlier resolution. To Joseph Warren of the Buffalo *Courier* he gave his written consent to accept the nomination if offered with the concurrence of other candidates.[11] Warren then obtained declarations of withdrawal from prominent aspirants. With these documents, Warren on September 8 met Tilden in Albany to persuade him to step aside for Church. With Warren were Jarvis Lord of Rochester, DeWolf of Oswego and other canal men, while Reuben E. Fenton waited in an adjoining room.[12] Fenton's plan was first to obtain Tilden's withdrawal, then have the Liberal Republican's nominate Church,[13] and finally to secure Democratic approbation. Warren bluntly told Tilden that he could not win while Church could, and asked him to step aside.

But Tilden had detected, better than Warren or any other political observer, the ground swell of public opinion. The more Warren explained, the more Tilden was convinced that he was spokesman for the gang that must be fought. John Kelly publicly announced that Warren, Lord and DeWolf profited from canal contracts and favored Church because he would help rather than oppose them.[14]

At length the conventions came. The Prohibitionists nominated Myron H. Clark for Governor. The Temperance Republicans opposed the renomination of Governor Dix. The Liberal Republicans denounced the Grant administration. Some delegates favored Tilden, others Dix, so they did nothing but approve the Greeley platform.[15] The Canal Ring tried to induce the Liberal Republicans to endorse Church, but Tilden's friends defeated the plot.[16] The Democrats met in Syracuse on Septem-

---

[8] Sept. 18, 1874.   [9] July 24, 1874.   [10] *Retrospections,* V, 154.
[11] *World,* Sept. 10, 1874.   [12] Alexander, III, 312.
[13] *Herald,* Sept. 9, 1874; Buffalo *Courier,* Sept. 11, 1874.
[14] *World,* Sept. 10, 1874; *Life,* I, 226.   [15] *An. Cyc.,* 1874, 610.
[16] Tilden Papers.

ber 16 in the largest State convention ever held, each Assembly district having sent three delegates. General Lester B. Faulkner was chosen chairman, and Seymour presented the platform which Manton Marble had drafted, with Tilden's aid, demanding specie payment, revenue reform, home rule, economy, a free press, and state supervision of corporations. Opposition was expressed to partial legislation and partial taxation, sumptuary laws and a third term for the President. Public office was a public trust, it declared, and there should be strict accountability. The hand of friendship was held out to the Liberal Republicans. Seymour, in a brief but forceful speech, placed Tilden in nomination, and loud cheers followed the announcement of his name. Amasa J. Parker was nominated as the representative of the conservative wing of the party—a compromise candidate among the supporters of various aspirants. Twice before he had been the nominee of the Democrats, but had been defeated. On the first ballot Tilden received 252 votes and Parker 128, giving the nomination to the former.[17] In the same city on September 23 the Republicans renominated Governor Dix by acclamation. The opposing candidates for Lieutenant Governor were William E. Dorsheimer and General J. C. Robinson.[18]

During the convention Tilden was in the city but kept himself secluded. On the evening following his nomination he was serenaded by a brass band. He was introduced as "the next Governor" by Attorney General Pratt, and made a brief speech. After thanking the people for the honor they did him, he asserted that a "peaceful revolution" was subjecting the nation to financial evils, dry-rot in business, shrinking incomes, and poverty. The inflation of paper money no longer inflated. "Our body politic has been over-drugged with stimulants." But taxes "put on new sprouts and grow"—the collector is as certain as death. "Incomes, profits, wages, fall; but taxes rise." This condition he had predicted six years earlier. Relief would come only from retrenchment, lowered tariffs and taxes, accountability of public officers, and reforms.

The Federal Government now threatened communication, transportation, education and the press. Unless these tendencies toward centralization were stopped, the institutions of the Fathers would change for the worse, and the most corrupt system of control would emerge. Civil liberty was endangered by Grant's "bad ambition" for a third term be-

[17] *An. Cyc.*, 1874, 611; Alexander, III, 314, states that Seymour wrote it.
[18] Alexander, III, 315.

cause it might result in the indefinite re-election of a President by patronage and corruption—an "elective, personal despotism"—the story of Caesar repeated! Thoughtful minds were seeking escape from these "overshadowing evils." Republicans saved the Union but had failed to reconstruct civil liberty and free institutions. "A change of men is necessary to a change of measures." Democrats, having the most men of sound ideas and political experience, must save the nation. The Democratic party "reformed itself in order that it might reform the country."

In the name of 500,000 voters, he concluded, "Come weal or come woe, we will not lower our flag," but work out a political revolution to restore the principles of Jefferson and Jackson at Washington. "Let us never despair of our country. Actual evils can be mitigated; bad tendencies can be turned aside; the burdens of government can be diminished; productive industry will be renewed; and frugality will repair the waste of our resources. Then shall the golden days of the Republic once more return and the people become prosperous and happy." [19]

This speech, tinged with rancor and a bit demagogic, was actually the prophecy of a new era in American history. It touched the hearts of the common man and the mind of the thinker. It explains why Tilden's nomination evoked enthusiasm among Republicans and Democrats alike. Seymour pronounced it "clear and able" but warned, "There are reasons why you should not make any more speeches." If he did, he should speak about national affairs, and not about himself. This would hold the "many Republicans who are disposed to vote for you for home reasons" and would not draw the fire of hostile journals. His true policy was to "look after organization." [20] He advised Tilden about the Granger vote and thought Kernan could hold the Irish. The State Committee should send out an address "strong in facts," but temperate in language reciting Dix's greed for office and the use of his political influence for certain corporations. Not trusting the regular mails, he asked, "How shall I address letters to you?" [21]

When the *Tribune* seemed to be "coming out for Dix," Seymour insisted that Tilden see Whitelaw Reid to "change his views." That paper seemed to waver at first, asserting that, while Tilden had accomplished great things in ousting the Tweed Ring and in reforming his own party, still many could not forget that he had "acted as counsel for some of the

[19] *Writings*, II, 10, Sept. 20, 1874.
[21] *Life*, I, 227.

[20] *Letters*, I, 337, 341.

greatest railroad corporations in the State" or was a "moral coward" in not going after the Ring earlier.[22] But on September 11, Reid told Dix that he intended to support Tilden, and it was not long before he virtually made the *Tribune* Tilden's organ. Indeed Tilden frankly acknowledged that his victory was due to the editor of that journal.[23] The nomination brought commendations galore—those from old friends being a delight to Tilden. Theodore Roosevelt was "sincerely glad" he had beaten "the old rogues." O'Conor, eyes-deep in the Ring cases, thought a "dog trot" would defeat the Republicans. Tilden was assured that there was no defection in New York City, and even Delos DeWolf of the Canal Ring promised to do everything possible for his election. Kernan expressed the situation accurately when he wrote, "Your nomination is well-received everywhere," and cautioned him to let only honest men handle the campaign funds.[24]

"There are no illusions in my mind in respect to public life," Tilden said. "I know that peace, content and happiness are only in a private station, and it is wholly exceptional in me to do what I am doing." Aware of his foes, he was resolved not "to stumble and fall" by failing to see the "sticks and stones in the path"—as Wright had once warned him.[25] He was willing to let the people idealize him. When Theodore E. Cook asked confidentially who really overthrew the Tweed Ring, he answered, "People *think I did it*—hence the Republicans can't make it an issue." [26] Soon the campaign was on—in the papers, on the platform, at the street corner, in the saloon and in the home—a vocal bombardment supplemented by printer's ink. Amasa J. Parker advised Tilden to go after the national administration.[27] If elected, the *Tribune* said, his office would be "distinguished alike for integrity . . . administrative skill and shrewd political management." [28] The *Times* rejoiced that he was not nominated by the "canal plunderers" and said that his party need not be ashamed of him. The *Post* congratulated the people of New York on his nomination. As the campaign progressed Seymour became more optimistic. On his return from Wisconsin he stopped off in Western New York to see some of the key men and reported that the sore-heads in the convention were placated and that one canal contractor would vote for Tilden because he did not want to be blamed for defeating him.[29] Young

[22] *Letters*, I, 339, 341.   [23] Cortissoz, *Reid*, 294.
[24] Tilden Papers.   [25] *Letters*, I, 337, Tilden to Birdsall, Sept. 19, 1874.
[26] Cook, *Tilden*.   [27] Tilden Papers, Oct. 3, 1874.   [28] *Letters*, I, 339, quoted.
[29] Tilden Papers, Oct. 16, 20, 21, 1874.

D. B. Hill worked for the whole ticket but said, "I fear that Mr. Tilden is the weakest name on it." [30]

It must not be assumed that Tilden's foes were frightened into inactivity by his nomination. On the contrary they put up a strenuous fight, both openly and under cover, hoping that with the aid of the Republicans he might be defeated. One of the earliest maneuvers was to persuade Tilden to accept campaign funds from the Tweed crowd, with the intent, no doubt, of discrediting him; for no sooner was he nominated than they tried to bargain with him through P. H. Cowan, a lawyer of Saratoga Springs. "Every one knows," Cowan wrote, "that without the aid of the personal friends of Tweed, the State ticket will be defeated by 40,000 majority." Tweed's friends can be made our friends. If they have your promise that you will pardon him, they will "put a half million into a fund for your success" and instruct their supporters in each county to further your election. Then you will have the whole party behind you. In addition he urged Tilden: "Let the temperance men be paid and their organization sustained by money, and success is certain." Although Cowan declared that he "never was a Tweed man" yet he felt that Tweed was punished sufficiently.[31] Remembering his long fight against the gang of corruptionists, Tilden's reaction to this "bold proposition" was characteristic—he flatly refused to consider any compromise and declared that he would not receive a dollar from any of the thieves or their open friends. Full well did he realize that his attack on the Ring was his best campaign asset. The upstate Canal Ring did not conduct an openly organized fight but worked underground.

The Democratic strategy was to center fire on Dix at Albany and Grant at Washington. The party press and stump speakers fired broadside after broadside against Dix. He was accused of nepotism and wastefulness. Altogether as a public official he had drawn $250,000.[32] As president of the Union Pacific Railroad when Oakes Ames' contract was made, his name was associated with the Credit Mobilier. It was not these charges, however, that defeated him but the apathy of his managers who acted as if they desired him to lose.[33] Furthermore Conkling and other leaders gave him only half-hearted support.

The bitter quarrel between Mayor Havemeyer and John Kelly, boss

[30] D. B. Hill to Theodore Miller, Sept. 21, 1874. Hill Papers, New York Public Library.
[31] Letters, I, 338, Sept. 21, 1874.
[32] Life, I, 233, Seymour to Tilden, Oct. 5, 1874; Tilden Papers, Purcell to Tilden.
[33] Dix, Life, II, 128, 149, 195.

of a reformed Tammany, turned many a vote to Tilden. Havemeyer accused Kelly of stealing $84,482 by illegal methods while sheriff, and Kelly sued him for libel. When Havemeyer desired to be re-elected Mayor, Kelly selected as the Tammany candidate William H. Wickham, a diamond merchant, who had been a member of the Committee of Seventy but who, O'Conor said, thought only of "making a pleasant thing for himself" out of the office of Mayor.[34] Kelly's candidate for Register was James Haynes who made half a million under Tweed; and, of the fifteen aldermen, nine belonged to the Ring and two of these had been indicted for fraud.[35] Kelly also appointed to a marshalship Richard Croker who had been attached to Connolly's office.[36] But Boss Kelly still applauded the reform pronouncements of Tilden and promised strong support from the metropolis. While there were no signs of a rift between these two strong political leaders, there were breakers ahead. When Havemeyer died shortly after Tilden's election, Kelly boasted, "Tammany is the only reform party in existence here today." Tilden must have smiled with satisfaction when another boss, Thurlow Weed, invited him to dine, ostensibly to consider a monument to Robert Fulton but in reality to discuss the political situation.

The election campaign was supervised by Tilden himself because he found it difficult to deputize others to do such work. Allen C. Beach, Chairman of the State Committee, from the headquarters in New York City, where he was in constant consultation with his master, sent out to party leaders a "plan of organization" for each election district and a questionnaire to be returned "as soon as possible." He told Tilden, "Our reports from all parts of the State are encouraging," [37] but that was not enough; there must be no guesswork. With his consummate cleverness as a manager, Tilden took the returns of his agents in all parts of the State and figured with the mathematical precision of a census taker just how the vote stood from time to time. To W. C. Hudson of the Brooklyn *Eagle* he showed a book containing the names of 50,000 Democrats, one or two in each school district, with whom he discussed the situation and to whom he entrusted his orders.[38] He was the commander in chief of a Democratic army and never for a moment in doubt as to the outcome.

In Tilden's scheme for winning an election, machinery was not

[34] *Life*, I, 245.   [35] Myers, 307.   [36] Alexander, III, 318–319.
[37] Tilden Papers.   [38] Hudson, *Rand. Recol.*, 46.

enough. The campaign must be one of education—the voters must be enlightened—hence publicity was a necessity. Not only were the newspapers supplied with information the voters should have, but special pamphlets were sent all over the State. For this work a staff of competent writers was employed and given specific instructions as to what to prepare. Among the leaflets distributed was one with the heading, "For Governor and Reform," which was a sketch of his father and himself with his record as a political reformer.[39] A second medium of publicity was the spoken word. Considerable attention was given to the selection of speakers, and their itineraries were carefully planned. There was no dearth of oratorical assistance from his political friends, among them being Seymour, Kernan and Abram S. Hewitt.[40] Dorsheimer was kept busy until illness compelled him to rest. Tilden himself followed Seymour's injunction not to make many addresses. Those he did deliver were carefully prepared, sent to the newspapers and in some cases printed in pamphlet form for electioneering purposes.[41]

Funds had to be raised for the campaign, and his papers, while not very revealing on this subject, indicate that generous donations came from his party associates. Naturally he himself contributed heavily. He watched the disbursements carefully and made certain that there was no misuse of money. The campaign as a whole was conducted on a higher level than was customary. As election day approached, Kernan predicted what Tilden already knew: "We shall carry the State. Your election is assured."

When the election returns were finally counted, it was found that Tilden had received 416,391 votes, a plurality of 50,317.[42] Beach, reflecting Tilden's own estimate, had predicted a victory by 50,000 and was quite proud of himself as a prophet.[43] Dix met with a heavy loss in contrast to his plurality of 53,451 in 1872. Clark, the temperance candidate, polled only 11,768 votes. Dorsheimer won the office of Lieutenant Governor by a plurality of 51,488.[44] Proud of the fact that his plurality was reported as 1,500 above that of Tilden, he called on Tilden and, after talking over the campaign, remarked, "By the way, Governor, did you notice that my plurality was 51,500 while yours was only 50,000?" "Yes, yes," Tilden replied. "You got the 1,500; I gave you the 50,000." [45]

[39] Tilden Papers.   [40] Nevins, *Hewitt*, 293.   [41] Tilden Papers, Oct. 1, 1874.
[42] *An. Cyc.*, 1874, 612.   [43] Tilden Papers, Nov. 11, 1874.
[44] *An. Cyc.*, 1874, 612.   [45] A. C. Stevenson, *Men I Have Known*, 394.

The Democratic triumph was much greater than appeared in the election of a Governor. To Washington were sent 18 Democratic Congressmen and 15 Republican. In the Legislature of 1875 there were 75 Democrats and 53 Republicans in the Assembly, and 18 Republicans, 12 Democrats and 2 Independents in the Senate. In New York City, Wickham, the Tammany candidate (reformed), was elected Mayor with 70,071 votes, Wales the Republican receiving 36,953 and Ottendorfer, Independent, 24,226. For Governor, New York City gave Tilden 87,623 votes and Dix 44,871. All the amendments to the State Constitution, including Art. II Sec. 2 on the punishment of bribery, were carried.[46] The certificate of his election as Governor dated December 16, 1874, was carefully preserved by him to the day of his death.

After the election of Tilden, Senator Bayard remarked that he would now give up trying to understand New York politics. Thurlow Weed explained the victory as the result of the "incapacity and persistent wrongdoing at Washington." [47] Governor-elect Tilden's interpretation was given in an interview with a representative of the *Tribune* on November 4. "The people are beginning to think that it is time to have a real peace in the United States." Ten years after the war, the systems of finance and taxation produced by that conflict still survived. These evils were aggravated by the treatment of the South with carpetbag dominion. The "illusion of a false prosperity" founded upon an "audacious system of robbery," unless stopped would bring ruin to the nation. Unnecessary and extravagant expenditure, fat jobs, the distribution of plunder to favorites, the blight of oppressive taxation, special privileges for "favored classes" and the waste of capital were as disastrous as in wartime. The people were now awakening to the real situation. "The first step toward a remedy of the disease is to obtain a true diagnosis of the malady." The election meant that the people were discarding their "present political doctors" in order to try new ones. With all the disadvantages of having no patronage to help them, the people had won a great victory.[48]

Tilden's explanation was significant because, couched in national rather than local terms, it seemed to point forward to 1876 rather than backward to 1871. His personal and party friends unanimously attributed his triumph to his reputation and managerial skill, yet one detects

[46] *An. Cyc.*, 1874, 612–613.　　　　[47] Barnes, *Thurlow Weed,* II, 505, 506.
[48] *Life,* I, 235.

in their felicitations a rejoicing over the victory of the reform cause. But the friends of Tweed and the canal profiteers were as silent as the grave. When Francis C. Barlow interpreted the election as "a national triumph" he was giving expression to a widespread feeling. Washington was stunned by the "November revolution"; and both Republicans and the poor were looking to Tilden as a savior. R. J. Wright of Indiana intended to call to present his congratulations in person, first at Albany, then at the White House. Kernan could talk of nothing but 1876. E. Casserly actually nominated Tilden and Hendricks for the national ticket. And Tilden's physician, Dr. A. Flint, Jr., asked him to arrest his march "toward the Chief Magistracy" long enough to eat "a simple and scientific dinner." [49] These illustrations are sufficient to show that the New York election of 1874 was interpreted as a forerunner of a reform administration in the national Capital.

At the Manhattan Club on November 5 a jollification was held at which Tilden was persuaded to make a short speech. He asserted that the triumph was "not a personal victory" and that the "beneficent consequences" would not be confined to a party or a class, but its blessings "like the dews of Heaven, will fall equally upon all the people." Thousands who lacked the moral courage to break away from their party ties "slept more tranquilly" the night after the election. He urged his partisans to act magnanimously toward their adversaries, because after all the triumphant party was only "a trustee for the whole people." The creators of the Republic had predicted that civil war would destroy it, and when the Civil War came many agreed with them. "We had to save our country from dismemberment first, and afterward its liberties from subversion." The breaking down of the two-term tradition might lead to election for life. This waste of war had been followed by ten years of waste in peace. The Southern policy had added to the evils. Only a change at Washington would save "the great traditions of American free government; and it is every man's duty to help restore the principles of Thomas Jefferson." [50]

The reception given to Governor Tilden and Mayor Wickham on November 19 at Delmonico's by the Young Men's Democratic Club was attended with simplicity and enthusiasm. Tilden was received by Townsend, Cox, Sterne, Cooper and Peckham, and like a father was introduced to his political children. In response to a toast the Governor-elect

[49] Tilden Papers, various dates.   [50] *Writings*, II, 21; *Life*, I, 237.

made some "remarks." [51] Only an opportunity to greet the young men would have called him out. The duties of citizenship had been too much neglected everywhere, and the remedy must come from the young voters. During the sectional controversies of past years "we almost ceased to educate young men to do their part in human society." In seeking a young man to serve the State in 1867, no capable man under fifty could be found. "Schools of statesmanship" were needed to prepare young men to carry on government. "Go on, young men; perfect yourselves in political education; go back to the original fountains of Democratic-Republican opinions. . . . Seek the application of the great principles of popular government to the problems that are before us. Seek above all to elevate the standard of official morality."

"Old men grunt; young men lift," he was wont to say when he wished to get something done. Hence he was eager to organize the young voters to take an active part in public life. We who are older will look in vain for "those to whom we can hand over these great trusts" unless they are found within the next few years. When he was a young man, public servants were honest. Then came gradually "the lamentable decline in official morality."

In periods of despondency "I still retained trust in the body of the American people with whom I began life . . . and never lost . . . my belief that the element of human society which seeks for what is good is more powerful, if we trust it, than all those selfish combinations that would obtain unjust advantages over the masses. . . . I see here to-night intelligent young men who will be able, if they trust in the people, to form for this city, for this State, and for this country a great and noble future." Thus spoke the earnest exponent of popular rule and of practical reform.

During the two months before inauguration, the Governor-elect was confronted by three problems—patronage, a home in Albany and the preparation of his message to the legislature. The question of patronage included first the selection of his own staff and secondly jobs for party workers. Charles Stebbins was appointed private secretary. The selection of a military staff of fifteen was more difficult, for men like Seymour, Kernan and Dana had candidates.[52] When completed it included Adjutant General Franklin Townsend; Tilden's personal physician,

<hr>

[51] Published in *World* and *Tribune*, Nov. 20, 1874, and included in *Writings*, II, 16, under title, "The Political Duties of Young Men."
[52] Tilden Papers, various dates.

Surgeon General Dr. Austin Flint, Jr.; and his nephew Colonel William T. Pelton.[53] Seymour professed to be fending off applicants for office and yet was continually asking for places for relatives and others. Kernan was pestered to get positions for party workers but spared Tilden as much as possible. Fairchild, Randall, Peckham, Earl and Parker asked for jobs for themselves and party friends, but Tilden was too experienced to be stampeded by these requests and sought to bring into State service men who were both loyal to his ideals and efficient.[54]

The task of finding a suitable Governor's Mansion was left to William T. Pelton, who by November 30 had rented a house that pleased Tilden at 138 Eagle Street for $8,990 annual rent and taxes. On the rear of the lot he built a commodious stable. Later this house, on Tilden's recommendation, was purchased by the State as the permanent Governor's Mansion. Meanwhile Tilden withdrew from boards of directors and honorary positions. He could not refuse certain social obligations, such as meeting distinguished visitors to New York—Lord Dufferin, Rt. Hon. W. E. Forster, M.P., Sir Farwell Buxton, and Professor Bonamy Price. He declined all invitations to speak except at the reception tendered him in the Manhattan Club on December 29. In a letter to John Kelly one gets a good picture of Tilden during this period: "In the interminable conferences with public bodies, committees and officers from November 5 to December 25, I did become very weary, and felt some exhaustion of nervous force and much indigestion." [55] Before the election Tilden had promised his support to Kernan for the United States Senatorship but it was not until both Seymour and O'Conor withdrew that Tilden felt easy in his mind over his pledge.[56]

Tilden's third problem, the preparation of his message, seems to have been the least of his worries. Seymour early advised that its keynote must be economy, beginning with the Executive Chamber.[57] The State departments sent data that might be used. Cox warned him not to forget the social problems. Not until the holidays did he take up the composition of the message, but he found it not only rested him but restored his "Physique." [58] Such was the man who was coming to the Governor's chair—tired out by meeting men but rejuvenated in dealing with ideas.

[53] McElroy and McBride, *Governmental Officers*, 15.
[54] Tilden Papers, various dates.   [55] *Letters*, I, 343, Feb. 28, 1875.
[56] Kernan Papers.   [57] *Letters*, I, 344.   [58] Tilden Papers.

NEW YEAR'S DAY, 1875, was set by law for the inauguration of Samuel
Jones Tilden as the "Reform Governor." The newly appointed Governor's staff and crowds of citizens patiently waited on December 31
to welcome him to the Capital. But with characteristic indifference he
slipped into Albany near midnight, recognized by only a few persons,
and took a common hack to his home.

January 1, like election day, was a good omen—clear, sunny and,
although the thermometer stood below zero, "exceptionally beautiful
and pleasant," when nature put on her holiday attire for a "matter of
the greatest importance." The city was full of relatives and friends, and
the hotels and saloons did a flourishing business. The people were bois-
terously joyous and imbued with the carnival spirit. Flags were flying
and the city was decorated. Many members of the legislature were on
hand, although its formal opening came the following week. The Governor's staff had arrived to induct their chief, their glittering uniforms
standing out in shining contrast to the black Prince Alberts and silk
hats worn by State officials and visitors. A stranger in Albany might
have imagined that a war rather than an election had been won.

At 9:30 in the morning the military staff drove from the Delavan
House to the Governor's Mansion, while the Grand Marshal, General
D. M. Woodhall, arranged the military parade. Led by a platoon of
police, it included the 9th Regiment, Klein's Band, the 25th Regiment,
Batteries A and B, Gilmore's Band, Jackson's Corps—all Democrats—
the Governor and his staff in carriages, Sullivan's Band, the 10th Regiment and the Cavalry of the 9th Brigade. From Eagle Street the procession moved up Madison to Dove, down Hudson to South Pearl, down
Orange to Broadway, and up State to the Capitol.

Meanwhile the Assembly Chamber filled with invited guests. At
10:55 Tilden, arm-in-arm with Governor Dix, entered amid wild applause. Turning to his successor, Governor Dix said, "Mr. Tilden: The
people of the State have called you to preside over . . . their government by a majority which manifests the highest confidence in your . . .
attributes of statesmanship." He added that Tilden's municipal reform

gave assurance that the State's interests would be "vigilantly guarded," and redound to "your honor and to the lasting prosperity of the . . . whole State." These were pleasant words from an old friend.

The two men had been for years political associates, intimate friends, and ardent supporters of Silas Wright. Rivals in an acrimonious campaign, they stood this day on the solid ground of mutual respect. Tilden replied, "Governor Dix: It is he who has completed a period of distinguished public service, and, having gathered all its honors, has nothing left to him but to lay down its burdens—it is he who is truly to be congratulated on this occasion." Then he paused in deep reflection, and continued: "I cannot stand in this hall to assume the chief executive trust . . . without my thoughts turning on him [Silas Wright], your friend and mine, and my father's, who held it in early manhood. I came here as an Assemblyman to sustain his administration." The memory choked him and he was unable to continue. In a faint voice he added: "In the interval, how vast and diversified have the interests become which are under the guardianship of the State administration. To build up this great Commonwealth in her polity and institutions until they shall become a greater blessing to all the people . . . is a work far surpassing any object of human ambition." He had hoped to pass the winter "in the cradle of ancient literature and arts." Congratulating his friend on his plans to visit Europe, Tilden revealed a tact and grace on this occasion which won general applause.[1]

To the oath administered by the Secretary of State, he responded in a firm voice, "So help me God," kissed the Bible, and now was the Governor of the Empire State. This was announced to the citizens of Albany by the firing of a salute of 21 guns. The Governor and his staff then proceeded to the Executive Chamber to receive for an hour the many visitors who wished to shake his hand. Meantime at the Executive Mansion Mrs. Pelton, his sister, who was to manage his household, and Miss Dickerson, Miss Adelaide Tilden, Miss Susie Tilden, and other relatives gave a cordial welcome to all guests who called during the early afternoon and evening.

"A distinguished representative and exponent of the Liberal-Conservative spirit enters upon the discharge of his duties," remarked the *Argus* in an editorial. Taking a wider geographical survey, it added: "As the result of the Revolution . . . the control of a majority of the States

[1] *Life* I, 239.

passes today into the hands of the Democracy." [2] The next day Governor Tilden remained at home to rest and to add last-minute corrections to his message to the legislature.

The legislature met on January 3, 1875, with the Republicans in control of the Senate and the Democrats of the Assembly. Jeremiah McGuire was elected Speaker, but not as Tilden's choice, and soon allied himself with Tammany and the Canal Ring. Thwarted by Tilden in attempting to play Santa Claus in building the Elmira Reformatory, he became vindictive and publicly denounced the Governor.[3] Lieutenant Governor Dorsheimer presided over the Senate and helped to offset the influence of Republican obstructionists such as Jarvis Lord and John Ganson.

Governor Tilden, as a reformer, knew that he had behind him an awakened public opinion and a friendly press. Every student of public affairs realized that he brought to his position a long training in professional politics, an expertness in public finance, an understanding of men, and a reputation for successful reform which had seldom been combined in the Governor of the State. He knew all the issues before the Commonwealth and the nation, and had positive convictions concerning their solution. For nearly half a century he had been identified with party politics and had been in touch with most of the statesmen of note. Intellectually, morally, and temperamentally he was qualified to make an exceptionably able Governor, but he thought so far ahead of his contemporaries that at times they were unable to comprehend his next move.

Tilden was so unpredictable that friend and foe awaited his message with concern. Seymour advised him to make it short—advice which Tilden always found it difficult to follow—and, anxious that the canal question be handled wisely, suggested a brief mention, to be followed later by a whole message on it.[4] O'Conor, fearful lest Tilden grow lukewarm as a reformer, reminded him that he must sustain "the revolutionary reform that made you Governor," and remember that "our friends" are the country's bitterest enemies.[5] Elected as a reformer, what recommendations would he make in his first public announcement? Would he be rash or discreet?

The message, prepared rather hastily, was listened to with profound

[2] *Argus*, Jan. 2, 1875.   [3] Buckman, *Tilden Unmasked*, 76; *Times*, Dec. 6, 1875.
[4] *Writings*, I, 23; Lincoln, *Messages*, VI, 719.   [5] Tilden Papers.

interest by the legislature and visitors. It was a masterful state paper written not only for the people of New York but for "our sister States" as well, because all were involved in "the benefits of an improved polity, of wise legislation, and of good administration." For this audience, Tilden reviewed first the problems of the State and then of the Federal Government in a document that contributed materially to his reputation as a reformer-statesman.

Tilden asked for appropriations to take the State Census, to study the poor laws and to send a commission to the Centennial at Philadelphia. Out of his extensive experience with the Tweed Ring, he declared that "the . . . most imperative of our duties" was to revise the laws so as "to provide criminal punishment and civil remedies for frauds by public officers." After the theft of millions of public money, the culprits went unpunished because the power to institute suits for redress against local corruptionists was in the hands of officials who themselves were in complicity with the wrongdoers. Tilden wished to transfer this authority to the Attorney General. The denial of genuine home rule to New York City, in the name of reform, was responsible for the frauds. Hence municipal independence with official accountability was the wisest solution of a problem that disturbed "all civilized people" and was "worthy of long-continued study" to reach "a safe and wise result."

Having in mind a later message dealing with the Canal Ring, Tilden merely remarked that the State, regarding the canals as a trust, was bound to protect them from spoliation and maladministration. He recommended a special commission of four to investigate and report on the whole situation. Meanwhile the strictest economy must be observed.

The final third of the message discussed the financial policy of the United States, because New York received 70% of national imports and 50% of all exports. Instead of financing the Civil War by compulsory circulation of irredeemable paper money, the Federal Government should have paid out treasury notes and redeemed them from loans and taxes with an ample sinking fund to meet its bonds. Under this plan the war would not have cost half what it did. Funds for resumption in gold and silver should be obtained from loans, taxes and the reduction of expenditures; and the time to begin was merely a matter of practical statesmanship.[6]

This penetrating analysis of Federal finance, followed by his sanction

[6] *Writings*, II, 23-74.

of the Thirteenth, Fourteenth and Fifteenth Amendments, and the injunction to "our Southern brethren" to rally "under the old flag with 'one Constitution and one destiny' " led many to think that Tilden had his eye on Washington in 1876. In a closing plea "to discard all memories of buried strifes," he urged all to join in building anew "the solid foundations of American government." The message revealed an "enlarged statesmanship," according to the Albany *Argus*.[7] Throughout the nation the press generally commented on it favorably as "an able State paper."[8] Individual praise included such phrases as: "Hurrah for your message"; "Wise and able"; "A sensible, straightforward message"; and "A businesslike document."

A considerable portion of the message dealt with municipal reform as one of his major objectives. This was no idle gesture but a purpose which he had steadily pursued for five years, and its consummation might be attained, he thought, first by continuing legal action against Tweed and other coadjutors in thievery; and second by obtaining legislation with teeth in it to correct the defects in municipal law.

O'Conor, ably assisted by Peckham, Barlow and Carter, was still directing the suits against the Ring peculators both at home and in Europe.[9] When Tweed's able lawyers secured his release during the same month in which Tilden was inaugurated, O'Conor rearrested him on a civil charge, in obedience to Tilden's order. The State's suits against the Ring leaders were now slowed down by conditions in New York City. Mayor Wickham, anxious to build up his own political machine, forgot about disagreeable reforms and co-operated less and less with O'Conor. To make matters worse E. Delafield Smith, an accommodating Republican, who had held the office of Corporation Counsel since 1871, now took the ground that the suits authorized by Attorney General Barlow in the name of the people were invalid—they could be instituted only by the City and County of New York. Consequently he treated O'Conor as if he had resigned and actually dismissed Peckham, Barlow and Carter and appointed Porter and Curtis to recover the stolen moneys.[10]

Then followed a movement to drive Smith and A. H. Green, the Comptroller, from office. Wickham encouraged these efforts because if they were successful he would control the patronage of both positions. O'Conor, not averse to the dismissal of Smith, strenuously opposed

[7] Jan. 6, 1875.
[9] Tilden Papers, O'Conor to Tilden, June 9, 1875.
[8] *Nation*, Jan. 14, 1875.
[10] *Life*, I, 243, Jan. 4, 1875.

the removal of Green, but he wanted the law department in honest hands and feared that the Mayor's appointee would be worse than Smith.[11] When Wickham removed Smith for failing to prosecute the claims against Tweed, Governor Tilden, at O'Conor's request, insisted that under the Charter he had the right to give his approval before the removal became valid.[12] In the end O'Conor himself drew up the charges on which Smith was dismissed and replaced by young William C. Whitney.[13] As for Comptroller Green, O'Conor suggested that he voluntarily resign "with flying colors," [14] but Governor Tilden stood squarely back of his old friend who served out his term. The newspapers hostile to Green then turned their guns on Tilden and taunted him with being false to his vaunted home rule principle.[15]

After these flurries, the Tweed cases dragged along through the year 1875 into 1876. The Watson estate settled for a sum over $590,000 and Elbert A. Woodwards offered to pay $175,000 for the "unconditional surrender of Tweed." [16] Tilden was severely criticized for pardoning "about nine out of ten men who were confessedly guilty" in order to use them as witnesses against Tweed, but the people generally applauded his management of a perplexing problem. He co-operated as much as possible with O'Conor and Peckham in the Ring suits and at the same time engineered through the legislature the following laws necessary to remove obstacles to an adequate punishment of official corruption:

1. The Act of February 17, 1875, made it a felony punishable by prison or a fine wrongfully to receive or to pay out public money, or wilfully to pay a false claim. The transfer of a bank deposit was deemed a "conversion." A jury might state the amount of the loss by fraud. If a trial showed the accused guilty of other crimes, he might be prosecuted for them.

2. The Act of March 12, 1875, authorized the people, through the Attorney General, to recover stolen public property by bringing suits within ten years in other States or in foreign countries to which the thieves might have taken their stealings.

3. The Act of May 20, 1875, enabled the Governor to suspend a State official during investigation and to direct the Attorney General to conduct a trial. If found guilty of misconduct, he could be removed with

[11] Life; I, 243, Jan. 4, 1875.   [12] Writings, II, 85, Feb. 3, 1875, 86, Feb. 5, 1875.
[13] Letters, I, 385, Aug. 9, 1875.   [14] Foord, Green, 154, 160.   [15] Tilden Papers.
[16] New York in Bondage, 141.

the concurrence of a majority of the Senate.

4. The Act of May 21, 1875, made provision for the payment of non-resident justices called to act in New York City in the First Judicial District.[17]

The enactment of these laws and the prosecution of the suits under them against the Tweed Ring constituted one of the two outstanding accomplishments of Governor Tilden's administration. He himself declared that these measures "providing judicial remedies against frauds affecting the public moneys or property" were of more value in "repressing the evils of municipal government than all the laws of the past twenty-nine years, in which the Constitution . . . has remained unchanged." [18]

That municipal reformation, to be thorough-going, must be founded on the Constitution and State statutes, Tilden had always maintained. Hence he sent a special message to the legislature on May 11 reviewing the history of local government after 1846 and describing existing conditions in 1875. The magnitude of the problem, he pointed out, was shown by the fact that the State had an aggregate value of $1,570,000,-000, raised $36,439,000 in taxes, and had a debt of $175,657,000. In contrast the people outside the cities paid a total of only one-third of the cities' taxes. This burden of city taxation was grave because it was due in part to fraud and mismanagement.[19] Hence he recommended the appointment of a commission to study the problem of city government and to report on a "general system" in 1876.[20] The legislature authorized him to name a bipartisan commission of not more than twelve persons. In dealing with an issue as important as this, Governor Tilden took particular pains to select men of sound character and recognized ability. He invited the well-known publicist, President Anderson of Rochester University, to head the commission. When Dr. Anderson declined to serve, Tilden named William M. Evarts as chairman. Other members were: Oswald Ottendorfer, W. A. Butler, J. C. Carter, Judge Lott, E. L. Godkin, Simon Sterne, Joshua Van Cott, Edward Cooper and Samuel Hand. The solution of the problem proved to be a more difficult one than had been anticipated, and in consequence their report on a reformed local government was delayed until 1877 when it was made in

[17] Laws of N.Y., 1875, Chs. 19, 49, 471, 491.
[18] Life, I, 250, note 2; Writings, II, 122, gives Message.
[19] Writings II, 120; Lincoln, Messages, VI, 825, 1024.
[20] Writings, II, 134; Lincoln, Messages, VI, 825, 844, 951.

the form of a constitutional amendment giving taxpayers the right to elect the board of audit.[21] This amendment giving the taxpayers only a more direct control over the purse was not submitted to the people, on the ground that it was an attempt to restrict suffrage,[22] as indeed it was. The report of the commission might be praised by James Bryce, but it was never popular in New York State, because it was regarded as an undemocratic and a backward step.[23]

One of the men who stood staunchly behind Governor Tilden in his reform of municipal government was Honest John Kelly of Tammany. Their relations were friendly if not intimate and Kelly was a guest at Tilden's home. Not infrequently in company with such men as Seymour and Kernan he called on the Governor.[24] Kelly's suggestions were not unwelcome and were often followed. For instance, in the appointment of a new Corporation Counsel to replace E. Delafield Smith, Kelly recommended Whitney, "an honest, high-toned gentleman, who will co-operate with you and do credit to himself." In the prosecution of the Tweed cases Kelly's advice was valuable and encouraging. Some of the longest and most confidential letters, which Governor Tilden wrote were to this Tammany boss, and it must have been gratifying to read, "Ring frauds will immortalize yourself, O'Conor etc." They had a cordial understanding about party matters and patronage. It was to Kelly that Tilden unbosomed himself about appointments and rumors of his "softening of the brain," "stroke," and excessive drinking. And to Tilden Kelly wrote: "May God spare you . . . until you have finished your tasks. Most men would have become disheartened at the many repulses." [25]

Since Civil War days Tilden's political philosophy and high party standards had made a deep impression on Cyrus H. McCormick who lauded his reformatory efforts and sent him in 1875 a copy of the Chicago *Courier* with an article on the "Jeffersonians." [26] Tilden approved of the name of the society, which "expresses in a single word what the country now needs. *That is a revival of Jeffersonian Democracy,* which for half a century formed the golden era of the Republic. . . . The regeneration will be in part a restoration of the reform ideas, systems and practices of Jefferson. I am glad to see you engaged in so noble a work." [27]

---

[21] *Life*, I, 266; Lincoln, *Messages*, VII, 134.   [22] Chester, *Courts and Lawyers*, II, 725.
[23] Doughtery, *Const. Hist.*, 270.   [24] Tilden Papers.
[25] *Letters*, I, 374, 376, Apr. 9, 1875; 343, 369.   [26] Casson, *Cyrus H. McCormick*, 77.
[27] McCormick Papers, July 25, 1875.

At the Hebrew Charity Fair Tilden made a felicitous address revealing his tolerant and sympathetic spirit. "It is now two hundred and twenty years," he said, "since the first little colony of your race and religion planted itself in New York City." Now there are seventy thousand in the city, all useful citizens, with high standards of "domestic and social morality," with respect for parents who take an interest in the education of their children, and with high personal virtues. He spoke of the persecution of their race, and referred to the generous treatment they received in England.[28]

On one occasion Governor Tilden went to New York City to inspect the National Guard. There he was accompanied by his military staff on horseback, few of whom were good riders. Tilden started up the street at a stiff pace, with his staff following. Soon some of the gaudily uniformed dignitaries, unaccustomed to such speed, fell off; others had their horses run away and were badly shaken up. Tilden arrived at the scene of the review with only a fraction of his staff. Riding easily and well himself, he set the pace purposely and greatly enjoyed the joke. He really had a keen sense of humor.[29] For winter riding and driving he had an expensive sealskin suit made, which resulted in the epithet "Sealskin Sammy." [30]

The first part of Governor Tilden's term was on the whole satisfactory. That he was on amicable terms with the legislature is shown by the fact that of the measures passed, 420 were signed and only 16 vetoed during the session. After adjournment of the legislature 212 bills were signed, 2 became law by lapse of time, and 38 were left unsigned. At the same time many individual items in the money bills were disapproved. The most important vetoes had to do with police justices and rapid transit railroads for New York City. From Tilden's point of view the principal laws secured were those having to do with a cleaner judicial system and a better form of city government. Governor Tilden entered upon his duties as a champion of civic reform under favorable circumstances. Crediting him with having cleaned up the Tweed gang, the people seated him at Albany. His political foes were silent and sullen, awaiting an opportunity for revenge. His message had flung down the gauntlet of combat to political grafters, and the shortcomings of

---

[28] *Writings*, II, 235, Dec. 7, 1875.
[29] Interview with Harry J. Cox of New Lebanon.
[30] Interview with Col. William Gorham Rice.

Grant's administration turned the eyes of forward-looking citizens to the new Moses in New York. Governor Tilden was fully conscious of this state of mind and charted his course for the remainder of his term accordingly.

GOVERNOR TILDEN's second major reform was the overthrow of the Canal Ring, composed of members of both parties who accumulated fortunes through fraudulent bills for repairing the canals. Co-operating with the Ring were "political parasites" forming a group of State officials, legislators, local officers, lawyers and judges who helped to have the inflated bills paid, passed laws favorable to dishonest contractors, and protected them in the courts. The small inner Ring consisted of Denison and Belden of Syracuse, the Lords of Rochester, Johnson of Fulton, and a few others. "Doc" H. D. Denison had served on the Democratic State Committee and was a hail-fellow-well-met who knew how to grease the palms of venal party colleagues. James J. Belden was a successful business man, a foe of drinking and a Presbyterian deacon. As a Republican, he handled the leaders of his party.[1] It was said that Denison won the Democrats with rum, and Belden the Republicans with unctuous hypocrisy.[2] Senator Jarvis Lord and his son Assemblyman George D. Lord, Republicans, had a host of friends and knew short cuts in getting false bills paid. Willard Johnson sat in the Assembly.[3]

These Canal Ring leaders made stealing from the State a business, pooled their interests and divided the spoils. Their dupes and tools in the outer group profited from sub-contracts, financial favors, legal fees, and appointments to office. The two groups combined in 1874 to oppose Tilden's nomination for Governor because they feared his sharp reform ax. For years he had known of their thievery and had felt their political power. He had no delusions about the difficulty of exposing and punishing them, because their dishonest dealings were hidden and the evidence destroyed.[4]

Knowing that it was necessary to have positive proof of guilt, Tilden quietly assembled evidence which would enable him to speak out boldly. In his message there were only indirect references to the Canal Ring. The passage of several months without action encouraged the Ring to send their friends to patronize the Governor. With suave compliments they told him how strong he was upstate and that he must not "weaken

[1] *Life*, I, 258.   [2] Cook, 183.   [3] *Civil List*, 1888, 414; *Life*, I, 259.
[4] *Life*, I, 258.

the party" in that region. But he was not deceived and bided his time. Meanwhile a trustworthy engineer, Elkanah Sweet, was employed at Tilden's expense to examine the work on the canals and study the records of the Canal Board to ascertain whether the contracts had been faithfully executed.[5] He investigated repairs for the previous six years, made his estimates, and compared them with the auditor's accounts. The Governor, making Sweet's report the basis of a special message to the legislature, was ready to fire his first shot.[6]

Following Seymour's advice, Tilden delayed his explosion until March 19, meanwhile going in person to the auditor's office to verify facts and figures. This "Canal Message" stated that a large part of the $11,000,000 spent during the past five years for extraordinary repairs had been stolen by the Canal Ring. "Intelligent, energetic, and persistent," the Ring operated through both parties and hoodwinked taxpayers to authorize useless works under the garb of improvements. Even necessary work cost much more than it should.[7]

The Constitution provided that contracts should go to the lowest bidders, but most contracts were artfully drawn to evade this requirement, and the cost exceeded from two to four times the amount of the contract. Bids for excavations varied from one cent to two dollars a cubic yard, hemlock lumber from three to thirty dollars a thousand feet, and oak timber from one to seventy dollars a thousand feet. Thus by tricky combinations bids might seem low but were really exorbitant. Small quantities were bid for at a low price and large quantities at a high price. By collusion contracts were changed to the contractor's profit. Ten contracts which should have cost $425,000 actually cost $1,561,000.[8]

To remedy these evils, Tilden declared, the engineer's report must honestly show the work to be done, and extra contracts must be let separately. The Canal Board's power to open and to reject bids must be enlarged. Canals must be managed like any business. An Inspector of Public Works must be appointed, but not by the Canal Board, and he must report to the legislature and Governor.[9] There should be an independent paymaster.

Tilden's declaration of war against the Ring created a sensation, for

[5] *Writings*, II, 97, 95; *Life*, I, 260.   [6] *Letters*, II, 406.
[7] *Ib.*, 357; *Writings*, II, 97; Lincoln, *Messages*, VI, 788.
[8] *Writings*, II, 105, 108.
[9] This office was created Apr. 30, 1875, *Laws of N.Y.*, 1875, Ch. 227.

the people knew that they had been paying it tribute. For the first time he made it clear how the stealing was done and dared to confront the thieves with their crimes. He became overnight a moral hero. Although representatives of the Ring were members of the legislature, they dared not vote against a concurrent resolution authorizing the Governor to appoint a Commission of Investigation.[10] Early in April he announced John Bigelow and Alexander E. Orr as the Republican members and Daniel Magone and J. D. Van Buren, Jr., Democrats. The commission was given power to subpoena witnesses for secret examination, to employ experts, and to use $30,000 appropriated for its work.[11] The first session was held on April 12 and Bigelow was made chairman.[12]

The Ring's friends at Albany sought to overshadow Tilden's commission by creating a Legislative Commission of Investigation, consisting of three Senators and six Assemblymen, empowered to employ counsel and to send for witnesses.[13] It met a few times and then sought to make the entire investigation abortive by inducing the Governor to combine the two boards. The plot was promptly exposed, however, and thereafter the legislative commission scarcely made a pretense of tackling the problem. On the other hand, the Governor's commission went to work in dead earnest.[14] Meanwhile, the legislature did little to aid the Governor in the overthrow of the corruptionists. On the contrary, special bills were passed for local canal improvements to favor the dishonest contractors, but these measures were speedily vetoed.

Meanwhile reverberations of the attack on the Ring came from all parts of the nation. Newspapers generally supported Tilden.[15] The Rochester *Chronicle* said that he weighed only 130 pounds, but that the Ring entertained the view of him that the boy did of the mule. Asked how much the mule weighed, he replied, "Well, I only weighed one of his hind legs and I calculate that weighed seven thousand pounds." The New York Chamber of Commerce praised his "bold and masterly exposure of the enormous frauds." [16] John Kelly advised, "Pursue the good work you have commenced, no matter where the rod will fall, either on friend or foe." [17] Civic bodies generally approved the reforms.[18] Thus encouraged, Tilden pressed the suits against the culprits and had

---

[10] *Laws of N.Y.*, 1875, 823.
[11] *Laws of N.Y.*, 1875, Chs. 91 and 634; *Letters*, II, 406.
[12] *An Cyc.*, 1875, 558.   [13] *Life*, I, 262.   [14] *Writings*, II, 296.
[15] *Nation*, Apr. 1, 1875.
[16] Bishop, *Chronicle of One Hundred and Fifty Years*, 185.
[17] *Letters*, I, 365, 367.   [18] Tilden Papers.

them squirming most uncomfortably. After the legislature adjourned, May 23, he hurried away for a rest—"disabled by boils so that I could not sit down." [19] Manning of the *Argus* wrote that since his departure Albany was "extremely slow and stupid," but he was "numerously remembered and, no doubt, prayed for. . . . The malcontents are restless, vituperative, mischievous and cowardly . . . they . . . make faces and tell what they intend to do at the next State convention. . . . Return to Albany as soon as you can." [20]

In the midst of these labors an agreeable surprise came to Tilden in the form of an honorary LL.D. from Yale University. He was informed that the President and Fellows had conferred this distinction on him at the "recent public commencement" and had enrolled him in the class of 1837 as an alumnus, in recognition of "the eminent public services which you have so abundantly deserved." [21]

While Tilden's commission was investigating the peculations of the canal contractors, he decided to make a tour of the upstate canal counties and thus carry the battle to his enemies. He left Albany on August 8 for Buffalo [22] where, at the home of Lieutenant Governor Dorsheimer, prominent citizens and a German delegation called to pay their respects. The Union Cornet Band and the Germans serenaded him at ten o'clock that night. Introduced by the Mayor, he thanked his German friends for their "almost unanimous support" at the polls.[23] He also appeared before the Board of Trade to discuss the canal problem.

The Governor left Buffalo by special train for Rochester, where he visited the Western House of Refuge and spoke to 412 boys. At the Osborn House he was greeted by prominent citizens.[24] Since no opportunity was given to discuss canal reforms, O'Conor wanted to know why Tilden did not "touch them up. . . . Is there a strong peculation group there? 'Begad, I begin soospec,' as the Frenchman said when he caught a man in bed with his wife." [25] In the afternoon he left for Syracuse where a large crowd escorted him to the Empire House, while cannon thundered forth a welcome.[26] After dining he said to the waiting throng that here in the center of the Canal Ring he was "glad to see that . . . reform . . . is awakening a deep interest. . . . Under your own eyes" frauds "have been carried on in open day by a combination that sought

19 *Letters*, I, 372, 383.
21 *Ib.*, 384, July 5, 1785.
23 Buffalo *Express*, Aug. 10, 1875.
25 *Letters*, II, 385.

20 *Letters*, I, 382, June 20, 1875.
22 *Writings*, II, 213.
24 *Writings*, II, 219, Aug. 11, 1875.
26 Syracuse *Standard*, Aug. 12, 1875.

to rule the State." He promised to protect the people's rights and to "punish those who have violated them." They had been told that this reform effort would fail and that "these great, rich and powerful culprits . . . would escape punishments for their crimes." But the cause would not fail. "With malice toward none, with charity for all," he said, "the work of reform must and shall go forward." [27]

Tilden then went to Utica where he dined with Senator Kernan. In the evening he was serenaded at his hotel and introduced by the Senator to a large audience. "I feel tonight," he said, "like a Grecian in the age of Demosthenes speaking to the Athenians." Our State, "first in the sisterhood of American Commonwealths," was setting an example for others. Through economy and reform, taxes had been reduced and a surplus left in the treasury. If honest men were sent to the legislature, there would be further reductions. "I am not of those who accept men who shelter under the Democratic flag . . . while they plunder the people." He favored everything for the public good and meant to "crush the spoilers of the State treasury." [28]

On his return to Albany he was given an ovation at each station and made brief addresses along the way. On reaching the Capital, he was escorted to the Assembly Chamber where ex-Mayor Lansing presented him to a throng of citizens whom he thanked for their approbation of his measures. This speaking tour was obviously for two purposes—to open "the anti-peculation campaign," and to launch a drive for party victory at the coming fall election. "Your speeches made the welkin ring," wrote O'Conor.[29]

So much had been accomplished that, when the autumn fairs opened, Tilden appeared on the platform in Elmira and Central New York. As the fall nomination conventions met, the Canal Ring was in a fighting mood to control the legislature and thus block the reform work. The Republican leaders felt, however, that they must divide the honors with the Governor in the reform crusade and yet charge him with insincerity and trickery. So at the Saratoga Republican State Convention on September 8, G. W. Curtis, chairman, induced that body to promise cooperation in the "correction of public abuses." Good men were sought for the ticket and the comptrollership was offered to John Bigelow, but he curtly declined it. A strong ticket headed by Frederick W. Seward as

---

[27] Cook, 213.   [28] *Writings*, II, 224.
[29] *Letters*, I, 384, Aug. 12, 1875.

Secretary of State was named.[30]

The Democratic State Convention was held on September 15–16 at Syracuse, with Judge Hezekiah Sturges in the chair. An anti-Tammany group headed by John Morrissey was refused seats. The national platform of 1872 and the State program of 1874 were approved. Governor Tilden's work was commended—honesty in public works and economy in expenditures. Liberal Republicans were invited to co-operate in reforming the State Government. John Bigelow was named for Secretary of State, Lucius Robinson for Comptroller, Charles S. Fairchild for Attorney General, Charles N. Ross for Treasurer, J. D. Van Buren, Jr., for Engineer, C. A. Walrath for Canal Commissioner, and R. R. Crowley for Inspector of State Prisons.[31] Considering the names on this ticket, there can be no doubt that Tilden dictated the entire slate and thus revealed his customary shrewdness in estimating men. Daniel Magone was chosen Chairman of the Democratic State Committee.[32]

The Liberal Republicans at Albany on September 22 gave hearty endorsement to Tilden's administration.[33] With the State tickets selected, Tilden continued his speaking tours by appearing at the fairs in Washington and Columbia Counties. For the latter he came up from New York City with a valet and a bundle of books. In addressing the three thousand people he mentioned his birth at New Lebanon, the associations of his youth, and his "first lessons" in patriotism. He boasted of descent from "a race of farmers," the governing class in the early days, and declared that "free institutions, government of the people, by the people, for the people, depends more largely upon the farming class than upon any other." The potato bug killed their crops, "But there is a bug far worse—and that is the tax-collector." Far too much of the earnings of society was consumed by government. There should be a stricter economy. If they elected the right man as their representative at Albany, the tax could be cut 50% in two years. Regardless of party they should unite to abolish peculation, to enforce frugality, and to preserve clean government.[34] After his address he was driven to New Lebanon, where a banquet was tendered him.

Governor Tilden then rushed to Utica to address the Central New

[30] Alexander, III, 325; Cook, 219; *An. Cyc.*, 1875, 562.
[31] *Ib.*, 326; *An. Cyc.*, 1875, 562.   [32] Cook, 219.
[33] *An. Cyc.*, 1875, 563; "Tilden has, as he desires to have, the lead of his own party and . . . of the Republicans." Elliott, *Uncle Sam Ward*, 557.
[34] *Writings*, II, 229.

York Annual Fair on September 30. Seymour, Kernan and an escort of troops conducted him to the grounds, where he addressed "fully twenty-five thousand persons." Unable to compete with "the illustrious dairy-man of Deerfield" or with the "ornate oratory of Roscoe Conkling," yet he begged to be heard as one who had a long ancestral line of tillers of the soil who "never submitted to arbitrary power." He grew up among farmers and he wished to speak to them about their own interests. Taxes, the fundamental issue, had increased five fold from 1860 to 1870 and now averaged about $700,000,000 a year—far too vast a sum to pay for government. Hence he asked all, regardless of party, to join in the demand for retrenchment. The farmers of the State could control the results if they would. The evils of corrupt government not only enriched the dishonest but also sapped public morality and if not checked would destroy the Republic.[35]

While in Utica Governor Tilden was a guest of Senator Kernan. The Senator's son, a lad of nine, without knowing that Tilden was occupying the spare room in his father's house, rushed into the room in the morning expecting to see his mother. Instead he saw a strange man, with a night-cap on his head and wearing a nightshirt that came only to his knees, just swinging his legs over the side of the bed. "In my surprise," he said, "and frightened, I rushed out of the room thinking that I had never seen a man with such thin legs." [36]

The Republicans made the campaign one of villification. Tilden's war record was held up to public gaze; his part in the National Democratic Convention of 1864 was denounced; his financial operations were slyly intimated to be crooked; his relations with Tweed in the earlier days were brought to light; his efforts to reform the management of the canals were minimized; and his slowness in joining the reform crusade for municipal government was pointed to as evidence of his dubious sin-cerity. He accepted the challenge and took the stump to carry the issue to the people. From one end of the State to the other he spoke to huge meetings, presenting facts which the farmer and the workingman could understand. The *Nation* explained:

"Tilden achieved his present success owing to his having, before anybody else of his class, understood the exact nature of the situation. He perceived sooner than his competitors that the time had come to stop preaching and

[35] *Writings,* II, 228; Cook, 214.
[36] Interview with Walter N. Kernan, Jan. 22, 1935.

to begin making arrests and drawing up indictments. He now finds, and his competitors find, that his acuteness has rendered him the highest service, and his enemies actually play into his hands." [37]

Roscoe Conkling, Seymour's brother-in-law, was in Europe during the summer of 1875 and hence did not attend the Republican State Convention.[38] Upon his return the activity of Tilden forced him to appear in Albany on October 13 and to take an active part in the remainder of the campaign. He admitted that reform was the dominant issue and thanked Tilden for the little he had done in that direction. But Bigelow came in for a severe drubbing for taking a place on the Canal Commission as a Republican and on the State ticket as a Democrat. The rift in New York City between Kelly and Morrissey almost lost Tammany the election, because the latter had the support of the Republicans. Indeed, to Kelly's discomfiture, Morrissey was sent to the State Senate from the old Tweed district. But in general the election left Tilden on the housetop while Conkling sat on the cellar steps.[39]

Governor Tilden was too wily a politician not to make use of his strongest weapon against his foes. The findings of the Canal Investigation Commission were not made public until they could be capitalized as political thunder. The members had taken off their coats immediately after assuming office. Their tremendous task was accomplished slowly, but Tilden was apprised of their discoveries—though only hints were given to the public—in a way which enabled him to formulate his campaign. The first report of the commission was submitted July 13, 1875, just a week before he started on his speaking tour in the canal counties. In all, the commission made twelve partial reports, the first in time to influence the election, and the last during the following winter.

Having discovered by November, 1875, that members of the Canal Board were guilty of misconduct, Tilden was disposed to suspend them from office, but Seymour advised that they be permitted to serve out their terms, ending January 1, 1876, because there would not be time for a full trial and the report of the commission would "of itself be a severe punishment for official wrongs." [40] This counsel Tilden followed. The commission made its full report on February 14, 1876, but continued to work till May. Efforts by the Ring to delay the investigation proved futile. The testimony, covering 3,000 pages, showed that the canal system

[37] Oct. 7, 1875.
[39] Alexander, III, 331.
[38] Conkling, *Life of Conkling*, 490.
[40] Tilden Papers, Nov. 13, 1875.

cost $28,500,000 more than it earned, and that the loss for the previous year was $650,000 or $1,500,000 if interest on the canal debt were added. The huge cost for repairs was due largely to frauds. The names of corrupt contractors and of accommodating State officials were given, together with concrete instances of dishonesty. The remedies proposed were to center responsibility, to remove offenders, and to pass laws to punish abuses.[41] After receiving this report Governor Tilden, on March 24, 1876, sent a second special message to the legislature reviewing the financial aspects of the canal system and recommending $400,000 to complete repairs and a like amount to deepen the Erie Canal to seven feet. He asked that the Canal Board be given power to redress all dishonesty; and that an appropriation be made to enable the State to punish corrupt contractors and guilty officials.[42]

As a result of this exposure, George D. Lord was indicted for bribery; T. C. Davis, a canal appraiser, for cheating; Alexander Barclay, for complicity; a number of canal employees, for corruption and dishonesty; and others were arrested. All but two of these men were Democrats. The frauds stopped, the service improved, and economies effected saved millions. The people gave Governor Tilden credit for his herculean task. In the fall election of 1875 his whole reform ticket was elected, but his personal and political enemies still controlled the legislature.[43] The political power of the Canal Ring was broken.

While Tilden was bending all his energy toward municipal reform and the elimination of the Canal Ring, he had to give attention to his health, never too robust. Fortunately he was constitutionally endowed to "concentrate on what seems of first importance, and defer with almost contemptuous indifference what can as well or better wait. This is the habit which had given me success in business and in the conduct of parties." [44] Defeated in the election "a small coterie of rogues" by "whispers" first circulated the rumor "that I had a softening of the brain; next that I had suffered a stroke; . . . then that I went to bed drunk every night; and at last . . . that I had lost my snap"—was unable to make removals or appointment, or "to make up my mind about anything." [45] To a Democratic friend Thurlow Weed said: "Did you know that Tilden had broken down? Yes, broken down deplorably; his mind all gone. His friends are in consternation. He drinks, they say

41 *Letters*, II, 407–428.   42 *Writing*, II, 301; Lincoln, *Messages*, VI, 991.
43 *An. Cyc.*, 1875, 564.   44 *Letters*, 344, 387.   45 *Ib.*, 343.

dreadfully, and neglects his business." [46]

Tilden's friends were not much alarmed by the report. A. S. Hewitt wrote him, "If your brain keeps on softening for a few months longer, I think you will arrive at a development which will leave no doubt in the public mind as to your entire fitness for a much higher position than you now fill." About a month later Bigelow said: "I have not heard much lately about the softening of your brain, but there are some inquiries for the kind of tipple you are partial to. The Tilden brand is just now rather the favorite." [47]

Tilden was no longer a young man. He was in his sixty-second year, slight of build, and his hair was turning gray. He rode horseback a good deal and enjoyed driving his spirited team of thoroughbreds, but otherwise paid little attention to exercise. He was exceedingly intemperate in work and performed feats that would prostrate a strong man. Bigelow remarked that he never met a man of Tilden's age with "a feebler comprehension of human physiology, or of the elementary laws of health." During his first winter in Albany he almost worked himself to death and exhibited the pale face, lusterless eyes, expressionless features and exhausted air "of a man pining in vain for sleep." Since admission to the bar he had been "an intemperate tea-bibber" and always resumed work immediately after leaving the table. Even while he was eating, the table was piled with papers; and visitors or secretaries constantly interrupted him. When friends remonstrated, he answered, "I can't help it; this work has to be done." There was no use in telling him that he might break down, for he paid no attention to the admonition. [48]

As he labored incessantly, so he saw no good reason why his clerks and other State officials should not work in the same intensive manner. His private secretary always had a bed in Tilden's home so he would be at hand day or night. When one of the assistant counsel of the Tweed suits seemed guilty of delay, Tilden called him to Albany to explain. The attorney said that he could not wholly neglect his private legal practice. "When you accepted this retainer," the Governor exploded, "you said that you would not permit your private business to interfere." The lawyer grumbled that he did not wish to have it reported that he was a man with but one client or one interest. "Sir!" Tilden screamed at him, "a man who is not a monomaniac is not worth a damn!" [49] When

[46] *Life*, I, 285.   [47] *Letters*, I, 351, Feb. 23, 1876; 361.   [48] *Life*, I, 284.
[49] *Ib.*, 285.

petulant or angry, sarcasm fell from his lips in a stream, and his pen could be equally sharp. As a rule, however, his deportment was restrained and dignified.

The four public buildings being erected by the State had to be watched in order to exclude graft. When the Elmira Reformatory building was taken out of the hands of a commissioner and put in charge of an architect, Speaker McGuire, Senator Bradley and Charles Walker, were led into the Governor's office by Steve Arnot, who was half drunk, and the demand made that the architect be turned out instantly to make a place for another man. Tilden's comment was, "I thought the Governor had better not abdicate his functions." [50] In filling vacancies of the State Board of Charities, he took care to satisfy Protestants, Catholics, and Hebrews.

In addition to all these matters, hundreds of letters had to be read and answered—a stream that grew in volume as Tilden was talked of as a candidate for President. Petitions for paroles and pardons had to be studied and answered. Invitations to dinners and other functions, if not accepted, must be handled diplomatically. For instance President Andrew D. White again invited him to the Cornell Commencement and G. W. Schuyler informed Dr. White that the Governor would be his guest. Typical of communications from John Kelly was this telegram: "Do not sign Assembly Bill . . . until I see you. I will be up." To refinance the *World,* Marble was loaned $45,000.[51] President Dickinson of the Delaware & Hudson Railroad insisted upon his presence to help open that line to Montreal.[52] He had to sit for his portrait; to appear before the Erie Investigation Committee to deny that he had received a fee of $20,000 from that road but to admit that he did accept $10,000 from the Cleveland & Pittsburgh Railroad for services.[53]

Governor Tilden's connection with the New York Elevated Railroad Company was made the occasion of criticism. A group of promoters, among them David Dows, who claimed to be a "leading Republican," won over a majority of the directors of the Greenwich Street Elevated Railroad in October 1869, reorganized the road as the New York Elevated Railroad Company and asked the legislature to sanction the transfer, but were defeated in 1872–73. The next year, by buying up votes, they got the bill through, but Governor Dix vetoed it. The "Dows

[50] *Letters,* I, 345.   [51] Tilden Papers.
[52] L. F. Loree, *A Century of Progress,* 253.   [53] Tilden Papers, Mar. 3, 1876.

Ring" in 1875 renewed their application to the legislature and had it passed. The defrauded stockholders of the early company and property owners who thought the road would injure their holdings begged Tilden to veto the bill, because it was unconstitutional and had been passed by bribery. Tilden acknowledged its unconstitutionality but signed it, on O'Conor's advice,[54] as a favor to Dows, who agreed to sustain its legality in the courts. There was a great public outcry against the act. The *World* on July 10 asserted that 65 votes had been bought in the Assembly at $100 each, and a lobbyist had been paid $10,000. The *Tribune* said there was reason for believing that the $10,000 had been spent on the Republican Senate. Tilden's compensation, it was alleged, was that David Dows prevented Orr from resigning from the Canal Investigation Commission as he threatened to do in October, 1875, and that Dows also gave public support to Governor Tilden's reform program.[55]

Governor Tilden enjoyed having as guests friends of his youth, such as Bigelow and Bryant, with whom he kept in close touch. A few weeks after his inauguration, he invited Bryant and his family to spend a week at the Governor's Mansion. A lifelong friendship existed between these two strong men; Tilden was a frequent guest in Bryant's city home and at his summer house on Long Island. Each sincerely appreciated the elements of greatness in the other and recognized the right to differences of opinion on the issues of the day. Tilden found it a relief to get his mind off politics long enough to discuss literature, history, and personal matters with his charming, well-informed visitor. Bryant found at the Governor's Mansion "a large household of nephews and nieces." [56] The legislature also received Bryant—an honor seldom paid to a literary man. Bryant was consulting Tilden about his will when the latter was called to Albany as Governor.[57] Indeed he leaned heavily on Tilden for all sorts of business advice.[58]

The bill signed by Tilden granting the Sisterhood of Gray Nuns the right to confer on graduates diplomas permitting them to teach in the common schools after filing their diplomas with the Superintendent of Public Instruction, created an uproar.[59] Religious newspapers as well as the secular press took up the discussion. The New York *Observer* recited the history of the measure and demanded its repeal. Ministers

[54] Tilden Papers, July 12, 1875.
[55] Buckman, B. E., *Samuel J. Tilden Unmasked, 1876*, 90–97.
[56] Godwin, *Bryant*, II, 362.　　[57] *Life*, I, 301.　　[58] *Letters*, I, 378.
[59] *Laws of New York*, 1875, Ch. 353, May 15, 1875.

denounced it from their pulpits. In its defense it was said that the Superintendent of Public Instruction could admit these graduates as teachers "only on examination," and that he had recognized the law as valid. "A Democrat but not a Catholic" warned Tilden, "The Gray Nun Act . . . signed by you is killing the Democratic Party in Albany." [60]

Methodist synods appointed committees to persuade the legislature to repeal the act. Dr. Howard Crosby, Chancellor of New York University, Tilden's own college, publicly pointed out the danger of "putting into the hands of those outside our educational matters the power to appoint teachers in our public schools, without being restricted by the requirements of the Department of Public Instruction." Baptists and Presbyterians also took action against the law.[61] The *Evening Post* thought that "the next Legislature ought to repeal it at once," and the *Tribune* declared, "This act is inexcusable." [62] In his message to the legislature on January 4, 1876, Tilden sought to throw the blame for the act on the legislature and explained that a later law of June 9, 1875, had removed all discretionary power of the State Superintendent.[63] Nast's cartoons ridiculed the law and *Harper's Weekly* criticized the Governor for not vetoing it as unconstitutional.[64] Tilden considered the law valid but left no opinion about its wisdom. This concession to Catholic friends caused him small concern. As a result of Protestant objections, the act was repealed and Tilden signed the repeal. Manton Marble's father was surprised that the Republicans had not made more of the issue.[65]

Tilden devoted the last days of December, 1875, to his second annual message. He conferred with the well-known political economist, David A. Wells, and received information on finance.[66] Wells advised him to "stick to the great principles" and not engage in "economic controversy." The message, communicated on January 4, 1876, to an unfriendly legislature,[67] was eagerly awaited throughout the country. His summary of the investigation of canals and recommendations for improvements did not disappoint his friends. He described the status of the new Capitol, the State humanitarian and penal institutions, and education; but the major portion of the message was devoted to recommendations for a reduction of the State debt and taxes, to a discussion of the causes of the business depression, due to the waste and misman-

[60] Tilden Papers.   [61] *Sun*, Dec. 20, 1875.   [62] Jan. 14, 1876.
[63] *Writings*, II, 268.   [64] Jan. 15, 1876.   [65] Marble Papers, Nov. 21, 1875.
[66] *Letters*, I, 191.   [67] *Writings*, II, 238; Lincoln, *Messages*, VI, 912.

agement of the Federal Government, and to an exposition on sound finance. Tilden assailed the "financial quackery" of the day, pronounced the claim that a new issue of legal tender notes would cure the business evils "illusory" and assailed the belief that the quantity of currency caused high or low prices as fallacious. Progressive views were advanced concerning savings banks and insurance companies, and a fling was taken at Republican misgovernment of the Southern States.

This message was written for the American people. The treatment of the financial and economic problems was masterful, and awakened wide interest. Tilden was fully aware that his constituency spread across the continent and that he was the spokesman for the elements hostile to Grant in both parties. David A. Wells expressed his "admiration" for the message and asked for "an early copy." [68] Praise for his treatment of the currency problem came from all parts of the country. The anti-administration press was loud in its commendation. But not a few men, even in his own party, believers in the magic of paper money, thought that Tilden was speaking for the bankers and rich corporations. Realizing that the public generally would wish to read his discussion of the money problem, Tilden had the message set up in booklet form and arranged for its distribution. [69]

Tilden always professed to be a friend of the working classes. So when the legislature passed an act requiring convicts and paupers in institutions in the metropolis to be put to work, he vetoed it on the ground that they became competitors of workers at a time of widespread unemployment. [70] This significant action was warmly applauded by the workingmen. [71]

After his nomination for President, Governor Tilden did not resign his office, but served out his full term to the end of 1876. As the campaign advanced, however, he spent more time in New York than in Albany, and State affairs suffered somewhat. The prosecution of the Canal Ring, municipal reform and the reorganization of finance and taxation were bequeathed to his successor, Governor Robinson.

[68] *Letters*, II, 395.   [69] Tilden Papers, T. B. Carroll, Jan. 7, 1875.
[70] Lincoln, *Messages*, VI, 982.   [71] Cook, 308.

POLITICAL eminence in the United States affords an occasion for flattering friends to hint at an open road to the White House. In 1868 a few friends had mentioned such a possibility to Tilden, and Welles recorded in his *Diary*, "Blair tells me that Samuel J. Tilden wanted to be the candidate . . . for President." [1] Following his attack on the Tweed Ring, even in distant California there arose a cry of "Tilden for President." [2] After his assault on the Canal Ring, the movement for his nomination attained an astonishing impetus, and Bigelow spoke of him as being "in the direct line for the succession to Grant." Abram S. Hewitt thought that "the public mind" was considering him "for a much higher position," [3] and similar expectations were expressed in dozens of letters. In August, 1875, the Springfield *Republican* published a friendly editorial on "Governor Tilden and the Presidency." After meeting Tilden at Saratoga Springs, O. H. Browning recorded in his *Diary*, "He is a candidate for the Presidency and if nominated I think I will support him."

In 1876 Tilden's name was a topic of common conversation all over the country, and everybody saw that it had to be reckoned with in the coming National Democratic Convention. Even from Oxford, England, Bonamy Price wrote: "I have closely watched your public career. . . . Never did a man deserve better of his country; and I fervently hope that the new year will bring the amplest recognition of this fact from your fellow-countrymen." [4] He was regarded by Seymour as the logical candidate of the Democrats, and his capable leadership was acknowledged even by members of his party who did not like him personally. For "sheer intellect," he had few superiors in political life, but unfortunately he was lacking in those human qualities—kindly sympathy, good fellowship, sociability, and warm-heartedness—which are valuable assets in the careers of public men.[5] Whitelaw Reid informed Tilden that William M. Evarts said, "Your nomination is almost if not absolutely inevitable." [6] Others were not quite so positive. For example, Levi H.

[1] Welles, *Diary*, III, 446.   [2] Tilden Papers, Nov. 27, 1871.
[3] *Letters*, I, 330, 351.   [4] *Ib.*, II, 399.
[5] Peck, *Twenty Years of the Republic*, 115.   [6] Tilden Papers, Apr. 2, 1876.

Brown of Watertown asked Kernan: "What is the prospect for Tilden? Would Seymour and Hendricks not be the strong team?" [7]

Now that Tilden seemed to be out of the running for the Governorship, his foes looked about for a candidate. They selected Church, who made strenuous efforts to win delegates and asked Kernan to round up supporters for him.[8] When Kernan replied ambiguously that he intended to work for the harmony of the party, Church fruitlessly urged him to write a public letter explaining just what he meant by "harmony." [9]

New York naturally was expected to take the initial step in promoting Tilden's candidacy. In an early effort to undermine his popularity, the Greenback Party held its State Convention at Syracuse on March 15, 1876, to protest against the Democratic position on national finance. It charged that Tilden was "controlled by the great money and corporate interests" and had no sympathy with the common people. At an adjourned meeting in New York City on June 1, representatives from 52 counties demanded that the Democratic Convention support the legal-tender notes, and that the pledge of Congress to resume specie payments on January 1, 1879, be repealed.

When the State Committee met to call the convention, it was voted unanimously that Tilden should be the Presidential candidate. The Democratic Convention met at Utica April 26, seated the Tammany men in the contesting delegations, listened to speeches by Kernan and Seymour, endorsed the reforms of Governor Tilden, proposed his name as President, decreed that the delegates to the National Convention should vote as a unit, but made no commitment on the money question.[10] It was significant, however, that when Tilden's name was voted on there was no applause or demonstration of any kind. The Democrats were forced by circumstances to accept his leadership but some did not refrain from expressing their personal dislike of him. Outside the convention, however, the newspapers, which more accurately represented the feelings of the people, revealed widespread approval. The only result was that his enemies were now exposed and could be more easily counteracted.[11] The people trusted Tilden for his stand on sound money and honest government and distrusted his enemies who wished to use political power for selfish purposes. Therein lay his strength as a leader of

[7] Kernan Papers, Apr. 15, 1876.   [8] Ib., Mar. 28, 1876.
[9] Ib., Apr. 3, 1876, and later.
[10] An. Cyc., 1876, 601–602.   [11] Tribune, May 27, 1876.

his party. Outside of New York such anti-Tilden sentiment as developed, aside from loyalty to local sons, came from "Western inflationists and communists." [12]

Now that the Tilden boom had been launched, he became wary about accepting any speaking engagements that had a political tinge, but two exceptions may be mentioned. As the guest of the New York Chamber of Commerce he responded to the toast "The State of New York" and declared that the Federal Government drew in taxes from New York far more than did the State and localities. Governmental evils could be cured only by a reduction of taxation—such, for instance, as the $4,-000,000 remitted to the city by the State. Three days later he addressed the Young Women's Christian Association, stating that his appointment of a woman to the State Board of Charities was "perhaps the solitary success of my whole life with the female sex." [13] In April there began a nation-wide campaign through paid advertisements in rural newspapers. Henry M. Alexander of New York City informed Tilden that the articles delivered by Pelton would appear in 1,200 local papers within ten days.[14] Bates and Lock of the metropolis were employed to manage the campaign. Rural papers were glad to get the work, which paid them $4 for each of five insertions beginning May 19. The Cincinnati *Enquirer* printed one of the copies furnished by the advertising agency and denounced it as an unfair type of pre-convention publicity.

A Newspaper Popularity Bureau, with a full staff of editors, writers, artists and "advertisement concoctors," was organized to promote Tilden's candidacy, and was managed by Goodsell Brothers. Favorable comments about him appeared in such papers as the *Tribune, Times* and *World* and then were copied elsewhere—all said to be the work of the resourceful publicity firm. Then appeared the *Daily Graphic,* which claimed the honor of having first nominated Tilden for President and was filled with clever "Tilden Cartoons," some of which were ridiculed by the *Times*. Somewhat later was established a Literary Bureau for publicity work with a paid staff of experts, which was perhaps the most efficient organization of its kind thus far employed in the nation. Behind the project was the idea of an educational campaign that would reach the masses of the voters through the mails and newspapers. Literally tons of reading matter of a high grade were sent all over the country and probably were a factor in the large popular vote for Tilden. The

[12] *Letters,* II, 430.   [13] *Writings,* II, 349, 352.   [14] Tilden Papers, Apr. 22, 1876.

letter by Clarkson N. Potter to Senator Kernan on "The Danger and Duty of the Democracy," advocating civic reform, the abolition of executive patronage and the election of 40,000 postmasters, is an excellent example of the character of the publicity issued.[15] Most of the circulars were issued in a handy size resembling railroad time tables, and printed in a variety of colors. The expense was borne in part by Tilden and in part by private subscriptions, notably $20,000 given by Edward Cooper.[16]

Tilden's papers for the early months of 1876 indicate that he and his backers were active in making a survey of public sentiment throughout the country. Democratic leaders in various States sent in reports and newspaper clippings; and these were studied by Tilden with the eye of a trained prognosticator. Trusted supporters such as Montgomery Blair served as scouts to test the attitude of men of local and national prominence. Favorite sons were urged on Tilden as suitable running mates. George L. Miller reported that, on account of "Wall Street and sound money," Tilden was strong in the South but weak in Ohio and Indiana. Henry Watterson asked Tilden to have the biographical sketch being prepared by Bigelow stress his States' rights utterances for consumption in Kentucky and the South, said the subordination of money to reform was creating Tilden sentiment, and was going to take a group of Democratic leaders to New York to meet the next President. From Virginia, B. F. Bland hoped to see Tilden made President as the "great representative of reform," and wanted to know whether the delegates should go instructed or not. A. C. Janin reported Louisiana safe but insisted on having $400 a week for the New Orleans *Democrat* or it would suspend publication.[17] John T. Morgan sent the good news that all but two of the twenty delegates were for the "strongest man in New York, an honest Democrat, who will attack fraud and corruption wherever he meets them"; and said that Church and Kelly deceived no one.[18] From far away California Gwin announced that Tilden was the best man, while Casserly said that the State was "Tilden all over." [19] Perry H. Smith telegraphed Tilden that the Illinois convention was for him.[20] D. A. Wells, after a conference with Tilden, doubted whether Connecticut would give him a full vote on account of Barnum, who, like Tweed, was a corrupt local politician,[21] but C. B. Beck was confident that "Tilden sentiment" was growing.[22] With such data at his command, Tilden had no difficulty in assuring himself of the drift of the political winds outside of New York.

But the anti-Tilden storm brewing in New York State endangered the national situation. Senator Kernan might report that Tilden could carry New York, Connecticut, and New Jersey, but his frequent conferences showed an uneasy state of mind. Loyal Magone might counsel, "conciliate Amasa J. Parker and make Judge C. E. Church Governor, and everything will be satisfactory," but Tilden was not a man to compromise with those he did not trust. From the outset he had anticipated hostility from the rogues within the party whom he had either exposed for wrongdoing or had refused to recognize as in good standing, and in spite of their opposition had won the endorsement of his party convention for the Presidency. By May the disaffection had become so menacing that Tilden's friends both in New York and outside began to ask whether he could carry the Empire State.

The original anti-Tilden Democrats were greatly strengthened when John Kelly, who had so enthusiastically supported Tilden and his reforms in 1875, grew lukewarm and then openly hostile. Judge James P. Sinnott was sent to placate Kelly and had a frank talk with him. Kelly felt that he was no longer under any obligation to help Tilden but would not put a straw in his way. "Tammany will help you, but Kelly has no interest in your nomination," Sinnott reported.[23] Tilden made no further effort to placate Kelly, who speedily led Tammany into the anti-Tilden ranks. By this time those who opposed Tilden included many high-grade Democrats, among whom were able and experienced leaders. After several secret conferences, about 120 prominent Democrats signed a circular, which was printed and widely circulated, stating that they were opposed to Tilden's nomination. One is not surprised to find on it disgruntled Democrats such as Judge J. F. Barnard, ex-Governor Hoffman, John Kelly, Fernando Wood, and Delos Wolf, but it is more difficult to account for the signatures of men like Chancellor J. V. S. Pruyn, S. S. Cox, August Belmont, Augustus Schell, H. Seymour, Jr., Erastus Corning, A. J. Parker, A. C. Beach, Littlejohn, Church, and Allen. Tilden might have won some of this group by making one of them Governor, but he refused to do so. While he had thwarted the ambition of some of these men, others had received political favors from his hand.

[22] Tilden Papers, May 19, 1876.   [23] Ib., Feb. 2, 1876.

The first hostile act was an attempt to break the unit rule adopted by the State Convention, but it failed. With his usual foresight Tilden had laid his plans securely and was adamant against compromise with his enemies, even when intimate friends advised it. The second part of the anti-Tilden movement was defeatist propaganda. The cry was raised that he could not carry his own State and hence would lose the election. But this was answered by pointing to his 50,000 majority over Dix in 1874. Theodore P. Cook, author of a semi-official campaign biography of Tilden, predicted, "You will be nominated on the second ballot," and urged that men like Spriggs be sent to St. Louis to counteract the propaganda of his opponents. He was admonished to "clean out the unclean Birds at Washington." The Union Clubs gave him staunch support, and in Rooseveltian style Robert B. Roosevelt advised: "You need me to conduct your campaign. You have too much experience and lack a little rashness. I could supply that deficiency. . . . Tilden's honesty and statesmanship dashed with Blaine's audacity and impudence would sweep the Union." Tilden attempted to placate A. C. Beach of the State Committee, who returned the icy reply that he wanted "to see the best man nominated"—and that man was not Tilden. To some plain talk from Tilden Beach said, "I never thought that you were dead a year ago . . . or that you got down on your knees to me—that's a lie." He blamed Tilden for defeating his aspiration to be Governor and for trying to prevent his election as a delegate. Even after Tilden's nomination was conceded, Beach curtly told him that he had reserved his right as a delegate to vote as he pleased.[24]

Tilden managed matters so adroitly that the Democratic-Republican State Committee was in the hands of trustworthy supporters. Daniel Magone of Ogdensburg, an able attorney, was made chairman—and a more devoted and faithful follower Tilden never had. E. K. Apgar became secretary, C. S. Fairchild, treasurer, and young D. S. Lamont, clerk. Other members were Fowler, Kelly, Manning, Beach, Gorham, Faulkner, Warren and Bookstover. Headquarters were taken in the Everett House in the metropolis where the National Democratic Committee was located.[25] It will be observed that, while the anti-Tilden faction was represented on the committee, they held no offices and were a minority. This was not an accident, for so far as was humanly possible, Tilden never left anything to accident.

[24] Tilden Papers.   [25] Ib.

Among Tilden's most loyal supporters were A. S. Hewitt and Edward S. Cooper, whose friendship ran back at least twenty years. Tilden had been associated with them in investments in Western railroads, in the Iron Cliffs Company in Michigan, in the Franklin Coal Company and the Phoenix Park Coal Company, in Pennsylvania, and in the Trenton Iron Company of New Jersey, in which he bought 50 shares during the war. Tilden had aided them in 1867 to acquire complete control of the last-named concern. As neighbors at Gramercy Park they exchanged calls and dinners. They contributed $10,000 to Tilden for his reform crusade in 1871, helped to reorganize Tammany Hall in 1872, and in 1874 they worked to elect him Governor; while he insisted on Hewitt's going to Congress. Both Hewitt and Cooper rejoiced at the prospect of Tilden's nomination for President.[26]

In April, Carl Schurz, Bryant, Woolsey, Bullock and Horace White, through H. C. Lodge, sent out invitations to a group of men, mostly Liberal Republicans, to attend a conference at the Fifth Avenue Hotel in New York City on May 16–17 for the purpose of selecting a suitable successor to President Grant.[27] Woolsey was made president of the convention of about 200 statesmen, scholars, lawyers, editors and business men from seventeen States, among them being Seelye, Sumner, Godwin, C. F. Adams, Higginson, Wells and Peter Cooper. The real purpose was not so much to select a Presidential candidate or adopt a platform as to prevent the nomination of an heir to Grant such as Blaine, Conkling, or Morton.[28] The resolutions adopted and sent out as "An Address to the American People" denounced corruption in public administration, and called on good citizens to support no candidate who would not pledge himself to carry out "genuine reform." The Republic must have a President "whose name is already a watchword of reform" and who has courage and fidelity. Many believed that the conference meant to support Tilden, and he himself had some reasons for believing that it would aid rather than injure his prospects. The *Argus* for weeks printed portions of the resolutions as if a part of the Democratic platform, perhaps as good strategy to win Liberal Republicans. The real purpose was merely to force the Republicans to nominate an anti-Grant candidate of high character; yet Adams, Lodge, Bryant, Wells, Godwin and others voted for Tilden.[29]

[26] Nevins, *Hewitt*, 158, 163, 262, 264, 274, 296.   [27] Oberholter, *Hist. of U.S.*, III, 260.
[28] Letter of Parke Godwin in *Tribune*, July 22, 1876.
[29] *Letters*, II, 404, 430; *Life*, I, 296; *An. Cyc.*, 1876, 779.

In the pre-convention campaign Tilden missed no opportunity to strengthen his position. When a citizen of Minnesota demanded proofs of results in the fight against the Canal Ring, the Governor personally explained how the system was broken up. When an Illinoisan asked whether he had fathered the peace resolution of 1864 pronouncing the war a failure, Manton Marble wired that Tilden opposed it and advised McClellan to discard it in his letter of acceptance.[30] Tilden relied on Bigelow to dissipate other false rumors, such as charges of dishonesty in business dealings. The *World's* lukewarmness had to be overcome, and also the hostility of the *Express,* which Augustus Schell, an "inflationist," had purchased.[31] To show what young men were thinking, reports were gathered of college commencements; and it was found that "reform" and "Samuel J. Tilden" ran like a purple thread through the baccalaureate sermons and addresses. A study of Fourth-of-July orations revealed that a demand for civic improvement was mingled with observance of the Centennial. Reform was in the air.

Not since the Civil War were the people so wrought up over the approach of national party conventions. The Republican Convention was held at Cincinnati on June 14, 1876, where 1,500 delegates—white and black, Liberals and Regulars—met to select a leader to replace Grant. Who would win—Blaine, Conkling, Morton, Bristow, Hartranft, Jewell or Hayes? After six ballots Hayes was nominated, and William A. Wheeler, of Malone, New York, was given second place by acclamation.

The Democratic National Convention met in St. Louis on June 27, 1876.[32] As the day approached, throngs from every State in the Union congested the streets, crowded the saloons and packed the hotels. On all sides Democrats were boasting that their innings were coming at last. Buildings were decorated with bunting and flags, and there was much excitement. Party leaders had gathered in advance. On June 21 A. H. Tremaine, R. W. Peckham, Daniel Manning, Samuel Hand, C. S. Fairchild and a dozen other Tilden supporters left Albany for the scene of contest.[33] Lieutenant Governor Dorsheimer had departed earlier with important instructions from Tilden.

Stubborn John Kelly's special train with his picture and 150 Tam-

[30] *Letters,* I, 434, June 15, 21, 1876.
[31] *An. Cyc.* 1876, 782; Stanwood, *Hist. of Pres.,* 320; *Retrospections,* V, 262, 266.
[32] Tilden had expressed a preference for Chicago.
[33] *Argus,* June 21, 1876.

many workers arrived shouting for Hendricks. Over Tammany's head-quarters was a banner stating, "New York, the largest Democratic city in the Union, is uncompromisingly opposed to the nomination of Samuel J. Tilden because he cannot carry the State of New York." Upstate allies of Tammany such as A. C. Beach, Colonel W. S. Church, S. S. Cox, Judge Allen, Erasmus Corning and John V. L. Pruyn were secretly active against Tilden. Other well-known New Yorkers were Kernan, Hewitt, Otendorfer, Wickham, Whitney, Marble, Magone, Purcell, West, Smith M. Weed, D. B. Hill, Belmont and Schell—all Tilden men except the last two. In a four-hour session on June 26, New York's Tilden delegates failed to win over their opponents, but did uphold the unit rule by a vote of 53 to 17. To clear the air Seymour positively refused to be a candidate.

The most dangerous opposition to Tilden's nomination came from the Western champions of paper money led by Hendricks. These soft money men were beaten in the Committee on Resolutions and on the convention floor, but with a better organization they might have made a formidable contest. Their strength was split among rival candidates. Belief in Tilden's triumph grew until no bets against him would be taken at any odds—even by Tammany men with rolls of bills bulging from their pockets. The ubiquitous John Morrissey wagered $10,000 that Tilden would be nominated and offered another $10,000 that he would be elected. Dorsheimer bet $1,000 with Van Buskirk that Tilden would carry New York, and Kernan was stakeholder. The demand of Demo-crats generally was almost irresistible, for to them he was a far-sighted man with a capacity for organization, who stood on his own record as an economist and reformer. "Old Usufruct" was the people's choice if not the politicians'. Bigelow was already figuring how the Democrats could match the $15,000,000 campaign fund which the Republicans could raise from its army of 300,000 officeholders.[34]

The weather was sultry, and the delegates took off their coats. A mili-tary band back of the chairman's desk played patriotic airs until the gavel fell for order. Augustus Schell, Chairman of the National Com-mittee, called the noisy delegates to order at 12:20 o'clock on June 27 and after a few words introduced Henry Watterson as temporary chair-man of the huge assembly of 5,000. He received an ovation as he was

[34] Kernan Papers, Dorsheimer to Kernan, Nov. 27, 1876; Bigelow to Kernan, Dec. 8, 1876.

escorted to the chair by Senators Barnum of Connecticut and Ransom of North Carolina. Watterson said: "We are called together to determine by our wisdom whether honest government, administered by honest men, shall be restored to the American people." He added that hard times, vacant houses, neglected fields, closed factories and idle hands were all about them. The cause? "Partisan misrule and sectional misdirection." The Republicans were not alone responsible. "With them rest the disgraces, with us the follies." Our financial system was a cheat; oligarchy ruled. They were here to make the people's fight for a free and honest government—for reform, home rule, economy and a chance for all men. "It is the issue, not the man, that should engage us"—to drive out the rings and robbers regardless of party.[35] After minor officials had been selected, the two-thirds rule was adopted and the Committee on Platform appointed, one member for each State, Dorsheimer representing New York.

At the afternoon session General John A. McClernand of Illinois was named permanent chairman. There were no contesting delegations. Judge Meredith, chairman of the Platform Committee, asked Dorsheimer of New York to read the report. A giant of a man with a deep voice and a fervid oratorical style, he read the document and brought the convention to its feet again and again with cheers and applause. The phraseology of the platform was from the pen of Manton Marble, but its thought and logic were Tilden's.[36] It based the whole campaign on immediate reform; reiterated faith in majority rule, supremacy of civil power, separation of Church and State, equality before the law, liberty of individual conduct, and popular education; and solemnly pledged the party to seek their realization.

Then followed nine planks, each beginning with the resounding phrase "Reform is necessary," which had an electric effect upon the huge audience as read by Dorsheimer's booming voice. "Reform is necessary" to rebuild the Union, to rescue it from a "corrupt centralism," to establish a sound currency and public credit, to abolish unjust tariffs, to reduce taxes, to stop the waste in public lands, to eliminate sectional strife and hatred, to improve civil service, to curb official crimes, and to bring "a change of measures and men" through a peaceful civic revolution.[37]

General Ewing then presented the minority report, which demanded

---

[35] *Century*, May, 1913.
[36] Rhodes, VII, 276; platform in *An. Cyc.*, 1876, 785; Alexander, III, 344.
[37] *Life*, I, 411; Stanwood, 374; *An. Cyc.*, 1876, 785.

the repeal of the act to resume specie payments in 1879. Dorsheimer said the issue was between "soft money and hard money" and must be settled by the convention. After an acrimonious wrangle, the convention, by a vote of 550 to 219, upheld the majority report for hard money and clearly pointed to Tilden as the national leader. The first battle had been won.[38]

The convention was called to order on June 28 at 11:05 A. M. and Father Brady offered prayer. "Mr. Kelly of New York," holding in his hand a paper signed by New Yorkers who opposed the nomination of Tilden, asked for the privilege of the floor to present it. His request was greeted with "applause and hisses." The chairman convulsed the audience by mistakenly recognizing him as "the gentleman from Maine," but upon being set aright as to Kelly's identity and the purport of his paper, he ruled its presentation out of order. Kelly then lost his temper and employed "minatory language towards several gentlemen." The year before he had supported Tilden and all his reforms, "purified" Tammany Hall and expelled the "scalawags." Now, however, he was determined to prevent Tilden's triumph.[39] After a good deal of quibbling the convention recessed until 2 P. M.

The convention was now ready to receive nominations. As the roll of States was called alphabetically, Delaware nominated Senator Thomas F. Bayard and Illinois presented Governor Thomas A. Hendricks. Then by mistake New York was called in place of New Jersey and the audience went wild with cheering and waving of hats, handkerchiefs and fans in a tribute to Tilden. The mistake was discovered and New Jersey proposed Governor Noel Parker.[40] As New York was called again, Kernan strode to the platform amidst thunderous applause, and said, "The great issue upon which this election will be lost or won is the question of needed administrative reform." If we have a man who has "laid his hand on dishonest officials," rooted out abuses, lowered taxes and inaugurated reforms, and if we are wise enough to select him as our leader, we will sweep the Union. Governor Tilden reduced the taxes of New York from $15,000,000 to $8,000,000. Our farmers and business men have faith in him and the honest people throughout the country want him for President. Deafening cheers punctuated this address and followed its conclusion. Tilden's nomination was seconded by Flour-

[38] Stanwood, 379.   [39] Reports in New York papers, June 29, 1876.
[40] Report of the Convention by D. S. Lamont in the Albany *Argus*, June 29, 1876.

noy of Virginia and Herndon of Texas.[41] Then John Kelly hurried to the platform, amid hisses and shouts of "Out of order!" Kernan begged that Kelly be heard and he urged the selection of a Western candidate to secure Indiana and Ohio in October in order to win New York in November. While he was speaking someone from the platform shouted "Three cheers for Tilden," but Kelly held the floor and finished his speech.[42]

Next followed two formidable candidates—the farmer-statesman, William Allen of Ohio, and General Winfield Scott Hancock of Pennsylvania. When Wisconsin pledged its delegates to Tilden, the oratorical fireworks ended without singeing anybody, and it looked like a free for all fight among Hendricks, Allen, Hancock and Tilden. On the first ballot Tilden received all the votes of 18 States and part of the votes of 11 more, making a total of 404½. Hendricks received 140½ votes, Hancock 75, Allen 54, Bayard 33, Parker 18 and Brodhead 16. Tilden lacked 87½ of the 492 votes necessary for a choice. Before the vote was announced, however, Missouri added 7 votes for Tilden, giving him 411½ on the first ballot. Allen and Hancock were virtually eliminated on this first ballot, leaving Hendricks as Tilden's only formidable rival.

The second ballot was like a Tilden deluge. Colorado gave him 6 votes, Georgia added 10, Illinois 4, Iowa and Kansas 2 each, making 467 —still 25 short. Then Iowa added 4 more, Illinois 2 and Missouri 21. By this time the convention was on its feet shouting, calling order and demanding the count. One mighty roar of applause swept the convention, the band played and bedlam let loose. Men leaped upon desks and chairs, yelled themselves hoarse. The chairman rapped for order in vain and at last the secretaries held up two fingers, thinking that in the change of votes Tilden still lacked two. These were quickly supplied, and the uproar started all over again. When the second ballot was announced Tilden had 508 votes, Hendricks 75, Hancock 60, Allen 54, Bayard 11 and Thurman 2. Additional changes raised Tilden's votes to 535 when Wallace of Pennsylvania, with a second from Indiana, moved to make the nomination unanimous. It was now nearly 8:30 and the convention adjourned.[43]

The next morning, June 29, the convention was called to order at

[41] Writings, II, 354.   [42] Newspaper accounts, June 29, 1876.
[43] An. Cyc., 1876, 785; Stanwood, 379, gives Tilden 417 votes on the first ballot.

10:25. Bishop Robinson offered prayer and the chairman read a telegram from Sedalia, Missouri: "Fired one hundred guns for Tilden.
Hope Hendricks will be Vice President." [44] Thomas A. Hendricks, idol
of the soft money Democrats, was tendered that honor unanimously.
After he had announced that he would not take second place, it took
considerable coaxing by John Kelly and others to induce him to play
second fiddle to Tilden. Some Western Democrats regarded him as a
liability instead of an asset and said that his name would be a "heavy
load to carry" and would be certain to lose Ohio.[45] John Kelly got the
floor long enough to tell the convention that, although he had done all
within his power to defeat Tilden, he pledged himself and followers to
co-operate in the coming campaign.

When a sympathetic reporter asked Tilden for an explanation of the
mystery of Kelly's hostility, he meditated for a moment, as if reviewing
past relations, and then whispered in reply that he did not know, "unless
it is that Kelly sees in me an obstacle to his ambition to become the
leader of the Democracy of . . . New York. . . . His opposition came
without warning and without anything, within my knowledge, leading
up to it." [46] This enmity of Kelly lasted until Tilden's death, a decade
later, and was extended to all his intimate friends. When Kelly was so
ingloriously defeated, the *Sun* facetiously suggested that he should go
home and hire out as a driver of an ice cart in order to cool off.

Local St. Louis sentiment favored Tilden and after his nomination a
grand ratification meeting was held at which the leading delegates predicted an easy triumph in the fall. This was a reward for "steady political work" in which Tilden was without a rival.[47] "The Tilden forces
were the most superbly organized body that ever attended a convention." The master mind was far away, but the fruits of his prevision were
apparent. He was also wise enough to permit individuals to believe that
they had engineered the nomination. For example Bigelow recorded in
his *Diary*, "I went to St. Louis and had the satisfaction of having Governor Tilden nominated on the second ballot." [48] Papers like the *Nation,
Sun, Staats Zeitung, Herald* and Rochester *Union* were enthusiastic
over the platform and ticket; but the *Tribune, Times* and *World* were
cool. The Republican press poked fun at the ticket—it was like two
horses tied together by their tails; it was a "Kangaroo ticket" with all

[44] *World,* June 30, 1876.
[45] *Nation,* July 6, 1876; Tilden Papers, Dr. R. Henning to Tilden.
[46] Hudson, *Recollections,* 88.   [47] *Nation,* July 6, 1876.   [48] *Retrospections,* V, 267.

its strength in its hind legs. The Tammany papers called the convention a "riotous mob" where drunken men knocked each other down and the platform was a "verbal scarecrow." Tilden thought he was now Sam Jackson Tilden but should be called "Slippery Sam." The New York *Express* remarked that Dorsheimer, who spent $10,000 at St. Louis, expected to be reimbursed with the Governorship. Whitelaw Reid was sorry that the addition of Hendricks to the ticket forced the *Tribune* to support Hayes but was glad that honest men had compelled the Democrats to nominate Tilden.[49] Henry Watterson wired Tilden, "Tell Blackstone that he wins in a walk," and took off his coat to work for his party paragon.[50]

Delegates returned home confident that the best man had won and that no one need apologize for the selection. As such bodies go, the convention was reasonably harmonious, with no threatening defection in the coming election. Disappointments over the defeat of favorite sons quickly disappeared. A clear-cut platform for reform and sound money had been adopted. The party occupied a strategic position and, for the first time in a generation, Democrats felt that national victory was within sight.

How did the rank and file receive the news? And what stand would the independent Republicans take? If we use as a measurement of public opinion the newspapers, ratification meetings, and the talk of the common people, the Democrats were ready to rally more enthusiastically behind Tilden than behind any leader since Jackson. Thinking men felt that, compared with Hayes, Tilden had a more penetrating mind, a more valuable experience, a deeper grasp of political science, greater natural ability, and a more comprehensive program. He stood as a symbol of the finest traditions of Democracy; and had a commendable record of accomplishment. With these assets would he win the election? Tilden himself, relying on his sagacity in interpreting the political skies, smiled inscrutably as if confident of victory, but was too cautious to give utterance to his convictions.

[49] *Letters*, II, 439.   [50] *Century*, May, 1913.

DURING the pre-convention activities and the hurly-burly of the gathering itself, with the entire nation excited to see what would be done at St. Louis, Tilden was living quietly at 138 Eagle Street, Albany. The even tenor of his customary course was undisturbed. He had held numerous conferences in New York City and at the Capital with political friends and strangers, who wished to confer with him or just to see him out of curiosity. Of course he was consulted about the platform and supplied the dominant ideas, although he let Marble write the document.[1] A deluge of letters had to be answered. And the business of the State could not be neglected.

On the day before the convention met, the Governor, in a communication to President Potter of Union College, withdrew his promise to be present at commencement. He had intended to give the young men a little sermon on "a high ideal of conduct," which he briefly outlined in his letter.[2] Clarkson N. Potter, who returned to Union for the exercises, said the letter "was well received" and expressed his joy over Tilden's nomination. "Heaven grant you may be elected. The country needs that, far more than you do or can desire it."[3]

While the convention was in session, Tilden was attending to his official affairs. On the day of his nomination he was busy with a lawsuit to which he was a party. James C. Carter of New York, handling the case for him, was his house guest. He and the Governor devoted themselves to "recalling and arranging the facts of the complicated transactions out of which this lawsuit grew." Save for the numerous telegrams which had to be answered, Tilden seemed to give little thought to the momentous decision pending in the Middle West. There was no radio to entice him to listen to details of the convention, and if there had been Tilden in all probability would have shut it off until the business in hand was concluded.[4]

A telegraph line had been run to the Executive Chamber to permit the Governor to keep in touch with St. Louis, but during the entire day he never set foot in the Capitol. However, swift-footed messenger boys

[1] Rhodes, VII, 276.   [2] *Argus*, June 29, 1876.   [3] *Letters*, II, 436.
[4] *Life*, I, 307.

were kept busy carrying telegrams to the Governor's home. Apparently the telegrams were carefully sorted in the Executive Chamber and only those of importance submitted to Tilden. Those were scanned hurriedly, and replies sent to such as deserved or demanded acknowledgment. One of the most significant messages came from B. Gratz Brown congratulating him on his nomination and declaring that his election was certain.[5]

After devoting a day to the organization of materials for the trial, Tilden took Carter for a drive late in the afternoon. He himself drove "the high-spirited horse" hitched to an open carriage. There was no allusion to the convention. "His conversation, animated and incessant, was upon false policies in government, the mischiefs of . . . overexpenditures, the true principles of taxation, the errors of protective tariffs, etc." The Presidency meant little to him, but the "chance of laying his reforming hand upon the multitude of abuses . . . aroused his enthusiasm." Eloquent and intense, he gave little attention to the horse, and Carter was "in constant fear of a catastrophe" such as occurred the next day, which cost the Governor $2,800 in damages. When informed that the hard money plank had been adopted, he chuckled. During the drive he knew from Dorsheimer's wire that balloting was in progress. When Carter suggested that a telegram announcing his nomination might be awaiting his return, he commented, "No, not until about half-past nine." At that hour he was taking a cup of tea with Mrs. Pelton, when W. C. Newell brought the news, "Governor, you have been nominated." He arose, shook hands with Newell, read the dispatch "in his usual quiet way," and received the congratulations of his sister and friends.[6]

Tilden's calmness was in sharp contrast to the excitement in Albany. All day crowds had hung about the newspaper and telegraph offices. When the final message came cheers were heard in the streets, and soon bonfires appeared all over Capitol Hill. The State House was illuminated, and shouting admirers with a brass band serenaded Tilden until he appeared and thanked his friends for the demonstration. Congratulatory telegrams poured in from all parts of the nation.[7] To the Jackson Corps, a Democratic organization of workingmen, of which he was an honorary member, he explained that the gaunt wolf of hunger was at

[5] Tilden Papers, June 28, 1876.   [6] *Atlantic Monthly,* Oct., 1892; *Life,* I, 310.
[7] *Argus,* June 28, 1876.

the door of every home because the "earnings of labor and the income of capital have been consumed or wasted in government expenditures." Taxes had increased four fold and exceeded earnings. Everywhere "abuses, peculations, frauds and corruption" in public life made Americans almost ashamed of their country. "Our centennial products are the evils . . . to escape which our ancestors abandoned their homes in the Old World and planted themselves in the Wilderness." So numerous and so unscrupulous had the officeholding class become that "the Government no longer exists for the people" but the people for the Government. "What is the remedy?" To this question a voice cried, "The election of Tilden" and there was vociferous applause. To his own question Tilden replied, "Reform," which was received with more cheers.[8]

Tilden knew how to appeal to the understanding and the enthusiasms of his constituents. Men closely associated with him were impressed by his accurate knowledge of men and of political science. When Carter expressed surprise that he had not affiliated with the Republicans, who included more men of culture and wealth able to understand his advanced ideas, he replied that they formed "a party of self-seekers" who wanted special laws to build up their fortunes and were not interested in a government for the masses. He felt that the Democratic Party was more easily guided "by the force of ideas," and consequently more likely to be entrusted with power in the future.[9]

Tilden's explanation of his selection as the candidate of his party was quite simple. To a group at the Executive Mansion he said: "The nomination was not made by the leaders of the party. It was the people who made it. They want reform. They have wanted it a long while, and, in looking about, they became convinced that it is to be found here (pointing to himself)." [10] Proof of the truth of this statement is found in the numerous telegrams and letters from men and women preserved in the Tilden Papers. They came from London and Paris, from most of the States in the Union, and particularly from the Empire State. His Southern admirers were most emphatic—"We are going to move Heaven and Hell. . . . I shall spend every damn cent I have . . . to beat Hayes." From California came the cheering comment, "What a blessing . . . to have you . . . in the White House." Congratulations from Republicans as well as Democrats poured in. Some interpreted the nomination

8 *Life*, I, 310–311.   9 *Ib.*, 308.
10 Report of Associated Press, in *Argus*, June 29, 1876.

as an act of Providence—"God is in this move"; and "Thank the Lord . . . that we have . . . reason to hail yourself as the coming President." [11] Promises to speak, write, and contribute came from all sides. Many begged him to speak out plainly on the money question.[12] Cyrus H. McCormick would take Hendricks' place if he declined to run; and volunteered to accept the portfolio of Secretary of the Treasury.[13] But Hendricks, instead of stepping aside, urged Tilden to speak in New York City the same day Hayes reviewed the Army in Philadelphia. And Hewitt wanted to know Tilden's views on the money measures in Congress.[14]

The soft money Democrats of the Middle West were much disgruntled over the nomination of "a Wall Street man." The *Enquirer* of Cincinnati believed that Tilden's nomination was a blow aimed at the West. The Evansville, Indiana, *Courier* bolted the ticket for a short time. The *Sentinel* of Indianapolis for some days revealed but little enthusiasm for Tilden. Hendricks wired Tilden from Cleveland that "thousands of votes" would be lost in Ohio unless the Democrats "urged a proper measure of repeal" of the Resumption Act. Tilden refused to make any concessions, and Hendricks, a week later, in his letter of acceptance, disregarding Tilden's position, openly advocated repeal.

Charles Francis Adams assured Tilden that "since the nomination of Governor Hayes, I have been prepared to give *you* a public and hearty support—I am even anxious to do it." However, the platform and Hendrick's utterances "make my position wholly untenable. . . . *You*, without any platform and with a nobody for a Vice President I could see my way to support aggressively. . . . Cannot you throw some of the weight off?" Can you not repudiate the "dishonest action of those in your party who are *not* your friends?" [15]

The next act in the drama was the official notification to Tilden of his nomination. The advance in communication had rendered this custom perfunctory, yet the practice was perpetuated under the belief that it possessed some psychological effect and was excellent publicity. So the convention had appointed a committee to bear the glad tidings, with John A. McClernand as chairman. He notified Tilden that on July 11 the committee would meet in New York City to perform its function.

[11] Tilden Papers, J. Van Schaack, June 30, 1876; Harriet D. Gallatin, July 1, 1876; R. E. Spinner, Newport, Ark.; E. Casserly, June 29, 1876; W. G. Boggs of the *Post*. [12] *Letters*, II, 439.   [13] *Ib.*, 440.   [14] Tilden Papers, July 6, 1876. [15] Tilden Papers, July 10, 1876.

Hendrick B. Wright of Wilkes-Barre informed Tilden that he was preparing the letter of notification and asked him for suggestions, which were forwarded. Nothing was left to chance—and Tilden was thus permitted to notify himself.[16] The carefully drawn document was approved on the 10th by the committee, and Tilden was asked to receive it at his home in New York City. He preferred the Governor's Mansion, but finally yielded and hurried to the metropolis. He was met about 9 P. M. at Gramercy Park by the committee, newspaper reporters and a number of friends.[17]

When Tilden entered the large parlor, McClernand made a few complimentary remarks, and Harris read the letter. Then W. B. Hanna of Indiana drew from his breast pocket an "eloquent" address which he read in a pompous voice, pledging the hearty support of his State to Tilden and Hendricks.[18]

Twenty busy days passed before Tilden completed his letter of acceptance. He knew what he wanted to say, and the form of a public document never bothered him. Had he resigned as Governor and given Dorsheimer a well-earned reward, his burden might have been lightened, but he did not choose to do so. His elder brother, Moses, passed away during this interval, leaving a financial mess on Samuel's doorstep.[19] Advice as to what should go into his acceptance was not lacking —and Tilden was not over-fond of advice. Hewitt urged civil service reform to "strike the public favorably," thought he and Hendricks should fix a date for specie resumption, felt the letter should deal with the South, and wanted to see the document before it was given out.[20] Others advised calling attention to the "alarming pauperism," and to public stealings. Tilden asked Hendricks to send him his letter of acceptance as Governor of Indiana, so as to avoid disagreements, and when they met at Saratoga Springs on July 26 Tilden read his letter to his team-mate.[21] Meanwhile the delay was causing considerable impatience, and Bigelow was polishing the style of the document.

The letter, containing three times as many words as the party platform, appeared on July 31. Some thought its verbosity weakened the convention's declaration.[22] Tilden attributed the business depression to

[16] Tilden Papers, July 3, 1876.   [17] New York City newspapers.
[18] Writings, II, 355.
[19] Mrs. G. W. Smith, Ms. Tilden Genealogy, Sept. 9, 1876, at age of 64.
[20] Letters, II, 442, 443.
[21] Tilden Papers, H. F. McDermott, July 18, 1876; C. H. Sanborne, July 22, 1876.
[22] Minor, Story of Dem. Party, 312.

the waste of capital since 1865. "Unscientific and ill-adjusted methods of taxation" in the past eleven years, amounting to $7,500,000,000, had brought more sacrifices to the people than receipts to the public treasury. He suggested an amendment to the Constitution which would compel distinct appropriations for the various departments. "An accessory cause" of business distress was the misgovernment of the South, with fraudulent bonds and confiscatory taxation. At the end of the war, there should have been a complete reconciliation among all citizens, regardless of color. He promised to use his power as President to protect citizens "in every political and personal right."

There should be a "resumption of specie payments on the legal-tender notes" to restore credit and a sound currency. But the Government must first make such notes as good as specie by creating a "central reservoir" of coin where individuals might exchange their notes. Hence to the $74,-000,000 of hard money should be added by purchase enough gold and silver for redemption. By stopping waste, reducing expenses, and refunding, the whole national debt could be paid "without cost to the people." To fix a day for resumption was a sham and might bring a fresh disaster. If elected President, he would by "gradual and safe processes" restore prosperity.

He promised complete reformation of the Federal Government from the Presidency down—an improved civil service, strict accountability of subordinates, abolition of unnecessary offices, elevation of the standard of appointments, reward of fidelity in public employment, and the disqualification of the President for re-election.

In concluding this labored document Tilden said that, while he had fulfilled his duties as a private citizen for forty years, yet he had never "acquired the habit of official life." When he accepted the Governorship, it was "to consummate reforms" to which he had devoted several years. Experience had taught him the difficulty of "working out a reform of systems and policies"; but, if summoned to attempt that work at Washington, he would "endeavor, with God's help, to be the efficient instrument" of the people's will.[23]

Although inferior to other political papers of Tilden, this document was commented upon extensively. If Bryant was disappointed with the weak treatment of civil service and Sidney Webster with the advocacy of a single Presidential term, Hewitt wrote from Washington, "Your

[23] *Writings*, II, 359, July 31, 1876. See comment of Rhodes, *Hist. of U.S.*, VII, 216.

letter gives general satisfaction, especially to the Southern members, who are loud in its praise." A railroad president believed it would win Republican votes, and Governor Bigler of Pennsylvania thought that it had deeply impressed the business men. It converted Ignatius Donnelly to Tilden's support. When the editor of the New York *Star* told Tilden that the letter was able but too long for the people to read, he replied tartly, "It was not intended for *people* to read."

Meanwhile there were other matters of importance to look after. General R. Brinkerhoff of Ohio, as a guest in Albany, was surprised to find that Tilden knew more about Ohio politics than he did, and said that Tilden's method of work was to deal with individuals rather than irresponsible committees.[24] Scandinavian and German newspapers were assisted, and means taken to win Negro votes. D. A. Wells and William Graham Sumner offered to write letters in support of Tilden. Henry A. Tilden was set to work organizing Tilden German clubs.[25] To hold as much of Tammany Hall as possible, advantage was taken of such invitations as that of the "Old and Young Men's General Committee of Tammany Hall" to address a meeting in the first senatorial district. Hundreds of callers had to be met individually and in committees. And all the machinery must be set up for waging the coming campaign. Tilden had never been an idle man, but the summer and fall of 1876 formed the busiest period of his entire life.

In the midst of all these happenings Tilden took time to answer a Southern friend who in 1872 had asked whether he "had entirely abandoned public life." Although he had given half his life to civic betterment, yet before he was elected Governor he had only served two terms in the Assembly and sat in two constitutional conventions. "I never destined myself for a public career." He accepted his "present trust" because he saw no other way to promote political reform. "I have felt gloomily the decay of all my early ideals of my country, and engaged in the effort to restore them . . . with no idea of any result to myself except of sacrifice. The logic of events has brought me into my present position." Their mutual friend, Martin Van Buren, would be "puzzled about me, for he told me near the close of his life, when he had observed me for thirty years, that I was the most unambitious man he had ever known." [26]

[24] Godwin, *Bryant*, II, 378; *Tilden Letters*, II, 440; Tilden Papers, August, 1876.
[25] Tilden Papers, Scott Lord, July 31, 1876.
[26] *Letters*, II, 448, John Bragg, Aug. 11, 1876.

TILDEN knew that a nomination, applauded by jubilant supporters, did not guarantee an election. There was no more intelligent political organizer than he in the United States. With forty years of first-hand knowledge, with long service on the State Committee, and with an extraordinary acquaintance among party leaders, he was competent to give wise advice on campaign management. But he was not content with the rôle of adviser and largely managed his own campaign with consummate skill and sagacity.

The Republicans had more able politicians in control of their cause than did the Democrats, but none so shrewd as Tilden. His lieutenants were of limited experience and moderate ability. Thurman and Bayard bore weighty names, but were not intimate with party mechanics. With few aides Tilden outlined, organized, and financed the movement. In the end this proved a disadvantage, because he had not surrounded himself with able generals who in the moment of doubt would fight to the last ditch.

A successful canvass involved four major problems. First, an efficient organization had to be built up. Second, publicity must be handled in an effective manner. Tilden was an expert publicity man and understood the psychology of advertising. In the third place, considerable attention had to be given to speakers. The hard and soft money areas, the bankers, the farmers, the laboring classes, the North and the South had to be reached by orators who could make the right kind of appeal. And, finally, funds must be raised to perfect the party machinery, to prepare, print and distribute the literature, and to pay the expenses of workers, speakers, rallies and parades.

While Tilden directed the canvass, theoretically and to a large degree practically, Abram S. Hewitt, a successful business man and now a member of Congress, was in official charge, by virtue of his selection as Chairman of the new Democratic National Committee. He was able and indefatigable, but a novice in politics. As the campaign progressed, Hewitt felt that Tilden did not give him the full confidence which he had a right to expect, and seldom conferred with him. Fortunately,

Hewitt did not openly resent this secretiveness, but, effacing himself and using the magic of Tilden's name, became the galvanizing force of the canvass.[1] It is evident that Tilden approved of the management of the campaign by Hewitt, for his only advice was to curtail expenditures; and the press generally commended the "sleepless vigilance" of the Democratic methods.[2]

In the machinery created to carry on the campaign, next to Tilden as the party head and to Hewitt as his commander in chief, the new Democratic National Committee functioned as a general advisory council. F. O. Prince, as secretary, kept the National Committee informed of what was going on. A smaller executive committee was the working body.[3] Headquarters were in the Everett House. The State Committee under Magone co-operated with it, and after August had its headquarters at the same hotel. Frequent conferences were held, and when Tilden put in appearance the excitement was intense. Supplementing these committees were others in each State and in thousands of localities. Thus the model perfected by Tilden in New York was extended to the nation, and it was a superb organization.

Tilden was one of the first party leaders to employ newspapers, pamphlets, and circular letters as effective publicity based on the psychology of advertising. Facts were repeated through the printed page and on the platform until they sank deeply into the popular mind. At Albany he had two rooms "filled with able and ready writers" preparing publicity. Feeling that there was more potency in truth than lies, he stuck to facts and avoided misrepresentations.

Hewitt agreed with Tilden that publicity was the first major problem, and this was rendered easy because the pre-convention machinery, which had brought about Tilden's nomination, was still intact. The staff of experts was available and could be quickly adapted to the new needs. Renamed the "Literary Bureau," it was housed at 59 Liberty Street, where a printing press was installed, and Colonel W. T. Pelton put in charge.[4] The primary purpose was to disseminate reliable information. Hewitt, afire to get the public appeal under way, wrote to Tilden, "I am already flooded with . . . propositions to conduct the campaign." Within a month he had "in preparation all the necessary documents"

[1] Nevins, *Hewitt*, 316.　　　　　　　　[2] *Tribune*, Oct. 23, 1876.
[3] Tilden Papers. Letterheads give names of Hewitt, Prince, Priest, Ham, Miller, Barnum, Ross, Ransom, Thompson, Scott and Bate, with W. S. Andrews as clerk.
[4] Tilden Papers; Nevins, *Hewitt*, 309.

for an assault on "the frauds and corruptions of the administration." [5]
He was hoping for "the best results" and that Congress would adjourn
so he could "organize the campaign." [6] During hurried week-ends in
New York City he supervised the preparation of a campaign textbook
of 750 pages portraying Tilden's ideas and exposing the scandals of the
Grant administration. For the first time in American party history such
ammunition was made available for party workers. This volume, which
Hewitt outlined without consulting Tilden, written by A. M. Gibson of
the *Sun* and other young Democrats, "determined the result of the
struggle." By the end of August a large edition was distributed. Its
accounts of lurid frauds and defalcations were not pleasant reading, but
were reprinted in thousands of newspapers, and gave the Democrats the
initial advantage. From the "Literary Bureau" emanated editorials,
news releases, broadsides and handy-sized circulars by bales, for newspapers and a gigantic mailing list. Democratic speeches were sent out
by the millions.[7]

Another phase of publicity work was the use of city and rural newspapers over the nation to interpret this literature in the interest of Tilden's election. This was done as quickly and thoroughly as possible, and
a card index prepared. Quite as important as the "Literary Bureau" was
the "Speakers' Bureau," under Colonel W. T. Pelton, which first cata-
logued all available men and women and then arranged schedules for
them in such a way as to meet local needs. The work of this agency necessitated close touch with the requirements of State and local committees.
Another part of the publicity work was the enrolment of Democrats in
local clubs to insure mass meetings for the speakers and impressive
parades. At Utica an "Uncle Sam Union Club" was organized on July 11
and soon there were six hundred such clubs in New York State alone.
Tilden Clubs, Hendricks Clubs, and Tilden and Hendricks Clubs soon
covered the nation, to furnish noise and enthusiasm. And finally there
was the "Bureau of Correspondence," personally directed by Tilden,[8]
which required a large staff to send out the printed matter and information requested, and to answer innumerable questions which poured into
headquarters. Typewriters had not yet come into use and all correspondence had to be done in long hand. Tilden sent to subordinates in
this bureau unimportant inquiries, but communications from persons of

---

[5] Tilden Papers, July 5, 1876; Aug. 6, 1876.   [6] *Letters*, II, 443.
[7] Nevins, *Hewitt*, 309, 310–311.   [8] *Ib.*, 313; *Nation*, Feb. 1, 1877.

consequence not acknowledged by him personally were answered by his own personal staff, on which were Bigelow, Dana, Marble and Randall as confidential advisers.

These activities required a large campaign fund. Edward Cooper, Hewitt's brother-in-law, was Treasurer of the National Committee and collected $150,000, Cooper and Hewitt being the largest contributors. When hard pressed for money, Hewitt and Cooper advanced "a very considerable amount" beyond their large subscriptions, and Tilden reimbursed them for that sum.[9] Thus the National Committee may have had as much as $200,000 for expenses. "Considerable sums were handed directly to Mr. Tilden"—the direct appeals to him for funds were numerous—and not turned over to Cooper—just how much cannot be ascertained. From such funds the expenses of the "Literary Bureau" and other agencies were paid. One also finds him sending to Indiana $60,-000,[10] and smaller sums elsewhere. As the October elections in Indiana and Ohio approached, Tilden appealed to men most able to contribute. Belmont placed in his hands $10,000 in $500 bills—"my contribution for Ind. and O.—you know how and where to use it." James Stokes gave $500; and E. N. Robinson, a broker, $1,000. But there is no record of the amount raised. So it may be assumed that he received directly an amount equal to the cash raised by Cooper. Among Tilden's papers is an account of expenses from January 4 to November 8, under two headings, "Political Expenses" and "National Democratic Committee"—the former aggregating $115,933.77 and the latter $136,122.88—a total of $252,056.65.[11] If Tilden received $150,000 from friends—a very generous estimate, although Hewitt thought it considerably more,—then his own personal contribution was approximately $100,000. This was a small sum for a man of Tilden's wealth and in accord with Hewitt's emphatic statement that Tilden did not "use a large private fortune . . . to secure his election." [12] Yet W. C. Whitney said that Tilden spent $150,000 in a non-Presidential year and much more in a Presidential year. In the item of over half a million mentioned above, printing cost more than $60,000; the Bureau of Correspondence $17,500; and activities under the direction of William T. Pelton $113,000. The total amount of money available for the campaign at headquarters seems to have been under

[9] Nevins, *Hewitt*, 312. On Oct. 15, 1878 Cooper gave Tilden a receipt in full for $11,000. Tilden Papers.
[10] Watterson, *Hist. of Manhat. Club*, 145.   [11] Tilden Papers.
[12] Nevins, *Hewitt*, 312.

$500,000. To that sum should be added the sums raised locally, which must have totaled a considerable amount.

Hewitt, as campaign manager, had no delusions about the imperative need of adequate funds. Zachariah Chandler, Republican National Chairman, in the face of protests from men like Schurz, was following the practice of taxing officeholders, and with satisfying results. Hewitt had no such resources to draw on. With the campaign confronting him, and only about $30,000 in the treasury, he became panicky, called Colonel Pelton into conference, and sent an oral appeal to Tilden. This was followed by a letter saying, "I am now embarrassed beyond all endurance." The campaign expenses would be $250,000. With that sum there would be hope of success; without it, failure. The danger was great. "I am forced by every sense of duty to make you comprehend it." [13] No one knew better than Tilden the legitimate costliness of a campaign and the imperative necessity of plentiful resources. He felt, however, that the money should come from a large number of Democrats who could afford to contribute rather than from the candidate; and that the National Committee should collect the money. On the other hand the wealthy Democrats thought that a man as rich as Tilden should finance his own campaign. As a result contributions from both sources were a disappointment to Hewitt, and he himself was not as active in raising funds as Chandler.

Tilden may not have responded to Hewitt's appeal as speedily or as generously as the latter hoped for, but he did give fairly large sums. Hewitt always felt, however, that Tilden's indifference to the financial needs of the campaign was open to criticism because it left the Democratic fund less than the Republican. Had ample funds been sent to Ohio and the South, the outcome might have been different. Yet "Uncle Sammy's bar'l" was the butt of many jokes. Nast depicted Tilden shaking bank notes out of a barrel into a ballot box with the legend, "Shotgun policy in the South and the barrel policy in the North." [14] Seymour told Tilden that the Republicans were relying on the "use of money" to defeat him and another knew that Chandler planned to carry States "by the *commercial element*." But Tilden was relying on ideas, not dollars, to win the contest.

Tilden tried to persuade Democrats in the various States to nominate their best men. For instance, in Massachusetts, he wished C. F. Adams,

[13] Tilden Papers, Sept. 2, 1876.   [14] *Harper's Weekly*.

Sr., to run for Governor, but Fenian sympathizers defeated the plan.[15]
New York Republicans selected Edwin D. Morgan, war Governor, denounced Tilden for "repudiating his pledge of specie resumption," and
claimed that they had led the way for reform.

But "true liberals" declared their intention to support Tilden's reform
program. Tilden gave particular attention to the State ticket because he
realized the danger of defection by Tammany and the Canal Ring. Preparatory work seemingly had smoothed the way for harmony at the
State Convention in Saratoga on August 30. Kelly and Morrissey had
adjusted their differences; the platform and election of delegates pro-
voked no discussion; and Tilden and Hendricks were endorsed.[16] When
it came to nominations for Governor, however, harmony walked out of
the hall. Tilden had selected Dorsheimer but, in characteristic fashion,
had not advocated his nomination openly.

Meanwhile other candidates were proposed—Seymour, Hewitt, Marble, Robinson, Potter, Church and Starbuck. Fairchild urged Tilden to
induce Hewitt to accept the honor, but Hewitt, knowing that Dorsheimer
was Tilden's preference,[17] refused to run unless personally recommended by Tilden; he was disqualified anyhow because of a residence
requirement.[18] Kelly was vociferous in support of C. N. Potter.[19] General Taylor preferred Manton Marble. Seymour had declared that on
account of age and health he was out of the race. Kernan, who leaned
toward Dorsheimer, suggested a conference to unite the party on a
candidate,[20] but without success. The leaders had finally agreed that
Dorsheimer should be retained as Lieutenant Governor and head of the
Canal Board.[21] Such was the confusion when the convention was ready
for nominations. When Tilden's lieutenants, in his absence, placed Dorsheimer's name before the delegates, it was a signal for hostility against
any Tilden candidate. The opposition yelled for Potter first, and then,
from all over the hall and the galleries, came the shout "Seymour! Seymour! We want a Democrat! Seymour!" So emphatic was the outcry
that the old Democratic war horse was nominated by acclamation. Dorsheimer had to be content with second place. The minor places on the
ticket were filled without any opposition.[22]

---

[15] *Letters*, II, 470, Oct. 25, 1876, 471; R. D. Rice, Oct. 27, 1876, 451–453.
[16] *An. Cyc.*, 1876, 602, 603; Alexander, III, 337.
[17] Tilden Papers, Aug. 1, 1876; Nevins, *Hewitt*, 310.   [18] *Retrospections*, V, 280.
[19] *Letters*, II, 462.   [20] Tilden Papers.   [21] Kernan Papers, Aug. 27, 1876.
[22] *An. Cyc.*, 1876, 604.

Although Seymour had wired a "peremptory refusal," a committee sent to notify him of the choice of the convention reported that he felt "constrained to obey the wishes of the people," and the convention adjourned. Seymour wrote Tilden that he could not accept because it would "dishonor my sincerity." Then he told Tilden frankly what he must do to conciliate the disaffected Democrats—nominate Potter or DeWitt C. West to remove the prejudice of those who think your policy "narrow, personal and proscriptive." [23] Seymour had already advised Kernan to have West nominated as a "peace offering" to harmonize all factions.[24] He told Tilden that, although West opposed his nomination, he was loyal now. Honest, able, and opposed to the Tweed Ring in 1871, his nomination would be regarded as a magnanimous act. You must do this or you "will be beaten in New York," and hence in the nation. The nomination should be made by the State Executive Committee, which Tilden controlled. Kernan informed Tilden that Seymour could not be budged and Seymour sent his positive refusal to the convention committee.

But on none of these points did Tilden take his venerable mentor's advice. He refused to accept Potter because Kelly supported him; he could not forgive West for opposing his nomination; and he thought it wiser to call a second convention than to have the State Executive Committee choose a candidate. Hoping that Seymour might be induced to change his mind, when Cooper wired, "What is Seymour's decision?" Tilden replied, "Not yet made." While Waterbury and others were certain that Seymour's withdrawal meant defeat, Roswell P. Flower expressed the opinion that Tilden was to be congratulated on Seymour's elimination.[25] The feeling was intense and speculation as to the results rife. Most of Tilden's supporters agreed with Flower that the decision to call a new convention was the proper procedure.

Taking advantage of an invitation from D. A. Wells to open the Social Science Association at Saratoga on September 5,[26] Tilden invited Bigelow, Kernan, Appleton, and others to confer on the gubernatorial situation. Dorsheimer was dropped, and a vain effort made to induce S. D. Babcock to run.[27] Finally Lucius Robinson was agreed upon, against strenuous opposition from Dorsheimer, Scott Lord, and Robert Earl. At a second convention on September 13, Robinson won the nomina-

[23] Tilden Papers, Aug. 31, 1876.   [24] Kernan Papers, Aug., 1876.
[25] Tilden Papers, Aug. 31.   [26] *Writings*, II, 374.   [27] *Retrospections*, V, 280–281.

tion over Potter by 80 votes on the first ballot.[28] Being the descendant of the Reverend John Robinson of Leyden, it was jokingly said that he was not quite so bad as Dorsheimer, a descendant of Martin Luther. An effort to persuade Bryant to take a place on the electoral ticket failed, but he intimated that he would vote for Tilden. After Seymour's withdrawal, John Kelly stepped aside to give him a place on the electoral ticket.[29]

With the State tickets made up by September, the field work got under way, although the printing presses had been humming for more than a month. McKinley stated that the campaign of 1876 was neither "exciting nor the enthusiasm of either party great" because the people were more interested in the Centennial; [30] and an eminent historian later asserted, "the Campaign was tame." [31] On the contrary, it was one of the most exciting political clashes in American history. Both candidates were clean, estimable men, with excellent records in private and public life, who wished to conduct the campaign like gentlemen. Both were able lawyers, but Tilden had the higher standing and wider experience. Both were men of means, but Tilden much the wealthier. Both had served their States as legislators and Governors, but Hayes had a longer public career and had sat in Congress. Both favored civil service reform, but Hayes more openly. In the Civil War Hayes won the rank of brigadier general, while Tilden had the opprobrium of being a "War Democrat." Both were men of culture; both loved and collected books and had enjoyed the refining atmosphere of a college, but Tilden was the more profound student of economics and political science. Both had struggled from lowly positions to stations of eminence. Both were past middle life—Hayes 54; Tilden 62. Hayes won the leadership of his party as a "dark horse," while Tilden's conspicuous leadership as a successful reformer forced his party to accept him as its standard bearer. Both were well qualified, and in the election of either Americans might well take pride.

Tilden's plan for an educational campaign to show the need of reform encountered stumbling blocks. Seymour told him plainly: "The word 'reform' is not popular with the workingmen. To them it means less money spent and less work." Hayes' hostility to the Irish and their religion must be played up or their vote would be lost.[32] So the cam-

---

[28] *An. Cyc.*, 1876, 604.   [29] *Letters*, II, 445; *Life*, I, 300, 462.   [30] *Speeches*, 648.
[31] Andrews, *The U.S. in Our Time*, 212.   [32] *Letters*, II, 470, Oct. 25, 1876.

paign changed from one of enlightenment to one of vituperation—
"Turn the rascals out." Words like blacklegs and crooks took the place
of reform. Grant was denounced as the Mephistopheles of American
government, and all the evils of public life were charged to the Republicans by stump speakers and party organs. The thousands of letters sent to Tilden revealed the high hope of Democrats to feed once
more at the public crib.[33]

From Michigan came the news that the superintendent of the New
York Iron Mine was "a strong Hayes man" and that the Iron Cliff
Company was a hotbed of Republicanism. Of course steps were taken
to change the situation in these industries controlled by Tilden. Senator Conover had deserted the Republicans and offered to turn Florida
over to the Democrats for "certain contingencies." Montgomery Blair
asked for more publicity money to carry Indiana and Ohio. Democratic enthusiasm was mounting, and the South was safe. Bets in Mil-
waukee that Tilden would carry Wisconsin and Ohio found no takers.
Alabama would go for Tilden and wanted him to attend the State
Fair.[34] And from Louisiana came a prophetic letter stating that the
Republicans were determined to carry that State by controlling the
Board of Registration and the Returning Board. It was possible for a
Negro to vote 22 times in the parish of Baton Rouge by registering
that many times, and repeaters could not be detected. The Supreme
Court had ruled that the verdict of the Returning Board was final, and
the election laws gave the Republicans all the advantage. It would be
a sad commentary on American liberty if a "handful of unscrupulous
carpetbaggers could determine the national election." Tilden was im-
plored to protect the rights of the whites.[35] If this pre-election warning given in September had been heeded, the result of the election
might have been different.

The back fire to check the Democratic conflagration was burning
briskly by September. Hayes' managers cared less for the triumph of
their leader than their political machine, and contended more for patronage than policies. If Tilden won, they would have to sit on the
back steps a long time before they were permitted to feed at the
public trough, and moreover big business might go over to the enemy.
Alarmed and desperate, they worked out a strategy consisting of two

[33] Tilden Papers.   [34] *Ib.*, A. W. Swinford, Aug. 2, Sept. 16, Sept. 26, 1876.
[35] *Ib.*, R. W. Knickerbocker, a native New Yorker, Sept. 1, 1876.

powerful assaults. One was against the Democratic Party, which was declared synonymous with Southern treason. The bloody shirt was the flag and symbol—a Holy Grail—which was carried across the continent in a crusade of freedom accompanied by patriotic music and the tramping of Union soldiers as a warning to rebels. "A bloody shirt campaign, with money, and Indiana is safe," wrote Kilpatrick to Hayes [36] who forgot himself when he urged Blaine to play up "a solid South, rebel rule, etc., etc., etc.," to lead the people away from "Hard Times." [37] All Democrats must be pictured as Copperheads, an emotional illusion successfully employed in three presidential campaigns. Such tactics caught older voters motivated by war psychology; the younger men and thoughtful independents merely smiled with the Democrats at this old trick.

The second part of the strategy, a surprise but not a novelty in politics, consisted of a barrage of vilification of Tilden. All the venom hurled at Democrats in general was directed with special vindictiveness at their leader. The instruments employed were printer's ink, the stump and the whispering gallery. The literary genius, artistic talent, and fervid oratory employed clothed the malignant attack on Tilden with dextrous finesse. Prose, poetry, cartoon, handbill, wit, sarcasm and buffoonery were used with telling effect. Disregarding the morality involved, and viewing the scheme merely as a psychological maneuver to discredit a man in the eyes of the public, it was admirable in concept and skillful in execution. It took a daring imagination to invent the plausible slanders and the ingenious misrepresentations. Facts and figures were deftly manipulated to serve as plausible proofs. And the principle of reiteration, which Tilden himself had invented for effective campaigning, was now used to discredit him. Even Schurz, who avoided the bloody shirt and did not approve of the lies about Tilden, declared that he was "too much of a demagogue—too much of a wire-puller and machine politician" to be depended upon as a "man of principle." In August, however, he feared that the independent vote would elect Tilden.[38]

The adroit mud-slinging attack on Tilden can be classified under three distinct headings—his Civil War record, his evaded income tax returns, and his connection with election frauds and railroad rings.

[36] *An. Cyc., 1876,* 411.   [37] Hamilton, *Blaine,* 422.
[38] Bancroft and Dunning, *Schurz's Speeches,* III, 259, 262.

In the review of his war record it was charged that he vindicated slavery, abetted secession, was responsible for Andersonville, rejoiced in Southern victories and was guilty of the blackest treason to the Federal Government. He was accused of sending out Copperhead literature and of refusing to attend Union meetings.[39] This was the earliest and the strongest charge against Tilden in alienating Northern voters, and was heard immediately after his nomination. When Tilden was asked whether he had said, "This war is a perfect outrage and I will lend no assistance whatever to its prosecution," his secretary replied that he had never used language so contrary to his patriotic attitude. So diligently was the accusation of disloyalty pressed that Marble had him telegraph a full statement from New Lebanon,[40] and Hewitt in the House of Representatives made a magnificent defense of his loyalty.[41] Through the *World* this speech was given wide publicity.[42] Lincoln's Secretary of War volunteered testimony upon Tilden's good conduct during the war.[43] Knowing that his war record would be under fire during the campaign, Tilden had Bigelow prepare a full statement of his war activities, to answer General Dix and to be sent out to all inquirers.[44] It was a convincing vindication, but it operated only as a partial check on Republican misrepresentations, which went merrily on. Even William M. Evarts, Tilden's classmate at Yale, said that if elected he would be "the phantom of Buchanan's likeness in the Presidential chair." [45]

The second charge against Tilden was that he falsified his income tax returns. A few days after his nomination, the Department of the Interior, of which Zach Chandler was the head, ordered Bliss to investigate his tax record. Acting on Bliss's report, the *Times* accused Tilden of defrauding the Federal Government of a part of his legitimate income tax in 1862 and subsequently, when money was badly needed to suppress the Rebellion. Although a wealthy man, yet his income was given as only $7,118—and in later years he made no return, leaving the amount to be determined by the Federal assessor. The *Times* showed that in 1862 he had sworn to receiving fees of $20,000 from a single railroad and estimated his income for that year

[39] *Harper's Weekly*, July 15 and Aug. 19, 1876.
[40] Tilden Papers, F. A. Flower, Aug. 3, Aug. 12, Aug. 15, 1876.
[41] *Cong. Rec.*, Aug. 14, 1876, 5636–5638.   [42] *World,* Aug. 25, 1876.
[43] Tilden Papers, Peter H. Watson.
[44] *Letters*, II, 453; *Retrospections*, V, 277.   [45] Cortissoz, *Reid*, I, 514.

MRS. YOUNGLOVE

DR. YOUNGLOVE

ELAM TILDEN

MRS. ELAM TILDEN

MARIE CELESTE STAUFFER
CORA E. SMITH

LAURA A. PELTON

CHARLES O'CONOR

DANIEL MANNING

LIEUTENANT GOVERNOR DORSHEIMER

TILDEN'S POLITICAL FRIENDS

NYMPHS TRYING TO LURE THE COY FAUN INTO PRESIDENTIAL WATERS

"Puck's" adaptation of Bouguéreau's famous picture

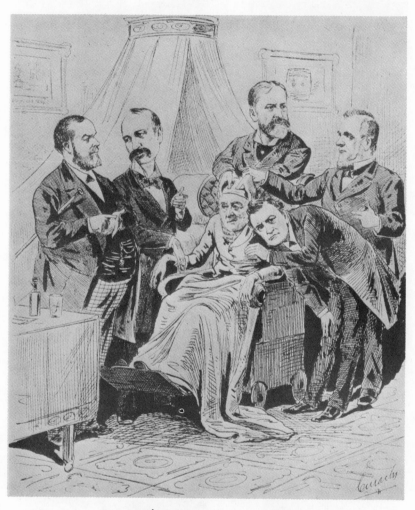

TILDEN'S POLITICAL ASSOCIATES

AN IMPORTANT MEDICAL CONSULTATION

Dr. Kelly—"The condition of the patient, in my opinion, is hopeless."
Drs. Cow, Randall, Church and Cooper—"So say we all of us."

FOUNDERING
From "Puck"

THE ONE HAPPY DEMOCRAT
From "Puck"

DESPATCHED

From "Harper's Weekly"

BETWEEN TWO FIRES

From "Harper's Weekly"

GREYSTONE, TILDEN'S HOME AT YONKERS, NEW YORK

THE PORCH AT GREYSTONE

THE FUNERAL OF SAMUEL J. TILDEN

LEAVING GREYSTONE
TILDEN'S BIRTHPLACE
AT THE GRAVE

From "Harper's Weekly"

SAMUEL J. TILDEN

Painting in the Trustees' Room of the New York Public Library

at $108,000. Later he paid a tax on an assessed income of $15,000, together with penalties for delinquency. On this record he was accused of fraud, perjury, and treason. By September Republican papers were printing alleged interviews with brokers indicating that Tilden had made enormous profits "on the street." [46]

This exposure created a sensation. Republican leaders were jubilant, Democratic leaders solicitous. "The income tax charge is doing a good deal of harm," wrote W. C. Whitney.[47] John Kelly, Dan Magone, and J. C. Spencer wired Tilden not to go to Philadelphia until the excitement subsided; and Kelly hurried down to Washington to see what could be done about it.[48] The president of the Pittsburg, Fort Wayne & Chicago Railroad refused to allow Bliss to examine the company books.[49] Hewitt asked for a certified copy of the income returns of both Hayes and Tilden, but the Federal Government refused the request.[50] Meanwhile Tilden said nothing and the *Nation* called his reticence "an ugly flaw."

As usual, Tilden proceeded to assemble facts to answer the charge. Judge James P. Sinnott, with the assistance of Tilden himself, Bigelow, and a few clerks, compiled the data for a defense in a letter to Hewitt denying twelve of the thirteen charges in the *Times*. Dorsheimer was also preparing a defense. Hewitt then issued a statement "To the Public" explaining that Tilden's income-producing property was largely in railroad stocks and bonds on which the tax was paid at the source; and that he also had had large losses in business, notably in the New Lebanon drug concern. The *Nation* now exonerated Tilden on the ground that his returns were as full as men of his class were accustomed to make; [51] the *Sun* printed a long vindication; and Bryant, incensed at the "shameful" attacks, promised to open the *Post* to a refutation of the "slander" and wrote an article himself which the managing editor persuaded him not to print.[52] These defenses satisfied friendly critics, but political opponents used the exposure with telling effect to the end of the campaign. No doubt many believed the insinuation and on that account voted againt Tilden.

Tilden's political foes also sought to blacken his personal character. He was accused of being a victim of paresis, a bluffing egotist, an in-

[46] New York *Times*.   [47] Tilden Papers, Sept. 5, 1876.
[48] H. R. Misc. Docs., 45 Cong., 3rd Sess., No. 31, Pt. 4, 328.
[49] Tilden Papers.   [50] Nevins, *Hewitt*, 320.
[51] Tilden Papers, Sept. 11, 20, 28, 29, 1876.   [52] *Letters*, II, 446, 466.

consistent hypocrite, false to his friends, immoral, dishonest and utterly unreliable. Parke Godwin said the Republicans called Tilden "a drunkard, a liar, a cheat, a counterfeiter, a perjurer and a swindler." [53] As a lawyer, he was a tool of corporations, bankers and Wall Street gamblers who made millions out of wrecking railroads and crooked business deals. In his Michigan mines he issued $4,000,000 in shinplasters with which the laboring people were defrauded. He was accused of secretly countenancing election frauds; and of being a party friend of Tweed, at whose robberies he winked until forced to take a stand against them. As a sham reformer he blustered about the Canal Ring but accomplished little. His alleged economy was a mere pretense, as proved by his falsified figures. The moral turpitude charged against him destroyed the fabric of the Ten Commandments.

The muckraking *Times*, unearthing "new rascalities of Tilden," discovered the "Brady Bend Swindle" in which he wrecked a railroad and a thriving community and tried to bribe a superintendent with $50,000 in stocks. Fraudulent registrations in Philadelphia were laid at his door because his name was found on a hotel register in that city. A campaign song spoke of "Sly Sam, the Railroad Thief." G. W. Curtis,[54] who regarded him as an "honest and intelligent" Democrat, called him "Usufructuary Tilden" after his nomination and filled his journal with satirical cartoons by Nast and Frost. The "Tweedle-dee and Tilden-dum" picture showed Tweed and Tilden as cronies in graft. Tilden and Hendricks were an ox and ass hitched to the Democratic plow. Tilden on a "Still Hunt" had a check for $5,000 sticking out of his coat tail; and, as a Copperhead on the shoulders of "Sinbad Reform," he was surrounded with posters depicting all the charges against him.

Samuel J. Tilden Unmasked by B. E. Buckman, a New York policeman, presented a garbled account of Tilden's reorganization of Western railroads,[55] and his alleged association with Oakes Ames, Tom Scott, and other railroad promoters, from which his fortune was derived. He was denounced as the original railroad ring organizer, the farmer's foe, a perfidious attorney, a sycophant of corporations, a corrupter of the press, a dangerous demagogue, an enemy of State schools

---

[53] "The Need of New Men and New Measures," printed by the Democratic National Committee.
[54] Editor of *Harper's Weekly*.
[55] Based on Parton's *Manual of Instruction for Rings*.

and the Erie Canal, a traitor to the Democratic Party, "a disgrace to the State of New York," and a "menace to the United States." Hence farmers, mechanics, laborers, Catholics and Irishmen were called upon to repudiate him at the polls. This diatribe was so ineptly overdone that it is doubtful whether it did Tilden much injury. The exposé of Tilden's connection with the reorganization of the Terre Haute, Alton & St. Louis Railroad in the Chicago *Tribune* did more damage because it was more truthful.[56]

Marble informed Tilden that the Chicago paper was attempting to ascertain whether he had amassed "a colossal fortune by sitting up with sick railroads and attending their funerals." Why not set forth "what you have done for railroads?" Thus you would take "the wind out of the sails of your slanderers. You dictate the material and I will work it up." [57] The idea pleased Tilden and soon favorable references to his railroad rehabilitations began to appear in the newspapers, and the "Literary Bureau" issued Document No. 8 on the subject. The *Nation* gave an accurate account of the reorganization of the Terre Haute, Alton & St. Louis Railroad and declared that all the holders of old securities made money. Hence Tilden was a railroad saver, not a railroad robber.[58] But these explanations about Tilden's railroad transactions never traveled rapidly enough to catch up with the lies. Republican newspapers and speakers did their best to connect Tilden with the scandalous Crédit Mobilier as legal adviser in its dealings with the Union Pacific. The *Sun* denounced the allegation as "false and ridiculous" and Judge James P. Sinnott, who had been in Tilden's law office from 1859 to 1872, testified that Tilden had no part in the organization of the concern. He had been asked in 1867 to give advice but had refused. He was consulted in 1869, however, by the exploited stockholders.[59]

There was no radio to broadcast this program of slander, but printer's ink, the platform and back stairs gossip were used to the limit. Columns and entire pages were devoted to one or another of these canards. Repetition had weight with the ignorant and those anxious to believe, who repeated the tales in all sorts of gatherings. The Republicans had brilliant campaign orators—Blaine, Garfield, Logan, Harrison, Evarts, Ingersoll, Curtis, Cameron, Sherman, Depew and

[56] Aug. 8, 1876.   [57] Tilden Papers, Aug. 22, 1876.
[58] Democratic National Committee, Document No. 8.   [59] Tilden Papers.

Mark Twain. Not all dipped their hands in pitch—Roscoe Conkling in his single address refused to utter a word against Tilden and Lowell lamented, "The worst element of the Republican Party has got hold of the canvass." [60] But lesser orators let their tongues run riot in the crusade of defamation. The campaign was not one between the two parties, nor between Hayes and Tilden, but between a handful of Republican leaders and Tilden.

Greeley was killed by such an onslaught in 1872, and Tilden might have succumbed under the storm of abuse in 1876 had he not been less sensitive, more experienced, and buoyed up by a fanatical zeal for decent government. Besides he had a profound conviction that the people knew he was fighting their cause and would defend him at the polls. At first he answered some of the charges himself. To a Minnesota man who said he could find no evidence that Tilden had accomplished anything in his assault on the Canal Ring, he sent a full explanation of what had been accomplished and what was being done. [61] Bigelow and Marble were kept busy refuting Republican exposures and all sorts of trumped-up charges. Some of Tilden's supporters, without encouragement from him, sought to repay his maligners in their own coin. There were scandalmongers aplenty among the Democrats, and Hayes was accused of stealing the pay of dead soldiers in his regiment. His letter to the American Alliance was exploited to prove that he was a foe of naturalized citizens. One muckraker sent Tilden a list of topics concerning Hayes which should be looked up as campaign ammunition. Among the items were: Hayes's tax returns for 15 years; his back pay after 1866; his army pay; his bequests from Birchard; legal fees not in his income tax returns; the value of his library, paintings, diamonds etc., not reported; his record as Congressman and Governor; and an answer to the question, "Did Hayes shoot his mother in a fit of insanity?" [62] A Democratic paper in Ohio accused him of frauds in his tax returns and the Chicago *Times* printed a document to prove that in 1874–76 he reported an income of $2,581 when it should have been $57,200.

Along with the billingsgate, the campaign was enlivened with popular songs and amusing stories. *The Tilden Illustrated Campaign Song and Joke Book* [63] had a tremendous sale. Tilden adorned the front

[60] Lowell, *Letters*, II, 176; Chidsey, *Conkling*, 207, Oct. 3, 1876.
[61] *Letters*, II, 434, June 15, 1876.   [62] Tilden Papers, J. S. Douglas, Sept. 25, 1876.
[63] Published by The American News Company and sold at a dime.

page and the title page presented the American flag. It contained fifty pages of songs and comical comments. "Hold the Fort for Tilden" had thirteen stanzas and a chorus of which the following are examples:

> See the rings, the combinations,
>   Whiskey, railroad, land;
> Wicked schemes for peculation
>   Rife on every hand.
>   Chorus
> Hold the fort, for we are coming,
>   Hear the people cry;
> Wave the answer back with fervor
>   By your help we'll try.

There were many songs on "Uncle Sam," and a parody on Yankee Doodle ran:

> Sam Tilden is a gentleman,
>   A true and honest man, sir;
> And when we call for honest work
>   He's just the chap to answer.
> He represents the very truths
>   That we have all been drilled in,
> And we couldn't have to lead us on
>   A better man than Tilden.

Petroleum V. Nasby convulsed both parties with his ungrammatical wit, as for instance, his final appeal to the Democrats to "Rally agin hard money in the West. Rally agin soft money in the East. Rally agin offishls uv a corrupt administrashun. . . . Rally agin the military power, which prevents us from killin niggers as we please. . . . Rally agin nigger in the concrete. Rally agin nigger in the abstract. Rally for victory and postoffices . . . P.S. I forgot to say we might ez well rally for reform."

After his speech of acceptance Tilden made only two nonpolitical addresses during the campaign—one at Saratoga on applied sociology; [64] the other on the Centennial at Philadelphia where he was given a tremendous ovation.[65] He sent out no statement under his own name until near the close of the campaign. Nevertheless he supplied materials for numerous addresses and pronouncements by his loyal lieutenants, and thus was conscious of keeping his ideas before the people continu-

[64] *Writings*, II, 374, Sept. 5, 1876.   [65] Cook, 328, Sept. 21, 1876.

ally. Key men from all over the nation conferred with him and went home to put his suggestions into operation. A mountain of mail had his general oversight; and every critical phase of the canvass received his consideration. Because he made no fuss, never flew into tantrums and revealed no nervous excitement, many people thought him indifferent, too secretive and unduly conservative; [66] but he had schooled himself to keep an eye on the fundamentals while ignoring the incidentals. Parke Godwin tried to induce him to go to the White Mountains for a good rest, but he refused to desert his post.[67] During the first part of the campaign he spent much time in Albany, but when it was well under way he stayed almost continually in New York City.

The most effective work was performed by Hewitt, Bigelow, Marble, Watterson, Dana, Randall, Magone, and Pelton, not through platform oratory but with the printed page and administrative machinery. The leading field speakers and workers were Kernan, Bigler, Barnum, Hendricks, Thurman, Bayard, Cox, Gwin, Miller, Prince, Casserly, Godwin, Hoadly and Montgomery Blair. Seymour professed to be too ill to participate. Among the minor speakers were Henry George, who worked in California and wrote a pamphlet on the campaign issues; [68] Joseph Pulitzer, who hurried home from Europe to take the stump; [69] Henry B. Stanton, husband of Elizabeth Cady Stanton, who was an advocate of Tilden's reforms; [70] Cyrus Hall McCormick, who contributed time and money; [71] Reverend John C. Kimball of the Unitarian Church in Providence, Rhode Island, who attacked the Republican "bloody shirt" campaign; [72] and General Franz Sigel, who labored to hold the German vote.[73] Taking the Democratic working staff as a whole, it was a capable group fired with an enthusiastic determination to win; yet inferior to the Republicans in executive ability.

After Congress adjourned, Hewitt directed the campaign from New York City in conjunction with Tilden, Bigelow, Marble, Dana and Pelton. Among those who made visits to headquarters for direction and inspiration was Henry Watterson, who spent several weeks there assisting in publicity and in outlining methods of campaigning in the West and the South. He saw a good deal of Tilden, and on one occasion, as Tilden, Marble and he were discussing the situation over sev-

66 *Tribune*, Sept. 19, 1876.
67 Tilden Papers, Aug. 15, 1876.
68 Tilden Papers, Aug. 22, 1876.
69 Seitz, *Pulitzer*.
70 Mitchell, *Memoirs*, 216.   71 Casson, *McCormick*, 165.   72 *Herald*, Nov. 7, 1876.
73 Tilden Papers.

eral bottles of old German wine, Marble asked, "Governor, what are we—Watterson and I—to have when you come into the Kingdom?" Tilden smiled and replied: "You boys don't want any offices. They would do you more harm than good. What you really want is big influence with the administration." [74] In such conferences a contemporary described Tilden as sitting on the edge of his chair as he leaned forward and whispered his words of wisdom. His drooping eyelid gave him the appearance of sagacity. He looked older than he was; his movements were slow; his utterance unimpressive; his mind deliberate, unexcitable and capable of personal detachment with power to make momentous decisions.[75]

As the final month of the campaign approached every nerve was strained. New York, Connecticut, and New Jersey were reported safe. All eyes were turned to Ohio and Indiana, which voted on local tickets on October 10. In Ohio the canvass was "lumbering along without much method or direction," as if the New York managers thought that State lost—"a great mistake." Some "judicious friend" should be sent there to stay till election.[76] Bigler was ill and could not go so Kernan was hurried out to help.[77] But Ohio went Republican by a small majority of 6,636 which might have been avoided if the Democrats had sent more men and money. As for Indiana, Barnum went with $60,000 to assist Hendricks and Voorhees and proved to be "just the man," while colored speakers were sent into the southern part of that State and Illinois.[78] As a result the Democrats won Indiana by a small majority of 5,084. The South was believed to be safe, but Tilden was warned that the real fight would be there, because Chandler and Tyner had decided to carry the Carolinas, Louisiana and Florida "by the commercial element." A Mississippian wrote Tilden "seventy-four of my old slaves will vote for you," and a number of leaders of the Southern Negroes were going to support him.[79] To win the foreign vote German, Swedish, French, and Bohemian speakers were employed.

The question of hard or soft money was a knotty problem in the contest and Tilden was told repeatedly that his stand for sound finance was losing him thousands of votes. He was adamant, however, and declared that he would rather lose a million votes than that "the me-

[74] Watterson, *Hist. of the Manhattan Club*, 145.   [75] Mitchell, *Memoirs*, 264.
[76] Tilden Papers, Thomas Ewing, Sept. 30, 1876.
[77] *Ib.*, William Bigler, Sept. 30, 1876.
[78] *Ib.*, W. E. Niblect to Hewitt, Oct. 7, 1876.   [79] *Ib.*, F. M. Shields, Oct. 22, 1876.

chanics, the servant girls and laboring men should be robbed of their earnings." [80] While Peter Cooper and the Greenbackers were almost lost sight of in the excitement of the campaign, yet those who supported soft money were mostly Democrats. The Grangers of the Northwest gave Cooper only a few votes and seemed to prefer Tilden to Hayes.

Near the end of the campaign the assertion of speakers like Blaine that, if President, Tilden would pay off Confederate war damages, was answered by a letter which Hewitt sent out before Tilden could change his mind about it.[81] It showed that the Fourteenth Amendment made it impossible to pay any rebel losses, and declared that Tilden would veto any bill seeking to reopen this question. It made the plea: "Let bygones be bygones; turn from the dead past to a new and better future." Robert Toombs might call it "infamous" and refuse to vote for Tilden,[82] but other Southerners commended it and said, "Not a single State in the South will be lost to our party." [83] Northern Democrats were delighted, and wanted it printed in blue and posted up everywhere.

In summing up this famous Presidential contest, it should be remembered that arrayed against Tilden were the regular Republicans whose convictions were rooted in the antislavery movement, who had loyally crushed the Civil War, and who had been in power at Washington since 1860—so long in fact that they felt they had a perpetual mortgage on the Federal Government. Allied with them were the "Boys in Blue" who professed to believe that only the Republicans could safely perpetuate the country which they had saved and would reward them with pensions. Of course not a few soldiers followed McClellan, Sigel, and Hancock, but they were under suspicion in their own communities. Most of the Liberal Republicans who in 1872 opposed the election of Grant turned to Hayes as reliable, honest and progressive. That portion of the business men who relied more and more for financial success upon a high protective tariff gave their votes to the man whose party was its champion and who stood for sound money. The friends of the Tweed Ring and the Canal Ring were implacable in their hatred of Tilden. Not many of them openly joined the Republicans, but they secretly stabbed him in the back and pursued a defeat-

[80] *World*, Aug. 26, 1876.   [81] Nevins, *Hewitt*, 314.   [82] *Am. Hist. Assn.*, 1911, II, 722.
[83] *Letters*, II, 472; Tilden Papers, D. J. Goodwin, Oct. 26, 1876.

ist policy. Boss John Kelly and his Tammany followers did some injury by their indifference. "I hope you smooth the ruffled feathers of the Tammany braves" came to Tilden's ears from all sides.[84] As prospects of a Democratic victory brightened, these recalcitrant members showed signs of hedging. "Judge Church has changed his tune within the last ten days," Tilden was informed.

Tilden's support came from various political, sectional, racial, and economic groups, mostly already within the Democratic Party, North and South, which in spite of factional discordances presented a remarkable unity throughout the whole campaign. Out of power for a generation, the leaders felt that they must either elect a President or be submerged. They thought the Republicans had supplied the petard for their own defeat. The Southerners had no other choice than to work for the election of Tilden, who represented a hope for their deliverance. Some bitter-enders like Toombs may not have expected "anything good from an old Van Buren Free-Soiler trained in Tammany Hall and Wall Street," [85] but the majority of Southerners gave him reasonable, some enthusiastic, support. Eight of the rebel States had recovered self-government, although still in a wretched economic condition. Five of them had safe white majorities. Would pressure from Washington compel the counting of the black majorities in the other three—Georgia, Alabama, and Mississippi? And, what of South Carolina, Florida, and Louisiana—the "unreconstructed" States still under the domination of the Grant administration? Time alone could answer these questions.

Independents in great numbers advocated Tilden's election, Charles Francis Adams, Sr., and his son Charles Francis Adams, Jr., both openly approved of him as a candidate.[86] Although James Russell Lowell found little to choose between Hayes and Tilden on their Southern policies, he said, "I rather sympathize with the Democrats," and voted for the latter.[87] Ottendorfer, Hoadley, and Lyman Trumbull [88]—in whose office William Jennings Bryan studied law—brought character to Tilden's cause. Professor W. G. Sumner, a Yale economist, created a sensation when he repudiated Hayes as "a creature of the machine" and lauded Tilden because he was "opposed by all the worst elements of his party" and endorsed by honest men, particularly young men of ideals; be-

[84] Tilden Papers, Manton Marble, Aug. 23, 1876.
[85] *American Historical Association*, 1911, II, 722.
[86] *Letters*, II, 452.   [87] Lowell, *Letters*, II, 174.   [88] White, *Trumbull*, 411.

cause he had not abandoned his stand for hard money; and because he was a man of skill, knowledge and achievement.

Sumner was quoted widely and won many Independents for Tilden. Young men all over the country—among them Henry Cabot Lodge, Charles Nordhoff, and Walter Phelps—were swept off their feet by the spreading wave of reform. Grover Cleveland wanted Bayard for President, but supported the party candidates. Some Independents, however, agreed with Bryant, who never told how he voted, that, although Tilden was "the most of a statesman, the soundest and most enlarged in opinions and . . . of the finest character," yet the Republican Party was the "most to be relied on." Others, like Whitelaw Reid, openly balked at Hendricks and the prospect of inflation, but endorsed Tilden personally.[89]

Hard times and the promise of reduced taxes carried many of the farmers into the Democratic camp. Economic distress, low wages, and the hope of improvement caught the mechanics and laboring men. A substantial group of bankers and promoters of railroads and mines, who cared more for internal peace and prosperity than they did for tariffs and who had a high regard for Tilden's business acumen, backed him. Men like Judge Stallo of Ohio, Koerner of Illinois, and General Sigel, Pulitzer and Dorsheimer of New York offset the influence of Schurz over the Germans. The Irish Catholics generally were loyal to Tilden through the influence of men such as Senator Kernan.

As the day of decision approached it was believed that all the Southern States, with the possible exception of South Carolina, would vote for Tilden, thus giving him 131 electoral votes. Thirteen Northern states with 129 electoral votes were conceded to Hayes. In the doubtful list were the important States of Indiana, Ohio, and New York, and the lesser States of Connecticut, New Jersey, Delaware, and Maryland. Campaign bets in New York City were reported to be five to two in favor of Tilden, and John Morrissey had difficulty in finding any takers for his $700,000 [90] at these odds. The excitement of the campaign went on—the huge gatherings by day and night, in halls and out of doors, the spread-eagle oratory of the Centennial year, the bonfires and pole-raisings, the parades with dripping torches and trans-

[89] Howe, *James Ford Rhodes,* 308; Tilden Papers, D. A. Wells, Oct. 24, 1876; Nevins, *Cleveland,* 75; Bryant to I. C. Derby, Aug. 28, 1876; Cortissoz, *Reid,* 322.
[90] Tilden papers.

parent banners, the shouting and rough comments, the blaring bands and boisterous songs. This in the North and West; the South was not in a mood for celebration—its future was too serious. The South stood dry-eyed, expectant.

THE Presidential canvass of 1876 ended on November 6, the date on which Governor Tilden issued his Thanksgiving Proclamation.[1] At the same time, as a symbol of Tilden's triumph as a political reformer, Boss Tweed was being brought back to New York a prisoner.[2] The eyes of the nation, however, were centered not on the fallen corruptionist but upon two men—one a military leader in the Buckeye State; the other a drab, colorless figure in the Empire State. Which would become President on the morrow? The decision in New York, with its large electoral vote, would answer that question, for it was generally believed that the candidate who won there would succeed Grant. With Tilden in the Governor's chair of that pivotal State, it seemed that he had an advantage. But Wheeler, a New Yorker, was popular, and some of the ablest Republican managers had devoted much time to the canvass.

While Tilden's habitual taciturnity precluded an expression of his judgment as to the result in either New York or the nation, his lieutenants were emphatic in their belief that victory was certain. One was so confident that he advised the coming President to prepare the party for the fulfillment of "our promises" and suggested that Kernan might make the initial address.[3] Kernan sent his congratulations and rejoiced that "The entire people will be blessed by the restoration of economy and honesty . . . and have the greatly needed reforms." [4] While some of the Ring's friends mounted the bandwagon,[5] Kelly still sulked. Outside of New York cheering messages were sent to Tilden. A Presidential elector from Louisiana denied the rumor that that State would not support the national ticket.[6] The National Committees of the two parties met in New York City on the evening of November 6 to send out last-minute instructions and to make their election forecasts. Hewitt and his colleagues were jubilant as they studied the final reports from the various States and were positive of the happy ending of the

---

[1] Not given in Lincoln, *Messages*, VI.   [2] Lynch, *Boss Tweed*, 401.
[3] Tilden Papers, E. K. Apgar, Nov. 3, 1876.
[4] *Letters*, II, 486.
[5] Tilden Papers, A. C. Beach for example; L. S. Martin, Nov. 2, 1876.
[6] *Democratic Campaign Book*, 1880.

campaign. Zach Chandler and his allies, at the Fifth Avenue Hotel, were clearly worried.[7] Meanwhile in the city and elsewhere the Democrats took the greatest pains to get voters to the polls and to watch the counting.[8]

Election day, November 7, broke with lowering skies and rain in New York State—a good omen of a Democratic victory upstate. The better morning papers cautioned the people to keep their heads cool, because "whichever of the two candidates is elected, the country will be safe." The election took place without any clashes or riots. At the Democratic headquarters in the Everett House Tilden supporters like Magone, Bigelow, and Pelton cheerfully declared that he would be elected, and the betting was about 100 to 80 in his favor. After voting Tilden went to the Everett House about noon where many friends came and went. He was driven home about four o'clock, in the best of spirits, and received congratulations from callers, among them "ladies of his social circle." Dressed in black, with a red flower in his buttonhole, he received them with dignity and a confident smile. A telegraph line had been run to his house. Over this as the day passed a flood of congratulations came from men like General McClellan, C. N. Potter, Senator Randolph, and Benjamin Wood. An excited group assembled in front of Tilden's home in Gramercy Park, cheering and waving hats and handkerchiefs, anxious to get a glimpse of the next President. Not minding the cold rain, crowds gathered in front of the Everett House and packed Irving Hall to hear the bulletins. The streets about the newspaper offices, clubs, and theaters were packed with people eager for the latest news. After dinner Tilden returned to headquarters to hear the returns, which early showed a triumph in the metropolis and the State. When victories were reported from New Jersey and Connecticut, there were indications of a landslide. As Tilden went home toward midnight, bedlam had let loose in Manhattan and across the Empire State.[9] When he carried New York it was believed that the election had been decided, and by midnight people went to bed convinced that he was President-elect. Governor Hayes retired feeling that he had lost the race, and recorded in his *Diary*, "From that time I never supposed there was a chance for Republican success." [10] Washington was wild with excitement when the returns indicated a Tilden

[7] Marble Papers, Lib. of Cong.
[9] New York newspapers.
[8] *Herald*, Nov. 7, 1876.
[10] Eckenrode, *Hayes*, 178.

triumph.[11]

On the morning of election day the National Republican Committee used the private house wire of Jay Gould to persuade President Grant, a guest of George W. Childs in Philadelphia, to send Federal troops to doubtful Southern States.[12] He ordered General Sherman to dispatch troops to South Carolina, Louisiana and Florida. Grant thought Tilden, having won Louisiana, was elected, but felt that Florida was doubtful and that South Carolina and Oregon had gone for Hayes.[13] James A. Garfield explained the Democratic victory as a result of the "combined power of rebellion, Catholicism, and whiskey" —antecedents of "Rum, Romanism, and Rebellion," the slogan that defeated Blaine.[14]

With sunrise on the day following the election, November 8, newspapers of both parties all over the country announced that Tilden was the next President; and Democrats prepared for a big celebration. In New York the *Tribune* conceded his victory and the *Evening Post* gave him 209 electoral votes to Hayes' 160. The *Herald* and the *Times*, however, refused to concede a Democratic triumph. The headlines of the *Herald* ran: "The Result—What is it? Something that no fellow can understand. Impossible to name our next President. The returns too meager." Florida, Louisiana and Oregon were conceded to Tilden; and, "Returns seem to indicate that Governor Tilden has been elected." Similar advice was cabled to the Rothschilds, and Belmont wired Tilden, "Wall Street evidently not frightened by Evarts's bugbear."[15]

The *Times* had attacked Tilden during the campaign with a bitterness explainable only by a fear that he was going to be elected.[16] Had it not been for the stubborn resistance of that journal, Tilden's election might have been quietly acknowledged.[17] Its managing editor, John C. Reid, still remembered his sufferings in Libby Prison, and his vehement partisanship was reflected in the policy of the paper. When about midnight of election day, Hewitt, overconfident and perhaps incautious, sent a messenger to the *Times* politely inquiring what majority it conceded to Tilden, Reid peevishly replied, "None."[18] Then about 3:45 A. M., while Reid and three other members of the

11 Perley, *Reminiscences*, II, 320.
12 Philadelphia *Ledger*, Sept. 5, 1885; Gibson, *A Political Crime*, 56–57.
13 McClure, *Recollections*, 100.   14 Caldwell, *Garfield*, 251.
15 Tilden Papers, Nov. 6, 1876.   16 Davis, *Times*, 131.
17 Nevins, *Hewitt*, 320.   18 Davis, *Times*, 136.

Times staff were deciding what interpretation to give the election returns in their first edition, Dan Magone, Chairman of the State Democratic Committee, sent from his headquarters the following dispatch: "Please give your estimate of the electoral votes secured for Tilden. Answer at once." [19] This indiscreet inquiry was interpreted by Reid and his associates to mean that the Democratic leaders were in a doubtful frame of mind, and this belief, coupled with reports that Oregon was Republican by a majority of 500, that South Carolina and Louisiana were claimed for Hayes, and that Florida was in doubt, induced them to accept Edward Cary's suggestion that the *Times* should announce in the first edition that the election was uncertain. Cary then prepared an editorial headed, "A Doubtful Election," which stated that after a heavy vote the result was indecisive and that it was feared "the shotgun and rifle clubs," would give the Democrats the victory. The loss of New York was conceded. Hayes was given 178 electoral votes and Tilden 175. Later returns were interpreted as still more favorable to Hayes, so when the 6:30 A. M. edition appeared, the editorial was more confident and the "shotgun" reference was omitted, while the vote became Tilden 184 and Hayes 181, counting Louisiana, South Carolina, and Oregon in the Republican column but leaving Florida in doubt.

At this point Reid went to the rooms of the Republican National Committee in the Fifth Avenue Hotel, found them deserted, and was on his way to the hotel office to get the number of Zach Chandler's room, when he ran into Committeeman W. E. Chandler disguised in goggles and a heavy military coat. Just in from New Hampshire, Chandler, a deckhand for the committee,[20] was worked up over the Republican disaster of which he had just read in the *Tribune*. Reid assured him that there would be no disaster "if you keep your heads up here." In W. E. Chandler's room the electoral returns were carefully studied State by State and the possibility of a Republican victory pointed out by Reid. "What should be done?" Chandler eagerly asked. Reid replied, "Telegraph immediately to leading Republicans . . . in South Carolina, Florida, Louisiana, California, Oregon and Nevada." Greatly relieved, Chandler said, "We must go and see Zach." With some difficulty they found Zach Chandler's room and he received them in his

[19] Tilden Papers, Nov. 8, 1876. Davis, *Times*, 136, states that A. P. Gorman sent the message, and Bigelow, II, 11, mentions Barnum.
[20] Davis, *Times*, 135.

nightdress. "Here is a gentleman who has news . . . and . . . suggestions," explained W. E. Chandler. "Yes, I know him. . . . What is it?"
said Zach. Reid then explained to the sleepy National Chairman, who,
lying on the bed, agreed. "Go ahead and do what you think necessary,"
he said.

Reid and W. E. Chandler hurried down to the hotel telegraph office,
found it closed, and after preparing the messages, drove to the main
office of the Western Union, where the following telegram was sent to
D. H. Chamberlain, Columbia, South Carolina: "Hayes is elected if
we have carried South Carolina, Florida and Louisiana. Can you hold
your State? Answer immediately." Variations of this telegram were
sent to trustworthy Republicans in Florida, Louisiana, Oregon and
California. The name of Zachariah Chandler was signed to the first
three telegrams and that of W. E. Chandler to the last two. The telegraph operator, refusing to charge them to the Republican National
Committee, was told by Reid to charge them to the *Times*.[21] This was
the "conspiracy" which John Bigelow so indignantly condemned; [22]
at most it was only the product of Reid's bitter partisanship combined
with the gambler's wish of the two Chandlers to win the election.

After receiving encouraging replies to these telegrams, the Republican National Committee, at 10:30 P. M. of the same day, November 8,
sent out this announcement: "Dispatches received at these headquarters report that Louisiana, Florida, South Carolina, Wisconsin, Oregon,
Nevada and California have given Republican majorities. There is
no reason to doubt the correctness of these reports and if confirmed the
election of Hayes is assured by a majority of one in the Electoral College." [23] There seems to be no contemporary proof that early on the
morning of November 8 Zach Chandler sent out a message claiming
185 votes for Hayes. On the contrary there is some evidence that the
first reports from the Republican chairmen in Louisiana and Florida
conceded these States to Tilden but that Chandler suppressed them.
The *Times* knew that the Democrats claimed Louisiana by 20,000;
the Republicans by 4,000. This news was sufficient to place that State
in the doubtful column at first; and then in the Hayes column. Knowing that the Returning Boards were in Republican hands in the three
doubtful Southern States, the Republican National Chairman felt

[21] *Times,* June 15, 1887. Reid's account.   [22] Life, II, 8–17.
[23] *Herald,* Nov. 9, 1876.

fairly confident in claiming them for Hayes.

As a result of the bold claim of the *Times* and Zach Chandler, the Democratic leaders were in a quandary. Manton Marble, resting at Bryn Mawr, Pennsylvania, after a strenuous campaign, wired G. W. Smith, Tilden's secretary, on November 8: "Is there any doubt? All sorts of reports here." Frantic questions poured into Tilden and the Democratic National Committee.[24] That Tilden himself was concerned is shown by the fact that, after a late breakfast on the morning following the election, he walked with his secretary to the Democratic National Headquarters and remained there until 2:45 P. M., talking with party leaders. To those who offered congratulations he replied in a dignified manner, "Thank you, sir," but if he made any comment, it has not survived. Upon his return to Gramercy Park in the early afternoon a crowd there gave him a hearty cheer. Believing that he had won, he said to a *World* reporter: "My election was due . . . to the issues. . . . I received a great number of Republican votes. . . . The election was decided in part on my record as Governor. . . . The closeness of the contest shows . . . the opposition I had to overcome. . . . I did not expect a large majority in the Electoral College." After a late luncheon he drove his team of "bright bays" in an open phaeton with a footman beside him to the home of his peppery friend, Charles O'Conor, and returned at 7:30 P. M. Half an hour later he entertained forty persons at what must have seemed like a victory dinner.[25]

On the second day following the election, November 9, the general situation was well summed up by a Mid-Western newspaper, "You could have told a Republican five hundred yards away yesterday morning by the length of his visage." But "our boys" began to brace up when the *Times* report and the bulletin from the Republican National Committee were sent out.[26] Other Republican papers over the country, following the lead of the *Times,* were claiming the count for Hayes. The *Herald* headed election news with "Neck and Neck! Who is it?" and its editorial, "Election a Doubtful Result," gave Tilden 184 votes, Hayes 151 and doubtful 34. Tilden was significantly silent, but Hayes gave an interview to a Cincinnati newspaper in which he was quoted as saying: "I think we are defeated in spite of recent good news. I am of the opinion that the Democrats have carried the coun-

[24] Tilden Papers.   [25] Newspapers of Nov. 8, 1876.
[26] Indianapolis *Journal,* Nov. 9, 1876.

try and elected Tilden." [27]

As soon as it became apparent that the election would be decided by the doubtful Southern States, plans were made by both parties to send their strongest leaders South. The Republican chiefs met in Washington on the night of November 8 and decided to send Zach Chandler to Florida by express.[28] Henry Watterson wired Tilden: "Our friends in La. need moral support and personal advisement. Have Bayard, Thurman, Barnum, Randall, McDonald, Dorsheimer, Kernan and others go to New Orleans at once. A strong demonstration will defeat the designs of the Returning Board. Beck, McHenry and I start tonight. You must reinforce us." From Florida Democrats came the appeals: "Need money to resist Radicals' pranks" and, "Need material aid to check Radicals." Coyle was hurried down to South Carolina.[29] After consulting with Tilden, Hewitt "caused letters to be sent" to leading Northerners, inviting them to go South for the purpose of insuring an honest count. Grant followed with a similar request to Republicans only.[30]

On November 10 the *Herald* used the headlines over election news, "Nip and Tuck"—Tilden still had 184 votes, Hayes had come up to 166 and 19 were undetermined. "Keep cool!" was the injunction people found difficult to follow. Tired out by the excitement, Tilden remarked, "The fiery zealots of the Republican Party may attempt to count me out, but I don't think the better class of Republicans will permit it." [31] Suspicious, apparently, of Secretary of War Cameron's order to General W. T. Sherman to send soldiers to Tallahassee, Florida, President Grant asked Sherman to "instruct General Auger in Louisiana and General Ruger in Florida . . . to see that the . . . legal Boards of Canvassers are unmolested in the performance of their duties. Should there be any grounds of suspicion of fraudulent counting on either side, it should be . . . denounced at once. . . . The country cannot afford to have the result tainted by the suspicion of illegal or false returns." [32]

On this third day following the election, Tilden kept his mouth shut except to his most intimate party associates. In the afternoon he took a long drive with John Bigelow to discuss the outlook. A contemporary

[27] Kent, *The Democratic Party*, 257.
[28] *Letters*, II.
[29] Tilden Papers, Nov. 9, 1876.
[30] Nevins, *Hewitt*, 326.
[31] *Herald*, Nov. 11, 1876.
[32] *Life*, II, 19.

described him at this time as, "A most accomplished and astute politician—less confiding and more distrustful than Grant—a man of modest, unobtrusive personality . . . stooped and hence looks smaller than he is—small smooth boyish face—round head bent with that sleepy droop in the left eyelid . . . caused by ptosis . . . small, delicate, utterly unobtrusive features . . . dressed with a plainness . . . like the pettiest clerk . . . so weak, so mild, so selfless, so uncombative . . . surrounded by political giants who bow before the modest little man with the cold, passionless, sagacious face . . . clear blue eyes . . . paled by age . . . fresh complexion . . . wrinkles about his eyes . . . pleasant small mouth wanting in sensual warmth . . . nose thin, small, bulging at the end, indicative of firmness . . . with wonderful self-control . . . no anxiety." [33] Tilden must have smiled to be reminded that Governor Marcy predicted that he would be President except for his "physical stamina. It is like putting a 200 horse power engine in a . . . craft built for only 100 horse power. . . . Tilden has too much mind for his body." [34]

An observing English visitor who just before the election spent an evening with Tilden beside the open fire in his study was deeply impressed by his views. "Political power is a trust," he said, "that should be fulfilled to the best interest of mankind." Human government might be the greatest good or the worst evil, but he hoped to restore the Jeffersonian state. The political idealism of his childhood had been dispelled by experience. He accepted public office at great personal sacrifice to reform corrupt civic practices and if sent to Washington he would continue the work of reform he had been doing in New York. His political foes assailed his motives and character because they were afraid of his leadership. He accepted the nomination for President only because he wished to garner the reform harvest which he had planted. He talked like a "statesman in his own house" and was "utterly free from pose or preparation." After some time he asked: "Have I tired you? I have never talked so much about myself to a lady before in my life." She was agreeably impressed by his personality and upon saying good-bye "begged him to win, because I have a lively new pink silk, Mr. Tilden, and I want to wear it at the Inaugural Ball." Laughingly he replied, "If those zealots do not prevent it, you shall

[33] *Herald*, Nov. 10, 1876.   [34] Tilden Papers, E. A. Doolittle, Nov. 8, 1876.

not only wear your pink silk but I have serious thoughts of making you my private secretary." [35]

As the deadlock continued the reactions of individuals and groups were significant. Not a few Hayes men believed that Tilden was honestly elected and should be seated. Among them was David Dudley Field who was so incensed that he deserted the Republicans and accepted a seat in Congress as a Democrat.[36] "Many of the more intelligent and influential Republicans" said openly that Tilden was entitled to the office of President,[37] and some of them put themselves on record in letters to him.[38] While intensely partisan Republicans naturally followed their leaders in seeking to exclude Tilden, Senator Conkling would countenance no fraud, thought Tilden should be aggressive and not "act upon the good-boy principle of submission"; and promised to render "hearty co-operation." [39] Garfield and Sherman feared Conkling would desert Hayes.[40] The Democrats generally assumed that there was no doubt whatever about Tilden's election and either charged the Republicans with a conspiracy to keep him out of office or asserted that Grant sought to eliminate both candidates so he might become dictator.[41] As time passed it was said, "Men here are desperate" and they insisted that Tilden act. "You are the only man who can . . . preserve the Constitution and the liberties of the people. . . . Three-fourths of the American people will sustain you. . . . Without action the case is hopeless." [42] "We all look upon you as our Savior. . . . You alone can rescue the country." Level-headed Kernan was "firm in the faith" that "right will prevail." [43] Tilden was reminded, much in his own words: "Courage is supreme wisdom now. You can arouse the people." [44] So much confidence did his followers have that they believed a stroke from his magic pen would settle the disputed election, curb the "bad men so conspicuous in the disputed States," and bring the "censure of honest and influential Republicans."

Those Democrats who did not permit their emotions to run away with them endeavored to view the situation realistically. Congressman R. B. Bradford wrote, "If you are not inaugurated, you'll never be President. . . . Nerve and resolution will win for you." Many persons

---

[35] Tilden Papers, Mrs. Florence D. Grey to Bigelow, Nov. 4, 1887.
[36] Field, *Life of D. D. Field*, 271.   [37] McClure, *Recollections*, 100.
[38] Tilden Papers, J. M. Strider, Dec. 20, 1876.   [39] *Letters*, II, 491.
[40] T. C. Smith, *Garfield*, II, 626.
[41] Tilden Papers, C. N. Ross to Tilden, Nov. 16, 1876; G. J. Pillow, Nov. 14, 1876.
[42] *Letters*, II, 489.   [43] Tilden Papers, Louis Schade.   [44] *Ib.*, J. M. Scovell telegram.

promised Tilden that they would attend his installation; some specu-
lated about his Cabinet; and prospective office seekers became solicitous. It was quite generally believed that a great legal battle was
ahead, and Tilden was flooded with advice as to the course to pursue.
A few persons suggested the wisdom of compromise and proposed that
he make Hayes his Secretary of State. The constitutional right of the
President of the Senate to count the vote was denied early by such men
as Bigler.

Influential men like Dana tried to persuade Tilden to take a positive, aggressive stand but found it difficult.[45] Indeed a wave of indignation spread across the country at his annoying inactivity. "Hundreds
of thousands came to regard him as a procrastinator." "Slow of movement, unimpressive of utterance, deliberate in judgment, unexcitable
of temperament, capable of absolutely personal detachment even from
a situation that greatly concerned himself, capable likewise of momentous decisions," still he found it difficult to make up his mind quickly.
His half audible "I'll see you later" merely meant that he wanted time
to mull things over.[46] He was forever holding conferences with small
groups—like Dorsheimer, Bigelow and Hewitt on November 14—or
with individuals such as C. F. Adams. When it was reported from
Washington that Tilden's managers "don't get below the surface of
things" and Dana was asked to "give Tilden a hint," he sent the letter
to Tilden, but nothing was done.[47] It was this dilatoriness that led Andrew D. White, who had known Tilden for some years, to remark that
he came within "a hair's breadth of the Presidency." [48] The same habit
of thought and action will crop out many times during the next few
months.

Hot-tempered Democrats were impatient with a policy of watchful
waiting. They wanted action coupled with a threat of force—a fair
count or a fight, as one Virginian put it. A Tennesseean warned Tilden
that he would be inaugurated only after a "bloody revolution." Either
fight or surrender was a reiterated theme. Nothing short of an earth-
quake would drive the Republicans out of office.[49] The excited state
of mind is revealed in the offer of Northerners and Southerners to recruit regiments, on the ground that "Our liberties are best preserved
by the sword." The militant spirit was to grow into alarming propor-

---

[45] Rosebaut, *When Dana Was the Sun*, 216.   [46] Mitchell, *Memoirs*.
[47] Tilden Papers.   [48] White, *Autobiography*, 125, 128, 174.
[49] Tilden Papers, Nov. 13, 1876; Nov. 14, 1876; Nov. 21, 1876.

tions during the next few months.

Disconcerting was the rumor that circulated in the North shortly after the election that the South was disposed to trade off Tilden's victory for local security and autonomy. A Congressman informed Tilden that he had just met fifty Democrats who declared that they would "abandon the Democratic Party if the Democrats failed to maintain their rights. . . . Lamar . . . would compromise to remain a Senator. . . . Suspect his intriguing with the enemy. . . . Eastern Democrats are too lukewarm." [50] From Washington came the news that there was serious danger of "defection among the Southern Democrats"—that Hayes men were "bidding high" and their offers were being considered.[51] Garfield wrote in his *Diary* that Young of Tennessee informed him that "if we could give such men as he good ground to stand on, fifty Democratic Congressmen would stand for Hayes." He told Hayes that Democratic business men were "more anxious for quiet than Tilden." [52] For example railroad men like Jay Gould, C. P. Huntington and Tom Scott were working to count Hayes in.[53] Under these conditions the best Democrats began to send Tilden advice about dependable constitutional methods for settling the disputed election, a theme that was much discussed during the coming months. One of the methods proposed was to hold great mass meetings of protest in the various States, which will be described later on.

That the majority of the people believed Tilden was President-elect is shown in the avalanche of telegrams, postcards and letters that poured in for months following November 7. Victory salutes were fired for months, and the composition of hymns and marches in his honor continued. The Democratic rooster appeared in homes across the continent and schoolboys sent cartoons of party triumph to their hero. Congratulations came from all classes—bankers and mechanics, railroad heads and farmers, college presidents and scrub women, and Union as well as Confederate soldiers. From Europe Julia Rothschild, Sir Robert Peel, Lord Hay and the American colony in Florence sent felicitations. The Oxford Union Society urged: "Like Hercules, cleanse the Augean Stables of the White House—like Pericles, show that Democracy does not mean unscrupulousness." [54] Seymour believed that Tilden had been elected.[55]

[50] Tilden Papers.   [51] *Ib.*, A. M. Gibson, Dec. 13, 1876.
[52] Smith, *Garfield*, II, 624.   [53] Tilden Papers, Dec. 13, 1876.
[54] Tilden Papers, various dates.   [55] Mitchell, *Seymour*, 532.

What was there about this little, sallow-faced, shambling dyspeptic that made him a popular hero? He had won no victory on the battle-field; he was not a magnetic orator; he had written no masterpiece in literature. Yet he was revered as a Moses leading his people out of bondage—as a Lincoln signing a new Emancipation Proclamation. The explanation of this mass psychology is that Tilden conquered through his ideas. His denunciation of corruption in public office, his demand for reformed government, his trust in the wisdom of democracy, his superb faith in American institutions as adequate to meet the needs of the nation, and his record in overthrowing the evil Rings made a powerful appeal to all types of people. They forgot that he was a past master in political psychology and in party mechanics, that he was a party man almost before he was an American, that he accumulated millions as a corporation lawyer, that he was cold-hearted, gruff and merciless, that he had no bosom friends and had never won the love of a woman, and that he was egotistical, opinionated and self-centered.

If the reader thinks this characterization of Tilden's appeal to the popular imagination is overdrawn, let him examine, for confirmation, the thousands of communications preserved in the Tilden Papers. The election in fact was just what Tilden described it to be—a tremendous peaceful revolution through the ballot box. Most Americans desired to forget the horrors and errors of the Civil War. They wished to oust the party that had taken advantage of its great record and its popularity to lord it over a fallen foe, to pilfer public funds, to gamble in patronage and to perpetuate its power. They wanted abuses corrected, hard times ended, taxes reduced, and the effectiveness of democracy demonstrated. They did not ask seriously whether Tilden and his party would fulfill their expectations, but their faith in his integrity and leadership led them to feel that a change would be both a relief and an improvement.

ALTHOUGH Tilden had received over a quarter of a million more votes than Hayes, yet under the American system of choosing a President by electors from the several States they had no direct influence on the actual count. The Republicans conceded that Tilden received from seventeen States 184 electoral votes, one short of the majority necessary to give him the decision. The Democrats conceded to Hayes in fifteen States 163 electoral votes. The electoral votes of four States were in dispute—1 out of 3 in Oregon; 7 in South Carolina; 4 in Florida; and 8 in Louisiana. If Tilden received a single vote from any one of these States he would be President, while Hayes needed the votes of all.

Who was to decide how the electoral vote in the three Southern States should be counted? South Carolina, Louisiana and Florida were still "unreconstructed," [1] and consequently under carpetbag rule backed up by the bayonets of Union soldiers. A State Board of Canvassers passed on the returns for Presidential electors. When selected, the electors then met, cast a ballot for President and Vice President, and sent a signed and sealed certificate of the choice to the President of the United States Senate. Since the Republicans dominated the carpetbag government of these States, they believed it would be possible to control the decision of the electors. The Democrats were depending upon the local whites to handle the situation so as to return Tilden electors.

In South Carolina the Board of Canvassers consisted of the Secretary of State, Comptroller General, Attorney General, Auditor, Treasurer and Inspector General, and the chairman of the Committee on Privileges and Elections of the State House of Representatives (who did not vote). These seven members were all Republicans; three were Negroes and three were candidates in the election. This board had power to receive and to canvass the returns for all officers except Governor and Lieutenant Governor, whose election was determined by the joint session of the legislature. It was the duty of the board "to decide all cases under protest or contest"; [2] and it assumed discretionary power. Under these

---

[1] These States from 1865 to 1869 had formally ratified the 13th, 14th and 15th Amendments but had failed to enact measures to protect the Negro in his newly acquired franchise.
[2] Act of Mar. 1, 1870.

conditions the Republicans were certain of the electoral vote of South Carolina.[3]

The Democrats, on the other hand, applied to the Supreme Court of South Carolina, composed of three Republicans, one a colored man [4] for a writ to compel the Returning Board merely to certify to the Secretary of State the persons receiving the highest number of votes, without exercising any judicial functions, and such an order was issued on November 17. The board did make such a report four days later, but denied that it was required to account to the court for its actions.[5] The report gave the Republicans all the electors and the Democrats enough Assemblymen to insure control of the joint legislature by which Wade Hampton was chosen Governor. It also mentioned frauds in three counties—a wedge for trouble. Would the Democrats be content with a local victory in the Governorship in exchange for the defeat of Tilden?

After consulting with national and local Democrats, the white leaders requested the Supreme Court to order the Canvassing Board to certify the election of Presidential electors and of all State Senators and Representatives and thus to assure the gubernatorial triumph. Then they asked for a full report to the court with all the papers on the returns of Presidential electors, hoping thus to save one Democratic elector or more.[6] The court delayed issuing the two orders, hoping that the time limit of ten days allowed the Canvassing Board would expire, after which all election records would go to the court. That was a shrewd scheme to save Tilden electors. On November 22, the last day of the session of the Canvassing Board, the first order was issued by the court. The board gave certificates to electors and to State and local officials, then adjourning before the second order could be served.[7]

Meantime Manton Marble and other Northern Democrats were on hand to advise the enraged State Democrats, and Governor-elect Wade Hampton expressed their indignation at the clever defeat of their plan.[8] Marble wired Pelton, "Three Republican affidavits proved frauds and forgeries." [9] The Democrats next tried to prevent the Republican electors from voting, but this also failed. Then they attempted to bribe one elector but in vain.[10] Finally on December 6 the electors met unhindered

---

[3] Haworth, *Hayes-Tilden Election,* 148–149.
[4] Allen, W. A., *Gov. Chamberlain's Administration,* 429.
[5] Haworth, 150.   [6] *Ib.,* 152.   [7] *Times* and *Herald,* Nov. 23, 1876.
[8] Haworth, 154; *An. Cyc.,* 1876, 725.   [9] Tilden Papers, Nov. 30, 1876.
[10] Haworth, 154.

and cast ballots for Hayes and Wheeler, which were duly certified and forwarded to Washington. The Democratic electoral claimants also met on December 6 and hurried their votes for Tilden and Hendricks to the President of the Senate. Their pretensions were rather flimsy. Neither at this time nor later before a Congressional Committee were the Democrats able to make out a good case for Tilden.[11] But national leaders felt that it was tactically important to claim South Carolina.

As early as November 14 Smith M. Weed telegraphed Democratic headquarters, "Best I can figure, Tilden will be 2,600 behind Hampton, and see little hope; shall keep up appearances."[12] The *Times* announced that Weed was there with a "barrel" and "mules." Weed wired, "Board demands $75,000 for two or three electors," and later, "Looks now as though $75,000 would secure all seven votes."[13] On the 17th he sent word: "Press everywhere. No certainty here. Simply a hope." But on the 18th he reported: "Majority of board secured. Cost $80,000. Send one parcel of $65,000; one of $10,000; one of $5,000. All to be in $1,000 or $500 bills. Have cash ready to reach Baltimore Sunday night." Pelton, after a conference with Edward Cooper at Tilden's house, met Weed in Baltimore, but without the money; and both hurried to New York to obtain it.[14] Tilden promptly quashed the plan. Hardy Soloman, pretending to represent the Returning Board, went to Baltimore to receive the money, but payment was peremptorily refused. Republicans later charged Weed and Marble with the attempt to purchase the vote of South Carolina, but the charge was never actually proved.[15] Tilden denied under oath that he had any knowledge of these negotiations.[16]

Louisiana's position differed considerably from that of South Carolina. The Republicans had nominated S. B. Packard for Governor while the Democrats selected General F. T. Nicholls. The Democratic platform approved the last three Federal Amendments, pledged a free election, and promised equal educational opportunities to blacks and whites. Meanwhile W. P. Kellogg, recognized by President Grant, and John McEnery both pretended to be Governor, but the former's authority was more generally recognized.

At the head of the election system was a State Returning Board of

[11] Haworth, 155.
[12] H. R. Misc. Docs., No. 31, pt. 4, 45th Cong., 3rd Sess., 133.
[13] To Henry Havemeyer, without cipher.
[14] H. R. Misc. Docs., No. 31, pt. 4, 45th Cong., 3rd Sess., 198.
[15] Andrews, 215.
[16] H. R. Misc. Docs., No. 31, pt. 3, 45th Cong. 3rd Sess., 196.

five members, chosen in 1873, but the only Democrat had resigned and his place had not been filled. Of the remaining four Republicans, two were whites and two mulattoes.[17] J. M. Wells, president, a carpetbag surveyor of the port, had been denounced as "a political trickster and a dishonest man" when in 1867 General Sherman had removed him as Governor. T. C. Anderson, a former Senator, was a corruptionist. L. M. Kenner was a colored saloon keeper who had been indicted for larceny. And G. Casanave was a colored undertaker with no high moral standing.[18] This board had power to inquire into elections and to reject the vote of any precinct or parish wherein force or fraud had affected the result. It could throw out but not add votes.[19] Considering its character and authority, the possibility of irregularities was great.

The Democrats conducted the election on November 7 in an orderly manner in the sections they were sure to carry so that the board would have no occasion to reject the vote in them. But in areas where Negroes and Republican majorities predominated, Democrats were guilty of terrorism so as to have the vote thrown out.[20] Colored speakers were employed to help conduct the Democratic canvass.[21] The choice of Presidential electors was subordinated to the election of State officers.

Republicans collected proofs of Democratic intimidation, appointed obedient registration officials, and instructed election supervisors to get out the full party vote. Successful efforts were made to increase the registration of Negroes and to decrease the illegal registrations of white Democrats.[22] As a result of the turmoil it was some days before the election results were known. On the face of returns, Democratic electors were chosen by safe majorities, so the State was claimed for Tilden. But Republicans replied that the Returning Board would put a different face on the situation.[23]

Meanwhile "visiting statesmen" from the North had arrived. Henry Watterson on November 8 urged Tilden to join Hayes in sending a committee of eminent citizens to Louisiana to guarantee an honest election, but Tilden preferred to send his own representatives.[24] So Hewitt invited leading Democrats and Republicans to go to North Carolina, Louisiana and Florida to see that "a fair count was made, and the returns honestly canvassed." President Grant issued a similar request to

[17] Haworth, 87–88, 98.
[18] *Ib*. His letters of 1877–78 in the Hayes Papers show that he was no ignoramus.
[19] *Ib*., 88.   [20] *Ib*., 89–90.   [21] *An. Cyc.*, 1876, 486, 94.
[22] Haworth, 94.   [23] *Ib.*, 95.   [24] *Century,* May, 1913.

twenty-five leading Republicans.[25] To Louisiana hurried John Sherman, James A. Garfield, W. D. Kelly, ex-Governor Noyes, J. A. Kasson, W. M. Evarts, J. A. Dix, J. A. Logan, Eugene Hale, M. S. Quay and Lew Wallace. Among the Democrats were J. M. Palmer, Lyman Trumbull, S. J. Randall, W. R. Morrison, J. R. Doolittle, Henry Watterson, J. B. Stallo, O. Ottendorfer, G. W. Julian, William Bigler, J. L. Carroll, F. R. Coudert and W. G. Sumner. Although the Republicans refused to co-operate with the Democrats, relations were cordial.[26] When a friend sent a demijohn of old Bourbon to Henry Watterson, he promptly divided it with his friendly enemies.[27] J. R. Doolittle said that at first the representatives of the two parties in conference agreed that all evidence should be submitted to an impartial committee, but Garfield disregarded this and was responsible for the schism that resulted.[28] It was discovered later that all of the Democratic telegrams passing over the wires of the Western Union were sent to the Republicans.[29]

On November 12 John Sherman wrote C. I. Wright of Chicago that his letter was not answered "because I felt the uncertainty of the election. . . . And now that the election is over results are as uncertain as before. . . . I fear the intimidation has been so far successful as to leave us a minority. . . . I have been invited by the President to go to New Orleans . . . but I see no good to come of it." [30] Wright replied: "Were I in the South I would fight for white supremacy." On the 16th Sherman wrote his wife that he had met the Republican representatives and that they were organizing, he being made chairman. Next day he was sorry that the Republicans had refused to co-operate with the Democratic visiting statesmen to settle the Louisiana dispute.[31] Sherman expecting to stay about a month, complained that Grant had "forced" him to go and that he was sorry he had come. The trip would cost him $400, a "dead loss," but the Republicans had done nothing to be ashamed of. By November 29 he believed that Hayes would be seated, but thought "It is a dangerous ending of our . . . contest to have it decided by the . . . doubtful votes of three States where fraud, murder and violence have prevailed for years. I have got the insight

[25] Nevins, *Writings of Hewitt*, 162, Nov. 9, 1876, I, 326.
[26] Haworth, 95–96.   [27] *Century*, May, 1913.
[28] Sellers, "James R. Doolittle," *Wis. Mag. of Hist.*, Dec., 1934, 180.
[29] Watterson, *Century*, May, 1913.
[30] Sherman Papers; *Recollections*, 454–455, gives a list of visitors.
[31] *Ib.*, Nov. 15, 1876.

into the history of politics here that alarms me for the peace of the whole country." [32]

Meanwhile Hayes wrote Sherman: "We are not to allow our friends to defeat one outrage and fraud by another. There must be nothing crooked on our part. Let Mr. Tilden have the place by violence, intimidation and fraud, rather than to undertake to prevent it by means that will not bear the severest scrutiny." [33] These were noble words, but there are other documents which show that Sherman was intent on a Republican triumph even at the price of an arrangement which was a close cousin to bribery. Rumors were afloat that the Louisiana electoral votes would be purchased for Hayes. When in 1895 Sherman wrote his *Recollections* he believed "that the probabilities were that Tilden was elected." [34]

At length the Canvassing Board was ready to begin its work. As a gesture of impartiality it invited five from each group of "visiting statesmen" to attend the open sessions at which parish returns were opened and examined. If unprotested, the returns were sent to a private room to be tabulated by clerks, all Republicans. When returns were protested, testimony was taken and written arguments were presented by attorneys of both parties. Prior to December 4, when the board met in secret to conclude its work, twelve public sessions were held. [35]

From the first the Democratic representatives realized that the cards were stacked against them. Watterson wired Tilden: "Well-organized plan supported by troops to cheat us in count of votes. Our majority 7,750." He urged that representative men be sent to watch Florida. [36] With Randall, Lamar, and Ottendorfer, he advised Tilden to make some proposal to Hayes to settle the disputed election. [37] James McQuade informed Tilden of Zach Chandler's boast that he would have four Southern States and concluded: "I am convinced they will count you out." [38] A Missouri delegate complained of the indifference of Northern Democrats. "The entire Democracy of the South feel more than ever that they are leaning on a bag of mush when they look for aid and comfort to the North." Montgomery Blair begged Tilden to "denounce the jobbery" by which he was being cheated out of the Presi-

[32] Sherman Papers, Nov. 24, 1876.   [33] *Ib., Recollections,* I, 559.
[34] *Ib.,* 453.   [35] Haworth, 99, 100–111.   [36] Tilden Papers.
[37] H. R. Misc. Docs., 45 Cong. 3 Sess., No. 31, pt. 4, 336, Nov. 14, 1876.
[38] Tilden Papers, Nov. 16, 1876.

dency.[39] Hewitt in a manifesto to the Democrats of the three Southern States urged them to stand firmly for their rights.[40]

The ugliest phase of the Louisiana situation now appeared—the attempt to dispose of the electoral vote by bargain or sale. D. A. Webber and James Anderson on November 20 wrote John Sherman:

"We have carefully considered the arguments advanced by you in our interview. Your assurance that we shall be taken care of is scarcely specific enough. In case we pursue the course suggested by you, we would have to leave the State. Will you therefore state in writing who we shall look to for the fulfillment of these promises?"[41]

On the same day Sherman replied:

"Neither Mr. Hayes, myself, the gentlemen who accompany me or the country at large can ever forget the obligation under which you will have placed us, should you stand firm in the position you have taken. From a long and intimate acquaintance with Gov. Hayes I am justified in assuming responsibility for promises made and will guarantee that you shall be provided for as soon after the 4th of March as may be practicable; and in such manner as to enable you both to leave La. should you deem it necessary."[42]

In the interest of fairness it should be said that a few years later Sherman under oath before the Potter Committee asserted that he did not believe he had written such a letter although he did not absolutely deny the possibility of having done so.[43]

There is ample evidence that J. M. Wells, head of the Returning Board, shopped around for a price and tried to play off one party against the other. To Senator West he wrote:

"Imprudent to write. . . . See you in Washington. . . . We hold destiny of the nation in our hands. . . . I fully comprehend the situation . . . and not with my consent shall this oppressed people be governed by . . . parolled prisoners aided by their white-livered cowards of the North. . . . Millions have been sent here and will be used in the interest of Tilden, and unless some counter move (is made), it will be impossible for me . . . to wrest its productive results. . . . See our friends and act promptly or the results will be disastrous. A hint to the wise is sufficient. . . . Strictly confidential."[44]

Getting no satisfactory response, apparently, Wells sent Colonel John T. Pickett, who had sold the Confederate archives to the Federal Gov-

[39] Tilden Papers.
[40] Nevins, *Hewitt*, 326, letter to Wade Hampton, Nov. 24, 1876.
[41] Letter submitted to the Potter Committee.
[42] Gibson, *A Political Crime*, 146.   [43] *Ib.*, 145.
[44] *Nation*, Feb. 8, 1877.

ernment, to Hewitt in New York City to promise a favorable decision for Tilden for $1,000,000. This offer, the third Hewitt received, was not accepted. Even when Wells cut his price to $200,000, no Democrat jumped at the bait, although Colonel W. T. Pelton did some dickering behind Tilden's back.[45] Just how much money, if any, Wells and his colleagues received has never been disclosed. Watterson asserted that a direct offer to sell the electoral vote for $250,000 was made to him, a statement confirmed by W. C. Hudson of the Brooklyn *Eagle*. A man named Rhodes, used by Tilden to smash the Rings, was in New Orleans and told Hudson that he was taking the terms of the bargain north to Hewitt, who refused to buy.[46] Elector Levissée said, "I have been offered today $100,000 to give my vote for Samuel J. Tilden, but I consider the right to vote for Rutherford B. Hayes worth more than that." [47] After Hayes' inauguration Wells became Surveyor and Anderson Deputy Collector of the Port of New Orleans; and Kenner got the deputy naval officership [48]—perhaps the only rewards received. Grant, informed by Wells' agents that the electoral vote was for sale, asked Hewitt, "Are you going to buy the Returning Board?" Hewitt denied such intent, but Grant believed there would be "an active competition for the purchase." [49] Hewitt declared fifteen years later: "Louisiana has determined the result of a Presidential election. The vote . . . was offered to me for money, and I declined to buy it. But the vote of that State was sold for money." [50] He refused the temptation because "the Democratic Party could not afford to take the responsibility" for anarchy and panic. The best men of New Orleans in an address to the nation declared that "a large majority of the honest votes" were cast for the Democratic ticket and deplored the frauds and lawlessness.

After the Returning Board went into secret session,[51] the Federal Marshal in New Orleans on December 3 wired Senator West (a Republican) at Washington: "Wells says Board will return Hayes sure. Have no fear." [52] The board on December 6 declared that the Hayes electors had majorities from 4,626 to 4,712, although on the face of the returns Tilden electors had majorities from 6,300 to 8,957. The difference had

45 Eckenrode, 190; Haworth, 111–112.   46 Hudson, *Recollections*, 72–77.
47 *An. Cyc.*, 1876, 491.   48 Haworth, 112.
49 *Letters*, II, 553; *Sun*, Mar. 7, 1877.   50 *Ib.*, 482, Nov. 12, 1891.
51 New York *World*, Dec. 2, 1876.
52 Morrison Report, 9.

been accomplished by throwing out 13,250 Democratic votes and 2,042 Republican votes.[53] These alterations had been made after John Sherman had received instructions in cipher telegrams and was told to stand "against the raging billows of Rebel Democracy." [54] After the decision of the board was made, Governor Kellogg gave the eight Hayes electors (including himself as one) certificates of election.[55]

On December 5 John McEnery, signing himself "Governor of Louisiana," certified the election of the eight Tilden electors (one being himself).[56] The Democratic Committee of Returns certified the same result. And the Democratic "visiting statesmen" in an address to the nation announced that the Democrats had won the State election in Louisiana and were entitled to the electors.[57]

Of course no such change from the detailed returns should have been made except on indisputable evidence of fraud open to any interested observer and by men of unquestionable honesty. As it was, Wells and his tools, ready to offer the prize to the highest bidder, in secret determined the Presidency of the United States.[58]

Although President Grant had said "that in his opinion there had been no fair election" in Louisiana,[59] yet John Sherman and eight of his Republican colleagues on December 6 wrote a letter to Grant, who presented it to Congress, justifying the decision in favor of Hayes, while of course the Democrats in a report to Hewitt denounced the Returning Board's verdict as arbitrary and dishonest. Sherman's rôle in Louisiana was one of mere political expediency, for he had no word of criticism of Tilden. Having served on railroad boards with him, he knew him well, and thought him a man of "singular political sagacity, of great shrewdness, a money-making man" who had acquired a fortune as an attorney of corporations but who had overthrown the Tweed Ring and stood for reform and honesty in politics." [60] The historian Rhodes was convinced that the truth about Louisiana was deliberately withheld from Hayes.[61]

In explaining the steps taken in Louisiana W. E. Chandler said that "there had been thrown into the ballot box over 7,000 more votes for the Tilden than the Hayes electors"; hence to make Hayes President

[53] Haworth, 113; Oberholtzer, III, 287.
[54] Haworth, 113; Sherman Papers, Dec. 7, 1876.
[55] Haworth, 114; An. Cyc., 1876, 489; Oberholtzer, III, 287.
[56] An. Cyc., 1876, 489; Haworth, 114.
[57] An. Cyc., 1876, 490; Times and World, Dec. 7, 1876.
[58] Rhodes, VII, 297.   [59] Letters, II, 553, Hewitt, Dec. 3, 1876.
[60] Sherman, Recollections, I, 551.   [61] Rhodes, VII, 300.

it "became necessary" for the board to throw out 7,000 Tilden votes "on alleged charges of murder, riot and intimidation in preventing a fair and free election." This required "undaunted courage," and the "national exigency" demanded it. Governor Warmouth acknowledged that, although Tilden electors had a majority of 9,000 or more votes, yet means would be found to return the State for Hayes.[62]

The historic fact seems to be that, as the election was conducted, Tilden carried Louisiana. The intimidations of the Democrats undoubtedly affected the voting, but not sufficiently to determine the result. W. R. Morrison reported that "thousands of colored persons voluntarily and actively supported the Democratic ticket."[63] Republican frauds in registration offset Democratic intimidations.[64] If there had been an absolutely honest election, with the Negro vote fairly recorded, it is not beyond doubt that the State would have gone Republican. But the outcome was determined by a dishonest and probably a bribed Returning Board. And this result was abetted by a group of Republicans who outwitted and outmaneuvered the Democratic visitors.

Under the Constitution three copies of the electoral vote had to be made out—one mailed to the President of the Senate, one sent him by messenger, and the third deposited with the United States district judge. The Republican messenger had his attention called by Senator Ferry to an irregularity in the certificate and hurried back to New Orleans to have it corrected. But two electors were absent, hence their names were forged to the new document in order to get it back to Washington in time. Had any Democrat discovered this forgery, Louisiana's vote might have been invalidated.[65] "But neither suspicion nor inspiration" opened this chance to the friends of Tilden.[66] And so the Republicans, with confidence, counted Louisiana for Hayes.[67] If he had known all the facts about the vote of this State, Rhodes believed he would have refused the Presidency.[68]

Recent studies of the election of 1876 in Florida show conclusively that Tilden had a majority of the votes and was entitled to the four electoral votes. "A fair election would have resulted in a more complete

[62] *Letters*, II, 539, to Mrs. Aaron M. Wilcox.
[63] Morrison Report.   [64] Rhodes, VII, 299.
[65] *Harper's Magazine*, Mar., 1907.   [66] *Letters*, II, 484–485.
[67] See "Letter to Matthews on the Unconstitutionality of the La. Return. Board" by C. E. Fenner; A. E. Burke, "Facts Rel. to the Election in La.;" and S. E. Chaile, "Intimidation . . . in La. in 1876."
[68] Rhodes, VII, 236. Cf. Schouler, *Hist. of People of U.S.*, VII, 327 n.

Democratic victory." [69] It must be remembered that Florida was not a black State like South Carolina and Louisiana, but had a safe majority of whites. But the State government was in the hands of the carpetbaggers. In the scramble to control the Presidential election, the Democrats used intimidation against black voters and the Republicans employed frauds in some sections. In other regions the two parties reversed their methods. If there is doubt that a fair election in Louisiana would have given the Democrats a victory, there is absolutely no doubt in Florida.

When, on November 8, Zach Chandler wired Martin, Chairman of the State Republican Committee, "Hayes defeated without Florida," the latter replied, "If Florida is important, authorize me to draw on you for $2,000." The same day W. E. Chandler was hurried to Tallahassee, where he was joined on the 12th by Governor Noyes, J. A. Kasson, Lew Wallace, F. C. Barlow and others, and telegraphed to local Republican leaders: "Render every possible assistance. Funds will be on hand to meet every requirement." He wired New York for $2,000 and two days later for an additional $5,000, these sums and others being promptly supplied.[70] Governor Stearns asked President Grant for troops, which were immediately furnished.

The Democrats acted even more quickly than the Republicans. As soon as W. E. Chandler was hurried to Florida by "special train," Tilden knew of it and rushed his representatives down.[71] Chandler complained that, when he reached Florida, he found "visiting Democratic statesmen" ahead of him,[72] among them Governor Brown of Georgia, C. W. Wooley, J. F. Coyle and Manton Marble. Both groups were well supplied with funds.[73] J. S. Floyd of Florida on November 14 informed Hewitt that $10,000 was needed to insure the State for Tilden and offered to give $1,000 himself, "not to purchase votes . . . but to send strong and honest men into every voting precinct," but Hewitt refused to do anything more for Florida than had been done.[74]

In the face of the carpetbag government, the Florida voters gave the Democratic tickets, both State and national, a small majority. The strategy of the Republican managers was to prove fraud in casting or

[69] Davis, W. W., *The Civil War and Reconstruction in Florida,* 1913, settles the case in favor of Tilden; Eckenrode's *Hayes* endorses the conclusions of Davis.
[70] Davis, 687–714; Gibson, *A Political Crime,* 65–67, shows that Chandler had at least $15,000 exclusive of what he took with him.
[71] *Letters,* II, 487, Quackenbos to Tilden, Nov. 10, 1876.   [72] Davis, 714.
[73] Haworth, 64–65.   [74] *Retrospections,* V, 285.

in counting votes so that the Board of State Canvassers would decide in favor of a Republican victory. The Democrats were determined to hold the triumph they had won at the polls. Both parties began to collect affidavits by the hundreds to prove the corruption and dishonesty of rivals.[75] This phase of the election was quite as crooked as the misuse of the ballot box.

The Board of State Canvassers was composed of Secretary of State S. B. McLin, a Tennesseean, who had deserted the Confederate Army and was now a "scalawag" Republican; Comptroller C. A. Cowgill, a physician and a carpetbag Republican; and Attorney General W. A. Cocke, a Virginia Democrat.[76] This board began its work on November 27 in the presence of the "visiting statesmen" of both parties, the Republican Governor, Stearns, and his Democratic opponent, G. F. Drew. It exercised authority to accept or to reject returns, received documents of protest, and heard witnesses.[77]

Though far away, Tilden kept a sharp eye on the Florida contest. Manton Marble and other Democrats were there to safeguard his interests. The secret telegrams published in 1878 between them and his managers in New York City show negotiations to purchase one electoral vote or more. From Tallahassee C. W. Wooley wired Henry Havemeyer December 1, 1876: "Board may make necessary expense of half a hundred thousand dollars. Can you say will deposit it in bank immediately if agreed?"

To Wooley was sent the reply: "Telegram received. Will deposit dollars agreed. Cannot draw before vote [of] member [is] received."

Wooley answered: "Select some one in whom you have more confidence." The response was: "All here have perfect confidence in you. No other has power and all applications declined. Stay and do what you telegraphed you could do."

On December 2 Manton Marble under the name of "Moses" telegraphed Colonel W. T. Pelton: "Have just received a proposition to hand over at any hour required Tilden decision of board and certificate of Governor for $200,000." And two days later Marble again wired

[75] Davis, 715, 716. W. E. Chandler reported, Nov. 18, that the Democrats had 7,600 votes, Republicans 7,445, and said that Hayes should be prepared for unfavorable results. Hayes Papers.

[76] Haworth, 64; Davis, 716.

[77] Haworth, 65. In Manton Marble's Papers are letters of Nov. 19, 20 and 27, dealing with Governor Stearns' exercise of power to canvass the vote. See *World*, Dec. 1, 1876; *A Secret Chapter*, 6.

Pelton: "Proposition received here giving vote of Republican of board, or his concurrence in court action preventing electoral votes from being cast, for half a hundred best U. S. documents." This was followed by: "May Wooley give one hundred thousand dollars less half for Tilden additional Board member?"

After some delay Pelton replied: "Proposition accepted if only done once."

Evidently the plan went awry, for Marble sent the discouraging communication: "Proposition failed. Finished yesterday afternoon responsibility as Moses. Last night Wooley found me and said he had nothing, which I knew already. Tell Tilden to saddle Blackstone." This was followed by Marble's report: "Radicals cut wires three times. . . . Board threw out Democratic counties wholesale and manufactured a fraudulent majority of 925. Attorney General Cocke filed protest."

Thus only through hesitancy and delay in New York was the intent to bribe Florida electors frustrated.[78] Tilden denied that he had any knowledge of these negotiations, and this denial was affirmed by Marble and Pelton under oath. The cipher used was one which Tilden had long employed in his business transactions, and to which Pelton naturally turned.[79]

While these secret efforts were being made to buy the Presidency, the Democratic counselors were attempting to obtain a victory by legal means. Fourteen of them presented to the Board of Canvassers an argument in support of the claim that Tilden electors had carried the State by 2,219 votes.[80] The Democratic legislature of Florida memorialized Congress to count the electoral votes for Tilden.[81] On the other hand the Republicans were equally alert in corralling the Florida vote for Hayes. At a private session on December 5 the partisan board converted the Tilden majority of 93 into a Hayes majority of 924, thus giving the State to the Republicans.[82] Next day the Hayes electors met, cast their vote for Hayes, and sent it to Washington; and the Democratic electors took similar action.[83] There seems no doubt that in any fair count Tilden would have had a small majority. General Francis C.

[78] Paine, *Thomas Nast*, 394–396.   [79] Tilden Papers; *McClure's*, May, 1904.
[80] "Argument etc.," 14, Dec. 4, 1876.   [81] Feb. 12–13, 1877.
[82] In 10 counties the returns were altered by Secretary of State McLin so as to give Hayes a majority of 909 in place of Tilden's majority of 86. *World*, Jan. 17, 1878. McLin did not scruple to lie and take bribes. Washington *Post*, Jan. 14, 1878.
[83] Haworth, 76; Davis, 728; Tilden Papers, Sam Pasco, Chairman Dem. Fla. State Com., Dec. 7, 1876.

Barlow, who went to Florida at the request of President Grant, was convinced that Tilden should have had a majority of from 30 to 55, and tried to persuade one of the Board of Canvassers to take that view of the case. He was disgusted with the outcome and became a suspect in his own party for expressing his opinion.[84] *Harper's Weekly* and other fearless papers praised him for his independent and truthful letter.[85]

The Board of State Canvassers, by a vote of two to one, had not only seated the Hayes electors but also had declared that the Republican Governor, Stearns, was elected. But G. B. Drew, the Democratic candidate, insisted that he had been chosen Governor and appealed to the State Supreme Court for a recount. The order was given; a recount was made; and Drew was declared elected. After he was sworn in, the new Secretary of State, the new Comptroller and the new Attorney General met as the new Board of State Canvassers and declared the Democratic electors chosen. The Democratic electors met at once, voted on January 19 a second time for Tilden, and sent their certificate, signed by Governor Drew, to Washington.[86] The decision now rested with Congress.

The Republicans then declared that the Tilden electors were certified after the day required by law. To show that this lack of punctuality "was cured by other evidence," Tilden prepared a long brief. The appointment of the Tilden electors, he contended, was in accord with the order of the State legislature. The report of the first canvassing board was "unlawful and untrue," because the board had exercised judicial powers not granted to it. By *quo warranto* proceedings instituted against the Hayes electors before they cast their votes on December 6, 1876,[87] they were ousted on January 25, 1877, and the three lists were transferred to the Tilden electors, who had cast their vote on December 6. Hence the votes of the Tilden electors should be counted. A formidable list of decisions and cases was given to validate the brief.[88] It should be said that McLin testified that W. E. Chandler promised that he and Cowgill "would be taken care of" if Florida went for Hayes. McLin was made justice of New Mexico; but Cowgill, who wavered, got nothing. McLin had the courage to confess later that his judgment

[84] Haworth, 68–74; Davis, 730.
[85] Jan. 6, 1877. In the Hayes Papers is a report of W. M. Ampt dated Dec. 22, 1876, giving the inside history of Barlow's defection and the counter-action to offset it.
[86] Davis, 728, 733–736.   [87] Tilden Papers, C. Gibson, Dec. 9, 1876.
[88] *Writings*, II, 454–481.

was misled. "The conclusion is irresistible," he asserted, "that Mr. Tilden was entitled to the electoral vote of Florida and not Mr. Hayes." [89]

As Louisiana and Florida became less certain, Democratic hope turned to Oregon. Both parties of that State recognized the election of three Hayes electors. But after the election it was discovered that one, J. W. Watts, was a deputy postmaster, which disqualified him. The possibility of winning this needed vote was seen by a few shrewd Democrats before Tilden and his advisers were fully aware of it. After being urged to rely on Oregon rather than the Southern States and asked, "Can't Oregon legislature fill electoral vacancy as Vermont has done?" Tilden went into conference with Dorsheimer, Bigelow, Hewitt, Cox and C. F. Adams.

Alive to this new opportunity, Pelton and Hewitt deluged Oregon Democrats with telegrams to have Governor L. F. Grover take the initiative in choosing a new elector. Congressman S. S. Cox cautioned Tilden to have all his telegrams to Oregon repeated back to him; urged him to send ex-Senator Hager and James Beard of California up to Oregon at once, with specific instructions from Dr. Gwin; and advised that telegrams be sent to Governor Grover, a Democrat, and Senator Kelly immediately.[90] On the back of Cox's letter in pencil is the following message, which was undoubtedly sent:

"Governor Grover:
Upon careful investigation the legal opinion is that votes cast for a Federal officeholder as elector are void and that the person securing the next highest number of votes is appointed. The board of canvassers should canvass accordingly and the certificate and return made out in conformity to this rule. Your official certificate will force the Congress to go behind the certificate and open the way for us to go into the merits in all cases." [91]

This telegram, sent by Hewitt on November 15, became the basis for Democratic action. When J. N. H. Patrick of Omaha was hurried out to Oregon by Dr. G. L. Miller of the Democratic National Committee, J. J. Doyle wired Hewitt: "Send better man. Everything possible being done." Upon reaching Oregon, Patrick engaged the services of a local Republican law firm at a fee of $3,000 and in cipher wired back to Pelton that $10,000 was necessary to win one of the Republican electors.

[89] Davis, 730–732.
[90] Tilden Papers, J. R. Chambers of Tennessee, S. S. Cox, Nov. 16, 1876.
[91] Haworth, 159.

Pelton drew $8,000 out of the bank and deposited it with Patrick's New York banker for use in Oregon. W. L. Scott of the Democratic National Committee promised to back Pelton to the extent of $20,000.[92] Patrick telegraphed Pelton in cipher on November 30:

"Governor all right without reward. Will issue certificate Tuesday. One elector must be paid to recognize Democrat to secure majority. Will take $5,000 for Republican elector."

The next morning a cipher dispatch signed "Gabble" stated:

"I shall decide every point in the case of post-office elector (the disqualified Republican) in favor of highest Democratic elector, and grant certificate accordingly on morning of 6th. Confidential."

Although Governor Grover denied sending this message, nevertheless he carried out the promise made in it. He certified the two Republican electors and also E. A. Cronin, the Democratic aspirant for Watts' place. But meantime Watts resigned as postmaster and then claimed to be the legally chosen third elector. When the two Republicans refused to act with Cronin, he filled their places with Democrats who joined him in casting two votes for Hayes and one for Tilden. But he refused to take these certificates to Washington until he was paid $3,000 for expenses. Meanwhile Watts, after his reappointment, met with the other two Republican electors and they cast three votes for Hayes.[93] Both returns were hurried to Washington to increase the confusion and doubt. Thus a genuine Democratic elector was not secured, and it seems that the check for $8,000 was returned untouched.[94] Hewitt admitted that Tilden had no right to the Oregon elector and explained that the claim to it was merely intended "to offset the palpable frauds in Florida and Louisiana."[95] The Republicans accused the Democrats of an attempt to steal an elector in Oregon.

In the political game played before the American public, Republican leaders were determined to win regardless of the methods employed. Aided by the Negro vote, carpetbag governments, venal local politicians, Federal troops, and masterful party strategy, they secured the three doubtful Southern States. The outwitted and defeated Democrats made the best of the situation by crying fraud and by selecting rump electors who voted for Tilden and forwarded their votes to Washington. Con-

[92] *Nation*, Feb. 1, 1877. [93] Haworth, 165.
[94] *Nation*, Feb. 1, 1877. Haworth states that $10,000 went to Patrick.
[95] Nevins, *Hewitt*, 327.

fident of victory, Zach Chandler remarked to Thomas Nast: "That 'Elephant' is safe. Would it not be well to put him on his feet, with one foot on the Democratic tiger, with Tilden upon one tusk and Hendricks upon the other?" Not only did Nast decline to follow that suggestion; he also refused to accept a check for $10,000 sent him by the Republican National Committee.[96]

In explaining the electoral count, Tilden asserted that under Grant the three carpetbag States "were pervaded by emissaries of the administration" under the supervision of a Cabinet member. "The civil service was never so audaciously and so unscrupulously used for electioneering purposes as in the late canvass." Military occupation was continued and in some cases extended. Troops and money needed to carry the doubtful States were supplied. The 100,000 officeholders were forced to contribute a large fund. The Army, without which there would have been no Republican Party in the three disputed States, was used as an electioneering machine. The scheme was to "carry the frauds as far back as possible" to make detection more difficult. In Florida "the expedients failed" and the county canvassers showed a small majority for Democratic electors. In Louisiana the failure was more conspicuous and gave Tilden electors a majority of over 8,000. Hence the canvassers of these two States were induced to make a false canvass. In Florida the State board had no authority to change the county returns, and the Supreme Court, composed of Republican judges, so ruled. Thus later frauds changed the actual results of the polls, and falsified the returns of two States and consequently the electoral votes.[97]

It will be observed that in the four doubtful States, South Carolina and Oregon belonged without much opposition to the Hayes column. The results in Louisiana, as judged by John Sherman and other Republicans, proved a justifiable Republican triumph. But Tilden to the day of his death insisted that indisputably Louisiana had given him an honest majority of which he was deprived by Republican machination. Some recent writers are not disposed to agree with Tilden's interpretation. Haworth, after careful study, declared that the election in that State was neither free nor fair; that intimidation was rife but used mostly by Democrats; and that an absolutely full election by whites and Negroes would have given a Republican majority of from 5,000 to

[96] Paine, *Thomas Nast*, 343, 349.   [97] Tilden Papers.

15,000.[98] But if the Negro vote had been curtailed and managed as it has been for the past half century, the State was unquestionably Democratic. Florida, which Tilden did not claim so stubbornly as Louisiana, is now generally conceded to have gone for him.

Thus by December 6, 1876, when the electoral votes were taken in the respective States, 184 votes were conceded to Tilden and 22 more were claimed by his managers, making a total of 206. To Hayes, on the other hand, was granted 163 undisputed votes; and the 22 votes in dispute counted by his supporters gave him 185 votes and the Presidency.

In this uncertain state of affairs Hewitt prepared an address to the nation "setting forth the facts as they then appeared . . . and calling upon the people to assemble in their several places . . . to protest against the frauds . . . and to express their determination that the people should not be robbed of their choice for President." It was submitted to Tilden on December 9. He struck out the call for public assemblies on Jackson Day because violence might result, and thought a sense of justice would show itself sooner or later. While the address was being copied Tilden requested that it be withheld altogether. Hewitt "absolutely dissented" from this policy of inaction, but complied with Tilden's wishes.[99] August Belmont, David Dudley Field, and other Democrats also urged Tilden to make a public appeal to the voters, but Tilden preferred to let the people work their own way out of the crisis. Henry Watterson was depressed and discouraged "by the tense quietude on our side." [100] Hewitt was not inactive, however, for he urged an Illinois Democrat to hold protest meetings in every school district. A Jackson, a Cleveland, or a Theodore Roosevelt would have taken the lead with an emphatic manifesto; but the calm and reflective Tilden was not a rough and tumble statesman who would run the risk of war for a party victory. Even when the Young Men's Democratic Club sent Simon Sterne to ask him to receive a body of serenaders and to take advantage of the occasion to assert his claim to the Presidency, he curtly replied, "It would not be decent." The *Tribune* announced that Democrats coming out of Gramercy Park remarked in despair: "Oh, Tilden won't do anything; he's as cold as a damn clam."

[98] Haworth, 119.   [99] Nevins, *Hewitt*, 330.
[100] *Autobiography*, I, 301.

As prescribed by the Constitution, the electors met in the States on December 6, 1876, cast their votes and hurried the results to the President of the Senate at Washington. But, as has been seen, two returns were sent from South Carolina, Louisiana, Florida and Oregon. Both parties claimed the victory and neither would give way.

Addressing the New York electors, Horatio Seymour called attention to the fact that the Republicans had made the point that the "solid South" would go for Tilden, but now they had to depend upon three Southern States to offset Democratic victories in the North to stand any chance of electing Hayes. To obtain the necessary votes, the Republicans negotiated with Southern politicians of doubtful honesty. "To elect men to govern the Union against the will of the people by unfair methods is revolution. Such plots involve anarchy, distress and dishonor." Hence Republicans must realize that the "heaviest responsibility" for a just decision rests with them, and an unjust triumph will prove a curse to them. "If fraud is suspected, it must be the work of others, not the Democratic Party." He charged the Republicans with using the Federal Government to win the election." [1]

When Abram S. Hewitt, as the spokesman of the Democratic Party, announced on December 13 that Tilden and Hendricks were elected,[2] the claim was denied by Zach Chandler, Chairman of the Republican National Committee.[3] Hayes believed that he was elected but "to the end of his life he had qualms." [4] Tilden died a decade later firmly convinced that he had been cheated out of the Presidency. Naturally all sorts of ugly rumors were afloat. The *Times* reported that Hayes had arranged a trade with Southern Democrats.[5] The Democrats were accused of attempting to bribe Returning Boards and even electors.[6] The *Nation* called upon some patriotic Republican to cast a vote for Tilden and thus settle the dispute, and the story was circulated that James Russell Lowell had declared his intention to do so. Lowell denied the report and had considerable difficulty in convincing earnest Republicans that he was not a traitor.[7]

[1] *Life*, II, 84.   [2] *World*, Dec. 14, 1876.   [3] *Herald*, Dec. 14, 1876.
[4] Eckenrode, 200.   [5] Dec. 3, 4, 5, 1876.   [6] *Times*, Dec. 7, 1876.
[7] *Nation*, XXIII, 322, 334.

With an excited nation confronted by a disputed election, what was Tilden's attitude? Did he sense the seriousness of the situation? Did he have a well-reasoned remedy? If so, what steps did he take to apply it? Was he tempted by the opportunity offered him to purchase the high office? Discreetly refraining from a public statement about the election, he kept his own counsel to an aggravating degree, as was his wont, but manifested an extraordinary diligence in scrutinizing every report and in leaving unchallenged no flaw in the case of his opponent. While sedulously avoiding manifestoes during this crisis, he did not assume a negative attitude. On the contrary his views "were perfectly defined and freely expressed to all who consulted him, long before the meeting of Congress in December." [8] That he clearly sensed the evil results that might develop from a fraudulent election is indicated by a statement found among his papers:

"Our Presidential election as made by the people has been subverted by a false count of the votes cast by the Presidential electors, founded on a substitution of pretended votes known at the time to be fraudulent or forged, and to have been manufactured for that particular use.

If a Presidential election should be next controlled by abusive or corrupt influence exercised by the Government upon the voters in particular States, and a vista be opened of Third Terms and Terms in indefinite series displaying the undisputed supreme mastery of the office-holding class in successive elections, our Government would have degenerated into a bad copy of the worst governments of the worst ages." [9]

Tilden's policy prior to the meeting of Congress may be described as "watchful waiting." He insisted upon his constitutional rights in every instance where he believed them to be violated. He refused absolutely to buy the one vote he needed, resisted every suggestion of violence, and vetoed all efforts of Hewitt and others to call protest meetings. It could not have been indifference and it was not timidity that induced him to oppose the aggressive suggestions of party associates. His high regard for forms of law, the Constitution, and the sanctity of precedent guided his conduct, and gave rise to criticism, to charges of hesitance, indecision and supineness, and to blame for the triumph of his political foes. This was not a period of idleness, because his days and nights were taken up with effective work in conferences, in confidential correspond-

[8] *Letters*, II, 528; Marble Papers; Marble, *A Secret Chapter*, 10.
[9] Tilden Papers, undated.

ence, and in the preparation of his case before the American people and Congress.

This case—a lawyer's, not a politician's—was simple and logical—to rely on the Constitution and "to stand firmly and inflexibly on the unbroken series of precedents formed by the twenty-two Presidential counts from 1789 to 1872." The feeling was general that the laws governing the choice of electors and the counting of the electoral vote must be examined thoroughly. Tilden himself took the keenest interest in these legal problems.

Unfortunately the Constitution and statutes were not clear on the problem that confronted the nation. The Constitution stated: "The President of the Senate shall, in the presence of the Senate and the House of Representatives, open all the certificates, and the votes shall then be counted." [10] Republicans contended that this plainly implied that in case two certificates were sent by a State, the President of the Senate must decide which one was valid before the votes could be counted. Hayes himself was of this opinion. The Democrats combated this interpretation because it made the President of the Senate the arbiter of a disputed election, which was clearly not intended by the framers of the fundamental law. They insisted that both returns of doubtful States should be thrown out, which would give neither candidate a majority and throw the election into the House of Representatives. This, being Democratic, would give the election to Tilden. [11]

To complicate matters, the 22nd joint rule of Congress, adopted in 1865, gave either branch of Congress the right to refuse to count the electoral vote of any State. Under this rule, in the count of 1873, the vote of Louisiana had been thrown out by the joint action of both Houses [12] and that of Arkansas by action of the Senate alone. Since this rule might operate favorably for the Democrats, the Republican Senate in January, 1876, refused to adopt it. [13]

With the intention of settling this problem, Tilden had all official records, debates, rules and laws on the counting of electoral votes from the election of Washington thoroughly examined. Bigelow, Marble and others did the work and placed the results before Tilden, who summarized them for publication. This study was printed in December, 1876, under the title *The Presidential Counts*, [14] placed on the desk of

[10] *Atlantic Monthly*, LXXII, 522.   [11] *Ib.*, 523.
[12] H. R. Misc. Docs., No. 13, 44th Cong., 2nd Sess., 357–408.   [13] *Ib.*, 782–794.
[14] *Letters*, II, 528, 556; *Writings*, II, 386. Published by D. Appleton & Co.

every member of Congress, and widely distributed. Bigelow wrote the "Analytical Introduction," [15] which was printed separately and used by the Democratic National Committee. Marble prepared the citations to authorities. The indefiniteness of the Constitution was frankly admitted. It was shown that in 1793 the two Houses, by concurrent resolution, prescribed the mode of counting, which was followed down to 1865. Subsequently a standing rule of Congress for counting prevailed in 1865, 1869 and 1872. The two Houses had invariably appointed tellers to make the count—two for the Lower House and one for the Senate.

In this survey, with citations to sources, Tilden contended: (1) That the two Houses had exclusive jurisdiction to count the electoral votes under their own rules and had exercised that power from the beginning of the Federal Government. (2) That the President of the Senate merely opened the votes and presented them to the two Houses for action, but had never gone beyond that limited function in a single instance. To allow him to count the votes would permit him to disfranchise a State, and even to elect himself President. (3) That the two Houses had authority to decide upon the legality of votes and might go behind the returns to do so. These unassailable arguments based on the records persuaded the Republicans to abandon their intention to have the President of the Senate count the votes.[16] To Tilden the preparation of this historical work did not seem like time wasted but a notable advantage in presenting his case to the only body clothed with power to act. Although Tilden supervised this investigation, he asked for facts and opinions from Sidney Webster, J. L. Douglas, C. N. Potter, A. C. Story, Charles O'Conor, S. J. Randall, Charles Mason and others. Information and briefs which Democratic lawyers, law students, and teachers of political science forwarded to him were carefully studied for valuable suggestions.[17]

During the survey, discreet publicity was fed to the press and extensively used. In consequence the whole country was discussing the issues involved, which was just what Tilden desired. Newspaper editorials and letters were carefully studied in order to get the drift of public opinion. Misleading statements were corrected so far as possible. George Ticknor Curtis wrote an article in the *Sun* to instruct the "public mind." [18] He explained the duties of State electors in casting their votes

[15] *Writings*, II, 385.   [16] *Ib.*, 384–452.   [17] Tilden Papers.
[18] Nov. 22, 1876.

and transmitting them to Washington. In counting them the President of the Senate merely broke open the seals in the presence of the two Houses, which had no authority to inquire into the legality of the appointment of electors or to reject any State's votes. If Hayes received 185 votes or more, he must be accepted, regardless of frauds in doubtful States. Congress might determine "the fact of the frauds," but that would not affect the "legally certified electors." Hayes would be President and his party would be responsible for the dishonesty. The Democrats could only use the ballot box to redress the wrong. The alternative would be anarchy.[19] This editorial aroused Tilden and his friends. Belmont, sent to persuade Curtis to "keep quiet," suggested that some attention from Tilden would appease his vanity and "silence his constitutional croaking." Barlow went to prevent Dana from repeating such political heresy.[20]

When the time was ripe, Tilden, insisting that the 22nd joint rule of 1865 must be the guiding principle, prepared two resolutions in December to put his ideas into operation and asked his subordinates not to act until they were adopted. These resolutions, when introduced, were sent to the Committee on the Privileges, Powers and Duties of the House of Representatives, appointed December 22, with J. Proctor Knott of Kentucky as chairman.[21] This committee expanded Tilden's two resolutions into the following five: (1) That the Constitution does not confer upon the President of the Senate the power to count the votes for President. (2) That he may only receive, preserve and open them. (3) That the Senate and House alone may "examine and ascertain the votes to be counted." (4) That in the exercise of this power the House is at least the equal of the Senate. (5) That no vote can be counted against the judgment of the House.[22] These resolutions did undoubtedly prevent the President of the Senate from counting the votes, but that was all. Had Tilden pressed hard for their adoption earlier, they might have accomplished more. His insistence on the validity of the 22nd joint rule of 1865, which had been in force in three Presidential elections, was not accepted by Hewitt and other members of his own party because joint rules only continued from Congress to Congress. But most important of all influences in weakening Tilden's plan of action was the rapid growth

[19] *Letters*, II, 492; Mitchell, *Memoirs*, 299.   [20] *Ib.*, 492, Nov. 23, 1876.
[21] *Cong. Record*, 197–199, Dec. 22, 1876.   [22] *Ib.*, Jan. 12, 1877.

in both parties of a feeling for the settlement of the disputed election by arbitration.

A second part of Tilden's policy was to keep in touch with the outstanding Democratic leaders. Great reliance was placed on S. J. Randall, Speaker of the House, who often conferred with Tilden and did his best to hold the loyalty of the recalcitrant Southern Congressmen. Because of his political skill, D. D. Field had been sent to Congress by Tilden as his representative,[23] despite the fact that he had been counsel for Gould, Fisk and Boss Tweed. Tilden's "most intimate friend" was A. S. Hewitt, spokesman for the party in the House. Hewitt and Belmont arranged for conferences of men like Bayard, Thurman and Ransom with Tilden that they might hear his "able argument." [24] Senator Thurman remarked that there were three courses: "We can fight; we can back down; or we can arbitrate." Tilden replied: "It will not do to fight. We have just emerged from one Civil War, and it will never do to engage in another; it would end in the destruction of free government. We can, therefore, only arbitrate." [25] Thurman left for Washington with the determination to arbitrate. Perhaps General Hancock reflected Tilden's mind most literally when he declared that the solution was "simple" because the machinery already existed. Congress in joint session should decide who was President-elect; if the two Houses disagreed, then the election of a President went to the House of Representatives and of a Vice President to the Senate. The people wanted a fair, lawful and "peaceful determination of this matter." [26] Colonel Pelton and Sam Ward served Tilden as messengers and were thought to have great influence with him. Some of these men Tilden never trusted fully—not even his own nephew—and some of them did not heed Tilden's wishes.

As the futility of Tilden's proposals became more apparent, the attitude of President Grant grew in importance, because it was felt that he might assume the power either to seat Hayes or to prolong his own term. Newspapers intimated that he was concentrating troops in the Capital for that purpose. To learn just what Grant's position was, Hewitt on December 3 had a long conference with him. Grant said that no man could take the office of President unless the people believed that he was fairly elected. He believed that South Carolina had gone for

[23] Field, *D. D. Field*, 270. [24] Tilden Papers, Belmont to Tilden, Dec. 22, 1876.
[25] Nevins, *Hewitt*, 335. [26] *Letters*, II, 506, Hancock to Sherman, Dec. 28, 1876.

Hayes, also Florida by a majority of 40, but that Louisiana had given Tilden a majority of from 6,000 to 8,000 on the face of the returns. He thought that because of irregularities the vote of the last-named State should be thrown out, in which case the House would elect the President. In case the two Houses came to blows, he would not interfere, unless either side called up an armed force, and then only to save public property. Hewitt was convinced that Grant believed that Tilden was elected.[27] To a reporter of the Brooklyn *Eagle* Grant declared that he would "not seat any man in the White House" but would be bound by the action of Congress whether the choice fell on Tilden or Hayes. Hewitt said to the reporter, "You went to the President and asked that question?" and laughingly exclaimed, "That is the cheekiest thing I ever knew a man to do." An acquaintance to whom the incident was related commented, "I am convinced that Congress will count Hayes in, rightly or wrongly" and he "will be seated in the White House." [28]

For a settlement, the people now looked to Congress, which met on December 4, and flooded that body with petitions and letters.[29] The Democrats had a majority of 74 in the House; the Republicans of 17 in the Senate. Both chambers were conscious of a solemn obligation. Without debate the House appointed committees of nine, fifteen and six to go to South Carolina, Louisiana and Florida, respectively, to investigate the recent elections and actions of the Returning Boards.[30] Next day the Senate authorized its Committee on Elections to investigate the same States and, in addition, Georgia, Alabama and Mississippi —and later Oregon. Theoretically these committees were supposed to review the facts, but in reality they were looking for proofs to strengthen their party's candidates. Weeks were consumed and some 13,000 pages of testimony taken in the doubtful States, the results being what might have been expected—to two sets of electoral certificates for South Carolina, Louisiana, Florida and Oregon were now added two conflicting reports from each House of Congress. The deadlock was only aggravated. Meanwhile the situation was discussed with increasing warmth throughout the country and the debates in Congress were acrimonious and extremely partisan, few statesmen being sufficiently patriotic to take a dispassionate view of the ugly condition.[31]

Perhaps the two most self-contained persons in the nation were the

27 Nevins, *Hewitt*, 337–341.   28 Hudson, *Recollections*, 82–84.
29 *Cong. Record*, 1877, Vol. V, 11–16.   30 *Ib.*, 90, Dec. 22, 1876. Cf. *Ib.*, 365–367.
31 Newspapers of the period.

chief figures, Hayes and Tilden, who while deeply interested kept their heads, restrained their public utterances, and comported themselves with dignity. The press, with a few notable exceptions, surrendered to propaganda. The pulpit and the teacher's desk were not immune. Typical of the pamphlet literature was Henry George's "Who Shall Be President?" He argued that the Chief Executive should be chosen by a lawful election and not by the Mexican system. The dispute should be settled by the Constitution, which in a dispute authorizes the House to act, and not by the *coup d'état* being fomented by the Republicans. "Mr. Tilden should not shrink. His long career shows anything but moral cowardice. . . . So plain would be the path of duty, hedged with fire and slippery with blood though it be," that he must follow it. Even if sworn in by a justice of peace in Albany he would be much more powerful in a few days than the illegally inaugurated claimant in possession of the Capitol.[32] Tilden was urged on all sides to hold public meetings to demand his right to the Presidential Chair,[33] and to organize Democratic lodges for the same purpose.[34] Bigler reported that the Pennsylvania Democratic State Committee wished to hold a convention to support him and said that the Philadelphia bankers who voted for Hayes would "be satisfied with you." [35] Even Republicans like D. A. McKnight forwarded advice to insure fair play.[36] Democratic meetings of protest were held in Ohio, Indiana and Virginia.[37] Watterson, depressed by the inactivity of the Democrats while the Republicans "were busy as bees," spent Christmas week with Tilden planning a mass meeting of 100,000 Democrats in Washington. His speech was written and toned down by Tilden. Watterson delivered the address, but the Republicans killed its effect with ridicule.[38] Optimistic Robert Toombs wrote: "I still think if the Democrats in Congress stand firm, show no symptoms of . . . compromising, Tilden—as poor a Democrat as he is—will be peaceably . . . inaugurated . . . as the true elect of the people." [39]

A national organ to lead the movement for Tilden's inauguration was established in Washington December 6, 1876—the very day the Electoral College met. Montgomery Blair was editor in chief of this daily *Union;* Black, Marble, Chamberlain and others supplied news articles;

[32] San Francisco, Jan. 8, 1877, 8.   [33] Tilden Papers.
[34] *Ib.*, Q. R. Chase of New Orleans.   [35] *Ib.*   [36] *Ib.*
[37] *Letters*, II, 524, 526; Indianapolis *Journal* and *Sentinel*, Jan. 9, 1877.
[38] *Century*, May, 1913.
[39] *An. Rept. Am. Hist. Assn.*, 1911. Toombs to Stephens, Dec. 28, 1876.

and W. W. Corcoran financed the paper. This "handsome and newsy" journal, in a tone that was at first moderate but later more vehement, insisted that Louisiana was Democratic, that only the House could count the vote for President, and that neither the Supreme Court nor an electoral commission could settle the dispute. Soon the largest morning daily in the District of Columbia, it was copied by Democratic papers over the land. Within a few months the *Union* reached the conclusion that the rich Democrats did not want Tilden and reform, feared war and the decline of prices if he were seated, and hence sold out to the Republicans.[40]

The *Sun,* representing Tilden's attitude, thought it better to submit to wrong "however gross, than to appeal to any but legal, constitutional and peaceful remedies,"[41] but hot-headed adherents threatened civil war if necessary to seat him. John Kelly's *Express* spoke of the "use of the sword," and the *World* said that if Hayes were installed many times

> Forty thousand American men
> Will know the reason way.[42]

"Tilden or blood" became the slogan among reckless Democrats.[43] On the other hand Union soldiers, hostile to Tilden, answered the Democratic propagandists with bellicose warnings. The *Herald,* while declaring: "There must be no violence. . . . This is not Mexico," charged the Democrats with having instituted the Rebellion and declared that the country would not tolerate any threat of "a disorderly or violent attempt to grasp power."[44]

The Democrats were more belligerent than the Republicans. The Democratic Veteran Soldiers Association of Union troops made a good deal of noise. Tilden and Hendricks "Minute Men" were enrolled and military organizations formed in eleven States. Generals Corse, Franklin and Hancock were mentioned as possible commanders in chief and Hewitt declared that a leader was agreed upon tentatively.[45] In mass meetings in three States wild orators like George W. Julian declared that "millions of men" would "offer their lives" for the "sacredness of the ballot" and urged "whosoever hath a sword, let him gird it on."[46]

---

[40] Smith, *Blair Family,* II, 483–485.   [41] Nov. 21, 1876.
[42] Nov. 16, 1876.   [43] *Times,* Dec. 19, 1876.   [44] Nov. 10, 1876.
[45] Rogers, "How Hayes Became President," *McClure's,* May, 1904, 77.
[46] Indianapolis *Journal,* Jan. 9, 1877.

Joseph Pulitzer asked the hundred thousand men expected at Watterson's Washington meeting to "come fully armed and ready for business." [47] Tilden was told that Company D, 35th Battalion, New York National Guard, half of them veterans, was ready for his call; that the South would follow the North in an armed uprising; that Democratic gatherings "pledged their lives and their fortunes" to see him inducted into office; and that political clubs were ready to be converted into armed regiments. Many officers and civilians volunteered their services in hundreds of letters. One man offered himself and five sons; another, 80 armed men; and it was reported that the New Hampshire farmers could scarcely be restrained. These examples show how easy it would have been for a militant leader to incite an outbreak.[48]

Although Senator Hoar asserted that, had it not been for "the bitter experience of a few years before, there would have been war," [49] yet these manifestations of belligerency should be regarded as the product of bitter party feeling. The assertion that war was imminent may be discounted. The South certainly did not want war and could not have been induced to take up arms to seat Tilden. Republican leaders in the North did not want war. The saner Democratic leaders in the North would not have gone to such extremities, and the most influential Democratic papers cautioned moderation. The people were greatly wrought up, it is true, but would have carried on nothing more serious than an oral war. Neither Hayes nor Tilden was disposed to countenance for a moment any suggestion for imitating administrative changes in Latin America. A good deal of the talk of war was mere bluster. Had Tilden been declared the winner, the country would have settled down peaceably to its ordinary pursuits, as it did under Hayes. In his emphatic but dignified expression of pacifism, Tilden was supported by the best men in his party as well as among his opponents.

The inauguration of Lucius Robinson as Governor of New York, on January 1, 1877, afforded Tilden an opportunity to make one of his few public utterances during this period. Escorting his successor into the Assembly Chamber, Tilden drew a manuscript from his pocket and briefly addressed him in the presence of a crowded room. After alluding to the valuable service he had received from Robinson as Comptroller, he said:

[47] *Century*, May, 1913.   [48] Tilden Papers, various persons and dates.
[49] *Autobiography*, I, 369.

"To recall the government of this State to the pure condition in which a generation ago you and I knew it; to remove the fungus-growths which in evil times had overspread its administration and legislation; to lighten the intolerable burdens of the people; to improve institutions and laws; systematically to call into the civil service, whether by appointment or election, men of higher ideals of official life, of better training and more general culture, thus utilizing a class inferior in the arts of political competition, but superior in capacities for public usefulness—these are noble objects. . . . Our support was an unfaltering trust in the people, if the prospect of real reform could be made visible. . . . The standard of official conduct has been elevated. . . . The public suspicion of legislative venality is disappearing, and the lobbies are disbanded. . . . I congratulate you, sir, that . . . with such favoring auspices you enter upon an administration which, I believe, will be fruitful of public benefit." [50]

This brief address elicited hearty applause. Governor Robinson replied that the people of the country had shown their appreciation of Tilden's services by giving him the majority of their votes for President. At that statement the audience shouted its approbation. Tilden had suppressed the lobby; he would not let it return. Tilden had "arrested gross abuses and wasteful expenditures" and had "restored a higher moral tone to . . . government." [51] He would cling stubbornly to that same high ideal. When Tilden left at 5 P. M. for New York City, only a few persons were at the station to see him depart. "He attracts few people," explained Bigelow, "and no one in Albany cares for him." [52] The colored porter might say jokingly that Tilden's trunks were checked through to the White House, but others were not so sure.

In characteristic indirection Tilden took advantage of Governor Robinson's Inauguration to address the nation on the political situation. The end of the Inaugural Message, dealing with the count of the electoral vote, was prepared by Tilden and reflected his interpretation of the situation at the beginning of 1877. It referred to the Presidential election as threatening "to prove an epoch of solemn portent in our history." For the first time in twenty-two national elections, he said, the votes are a "subject of controversy." The Houses of Congress had repeatedly passed on "the authenticity and validity of electoral votes," but no election had ever "turned upon the questionable votes." Tilden had 184 undisputed votes; Hayes 165; and 20 were in dispute from four doubtful States which had sent two sets of returns which awaited "the

[50] *Writings,* II, 483.   [51] *Retrospections,* V, 385.   [52] *Tribune,* Jan. 2, 1877.

action of the two Houses . . . whose duty it is to verify, ascertain and count the electoral votes." Louisiana's government, imposed by military force and condemned by Congress as illegal in 1873, created the Returning Board which had reversed the vote of the people in 1876. Such a board neither the Federal Government nor the State had power to set up, because the Constitution declares that "the State shall appoint" electors. In South Carolina a State Board fabricated a canvass in disobedience to the State Supreme Court; and Federal troops decided who was elected to the legislature. Such a military interference violated the Constitution. In Florida a Board of State Canvassers, with only ministerial powers, had assumed authority to reverse the choice of electors as shown on the face of returns, in disobedience of the judicial tribunal. These measures in the doubtful Southern States were counseled by a member of the President's Cabinet (Zach Chandler) who was Chairman of the Republican National Committee and co-operating with "some of his colleagues in the Cabinet."

The President of the Senate had power only to "open" certificates, Tilden went on, and not to determine their validity. No such officer had ever acted otherwise in all past elections. The mode of counting had always been prescribed by the two Houses, and the President of the Senate merely carried out their wishes. The people would never consent to have their representatives stripped of this power by a deputy of the Senate. The State of New York, he concluded, would in nowise agree to such "revolutionary expedients." [53]

Tilden and the Democratic leaders still had hope of winning Florida through "legal proceedings." The Chairman of the Florida Democratic State Committee was in New York City consulting Hewitt, who expressed doubt to Tilden whether the Florida Supreme Court could be relied upon for a favorable decision. After consulting Tucker, Field and Payne, Hewitt suggested that it might be better to rely upon the Florida legislature, and urged Tilden to send Colonel Sellers and Bidelle to Florida to conduct the Democratic case, because the Florida lawyers were "not up to that kind of business." Knowing Tilden's tendency to procrastination, Hewitt warned, "Time is of the essence of success." Meanwhile Marble was working with Wilkinson Call, R. B. Helton and Governor G. F. Drew for favorable action, and C. N. Potter was put in charge of the Florida *quo warranto* action.[54] Tilden's own brief on "The

[53] Lincoln, *Messages*, VII, 32.   [54] Tilden Papers, Jan. 8, 1877.

Florida Electoral Vote" [55] was an exhaustive review of the legal possibilities of saving the four electoral votes.

As the controversy drifted into 1877, the nation became more sharply divided into two hostile political camps. Democrats charged the Republicans with a brazen conspiracy to steal the election, and the Republicans returned the compliment. Congress reflected the schism, and able leaders were seeking a satisfactory way out of the deadlock. In the doubtful Southern States two rival governments had been set up and the people were in a turmoil of passion. Tilden continued to place his faith in constitutional provisions and precedents, and demanded that the House stand on its right to count and to deny the pretensions of the President of the Senate. R. M. McLane reported that he had consulted Randall and Knott and that they would follow Tilden's advice.[56] Belmont was trying to persuade Senator Bayard and others to do the same, and thus compel the "Jacobins of the Republican Party to show their colors." [57]

Outside Congress the one absorbing topic of discussion was the question: Who will be inaugurated on March 4? Tilden was encouraged by hundreds of communications to "stand firm" against "gambling politicians." Many different suggestions were made for settling the dispute —to let the Supreme Court decide, to have both candidates withdraw and then hold a new election, to have Tilden and Hayes each choose an arbiter and these two a third, to call a "Joint Convention," to set up a special tribunal. In fact, every scheme under the sun was proposed except a trial by combat. These personal letters were supplemented by editorials, articles in newspapers, and pamphlets, which taxed Tilden's mailmen. Meanwhile out of all this discussion was gradually evolving a disposition to resort to compromise which had the support of the best men in each party.[58]

[55] *Writings*, II, 454.
[56] Tilden Papers, McLane to Belmont, Jan. 4, 1877.
[57] *Ib.*, Belmont to Tilden, Jan. 8, 1877; Marble Papers, Lib. of Cong., Dec. 31, 1876.
[58] See *Cong. Record*, 72, for petitions to Congress to settle the dispute.

IN 1800 a law had been proposed to create an electoral council of six Senators, six Representatives and the Chief Justice of the Supreme Court to settle disputed Presidential elections, but it did not pass. As recently as 1875 Oliver P. Morton had suggested a law to define the method of counting doubtful electoral votes, but it also failed of passage. Soon after November 7, 1876, J. G. Phillips of Illinois suggested to John Sherman a commission of twelve men selected from members of Congress and the Supreme Court to decide the issue.[1] The newspapers were filled with proposals, some erudite, and some intemperate. Grant's private secretary, D. D. Come, insisted that Grant was the father of the Electoral Commission, and that it was Hewitt and Randall who were won over to the idea that put Hayes in the White House.[2] Certain it is that by the time Congress met some leaders of both parties had arrived at an understanding that they would attempt to adjust the dispute.

The New York *World,* spokesman for Tilden, consistently opposed any extra-legal body to pass on the doubtful electoral votes, and later charged up to the Electoral Commission all the ills that befell the Democratic Party. It should be remembered, however, that the *Tribune* and the *Times* were just as vehemently hostile to it but for very different reasons. The *Herald* alone of all the metropolitan newspapers favored it.

On December 7, in the House, George W. McCrary of Iowa, a Republican, moved a committee of five to act with a similar Senate committee to prepare a bill or a constitutional amendment to remove all doubt about the election.[3] Hewitt amended the motion by proposing a tribunal with power to decide, his purpose being to show that the Democrats wished to settle the dispute in a peaceable manner. The Judiciary Committee of the House to whom the resolution was referred, recommended increasing the committee to seven, and the Senate concurred in appointing a similar committee.[4] On December 22 the House named Henry B. Payne, of Ohio, chairman, at Tilden's request, Eppa Hunton, A. S. Hewitt and W. M. Springer, Democrats; and McCrary, G. F.

---

[1] Tilden Papers.
[2] Washington *Post,* Sept. 13, Nov. 8, 1885. Cf. McClure, *Recollections,* 272.
[3] *Cong. Record,* V, Pt. 1, 91, 92.   [4] *Ib.,* 197–199, 221.

Hoar, and George Willard, Republicans. The Senate appointed G. F. Edmunds, chairman, O. P. Morton, F. T. Frelinghuysen and J. A. Logan, Republicans; and A. G. Thurman, T. F. Bayard and M. W. Ransom, Democrats. When Logan declined, his place was filled by Roscoe Conkling.[5] Thus in the joint committee each party had seven members. While moderate men of both parties were talking of compromise with honor, the Democrats were more disposed to mediation than the Republicans, who felt that law and force were on their side.

During the Christmas holidays, before any important sessions were held, leading Democratic Congressmen and Senators conferred with Tilden as to the wisest course to follow. "He was frank, open and earnest in his conversations with them . . . in advocating the making of an issue first in the House and then in the Senate." As the initial step he advised a resolution in the House asserting the exclusive right of the two Houses, acting concurrently, to count the electoral vote and to decide, in case of two returns, which should be valid. That issue, he thought, should be debated in Congress and before the country. The menace of usurpation by the Republicans in threatening to have the President of the Senate decide the election "would break down in process of execution." Tilden himself accepted a simpler statement which Chairman Knott presented; [6] but it had little influence. Senators Bayard and Lamar, calling on Tilden at his request, were shown his compilation on the electoral count, but he "gave no intimation whatever of his intentions." [7] Watterson, Bigelow and Marble were at Tilden's home on Christmas day, when Tilden informed them that Hewitt, Bayard and Thurman had united to create the Electoral Commission.[8] Thus it is clear that there appeared in Congress two plans—one to follow the Committee on Privileges for a decision within that body itself; the other to encourage the Committee on Electoral Count to create a new agency outside of Congress. Tilden knew of both but favored the former.

After New Year's day, 1877, the two committees on the electoral count began their labors separately. The discussion intensified the feeling that only some kind of tribunal could adjudicate the disputed returns. The House committee met on January 3 and 10. When Democrats, with Tilden's wishes in mind, proposed to limit the action of the President of the Senate to opening the electoral returns, the Republicans

[5] *Cong. Record*, V, Pt. 1, 258, 766 ff.
[6] Tilden Papers, II, 529; Marble Papers, Library of Congress.   [7] Spencer, *Bayard*, 261.
[8] *Saturday Evening Post*, May 3, 1919.

objected.[9] Finally, after a good dinner, McCrary presented a printed bill providing for an Electoral Commission, consisting of the Chief Justice and four associate Justices chosen by lot, which Grant had suggested and Conkling had prepared.[10] This suggests that the Republicans had fixed upon such a scheme at an earlier date than has been supposed.[11] While the committee agreed upon the principle, certain features were objected to and a second printing was ordered, and at another meeting a third draft was authorized. Meanwhile the Senate committee had been working on the same problem and had arrived at a similar conclusion.[12] The contention of Bigelow and Marble that Tilden was kept in the dark about the development of the Electoral Commission scheme is not borne out by the facts.[13] He knew about the various proposals, was aware that the bill creating the committees on electoral count contemplated a "tribunal," and on Christmas day told intimate friends that certain Democratic leaders in Congress were committed to an Electoral Commission.

Hewitt on January 9 sent Tilden the third draft of the bill to provide for counting electoral votes as agreed upon in the Senate committee, enjoined absolute secrecy, said he would confer with him soon, and asked him to wire in cipher his views about the choice of judges. J. R. Tucker wrote from the Capital that Tilden's telegram and letter urging the House to take a decisive stand had been received. "Speaker Randall and I have decided to stress the points on which the contest must rest and I send you a copy. If satisfactory telegraph Randall 'All right.' . . . Hope our departure from your suggestions will not be regarded as any abatement of respect we feel for your opinion." The next day W. C. Whitney hoped Tilden would force a modification of "the resolutions" in order to preserve the constitutional right of the two Houses to participate equally in the count—that is "all we want" and the country is with us.[14]

The two committees were now ready to summon a joint session, which was held on January 12 and continued for the next five days. At the first session Senator Edmunds reported in favor of a tribunal of thirteen made up of nine members from the two Houses and four Justices of the Supreme Court. The nine members were to be selected by having

[9] M. H. Northrup, "A Grave Crisis," *Century*, XL, 923; Nevins, *Hewitt*, 348.
[10] Rhodes, VII, 314.   [11] Nevins, *Writings of Hewitt*, 166.
[12] Rhodes, VII, 318; Senator Edmunds also presented a plan. Nevins, *Hewitt*, 344.
[13] *Life*, II, 74; Marble, *A Secret Chapter*, 15.   [14] Tilden Papers, Jan. 9, 10, 1877.

each House name five, then dropping one by lot.[15] The sessions were kept so secret that even Senators Barnum and Kernan knew nothing about the "electoral contrivance" under consideration in the Senate committee.[16] Manton Marble recorded in his notes: "Jan. 12. Democratic Senators not of Senate Committee unaware of counterplan by that Senate Committee—Barnum and Kernan. Democratic Representatives of House Committee unaware of counterplan by Senate Committee." [17] It was not true, as Marble and others stated, that Tilden was kept in complete ignorance of the measure until January 14,[18] because Hewitt on January 12, upon learning in the afternoon of the proposal of the Senate committee in the joint conference, sent Tilden the latest draft of the secret "Electoral Bill," together with "documents and information" about the work of the two committees and again warned him that they were "strictly confidential." [19]

The following day, January 13, at the second joint meeting, the House committee accepted the plan of the Senate committee in principle, but insisted upon applying the mode of reduction by lot to the judges. Before the day ended the joint committee agreed upon a tribunal which had the assent of all members except Morton and Springer.[20] This scheme provided for a commission of fifteen members—five from the House, five from the Senate and five from the Supreme Court—the judges to be determined by putting the names of six senior justices in a hat and then drawing out one.[21] Because of Springer's insistence on delay, decision was postponed till the 15th. Secrecy was imposed on all members of the committee. Hewitt then hurried up to New York to consult with Tilden over the Sabbath.[22] Meantime on Saturday evening, January 13, Marble called on Tilden and found him examining the McCrary House Bill and accompanying papers which Hewitt had rushed on to him. They "sat late into the night" analyzing the documents and discussing the situation. Marble was invited to return on Sunday, when Hewitt himself would be present to explain the measures proposed.[23]

At the Sunday morning conference, January 14, Tilden, Hewitt,

[15] Rhodes, VII, 314.
[16] *Letters,* II, 530.
[17] Marble Papers, Library of Congress.
[18] Marble, *A Secret Chapter,* 15.
[19] Tilden Papers, Jan. 12, 1877.
[20] Rhodes, VII, 314. W. E. Chandler on Jan. 13, 1877, wrote Hayes that he favored the Electoral Commission but thought the Democrats might not. Some Republicans worried over Louisiana, others over their future if the Democrats won, and still others over what Hayes would do for friendly Southerners. Hayes Papers.
[21] Haworth, 198.
[22] *Letters,* II, 530.
[23] Marble, *A Secret Chapter,* 15.

Cooper and Potter were present. Other persons "came and went during the day" and Marble may have been in the house. But the "consultation" was "personal" between Tilden and Hewitt.[24] It is possible that there was a second conference in the afternoon which lasted until near nine in the evening and which Marble attended.[25] Tilden later declared that at this meeting with Hewitt he received "his first information that the other measures [in the House] had been abandoned, and that the subject upon which he [Hewitt] wished to confer was the Electoral Bill." [26] Yet Marble and Bigelow erroneously asserted that Tilden had been kept in ignorance of the secret, extra-constitutional device.[27] Perhaps he had not received "from Mr. Hewitt's lips" an account of the measure, but Hewitt had sent him a copy of the proposed bill and an explanation of what had taken place. And now he had made clear the whole situation in Washington.

Before waiting for Tilden to read the "new bill," Hewitt told him that the Democratic members of the Senate committee—Bayard and Thurman—"were already absolutely committed to this bill" and would concur with the Republican members in reporting it to the Senate whether the House should agree to it or not.[28] Of course the Democrats on the House committee, of which Hewitt was one, being in the majority, could have killed the bill had they wished to do so. Moreover, Payne, the chairman, had been designated by Tilden himself and must have known his wishes.

After receiving this information from Hewitt, Tilden asked, "Is it not rather late, then, to consult me?"

"They do not consult you," answered Hewitt. "They are public men and have their own duties and responsibilities. I consult you."

They proceeded then to study the bill and to discuss its provisions in detail. Hewitt pressed upon Tilden the difficulty which the House committee would face if it attempted to carry out an independent policy without the support of the Democratic Senators. "I can't advise you to agree to the bill," Tilden said, "but I will advise you as to details." As to the elimination of one of six judges by lot, in order to obtain the requisite five, he declared emphatically: "I may lose the Presidency, but

[24] Nevins, *Writings of Hewitt*, 167, 185.   [25] Marble, *A Secret Chapter*, 15.
[26] Letters, II, 530; Marble, in *Sun*, Aug. 5, 1878.
[27] Nevins, *Hewitt*, 392; *Life*, II, 75; *Letters*, II, 530.
[28] *Letters*, II, 530; *Life*, II, 75; *Sun*, Aug. 5, 1878; Nevins, *Hewitt*, 352.

I will not raffle for it." If arbitration were adopted, he thought the tribunal should be fixed in the bill and not be left to "chance or intrigue." [29] The duty of the arbitrators to "investigate and decide the case on its merits should be made mandatory." The element of gamble should be eliminated. "If you go into a conference with your adversary," Tilden continued, "and can't break off because you feel you must agree to something, you cannot negotiate—you are not fit to negotiate. You will be beaten on every detail." Hewitt then said that there was danger of a "collision of force" with President Grant. These rumors Tilden thought exaggerated and asked: "Why surrender now? You can always surrender. Why surrender before the battle for fear you may have to surrender after the battle is over?" [30]

Pressed by Hewitt to agree to the bill if it were modified so as to "fix the five judges by a positive provision," Tilden "firmly declined." The session of the joint committee called for that evening at Senator Bayard's home did not materialize because Hewitt wired that Tilden refused to give his "adhesion" to the project. Tilden condemned the "proposed action as precipitate.[31] It was a month before the time for the count, and he saw no reason why there should not be an opportunity afforded for . . . consultation. . . . He treated it as a panic in which they were liable to act in haste and repent at leisure. He did not ask any time for himself . . . to decide what he would do . . . but he advised more deliberation upon the part of those who were to act in Washington. He believed in publicity and discussion, and a wider consultation. He had an inherent and incurable distrust of the scheme. . . . Mr. Tilden also disapproved of the secrecy with which the proceedings were shrouded. . . . No argument or persuasion could extract from him a word of sanction to the scheme. If, however, it was to be adopted . . . he manifested a desire that the provisions of the bill should be made to operate as much good and as little mischief as possible. . . . He was willing to advise . . . in respect to specific provisions, but took care, in doing so, not incidentally to adopt the bill." [32]

These quotations from Tilden himself must be accepted as a positive and truthful statement of his attitude toward the proposed tribunal. He regarded it as a hasty, inept, and doubtful agency, and consequently

---

[29] *Letters*, II, 350.   [30] *Ib.*, 531; Nevins, *Hewitt*, 353.
[31] *Letters*, 532; Marble, *A Secret Chapter*, 18–19, gives quotations with variations. Compare Nevins, *Hewitt*, 352–353.
[32] *Letters*, II, 532; Marble, *A Secret Chapter*, 15–16.

refused to give it his sanction. At the same time he recognized the right of experienced and patriotic Democrats, who approved the bill, to act upon their own judgment, and was not disposed to make their course the subject of criticism. If they decided to proceed on their own responsibility, he expressed a willingness to co-operate as to details. According to H. B. Payne, Hewitt returned to Washington under the impression that Tilden was not unalterably opposed to some scheme for a tribunal.[33] "We parted, therefore," Hewitt wrote, "without any distinct approval or disapproval on the part of Mr. Tilden, but with the distinct understanding that I was to secure if possible the modification of the Six Judge Plan . . . and for the substitution of some other mode of selecting the judges which might be satisfactory to Mr. Tilden." If he absolutely disapproved of the bill, Hewitt told Tilden, it would not be passed; if he did not, it would be.[34] Tilden told Bigelow that Hewitt had been sent to him "not to consult me about it, but to get my approval of it," and that Bayard, Thurman and Ransom had made up their minds "whatever his advice or wishes might be." [35] Many Democrats believed incorrectly that Tilden had sanctioned the tribunal.[36]

Judge C. P. Daly thought the Senate committee would be justified, in view of Tilden's indecision, in presenting its plan at once, and advised the House committee to concur unless Tilden interposed an absolute veto. Daly called on Tilden at Hewitt's request that same Sunday night and in a long walk discussed the situation with him. Daly states that Tilden expressed grave doubts as to the wisdom of the proposed tribunal, but distinctly said that he was not willing to assume the responsibility of disapproving arbitration. The selection of judges, however, Tilden thought should be modified. "He did not express any disapproval of the principle or the policy of the bill but confined his criticisms to the details." [37]

Although an arbitration court did not emanate directly from Tilden, yet he advocated the principle involved and had used it to settle business disputes.[38] His belief was that the Constitution and precedent clearly pointed a way out. The plan of a tribunal came from Congress. Thurman

[33] Rhodes, VII, 316.   [34] Nevins, *Hewitt*, 353.   [35] *Life*, II, 76.
[36] Wilson, J. H., *The Life of Charles A. Dana*, 442.   [37] Nevins, *Hewitt*, 354–355.
[38] H. K. Enos, a New York City banker, averred that as Congress was assembling, in the presence of C. N. Jordan and I. C. New, Tilden said: "The proper way to settle the question would be to leave it to a Court of Arbitrament, but unfortunately the Republicans . . . will not take the risk of this equitable manner of settlement. It will have to be settled by the Courts." Hewitt Papers, Enos to A. S. Hewitt, Feb. 15, 1888.

believed that in his interview with Tilden the latter had acquiesced in the principle of arbitration; Bayard,[39] Hewitt, and other Democratic leaders were of the same opinion. The historic fact seems to be that when Tilden understood the mood of Congress and the decided drift there toward an amicable settlement through compromise, he yielded tacit consent to the judgment of the Democratic leaders, even though it was contrary to his own conviction. His objection to the six judge plan was wholly justifiable because it was certain to throw the decision to Hayes.

On the day Hewitt was in conference with Tilden, Charles Francis Adams was in the city to "talk over . . . the great cause." Unable to see Tilden, he submitted to him by letter a solution of the difficulty. He proposed that the two Presidential candidates should "agree on a practical way out . . . and unite in jointly recommending it to Congress and the country"; and thought its adoption by Congress was "inevitable." Evidently what he had in mind was another election, for nothing but "an appeal to the ballot . . . the simple, fundamental, democratic appeal to the great tribunal," could satisfactorily settle the question.[40] Although others had made a similar suggestion, there is no evidence that it elicited any favorable response from Tilden.

Meanwhile, news of the proposed Electoral Commission leaked out. The *Times* decried the "Dice-Box vs. Ballot-Box" method and said Hayes and Tilden might as well draw cuts.[41] There was a popular outcry and some Democrats said they would not "consent that the great office of President should be raffled off like a Thanksgiving turkey." [42] Payne told the joint committee that a bill embodying the lottery feature could not pass the House [43] and proposed that the five judges be chosen outright.[44] Hewitt agreed that the "Senate bill would not pass the House" and said:

"I have had little to say in this discussion. Owing to my peculiar relations, I am unjustly supposed to speak for another. But my personal views are not . . . necessarily in harmony with those of the person for whom I am supposed to speak. I have great hopes of bringing our present plan to a point where both committees may agree. A plan has occurred to me which at the proper time I will submit." [45]

[39] Spencer, *Bayard*, 262.
[40] Tilden Papers, Jan. 13, 16, 1877.
[41] Jan. 13, 1877.
[42] Northrup, *Century*, Oct., 1901, 929.
[43] *Ib.*, 315, Jan. 15, 1877.
[44] Rhodes, VII, 315.
[45] Northrup, *Century*, Oct., 1901, 928–929.

Payne's suggestion did not seem acceptable to the Senate committee, because Hewitt telegraphed to Edward Cooper: "The Senate committee will probably reject five- and report six-judge plan immediately. Our Senators feel committed to concur. House committee will not concur, and for present will not report." After consulting with Tilden, Cooper wired back: "Procrastinate to give few days for information and consultation. The six-judge inadmissible." [46] Perhaps the biggest mistake Tilden made was in not issuing a clear-cut proclamation to the American people giving in unmistakable language his unalterable opposition to an extra-constitutional tribunal of arbitration. This he refused to do and consequently many persons believed that he was not averse to such an arrangement. Both Hewitt and Payne professed to believe that Tilden was so set on a pacific solution of the problem that under certain conditions his endorsement might be obtained. In the House the irreconcilable Democrats from the first opposed an Electoral Commission, but Randall and Hewitt both fought them and prevented their taking action.[47] Outside Congress a number of newspapers followed the New York *Sun*, which opposed the Electoral Commission because Dana was convinced that Tilden had been elected President.[48] If Tilden had come out unequivocally against the tribunal, both in principle and in fact, it seems probable that the Democrats in Congress would have defeated it. Indeed to F. F. Marbury he boasted, "Why, if I were so disposed, I could kill this bill by the mere wave of my fingers." [49] But he refused to accept that responsibility.

After his Sunday conference with Tilden, Hewitt's remarks before the joint committee might indicate that the consultation had not been entirely harmonious. Still he was hopeful of a solution that would give Tilden the decision. In the joint committee on January 16, Payne presented a bill which he and Hewitt had drawn up proposing a commission consisting of five members from the House, five from the Senate and five definitely named senior members of the Supreme Court.[50] Hewitt, knowing Tilden's objection to the use of chance in creating a tribunal, argued strenuously for the arrangement. McCrary said the House had originally stood for a decision by five justices alone, whereupon Hewitt

[46] *Letters*, II, 533, Jan. 15, 1877.
[47] Rogers, "How Hayes Became President," *McClure's*, May, 1904, 84.
[48] Wilson, *Dana*, 444.   [49] Nevins, *Hewitt*, 354.
[50] Rhodes, VII, 317; Northrup, *Century*, Oct., 1901, 930.

remarked that he would still favor such a court. He had investigated Justice David Davis and was convinced that he was a "neutral." Finally, he expressed a willingness to let four designated judges choose a fifth. Thurman was positive that the Supreme Court judges would not be partisan; and Bayard, admitting that Davis was more of a Democrat than a Republican, thought party bias was being stressed too much.[51] "Uncle Sam" Ward, on cordial social terms with Democratic leaders in Washington, reported to Tilden that both Ransom and Bayard were "grave and Bayard was angry" over the situation; and that the Republicans feared Tilden's "daylight policy." [52]

Through Edward Cooper, Hewitt reported to Tilden what had happened:

"After protracted negotiations Senators receded from six-judge. Declined five-judge and offered four senior associate justices who are to choose the fifth judge excluding Chief Justice. Our Senate friends earnestly favor acceptance, because they don't believe it possible to pass over Field. The Democrats on the House committee believe this is the last chance of agreement. . . . If we decline Senate committee will report their original plan to which our friends are committed. Telegraph your advice."

This message was sent late on the 16th after the discussions in the joint committee had ended. In the evening Tilden summoned Marble, Cooper, and "several other gentlemen" to his library to consider the news brought over the wire. "The situation was freely canvassed." Then Tilden dictated a telegram to be transmitted in cipher. As a result it was not sent out until two o'clock that night, and was as follows:

"Be firm and cool. Four-judge plan will not do. Perhaps worse than six. Complaints likely to arise of haste and want of consultation with members, and embarrassment in exercise of their judgment after plan is disclosed by premature committal of their representatives. There should be more opportunity for deliberation and consultation. Secrecy dangerous; probably mistake in itself, and if it results in disaster would involve great blame and infinite mischief." [53]

The telegram was not addressed to Hewitt but was soon in his hands. It took him and General R. C. Taylor more than an hour to decipher it. It probably went to Colonel Pelton and reveals Tilden's continued hostility to the commission idea. To offset this negative attitude he had

[51] Northrup, *Century*, Oct., 1901, 930–931.   [52] Tilden Papers, Jan. 16, 1877.
[53] *Letters*, II, 533, 534.

nothing of a constructive character to suggest and thus put Hewitt in an exceedingly difficult position. Yet Hewitt told Taylor that he would never agree to any arrangement that Tilden flatly opposed.[54]

H. W. Potter wrote: "I was at the rooms of the National Committee on the night before the appointment of the Electoral Commission. . . . Went with P. B. Olney to Tilden's house and found Tilden, Belmont and Marble in the Library. Belmont was advising a telegram in reply to the news of the Electoral Commission. Tilden said: 'Mr. Belmont, individually I do not care the snap of my fingers for the Presidency, and will not consent to raffle for it.' " [55]

On the evening of the 16th Hewitt summoned the Democratic advisory committee in Congress. All but one of the twenty-three members answered the call. After a long discussion, all of the Senators and some of the Representatives favored the four-judge plan. Among the Congressmen objecting was Watterson, who told Hewitt that he had lost all by failing to call out the people, and that now nothing was left but to take the best terms they could get. "The only effect of the Electoral Commission Bill," he avowed, "will be to put Mr. Hayes into office with a color of title, whereas otherwise he will have to be inducted by the Senate, General Grant, and the Army." No action was taken to bind the committee. Hewitt stated that Conkling used his influence to induce the Republicans to abandon the "lot" feature in the bill.[56] Hewitt was disposed to be impatient with Tilden's dilatoriness—except when they were discussing their common foe, dyspepsia [57]—and therefore during these momentous days, unfortunately, lost his confidence almost completely. For guidance Hewitt relied more and more on the Democratic leaders in Congress, with results that were far from satisfactory.

Consideration of the Electoral Commission Bill continued on January 17, when Payne announced that the House committee would not accept the Senate committee's proposal because it classified Davis as a Democrat.[58] Hewitt agreed with Payne, was anxious over the situation, and had not slept a wink because of worry. "I have felt," he said, "that if an agreement failed, I would be charged with the responsibility." He then proposed that Clifford and Swayne, as senior judges, each select another judge, and that these four choose a fifth. The Senate committee rejected

[54] Nevins, *Hewitt*, 359.   [55] Tilden Papers. Potter to Bigelow, Feb. 22, 1879.
[56] Nevins, *Hewitt*, 352, 359; *Writings of Hewitt*, 183; *Century*, May, 1913, states that Watterson was the only member who opposed the Electoral Commission.
[57] Mitchell, *Memoirs*, 264.   [58] Rhodes, VII, 318.

Hewitt's plan and set forth a counter-proposal to select four judges from the first, third, eighth and ninth circuits, who would agree upon a fifth judge. Springer was also hostile to Hewitt's proposal because it "flavored of the dice-box." [59] Finally, toward evening, the House committee, with the sole exception of Eppa Hunton, accepted the Senate committee's solution.[60] Members of the joint committee were elated at the agreement. Hoar declared it the happiest event in American history; Thurman said it would be hailed with joy from ocean to ocean; and Hewitt thought that it was "worth five hundred millions to the country at once." [61] In the end, on January 18, the recommendation was signed by all members of the joint committee except Morton, who told Hewitt that it "was equivalent to the abandonment of the contest by the Republican side." [62] Thus out of discussion and compromise the Electoral Commission was evolved.

On January 17, Colonel Pelton was hurried to New York with the bill as agreed upon, to obtain Tilden's "approval or rejection." He returned to Washington on the morning of the 18th and reported to the House committee that Tilden regarded the amended measure "as a great improvement upon any previous proposition, and advised its adoption by the House committee." Thereupon General Hunton signed the report, although with reluctance. The Democrats were jubilant because they believed that with Judge Davis as the fifth justice "the victory was won."

In 1879, H. H. Smith asked Pelton for details of his conference with his uncle about the Electoral Commission Bill. Pelton replied that, upon his arrival with the document, Tilden sent for "two or three old and trusted friends" with whom he discussed details. As a result, he concluded that "it was advisable to accept the bill, objectionable as it was in almost every respect." He proposed several amendments at first, "but finally decided that it was inexpedient to make any formal suggestions." The report of Pelton to Hewitt, Hunton, Springer and others brought about their approval of the bill in the House. When Simon Sterne protested acceptance of the bill, Tilden asked sharply, "What is left but war? He was determined to protect the Democratic Party from the charge of a lack of patriotism." [63]

On the evening of January 17, after conferring with Marble and "several other gentlemen," Tilden prepared a final telegram. It was

[59] Northrup, *Century*, Oct., 1901, 931.   [60] Rhodes, VII, 319.
[61] Northrup, 932.   [62] Nevins, *Hewitt*, 365.   [63] *Ib.*, 361–363.

sent over to the committee room at midnight to be translated into cipher and sent to Washington, probably to Pelton. Meanwhile Pelton was on the train bound for New York. After learning from Pelton of the agreement on the Electoral Commission, Tilden very likely instructed him to suppress the telegram or Pelton may have withheld it on his own initiative. Tilden himself testified: "It was not addressed to Mr. Hewitt and therefore was not seen by him." [64] Hewitt also asserted that he never saw the telegram and believed that it had been suppressed.[65] Its value consists in showing Tilden's views, and therefore it is given below:

"No need of hot haste, but much danger in it. Some days' interval should be taken; the risk of publicity harmless. No information here . . . which could justify abstinence from condemning such an abandonment of the Constitution . . . and of the rights of the two Houses and of the people. . . . We are overpressed by exaggerated fears and forget that the other side will have greater trouble than we unless relieved by some agreement. They have no way out but by usurpation; are bullying us with what they dare not do. . . . So long as we stand on the Constitution and settled practice, we know where we are. . . . Only way of getting accessions in the Senate is by House standing firm—and judicious friends believe in that case we will go safely through. . . . Though details may be properly discussed, final committal by House committee should be firmly withheld." [66]

When in 1878 prominent Democrats like Watterson, Marble and Bigelow were discussing the vindication of the wrong of 1876, they thought that Tilden's chances in 1880 would be strengthened if it could be shown that he never consented to the Electoral Commission but was the victim of fraud and Democratic disloyalty. Watterson, on his way east, stopped at Washington, where he was excluded by Hewitt from a congressional Democratic caucus. Resentful of this treatment, he went on to New York, where he was soon posing as the mouthpiece of Tilden in letters to the *Sun* and other papers in which he denounced Hewitt, Bayard, Thurman, and Randall for consenting to the Electoral Commission against the expressed wish of Tilden. Manton Marble took up the war cry in a long letter in the *Sun*.[67] He portrayed Tilden as the great, fearless leader betrayed by his followers, quoted Tilden's own words to prove his charges, and gave to the public certain telegrams which Tilden had sent. Tilden, in dictating the material for a part of this

[64] *Letters*, II, 534. See *Life* for difference in date.
[65] Nevins, *Hewitt*, 393–394; *Writings of Hewitt*, 189.
[66] *Letters*, II, 534–535, Jan. 17, 1877, Midnight.
[67] Aug. 5, 1878.

letter, had insisted on a footnote reading, "Please state that I have never questioned the good faith and patriotic purposes of Mr. Hewitt, or of any whose counsels and guidance he thought it his duty to follow." Hewitt at once denied Marble's allegations and asserted that the telegram beginning "No need of hot haste" was suppressed with Tilden's own knowledge, or by his positive order.

Marble used this telegram, apparently with Tilden's knowledge if not his consent, without giving all the facts, to make it appear that Tilden had condemned the Electoral Commission, had sought through Hewitt and other Democratic leaders to prevent its creation, and had consistently demanded the settlement of the dispute through constitutional means. Marble's implication clearly was that Hewitt had given his support to the tribunal which deprived Tilden of the honor to which the people had elected him. So irritated was Hewitt by this misrepresentation that he prepared a letter asserting that Tilden tacitly if not publicly favored the commission but was persuaded by friends not to make it public. When in 1895 Bigelow's *Life of Tilden* appeared, repeating the charges made by Marble and reprinting the telegram,[68] Hewitt prepared his "Secret History," denying Bigelow's interpretation, which Allan Nevins has given to the public for the first time. In Tilden's *Letters*, edited by Bigelow in 1908, the telegram appears again with an accompanying memorandum dictated by Tilden.[69]

On January 17, 1877, a sketch of the Electoral Commission Bill was printed in the New York papers. The *World* reported substantial agreement in the joint committee and general rejoicing. Senator Edmunds explained the decision of the joint committee to the Senate and the bill was ordered printed. A week later Payne reported it to the House.[70] While there were expressions of disapproval of the measure, Tilden himself gave no public utterance that might indicate his hostility. His silence was interpreted as acquiescence. His real opinion about the contrivance was known, not alone to Marble, Potter, Bigelow and Pelton, but to Hewitt, Payne, and other Democrats on the House committee. They felt, however, that, with certain modifications for which they worked diligently, his assent could be obtained. Hence they had been induced to accept an altered form presented by the Senate committee and affixed their signatures to it.

[68] *Life*, II, 79.   [69] *Letters*, II, 534.
[70] *Cong. Record*, 930; Edmunds, "Another View of the Hayes-Tilden Contest," *Century*, June, 1913, 197.

In this crisis Tilden's own plan was very simple—far simpler than his party understood. That solution was "to stand firmly and inflexibly on the unbroken series of precedents formed by the twenty-two Presidential counts from 1793 to 1872." The House must assert the exclusive, constitutional right of the two Houses, acting concurrently, to count the electoral vote and to decide what votes should be excluded.[71] If neither candidate obtained a majority of all the votes, then the House should elect the President and the Senate the Vice President. If under these conditions, Tilden were elected by the House, he said, "I will go to Washington and take the oath if I am shot the next day." [72] In 1878 a *World* reporter called Tilden's attention to the story that he said he would take the oath of office at City Hall in New York and that President Grant intended to arrest him if he did. Asked whether that thought had occurred to him "at any time," he musingly replied: "At any time? Certainly—if the House had declared me elected. Then I should have had a certificate—a title. But after the electoral scheme, which I always opposed, was complete . . . I never entertained the idea of taking the oath of office either in Washington or in New York or elsewhere. It would have been ridiculous. I had no evidence of title then—no claim—no warrant." [73]

In his own mind Tilden stood on the fundamental law of the land and spurned an extra-constitutional device. The utmost concession that Hewitt could get from him was that, if Congress was determined to try the experiment of arbitration, he would not only not oppose it but would give advice as to details. When his own party leaders departed from his advice and created the electoral machinery, Tilden gave reluctant assent but made it clear that responsibility for the outcome rested on their shoulders and not on his. Perhaps it is idle to speculate on what would have happened had Tilden come out with a public disavowal, but it is conceivable that the result would have been different. Blaine told Bigelow that, if the Democrats had taken an unalterable stand, the Republicans would havé backed down.[74] In after years Tilden at least had the consolation of an excuse for using one of his pet phrases: "I told you so."

Tilden would have been happy to be seated by the House without arbitration. Hayes also bitterly objected to the tribunal and clung to the

[71] *Letters*, II, 529. [72] *Life*, II, 82. Quotation from Watterson.
[73] *Letters*, II, 577. General Woodford to Mr. Mines, quoted from *World*.
[74] *Life*, II, 74, note.

alleged right of the President of the Senate to count the vote. But Congress believed adjudication imperative—and both Tilden and Hayes reluctantly acquiesced. Hewitt always maintained that a stubborn Democratic opposition would have been hopeless; that Tilden could not be inaugurated without a resort to arms; and that the course followed was the only wise one.[75] The *Nation* declared that the Democrats had no choice in the matter. Certain it is that the leaders of his party felt themselves justified in not heeding Tilden's advice. Some, aspirants for the Presidency, would not go into mourning over the defeat of a rival. Others believed that they were finding an honorable way out. And still others were convinced that this course was the only chance for victory. Did not the President of the Senate have all the returns in his hands and might he not declare Hayes elected and ask Grant to see that he was inaugurated? If in the face of such action the House elected Tilden, might he not be declared a traitor? Would the people give him sufficient support in a resort to force? Besides, was it not highly probable that out of all the disputed votes Tilden was quite certain of getting the single vote that would seat him? And was there not the chance of obtaining, as the man holding the decisive vote, Judge Davis who, although an Independent, was believed to have Democratic leanings?

The bill creating the Electoral Commission, signed by all the joint committee except Senator O. P. Morton,[76] provided:

1. That the two Houses should meet in joint session on the first Thursday in February in the House of Representatives, the President of the Senate presiding.

2. Objections to returns from States where there was a single certificate had to be made in writing and signed by at least one member of each House. No vote or votes could be excluded except by concurrent action.

3. In cases where more than one return had been received, they were to be opened, read and then submitted with all papers to the Electoral Commission, which "shall proceed to consider the same" and to decide by a majority what votes are "provided for by the Constitution." This decision was to stand unless an objection signed by five members from each House should be sustained by the separate vote of each House.

4. The joint meeting of the two Houses was not to be dissolved until the count was completed; and there was to be no debate. At separate

[75] Nevins, *Hewitt*, 363.   [76] Haworth, 204.

sessions debate was limited to two hours.

5. The right to question in the courts the title of any person to the Presidency was in nowise restricted.[77]

This report, promising an end of the dispute, was received with satisfaction in all parts of the nation. Hendricks publicly expressed his gratification. "A large portion of the press" approved of the arrangement.[78] The *Times* feared that some Republican on the commission might double-cross Hayes.[79] "The Republican Party has not gained strength since the election," said *Harper's Weekly,* and "could not survive the inauguration of a President whose title should rest on a grave moral doubt."[80] A majority of Democrats supported the bill. Most Republicans opposed the measure because it seemed to increase the Democratic chances of victory. Although Grant used his influence to have the bill passed,[81] Hayes regarded it as unconstitutional.[82] Congressman A. E. Stevenson never regretted being "an earnest advocate" of the tribunal as "an imperative necessity" even though it shut its eyes to the light of truth.[83] Lamar prepared a speech against it, but never delivered it. Convinced that Tilden could not be seated without force, he regarded the tribunal as the only "peaceable solution."[84] That Bayard and Thurman, for whose judgment Hewitt had a high regard, stubbornly promoted the commission under the honest belief that it would result in a triumph of their party, one cannot doubt. When Randall and Watterson remonstrated with Bayard, he replied angrily, "If you do not accept this plan, I shall wash my hands of the whole business, and you can go ahead and seat your President in your own way."[85] Watterson himself finally consented to the commission.[86] Bayard was reported to have said, "This is the first day I have had any hope of Tilden's election."[87]

Senator Edmunds, in presenting the bill on January 20, made a powerful nonpartisan plea for the device and urged its passage as a wise and fair measure.[88] Senator Morton made a bitter partisan attack on it as a "contrivance for surrender."[89] Conkling, in an eloquent address that captivated the galleries, supported the plan,[90] after Sherman, reflecting Hayes' view, had expressed disapproval.[91] Bayard and Thur-

[77] *Cong. Record,* 713.   [78] Haworth, 207.   [79] Davis, *Hist. of N.Y. Times,* 141.
[80] Jan. 13, 1877.   [81] Haworth, 210.   [82] Sherman, *Recollections,* I, 561.
[83] Stevenson, *Men I Have Known,* 14–16, 78.   [84] Mayes, *Lamar,* 302, 440, 699.
[85] *Century,* May, 1913, 18.   [86] *Ib.,* June, 1912, 199.
[87] Tilden Papers, "E.G.L.," Jan. 21, 1877.   [88] *Cong. Record,* 1877, Vol. V, 767–771.
[89] *Ib.,* 799–801; Foulke, *Life of Morton,* II, 443–452.
[90] *Ib.,* 825–831, 870–878.   [91] *Ib.,* 820–825.

man defended the compromise, while Blaine denounced it.[92] The bill passed the Senate on January 25 by a vote of 47 to 17.[93] The 47 ayes were made up of 26 Democrats and 21 Republicans; the 17 noes were all Republican except one.

On January 25 the Electoral Bill was introduced in the House by Payne and discussed by McCrary, Lamar, Springer, Watterson, Hunter, and Hewitt, who considered both the legality and the wisdom of the proposal. Hewitt declared that the tribunal would avoid a national schism. Others said that this adjustment was the only hope of a peaceful solution. Among those who opposed the measure were Hale, Knott, Monroe, Townsend, Hurlbut, Kasson and Garfield. The bill passed on January 26 by 191 to 86.[94] The bill carried by the combination of a majority of Democrats—over 8 to 1—with a minority of Republicans—a total of 186 Democrats in the two Houses and 52 Republicans.[95] This shows that it was a Democratic measure, which caused the *Times* to be "cast in gloom." Republicans like Garfield were convinced that the tribunal meant the inauguration of Tilden.

While Congress was discussing the bill, the expectation that Judge David Davis would be the deciding judge led Democrats to favor the measure.[96] Uncanny B. F. Butler asked a *Sun* reporter, "What is the news?" The reporter replied that Senator Morton was making a speech. "No, no! I don't mean that. I mean what is the news from Springfield?" When the reporter looked puzzled, Butler continued, "Springfield— Springfield, Illinois! That's the place you want to watch!" He had outguessed Washington politicians.[97] Davis had helped to organize the Republican Party and had supported Lincoln, who put him on the Supreme Court in 1862. When the Rebellion was over, like Tilden he defended the policy of President Johnson.[98] In 1872 and 1876 men like Judge S. J. Field, O. H. Browning [99] and Singleton suggested him as the Democratic candidate for President. He "spoke freely of Tilden . . . and not in complimentary terms." [100] Tilden regarded him as an upright and conscientious man but was not on intimate terms with him.[101]

---

[92] Cox, *Three Decades*, 656.   [93] *Cong. Record,* 1877, Vol. V, 913.

[94] *Ib.*, 930–948, 1007, 1050.

[95] *Ib.*, V, 913; Nevins, *Hewitt*, 364; Eckenrode, 210; *Rhodes*, VII, 261.

[96] Koerner, *Memoirs*, II, 619–620.

[97] Mitchell, *Memoirs*, 301–303. Butler refused the *Sun's* offer of $2,500 for an opinion on the situation because he was a member-elect of Congress.

[98] Stryker, *Johnson*, 410.   [99] Browning, *Diary*, 308, 438, 446, 521.

[100] Hayes Papers, W. H. Smith to Gov. Hayes, Feb. 17, 1877.

[101] Gibson, *A Political Crime*, 39.

As early as January 13 Tilden knew that "Davis would be the next Senator" of Illinois [102] and should have passed the word on to Hewitt as an additional argument against the commission, but there is no evidence that he did so. Although the Chicago *Tribune* had announced that the Democrats in caucus had selected Davis,[103] Hewitt inexcusably took no pains to ascertain definitely whether Davis would serve on the tribunal if chosen. With the support of Governor Palmer, Cyrus H. McCormick, and Granger votes, Davis was chosen Senator shortly after the Senate had passed the Electoral Bill [104]—a coincidence noted at once by the New York *Tribune,* which announced that he was now eliminated "as the odd member of the proposed tribunal." [105] When Hewitt heard the news his countenance dropped.[106] Judge Davis received congratulations and said he would be glad to get off the bench although he would not resign until after March 4.[107] At a dinner following Davis' election, Washburn remarked, "Well, we have saved our son." "Yes," replied Captain Parish, a Republican Greenbacker, "but we have lost Rome." "What?—What do you mean by that expression?" asked Washburn. "I mean," said Parish, "that Davis will not serve on the commission and Hayes will win." [108] Thus the Illinois Democrats, to win a State victory, defeated their party in the nation.[109]

Grant signed the bill creating the Electoral Commission, feeling that it settled "a gravely exciting question." [110] The next day the House chose as members Payne, Hunton and Abbott, Democrats, and Hoar and Garfield, Republicans; while the Senate selected Edmunds, Frelinghuysen and Morton, Republicans, and Thurman and Bayard, Democrats. At the same time the designated judges—Clifford and Field,[111] Democrats, and Strong and Miller, Republicans—offered the fifth place to Senator-elect David Davis, but he promptly declined to act. To settle all uncertainty, he gave Judge Strong a written assertion to

---

[102] Tilden Papers, H. H. Finly's telegram to Tilden and Pelton, Jan 25; Browning, *Diary,* II, 470, Jan. 17, 1877, thought either Davis or Singleton would be elected.

[103] Jan. 13, 1876. How when Gen. Logan and Gov. Palmer were deadlocked, the latter threw his support to Davis is explained in Palmer, *Recollections,* 1901.

[104] Browning, *Diary,* II, 438, 470.   [105] Jan. 26, 1876.

[106] Milton Northrup in *Century,* Oct., 1901, 933.

[107] *The Pantagraph,* Jan. 27, 1877; J. W. Fell to Gov. Palmer, Jan. 15, 1877.

[108] *Ill. Hist. Soc. Trans.,* 1909, 88, 188–189. Articles by J. T. Campbell and J. M. Davis.

[109] Logan, *Reminiscences of a Soldier's Wife,* 360–361, charged the use of bribery to seat Davis.

[110] *Cong. Record,* 1081, Jan. 29, 1877.

[111] Hill, "The Hayes-Tilden Contest," *Harper's Monthly,* March, 1907, 562, states that Justice Field voted for Hayes but gives no proof of it.

that effect; while he also told Judge Clifford that "under no condition would he go on the commission," and that even if unanimously chosen he would "decline the honor." [112]

Like Tilden, Davis distrusted the commission as a dangerous experiment which might imperil free government. Besides, he was unwilling to assume a responsibility which, however honestly exercised, "would subject him to misrepresentation . . . by the defeated party." [113] Democratic leaders knowing of his Southern birth, of Republican criticism of his court decisions, and of his political independence, counted on him for a favorable settlement. When a Democratic Congressman remarked that he would have been useful to his party as a member of the commission, "he made no reply." [114] Had Democrats known that he would not be the deciding judge, many would not have voted for the Electoral Commission. His acceptance of the Senatorship brought down on his head a "storm of abusive epithets," [115] for it was realized that, although his election did not disqualify him from serving on the commission, the matter was definitely settled.

Hewitt expressed "the surprise and disappointment" of his party. Instead of acknowledging his own blunder in not checking on a man as uncertain as Davis, he accused the Republicans under Senator Morton of engineering a plot to keep Davis off the commission,[116]—though Morton's papers do not substantiate the charge. R. B. Brown stated that the Republicans deliberately sought to eliminate Davis and that to Justice Noah N. Swayne was assigned this delicate task. After his election as Senator, Davis, having his customary Sunday supper with Swayne, said: "These fellows want me to get off the bench. . . . Our children have married and I want you to tell me whether I should . . . take this place." Swayne replied, "Davis, I think you should accept . . . and resign at once." Davis then declared, "You are my friend and I will take your advice." [117] A satisfactory explanation of Davis' action involves manipulations by Republican leaders like Swayne in Washington and Joseph Medill in Chicago; slow-witted Democrats like Cyrus H. McCormick, the Illinois Democratic Chairman, and overconfident Democrats like Hewitt in Congress; but mainly Davis' lack of intense party loyalty. "I can say without the least reserve," said Davis, that

---

[112] J. E. Harvey to Mrs. David Davis, March 7, 1887.
[113] Ib.   [114] The Pantagraph, Jan. 27, 1877.
[115] Dict. Am. Biog., V, 111.   [116] Nevins, Hewitt, 366; Writings of Hewitt, 171.
[117] Brown, "How Tilden Lost the Presidency," Harper's Weekly, July 30, 1904, 1171.

the Senatorship "came to me entirely unsought and unexpected. . . . I accepted because I had been anxious for two years to retire." [118] Davis stated the case accurately.

Was the Democratic cause irretrievably lost? Might not one of the three remaining justices be sufficiently impartial to give Tilden a chance of victory? Swayne, in his youth a Democrat, was unavailable because Tilden distrusted him. Hewitt consulted Conkling about Hunt, but Conkling thought Hunt would be unconsciously "unjust to Tilden." There is no evidence to show whether or not Hewitt consulted Tilden. Bradley alone remained available in Hewitt's eyes. He had known Bradley for many years in New Jersey, and Tilden shared Hewitt's confidence in him. John G. Stevens was sent by Hewitt to ascertain whether Bradley could decide the issue without party prejudice, and the report was "entirely satisfactory." [119] Judge Bradley had presided over a Southern circuit and his decision had pleased the Southerners. He had also shown a lack of sympathy with the radical Republicans.[120] The Democratic *World* applauded his selection and said that he was unsatisfactory to the Republicans.[121] Webb Hayes wired his father: "The Judge, it is Bradley. In Washington the bets are 5 to 1 that the next President will be Hayes." [122]

Thurman, Bayard and Hoar scouted the idea that justices of the Supreme Court would act from partisan motives; but John Sherman and others believed that they would, and that consequently the final decision would rest on Bradley.[123] The Democratic justices, Clifford and Field, both assured Hewitt that reliance could be placed upon "the radical fairness" of Bradley and declared it absurd to think that partisanship would influence his actions.[124] However there was some opposition to Bradley's appointment. McLane wrote Tilden, "Few of our friends wanted Judge Bradley as the fifth judge," but I am "better pleased with the Compromise." [125] J. B. Stillson of the *Herald* congratulated Tilden on the make-up of the Electoral Commission and did not see how he could be defeated.[126]

The fifteen members of the Electoral Commission in whose hands was placed the determination of the Presidential election of 1876 were all

[118] Gail Hamilton (Mary A. Dodge), *J. G. Blaine,* 424, Walker to Blaine, Jan. 26, 1877.
[119] Nevins, *Hewitt,* 367.   [120] Rhodes, VII, 328.
[121] Feb. 1, 1877; *Atlantic,* LXXII, 529; Nevins, *Hewitt,* 368.
[122] Minor, *Story of the Dem. Party,* 319. At 2 P. M., Jan. 31, 1877.
[123] Rhodes, VII, 328.   [124] Nevins, *Hewitt,* 368.
[125] Tilden Papers, Jan. 31, 1877.   [126] *Ib.,* Jan. 29, 1877.

lawyers except one—General Eppa Hunton. Seven of them were or had been judges and knew the character of evidence. Ten of them were college graduates—Harvard, Rutgers and Williams each having two; and Miami, Hamilton, Yale and Transylvania one. To their judgment was left one of the most momentous political questions that any official body in the Republic had ever been called upon to decide in time of peace.

ON February 1, 1877, the two branches of Congress met in the hall of the House for the count. The diplomatic gallery was filled by the Ministers of foreign lands and the other galleries were crowded. On the floor were many distinguished guests and visitors, among whom one might notice Justices Field and Miller, of the Electoral Commission, Jeremiah S. Black who had sat in Buchanan's Cabinet, J. D. Cameron, Secretary of War, George Bancroft, the historian, General Sherman, and Charles O'Conor. As the clock struck one, the doorkeeper of the House announced the Senate, whose members entered the hall. Ferry, President of the Senate, took the Speaker's chair, Randall sitting at his left. The tellers, secretaries and clerks occupied seats below the Speaker's desk. Ferry called the joint session to order, and one of the most important meetings in American history began.[1]

The votes of the States were announced in alphabetical order. The certificates of Alabama, Arkansas, California, Colorado, Connecticut and Delaware were opened and counted without incident. Florida was called next, a hush passed over the great hall, and all eyes were directed toward the presiding officer, who said:

"The Chair hands the tellers a certificate from the State of Florida, received by messenger, and the corresponding one by mail." [2] The teller read the certificate giving four votes to Hayes and Wheeler. The Chair then handed another set of certificates to a teller, and he announced four votes for Tilden and Hendricks. Then Ferry asked, "Are there any objections to the certificates from the State of Florida?" Field of New York objected to the first certificate and his objection was read. Sargent of California and Kasson of Iowa objected to the second certificates. "Are there any further objections?" asked the Chair. There being none, he said that the papers would be sent to the Electoral Commission for decision. The Senate then withdrew.[3]

The Electoral Commission meanwhile had met on January 31 in the Supreme Court room, with the venerable Justice Clifford in the chair, and organized by electing its officers. The members crowded about a

[1] Haworth, 222.   [2] *Proceedings*, 10–24.   [3] *Ib.*, 24–28.

table as if they were lawyers appearing before the Justices of the Supreme Court or a group of railroad directors. The chairs of the Justices,
empty and ominous, looked down upon them. There was little room for
visitors, and the most conspicuous object in the room was the cuspidor.[4]
The tribunal was a body of eminent Americans, and the array of counsel
for each party equally prominent. Foremost among the Republican
lawyers were W. M. Evarts,[5] E. W. Stoughton, Samuel Shellabarger,
Hayes' personal representative, J. A. Kasson, and Stanley Matthews.
Evarts had collaborated with Tilden in legal cases and as recently as
April, 1876, had accepted a retainer for a Western railroad case. In
Tilden's behalf appeared Charles O'Conor, Jeremiah S. Black, D. D.
Field, Montgomery Blair, George Hoadley, J. A. Campbell, Lyman
Trumbull, W. C. Whitney, R. T. Merrick and Ashlen Green.[6] O'Conor
urged Tilden to employ C. N. Potter because he wanted to be "used"
and knew so much about Louisiana. Tilden's counsel had been busy for
a week on briefs. Field was "determined to conduct the case." Green was
working on the question, "Could the Commission go behind the returns?" and Merrick was looking up the Florida case. Whitney was to
check up the facts. The opinion prevailed that the commission would go
behind the returns.[7]

The hearing on Florida continued from February 2 to 8. D. D. Field
opened for the Democrats by showing that in an orderly election Tilden
electors had been chosen, but by "jugglery" a false certificate, signed by
an ex-Governor, had been sent to Washington by the Republican electors. Hence, he argued, the commission could go behind Stearns' certificate and overthrow the fraud. Kasson presented the Republican case by
asserting that the tribunal could not go behind the certificate of the
Governor of Florida because that would violate the rights of a sovereign
State, and that the certificate of the Democratic electors was irregular
because it was signed by an officer not recognized by either national or
State law as having the right to certify.[8]

On the following day O'Conor read a learned paper offering legal
proofs of the Democratic contention.[9] After some wrangling, Evarts objected to the proofs offered, and each side was allowed two hours to discuss the abstract question whether the commission should receive evi-

[4] Picture in *Harper's Weekly*, Feb. 17, 1877.
[5] Dyer, *Public Career of W. M. Evarts*, 174.
[6] Haworth, 225.
[7] Tilden Papers, Feb. 1, 1877.
[8] *Proceedings*, 35–45, 54–64.
[9] *Ib.*, 64.

dence. Merrick opened the argument for the Democrats in a speech of much merit, and was followed by Matthews who held that the commission's sole business was to decide this question: "Which set of electors is entitled to act for Florida?" Evarts concluded with an answer to O'Conor's paper in an able speech which was commended by Hayes.[10]

No attempt had been made in advance to decide the important problem of going back of the returns, yet that was the very point on which adjudication must be made. Hewitt, in his secret memorandum, states that when the joint committee first met it was generally agreed that the arbitral body should have power to go back to the sources, in order to arrive at the truth about the disputed election. Edmunds alone refused to subscribe to that principle. Later the Republicans denied that they had ever taken such an attitude. On such a vital issue it was unfortunate that Hewitt and the Democratic leaders could not have had a commitment put into the record instead of merely hoping that Bradley would decide in their favor.[11]

Before the decision on Florida was reached on February 8, it was whispered among the Democrats that Judge Bradley would vote with the Democrats on the commission. Consequently there was rejoicing among the supporters of Tilden.[12] It was said that he had prepared a written opinion in favor of Tilden, but that during the night Republican leaders and railroad magnates pressed him so hard that he changed his mind and voted against Tilden. In a public letter Bradley did not deny that he had written a statement favorable to Tilden—that, he felt, was no one's business, and a common practice with judges—but he declared that his vote was the result of his own "deliberations" uninfluenced by outsiders. "No one called at my house that evening—the whole thing is a falsehood." He denied reading an opinion to Judges Clifford and Field, and doubted whether he had expressed one orally. He wrote and rewrote the arguments on both sides, and finally composed a short statement refusing to go behind the returns in Florida. This he read before the commission. He denied that there was any conspiracy and was confident that the decision was right.[13] Judge Stephen J. Field believed that Bradley's opinion and some of the comments about his change of mind shortly before the vote on Florida justified the caustic comments of the

---

[10] *Proceedings*, 117–118.   [11] Nevins, *Hewitt*, 370.
[12] Haworth, 233.
[13] *Letters*, II, 568. Letter of September 6, 1877, in Newark *Advertiser* was reprinted in the *Sun*.

press.[14] Senator P. J. Stockton of New Jersey visited Bigelow and told him that Judge Bradley was "not particular about the means with which he compassed his ends." [15]

The publication of Hewitt's "Secret History" throws some additional light on Bradley's action at this crucial period. On the night previous to the decision of the Florida case, John G. Stevens, Hewitt's house guest, visited Bradley at his home. About midnight he returned to Hewitt's house and told Richard Taylor and Senator Gibson, who, with Hewitt, were waiting for his return, that he had just read Bradley's opinion in favor of Tilden electors in Florida. Hewitt attended the meeting of the commission on February 8 without the slightest intimation that Bradley meanwhile had changed his mind. But after Stevens left Bradley, Senator Frelinghuysen and Secretary Robeson visited Bradley, and their entreaties, supplemented by Mrs. Bradley's prayer, induced the Judge to change his opinion. When the final test came, he favored the Hayes electors and refused to sanction going behind the returns.[16] This was a fatal blow to Democratic hopes.

That the Florida case was regarded as crucial is shown by the fact that the two Democrat Justices, Clifford and Field, both wrote out opinions which, after presentation to the commission, were printed. However, their arguments had no effect on the steam roller, and the "8 to 7" decision prevailed.[17] Justice Field was firmly of the opinion that Bradley's "change of views" was sudden and due to mysterious influences.[18] Senator Edmunds, more than once, had to stiffen Bradley's indecision,[19] and the railroad lobby may have been a factor.[20]

On February 8, 1877, the Electoral Commission voted 8 to 7 not to receive evidence by going behind the State returns; and two days later, after arguing the case for hours behind closed doors, decided by the same strictly partisan vote that Hayes electors in Florida should be counted.[21] Democrats at once denounced Bradley as an "unjust judge," and accused him of accepting a bribe. Tilden informed Bigelow that a Commissioner's vote was offered him for $200,000, but there is no further proof of it.[22] Showing an anonymous letter alleging that Bradley received $100,000 for his decision, Tilden remarked sarcas-

[14] *Letters*, II, 567, Field to Tilden, Dec. 11, 1877.   [15] *Retrospections*, V, 298.
[16] Nevins, *Hewitt*, 371–373.
[17] Remarks of Mr. Justice Clifford, etc., Washington, 1877. Remarks of Mr. Justice Field, etc., Washington, 1877.
[18] Tilden Papers, Field, Dec. 11, 1877.   [19] Stealey, *Forty Years*, 269.
[20] Nevins, *Hewitt*, 373.   [21] *Proceedings*, 138, 198.   [22] *Life*, II, 95.

tically that $200,000 "seems to be the standard figure." [23] Bradley in his own home told J. M. Scoville that the "commission would decide in favor of Tilden." [24] The simplest explanation of Bradley's action is that his judicial impartiality was submerged in partisanship and his vote was what his party expected.

When the Louisiana returns were presented in joint session, Conkling, confident that Tilden had been elected, was present but made no remarks. When the Houses met separately on the following day, it was expected by the Democrats that he would make a plea for the rejection of the Hayes electors. Hewitt, Barnum and other Democrats felt that they had a confidential understanding with him on this point. They had, at Conkling's request, refrained from objecting to a Hayes elector from Illinois who was a postmaster, in order to strengthen their position in the case of Louisiana.[25] However, the next morning Conkling was absent from the Senate. Days before the Springfield *Republican* said that Conkling had enough influence to defeat Hayes.[26] George Hoadley was certain that Conkling would "seat the Sage of Gramercy Park." But the Republican who was to make a Democratic President hurried over to Baltimore while the Louisiana case went to the Electoral Commission, where the decision was given to the Hayes electors on what are now known to have been forged returns.[27] Conkling's promise was broken partly because he was frightened at the Republican attacks and appeals, and partly by his own fickleness. Later the Brooklyn *Eagle* declared that he would have been supported in the Senate by a vote of 37 to 32.[28]

Though Tilden's best claim was perhaps in Florida, most Democrats then put their hope in Louisiana. McLane wrote Tilden "we have a better case in Louisiana and Oregon than Florida" and Judge Story refused "to accept any return whatever" from Louisiana.[29] Democratic counsel claimed before the commission that no State law designated the manner of appointing electors, that Democratic electors received a majority of the votes, that Kellogg's certificate was void because he was not Governor at the time, that the canvass of the Returning Board was illegal. Furthermore, two alleged electors, as Federal officeholders, were ineligible, while three others held State offices. And at the time of the election, the State had no republican government. In rebuttal

[23] *Retrospections*, V, 302.   [24] Tilden Papers, Feb. 10, 1877.
[25] Nevins, *Hewitt*, 375.   [26] Jan. 10, 1877.   [27] Nevins, *Hewitt*, 376.
[28] Feb. 22, 1879.   [29] Tilden Papers, Jan. 25, 1877.

Republican counsel held that the Tilden electors' certificate was signed by McEnery who was not Governor, that the Returning Board's decision was final, and that no fraud had been proved. Again the commission ruled that evidence could not be introduced, and, on February 16, by an 8 to 7 vote, gave Louisiana to Hayes.[30] Pelton reported to his uncle:

"Tribunal ruled out all evidence. . . . Most outrageous proceeding . . . great indignation manifested on all sides. . . . House will recess till 10 Monday. . . . The fight must be made in the Senate and we shall show C.[31] that he will receive our support. . . . If you have anything to suggest, send by messenger Saturday night. . . . Caucus then; if you have any suggestions for it, telegraph me." [32]

The commission's report was made to the two Houses on February 19, and the eight electors were counted for Hayes [33] amid shouts of "fraud" and "conspiracy." In the House, Pierce and Seelye, Republicans, refused to vote with their party. "The Grand Fraud of Gramercy Park" and his party, said a Republican, "had the impression that they could buy every man they could not frighten or delude." [34]

The Louisiana decision brought forth a storm of angry protests. A Maine man wrote "A Nation's Disgrace." [35] From New Orleans came the information, "The decision overwhelms us here with astonishment and sorrow." A number of persons wanted the commission abolished; some urged Tilden to write an open letter to the commission denying the validity of its action; and a follower of Andrew Jackson protested, "I would never submit to this damnable fraud." There were demands that Tilden should declare himself President. The more moderate suggested that he carry the contest to the Supreme Court. Militant hotheads bobbed up again to offer Tilden their fighting services.[36] Some of Tilden's supporters could not understand why he consistently opposed the use of force to establish his rights. Edward Livingston wrote: "I am puzzled to think he did not favor an uprising. . . . *I did.* Was it because he was wiser that he did not speak when he might have said, '*Vous qui m'aimez suivez moi.*' I hope so." [37] While Tilden maintained his customary silence after learning of the Louisiana decision, Bigelow recorded that he now showed "a disposi-

[30] *Proceedings,* 212–217, 243, 416–422.   [31] Probably Roscoe Conkling.
[32] Tilden Papers, undated, signed "W.T.P."   [33] Haworth, 244.
[34] *Cong. Record,* 1686.   [35] Written by B. F. Smith, in Tilden Papers.
[36] Tilden Papers, various persons.   [37] *Letters,* II, 565.

tion to consult" but sought the advice of others "before he expressed his own." He was one of the most difficult of men to get an opinion from; Governor Robinson, the easiest—the former was born to rule; the latter to serve.[38]

On February 19, the counting of the electoral vote in the joint session continued until Oregon was reached. Objections sent the vote of that State to the commission. The Democrats held that Postmaster Watts was ineligible and hence under the law Cronin, as next highest on the list of electors, should take his place. Further, he was certified by an unquestioned Governor. Republicans combated the claim and maintained that Watts' resignation and re-election were valid. The Democrats offered to drop Cronin if the Republicans would drop Watts, but in vain. By a party vote of 8 to 7 the three electoral votes of Oregon were given to Hayes. In the joint session there was the usual objection and separate votes by the two Houses but no change. In the House there was an outburst of feeling against Tilden among Western Democrats. "We of the West," said Le Moyne of Illinois, "are done in with the domination of New York. . . . If Mr. Tilden either directly or indirectly consented to the purchase of a Republican elector, he deserves double condemnation from every man who supported him." [39]

On February 26, South Carolina was reached in the count and objections sent the case to the commission. Democrats made no attempt to defend the Tilden electors but argued that the vote should be thrown out. Republicans defended their own certificate and submitted their case without further argument. Jeremiah S. Black had the last word for the Democrats and he flayed the commission without mercy.[40] South Carolina was added to the Hayes list and reported to the joint session on February 28.[41] The count of Vermont followed. Hewitt created a commotion when he attempted to force Ferry to receive a sealed certificate of Democratic electors for Vermont. Objections to the regular Vermont return forced the two Houses to separate.[42] The Senate voted unanimously to count Vermont for Hayes, but in the

---

[38] *Retrospections*, Feb. 17, 1877, V, 302.

[39] *Cong. Record,* 1913. Hewitt in exasperation accused Hoar of saying that proof would be admitted. This Hoar denied and accused Hewitt of having "a screw loose." Before his death Hoar prepared a statement to be made public when Hewitt's "Secret History" appeared, reflecting on Hewitt's veracity. Haworth, 259, note 3.

[40] *Proceedings*, 694–699. [41] *Cong. Record,* 1992–2002.

[42] *Proceedings*, 712–717; Nevins, *Hewitt,* 383.

House the pent-up fury of the disappointed Democrats broke forth in one of the most boisterous sessions ever held.[43]

Following the decision on Louisiana a filibuster by Democratic Representatives had been brewing, to prevent the completion of the count before March 4, thus hoping to gain some advantage. These filibusterers consisted of two factions, one, numbering about forty, consisted of Watterson's followers, who were determined to prevent the inauguration of Hayes at any cost; the other, made up chiefly of Southerners, were determined to force a promise that the Southern States would be entirely emancipated from carpetbag rule. This formidable dual alliance in the House was strong enough to delay the count. But Hewitt, Springer, Cox, Clymer, Lane and Randall wished the count to be concluded before March 4, even if it meant the triumph of Hayes. Hewitt professed to see that the only way to bring about this result was to appease the Southerners by granting their wishes. Hence he deliberately joined them in the filibuster—to save the nation from a fratricidal war. His immediate purpose was to force the Republicans, after they had given Louisiana and South Carolina to Hayes and thereby also restored carpetbag government, to assure white autonomy there.

To meet this situation, after two preliminary conferences at the Capitol, Matthews, Foster, Dennison, Garfield and Sherman met a group of Southerners—General Taylor, J. B. Young and E. J. Ellis— in Evarts' room in Wormley's Hotel on February 26 and 27. Hayes was in touch with his agents, and Hewitt was shown all the telegrams that passed between them. Finally on the 27th Matthews and Foster signed a definite promise that Hayes would restore self-government to the South. Until this promise could be made sufficiently satisfactory to the South, Hewitt permitted himself to be used as a tool to delay the final count an additional day. This was brought about, as has been shown, in connection with Vermont. On March 1 the House was jammed, and nearly all the Senators were present as spectators. The Democratic Vermont certificate which Hewitt had tried to force Ferry to accept had strangely disappeared. The House now demanded its return; and, when Randall ruled that the debate on Vermont should proceed whether the missing document was found or not, it mysteriously reappeared in Hewitt's hand.[44] The whole House was in

[43] *Cong. Record,* 2002–2004, 2027, 2032.   [44] Nevins, *Hewitt,* 382–385.

a turmoil, and some Representatives even grabbed their revolvers. Speaker Randall did not lose his head in the confusion, however, and at length quieted the members sufficiently to permit Congressman Levy of Louisiana to state that Hayes' "policy of conciliation toward the Southern States" was so satisfactory that he would no longer block the electoral count. He called upon his fellow Southern Representatives to follow his example.[45] This was just what Hewitt wanted, and approval of the second Vermont return was lost.

The final act in the drama now occurred. The votes of Virginia and West Virginia were quickly counted. Objection being made to Wisconsin, on the ground that one of the electors was a pension officer, the Houses again separated. The Senate without debate discarded the objection. In the House a last stand was taken by the irreconcilables. Mills of Texas moved that the House proceed to elect a President,[46] but no vote was taken on the resolution. "Nothing can postpone the regular election of Hayes beyond tomorrow," wired Evarts to Whitelaw Reid.[47] Randall thwarted the tactics of further delay. The end of the dramatic scene came in the early morning of March 2 when Blackburn of Kentucky said: "Mr. Speaker, today is Friday. Upon that day the Savior of the world suffered crucifixion between two thieves. On this Friday constitutional government, justice, honesty, fair dealing, manhood and decency suffer crucifixion amid a number of thieves." Williams of Wisconsin jumped to his feet answering, "This is not only Friday, but hangman's day; and there could be no more fitting time than just after the hour of midnight . . . that this bogus, pretentious bastard brat of political reform, which for the last twelve months has affronted the eyes of gods and men, should be strangled to death, gibbeted higher than Haman." [48]

A telegram to Randall from Tilden announced to the Democrats that he was willing to let the count be concluded.[49] The House voted Wisconsin for Hayes. At four in the morning the Senate marched into the hall, and ten minutes later Ferry announced to the crowded galleries and to the nation that Hayes and Wheeler were "duly elected." [50] There was a sigh of relief but no resounding applause from the victors. Hewitt collapsed and was taken home by his friends.

[45] Eckenrode, 229.
[46] *Cong. Record*, 2049, 2055–2056.
[47] *Tribune*, Mar. 1, 1877.
[48] Haworth, 280–281; *Cong. Record*, 2061.
[49] Nevins, *Hewitt*, 385.
[50] Haworth, 282; D. D. Field, "The Votes That Made the President," N.Y., 1877.

When the House considered what its final statement for the record should be, Tilden suggested: "Deplore subversion of popular will—Appeal to conscientious Republicans to right the wrong—Warn all instigators—Confidence in Patriotism of the people."

On March 3 the outwitted Democrats in the House made a last desperate but futile gesture by voting that Samuel J. Tilden had received 196 electoral votes and "was thereby duly elected President." [51] Ten Congressmen signed a telegram telling Tilden that these resolutions made him President. But Tilden paid no attention to such a post-mortem claim. He was the immovable rock of the peace party and gave his orders to Randall as his chief lieutenant in Congress. Hewitt had lost Tilden's full confidence and got his knowledge of Tilden's wishes from Randall.[52] The Washington *Union,* Tilden's official national organ, denounced the Democratic leaders for weakness in compromising, decried all appeals to arms, and demanded a lawful settlement. Its conclusion was that the Democratic politicians did not want Tilden for President because he was a reformer of the Silas Wright type; and they did not want a reduction of taxes or a cut in expenses, so they surrendered to the Republicans. Its editor declared that "there never was any intention to inaugurate Tilden. The House was controlled from the start by Tom Scott & Jay Gould." [53] The *Union* suspended publication on March 3 and its swan song was:

"Fraud has triumphed, and triumphed through the treachery of Democrats. Honest men of irresolute natures and dull perceptions have assisted, but corruption led the way."

The Cincinnati *Enquirer* in bold-faced type commented:

"It is done. And fitly done in the dark. By the grace of Joe Bradley, R. B. Hayes is 'Commissioned' as President, and the monster fraud of the century is consummated." [54]

Old Simon Cameron groaned, "Boys, this is a hell of a time!" When Tilden heard of the final action, he smiled, said it was what he had expected, and spoke of a horse he had bought that day. In the evening he attended a reception at the home of Parke Godwin,[55] who facetiously wrote the name of R. B. Hayes as "Returning Board

[51] *Cong. Record,* 2226; *Letters,* II, 577.
[52] Nevins, *Hewitt,* 380.
[53] Smith, *The Blair Family,* II, 484.
[54] March 2, 1877.
[55] Smith, *The Blair Family,* II, 485.

Hayes." [56] The *Sun* appeared in mourning on March 3 and, when Hayes appeared in New York City, printed his picture with "Fraud" across his forehead. Justice Nathan Clifford was so incensed over the decision that he never set foot inside the White House during Hayes' term of office.[57] Although given many opportunities, Hewitt refused to make the acquaintance of President Hayes.[58]

The Democratic minority of the commission drew up a protest against the verdict of the Republican majority. It set forth clearly the "partisan violence against law and morals by which the majority awarded the election to the defeated candidate." [59] Thus this political game, in which Tilden's initial advantage was changed by the commission to favor Hayes, came to an end.

George Hoadley remarked: "With the exception of General Barlow, H. L. Pierce of Boston, Professor Seelye of Amherst, and about one-quarter of Roscoe Conkling—making three and a quarter—no one in the Republican Party lifted up his voice against the infamy." [60] Stanley Matthews told a reporter of the Washington *Post* that he would like to see Tilden run in 1880 because he was anxious to ascertain whether he could "be elected *again*." [61] Justice Samuel F. Miller, before creditable witnesses, confessed that Tilden had been elected in Louisiana.[62] Justice William Strong was reported to have said that Tilden had won the election.[63] When Garfield was asked by Carter H. Harrison how he could vote that the Louisiana returns were not false, he replied, "Carter, if you had the cards, wouldn't you play them?" [64] And that was the view taken generally—the election of 1876 was a game, and a dirty game, in which the players were determined to win, honestly if possible, but win.

In the midst of the acrimonious charges, it was proposed to examine the bank accounts of Tilden and Zach Chandler to determine whether money influenced the election. But the Associated Press announced that committees of the two Houses had agreed not to make such an investigation.[65] When a rumor circulated in Washington that Tilden's friends were protecting him by this compromise, he telegraphed Kernan:

[56] Mitchell, *Memoirs*, 298.   [57] *Ib.; Dist. Am. Biog.*, IV, 218.   [58] Nevins, *Hewitt*, 389.
[59] Bangor *Commercial*, Oct. 29, 1891; *Life*, II, 397, gives the document.
[60] Watertown *Despatch*, Mar. 5, 1879.   [61] Washington *Post*, Mar. 13, 1879.
[62] *Sun*, Aug. 20, 1879.   [63] Utica *Observer*, Aug. 20, 1879.
[64] Senator Doolittle at Iroquois banquet, Chicago, Apr., 1884.
[65] Feb. 21, 1877.

"I reject the utterly false imputation that my private bank account . . . needs to be concealed. . . . A transcript of entries of private business, trusts and charities . . . has been taken with my knowledge to Washington."

He asked a sub-committee to examine him in New York City, and his banker, Ellis, a Republican, declared there was nothing compromising in his account.[66] Kernan notified him that no order had been issued to summon him before the Senate.[67]

Tilden felt that his case had been badly managed and that disloyalty was a factor—and he was not alone in this conviction. "The defeat . . . is due measurably to the manipulation of inexperienced and overconfident directors. . . . There has been too much willingness to compromise, and Senator Kernan . . . has acted unwisely. . . . You were slaughtered in the house of your friends" by conceited inexperience and "an over-weening confidence." Louisiana was "unskillfully handled" and the North and West were peeved by the selection of "new men, personal favorites," to run the campaign.[68]

The popular reaction may be observed in the deluge of letters and telegrams carried to Tilden's home. The query uppermost in the minds of those Southerners not a party to the bargain with Hayes was best expressed by W. C. Harrison of New Orleans: "Will the Democrats see a Usurper in the chair of Washington? . . . Say, No! Never!! in tones that will resound from Ocean to Ocean. If you say the word, 50,000 Louisianans will take up guns for you." Many Northerners agreed with J. M. Scovel of Philadelphia who wired: "Counsel resistance. We dare not submit to fraud." Level-headed supporters advised an appeal to the highest courts and thought a public fund should be raised to prosecute the case. "A poor homesteader" offered to give his "last dollar" for that purpose. Some urged the use of *quo warranto* proceedings. Others insisted upon Tilden's taking the oath as President. Alexander Long believed that he should go to Washington to give direct leadership to the party. A Texan Negro prayed that a "Right Jehovah will sustain you." Uncle Sam Ward proposed an address to the American people against "the partisan treachery of a *Pie poudre* Court which has deprived you of the satisfaction of serving them." A large number of persons advised Tilden "to repair the past in the future" by running in 1880.[69] Keen disappointment in the ju-

[66] *Life*, II, 222, Feb. 21, 1877.   [67] Tilden Papers, Feb. 22, 1877.
[68] *Letters*, II, 542, Thomas Cottman of La., Feb. 22, 1877.
[69] Tilden Papers, various dates.

dicial temper of the commission was expressed by men like General McClellan and A. E. Orr.[70] Charles Francis Adams complimented Tilden on "the calm and dignified manner in which you have passed through the great trial." [71] And not a few Republicans condemned the methods by which he was deprived of an office to which the people had elected him.[72] Men like Horace White and Roscoe Conkling voted for Hayes but were convinced that Tilden had been elected.

Hewitt and Randall were severely criticized as "weak-kneed Democrats" who were not equal to the superior type of leadership required.[73] McClernand scouted Hewitt's fear that the Republicans would have resorted to arms to uphold a fraud because the "business of the country" would not have supported such action.[74] R. M. McLane of Baltimore regretted that "our friends were ever beguiled into the Electoral Commission scheme" and believed that a firm stand by the House would have seated Tilden.[75] Saying, "The long agony is over—a thief is President," a Philadelphian laid the defeat to Hewitt's "timid, vacillating, halting, hesitating course." A resolute man could have saved the fight—and Randall's conduct was contemptible.[76] "We had a first-class case," was the comment of Alexander H. Stephens, "but we lost it by imperfect pleadings." [77] Watterson and other Democrats, eye-witnesses in Congress, were of the opinion that Hewitt's inexperience, egotism and ineptitude gave the Presidency to Hayes. To the few Democrats who knew that Hewitt was a party to the bargain between Southerners and Republicans, his action was denounced as little short of treachery.[78] Yet Hewitt boasted that he did more to restore self-government in the South than Tilden could have done, and that he was more instrumental than any other person in creating the Electoral Commission.[79]

"I spent three days in forming a letter for Mr. Tilden, saying to the American people that he believed himself to be the President-elect, and that on the fourth day of March, eighteen seventy-seven, he would come to Washington to be inaugurated," said Hewitt in 1886, after the death of Tilden. That proclamation proposing a *coup d'état* he took to New

---

[70] *Ib.; Letters*, II, 546, 547.   [71] *Letters*, II, 548.
[72] Tilden Papers, M. H. Ellis of Yonkers and others.
[73] *Ib.*, F. M. Childs of Vermont and others.   [74] *Ib.; Letters*, II, 545.
[75] *Letters*, II, 545.   [76] Tilden Papers, A. R. Schofield.
[77] Johnston and Brown, 537.   [78] Watterson, *Autobiography*, 408.
[79] Nevins, *Hewitt*, 389.

York City and did everything he could to induce Tilden to sign it. D. D. Field also employed his persuasive powers. But Tilden refused to sign the paper, and thereby in Hewitt's opinion "threw the Presidency away." Tilden's reasons were committed to writing and sent to Hewitt. Remembering that it took him six weeks to persuade Tilden to sign the letter on the Southern debt situation, the conclusion of Hewitt was that Tilden "was lacking in the courage necessary for the trying situation of that time." [80] In his later "Secret History," Hewitt remarked, "The habit of Mr. Tilden's mind was to criticize and postpone, not to decide." Keenly aware that the great responsibility was his alone, Tilden was less impetuous than his party advisers. He was absolutely adamant in refusing to plunge the nation into another fratricidal war, which he was thoroughly convinced Hewitt's proposal invited, and stood firmly upon the adequacy of the Constitution to safeguard his rights.

To justify his own course in connection with the commission Hewitt later asserted that civil war was more imminent "than was even at that time supposed. The Democratic forces had been organized in fifteen States and were composed chiefly of veterans . . . who were . . . ready once more to take up arms and move on Washington in defense . . . of Governor Tilden. . . . Even the Commander in Chief had been selected." The Democratic Governors were ready to act,[81] Hewitt asserted, and a public manifesto from Tilden would have unleashed the dogs of war. No one realized this serious condition more clearly than Tilden, but all his influence was exerted to keep the peace. There is ample evidence in the Tilden Papers to show that individuals and groups were ready to employ force to seat Tilden, but for the most part the offers to fight came from irresponsible persons. "There is some evidence, however, that McClellan seriously considered the formation of militant Democrats to oppose by force the seizure of the office by the Republicans, and to face even the horrors of another Civil War." [82] Although General McClellan in the East and General J. M. Corse in the Middle West gave ear to those who urged force to seat the President-elect, yet Hewitt's exaggeration needs to be toned down. There are no communications from any of the Governors of the "fifteen States" indicating that they were ready to follow Tilden's lead in declaring war. The show of militancy was mostly talk such as may be heard in periods of great ex-

[80] Quoted in *Public Opinion,* 1886, 504.   [81] Nevins, *Hewitt,* 380, 387.
[82] Myers, *General McClellan,* 492.

citement, and at no time was there serious danger of an appeal to arms.

Meanwhile Southerners proceeded "to pluck the flower of safety out of the nettle of danger," while Tilden and Hewitt were arguing over pronunciamentos, and traded off the defeat of Tilden for the autonomy of Louisiana, South Carolina and Florida in white hands. In commenting on the Hewitt plan, the Chicago *Times* thought it was "the far-looking sagacity of the crafty old politician" that sensed the wiser course and saved the nation from a civil conflict of the Latin-American type. It is not true, then, that Tilden willfully "threw the Presidency away." On the contrary, his chances of obtaining that high office would have been lessened by war while his name would have become infamous in American history as either the victim of selfish ambition or the tool of a hungry, office-seeking party.[83] In an appeal to force, the chances of victory were all with the Republicans.

The Democrats who favored war in 1876 found it difficult to forgive Tilden for refusing to take their advice, and others with party or personal grudges joined in the outcry against him. Even his own brother Henry used denunciatory brimstone in castigating his pacifism. This point of view was summed up in the New York *Star:* "He was the leader of his party but he refused to lead . . . he had no counsel to give . . . he was speechless and without resource." He spent his later years trying "to make his countrymen forget his recreancy.[84] . . . He left no impress of a noble character." [85]

On the other hand it may be safely said that the wiser leaders and the vast majority of the rank and file of the Democratic Party, while convinced of his legitimate election and his exclusion from the Presidency by fraud, commended his refusal to appeal to arms to vindicate his claim. Being neither a Cromwell nor a Bonaparte, he subordinated his personal considerations to the welfare of his country.[86] His "dignified silence saved the nation from the slightest turbulence" and his high patriotism was shown in his self-restraint.[87]

Confronted by the loss of the Presidency after winning the election and angered at Tilden's pacific course, Hewitt, blamed for defeat,[88] on March 3, 1877, resigned the chairmanship of the Democratic National Committee in a letter summarizing what had happened. He had said

[83] Quoted in *Public Opinion*, 1886, I, 504.   [84] N.Y. *Star,* Aug. 5, 1886.
[85] *Indianapolis News*, Aug. 5, 1886; *Harper's Weekly*, Aug. 14, 1886.
[86] N.Y. *Com. Bulletin*, Aug. 5, 1886.
[87] Springfield *Republican*, Aug. 5, 1886.

privately, "I prefer four years of Hayes' administration to four years of civil war," and was willing to stand on that statement. He denied that his action was affected by his ownership of U.S. bonds, for he owned none. He looked to the future for vindication. While claiming credit for Tilden's election, he felt no more responsibility for his defeat than other Democrats in Congress.[89] This letter, in a way, was a confession of failure; and was so interpreted by Tilden and some of Hewitt's colleagues.

[88] J. A. McClernand wrote Tilden, "If the chairman of our national committee had not . . . hesitated at a decisive moment . . . the spirit and courage of the Democracy . . . would have precluded . . . the electoral commission and its decision." *Letters*, II, 545.

[89] *Ib.*, 549–553.

UNDER a clouded title, not confident of the affection of the people, and with "a slight timidity," [1] Hayes went to Washington for his Inauguration. He was the guest of John Sherman, but was sworn in on March 3, just before a state dinner tendered by President Grant. The cheering of 30,000 people at his Inauguration on March 5 brought comfort to him. He selected a strong Cabinet, and his Inaugural Address was devoted largely to a sympathetic discussion of the Southern problems. Although confronted by hostile Democrats who controlled the House for four years and the Senate two, and by an unsympathetic group of Republicans, his administration was enlightened and able. But, like John Quincy Adams, he was a lonely President who leaned on his sympathetic wife [2] and found solace in recording his lofty purpose in his diary.

No man realized more fully than Hayes his indebtedness to the South for his high office. Individuals in Dixieland might profess keen disappointment over Tilden's defeat, but the Southern people as a whole did not feel deeply grieved. For more than a decade they had suffered under carpetbag domination—and now there was prospect of relief. While some Northern Democrats had sympathized with the South during the Civil War, the great majority, like Tilden, were Unionists. Tilden's supporters in the South cared little for his reform program except as it included a restoration of civil rights.

Southern Representatives revealed a willingness to desert him if they could thus save the autonomy of their own States. To them it was more important to end misrule in Louisiana and South Carolina than to elect a Northern Democrat. If they could not get home rule from Tilden, they might get it from Hayes. Convinced that Hayes would win after the Florida decision, B. H. Hill of Georgia "solemnly pledged" his forty-two ex-Confederate colleagues "upon their sacred honor to oppose all attempts to frustrate the counting of the votes for President," ostensibly to prevent "a second civil war" but in reality to pave the way for favors from the Hayes administration.[3]

[1] Eckenrode, 236.
[2] At Garfield's funeral Henderson of Illinois said, "I hope we shall never see a man again in the White House so thoroughly incompetent as President Hayes," but gallantly remarked that he would vote for Mrs. Hayes for the second term. Howe, *Rhodes,* 308.
[3] Baltimore *Evening Bulletin,* Aug. 22, 1878.

"If we should lose the national government, we may be able to save Louisiana," said Lamar. Elbow-deep in the plot, he wrote: "We do not want offices, but we do want to get our States and our people free from carpetbag government." Later, when President Cleveland gave Lamar a place in his Cabinet, Tilden was urged by his friends to prevent the appointment. Alexander H. Stephens approved of the bargain made with the friends of Hayes. Major Waldron carried the bargain a step further, when he presented to W. H. Smith of Chicago a request of "some Southern men" who had just caucused at Senator Alcorn's home that ex-Senator Key of Tennessee be made Postmaster General in Hayes' Cabinet, because this would induce five Southern States to support his administration. More than that, Southern Congressmen would assist in making Garfield Speaker of the new House. Smith hurried this information to Hayes so that he could communicate with Garfield and others.[4] If the Southerners deserted Tilden, it was only after they believed it no longer possible to save him. At the same time it should be pointed out that in this bargain the Republicans deserted the Negro, perhaps also because they believed his case hopeless.

Hayes' papers show conclusively that he knew what was going on and was by his own consent committed to the agreement which insured his triumph. The best that can be said for Hayes is that he faithfully carried out the terms of the bargain. With admirable courage on April 20, 1877, he ordered the troops withdrawn from the Louisiana State House, and four days later Nicholls took over the State Government, despite the declaration of Packard's friends that, in seating Nicholls, Hayes impeached the legitimacy of his own title.[5] On the day the troops were withdrawn from Louisiana, Hewitt gave a dinner in New York for Tilden, Bayard, and others. Upon hearing the news by wire, the defeated Democrats gave three cheers for the triumph and all its implications.[6] To Tilden the freedom of Louisiana was not only good news—it was a partial vindication, because the emancipation of the South was one of his major objectives in standing for the Presidency.

Aware of the "bargain," many Democrats wished Tilden publicly to expose the deal. Montgomery Blair hoped that he would feel it to be his duty to "speak out on this matter" just as Jackson did in 1824–25 when

    [4] Hayes Papers. W. H. Smith to Hayes, Feb. 17, 1877.
    [5] Telegram of U.S. Marshal Pitkin to Gov. Packard, Mar. 2, 1877. James G. Blaine made a similar statement to Bigelow on June 6, 1877. *Retrospections*, V, 319.
    [6] *Letters*, II, 353.

he was "traded off." On some "early and suitable occasion," he urged, "denounce the jobbery by which the President elected by the people was deposed." [7] Some newspapers were equally outspoken. Tilden knew of the dickering and must have realized its possible effect on his claims to the Presidency, but he did not choose to speak.

If Southern leaders, for local advantages, sacrificed loyalty to the party that had befriended them, these were not the only special interests that put forth every effort to keep Tilden out of the White House. Bankers, insurance companies, industrial leaders, heads of transportation lines, speculators, and promoters opposed Tilden's election. They feared that a Democratic victory meant reform, regulation, inflation and inexperience. Montgomery Blair expressed the opinion of many clear-headed observers when he charged that the railroad men sold Tilden out.[8] "When I saw the Presidency sold . . . to the railway jobbers," he said, "I wanted to be in Congress to defeat the fraud. It is no secret that Tom Scott and Jay Gould were the fowlers," and they got the bird into the net with the "hundreds of millions involved." While money was used to form the Electoral Commission, not "all who voted for the commission were bribed." [9] The Southerners had other things in mind, and some of them "would again job over your election if left in their places." A few wealthy men advocated Tilden's elevation to the Presidency—Cyrus H. McCormick, Belmont, Edward Cooper, and Hewitt. Belmont found party funds so low when the commission was being formed that he urged the closing of "Headquarters and Committee Rooms" in New York City, the disbursement of funds "under the sanction of the only person whom the committee seems thus far to have looked to for funds," and an endeavor to "see to what extent your friends will . . . bear their share" of the cost of seeing the contest to a conclusion. He promised to "respond to the extent of my ability." [10] Heavy counsel fees and other expenses involved in defending Tilden's rights before the Electoral Commission seem to have been met out of his own resources, but he did not deem it wise to supply money for general political purposes. So far, therefore, as money was a factor in the count, the Democratic leaders were at a disadvantage. Hewitt declared that if Tilden had supplied $25,000 for legitimate expenses in Florida and Louisiana, "his election would have been assured." [11] Without doubt money

[7] Tilden Papers.   [8] The *Union*, Dec. 14, 1876.   [9] Tilden Papers, Jan. 23, 1877.
[10] Tilden Papers, Jan. 26, 1877.   [11] Nevins, *Hewitt*, 313.

was a decisive factor in Tilden's defeat.

If Tilden could not rely on all Southern Democrats, Hayes could not rely on all Northern Republicans. Conkling, embittered by his defeat in the nominating convention, openly confessed his belief that Tilden was elected and should be inaugurated. Hewitt and others with whom Conkling was on intimate terms believed that, although the "putative father" of the Electoral Commission, he had been excluded from the tribunal because his "preference was supposed to be for Tilden." [12] He had demolished the Republican claim that the President of the Senate had a right to count the electoral votes, and the Democrats were hopeful that he would lead a group of Republican Senators to stand for an honest count.

The widely circulated report that Mrs. Kate Chase Sprague persuaded Conkling to give up the plan in revenge for Tilden's opposition to her father's nomination in 1868 seems to be unfounded.[13] Nor does there seem much ground for Whitelaw Reid's statement that Conkling's friends, by preventing the count before March 4, planned to elect him President of the Senate and thus to install him as Grant's successor. Although convinced of Tilden's election, he was careful not to say so publicly or to leave behind him any written record.

If Tilden had cared to carry the contest further, on the strength of this irregular election by the House, he might have taken the oath of office either in New York City or in Washington. John Bigelow, asked whether Tilden ever entertained any idea of taking the oath of President, declared that in the book on *Presidential Counts* Tilden had clearly stated the circumstances under which it would be lawful to take the oath, and that he never departed from that position. He would have taken the oath if Congress had counted the electoral votes and declared him President—a course he strongly advised; or if the House, on the failure of the Electoral Colleges to cast a majority vote for a candidate, had elected him President, voting by States as the Constitution prescribed. Neither contingency arising, Tilden did not feel in duty bound to take the oath. The election by resolution, on March 3, was not in accordance with the Constitution and "created no warrant of authority to Mr. Tilden to take the oath of office," and he never at any time thought of taking the oath illegally. Nevertheless, rumors that he would be

---

[12] Nevins, *Selected Writings of Hewitt*, 172.
[13] *Letters*, II, 513; Phelps, *Kate Sprague*, 249; Chidsey, *Conkling*, 233.

sworn in spread.

Hundreds of Democrats all over the land demanded that Tilden take the oath of office on the strength of the House resolutions, but he refused to be stampeded into any such rash action. Dorsheimer thought Tilden made a great mistake in not taking the oath of office. Men like Smith M. Weed, Manton Marble and Edward Cooper were quite incensed when he refused to make an open fight for the Presidency after they were convinced that he had been elected. Marble spoke emphatically in a personal conference. Tilden flared up and used some ugly words which hurt Marble's feelings and caused him to slam the door in Tilden's face. No sooner had they parted than Tilden sent the following note of apology: [14]

Dear Marble,

I was truly sorry to have wounded you, and ought not to have fallen into a worry which for the moment absorbed me and was exaggerated by physical causes, and did not let me see how I was touching you.

I had hoped to avoid care about this thing at a time of such demands on me, but we must make the best of it. You know I have the most affectionate kindness for you. I must ask you to dismiss the recollection of momentary impatience. You can help. Come down this evening soon after—immediately after—your dinner.

Watterson was one of Tilden's followers who believed him infallible and had a genuine affection for the "dear old bachelor," so genial, scholarly, and public-spirited. Of one thing Watterson was positive— Tilden refused to buy the Presidency, although three offers were made. Reviewing the contest in 1913, he was certain that "the whole truth" about it would never be known and that secrets involving the veracity of the dead would "remain a sealed book." Under the lash of party spirit, he said, men did what they would not do in saner moments. At a Washington dinner attended by President Cleveland, two Democrats and two Republicans, who had sustained confidential relations with Hayes and Tilden, in gay banter divulged startling secrets. Cleveland remarked, "What would the people think if they could hear these men?" One of them humorously replied, "If anyone repeats what I have said, I will denounce him as a liar." [15]

Senator Francis Kernan, always level-headed and wise, wrote Tilden from Washington on March 12, 1877, that he wanted to talk over the

[14] Tilden Papers.   [15] *Century,* May, 1913.

whole situation with him. "You were clearly and fairly elected by the people and Hayes has been counted in." Democrats were finding fault with what was done but he was of the opinion that the Democrats in Congress had "acted patriotically and wisely." In the threatened deadlock, the Senate would have declared Hayes elected and "the House would have elected you President—and civil war would probably have been the result. . . . My judgment was and is that what seemed a reasonably fair tribunal to decide the question involved was better than the risk of evil to our people and our system of government. Civil war is the last remedy of a people for political wrongs." Standing on the Democratic doctrine of States' rights, Kernan admitted to Senator Hoar that the commission had no right to go behind the State tribunals—and thus incurred the ill will of his excited colleagues. Senators Thurman and Bayard had made the same acknowledgment.[16] Yet the spokesmen of the two parties seemed to have changed places on the question of State and Federal authority. The Democrats insisted upon invading the prerogatives of the States to determine the honesty of the electoral count in three Southern States; on the other hand the Republicans stoutly upheld the rights of the three Southern States in settling the matter locally, so eager were both sides for the prize that neither one seemed fully aware of this strange anomaly.

In a public letter to Joseph H. Choate, John Bigelow reviewed the case from the point of view of its constitutionality. He argued that in creating the Electoral Commission Congress unwarrantedly assumed power to supersede the Twelfth Article of the Constitution by the creation of a body to usurp the power vested exclusively by the Constitution in the lower House. Further he maintained that nowhere in the Constitution was the Supreme Court, a majority of whom served on the commission, authorized either directly or indirectly "to meddle with the counting of the electoral votes for the Presidency." Yet it was a justice of the Supreme Court who seated Hayes and excluded Tilden. Justice Bradley was selected to exercise political power and did so. He assumed that the commission's powers were "precisely those . . . which the two Houses of Congress possess in the matter submitted to our consideration." In this statement the learned Justice, in the language of Uncle Remus, "dropped his molasses jug." When the two Houses could not agree about the electoral vote, Congress, acting jointly, ceased to have jurisdiction

16 Rogers, "How Hayes Became President," *McClure's*, May, 1904, 84.

over the question or to have authority to confer upon an extra-legal tribunal power to act. The Constitution specifically directed the House of Representatives to "choose immediately by ballot the President." And Justice Bradley himself asserted that the commands of the Constitution must be implicitly obeyed.[17]

What were Tilden's own reactions to the outcome of the Electoral Commission? Bigelow, who was at Tilden's home on March 4 and for the following week, has recorded:

"It was impossible to remark any change in his manner, except, perhaps, that he was less absorbed than usual and more interested in current affairs. . . . He has not been so cheerful at any time during the last three years as since the 4th inst. . . . His notion of being President meant a life of care, responsibility and effort . . . a fearful struggle. When his election was out of the question, he was naturally more sensible of his escape from the giants which he had seen in his path than the honors which might have been his, but were worn by another. . . . He regards Thurman and Bayard as chiefly responsible for his miscarriage." [18]

Mrs. G. W. Smith, wife of Tilden's confidential secretary, saw a great deal of him and said: "The Presidential contest against R. B. Hayes in 1876 proved to be a great strain on him . . . and was the beginning of his break. . . . The result was a distinct shock to him, and from that time on, *paralysis agitans* grew on him." [19] Mrs. Pelton, his devoted sister, on March 3, said to him, "You know, Samuel, I think William was much more bent on going to Washington than you were—and he takes it more to heart." Tilden replied, "Yes; he has been counted out, too!"

In reviewing the events of the previous eight months was Tilden conscious that the consequences were due in part to his own shortcomings as a party leader? The Republicans believed that he directed his own campaign, but the Democrats were confused about the leadership. Ostensibly Hewitt was conducting the canvass; Colonel W. T. Pelton seemed to be Tilden's immediate spokesman; Marble, Weed, and Havemeyer took it upon themselves to conduct negotiations without the knowledge of either Hewitt or Tilden; and Bigelow acted as a superior private secretary and adviser. Yet to none of these did Tilden delegate full responsibility for directing the campaign. Hence in crises they hesi-

---

[17] Bigelow, *The Supreme Court and the Electoral Commission,* 1903. See Goode, *American Law Review,* XXXVIII, 174; Gibson, *A Political Crime,* 39.
[18] *Life,* II, 110–111. [19] Yonkers *Herald,* Feb. 12, 1930.

tated, asked for instructions, and were nonplused by the lack of specific orders. Tilden himself revealed an irritating hesitancy and secretiveness, inconsistent with good generalship. He sent out unsigned telegrams, delayed definite answers to plain questions, postponed decisions on important issues, refused to take into complete confidence those who had a right to expect it, treated his best friends as if they might become his worst enemies, cast suspicion on other outstanding leaders in the party, and, worst of all, shifted blame for his own actions and inaction on his innocent subordinates.

When the decision was thrown into Congress, Tilden dropped into the background, being less qualified for a contest based on emotion than for one directed by brains. Democratic Senators and Representatives then took the initiative and pretty much ignored his advice. They were out-maneuvered, and induced to accept devices for settling the controversy which they believed were public-spirited in purpose but which were really intended to make possible a specious type of trickery. America owes Tilden a debt of gratitude because, when a turn of his hand might have set the citizens of the nation flying at each other's throats, he remained calm. Instead of calling his followers to defend his claim by war, he did everything within his power to still the uprising and accepted the verdict, knowing full well all the forces that lay behind the decision. It was a magnanimous surrender, wholly in keeping with his fixed principles. If he lost a political triumph, he gained a greater ethical victory. Fortunately there were Americans who appreciated this. As one wrote: "The whole world knows that your title to the Chief Magistracy of this Country is perfect, and yet you are willing out of pure patriotism to yield your undoubted right." [20]

Early in December, 1876, Tilden was convinced that the Republicans were determined not to permit a fair settlement. To H. K. Eno of New York and John C. New of Indiana he expressed this conviction with the remark: "I think I can retire to private life with the consciousness that I shall receive from posterity the credit of having been elected to the highest position in the gift of the people without any of the cares and responsibilities of the office." Hewitt was of the opinion that, while Tilden was disappointed, yet he "felt a profound sense of relief from the dangers of the situation." If the count had not been completed and if Hayes had been seated on March 4 by the Senate, or by Grant, or by General

[20] Tilden Papers, Oscar Keen of Newark, N.J., Apr. 18, 1877.

Sherman, Tilden would have been placed in a most embarrassing position. He would have been compelled either to accept a clouded title from the House or to submit humiliatingly to the usurpation of the office to which he was legally entitled. Tilden was constitutionally hostile to violence and incapable of effective leadership under such conditions. On the whole, Hewitt believed that he was "satisfied with the result" and consoled by the prospect of vindication in 1880.[21] In the *Sun* office Tilden asserted: "I will never be a party to any course which will array my countrymen in civil war against each other." Thousands may have thought him a whisperer and a procrastinator—a man whose method of approach was "a bit furtive and slantindicular" but in reality he was motivated by the highest patriotism.[22]

Tilden's first utterance after the inauguration of Hayes is found in a letter to C. F. Adams. Dated April, 1877, it was a reply to Adams' letter of March 5 written without "the bias of partisanship, passion or interest."[23] Instead of being conscious of "the great trial" to which Adams alluded, Tilden averred that he had no feeling "of desire or regret, separate from the public cause I have represented," which he regarded as the greatest in "this generation of Americans." Then followed a review of the creation of the Union and the evils that had grown up in it. "To curb and correct these evil tendencies . . . to restore . . . the best ideals of our early history, and to remove the fungus overgrowths engendered by civil war" was his first object. Supplementing that was to come "a general reform of administration," the reduction of taxes, a revival of industries, a cordial "reconciliation between estranged populations and classes" and the removal of "unfounded distrust and fear of each other." That was the work he expected to accomplish as President. The decision of the Electoral Commission showed how far the country had drifted away from the "theory of our government" and the difficult task of its restoration.

The Republican Party had perpetuated its power by "corrupt influence," by unscrupulously using the civil service for electioneering purposes, by exacting campaign funds from contractors, jobbers, and business men, and by using the Army to decide elections. But in the face of all these odds, added Tilden, public opinion, by a majority of 260,000 and an electoral majority of 23 votes, demanded better government.

[21] Nevins, *Hewitt*, 380.　　　　　　　　[22] Mitchell, *Memoirs*, 262, 300.
[23] *Letters*, II, 548. Bigelow states that it was never sent.

California was carried by fraud, as were several other States. Then "came the after frauds: the change of the actual result declared at the polls, by governmental influence falsifying the returns of two States and falsifying the count of the electoral votes." [24]

The same month Tilden turned from politics to a study of the life of Oliver Cromwell. With deep interest he read Carlyle and other authors and was impressed with Cromwell's "moderation, sagacity, and general superiority." To old friends who called he talked much about Cromwell's experience as compared with his own. [25] Not until June 13, 1877, when the Manhattan Club tendered a complimentary dinner to Hendricks, did Tilden make an address. He was given a vociferous ovation. Remarking that he too was expecting to visit the Old World, he said, in a voice so faint he could scarcely be heard:

"Everybody knows that, after the recent election, the men who were elected by the people as President and Vice President were counted out; and the men who were not elected were counted in and seated. If my voice could reach throughout our country and be heard in its remotest hamlet, I would say: Be of good cheer. The Republic will live. The institutions of our fathers are not to expire in shame. The sovereignty of the people shall be rescued from this peril and re-established." [26]

Tilden and Hendricks were called out on the steps and cheered. Watterson wrote: "Your Manhattan speech perfect. . . . Last three months depressed beyond power of expression. . . . The time will come when the country will recognize how much it owes to your abstinence." [27]

In the middle of July, 1877, Tilden "talked very freely" with a reporter of the *World* about the Electoral Commission. He said he had never felt "any real confidence" in the arbitration of a question of so much moment by a body of that kind. The issue involved not only the Presidency but also the vast patronage that went with it. The Republican leaders were too anxious to retain this power "to yield any point in an arbitration." The decision of the commission was what might have been expected, considering the stake. Furthermore, he never liked the principle of the scheme. The appeal for a decision should not have been from the 369 representatives of the people to 15, one of whom was selected by chance—perhaps by trickery—but to the 8,000,000 voters through a new election. He distrusted the secrecy and haste of the com-

[24] *Life*, II, 108.   [25] *Retrospections*, V, 315.
[26] Given in New York *Sun*, June 14, 1877.   [27] Tilden Papers, June 13, 1877.

mission. But the plan did appeal to the business classes who wanted a settlement at any price, and, since the joint committee of the two Houses presented it, it became the "only representative of the public desire for peace." He believed that the truth about Louisiana would come out just as the truth about the Canal Ring did.[28]

While Tilden thus expressed his condemnation of the Electoral Commission, he was too discreet to criticize, publicly, those Democrats who were responsible for its creation. However, persons close to him asserted that in private conversation he held Thurman, Bayard, Lamar, Randall and Hewitt responsible for his defeat. W. O. McDowell, for instance, testified that Tilden said, "I would have been President but for Abram S. Hewitt; he deceived me." [29] Simon Sterne declared that Tilden shifted the blame for the decision of the tribunal to Hewitt, whom he accused of being "headstrong and unmanageable." [30] If Tilden thus accused the Democratic leaders in Congress, he was not alone in that opinion. Hundreds of his followers made similar charges in letters still found among his papers. Indeed, a barrage of vituperative resentment was showered upon these leaders by excited and vindictive champions of Tilden, who lost their balance under the burden of disappointment. The accused men denied the charge of defeatism and countered with the assertion that Tilden had given express approval to the tribunal. Then Bigelow, Marble and especially Watterson poured out the vials of their unreasonable wrath on the heads of those Democrats who favored arbitration. The controversy over whether Tilden did or did not endorse the Electoral Commission reached its climax in 1878, when his friends were presenting him as the strong, silent, popular leader who, having been robbed of his crown, must seek vindication in 1880. Neither side was wholly right. But Tilden never lost his head, and such criticism as he offered on the course of Hewitt and others was moderate and reasonable. His protagonists attributed to him censures that were harsher than those he ever made himself. Moreover, he continued on friendly if not confidential terms with Hewitt to the day of his death.[31]

Recent historians have been disposed to say that it was far better for the nation that Hayes instead of Tilden was seated in the Presidency, because the Republicans would not have permitted the latter to be installed.[32] For good reasons one may doubt that surmise. There is little

[28] *Letters*, II, 560–562.   [29] *Sun*, Feb. 10, 1889.   [30] *Times*, Aug. 9, 1886.
[31] Nevins, *Hewitt*, 390, gives the best account of the controversy.
[32] Eckenrode, 233. Cf. Mitchell, *Seymour*, 528, 532.

reliable evidence to show that Republicans would have resorted to force to keep him out of office. Most of such blustering talk was by Democrats. There were enough honorable Republicans to prevent such a disgraceful movement. Moreover, Hayes was a man who would have accepted a decision against him like a gentleman—just as Tilden did. It must also be remembered that the House was Democratic and would have been a powerful factor in the situation. With Northern States like New York, Indiana, Connecticut and New Jersey supporting him, with a number of other Northern States almost equally divided in their allegiance, and with the South to be counted on, it seems extremely unlikely that an announcement favorable to Tilden would have been interfered with by the party in power.

Hewitt was accustomed to say that Hayes did more to restore Southern self-government and sectional harmony than Tilden could have done.[33] One may question such a sweeping statement, and look at the facts. The four major problems confronting the nation in 1877 were: reformation, home rule in the South, currency, and economy. That Tilden would have gone much farther than Hayes did in the correction of abuses in the national administration is clearly demonstrated not alone by the platform on which he stood but also by his record of actual achievement in the Empire State. That he would have handled the Southern problem quite as intelligently and more sympathetically seems certain. Besides he had the confidence of a large majority of the Southern people, and would have received their hearty co-operation in such compromises and adjustments as were necessary. On public finance and national economy Tilden had no superior in his day. The currency problem would have been handled with due regard for business and employment, and for sound monetary principles. That he would have effected economies in the national budget cannot be doubted in view of his accomplishments in New York. With the House behind him he would have obtained at least as much in the direction of civil service reform as Hayes did. If Hayes' administration worked a "revolution" in American government, as his latest biographer maintains, Tilden as President would have effected a significant transformation.

In planning his program, Tilden gave considerable thought to the creation of a capable Cabinet. Although he deplored the scarcity of able Democrats, he talked freely at times about those to whom portfolios

[33] Nevins, *Hewitt*, 389.

would be offered.[34] He had in mind Charles Francis Adams for Secretary of State, an honor for which Bigelow was also a candidate; Charles O'Conor for Attorney General; David A. Wells for Secretary of the Treasury; and Lyman Trumbull, William Graham Sumner, Manton Marble, and Abram S. Hewitt for other posts. G. W. Smith expected to be provided with a good position.[35] John J. Cahill has always held that had Judge David Davis played the rôle expected of him, he would have had a seat in the Cabinet and might have been Tilden's successor, an opinion in which Daniel Manning concurred.[36] While discussing Cabinet possibilities with one old party friend, Tilden completed a tentative slate. Surprised that his own name was not on the list, the old Democrat turned to Tilden and asked, "Where do I come in?" Tilden leaned over, put his hand confidentially on his friend's arm, and said in a whisper, "You, my good friend, you will have great influence with the administration." [37]

More than sixty years have passed since the disputed election of 1876 and many new sources have been made available. A review of the case today makes it evident that a legal judgment hinges on the simple issue of the vote of the Negro. If under the new amendments to the Constitution the colored man had a right to vote, then in South Carolina and Louisiana the Hayes electors had a clear majority. But this interpretation was invalidated by Hayes himself, who almost immediately disfranchised the blacks by restoring the dominance of the whites. And from that day to this little effort has been made to meddle with the franchise in the South. Hence historians of the South look with complacency on the seating of Hayes, while the cry of fraud in 1876 is left entirely to Northern Democrats. In the doubtful States both parties were guilty of acts which prevented a full and a free election. The laws to prevent frauds were not enforced because both parties found it disadvantageous to enforce them. A fair election with Negroes duly protected would have given South Carolina and Louisiana to Hayes, and Florida to Tilden. Under the unfair election Hayes got all three States, but the protesting Democrats sent their challenging certificates to Washington. Although Hayes as President was undoubtedly the beneficiary of fraud, yet, had Tilden triumphed, he too would have been the beneficiary of fraud. The difference was not one of fact but of degree.

The verdict of historians like Rhodes, Schouler, and Dunning has

---

[34] Parker, *Recollections*, 389.
[35] G. W. Smith Papers.
[36] Interview with Cahill, May 10, 1931.
[37] Related by Dr. Richard E. Day.

been that Tilden was entitled to the electoral votes of Louisiana and hence to the Presidency. Davis, Eckenrode, and Nevins give him the electoral votes of Florida and thus strengthen his title to that high office. Prominent contemporary Republicans believed that he had won. Consequently this question may be regarded as settled. So universally accepted is the verdict that this interpretation is now taught in the schools as a finality. The election of 1876 was a test of the people's ability to purify political life and to reform party practices. Though deprived of a victory won at the polls, Tilden's patriotic conduct under a keen sense of injustice was a triumph for law and orderly government. Well might Hewitt boast that "we have proven to the world that we are capable of self-government."

IN the disputed election Tilden lost more than the Presidency—he emerged from the strain with a shattered constitution. His left hand had been rendered almost useless by arthritis. "Numb palsy" or *paralysis agitans* afflicted him and increased in violence during the rest of his life. His gait was slow and shuffling, and his face had a yellowish, unhealthy appearance. Physically he was an old, broken man; but his mind was still keen, and all his faculties at instant command. For years his voice had been affected, and now was little above a hoarse whisper. The most remarkable thing about him was his eyes, which instantly revealed his emotions—merriment, sympathy, anger, dissent, and approbation. In his youth he expressed his lack of faith in doctors, but now he went to the other extreme and was always looking for some new nostrum for an unruly stomach or an aching head or swollen joints or trembling hands. All his life he relied inordinately on drugs, and his notebooks are full of prescriptions. At this period he became interested in the curative properties of electricity and read much in the literature on the subject.[1]

After the inauguration of President Hayes, Tilden's medical adviser, Dr. Austin Flint, insisted upon rest and moderate exercise. He discussed various plans for a vacation but found it difficult to arrive at a decision. W. B. Lawrence reminded him of a promise to spend the summer at his seashore home at Newport, but it does not appear that he filled the engagement.[2] Instead he went to Sea Girt, New Jersey, to recuperate, and by July was "looking remarkably well." [3]

After the restful trip to Europe in 1873, Tilden had planned to repeat the experience in 1875, but found it impossible to escape the burdens of his office. Again on February 9, 1877, he discussed a foreign tour with Bigelow [4]—an indication that he had given up all expectation of becoming President. As the weeks passed he seemed more anxious to forget the nerve-wracking experience he had gone through to get the rest he needed from travel and to consult specialists in Europe about his afflictions. Furthermore, he longed to continue his genealogical research in England. Evidently he and Bigelow talked the matter over repeatedly.

[1] Tilden Papers, Dr. A. Flint, Dec. 1, 1878.   [2] *Letters*, II, 555.
[3] *Ib.*, 560; *World*, July 17, 1877.   [4] *Retrospections*, V, 213, 298.

When Bigelow visited him at Sea Girt on July 4, he announced that nothing but "extraordinaries" would prevent his sailing on July 18. He was expecting to consult Robinson about State affairs, but the latter could not come on account of sore eyes.[5]

With his customary thrift Tilden had turned to a business acquaintance, Cyrus W. Field, to arrange for his steamship reservation. The latter wrote him: "I have secured for you in the S.S. *Bothenia,* sailing July 4, the two staterooms marked on the enclosed plan—the best on the ship. I sail on July 18 on the *Scythia.* The Cunard Co. will transfer you if you desire." [6] Tilden insisted that Bigelow should accompany him but did not offer to pay his expenses.[7] In the end, Tilden, with Bigelow and Field, departed quietly on July 18. The newspapers of July 19 commented briefly on Tilden's trip abroad. From Drexel, Morgan & Company he took a letter of credit for £5,000 or 126,250 francs. Against this he drew the following sums: August 23, £100; September 16, 2,000 francs; September 28, 4,000 francs; October 6, 4,000 francs; October 11, £50; and October 12, £50—thus exhausting but a small part of the letter.[8]

At Tilden's request there was no demonstration on his departure. Mrs. Pelton, Colonel Pelton, Henry A. Tilden and some friends were at the boat to say good-bye. Tilden wore a dark business suit and seemed well. Numerous reporters were on hand; as were also Mayor Ely, Smith M. Weed, A. H. Green, D. D. Field, E. K. Apgar, Dr. Austin Flint, Judge Sinnott and about three hundred others. Tilden occupied Stateroom 443. There were no flowers in it. A seat was arranged for him at the captain's table. As the steamer departed at 11 o'clock in the forenoon he bowed and waved farewell to friends and relatives. William Gorham Rice, representing Governor Robinson, was present to wish him *bon voyage.*[9]

Some of the Democratic leaders advised Tilden against going to Europe at this particular time. A. C. Beach wrote, "It would be as well for you not to go to Europe at present," because the whole American diplomatic force would be instructed to prevent any demonstrations in his favor on the other side. This, Beach feared, might weaken Tilden's candidacy in 1880.[10] A. S. Hewitt had already gone abroad and appar-

---

[5] *Retrospections,* V, 324.   [6] Tilden Papers, June 19, 1877.
[7] Statement by Poultney Bigelow.
[8] Tilden Papers, July 17, 1877. Letter of Credit still preserved.
[9] *World,* July 19, 1877.   [10] Tilden Papers, June 7, 1877.

ently Beach saw political danger in Tilden's following his example.

After thirteen restful days on the broad Atlantic, which Tilden greatly enjoyed, he and Bigelow landed at Queenstown, July 27, in order to gain a glimpse of Ireland. The London *Times* announced on July 30 that Tilden had disembarked. So many of his personal and political friends were Irish that he was anxious to visit some of the famous spots and obtain a first-hand view of social and economic conditions. His route took him from Cork to Blarney Castle and then on to Killarney. Here Tilden and Bigelow stopped at a tavern for luncheon. The proprietor stepped forward and greeted them by name. Tilden demanded in surprise, "How do you know us when we have never been here before?" Their host replied: "My name is Brooks. I used to be a copyist in your office in Wall Street." Tilden, greatly pleased by the incident, bombarded his former employee with innumerable questions about conditions in Ireland.[11] From Killarney he proceeded to Dublin, July 30. Bigelow has left a vivid description of this brief visit to the Emerald Isle.[12]

On August 1 they crossed to England, stopped at Eton Hall and Chester, and reached London on the 3rd. Hewitt had written Tilden at Queenstown that he would be in London but would leave shortly for Paris. He informed Tilden that Mrs. Stanly of 37 Whimple Street was very desirous of seeing him; that Sir Curtis Lampson, a partner of J. J. Astor, would invite him for a visit in Kent "near the home of your ancestors," but he must remember that Stanly and Cyrus Field "are not on good terms"; and that Lady Waldegrove, owner of "Strawberry Hall," former home of Horace Walpole, would ask him down there. "Go, by all means," Hewitt urged, "for there you will meet the whole Liberal Party." [13]

Tilden spent over a week in London at the Buckingham Hotel, cared for by his valet Louis. The courtesies of various clubs were offered him, the Athenaeum inviting him for a month; but in his need for special foods and sleep he had little use for them. So far as his "ascetic life" permitted he accepted some of the numerous social engagements arranged for him. He called on Minister Edwards Pierrepont, who gave him a dinner on August 7,[14] accepted an invitation to lunch with W. E. Forster, whom he had met in New York in 1868, and spent the evening with Lord

[11] *Retrospections,* V, 298. [12] *Life,* II, 121. [13] Tilden Papers.
[14] *Retrospections,* V, 299. There he met Lord Chancellor Cairnes, Courtlandt Parker, John Russell Young, Hoppin, Jackson and Beckwith.

Houghton and his son at the Cosmopolitan Club. He deeply regretted not meeting Bright. The general manager of the Metropolitan Railroad invited him to make a tour of inspection. Of course the Houses of Parliament, the birthplace of the Duke of Wellington, and other places of interest were visited. He went down to Roehampton to see the country estate of J. S. Morgan, the London banker, with whom he deposited $200,000, and also met Baron Hübner.

To avoid public attention, Tilden and Bigelow, on August 11, went up to Scotland, where ten days were spent in visiting Edinburgh, Melrose, Abbotsford and Dryburgh. Tilden met Robert Wallace and other distinguished gentlemen but pronounced the Scottish weather a failure.[15]

Upon returning to London on August 22, Tilden found among his letters one notifying him of election as an honorary member of the famous Cobden Club, which he acknowledged because he was happy to have his name associated with that "illustrious statesman." [16] The Caxton Centennial Exhibition was viewed on the 23rd and the next day he went to Canterbury for a week with the Tyldens. To his favorite sister, Mrs. W. T. Pelton, he wrote a glowing account of the visits to kinsmen, to the old Tylden manor house, and to the churches in which his ancestors worshiped. This experience was one of the bright spots of his summer abroad.[17] He had some of his English relatives dine with him in Canterbury and later sent the young ladies presents from Paris.[18] Upon learning that Sir William Tylden, a distant relative, had served as an English admiral in the War of 1812 off the coast of Florida and Louisiana, he borrowed his diary to take home. Later John J. Cahill copied it, leaving blank spaces for the sketches in pencil and water colors of the original. Mrs. G. W. Smith reproduced these in the copy, together with a "tinted carte-de visite photograph of Sir William." So delighted was Tilden with her work that to the day of his death he sent her a check for $50 each Christmas.[19]

On August 30 Tilden hurried back to London and then went to Lowestoft on the east coast to consult Dr. Garrod about his ailments. To his sister he wrote that this specialist in gout, rheumatism, and arthritis, whom he had already seen once in London, was doing him good. He proceeded, as when a young man, to give a full diagnosis of his condition. He expected to remain until October; his health was "im-

---

[15] *Life*, II, 129; *Sun*, Apr. 11, 1933.   [16] Tilden Papers; *Tribune*, Aug. 14, 1877.
[17] Mrs. G. W. Smith, Ms. Notes. This English branch spelled the name with a "y."
[18] *Life*, II, 131.   [19] Mrs. G. W. Smith, Ms. Notes.

proving all the time"; he was taking "more exercise and growing stronger"; but he would have to be careful "and continue the process for a year or more." The letter concluded with a detailed account of his exploration of the ancestral home and affectionate regards to "Willie, Gussie, Laura, yourself and all." [20]

In London Tilden learned of the triumph of John Kelly and Tammany over his friends in the State election.[21] There he and Bigelow met Hendricks and Hewitt, dined with them, took long walks, and talked over the campaign of 1876. It pleased Tilden to have Manning write Bigelow: "The Governor's hold on the regard of the people is stronger than ever. . . . It is amusing to hear our old enemies talk glibly of the views and wishes of Mr. Tilden." [22] Meanwhile Hewitt and his sick wife went to Paris, where at Bigelow's request they took rooms at the hotel where he and Tilden expected to stay. The intention to remain longer with Dr. Garrod was changed by the death of Thiers; and, with Bigelow, Tilden hurried over to Paris to attend the impressive funeral. "We met daily as usual," wrote Hewitt in 1895, "and saw many interesting men and places in common." [23] Tilden had a long talk with Gambetta on politics and dined with Louis Blanc, who recounted the career of Napoleon III. When Bigelow introduced him to Victor Hugo and explained how Tilden had waived the Presidency by submitting to the decision of the Electoral Commission, the great Frenchman shook his head in perplexity and remarked, "That is not the way we do things here in France." [24] Tilden had the Hewitts and Crawfords to dinner frequently and remained a month in Paris while Bigelow went to Berlin.[25]

The Hewitts had intended to return home on September 15, but as they decided to remain with Tilden it was not until October 8 that Tilden, Bigelow, and they crossed the English Channel in a terrible storm. Tilden, drenched to the skin, had a chill and a slight congestion of the lungs. In their hotel in London, Bigelow found Tilden "standing before the fire with his legs bare and his short coat and hat on, waiting for a bath." But he had heard about the new State ticket and was "quite gay and talkative." He insisted on "drinking so much stimulant of one kind or another—coffee . . . tea . . . brandy—that I do not hope for his restoration until he gets to sea," commented Bigelow in his *Diary*.

[20] Tilden Papers.
[21] *Life*, II, 130.
[22] *Retrospections*, V, 351, 353, Sept. 19, 1877.
[23] Nevins, *Hewitt*, 391.
[24] *Life*, II, 111.
[25] *Retrospections*, V, 351.

Pelton cabled that he thought Tilden should remain away until after election.[26] But Dr. Garrod took such good care of him that he was able to sail for home with Bigelow and the Hewitts on October 12, aboard the *Scythia*. They reached New York on the 25th, after a stormy passage which Tilden did not seem to mind. This long and cordial association with Hewitt corroborates his vehement denial that Tilden felt any grievance against him as the former Democratic National Chairman.[27] The trip had done Tilden good, according to the New York *Herald*, which significantly reported that John Kelly had taken out of Tilden's hands the direction of Democratic State politics.[28] On the contrary, Bigelow asserted that Tilden's hope of improved health was not realized. He had less control of his left arm and hand; his tremulousness had become more noticeable, and his vocal organs "were losing their flexibility." Though gravely concerned over his physical condition, he stubbornly refused to acknowledge that his usefulness had passed. Tilden asserted later that one reason for his early return was to dispose of the annoying income tax case which the Federal Government was still pressing against him.[29]

Some years later, when Bigelow wrote the life of Tilden, he recalled that Tilden could not accept responsibility for any decision unless satisfied that his conclusions, based on an exhaustive study of details, were sound. As an illustration Bigelow cited the crossing from England to France. "At what hotel shall we stay in Paris?" Tilden asked. Bigelow named three or four of the best, any one of which would be excellent. But Tilden was not satisfied. One of them *must* have distinct advantages over the others. He had his valet bring one of his bags, and from it took "a small library of guidebooks and maps." Going across the Channel and up to Paris he spent most of his time studying the details about several dozen first-class hotels. Finally, for reasons entirely satisfactory to himself, a hostelry was selected.[30]

Before sailing for home he had a letter from that brilliant but eccentric writer and reformer, Kate Field, then in Paris. She told him about an American woman who had been deserted by a wicked husband and was left stranded without a penny. "I am poor or I wouldn't beg for her. . . . Have raised £4 and want £50 to get her home." [31] Tilden responded generously to cases of genuine need, particularly when pre-

[26] *Retrospections*, V, 361, 363.   [27] Nevins, *Hewitt*, 391.   [28] Oct. 26, 1877.
[29] *Life*, II, 168, 236.   [30] *Ib.*, 377.   [31] Tilden Papers, Oct. 1, 1877.

sented by a woman, and one may assume that he answered this plea for help from a compatriot.

Among those who greeted Tilden at the dock were Mayor Ely, Wickham, Schell, Agnew, Clinton, Beach, Havemeyer, Cooper, Dr. Flint, Olney, Whitney, Ingersoll, King, Andrews and Van Wyck.[32] Schell asked the crowd to give three cheers for the returned leader who was still the master mind of the Democratic Party. On the following evening he was given a serenade by the Young Men's Democratic Club. He was much pleased by this attention, and from the steps of his home delivered a significant address known as the "Indian Corn Speech" because he predicted that the 60,000,000 bushels of corn imported by Great Britain would be greatly increased to give British workmen cheaper food and American farmers a better market. But he contended that "our barbarous revenue system" must be relaxed, for we should no longer "legislate against the wants of humanity and the beneficence of God." [33] He remarked that his "summer excursion" had repaired, as much as three months could, "the waste of six years consecrated to an effort for governmental reform in the city, State and nation."

This address, which must have been more or less extemporaneous, was a masterful survey of the campaign of 1876 with a perspective of nearly a year behind it, and based on reflection after a heart to heart talk with Hewitt. After calling upon his hearers to support the State Democratic ticket, he took up "the greatest political crime of our history, by which the result of the Presidential election of 1876 was set aside and reversed." At this point a voice in the audience cried out, "We know you got robbed!" Tilden replied, "I did not get robbed. The people got robbed . . . robbed of the dearest rights of American citizens." Then he explained the historical origin of those rights, remarking that in the early days there were no Louisiana and Florida "Returning Boards" to deprive citizens of their rights. He pointed to the rise in the last twenty years of "a vast officeholding class" and of political corruption, which had almost destroyed the balance of our complex system. Public opinion in 1876 had to have the approval of two-thirds of the people in order to obtain a majority of the votes at the election. If this autocratic tendency were not arrested, our democratic methods would be destroyed. Let the Federal Government control corporations, assume jurisdiction over riots, increase the Army, and ignore the prerogatives

[32] New York City newspapers.   [33] *Life*, II, 142; *Writings*, II, 485.

of the States, and a Third Napoleon might emerge in America. In the canvass of 1876 the Democratic candidates "were counted out, and a great fraud triumphed, which the American people . . . will never condone. . . . It stabbed the very foundations of free government. . . ., I call upon you to unite with me in the defense of our sacred . . . inheritance. The government of the people must not . . . become only an empty name.

"Young men! . . . we who have guarded the sacred traditions of our free government will soon leave that work to you. . . . Whether our institutions shall be preserved . . . will depend on you. Will you accomplish that duty, and mark these wrongdoers of 1876 with the indignation of a betrayed, wronged and sacrificed people? I can do no better than to stand among you and do battle for the maintenance of free government . . . for the cause I have represented, which has embraced the largest and holiest interests of humanity." [34] The *Tribune* reported that he said, "I swear in the presence of you all, and I call upon you to bear witness to the oath, to watch, during the remainder of my life, over the rights of the citizens of our country with a jealous care. Such a usurpation must never occur again." [35]

This address, interrupted by prolonged applause, was a clarion to a dispirited party. Letters deluged Tilden, congratulating him on his manifesto. Watterson thought the speech good with one exception—it did not castigate the traitors in his own party.[36] Hatred of the Electoral Commission was revived in numerous letters many of which Tilden answered personally. The tiresome personal conferences about State and national politics were resumed. Invitations to make addresses, to attend public functions and to be a guest at a luncheon or dinner came by every mail. Most of these were courteously declined. Occasionally Tilden departed from this rule, as for instance when a dinner was given to Junius S. Morgan by Cyrus W. Field on November 8. Morgan was a Connecticut boy who succeeded as a banker in London. Tilden presided at the banquet, found himself in a reminiscent mood and made a felicitous speech.

Looking around at the hundred business magnates assembled at Delmonico's Tilden said,

[34] *Life*, II, 142; *Writings*, II, 485.   [35] *Letters*, II, 562, Oct. 26, 1877.
[36] Tilden Papers, Nov. 5, 1877.

"I went down to Roehampton last summer to see the beautiful country house of my friend Mr. Morgan, a few miles out of London. He was well pleased to show me about everywhere. . . . No man could help being delighted with what I saw, and he was curious to know what were my impressions. Well, I had, while inspecting with pleasure the appliances of comfort and luxury, been thinking how much, after all, he got for himself out of his great wealth and great business . . . and said to him: 'I don't see but what you are a trustee here; you get only your food, your clothing, your shelter.' Of course a man may have some delight in a sense of power, in a sense of consequence; but I rather thought his coachman beat him in that particular."

Tilden also recalled that when he was "quite a young man" he was consulted about a will by Martin Van Buren—"a great statesman and a great thinker"—who was disposed to leave his property to his grandchildren rather than his children. Tilden advised:

"It is not well to be wiser than events; to attempt to control the far future, which no man can foresee; to trust one's grandchildren, whom one does not know, out of distrust, without special cause, of one's children, whom one does know."

A few weeks later Tilden was informed that Van Buren had abandoned the complicated trusts to tie up his property and left it all to his direct heirs.

Tilden called attention to the economic principle "that every man who, by any effort, reduces the cost or increases the fruits of any service demanded by society, to that extent enlarges the results of its exercise." These men are working not for themselves but for the general public. "Even personal accumulations, after the owners have left them, sink into the mass which society in the aggregate owns, and undergo a fresh distribution." He hoped that all men of wealth had discovered that "there is something better than money, and that is the merited esteem of their fellows; and that there is something better than the merited esteem of their fellows, which is a consciousness that human society is better because we have existed." [37] This must have been a startling doctrine to selfish captains of industry, and is evidence of the advanced position Tilden, himself a man of wealth, took in viewing the economic civilization of that day after contending for years that Government must not control corporations. Cyrus W. Field wished

[37] *Writings*, II, 494.

to print the addresses but it took him ten days to get a corrected copy from Tilden.[38]

When Bayard Taylor was appointed Minister to Germany, Whitelaw Reid induced Tilden to attend a small dinner in his honor at the Union League Club, and asked him to persuade O'Conor to be present, promising that reporters would be strictly excluded. Tilden replied, "I proposed going to Philadelphia, Pittsburgh and Cleveland tomorrow on business but will defer and place pleasure before business. . . . O'Conor is inflexible." [39] This note indicates how Tilden was still giving general oversight to his extensive properties in 1878. He denied that he was directing Governor Robinson's policies and refrained from making any requests of him.[40] When a rumor sprang up that he was a candidate for the United States Senate, he soon put a stop to it. He was not too busy for the performance of trivial courtesies such as helping to erect flagpoles in Gramercy Park,[41] exchanging delightful letters with his English kinsmen,[42] sending his nieces abroad, and helping young men, who came with letters of introduction, to get a start in the metropolis.[43] He recommended St. Clair McKelway for an editorial position on the Albany *Argus*. Mrs. C. Adele Fassett, who wished him to sit for a life-sized portrait to go into her picture of the Electoral Commission, was accommodated.[44] A call was made on Governor-General Dufferin in Ottawa. "Involuntary engagements" forced him to decline an invitation to attend the Louisville Industrial Exposition, but he sent a long letter. Among his callers were H. A. Richmond, who wished a loan; carpetbag Governor J. J. Moses of South Carolina, whose fare was paid to New York for an interview; the eccentric Dr. Mary Walker, who wanted legal advice; Dan Manning and Judge G. F. Comstock, who were desirous of discussing the State political outlook; Randall, who wished to survey the national situation; and of course more intimate friends. Horatio Seymour was thanked for his article in the *North American Review* and congratulated on his health. A useful set of Johnson's *Encyclopedia* was sent to Emily J. Raynor for a Christmas present. Although Tilden kept no diary, his carefully preserved correspondence serves that purpose admirably.[45]

Democrats refused to allow the frauds of 1876 to be forgotten either in or out of Congress. The *Sun* printed "The Fraud Laid Bare," J. E.

[38] Tilden Papers.   [39] *Letters*, II, 572; Tilden Papers.   [40] *Ib.*, 573.
[41] Tilden Papers.   [42] *Letters*, II, 570.   [43] *Ib.*, 572.
[44] Tilden Papers; Barry, *Forty Years*, 20–23.   [45] Tilden Papers.

Anderson's testimony, and Marble's letter on the Electoral Commission. By keeping the question alive it was hoped that Hayes' title would be still further clouded, and thus assure a Democratic victory in 1880. After a hard-fought struggle in the House, Clarkson N. Potter, with Tilden's approval, had a special committee appointed on May 20, 1878, to reinvestigate the frauds and corruption of the recent election. Potter was chairman and his Democratic colleagues were Hunton, Springer, Stenger, Morrison, McMahon and Blackburn. The Republican members were Reed, Butler, Cox and Hiscock.[46] A motion that no "subsequent Congress . . . has jurisdiction to revise the action" making Hayes President was carried in a Democratic House on June 24 by a vote of 215 to 21—Cox, Hewitt and Springer opposing the measure.[47] While this action had no direct connection with the Potter Committee, it did in a sense block its purpose.

For the first six months after June 1, 1878, the committee confined its work to a thoroughgoing review of the facts connected with Florida and Louisiana. Over two hundred witnesses, white and black, were called to testify, and some of them were roughly handled. The results were indecisive, however, as might have been expected from a political investigation. It was pretty much a case of the pot calling the kettle black. But the general effect on the country seemed to be to strengthen the conviction that Tilden had been elected. There was ample proof of fraud, intimidation, irregularity and offers to sell the electoral votes of South Carolina, Florida and Louisiana to the Democrats. The findings were given to the nation by the jubilant Democratic press.[48] Hewitt closed the debate and was thanked by Tilden.[49] The report raised the hopes of the Democrats that something might still be done to seat Tilden. Magone wanted public meetings held to back up the Potter resolusions. Dr. G. L. Miller of Omaha asked Kernan to tell him about the future.[50] Marble's letter attempting to place the blame for Tilden's defeat at Hewitt's door found many supporters. J. W. Buford of Tennessee found the tendency to criticize Tilden "for the late Presidential fiasco" completely answered. Arphaxed Loomis of Little Falls, New York, remarked that "moral courage and firmness from the start in the House" would have saved the day, but "timid counsel prevailed. Your friends consented to arbitrate whether your coat belonged to

[46] Haworth, 308; *Cong. Record,* 45 Cong., 2nd Sess., 3438.
[47] *An. Cyc.*, 1878, 167.   [48] Haworth, 314; Report printed Mar. 3, 1879.
[49] Nevins, *Hewitt,* 396.   [50] Kernan Papers, Mar. 1, 1878.

you or Mr. Hayes" and confided too much in the other side. "I am glad to learn that you gave no assent to the arbitration, but took your stand on the true, legal and constitutional ground. . . . It was too late to revolt" when the legally created tribunal made its decision.[51]

Visiting Florida and Louisiana the Potter Committee found witnesses who gave amazing testimony. S. B. McLin of Florida admitted that, in giving Florida to Hayes, his honest judgment had been broken down by party zeal and promise of reward, and that Republicans confessed wholesale ballot-box stuffing. In Louisiana, Republican election officials swore that John Sherman gave a written promise of good Federal jobs, and Negroes admitted the untruthfulness of their 1876 affidavits concerning violence and intimidation. In both States, it was found that those who gave the electoral votes to Hayes had received Federal offices.[52] In consequence there was a new outcry against the crime of 1876 and a hopeful look toward 1880 for a demonstration of justice.

[51] *Letters,* II, 575, Aug. 4, 1878.
[52] See Gibson, *A Political Crime,* for a full statement.

Chapter XXXIII   The Cipher Telegrams and Income Tax

DURING the canvass for minor State officers in 1878 there came the explosion of a bombshell in the Democratic camp. Beginning on October 7 and continuing for some days, the *Tribune* published the "cipher telegrams" and their translations. Republicans set forth the exposure to discredit Tilden. Over the Florida dispatches was the heading, "True Story . . . Told for the First Time," and the assertion that Tilden's confidential agents Manton Marble and J. F. Doyle had dickered to buy an elector's vote for $50,000. The South Carolina telegrams appeared on October 16. Three days later there was printed an *Extra* of forty-four pages which explained the whole system. These telegrams have an interesting history. Under a subpoena from the House Committee on Louisiana and from the Senate Committee on Privileges and Elections, the Western Union Telegraph Company, on January 25, 1877, delivered about 30,000 telegrams in cipher which the two National Committees had sent and received relative to the election. It has been said that William Orton, president of the telegraph company, a tricky Republican, permitted his party friends to extract some telegrams before turning them over to the committees.[1] The telegrams relating to Louisiana went to W. R. Morrison, a Democrat, who was chairman in the House; and those relating to Oregon and other doubtful States, to O. P. Morton, a Republican, in the Senate. Morrison returned the dispatches to the telegraph company, but Morton retained his until Hayes was inaugurated, when they were sent back after a number had been secretly abstracted, and all burned by order of the Senate committee, but not before the theft had been discovered.[2]

About a year later some 750 abstracted telegrams were in possession of George E. Bullock, a protégé of Morton, who in turn transferred them to Second Assistant Postmaster Brady, who had copies made. From him some copies and originals went to the *Tribune* and were given to the public. Others were given to William E. Chandler. The rest were turned over to B. F. Butler of the committee. If all the telegrams had been known, it seems probable that Republicans would have been quite

[1] McCulloch, *Men and Measures,* 420; *Dict. Am. Biog.,* XIV, 65.
[2] For details see H. R. Misc. Doc. No. 42, 44th Cong., 2nd Sess.

as much compromised as Democrats.[3] The cipher telegrams as selected and printed by the *Tribune* show: first, that Manton Marble and C. W. Wooley were in touch with W. T. Pelton and Henry Havemeyer concerning the purchase of one or more of the Florida electoral votes, but that the effort failed; and, secondly, that Smith M. Weed was conducting a similar negotiation in South Carolina, which was not consummated.[4]

These cipher dispatches produced an uproar and enabled the Republicans to point the finger of condemnation at Tilden, who was held responsible for the activities of Pelton, Marble, and Weed. Democrats at first refused to believe the telegrams genuine; and when that could no longer be maintained, they denounced the manner in which they had been obtained and denied their significance. Some of Tilden's foes within his own party contented themselves with the assertion that now he was eliminated from the race in 1880. Hewitt had been kept in ignorance of the messages about the purchase of electors for Tilden, although he knew that votes were on the market. He was told that unscrupulous Democrats had actually raised the $200,000 demanded, but that Tilden promptly intervened and stopped the deal. Governor Wells told Hewitt that the offer rejected by the Democrats had been accepted by the Republican managers, who agreed to pay the cash after Hayes was inaugurated. Part of it was actually paid.[5] In Congress Hewitt not only denied all knowledge of the telegrams but also declared that none of them were shown to Tilden. Pelton, he said, held no office with the Democratic National Committee. He invited the fullest examination and investigation in order to vindicate Tilden. Hale of Maine made a sarcastic plea to give a chance to "that simple-hearted old man in New York" to explain how he was betrayed by those about him. B. F. Butler, who had a large bundle of the messages in his possession, begged his colleagues not to press the investigation because it would stir up for both parties "something that had better not be seen, felt, or smelled." [6]

On the day the telegrams first appeared Bigelow found Tilden indignant that the men whom he trusted to help conduct the campaign had kept him in ignorance of these compromising documents. Bigelow had never seen him "more completely overcome" and remained several days to cheer him up. Tilden believed that the Republican administra-

[3] H. R. Misc. Doc. No. 31, 45th Cong., 3rd Sess., IV; *An. Cyc.*, 1878, 717.
[4] Haworth, 318, 319.   [5] Nevins, *Hewitt*, 397.
[6] *Cong. Record*, 1879, Vol. 8, Pt. 3, 610–611.

tion had resorted to this exposure to offset the Potter investigation. He felt forced to make a public defense, and with Bigelow's help did so in a letter to the *Herald* on October 16, 1878.[7] "I have no knowledge of the existence of these telegrams," he affirmed, "nor any information about them." More specifically, he denied knowing of the offer of the Florida Board of Canvassers, or that of South Carolina, to sell certificates to Democratic electors until long after December 6. No offer to buy such votes "was ever entertained, considered, or tolerated by me or anybody within my influence by my consent or with my knowledge." It was commonly known that these votes were for sale, and McLin, chairman of the Florida Canvassing Board, admitted it before the Potter Committee. Likewise the Louisiana electoral votes were repeatedly offered to Hewitt by the agent of J. M. Wells, but Hewitt declined to purchase them. But all these offered votes went to Hayes. From fixed principle, Tilden would not accept the Presidency if he had to buy it. Congress had refused to right the wrong, and "the monstrous conclusion" was reached that one man on a State Returning Board elected the President of the United States. Tilden denounced the "pretexts for taking from us the Presidency to which I had been elected and vesting it in one who had not been elected. . . . The attitude which I unavoidably occupied toward this transaction has been a constant though silent reproach. In it will be found the motive for the groundless imputations which have furnished the occasion for this statement."[8]

Tilden took no pains to conceal from Bigelow his "indignation with Pelton. . . . He says Pelton shall never live under the same roof again with him. Pelton left New York in June and has not been in Gramercy Park since. He is now in Canada."[9] C. F. Adams was delighted to know that Tilden was "not a fool, much less a rascal," and thought Pelton "little better than a circus clown."[10] The *Herald* called him an "indiscreet and bumptious young man . . . an empty, self-sufficient sister's son . . . who took unwarrantable liberties with Mr. Tilden in a foolish hope of serving him. The bribery dispatches were egregious acts of folly. . . . Weed went from South Carolina to Baltimore to get $55,000 to bribe . . . canvassers but there is no evidence that Pelton met him there." Watterson wrote Tilden that the ciphers "made a great impression" and not having any cue he adopted the

---

[7] *Life*, II, 175; *Retrospections*, V, 398.   [8] *Nation*, 17:250; 18:112.
[9] *Retrospections*, V, 398–399.   [10] *Ib.*, 401.

"dangerous policy of suppression." [11] He begged for a word as to what to do. Later he was discouraged as to the outlook of the party and saw enough dejection "to make a cat howl."

The Republicans now demanded that the Potter Committee investigate the cipher telegrams, and of course the Democrats objected. So widespread was the insistence, however, that on January 21, 1879, the Democratic House gave way and instructed the committee to look into the disclosures.[12] The first step was to discover how the *Tribune* gained possession of the documents and if possible to unearth incriminating Republican dispatches. Hence some of the officials of the telegraph company and certain Republicans were examined in Washington, but nothing disreputable was brought to light. It seems probable that if there were Republican messages suggesting questionable methods they were destroyed.[13] The next step was to proceed to New York City for the purpose of widening the inquiry.

It was natural that Tilden should seek to avoid the ordeal of appearing before the committee. A resolution to permit him to be represented by counsel was tabled on January 22, 1879. Consequently on February 7 he asked permission to appear before the sub-committee which was continuing the investigation at the Fifth Avenue Hotel to "submit some testimony" which he deemed "pertinent to the inquiry." Hunton, chairman, Springer and Stenger were Democrats; Reed and Hiscock, Republicans. By special arrangement Tilden appeared on the 9th to undergo an experience which only a man with nerves of steel and a determination to vindicate his honor would endure. The *Herald* gave a graphic description of the scene.[14]

Tilden, dressed in black, appeared in company with his brother Henry and Bigelow. His solemn face was imperturbable and sphinx-like. "He seemed to have aged considerably, and . . . looked quite ill and feeble," and as usual was suffering from a cold. It was a "painful spectacle to see the slow, halting, lame walk with which he passed the table and reached his seat. His figure was stiffly drawn up and seemed incapable of bending, as though . . . from a paralytic contraction of the limbs." Though every eye was on him, not a muscle of his face relaxed as he shook hands with the members of the committee. Then he took off his "elegant, silk-lined overcoat," seated him-

---

[11] Tilden Papers, Oct. 14, 1878.   [12] *Cong. Record,* 608–612.
[13] H. R. Misc. 45, Cong. No. 31, vol. 4, 3; Haworth, 323.   [14] Feb. 10, 1879.

self at the table and thrust a handkerchief into his breast pocket.

Sitting erect in his chair, for more than two and a half hours he gave his testimony in a calm, quiet manner, never changing expression and speaking in a hoarse, almost inaudible voice. As he came to the corrupt negotiations alluded to in the cipher dispatches, his voice rose suddenly to a dramatic and vehement intensity, his face flushed with deep feeling, his lips twitched, and one of his hands trembled "in a most painful manner." When he called on Heaven to witness his innocence of all knowledge of the ciphers, he struck the table "heavily" with his clenched fist and there "was a sympathizing outburst of applause." When Reed questioned him about "corrupt attempts," he asked dryly, "Attempts to sell or buy, which?" and there was a ripple of laughter.[15]

Of the cipher telegrams relating to South Carolina and Florida, Tilden said under oath:

"I did not recognize . . . a single one; the contents of no one of them . . . was communicated to me in any manner. . . . I had no . . . suspicion that such a correspondence . . . had existed until . . . the publication. No offer . . . in behalf of . . . the Returning Board of South Carolina, of the Board of Canvassers of Florida, or of any other State, was ever entertained by me . . . in any manner whatsoever."

His first knowledge of such negotiations was when Edward Cooper told him that Colonel Pelton, having received an offer to sell certificates to Democratic electors, was in Baltimore. "I immediately said that no such offer should be entertained . . . that not a cent should be furnished for any such purpose," and Pelton was immediately recalled to New York. "I did not . . . know that Mr. Smith M. Weed was there. . . . I had not seen him after the election." Tilden asserted that he knew nothing whatever about the Florida offers until after December 6, 1876, when Marble informed him that the vote of Florida was for sale but had been declined. Pelton assured him that all offers had been refused.

Tilden also vowed that he had never seen any of the Oregon dispatches except one from Governor Grover, stating that he would give the certificate to a Democratic elector. He acknowledged that some of the telegrams had been addressed to Pelton at "my residence" but

[15] Text of testimony in *Life*, II, 182.

so far as he knew none of them were ever delivered there. "At any rate, they never met my eye."

As for the visiting statesmen hurried South to guard Democratic interests, Tilden declared that he neither selected nor sent them, nor did he communicate with any of them. "The idea that they were my personal agents in any sense has no foundation in fact." From November 7 to December 6, 1876, "I maintained a uniform attitude . . . under no circumstances to enter any competition to obtain . . . the certificates . . . of the disputed States." Never for an instant did he think of seeking them "by any venal inducements, any promise of money or of office." To the people who elected him, he owed "every honorable sacrifice" but not a surrender of "one jot or tittle of my sense of right or personal self-respect." He was resolved that if the Chief Magistracy of his country was auctioned off, he would not be "among the bidders" but would appeal to the people to "reassert their great right . . . to elective self-government."

As a lawyer Tilden knew that when he asked to testify, his political foes would seek to humiliate him and blacken his character. Reed and Hiscock used every possible device to extract damaging admissions and to make it appear that he was dissembling, but he came through the fire unscathed. He did admit, however, that intimate associates such as G. W. Smith, Pelton, Smith M. Weed and Marble deceived him in conducting reprehensible negotiations. Pelton, in particular, whether rightly or wrongly, was made the scapegoat for the incriminations of Democratic leaders. Tilden had objected to his serving as secretary of the National Committee and in an "outburst of displeasure" had reproved him for his action at Baltimore as an "inchoate offense" for which "public opinion may punish him." Goaded too far by the probing of Hiscock, Tilden exploded: "I declare before God and my country that it is my belief that the votes and certificates of Florida and Louisiana were bought, and that the Presidency was controlled by their purchase."

Pelton and others may have thought that they were merely fighting fire with fire, or money with money, but he had "an entirely different code of ethics" and scorned to defend his "righteous title" by acquiring "a felonious possession." When asked whether he thought that there was evidence that the Returning Boards were bought, he replied, "I think so." Asked to point it out, he said, "McLin of Florida . . .

testified that he gave a false certificate . . . influenced by the promise of office" and was immediately appointed to a judgeship in New Mexico. This assertion was doubted and Tilden called for the record. After examining it, Hiscock dropped the subject. Then Tilden flared up: "Now, gentlemen, I believe that I am competent to be the custodian of my own honor. . . . You have been pursuing a course of examination . . . to ascribe to me some failure of duty, and you have intruded yourself into my domestic and family relations."

He had received a terrible grilling, but he came through the ordeal with his honor unimpeached. The best men in both parties were now satisfied that he had not used his wealth to buy the election.

Four days after Tilden gave his testimony, Bigelow found him "in a state of unusual irritability." President Ellis of the Third National Bank had asserted that the day before Weed's departure for the South he had held an hour's conversation with Tilden in the bank. If true, that would convict both Tilden and Weed of perjury. Tilden sent for Weed, and, after checking up on their movements, discovered that neither one was in the bank on the day mentioned. Tilden drove to the bank and presented the proofs to Ellis, who publicly acknowledged his mistake. This incident illustrates Tilden's foresight. For years he kept the files of all the newspapers. With his staff of clerks he was able to recall his activities on the day in question and present a complete record of his activities. Since the election he had also employed several eminent and costly lawyers to defend himself against the persecutions of his political adversaries.[16]

Democrats who disliked Tilden's reform program smiled with satisfaction at his discomfiture, but his friends were not slow to praise his courage. "I am delighted with your speech," wrote Hewitt, who had been present; "you never did better."[17] Others congratulated him for refuting "the slanderers" like a statesman and gentleman. "Let us hope that the bucket of political swill is almost empty."[18] John Kelly's comment would not look well in print.

Manton Marble, Smith M. Weed, and Colonel W. T. Pelton were also examined in New York City. Marble was exceedingly guarded in his admissions and insisted that the messages he signed were sent out merely as "danger signals";[19] but his reputation was badly scotched.

---

[16] Bigelow's *Diary*, quoted in *Life*, II, 220, 221.
[17] Tilden Papers, Jan. 25, 1879.   [18] *Ib.*, A. S. Southworth.
[19] H. R. Misc. Doc. No. 31, 45th Cong., 3rd Sess., IV, 114–166.

Weed did not deny the essential charges against him, but justified his acts on the flimsy excuse that he was seeking to recover "stolen goods from thieves." Both had defective memories and revealed ignorance of the keys to the telegrams. They agreed that Tilden was not a party to their own wickedness and was entirely innocent of what transpired.[20]

Next to the testimony of Tilden, that of his nephew attracted most attention. If Tilden was the hero, Pelton was the black sheep. Hesitant and perplexed, he replied in a "loud, hard, and rather grating voice" and "jumbled his words." He sat easily with his legs crossed, "picking his teeth . . . blinking his hard eyes" as he kept looking at the telegrams in his hands. When Reed and Hiscock gave him a merciless cross-examination his voice sank very low. He acknowledged having charge of the funds of the Democratic National Committee and sending the incriminating telegrams, but emphatically denied that his uncle knew anything about them. As a result he stood disgraced before both the public and Tilden. The press was unmerciful in its condemnation of Pelton for his efforts at corruption and for his deceit. Tilden denied him his home, but gave him an allowance. His last days were spent in dissipation. Tilden went to see him at the Everett House before he died on July 8, 1880, and made peace with him.[21]

One who cares to study the efforts of the Potter Committee to settle a second time what had been once decided, may spend many hours over the 3,000 printed pages of the report. It reveals a disgraceful chapter in American political history. Montgomery Blair urged Potter to make the report purely political—not to get new laws but to get justice; and to make the question the issue in 1880. As a matter of fact, the report was submitted to Tilden for corrections up to the last minute before its presentation. He in turn asked J. S. Black to help Potter with his "forceful logic and masterly statement of conclusions." Whitney was also consulted and presented a "résumé" which Hewitt and others thought should not be included. "I am spending the Sabbath," Potter wrote Whitney, "in digging out the ox of a cipher. . . . General Haton's key being out of town makes this the more difficult." [22] The report left neither party blameless, but was decidedly favorable to Tilden. General B. F. Butler's minority report also turned

---

[20] Haworth, 166–221, 221–272, 324.
[21] Mrs. G. W. Smith, Ms. Notes; see *Saturday Evening Post*, May 3, 1919; *Retrospections*, V, 402.
[22] Tilden Papers.

the scales in Tilden's behalf. But when they gained control of both Houses of Congress in 1879, the Democrats themselves refused to re-open the question of unseating Hayes. Indeed, the two partisan reports were intended merely as the preliminary bout in the campaign of 1880.[23]

As a result of the cipher telegrams the Republicans won an advantage which probably gave them the national election of 1880. Much of the public became convinced that the millionaire candidate for the Presidency had permitted his party directors to dip into his purse to win a decision for the party that was willing to pay the highest price. Thurlow Weed believed that the messages rendered Tilden's "complicity beyond doubt or question." [24] Some Democrats were likewise persuaded of Tilden's guilt. Dorsheimer wrote to Kernan:

> "This exposure with regard to Tilden sickens me. What do you propose to do? You and I both pledged ourselves for him, not only as to his success but as to his character and honor. I feel mortified and ashamed to a degree I cannot express. Where and when can I see you? I feel that the party as a whole through its committee, and you and I on our own account, should do what the case requires if it is possible. Tilden was a party to these disgraceful proceedings." [25]

After the publication of the messages W. H. Barnum summoned Democratic leaders to a conference in New York City, where they decided to divert attention from the dispatches to the issues of the political campaigns in the various States. William Purcell, State Chairman of New York, and Augustus Schell were expected to carry out this plan in the Empire State.[26]

Tilden's Democratic friends held that he had emerged from the trying ordeal unscathed, while on the other hand it had been proved that the Returning Boards of doubtful States might have been purchased for amounts that would have been but a drop in the bucket for him. Yet not a single elector was bought by the Democrats—Hayes got all the votes and rewarded the manipulators with office. Republicans denied that the Returning Boards were for sale; that Tilden's agents failed to buy them not because of reluctance to commit an immoral act but because they could not get them; that Tilden had used one of the ciphers in his business; that he continued on confi-

23 An. Cyc., 1878, 712.   24 Barnes, Weed, II, 546.
25 Kernan Papers, Oct. 11, 1878.   26 Ib., Oct. 21, 1878.

dential terms with Pelton, Weed and Marble after the exposure; and that, though personally guiltless of attempting bribery, still he was responsible to an extent for the acts of his managers. The general effect, therefore, was to cast a shadow over Tilden's leadership as a great reformer. Even Bigelow thought that the ciphers connected "so many persons more or less near to Tilden with plans to purchase votes of electors as to place his renomination in some uncertainty." [27] And Hewitt, who had urged Tilden's re-election "even if he had to be carried to the White House in his coffin," now questioned his availability in 1880.[28]

For Tilden it never rained but it poured; his troubles never came singly. He might regard himself as President-elect, but his party foes were determined not only to cloud that title but to close every avenue for acquiring any other. His relatives added to his difficulties instead of alleviating them. "The poor man was tried without end." [29] Pelton had dabbled in Elevated Railroad and Erie Railroad stocks, possibly in Tilden's name, and the latter was called upon to make his promises good. To get his brother Henry and Pelton out of financial difficulty, Tilden was forced to pay a guarantee of between $50,000 and $75,000. Henry, in a complaining mood, said Pelton owed him $10,000, thought Hayes should give Pelton a first-class mission because "he did so much to put him where he is," vowed to devote the rest of his days to his own affairs and "not to politics or to politicians," and declared he had attended his last convention.[30] If Henry had included a resolve not to ask Samuel for any further financial assistance, the latter would have uttered a hearty "Amen."

Many were the annoyances of this period of Tilden's life, but the worst was that connected with his income tax. The effort of his political foes to discredit him for having evaded his obligation to the Federal Government during the Civil War and later was launched for purely political purposes, and was nursed along for nearly six years as a painful thorn in Tilden's flesh. During all that time it was excellent propaganda for Republicans and hostile Democrats alike, and was used with telling effect. As has been seen, the charge was used in the campaign of 1876 and was not allowed to rest after the inauguration of Hayes. Colonel George Bliss began a suit shortly after the elec-

[27] Retrospections, V, 397.   [28] Nevins, Hewitt, 399.
[29] Retrospections, V, 402; March 21, 1879.
[30] Tilden Papers, Henry A. Tilden to G. W. Smith, June 5, 1879.

tion, partly for political reasons and partly because he honestly believed that Tilden had evaded his tax. Considerable publicity was given to the case, and it was prolonged several years without any serious effort to bring it to an issue. During the sessions of the Electoral Commission a writ of *capias* was served on Tilden, demanding $150,000 as back taxes and penalties; and on April 14, 1877, the complaint was filed giving details on which the claim was based—details gleaned by "roaming commissions" in Boston, Pittsburgh, Chicago, and Marquette.[31]

Tilden came home from Europe in October, 1877, to dispose of the case and prepared long "Memoranda" for his counsel. These attorneys, Charles F. Stone, Thomas Harland, A. J. Vanderpoel, and James Emott, prepared a lengthy defense, maintaining that he had made returns and paid the taxes levied by the assessor.[32] The Federal Government answered the demurrer, and an assessor of 1863 testified that Tilden refused to fill out a blank or answer questions because he declared the income tax unconstitutional.[33] Judge Blatchford, "sometimes a judge but always a politician," decided against the demurrer. Tilden then determined to have the Supreme Court review the case, but was told that judgment must first be given in an inferior court.

For assistance in this annoying case it was natural that Tilden should turn to his lifelong friend, Charles O'Conor. In March, 1879, he sent O'Conor a substantial retainer to handle the defense, but O'Conor promptly returned it with the curt comment, "I never accept retainers." Tilden then sent him a succinct statement of the issues involved on which he desired advice and enclosed the government's Bill of Discovery for filing in the U.S. Circuit Court. O'Conor wanted all the papers in the case but Tilden insisted upon an opinion as to whether, if a plea were made on the Bill of Discovery and it were overruled, the decision would constitute an action appealable to the Supreme Court.[34] The case was not one to O'Conor's liking, but he did give the opinion desired. In the end, however, the defense was transferred to the firm of Vanderpoel, Green and Cuming.[35]

Meanwhile the prosecution was not idle. W. P. Healy of Marquette, Michigan, was gathering data for a trial in May, 1879, and Federal

[31] *Life*, II, 231, 236, 239.
[32] "Points for Defendant on his Demurrer," 64 pp., and "Additional Points," 27 pp.
[33] *Mail and Express*, June 25, 1894.   [34] *Letters*, II, 584–586.
[35] *Life*, II, 237.

agents were examining the records of numerous railroads to find proof of guilt.

The Bill of Discovery, prepared under Stewart L. Woodford, alleged that for 1862–71 Tilden was indebted to the Federal Government more than $5,000 for income taxes, that the returns for 1862–63 were not true statements, and that no returns were made for 1864–71. The court was requested to compel Tilden to answer 472 questions.

Thomas Harland informed Tilden on August 14, 1879, that the Federal attorneys, Hill and Herrick, refused to suspend the taking of depositions until a decision was reached on the Bill of Discovery, and said that they would be ready for trial in November. However, Harland was confident that the Government would not really be ready at that time. "Webster tells us that they have no evidence at all," he reported, but they might call Tilden as the principal witness. Hill spent three days in Boston trying to get witnesses to the Union Pacific vouchers, but did not succeed. "I think we'd better put the case on the November calendar and oppose delay—it may force them to drop the case." Then he asked Tilden to have his secretary send him a check for $250. W. O. Bartlett's receipt for $25,000 in full for professional services was given on March 3, 1880. By this time many persons agreed with R. B. Roosevelt, who exclaimed, "The income Tax case is outrageous . . . deceives the people . . . and is kept going by the Republican press. . . . Why not get a list of Republican delinquents?" [36]

In 1881 Tilden seems to have appealed to W. C. Whitney to negotiate for the services of Elihu Root in the Income Tax case for October 27, Whitney wrote:

"Dear Governor:
I have arranged with Mr. Root for a retainer of $1,000 which will be satisfactory and if you give him a check for that amount it will be right." [37]

After receiving this information, Tilden invited Root to visit him at Graystone. Root called, formal greetings were exchanged, and after a discussion of a few commonplace matters, Tilden whispered to his secretary, who disappeared and returned with the check. This Mr. Tilden took and placed in the hand of Root saying, "This is your retainer; you are now pledged to secrecy." Then he proceeded to explain

---

[36] Tilden Papers, Mar. 3, 1880.   [37] Tilden Papers.

the details of the case at great length, showing him the documents relating to it. The greater part of the day was consumed in a discussion of the points involved. Tilden never did things by halves. While Root's name does not appear in the surviving data on the case, no doubt he gave valuable advice which led to an eventual settlement.[38] After a visit to Washington for the purpose of consulting the authorities about compromising the case, J. S. Black made a none too favorable report.

On December 3, 1881, five years after suit had been instituted, A. J. Vanderpoel, Tilden's counsel, renewed the suggestion that the United States discontinue the action on the promise of his client's paying costs.[39] Four months later Tilden again offered to pay expenses, Government counsel fees, and a tax on an assessed income of $15,000 a year. At length, on October 11, 1882, Edwards Pierrepont, special counsel for the United States, in a recommendation to Attorney General Phillips, gave hope that the case might be dismissed on payment of costs not to exceed $15,000. He called at Gramercy Park to discuss the matter with Tilden. Pierrepont and General Woodford, Federal District Attorney, both advised President Garfield "that the action ought to be dismissed" because it was the "only one in the entire United States which has been prosecuted."

After the red herring had been dragged around for years for political purposes, on October 23, 1882, the Government, by an order of the Circuit Court of the United States for the Southern District of New York, ordered the case "discontinued without costs to either party as against the other." [40] Thus ended one of the most notorious political cases in American history.

Altogether it cost Tilden a small fortune to settle his Income Tax suit with the Federal Government. Smith M. Weed wrote Bigelow that Tilden had to pay $45,350 to "be released from the fangs of these harpies." The firm of Whitney & Barnum on Tilden's behalf paid to G. R. Raum, Commissioner of Internal Revenue, $5,000, and to counsel for the Government: Garfield $5,000 and Edwards Pierrepont $10,000. Tilden paid Vanderpoel, Green and Cummings for services $10,-660.22.[41]

Notwithstanding such thorns, Tilden found life on the whole during

[38] Report of interview by Allan Nevins with Elihu Root.
[39] *Life*, II, 237, to Hon. Edwards Pierrepont, special counsel.
[40] *Ib.*, 239, 259.
[41] Tilden Papers, Jan. 29, 1883.

1878 and 1879 fairly pleasant, and had more leisure for books, pictures, and friends than at any time during the previous twenty years. His last downtown law office was at 20 Nassau Street. Although his legal business had largely been delegated to others, he was seen there frequently to direct matters of importance. When he discontinued his business he left his law library to Judge Charles F. MacLean, who later claimed the books as a gift and was permitted by Tilden's executors to keep them.[42] Until 1879 Tilden lived at 15 Gramercy Park, but in that year bought the adjoining house at No. 14 and had the two remodeled into one building. There he lived with his sister, Mrs. Mary B. Pelton, and for much of the time Andrew H. Green, his crony for many years. Colonel William T. Pelton's wife and daughter were also members of his household. He employed a valet, a butler, a maid for Mrs. Pelton, and five household servants. The additional space was used for his library, now greatly augmented. His private secretary and his wife, Mr. and Mrs. G. W. Smith, also resided at 14 Gramercy Park until 1879. Among the interior decorations were marble busts of Cicero, Cromwell, and Tilden by the sculptor Kitzen. He had a stairway constructed from his bedroom in number 15 to his valet's room in number 14; but there was no "secret stairway" leading into the basement through which politicians and unchaperoned women might come and go unseen.[43] Tilden lived the life of a cultured man of wealth, enjoying his books and callers, going out to a social gathering occasionally, and entertaining friends at luncheon or at a formal dinner.

[42] Mrs. G. W. Smith, Ms. Notes.
[43] Building sold to National Arts Club.

DURING the spring of 1879, with the hope of improving his health, Tilden began to look about for a summer home. It was his intention to spend the warm months amid quiet rural surroundings and to occupy his Gramercy Park house only during the severe winter months. Learning that John T. Waring's splendid estate overlooking the Hudson at Yonkers was for sale, he instructed his agent to get a refusal of the property. The furniture, he thought, might be obtained for $15,-100—perhaps less.[1] For the stone mansion, outbuildings, gardens and 63⅓ acres, the owner had spent $327,000. Tilden and Bigelow visited the place on July 11 and were so favorably impressed that Tilden leased it, with an option for purchase, and before the lease expired bought it for $150,000.[2] Soon 48 adjoining acres were added, at a cost of $78,000, and more than $166,000 was expended in improvements, making the total outlay $394,000.

To this country home, only three miles from New York City, he removed his household and a portion of his well-stocked library. He quickly became attached to Graystone [3] and greatly enjoyed the spacious mansion, the beautiful grounds, and above all the quiet seclusion he did not have in the metropolis. The rôle of a country squire, entertaining relatives and friends with a "generous hospitality," brought improved health and a keen satisfaction.

Tilden took his life as a gentleman farmer as seriously as he did everything else. At a cost of $5,450 he imported a cow from the Isle of Jersey and a bull from Guernsey. Among his pedigreed cattle was another bull which came to him with the name of "Dido," causing him considerable amusement—and some trouble in having the name changed. With much pride he loaned "Dido" for exhibition at the Hudson fair and other places. His cows were given such fancy names as "Lady Elise" and "Marie Celeste," the latter after a favorite friend in New Orleans. Nor did he ever fail to show his visitors his Sago palm,

---

[1] Tilden Papers. Mr. Trevor of Yonkers was his agent. June 6, 1879.

[2] *Retrospections,* V, 410.

[3] G. W. Smith explained that John T. Waring spelled the name "Greystone" but Tilden changed it to "Graystone" by which name it has since been known.

which was 200 years old and had formerly belonged to George Washington.

The citizens of Yonkers gave this eminent statesman a cordial welcome. William Allen Butler expressed delight at having him as a neighbor in "the most desirable suburb of New York" and predicted that the "semi-country life" would greatly improve his health. "The life I am leading," he wrote, "with outdoor exercise and physical activity alternated with rest, has left me little time for correspondence after I get through with other calls upon my attention." [4] The removal to Graystone probably prolonged Tilden's life by several years and brought him many joys which would not have been his in the city.

When Tilden took up his residence at Graystone he was wont to say that he no longer assumed responsibility for the leadership of the Democratic Party and had no time for anything except "the burden of private business." [5] But he was unable to escape. Members of his party were determined to regard him as the real leader, both in the State and nation. He regarded himself as President-elect but excluded by fraud from the office. His followers continued to address him as President and public resolutions made the same designation. His opinions were sought on public questions and given generously—with reservations. Invitations to address public gatherings were politely refused, usually with comments intended to be read and given to the press. In his semi-retirement the Sage of Graystone was a more commanding figure in politics than he had been as Governor.

Politically the year 1879 in New York was important. A Governor was to be chosen, and, since the following year would witness the election of a President, the eyes of the nation were on the Empire State. Lester B. Faulkner, Chairman, and young Dan S. Lamont, clerk, of the Democratic State Committee looked to Tilden for suggestions. The outlook was none too favorable, for the legislature was Republican and Conkling had been re-elected United States Senator. The Democratic Party was split into two factions—one led by John Kelly, Tammany, and the remnants of the upstate Canal Ring; the other following Tilden and Lucius Robinson. This breach between Tilden and Kelly attracted nation-wide attention, for a feeling prevailed that the election of 1880 would turn upon the vote of the Empire State. Tilden's friends did not conceal their perturbation. Robert B. Roosevelt, who was ever-

[4] *Letters*, II, 577, 586.   [5] Tilden Papers, to E. R. Mead, Feb. 20, 1879.

lastingly importuning Tilden to have him named to "a foreign mission," warned: "Kelly never forgives. . . . Ely says he is a wonderful dissembler and hypocrite. . . . He hates you as the Devil hates holy water. . . . One good push will tumble him out of Heaven and power."

The most important problem was the selection of a candidate for Governor—if possible one who could harmonize the two factions. Some of Tilden's most ardent admirers believed he should be drafted for that office. But he did "not think it fit to run for Governor" for three reasons: first, because of his health; second, because as President-elect he could not accept the Governorship; and third, because he was pledged to support Governor Robinson.[6] As early as June, Robinson was "anxious and determined" to have a renomination, and Tilden was told that a hint from him that Robinson should not run would "be ill received and do harm." [7] But Tilden's customary caution about an early commitment encouraged considerable opposition to Robinson's candidacy.

As usual, other aspirants bobbed up to complicate the situation. S. E. Church was willing to be a candidate and wrote Kernan, "I have tried through mutual friends to get Tilden to consent to some fair thing." He believed he could reconcile the two warring factions in the party.[8] Dorsheimer was also hoping that the political lightning would strike him. Hurlbut and others strongly favored Robinson. But John Kelly with his Tammany backers and his rule or ruin policy went to the Democratic State Convention at Syracuse on September 11—eight days after the Republicans had nominated A. B. Cornell—determined to thwart Robinson and Tilden. After a platform had been adopted, Augustus Schell declared that Tammany would not support the renomination of Robinson and with his followers marched out of the hall. Under the chairmanship of D. D. Field, the Tammany delegates then nominated Kelly for Governor by acclamation. The regulars renominated Robinson.[9]

Kelly's bolt created a national sensation. Some Democrats wished to attack Kelly in the press; others urged Tilden to have one or both candidates resign. Springer of Illinois advised Tilden: "Let Robinson decline . . . and Kelly will follow. . . . Then let Potter be nomi-

[6] *Letters*, II, 586.   [7] Tilden Papers, E. K. Apgar, June 9, 1879.
[8] Kernan Papers, Church to Kernan, Sept. 5, 1879.   [9] Alexander, III, 416–424.

nated . . . and you will get the credit. . . . You must now assume the command of our party in New York and save the State and nation from Republican rule. . . . Then we shall have victory this fall and in 1880"—and you would show that you can carry your State.[10] McClernand thought the "diseased members of the party have fallen off" but would repent and return. The defection of the egotistic Dorsheimer was no surprise. Tilden was advised to force Senator Kernan to come out for Robinson.[11] Republican journals praised Kelly, and Republican "Scratchers," led by Curtis, refused to vote for Cornell because of his mismanagement of the New York customhouse. Conkling was silent on the State ticket and there was talk of a secret bargain between Kelly and Cornell. Kelly's speeches denouncing the "old humbug of Cipher alley" and "Sore eyes" Robinson were applauded by Republicans, but pronounced "failures" by the *World*.[12]

Although Kelly's plan was to defeat only the head of the ticket, every Democrat, except C. S. Fairchild, the nephew of Horatio Seymour, was slaughtered by his 77,566 votes. The Republican victory was charged by some to a decline in the popularity of Tilden, who took little part in the campaign. But he emphatically asserted that the "dissension" of 1879 "cannot be continued or repeated in 1880." [13] Robinson's defeat was laid at the door of Field, Schell, and Dorsheimer as well as Kelly. Montgomery Blair informed Tilden that Kelly had been aided by hostile Southern Democrats and was "the tool of the man who sold us out in 1876–77 . . . but we can fix things by 1880." The Tilden column had "wavered just a bit after the election but is stronger again now." He wanted the *Sun* and *Argus* to "hit the Kelly traitors. . . . You are too mild with them. . . . Speak out in your own way." [14]

After the defeat of 1879 Tilden began to express doubt as to whether he should be a candidate for renomination for the Presidency in 1880. From the moment it became evident that he would not be seated in the White House, his party friends assured him that four years later the people would make certain of his vindication. There can be no doubt that Tilden himself wished to prove by his re-election that the country had been fraudulently deprived of its selection in 1876,[15] but he made no open campaign for the honor. Because of his reticence

[10] Tilden Papers, Sept. 12, 1879.   [11] *Ib.*, Magone, Sept. 22, 1879.
[12] Oct. 11, 14, 16, 17, 1879.   [13] *Letters*, II, 594.
[14] Tilden Papers, Nov. 19, 1879, Jan. 22, 1880.   [15] *Life*, II, 264.

the newspapers kept alive a rumor that he would not be a candidate. In consequence, thousands of letters from individuals and organizations all over the land begged him not to withdraw and declared that his re-election would be indisputable. One admirer wrote, "Democrats owe you more than any other living man. . . . The young men hold you in their hearts as the real leader. . . . You can name the man in 1880. . . . We must put down the Zach Chandler-Hayes-Mexican manner of making Presidents." [16] Reports of Tilden's hesitation brought appeals not to desert the ship. "You should take the candidacy even if you should resign the day after your election." [17]

As months passed without any positive announcement by Tilden of his candidacy, the Democratic newspapers seemed bent on drafting him for the race. The Baltimore *Telegram* kept Tilden's name at the head of the ticket from 1876 to 1880.[18] The New York *Sun* printed a series of articles by J. S. Black defending Tilden's title, while Dana's editorials kept him before the public eye. Indiana papers, believing that Tilden would carry New York, declared that he would be the strongest candidate in that state.[19] In California 75% of the voters were reported for him. After a careful survey S. J. Randall and others assured Tilden that the entire South would support him.[20] Wisconsin was advocating Tilden and Hendricks. Although Dan Magone was uncertain of Kelly, he was positive that Tilden would carry New York. The old political sage, Thurlow Weed, believed Tilden would be more popular than Grant.[21] Nearly every mail brought admonitions like "Stick! Stick! Stick!" "Falter not." "I endorse your paper in blank— you fill it in." [22]

Obsessed with the idea that the railroad interests and great corporations defeated Tilden in 1876, no man worked harder for his renomination than Montgomery Blair. To men all over the land he wrote that Tilden alone could bring victory to the party in 1880, and by December of 1879 he was convinced that Tilden would win. In close touch with Bigelow and other supporters, he was promised funds to subsidize newspapers in Tilden's interest. When Bigelow informed him that Tilden would not run, Blair refused to believe it and worked all

---

[16] Tilden Papers, J. M. Scovill, Nov. 19, 1879.
[17] *Ib.*, Montgomery Blair, Jan. 2 1880.
[18] Tilden Papers, M. Blair, Apr. 5, 1879.   [19] Tilden Papers.
[20] *Ib.*, numerous letters.   [21] Barnes, *Thurlow Weed*, II, 546.
[22] Tilden Papers.

the harder. He won over Greenbackers like Cary of Ohio, and had the
Maryland legislature pass a resolution authorizing the State Attorney
General to institute action before the Supreme Court to induce that
body to declare the decision of the Electoral Commission void and to
seat Tilden.[23]

Tilden's reticence was offset by the loquacity of Bigelow, who took
it upon himself to explain just what his illustrious mentor's attitude
was. Typical of many communications was his letter to an inquiry
from Michigan as to whether Tilden would "be in the field for the
Presidency in 1880." He replied that no one, not even Tilden himself,
could answer positively. As President-elect and hence "clothed with
certain responsibilities to his party" he was like a victorious commander who had defeated the enemy but had not yet realized the fruits
of his triumph. He could not desert his soldiers before the foe without
a leader. The Republicans were trying to drive him out of public life
by defaming his character and by persecution. He "could easily accommodate himself to the choice of any good man for the Presidency,"
but he would not make the slightest concession involving his personal
honor. To take another candidate would be an admission that he was
not elected in 1876, and that the charge of his attempt to buy electoral
votes was true. These calumnies would strengthen his candidacy but
would be fatal to any other nominee. "It is, therefore, a vital necessity
for the party to vindicate itself no less than Tilden." [24]

When this letter was shown to Tilden he said that the time had not
"yet come" to send it.[25] Seven months later, when invited to address a
mass meeting in Baltimore, while not revealing his own intention,
Tilden did declare that the issue "created by the subversion of the
election of 1876 was the most transcendent in our history." This reversal of the votes of the people, if successful, will be "fatal to the system of elective government . . . and every effort of the people to
change the administration will be nullified. The government, elective
in form, would become imperial in substance precisely as did that of
Rome. Such an issue, involving the very existence of our free government, is not to be belittled into a personal grievance—it is to be dealt
with as a great public cause." [26]

Up to the spring of 1880 Bigelow's shrewd interpretation of the

[23] Smith, *Blair Family*, II, 486–491.   [24] *Letters*, II, 578.
[25] Tilden Papers. Note on the original.
[26] *Letters*, II, 587, to John Gill, Jr., Sept. 27, 1879.

logic of events seems to have been accepted by Tilden. Bigelow wrote in his *Diary* May 12, 1880, "Mr. Tilden has finally determined, I believe, to be a candidate for the Presidency." Tilden, however, kept his own counsel and made confidants of few if any. There were times when he expressed doubts whether he was physically equal to the terrific drain on his strength which a campaign would entail. In preparing an annoying law case with Bigelow's help, he found himself confused and unable to concentrate. Vexed by this manifestation of old age, he said, "Let us go and take a ride." After a long silence, he spoke of the decline of his intellectual vigor and physical endurance, and in a "querulous tone" exploded, "If I am no longer fit to prepare a case for trial, I am not fit to be President of the United States." Then he looked at his companion as if he expected an earnest contradiction.[27] Bigelow replied, "No one has a right to ask you to accept such a burden at the risk of your life, and there is no use to disguise the fact that there is nothing that would more imperil your health than the inevitable excitement of a canvass for the Presidency and the first six months' service to which an election would expose you." At that time, Bigelow believed, Tilden was convinced that he did not wish to be a candidate. "It takes all my time to live," Tilden reflected, irritated by all the hygienic precautions imposed upon him by his physicians.[28]

The lawsuit mentioned above was one brought against Tilden and other officials of the Terre Haute & Alton Railroad by investing stockholders who alleged that they had lost $400,000. Tilden felt that the claim was unjust and that he was certain to win the suit if he could prepare the case, but he lacked the strength requisite to assemble and organize the data, and it was "fretting the life out of him." Bigelow advised him to settle the suit regardless of cost, and he paid $100,000 to compromise the claims and thus avoid the notoriety of a public trial. About the same time the income tax suit was set for trial and this so "completely unsettled him for several weeks" that his friends feared that the continued excitement "would soon destroy him." [29]

Notwithstanding Tilden's ill health, he postponed a public decision about his candidacy. This silence was interpreted as assent by his Democratic supporters, who in person and by letter told him that he alone could hold the party as a unit. Democratic newspapers generally refused to mention any other candidate. Some found their loyalty severely

[27] *Letters*, II, 597, 598.   [28] *Life*, II, 265.   [29] *Letters*, II, 598.

tested by his noncommittal attitude, and wanted him to take an emphatic stand. For example, J. Proctor Knott wrote, "The party expects Mr. Tilden to come to the front, or make up his mind to occupy a quiet position in the rear rank for the future." The general feeling is "that his indisposition to take bold and decided grounds at the proper time was mainly the cause of our being robbed of the fruits of the victory we had won." If he refused to direct the party, Democrats would look for a new leader.[30] Seymour was reported as thinking less of Tilden as a candidate than he once did. Watterson found the "politicians of the South against our ticket," but never doubted Tilden's "staying and wearing qualities." [31] Bayard and Thurman were sulking in their tents. Hendricks and his friends were bitter and would stop at nothing. Kelly's hostility was not taken seriously and many thought it would help more than it would hurt Tilden. Since these anti-Tilden sentiments were sporadic and not a part of any concerted movement, they received little consideration. Tilden himself knew that the party was fairly solidly behind him.

The clamor against Tilden came not from Democrats but from fearful Republicans, who used the country press to slander him.[32] One of them wrote: "Tilden is not only dead, but stinks like a rotten corpse. He is not working for himself, I hear, but wants to throw his mantle over Sam Randall." [33] The *Times* continued to assert: "Tildenism is personalism, which is false to Democracy and dangerous to the Republic. . . . The Democratic Party does not want any such moneygrabber, railroad wrecker, and paralytic hypocrite at the helm of the State." [34] A sample of the anti-Tilden Republican literature which covered the country was McLaughlin's *Tilden Memorabilia,* which took as its theme "Keep old men out of the Presidency." He was senile and avaricious; by turning the election of 1876 over to Pelton, Marble, and Weed, he had betrayed Democracy in its triumph. The cipher dispatches were a "monumental infamy." If Tilden himself was not guilty, he "hired others to cheat for him." He is not a great lawyer but merely a "crafty and unscrupulous railroad attorney." So malicious and untrue was this pamphlet that nobody paid any attention to it. But when the New York *Star* announced that Tilden would withdraw

30 Black Papers, Lib. of Cong., Knott to Black, Mar. 14, 1878.
31 Tilden Papers, Jan. 23, 1879.   32 *Ib.,* S. L. Southard.
33 Barnes, Carlisle, 47, Moor to Morrison, Jan. 12, 1880.
34 Apr. 21, 1880.

as a result of a caucus in Washington, many inquirers wanted to know the truth about the canard.[35] The prolongation of the income tax suit was perhaps the most effective bolt the Republicans had in their quiver.

As the early months of 1880 passed and the day of nomination approached, Tilden's silence continued, filling the party leaders with nervous anxiety. The National Executive Committee on February 23 at Washington called the National Convention to meet on June 23 at Cincinnati. The selection of delegates clearly indicated the popular choice. McClernand believed "the old coach stands ready to be hitched to, and that done, a safe and prosperous journey lies ahead." He urged Tilden to "lead the way in a speech . . . that would ring throughout the land." [36] Senator B. H. Hill of Georgia bluntly wrote, "You have no right to deny the Democratic Party the privilege of presenting your name to the people. . . . For three years the Republicans have been laboring to destroy your good name. . . . Certain Democrats aided them in committing the great fraud, and they have been aiding them to destroy you for the same reason. . . . I feel anxious to atone for the wrong I helped to consummate." [37]

The State Democratic Convention at Syracuse on April 20, 1880, was regarded as a decisive factor, for it would indicate whether or not Tilden could carry the Empire State. The Democratic State Committee met in New York City in March and endeavored to "patch up a peace with the Tammany bolters," but without success. The *Nation* discovered that four members of the committee were "unalterably opposed" to Tilden.[38] Many Democrats agreed with D. B. Hill of Elmira that unless the factions in the party were unified the Tilden cause was lost.[39] Tilden alone seemed unconcerned, because his experienced eye saw that as a result of the hard work of his lieutenants he had control of the convention. The wisdom of his noncommittal policy was now demonstrated in an unprecedented rally to force his nomination.

Faulkner called the convention to order, and a roll call to test the character of the Committee on Credentials revealed 295 votes for Tilden and only 80 against him. John Kelly opened his eyes with surprise. In 1876 the reform Governor had mustered only 201 out of 375 votes; now he was stronger than ever.[40] The convention refused the overtures

---

[35] Tilden Papers, Charles Howard, Apr. 5, 1880.   [36] *Letters*, II, 590.
[37] *Ib.*, 595.   [38] Apr. 1, 1880, 244.
[39] Tilden Papers, to Manning, Apr. 14, 1880.
[40] Alexander, III, 449.

of the Kelly faction for party harmony, endorsed the principles set forth at St. Louis in 1876, declared the "momentous issue" to be the vindication of the "right of the people to exercise . . . an elective self-government without . . . fraud or force"; vowed that the "odius crime of 1876" must be destroyed; and asserted that the party continued to feel "confidence in the character, fitness, and ability of that distinguished citizen of New York" who had been defrauded of the Presidency. Four delegates at large were chosen—Faulkner, Robinson, Pratt and Peckham. Then came the master stroke which manacled the Kelly delegates. It was voted that the New York delegation should vote as a unit and that any delegates refusing to do so would lose their seats.[41] Despite the alleged "senility and decrepitude" of Tilden, the *Nation* believed that he had helped to draft this iron-clad provision.[42]

Moved by anger and chagrin, the Kelly Tammanyites held their own rump convention in New York City over which chameleon Dorsheimer presided as temporary and Amasa J. Parker as permanent chairman. They declared that the deplorable schism had resulted "almost solely from the determined and persistent efforts of one man to secure the Democratic nomination to the Presidency," that he was responsible for the defeat of 1878 in New York City and of 1879 in the State, that he had degraded the party into a machine run for one man and his followers, and that he was unfit for the Presidency and his election would be a national calamity.[43] Tammany delegates were then chosen, and Kelly vowed that he would stab Tilden as he had stabbed Robinson. "Tilden," said he, "was elected by the votes of the people, and he had not sufficient courage after he was elected to go forward, as a brave man should go forward, and say to the people of the country, 'I have been elected by the votes of the people, and you see to it that I am inaugurated.'"

Hewitt and other Democrats felt outraged at this defection of Kelly and his determination to defeat Tilden and to ruin the party harmony.[44] But Tilden's hand was on the party engine, whether he had in mind his own nomination or that of someone designated by him. It is difficult to say how much influence this split in the Democratic Party in New York had on Tilden's final decision—less perhaps than has been supposed. Sphinxlike, he still kept his purposes to himself. He knew

[41] *An. Cyc.*, 1880, 574.   [42] Apr. 21, 1880.   [43] *Times*, Apr. 21, 1880.
[44] Nevins, *Hewitt*, 435.

that he could carry New York; he believed that he could be nominated; he was convinced that the people would re-elect him; and he had not for an instant lost sight of the significance of the contest of 1880. But one thing caused him to hesitate—his health. Could he afford to pay the price? He could not make up his mind—and meanwhile his secretary was sending out to men like Dan Magone and Tom Spratt the old county lists, in order to have new rosters made of those who were trustworthy and zealous—at least ten or fifteen in each district—for publicity purposes.[45] Ambitious young Democrats like Alton B. Parker soon informed him that the lists were completed. There is evidence likewise in Tilden's canceled checks that he was making liberal contributions for party purposes both in New York and nationally.

Few statesmen of the century could determine more accurately than Tilden the drift of public opinion. The mighty ground swell of denunciation of the Electoral Commission, which he measured with a practiced eye, reinforced his conviction that in 1880 he could sweep the country. There is no doubt that he expected to be the leader of his party, although at no time did he publicly announce his candidacy. Both experience and inherent caution warned him against such a course. Nor was there any need of such action. On all sides it was admitted that Tilden alone could win a Democratic victory.

It was a difficult decision that confronted Tilden in June, 1880. To run, and thereby put his life in jeopardy; or not to run, and thus see his party lose the first chance of a real victory in nearly a quarter of a century—that was the question. Had he been younger or stronger, there would have been but one answer. No one doubted that he could have the honor of the nomination, and few that the people would elect him.

[45] Tilden Papers, Mar. 17, 1879.

THE decision which Tilden realized he would have to make in 1880 was postponed to the very last. What that decision was to be could only be guessed by those who professed to know Tilden's mind. Every effort to elicit some positive statement was met with evasion or an ambiguous reply. G. L. Miller, a staunch political friend for years, walked with him for hours in a fruitless effort to obtain a decision.[1] Before sailing for Europe, J. S. Black called on Tilden [2] to obtain letters of introduction and asked categorically whether he would be a candidate. He received the evasive reply: "I take no part in the matter. I hold myself perfectly free." No wonder that W. C. Whitney spoke of the situation as "muddled" and explained:

"One of the peculiar weaknesses of Mr. Tilden as a political leader is that he gives his whole confidence to no one, not even to those on whom he must rely for the execution of his plans. He has reserves in everything he says and he expects his supporters to guess his intention. And if we do not guess accurately, he is angry. He lost the Presidential seat by just such methods. By withholding his confidence from those who represented his interest in Washington he weakened them with Democratic Senators and Congressmen who at first were willing, if not anxious, to submit to their lead." [3]

The New York *Herald* editorially urged that if Tilden were a candidate, he should say so. Seymour had declined with an emphatic negative; but "Mr. Tilden is incapable of doing the simplest thing without a mask." [4]

While there were many shades of opinion, Democratic leaders in general were divided into three groups. In the first class were those like Manning, Blair, Bigelow, Faulkner and Watterson who believed that Tilden really wished to be nominated but would not turn his hand to gain an honor which he felt his party owed him. The rank and file of the party also held this view which was expressed by the New York *Sun,* and by other Democratic papers. Though Hewitt had cooled in his devotion to Tilden and was convinced that his bodily infirmities

---

[1] Smith, *Blair Family,* II, 490.
[2] Black Papers, Library of Cong., Apr. 24, 1880.
[3] Hudson, *Recollections,* 106–108.   [4] June 17, 1880.

"might compel him to decline to be a candidate," yet he testified, "His intellect is unimpaired," and thought he would appreciate a nomination by acclamation. If given, he might be induced to run.[5] A second group were convinced that Tilden did not wish to be the candidate but felt that he should be allowed to dictate the nominee. Conspicuous among these was W. C. Whitney who understood that Tilden had expressed a preference for Henry B. Payne.[6] In this class were also the friends of S. J. Randall who regarded himself as Tilden's political heir. The third group consisted of those who openly opposed Tilden or believed him "unavailable." Three New York Democratic newspapers were hostile. John Kelly proclaimed on all occasions, "With Tilden we cannot win," because he would lose the Republicans who were hostile to Hayes. Independents were uncertain and some Democrats were disgusted over the cipher dispatches. Senator W. M. Gwin gave his support to Judge Stephen J. Field. "Tilden is dead," said Robert Toombs.[7] In this last group were found supporters of Ewing, Thurman, Bayard, Hendricks and Hancock, who said that the Democrats had the strongest issue but the weakest candidate.

Confident of Tilden's nomination, the Western Union Telegraph Company asked permission to put in a wire for his exclusive use.[8] The *Herald* conceded him 184 votes on the first ballot,[9] and *Harper's Weekly* predicted, "There is no reason to doubt that Tilden will receive or control the nomination." Tilden himself opposed the nomination of Thurman, Bayard, Hendricks and Seymour. With his extraordinary ability to interpret public opinion he was aware that a unanimous nomination would be difficult, if not impossible. He did not possess the strength to build up his fences across the land. Some New York delegates were ready to bolt at the first opportunity, and in New Jersey, the South and the Southwest there was open antagonism.

Before the New York delegates set out for Cincinnati, Tilden confided to Manning and Smith M. Weed, his personal representatives, that he was not anxious for the nomination and that, unless it came to him with a unanimity that would insure victory, he would not accept. He also made it clear that in his judgment this would not happen, and therefore he was out of the race. His first choice, he told them,

[5] *Herald*, June 14, 1880; Nevins, *Hewitt*, 435.
[6] Hudson, *Recollections*, 106–108.
[7] *An. Report Am. Hist. Assn.*, 1911, II, 741. Toombs to Stephens, Apr. 25, 1880.
[8] Tilden Papers, June 14, 1880.   [9] June 18, 1880.

was Payne and his second Randall. He would explain his position and his wishes in an explicit letter which his brother Henry would take to Cincinnati a few days later.[10]

This letter to the New York delegates, dated June 18, was to be read at their first meeting. After reviewing the reforms he had accomplished as Governor, Tilden devoted most of his letter to the miscarriage of the peoples' will in 1876–77:

"I was . . . elected to the Presidency absolutely free from any engagement. . . . I did everything in my power to elevate . . . standards. . . . I refused to ransom from the Returning Boards . . . the documentary evidence . . . for the perpetuation of a false count. The constitutional duty of the two Houses . . . was never fulfilled. An Electoral Commission for the existence of which I have no responsibility, was formed. . . . Its false count was not overruled. . . . It counted out the men elected by the people and counted in the men not elected. That subversion . . . involved the vital principle of self-government.

The failure to install the candidates chosen by the people . . . has left me . . . the involuntary but necessary representative of this momentous issue. As such . . . I have steadfastly endeavored to preserve the Democratic Party. . . . The supreme issue is whether this shall be a government by the sovereign people through elections, or a government by discarded servants holding over by force and fraud. And I have withheld no sacrifice . . . to uphold . . . the great party which alone under God can effectually resist their overthrow.

Having now borne faithfully my full share . . . in the public service . . . I desire nothing so much as an honorable discharge. I wish to lay down . . . even *quasi* party leadership, and to seek the repose of private life. In renouncing my renomination . . . it is a renunciation of re-election. . . . To those who think my . . . re-election indispensable to an effectual vindication of the right of the people to elect their own rulers . . . I have accorded as long a reserve of my decision as possible, but I can not overcome my repugnance to enter a new engagement which involves four years of ceaseless toil.

The dignity of the Presidential office is above a merely personal ambition, but it creates in me no illusions. . . . I said four years ago: If summoned by the suffrages of my countrymen to attempt this work, I shall endeavor, with God's help, to be the efficient instrument of their will. Such a work . . . is now, I fear beyond my strength. With unfeigned thanks for the honors bestowed upon me; with a heart swelling with emotions of gratitude to the Democratic masses for the support which they have given to the cause I represented . . . I remain, Your fellow citizen." [11]

[10] *Letters*, II, 598, 601; Alexander, III, 455, states that Manning had the original and Henry only a copy. This was an error. The letter was printed in pamphlet form and widely circulated by Tilden.
[11] *Writings*, II, 501. Printed as a campaign pamphlet.

While Henry A. Tilden was on the way to the Convention with this letter Whitney wired him to ask whether his brother was a candidate, and got this reply, "I don't know." [12]

This letter was written after Tilden had held a series of conferences with Democratic leaders from various States. Many delegates, even from the South, went to Cincinnati by way of New York to have a word with the "Sage of Graystone." At one of these conferences it was decided to print for distribution at the Convention a series of twelve questions that would make Tilden the inevitable candidate. A telegram was sent to Henry B. Payne of Cleveland, Ohio, asking him to accept second place on the ticket with Tilden, and his consent was obtained. F. O. Prince, Secretary of the Democratic National Committee, hurried from New York to Cincinnati and upon arrival stated that Tilden most certainly was a candidate.[13] But New York delegates who arrived on June 17 seemed a bit uncertain about Tilden's acceptance of the nomination.

Such were the conditions under which Tilden's letter was written. What was its real object? Did he honestly wish to withdraw, or was the letter a clever play to force the convention with greater unanimity to draft him for the race? Or, knowing that he was beaten, did he employ this method of saving his dignity and self-respect? The letter was certainly tactful and clever. After reciting his fitness for the high honor, he renounced a renomination and a certainty of election and said he desired "an honorable discharge." John Kelly declared it was a direct bid for the nomination. Had Tilden determined to decline absolutely, quite a different sort of letter would have been written. The evidence seems fairly conclusive that he expected the nomination as a personal vindication and also to strengthen his party in the approaching election; and the letter appeared rather a bid for such an endorsement than a refusal. Once renominated, however, he might use his letter as a pretext to decline the high honor without diminishing his fame or injuring the party, because it would enable him to pick his successor.

Henry A. Tilden, reaching Cincinnati at midnight on Sunday June 20, was met by Smith M. Weed and George C. Green. "Everyone expected a letter" and there was a rush "to know all about it." Henry

[12] Hudson, *Recollections*, 108. See Alexander III, 455, who mistakenly says that Manning took the original.

[13] *Times*, June 16, 18, 1880.

gave the letter to Manning, as instructed, and asked him to present it to the New York delegation but not to make it public until read in the convention. Manning, Weed and Barnum immediately issued a special call to the New York delegates to meet at 10 that same Sunday morning. A permanent organization was effected with Manning as chairman. He informed the delegates of the arrival of Tilden's letter, asked Peckham to read it "and gave it to the press." [14] It produced "a marked effect" and the delegates adjourned until ten the next morning, Monday, June 21, when they voted regret at Tilden's action and decided that New York would not present his name.[15] An editorial in the *Argus,* which must have had Manning's approval, stated positively that Tilden's letter must be accepted as final.

Tilden's brother Henry also understood the letter to mean his self-elimination. "I am glad you are out," he wrote, "now they have no one to grumble about and fight. . . . Those who are against us accept it as final; the moderate men, who have doubted if we could carry the State, want it reserved and not acted upon as final; then there are our friends, who say it shall not be regarded, and must come before the convention for final action." [16] D. S. Lamont wrote that the letter was the "ur :versal topic of conversation"; that it set moving the tide for the 1876 ticket; and that the general disinclination to heed it was growing. Conditions among the delegations were chaotic; the New York delegates were besieged with questions; the feeling against Tammany was bitter; and Tilden possessed "the hearts of the Democracy." Yet there was some disposition to accept New York's lead.[17] The New York *Sun* asserted that Tilden's friends were acting on the hypothesis that he would not be a candidate. Montgomery Blair said: "The withdrawal of Tilden seems to have confounded everybody, friends and foes. It is difficult to get on with him, but I think it will be found more difficult to get on without him." [18]

Comments upon the letter varied. An Illinois delegate wept; a whiskered Missourian said, "Damned if the óld man ain't a trump after all"; Apgar remarked, "Very strong"; McClune, "It will nominate Tilden"; Kingsley, "Able"; Fox, "Glorious—he means what he wrote"; Cooper, "A specious document"; Fellows, "Quite explicit"; and others, "No one can fill his shoes" and, "Sly, devilish sly, sir."

[14] *Letters,* II, 601.   [15] D. S. Lamont in *Argus,* June 21, 1880.
[16] *Letters,* II, 602, H. A. Tilden, June 21, 1880.
[17] Letter to *Argus,* June 21, 1880.   [18] Smith, *Blair Family,* II, 590.

Watterson declared that if he and others had not vehemently protested, Tilden would have written the letter months before.

Henry reported that the sentiment for the "old ticket" was increasing and no one could tell where it would end. Knowing that Tilden's preference for Payne had been wired to Randall, Henry and Manning had decided to "force a fight on Payne." Payne was opposed, however, because of his "Standard Oil connections," and the Brooklyn delegates were urging Pratt, who represented the mining interests. Hughes and Faulkner were "sour" because they had not been "fully consulted." "Hewitt is in"; Green thinks "lightning may strike him"; and, "The Tilden men are cheered and have all the sentiment." In a postscript he asked, "Shall we make a fight for anybody, or wait for developments? Answer, yes or no." [19] In reply Tilden wired Henry, "Do nothing. Don't meddle." [20]

Henry and G. W. Smith had arranged to exchange telegrams under a crude code in which such terms as Oyster, Fish, Cheese, Milk, Pork, Turnips, Flower, Peas and so on were given to prominent men. Tilden was Oyster and Henry signed himself Beans. Quite a number of these telegrams passed back and forth. The following is a sample: "Beef has got a resolution through committee on Oyster admirable and ringing which will be read. Will give me a copy to wire you tonight. Beans." Another ran, "Duck (Kingsly) says they will not go Cheese (Payne). Offers Hewitt privately to Squash (Green) who wants second what next statesman plenty Carrot (McLaughlin) means any one Turnip (Whitney) having a talk with him. I Can't go Duck (Kingsly). All this will turn to Oyster (Tilden) in the end. How are we to act? Answer. Beans." [21] Smith, as Tilden's private secretary, must have consulted him about these messages.

Meanwhile some delegates declared that Tilden had withdrawn in favor of Payne, and others that he had not. One group of Tildenites believed it would be unwise to nominate him under the circumstances, while another boasted, "We count on the absolute support of 305 delegates on the first ballot." When Tilden's letter was printed on June 21, it spread confusion over the nation and was the sole topic of conversation. It was called "Tilden's Valedictory" and the "Pretended Withdrawal."

The convention opened at 12:45 P. M. on June 22, when Barnum,

[19] *Letters*, II, 601–603.   [20] Tilden Papers.   [21] *Ib.*

Chairman of the National Committee, called it to order and presented Judge George Hoadley, Tilden's lifelong friend, as temporary chairman. A reference to Tilden in his short, spirited address brought tumultuous cheering. Lamont wired the *Argus,* "John Kelly received the worst punishment . . . ever dealt out to a politician." He attempted to address the convention but was greeted with hisses as a traitor and shouts of "Sit down!" He turned pale as he listened to demonstrations in Tilden's honor. Everywhere—on the streets, in the hotels and at the clubs—the mention of Tilden's name was the occasion for hurrahing. But Lamont was positive that all discussion as to a nominee was guesswork.

On June 23 the Committee on Credentials reported the exclusion of the Tammany delegates amid great applause. Senator J. W. Stevenson of Kentucky was chosen permanent chairman. He was escorted to the chair at 1:45 P. M. and made a brief but fiery speech with pointed references to the campaign of 1876. Meanwhile the New York delegates held a caucus to decide upon a candidate, and voted 36 to 34 to cast the 70 votes for Payne of Ohio, Tilden's preference.

Nominations were declared in order and as the roll was called California proposed the name of Field; Delaware, Bayard; Illinois, Morrison; Indiana, Hendricks; and Ohio, Thurman. When New York was called there was excited cheering, but the Empire State presented no candidate. Tilden had insisted, perhaps for strategic purposes, that his nomination should come, if at all, from some other State.[22] A telegram confirmed these oral instructions,[23] but his closest friends made no effort to induce another State to nominate him. Pennsylvania had no candidate, but one delegate nominated Hancock, which aroused an unexpectedly enthusiastic endorsement and brought a second from Virginia. The first ballot followed, Hancock receiving 171 votes; Hendricks 49½; Bayard 153½; Tilden 38; Thurman 68½; Field 65; Randall 116; Morrison 62; Payne 81; Ewing 10, McClellan 8 and others those remaining. New York cast her 70 votes for Payne. Tilden's 38 votes came from the following States: Pennsylvania 15; Missouri 7; Kentucky 5; Nevada 3; Massachusetts and Oregon each 2; and Michigan, Mississippi, North Carolina and Rhode Island each 1. There being no nomination, the convention adjourned. Although a majority of the New York delegates were ready to vote for Payne on

[22] *Times,* June 24, 1880.   [23] Tilden Papers.

the second ballot, there was so much feeling that W. C. Whitney, Payne's son-in-law, positively withdrew his name. It was then decided to cast New York's 70 votes for Randall.[24]

During the night the Hancock boom continued to grow. When on June 24 the second ballot was taken, Hancock received 320 votes on the first roll call, but so many changes were being made that a second roll call was ordered. This resulted in 705 votes for the General. Tilden received 6 votes, but 5 of them swung to Hancock, leaving him with a single vote from Iowa. When it was announced that Hancock was the standard bearer, the huge audience of 10,000 stood up to sing "America." At the request of Parker, Schell and Comstock, John Kelly was accorded the platform to promise support to the ticket and to beg for a reconciliation with the regulars. He shook hands with J. R. Fellows as a token of a buried hatchet, and that night the Tammany braves, boasting of the "downfall of the Old Man," serenaded the regulars at the Grand Hotel. William H. English was quickly put on the ticket as Hancock's running mate. Barnum immediately sent news of Hancock's nomination to Tilden who telegraphed Hancock, "I cordially congratulate you on your nomination."

In the midst of the balloting, Manning wired Tilden on June 23, asking whether he would yield to the pressure for his nomination that his letter had stimulated. Bigelow insinuates that this "indiscreet" message was sent for the purpose of eliciting a negative reply, which was the only one that could be given under the circumstances. Tilden's answer was sent the next day, too late to affect the results one way or the other,

"Received your telegrams and many others containing like information. My action was well considered and is irrevocable. No friends must be allowed to cast a doubt on my motives or my sincerity." [25]

Whatever one may think about the ambiguity of the letter, there was was no equivocation in this reply.

Tilden had little to complain about so far as the New York delegates were concerned. No effort had been spared to make the vote solid for him, if the assertions of Whitney, Apgar, Marble, Cooper, Hewitt, Green, Manning and Peckham may be relied upon. At Cincinnati, however, their hopes were shattered by the conditions they found. Ken-

[24] Albany *Argus* and New York City newspapers.
[25] *Life*, II, 272.

tucky and Iowa were determined to nominate Tilden and his letter seemed to strengthen his support in other quarters, but dangerous opposition had developed. More significant still was the fact that his New York friends in the main were convinced by this time that he wished to withdraw, and consequently they became confused and indifferent to an aggressive fight.[26]

If Tilden was actually indulging in a stroke of "finessing," he played it too fine and lost. If his specious letter was merely a bait, as many believed, it proved to be the wrong sort to catch the fish. The New York delegates lost influence in the convention when Tilden was dropped, because their support first of Payne and then of Randall was unavailing. About all they accomplished was the exclusion of the Tammany delegation. The simplest and most accurate explanation of Tilden's attitude was given by him to a *Herald* reporter:

"Do you not believe you could have been nominated and elected this time?"

"I do. But I did not feel able to enter upon five years of hard, exhausting labor." [27]

Of the fourteen planks in the short platform presented by Watterson, the reform of civil service was the only one of the reforms in the platform of 1876 given prominence. The seventh dealt with the "great fraud of 1876–77" as a "deadly blow at our system of representative government" and claimed credit for saving the nation from civil war in 1877 in the faith that the people in 1880 would punish the crime as a "sacred duty." The ninth and longest, inserted by Watterson, stated,

"The resolution of Samuel J. Tilden not again to be a candidate for the exalted place to which he was elected . . . and from which he was excluded by the leaders of the Republican Party, is received by the Democrats with sensibility, and they declare their confidence in his wisdom, patriotism and integrity . . . and they . . . assure him that he is followed into retirement he has chosen for himself by the sympathy and respect of his fellow citizens." [28]

This resolution, printed on a roll of parchment, was presented to Tilden by the committee sent to notify the successful candidates.

A *Herald* reporter found Tilden receiving a visit from Bigelow and "two ladies from New Orleans"—probably Celeste Stauffer and her

---

[26] Alexander, III, 457.   [27] June 26, 1880.
[28] *Life*, II, 272; Stanwood, 367.

mother. He was dressed in an ordinary business suit, dark tie and tall white hat. His step was quick but one leg dragged a bit and his body was bowed. His left hand and arm were useless, and his hands trembled quite noticeably. His left eye was dull and lifeless, but his right eye twinkled with merriment and intelligence. His round boyish face was sallow and wrinkled. His voice was a childish treble—all "pipes and whistles"—and he spoke with physical pain. Although a broken feeble man physically, his brain was alert. "I feel that I shall be quite well again," he said, "before the summer is over." While refusing to comment on the convention, he said that he had not sought renomination, that his letter contained no double meaning, that he had given Manning his decision verbally, and that he would support Hancock.[29]

Dana's editorial in the *Sun* predicted, "Mr. Tilden's name will rank with the names of Washington, Jefferson, Madison, Jackson and Lincoln. A truer and purer patriot is not to be found among them all." [30] This eulogistic admiration was sincere and uninfluenced by loans from Tilden, at one time as high as $45,000, to finance the *Sun*.[31] Manton Marble, deeply disappointed that his political mentor was not renominated, expressed his personal disgust at the selection of Hancock and attributed the outcome to Bayard and Hendricks.[32]

A few hours after the convention adjourned Whitney commented:

"Yes, it has gone as I foresaw, but not as I hoped. If Mr. Tilden had been frankly out two weeks before the convention met, we could have nominated Payne. But Tilden wasn't out even when he wrote that letter. No, that letter was written to be read in the convention, and Tilden believed that if it had been the convention would have been swept into a stampede for him. It was a very cunning thing. If the convention was determined to nominate someone else, then the result would go down in history as the consequence of Tilden's withdrawal. If in the reading of the letter in the convention it had had the effect intended, then history would say that the party refused to let him withdraw. . . . I conclude that there is an uncomfortable hour in prospect for both Henry and Manning. From the Tilden standpoint they have blundered woefully. However this ends Tilden. Anyhow, the old man is now nearly a physical wreck." [33]

Later on during the campaign Whitney said that no one knew from anything Tilden had stated what he did want. "Anyway, he got the candidate he didn't want."

[29] June 25, 28, 1880.   [30] June 25, 1880.   [31] Tilden Papers.
[32] Marble Papers.   [33] Hudson, *Recollections*, 110.

Manning, toward the end of his life, asked whether Tilden actually wished the nomination, replied:

"Your question cannot be answered by me. I think Mr. Tilden's ambition led him to desire the nomination, but he acquiesced in the result as the better end, in view of the consideration that he was physically unfit to undergo the turmoil of another compaign. And that was the opinion of his best friends prior to the meeting of the convention." [34]

The *Nation* asserted that Tilden's confidants had long anticipated his withdrawal. Without a circle of able adherents, he had to rely too much on himself and was "utterly wanting in the . . . decision necessary to win respect as a reformer. He put so much craft in his good works that people were uncertain about his real aims. His financial operations created distrust." Democrats clung to him to get $500,000 for the campaign which nobody else would finance. [35]

Smith M. Weed, ever faithful to Tilden's interests, wrote him from Cincinnati:

"It was very apparent to anyone that it was not possible to nominate you, even if you would have taken it, as I know you would have not. The element that sold you out in Washington in 1877, with those who were *honestly* fearful you could not win, were enough to defeat you under any circumstances; and yet the fear that we meant to try to do it prevented our being able to. . . . Injudicious friends . . . of our own delegation absolutely destroyed our influence in the convention. The Brooklyn people did not want you. . . . Had . . . Manning spoken your wishes, we could have nominated Mr. Payne. . . . Randall acted bad, and talked bad, and yet, under your advice . . . I named him as our second choice. . . . I feared Hancock's nomination, but . . . not . . . so early. Had your letter been there Saturday morning, and had we all acted together—i. e. your friends—we could have nominated Payne. I don't think we could have nominated Randall. . . . The old dictation of the South was prevalent without the old intellect. . . . I hope Hancock will . . . be your friend, and . . . that you will help him through." [36]

Cassius M. Clay told Tilden that the congressmen defeated him. [37]

Letters and telegrams from loyal supporters lamented that the "hopes of millions" were buried by the convention, [38] congratulated him on his "escape from the Hell of Politics," [39] and begged him not to leave them "without a principle." The National Democratic Com-

[34] Hudson, *Recollections*, 111.   [35] June 24, 1880.   [36] *Letters*, II, 599, June 25, 1880.
[37] *Ib.*, 600, June 26, 1880.
[38] Tilden Papers, W. S. Cook of Mobile, Ala.
[39] *Ib.*, George Dunn of Louisville, Ky., June 25, 1880.

mittee was denounced for abandoning "the idol of the masses." Dana, Randall, English and Hancock called to discuss the situation. Hancock had the wisdom to ask Tilden to correct his letter of acceptance, and the latter inserted the paragraph urging the restoration of fraternal feelings, the growth of a merchant marine, the extension of commerce with neighbor nations, economical national expenditures, and the protection of every individual in his natural right to the "fruits of his own industry." [40]

A Princeton professor expressed his admiration for Tilden who was "covered with merited honors and persecuted with unmerited obloquy," and thanked him for saving his earnings, together with those "of a multitude of poor men." They rejoiced in the downfall "of that wicked and treacherous conspirator, John Kelly. . . . You are esteemed and loved for your integrity, pureness, patriotism and moral courage. . . . History will do you justice. . . . May your precious life and health be spared." [41]

The Kellyites on July 1 issued a stirring justification of their revolt against Tilden for using "the power and prestige of a great party for personal ends," and declared ironically that "the machine had no place in Democratic politics." They promised to work for Hancock and English.[42] Nast's sarcastic pencil put Tilden's letter on a lightning rod with the legend below: "Can't they see a joke? Catch me believing in lightning rods again." An editorial remarked that Tilden would "hardly be remembered as the model of republican virtue." [43]

At the Democratic ratification rally on July 27 in the Academy of Music, Tilden presided and was given three cheers and an ovation. In a hoarse voice he declared that there must be a change in the Federal Government both for necessary reforms and as a retribution for the "crime of 1876." Tilden introduced Randall, Thomas Ewing and J. R. Tucker, who made addresses predicting Hancock's election. The *Times* remarked that the greeting of Tilden by the people showed that in their esteem he stood with Jefferson and Jackson, but the *World* said that his appearance was "ridiculous" and his speech "in wretched taste." [44] He took no part in the campaign but contributed to it substantially. With funds low by the end of August, Barnum, Chairman of the Demo-

[40] *Letters,* II, 604, July 27, 1880.
[41] *Ib.,* 607, Dr. Alexander T. McGill, Nov. 27, 1880.
[42] *Nation,* July 29, 1880.   [43] *Harper's Weekly,* July 12, 1880.
[44] *Nation,* Aug. 5, 1880.

cratic National Committee, and W. L. Scott wrote Tilden that they were working for harmony and needed money to insure victory. Their request did not go unheeded. As a personal favor he had already sent Montgomery Blair $1,000 for election expenses, and Randall and others were supplied with funds for a pre-convention canvass. Whitney also told Tilden that he was "trying to keep the machine grinding" but needed $10,000. "I put you down for $1,000. . . . It must seem rather jolly to find the time come when you don't have to pay it all." [45] It was said that, all told, he contributed $25,000 to the Hancock-English canvass.[46] R. T. Merrick bluntly informed Hancock, "You will be beaten unless you use the economic advice of Wells and Tilden"; and to Tilden he wrote: "Unless you come to our relief, we are defeated. That is the general feeling." [47]

In the election on November 2, Garfield's plurality over Hancock was only 3,033 votes but in the Electoral College Hancock lost by 59 electoral votes.[48] Garfield did not receive the electoral vote of a single Southern State and Hancock had only 25 votes from the North. The Senate was tied, but the Republicans had a good majority in the House.[49] Many Democrats, affirmed that Tilden would have won a decisive victory.

Many persons were more interested in the exodus of Hayes on March 4, 1881, than in the Inauguration of President Garfield. Tilden was greatly amused at the comment of one rough wit who commented, "Mr. Hayes came in by a majority of one and goes out by unanimous consent." The *Herald* thought that Hayes had given the country four years of peace and avoided scandals, but had violated his pledge for civil service reform, appointing "dozens and dozens" of corrupt men in the South for political services; and it feared that disclosures would force him from office "a disgraced man." There was a general "contempt and dislike" for him because he deceived his party.[50] The Washington *Post* carried a similar article. Tilden replied to the editor of the latter:

"You are entitled to great credit for your faithful vindication of the . . . interests of the people in respect to the election of 1876. I never considered the question as at all personal to myself. It seemed to be a duty cast upon

[45] Tilden Papers, Aug. 26, 1880.
[46] Mrs. G. W. Smith, Ms. Notes. She saw the canceled checks.
[47] Tilden Papers, Oct. 14, 1880.   [48] Stanwood, 373; *An. Cyc.*, 1880, 702.
[49] *Argus Almanac*, 1881, 18, 21.   [50] Mar. 5, 1881.

me by events to represent the public grievance until . . . the people had an opportunity to take the matter into their own hands. That duty was very onerous, and . . . prolific of nothing but sacrifices; and though I would not retire from it, I was glad when it was completed, and I was discharged from the responsibility for all consequences of the violation of the elective principle." [51]

Montgomery Blair explained the defeat of the Democratic ticket on the ground that "neither the reform issue nor the fraud issue" had been made paramount in the canvass. The abandonment of the "man of ideas" for Hancock changed the issues. The result, he knew, was a surprise neither to Tilden nor to any other man with his eyes open. He hoped the party was taught its "salutary lesson" and began immediately to write to Randall and others about the reorganization of a "Tilden party" for the race four years hence.[52] The Democratic enemies of Tilden attributed Hancock's defeat to the fact that his campaign was managed by Tilden men.[53]

Tilden did no speaking, because of his weak voice, but on numerous occasions, when urged to attend banquets and public meetings, used his pen to prepare communications that might be read and given to the press. A typical example was the request of the Young Men's Democratic Club for an address. He extended his cordial sympathy with their efforts to elect Hancock and said:

"As the canvass advances, every day renders more manifest the duty to promote that result incumbent upon all who believe in the traditions of free, constitutional, representative self-government as illustrated in the better days of the Republic. One Presidential election, as made by the people, has been subverted by a false count of the votes cast by the Presidential electors founded upon a substitution of votes known to be fraudulent or forged. If the next . . . election should be controlled by corrupt influence exercised by the Government upon the voters in particular States . . . our government will be degenerated into a bad copy of the worst governments of the worst ages." [54]

The question whether Tilden did or did not wish the nomination in 1880 cannot be answered positively and unconditionally. For four years Tilden was dominated by a conviction that he was the embodiment of the Democratic cause which would be vindicated by the people in 1880.

[51] *Letters*, II, 616; Mar. 26, 1881.
[52] Tilden Papers, Blair to Tilden, Nov. 10, 1880.
[53] Hudson, *Recollections*, 114.   [54] *Letters*, II, 606, Oct. 26, 1880.

Those four years took such a toll of his vitality, however, that as the time for a definite decision approached he became doubtful of his strength to stand the ordeal. This physical condition accentuated his natural habit of indecision and caused him to leave his supporters in doubt. He wanted the nomination if it might come to him unsought and with great unanimity, as evidence of his party's faith in him and as a justification for his submission to a wrong in 1876. Then he might resign the honor, escape the hardships of a canvass, and designate his heir. When forced at last to reveal his wishes, his letter definitely removed him from the contest.

THE nomination of Hancock relieved Tilden of a tremendous strain. While his name was still good front-page news, he now had more leisure than for some years. He was free to give more attention to his recreations, to his country estate, to business matters, and to his heavy correspondence. A man of his extensive investments was obliged to devote considerable thought to them, even though he had delegated to subordinates responsibility for looking after details.

Requests for financial assistance were incessant. Loans were made to Richmond, Watterson, Dana, and A. M. Gibson. J. T. Spriggs was refused $30,000 because Tilden was curtailing his loans. The eccentric Dr. Mary Walker wanted a secret loan of $1,000 to take care of the mortgage on her home. Whitney had Tilden arrange for him a bank loan of $80,000. Hewitt presented bills left over from the campaign of 1876.[1] Tilden's secretary wrote that so many solicitations came by mail and personal application that it was not "possible for him to grant them." [2] When W. A. Wilkins insisted upon a loan, he was sent a check for $250 as the least expensive way out.

In like manner legal and business matters continually intruded. Edwards Pierrepont asked for assistance in settling the estate of Mayor Havemeyer. Dana wanted an opinion in a railroad case. Though Tilden declared at the beginning of 1881, "I am not troubling myself much about business," yet he wrote Sidney Dillon about railroad investments [3] and, out of a "cordial friendship," let David Dows know that he was disposing of New York Elevated Railroad bonds because it was "prudent"—a tip Dows appreciated.[4] When Alexander Long begged him to help finance the Cleveland Railroad, Tilden had "temporary indigestion" and could be of no service. Jay Gould kept bobbing into the picture and sent a report about the Mexican Central Railroad. At Manning's request Tilden sent C. N. Jordan the names of reliable contractors to work on the Ontario & Western Railroad. One little business transaction afforded Tilden a good laugh. He was accustomed to have

---

[1] Tilden Papers, Jan. 12, 1880, and later dates.   [2] *Letters* II, 614, Feb. 21, 1881.
[3] Tilden Papers, Nov. 19, 1879, and later.
[4] *Letters*, II, 618, Apr. 22, 1881.

his clothes cleaned and repaired by Geral, Loockwood and Company at 176 Fifth Avenue, and let his account run until several dunning bills had been sent. On one occasion he received a letter which to his surprise contained not a dun but $13 in bills left in his pockets. This example of honesty supplied him with many a sermonette. He refused to invest $30,000 in his old friend J. L. O'Sullivan's fiber factory,[5] but was deeply interested in the making of a rotary engine.[6]

While Tilden was not a habitual dabbler in Wall Street, yet his secretary made regular reports to him about the market and there are indications that he operated through stockbrokers. As late as 1885 J. E. Simmons, a New York stockbroker and brother of Dr. Simmons, wrote that he had sold Tilden's West Shore stock for $50,199. There are "lively times in the stock market. . . . I will come up and see you when you are in a mood to talk stocks. . . . I may make some helpful suggestions." Tilden's check book shows that he was still dealing in large blocks of railroad stocks and looking after his investment in iron ore mines.

Tilden now withdrew from the various boards of directors on which he served and from trusteeships. For example on January 29, 1885, the Winona & St. Petersburg Railroad accepted his resignation as trustee of the second mortgage loans. On April 1 he withdrew as trustee of the Chicago & Northwestern Railroad. In May he was released from his obligation to the Peninsula Railroad. And similar action was taken with other business concerns.[7]

While always interested in American history, Tilden had reached that time in life when anniversary observances appealed to him. He was pleased to be invited to the centennial of the Battle of New Orleans, even if he could not be present.[8] He presided at the celebration in Tarrytown of the anniversary of the capture of Major André and presented Chauncey M. Depew as orator of the day. He was invited to attend the centenary of Washington's association with Newburgh and to use his efforts to obtain funds from the State and the Federal Governments.[9] The celebration in 1882 of the grant of the Dongan Charter to Albany, attended by President Cleveland, with Governor Hill the orator of the occasion, would have found Tilden present had he been sufficiently robust. He had to be content to write a letter recounting Al-

[5] Tilden Papers various dates.   [6] Ib. Patent among his papers.
[7] Ib., various dates.   [8] Ib., Nov. 13, 1880.
[9] Ib., Apr. 4, 1882.

bany's memorable history,[10] and a communication for inclusion in the bicentennial issue of the *Argus*. When Governor and Mrs. Morgan invited him to a reception to meet President and Mrs. Hayes, he sent regrets to their "R.S.V.P." [11] To the Cotton Exposition at Atlanta went a review of recent industrial changes,[12] and to the Southern Exposition at Louisville some of his choice works of art.[13] He was unable to respond to a toast on Jackson's Birthday in Chicago, but wrote a disquisition on political reform.[14] He joined the New York Free Trade Club, both to support a good cause and to encourage a young friend, Poultney Bigelow.[15]

Like other well-known men of wealth, Tilden was appealed to for a contribution in nearly every effort to raise funds for public and private memorials and projects. He sent $100 to help erect a monument at Scituate, Massachusetts, in honor of the pioneers, among whom were his ancestors, contributed $250 for a memorial to William Cullen Bryant, gave $100 toward a McClellan monument, and sent $1,000 to the fund for Mrs. General Hancock. He paid the Grant Monument Association $250.[16] Parke Godwin asked him to head the list of subscriptions for the Statue of Liberty on Bedloe's Island with $10,000— the same sum being asked of Vanderbilt and Astor; but Tilden replied, "My impression has been, and still remains, that other objects ought to have a preference; and those will suffice to consume all I shall at present devote to such purposes." [17] He never hesitated to criticize the merit of a project. When Bishop William C. Doane made repeated requests for help in building the Cathedral of Albany, he explained that there were "many requests more urgent than yours." To W. A. Butler, who urged a bequest to the Law School of New York University to help poor students, he replied, "I am not prepared to say anything on the subject."

Women were much more successful than men in obtaining from Tilden contributions for good causes. He sent $1,000 to the Women's Hospital in 1882, and two years later Susan F. Colgate thanked him for his donation to the Westchester County Home. To the Temporary Home he gave $100 occasionally. To Mrs. J. S. Lowell who asked for a subscription for the Charity Organization Society he replied that he

[10] Banks, *Albany Bicent.*, 68, July 19, 1886.   [11] Tilden Papers, May 15, 1880.
[12] *Writings*, II, 510; *Sun*, Dec. 26, 1881.   [13] Tilden Papers, 1883.
[14] *Writings*, II, 514, Mar. 11, 1882.   [15] Tilden Papers, Mar. 18, July 12, 1882.
[16] *Ib.*, Sept. 4, 1884.   [17] *Letters*, II, 625, 629.

received "thousands" of begging letters and that to "comply with their requests would overmatch the journalistic exaggerations" of his fortune. Nevertheless he asked her to call to explain her plans. The elucidation evidently was satisfactory, for he invited her to "come in person to collect" his donation. He had not had the pleasure of seeing her for "almost seven years" and did "not like to throw away this occasion." [18]

Cases of real merit that touched Tilden's heart elicited a generous response. For example when H. A. Richmond informed him that the friends of David Grey, editor of the *Courier,* who was ill, were raising $5,000 for him, Tilden promptly sent a check for $500. Henry B. Dawson, historian and editor of the *Magazine of American History,* thanked Tilden for saving his "home from foreclosure," for it and his books were alone left to comfort him and his wife. College presidents were handled rather roughly. When one of them offered, in return for a substantial gift, to name a building in his honor, Tilden told him curtly that it would be "a calamity to be published as a philanthropist." Dr. John Hall of the University of the City of New York wanted an endowment to support worthy students, but Tilden courteously declined. Dr. C. N. Potter was given permission to present the needs of Union College,[19] and accorded a courteous hearing. W. O. M'Dowell was one of the first persons to advise Tilden to use his wealth either to build a great Graduate School of Political Science at Graystone or to put it all into a gigantic library.[20]

Perhaps nothing afforded Tilden more genuine pleasure than to make a present to some friend of whom he was fond. To Dana he sent a box of rare Steinberger wine of the 1868 vintage, which cost $84 gold a case. Dana pronounced it "one of the very noblest products of nature"—and paid the interest on a loan, but Tilden told him "not to hurry" about the principal.[21] Tilden was pleased with the financial success of the *Sun* and as late as June 8, 1886, Dana was seeking to increase his loan. S. J. Randall did not hesitate to ask Tilden to give financial aid to his friends.

Tilden was conscious that he was growing old. In his letters there are numerous allusions to his youth and to the changes that come with the sunset of life. His time, he noticed, was taken up with "little things" relating to himself and everybody else. Like Jefferson in his retirement,

[18] Tilden Papers, Dec. 18, 1882, and later.   [19] *Ib.,* Sept. 17, 1882, and later.
[20] New York *Press,* Aug. 19, 1906.   [21] *Letters,* II, 623; Tilden Papers, June 30, 1883.

he preferred to read solid literature and the newspapers. Life became more mellow and he gave more attention to the performance of kindly deeds. To a neighbor of eighty, "who consumes less than fifty cents' worth of food a day out of an income of $1,500," he advised a quart or two of the best quality of milk plus 25% of cream. He would rent him a good cow, "and change it as often as necessary," or sell him one.[22] He congratulated Peter Cooper on his "marvelous health and strength," and, while he could not dine with him and his friends, he sent "best wishes." [23] He reminded George Bancroft that he had not seen him in five years.[24] To one who asked for the location of a Jackson quotation, he gave it and said:

"I well remember the document and the occasion. Although I had not yet reached my majority for several years, I addressed the people of my native town night after night on the subject, besides causing a copy to be put in the hands of every voter, and changed the vote 20%." [25]

The assassination of President Garfield affected Tilden profoundly. At a public meeting in Yonkers he drew up the resolutions adopted. Such a tragic event, twice within sixteen years, he wrote, was a deplorable event in our national history. . . . Such treason against the elective sovereignty of the people tends to encourage future attempts to subvert the Chief Magistracy of the Republic by criminal violence, under . . . increasing temptations to personal resentments and private malignity . . . incident to the ever-growing power and patronage of the executive office. . . . Good citizens ought to join in every wise measure for limiting these temptations, and for restoring . . . every moral security which heretofore surrounded the First Citizen of the Republic as he moved without guards among the people.[26]

Party leaders continued to look to Tilden for substantial support, and when Edward Cooper in 1881 informed him that the State Committee could raise no funds, he testily replied:

"It could scarcely be expected to foray on one man for the whole supplies desired. I am subject to a continual running fire for contributions. To deal . . . with the applications now before me, or sure to come, will be as much as ought to be expected from me. . . . Of course nobody will give or take any trouble to collect money, if all that is necessary is to ask one man. I do not just now feel very affluent. I have given away so much this year, and have been led into such large expenses that I am entrenching upon my capital, and

[22] Tilden Papers.   [23] *Ib.*, Feb. 12, 1880.   [24] *Letters*, II, 618.
[25] Tilden Papers.   [26] *Letters*, II, 619.

do not feel as indifferent to unnecessary extravagances as I might under other circumstances." [27]

Cooper, accustomed to such a complaint from Tilden, then asked him to give $5,000 to match the donations of Whitney and himself, a request that was not refused.[28]

When Tilden learned of the illness of Montgomery Blair in the summer of 1883, he sent some health maxims and "a young Holstein calf" to cheer him up. Tilden was "deeply afflicted" by Blair's demise in July. The passing of O'Conor less than a year later was a heavy blow. In commenting on his life, Tilden said that O'Conor "was the greatest jurist among all the English-speaking people. He carried the best spirit of philosophical inquiry into every professional investigation. . . . He had a vast mass of information on every professional subject. He was a man of lofty integrity and honor, and scorned all idea of making his professional abilities the means of acquiring money."

As the time approached for the nomination of a Governor in 1882, Tilden made it clear that he would not under any circumstances be a candidate himself and that he wanted the nomination of the best man. L. E. Chittenden, who had met Tilden at Van Buren's table thirty-four years previously, wrote, "You can defeat Cornell with an anti-monopoly candidate." [29] D. B. Hill told Tilden that, ever since he had asked him early in 1875 "to take hold of my district and make it right," he had held it for the party. Now he "would very much like the Democratic nomination for Lieutenant Governor," and a good word from you "will settle the question." It seems very likely that "the good word" was spoken.

While Tilden hesitated to commit himself for Grover Cleveland, the latter's excellent record for reform as Mayor of Buffalo won his admiration. Tilden was very close to Dana and probably inspired this editorial in the *Sun:* "Grover Cleveland is a man worthy of the highest public confidence. No one can study the record of his career . . . without being convinced that he possesses . . . sound principles . . . and courage to do what is right, no matter who may be pleased or displeased." [30] The nomination of Cleveland and Hill elicited a letter from

[27] *Letters*, II, 621.   [28] Tilden Papers, Oct. 31, 1881.
[29] *Ib.*, July 4, 1882.
[30] It is asserted in the D. B. Hill Papers that Tilden asked Hill to run for Governor as the "poor man's" candidate and offered to finance his campaign.

Tilden giving his unqualified approval of the ticket. He felt that the large class of "independent voters" who helped him "elevate the standard of official morality" and had held the balance of power in every subsequent contest would "determine . . . the approaching election." To these voters he said, "I cordially commend the support of Grover Cleveland." He contributed to the campaign fund. The next year he gave $100 for the city election and $1,000 to help the State election.[31]

Cleveland was a self-sufficient executive who did not ask advice from former Governors, but through Manning he did consult Tilden about laws dealing with corporations and other matters. Nor did Cleveland confer with him about his appointments, and Tilden was careful to make no requests. Eight months later D. S. Lamont, Cleveland's secretary, announced that the Governor would accept Tilden's invitation to visit him at Graystone.[32]

Tilden's bachelorhood, like that of Cleveland and Hill, was the occasion for considerable merriment among his acquaintances, and crops out in numerous letters. When W. F. Allen sent a widow to consult him about her investments, he could not resist warning him that she was a "charming lady." Mrs. Mabel Osgood Wright gives a vivid picture of meeting Tilden in Scribner's bookstore. She describes him as "the astute lawyer, famous for his routing the Tweed Ring and the Canal Ring. He was very dry and immobile . . . in fact [he] gave me several books and a colored Audubon print. Occasionally a twinkle would flash from his heavy-lidded eyes that at other times seemed closed at the outside corners, as if to prevent anyone from possibly reading his thoughts or getting an opinion in advance. In appearance he looked very much like an old-time farmer come to a county fair, rather than a New Yorker and politician who had been Governor." Frequently he called on Mr. Wright to play chess or billiards. There he noticed golden-haired Emma Wright and began to court her. One night there was no preliminary game of chess, so Tilden drew up to the comfortable fire, took off his shoes and toasted his feet while waiting for the blond lady to appear. The heat put the elderly swain to sleep. When she came down, she heard his snores, saw his stockinged feet, turned and fled. She married the nephew of an Italian Cardinal; the sequel of Tilden's waking is not disclosed.[33]

---

[31] Tilden Papers, to Manning, Oct. 5, 20, 1882.   [32] *Ib.*, Jan. 10, Sept. 20, 1883.
[33] Wright, *My New York*, 222–224.

In his old age Tilden found pleasure in women's society. His papers show that he was on friendly terms with actresses, singers, artists, and authoresses. He enjoyed sending them books, flowers, fruit and other gifts; he attended their public performances, and at times assisted them with financial aid. To his female relatives he was a bountiful Santa Claus. He was exceedingly fond of his only surviving sister, Mrs. Pelton, and kindly disposed toward the widows of his brothers Moses and Henry. R. D. Buchanon thanked him for his "generous offer to cancel the loan made a year or more ago . . . at Addie's suggestion." [34] Addie was the adopted daughter of Moses and had been given an expensive wedding at Graystone. Henry's two daughters were supplied with money for clothes and travel, and sent abroad with a chaperon. Tilden took pains to have them visit their English cousins in Kent, with whom he had kept up a pleasant correspondence. Tilden never tired of having young folks about, particularly girls. He took pleasure in conversing with them and in showing them gallant courtesies. Miss Mary M. Butler of Yonkers remembers calling with her sister on Tilden, then a trembling old man. He asked them cordially, "Do you like apples?" Of course they replied in the affirmative. "Well, come with me," he said, taking them to his well-stored cellar. "Fill your basket with these. They will keep your sweet mouths filled for a long time." [35] He understood young people and never assumed an aloof attitude toward them.

Prior to 1876 Tilden was deeply attached to Augusta D. Dickinson, a collateral relative in New Jersey. At the same time she was courted by Colonel W. T. Pelton, Tilden's nephew. Although greatly admiring Tilden she felt that he was her father's contemporary and that she could not burden herself with the care of another old man, so she chose Pelton and became his second wife. Pelton took her to live in Tilden's home, where she died in childbirth. Tilden "sincerely mourned her" and her memory caused him to show leniency in dealing with his irresponsible nephew.[36]

Nor did Tilden forget the wives of his contemporaries. The most beautiful illustration of this thoughtfulness was offered by his gift to Mrs. William Cullen Bryant. While he was visiting her she casually remarked, "A bamboo settee is my only want." Upon reaching home

[34] Tilden Papers, Oct. 5, 1882.   [35] Interview in 1934.
[36] Mrs. G. W. Smith, Ms. Notes.

Tilden wrote out an order to have it sent, put the letter in his pocket, and then forgot all about mailing it until he found it when packing to leave the city. He wrote Mrs. Bryant a charming note explaining his absent-mindedness and expressing the hope that the settee had arrived to explain "its own advent." He added, "I could not resist the impulse to supply . . . your *only want*. . . . I shall, doubtless, at some period not yet distinctly foreseen, share its benefits. . . . I am forever your debtor." She sent her "best acknowledgments" and said jokingly, "I wish I could as easily send you in return the thing you most want for your future household, or even tell you where to obtain it." [37]

Pleasant social contacts with women continued throughout Tilden's life. Anna Dickinson, well-known orator and novelist, wrote him about her "work and present need," and thanked him for a courteous refusal of a loan for $5,000. Margaret J. M. Sweek sent a word of appreciation for her visit at Graystone. Kate Field recalled the "charming dinner" he gave her in Paris and sought to interest him in her "causes," among them the "Mormon Monster." Nellie Hazeltine of St. Louis explained gossip that connected her name with his, invited him to pay her a visit, and came East to meet him. Katrina Lombard was "surprised and delighted" with his "lovely remembrance" of her on Christmas. Mary Margaretta Pryer thanked him for a "beautiful and timely" clock.[38] A story was circulated in Albany that to a pretty actress who appeared in that city he sent flowers and a check for $1,000.[39] Indeed so numerous were these attentions to attractive women that rumors of a marriage were not uncommon in the newspapers.[40] In a sympathetic mood he loaned Leonard Jerome $10,000 so that his daughter might marry Lord Randolph Churchill—and had trouble in collecting the debt.[41]

Sarah Jewitt, the actress, and her mother—"good Democrats"— were among Tilden's intimate friends. "Don't forget," Sarah wrote, "that among my pleasant thoughts, I have pleasant ones of you always." Her friendly notes covered a period of four years, and Tilden usually reserved a box at all of her performances. He was a patron likewise of the popular operatic star, Christine Nilsson, "a beautiful blonde, slim and graceful"—the typical Marguerite—a favorite in the

[37] *Letters*, II, 604, 605.
[38] Tilden Papers, June 6 and July 14, 1883 and later dates.
[39] Statement of William Gorham Rice. [40] *World*, Feb. 4, 1880.
[41] Letter of Mrs. G. W. Smith, June 9, 1931.

family of Parke Godwin, who wrote Tilden: "Christine is coming to-night to have some fun with the young folks. Can't you stop in and help?" [42] Mrs. Doremus persuaded Tilden to give her a public reception, and he did so in grand style.[43] He enjoyed her performances, and she sent him "A thousand thanks for the delicious wine." Cora Elise Smith of New Orleans was a congenial friend. He sent her books and fruit and frequently had her for dinner. She thanked him "a thousand times" for his "beautiful coffee cups," and valued the "good wishes and affection" that sent them.[44] She married the Earl of Stafford and later one of the wealthy Cunards.

In 1876 it was reported that Tilden might marry the twenty-four-year-old Leila Morse,[45] daughter of S. F. B. Morse, whose tangled estate he had settled. After her marriage to a musician named Rummell five years later, she continued a delightful correspondence with Tilden, sent him from Berlin a picture of herself and child marked "To Uncle," destroyed his letters marked "private," and begged him to spend the winter on the Mediterranean where she could see him. On one occasion she wrote, "I am working on the 4th pair of your silk stockings. Is not that doing well?" [46]

On the steamer returning from Europe in 1877 Bigelow introduced to Tilden a "bright, vivacious young lady," Miss Marie Celeste Stauffer of New Orleans. Thereafter with her mother she made frequent visits to New York City and informed Tilden that they might spend a few days at Graystone. With his usual caution Tilden would then dictate a note to Andrew H. Green inviting them to his home, and the latter would escort them up on the yacht. Thus "Miss Stauffer could never show a letter written to her by Tilden." [47] These visits ripened into an intimacy which gossip called an engagement. "Everyone is talking of your engagement to Miss Stauffer," said his niece, Susan Tilden. "What shall we say? Do you intend to marry her?" Tilden closed his eyes and replied, "I have compromised with her." "What do you mean?" asked Susie. "By leaving her something in my will," he answered. She was in Europe when he died, and expressed her admiration and affection for him. Although he bequeathed her $100,000, she complained of the "paltry sum." Her letters were exchanged for those

[42] Tilden Papers.
[43] Mrs. G. W. Smith, Ms. Notes.
[44] Tilden Papers, Dec. 30, 1881.
[45] *Tribune,* Nov. 13, 1876. See Feb. 3, 1880.
[46] Tilden Papers.
[47] Mrs. G. W. Smith, Ms. Notes.

written her by Green. She married Charles Eastwick and still survived when this account was written. Tilden would have married Miss Stauffer in 1880 had not Bigelow convinced him of the absurdity of such a union on account of his health and the disparity in their ages.[48] Her signed pictures—one taken in color in New Orleans and another in Paris—were cherished by Tilden to the end of his life.

John Bigelow, who knew Tilden for fifty years as intimately as any of his associates, spoke of him as a celibate, and declared that on two separate occasions Tilden assured him "that he had never had any acquaintance or relations with the female sex, of which he would have hesitated, from motives of delicacy, to speak with his mother or his sisters." Yet his extant papers contain a few mysterious passages with possibilities of interpretation that might modify Bigelow's sweeping statement. Bigelow was confident that "the affection side of his nature would have been more developed and his personality more generally attractive" had he been happily married. But had he taken a wife, Bigelow thought, he would not have been "so great a force in the world" or have lived so long, an assertion that is at least debatable. The love of a sensible companion, the affection of children and the cheering influence of a family fireside might have gone far to offset some of the more disagreeable phases of his character.[49] There were certainly a number of rumors of his marriage. He himself "often thought of marrying" and had no aversion to matrimony. He never married only because he was never violently attached to any woman and "never felt the need of a wife." His health, law, politics, and business absorbed all his energies.

[48] Letter of Mrs. G. W. Smith, Feb. 5, 1934.   [49] *Life*, II, 372–373.

THE election of Garfield permitted friends of Tilden to say that, if renomination had been forced on him in 1880, he would have won the election. Though many Democrats honestly doubted this assumption, the conviction grew that victory could come in 1884 only with Tilden as the national party leader. Dr. G. L. Miller and Montgomery Blair early initiated a campaign for that purpose. "If you hold your own . . . you will surely run and I will be in the convention for you," [1] predicted Randall, who was in constant touch with Tilden and received a check for political purposes.[2] Representatives of the Chicago *Times* and the Washington *Post* were promoting Tilden's nomination, but when a Texan proposed to start a paper for the same purpose, he was informed that "Tilden has no desire . . . to again quit his home, his books, and his private pursuits." [3] Democrats generally regretted the Electoral Commission and wished to make amends by electing him in 1884.[4]

Watterson had not seen Tilden for a year, but accepted an invitation to visit him in June, 1883. "His name is at this moment upon the lips of politicians of every class all over the country," he wrote. He was gratified to find Tilden well and enlarging his Gramercy Park house. Tilden took his guest all over the place and discussed architecture like a professional. At length Watterson asked, "Governor, don't you think we have had enough of this?" Tilden smiled and replied, "If you are tired we will go downstairs." Watterson described him as the man of 1876—"low voice . . . eyes bright . . . cheeks rosy . . . intellect sinewy and clear . . . wit incisive." He led a busy life at Graystone, with "no end of pigs, poultry and blooded stock. . . . I had to be dragged over his farm, and the devices of the old gentleman put slyly forth to trap me into some unguarded treason to the butter and eggs of my blue grass country were many and ingenious. . . . The Governor's farming is like everything else he undertakes, thoroughly well done. I asked him whether he tried to make

---

[1] Tilden Papers, Apr. 1, Dec. 12, 1881.   [2] *Ib.*, Oct. 17, 1882.
[3] *Letters*, II, 623.   [4] Tilden Papers, M. H. Bovee.

any money out of it. 'Oh, no,' he said. 'It is easier made some other way.' "

There was not even a "ghost of a politician" at Graystone, he continued, "while I was there. . . . Surrounded by his nieces and his books, the old statesman and philosopher was reserved in his conversation . . . but simple and cordial in his hospitality . . . and an attentive and wise observer of affairs." He talked of "everything from Thomas à Kempis to Thomas A. Hendricks. . . . No power on earth could induce him to accept the Presidency." Yet not long after this statement Watterson asked Tilden to invite Randall to confer with them "before any fighting begins."

Although a septuagenarian, Tilden was still a power in New York politics. Upon learning that his nephew, S. J. Tilden II, was going as a delegate to the State Convention, he advised against it because "it is not desirable to put up another lightning rod." [5] He also advised his namesake not to run for the State Senate or to take a place on the State ticket but to aim at "pecuniary independence, safety and comfort. . . . *I can tell you things which I cannot write.*" [6]

With the advent of 1884 Tilden was fairly flooded with demands that he stand once more. McCormick read his doubtful letter to a group of important business men at his home, and all, even the Republican family physician, vowed that they would vote for him. "You have in no case been found to say positively that, if nominated . . . you would not accept. . . . Should I say anything publicly?" Trumbull commented: "The Democracy all over the land are looking to you . . . to lead them. . . . Elected once . . . you can be again." [7] Prominent Democrats wrote, "Your declination is inadmissible," and, "Think . . . before positively saying 'No.'" A Republican for thirty years begged him to accept the nomination. One loyal supporter gave up all hope of ever seeing a Democratic President if he refused the office. The people "are of one voice," declared Randall, "that you must be our candidate." Springer expressed enthusiasm for the "old ticket." States from the West and South announced that their delegates were pledged to him. Clark Howell of the *Atlanta Constitution,* who had "hoisted his name for the nomination," after a conference mournfully announced, "Tilden will not run," and reported him as

[5] Tilden Papers, to Henry Tilden, Sept. 20, 1883.   [6] *Life,* II, 315; *Letters,* II, 695.
[7] *Letters,* II, 638, 642.

saying, "I am physically unfit to be President." But such indirect statements were unacceptable to those who vowed that: "unless satisfied you will be incapable . . . of the duties of the office, sensible men . . . will not ask your consent. We will fight the battle of '76." [8] It was remarkable that eight years after Tilden had lost the Presidency, he still drew so much valiant support for continued leadership.

Tilden made few public utterances during the early months of 1884. When the Iroquois Club of Chicago invited him to attend their banquet and respond to the sentiment, "The Federal Constitution," he sent a written response that was significant. The task of restoring the Government "to its original character is not yet accomplished." Myriads of officeholders and monied allies fought for control. No reform was possible so long as a party with false doctrines perpetuated existing abuses. The first step must be a change of administration. "I do not despair of ultimate deliverance. Though I can no longer aspire to be one of the leaders in this great work, I bid those upon whom this august mission may fall, Godspeed." [9]

By this time it had become apparent that the odds were greatly against Tilden's being the standard bearer. Watterson in a long editorial announced, "The public career of Mr. Tilden is ended." Although he had no "dream of any other possible leader" until Tilden laid upon him a definite command, he felt that the call in 1884 came too late—four years earlier he would have swept the country. The *Nation* saw in this Tilden boom merely an attempt to use him as a stalking horse to line up delegates who could be swung to some favorite candidate.[10] Magone informed Manning that Tilden should "not authoritatively decline" until after delegates were elected to the State Convention because his name would aid in having honest men chosen.[11]

The importunities that had been showered upon Tilden buoyed him up and improved his health. But he realized that he had only half a body, and that, badly shattered; that his mental powers had so slowed down that he depended on secretaries and friends to prepare his political addresses. Many a man in his senility would have grasped the high honor when a mere affirmative word would have brought it to him. If renomination was doubtful in 1880, unquestionably the road was open in 1884, and it led directly to the White House. Realizing

[8] Tilden Papers, W. S. Groesbeck, Apr. 29, 1884. [9] *Writings*, II, 519, Apr. 11, 1884.
[10] May 29, 1884. [11] *Letters*, II, 641.

that he could not run the race, he decided positively that he would not enter it. Bigelow urged him in May to make the announcement before the delegates to the State Convention were chosen, in order not to disappoint them.[12] But Washington friends urged delay, and he was awaiting a favorable pretext.

For once Tilden did something unexpected—he definitely withdrew from the Presidential contest and made the announcement public before he intended to. Convinced that he was eliminated by his physical condition, Dan Manning and a few other far-sighted New York Democrats were grooming Cleveland as the choice of the Empire State. Manning, Chairman of the Democratic State Committee, fearing that the New York delegates could not be held as a unit for Cleveland unless Tilden formally declined, with Cleveland's approval went down to induce Tilden to make public his refusal. He called on Bigelow on June 8 and the next day both went to Graystone to explain the situation. He told Tilden that he came at the request of Cleveland and assured him that he "should have a practical influence in the selection of the Cabinet, and particularly should name a member from the State of New York"; that Cleveland would "regard Mr. Tilden's friends as his friends, and, if elected, have as nearly as possible a thoroughly Tilden administration." [13] Manning asked Tilden to issue at once, before any more delegates were elected to the State Convention, a statement that "he would not be a candidate."

Bigelow, knowing that a "manifesto" had already been written, heartily endorsed Manning's request. Tilden had intended, as "a matter of delicacy," to delay its publication until after his name had been presented to the State Convention. But at Manning's urgence he "acceded to Mr. Cleveland's wish, sacrificed the preference and pride of my friends, and gave my letter to the press immediately." [14] In this renunciation, Tilden first quoted a large part of his communication of June 18, 1880. Four years only strengthened the considerations that induced his withdrawal from public life then. The unanimous appeal of the Democratic masses "to serve them once more" would inspire him to do anything consistent with his "judgment of duty." He took the nomination in 1876 because the people believed he could do at Washington what he had done at Albany. With the "idea that every

12 *Life*, II, 281. 13 *Letters*, II, 647, 676, 678.
14 *Ib.*, 676, letter to Manning, June 10, 1884.

power is a trust and involves a duty," he meant to redress the evils of twenty years of war and bad government. The task which he was now asked to take up would consume five years—and he had no illusions about the burden involved. Hence the considerations which caused his withdrawal in 1880 had become imperative in 1884—he lacked the "physical strength to carry through" the obligation. With declining powers, he doubted his ability to accomplish the reforms expected. "I am, therefore, constrained to say, definitely, that I cannot now assume the labor of an administration or of a canvass." He was consoled by the reflection that neither the party nor the Republic was dependent upon any one man for successful progress. "I but submit to the will of God in deeming my public career forever closed." [15]

This valedictory to his party and to the nation was eagerly read and widely commented on in the press. While Bigelow thought it was not strong enough "to keep your name out of the convention," Ewing expressed his "sincere admiration of the dignity and magnanimity of the utterance." [16] Some admirers begged him to recall it; others read it with deep regret; and many said that it made no difference—he would be renominated anyhow. The *Times* remarked: "Mr. Tilden . . . puts away a Presidential nomination he might have had, an act which has few precedents in the history of parties in this country. That act is extremely creditable to the good sense and to the clear perception of Mr. Tilden." [17] Twenty-two States had chosen delegates before the letter was printed on June 12, and all but two were for Tilden's nomination.[18] Of the fourteen States that elected delegates after June 12, nine made him their first choice and five expressed a preference for him. Had he been physically fit, his nomination would have been assured.

The Democratic National Convention met in Chicago, where the Republicans had nominated Blaine shortly before. As the delegates gathered, New York had two avowed candidates—Grover Cleveland, whose interests were in the hands of Manning; and R. P. Flower who had the support of John Kelly and Tammany. But high above all favorite sons loomed the Sage of Graystone. His abnegation seemed to increase his popularity and bring unity out of chaos. There was

[15] *Letters*, II, 648.
[16] Tilden Papers, *Memoranda Concerning Mr. Tilden's Reply to the Presidential Nomination in 1884*, 36.
[17] June 12, 1884.   [18] *Life*, II, 284.

much excited talk of ignoring Tilden's letter and nominating him by acclamation. So far did this determination go that W. H. Barnum, Chairman of the Democratic National Committee, telegraphed Tilden on July 4, "Will you accept an unanimous nomination from the Convention?" At the same time Manning wired, "It seems absolutely that you should answer Barnum's telegram." The next day Tilden replied to Barnum, "Your inquiry was explicitly answered in the negative by my letter of June 10th to Mr. Manning." That Tilden suspected, in the face of his emphatic words, that he might be honored with a nomination is shown by a pencil note on the telegram, "If the convention should nominate me, I should consider it as intended merely to acquit the Democratic Party of any shortcomings in respect to the fraudulent possession of the government in 1876, and with the knowledge that I would not accept the nomination." [19]

Manning and the supporters of Cleveland now proclaimed him as Tilden's choice and the embodiment of Tilden's principles. As President, they asserted, he would seek Tilden's advice and carry out his policies.[20] But Randall and his followers made a similar claim to Tilden's support.[21]

The convention was called to order by Barnum on July 8. Temporary Chairman Hubbard's mention of Tilden brought the huge audience to its feet with tremendous applause and waving of hats and handkerchiefs. The appeal of W. F. Vilas, permanent chairman, on July 9, to the young men to stand for reform was received with enthusiasm. The platform expressed regret that "the venerable statesman," because of "failing strength," was unable to lead the party, but promised that his "principles" would be carried on. On the second ballot Cleveland was nominated and Hendricks became his team-mate.[22] When Carter Harrison expressed the regret that the "Old ticket" was not before them, the applause was vociferous.

Before adjourning, the convention resolved that "though fraud, force and violence" deprived Tilden and Hendricks "of the offices conferred on them . . . in 1876, they yet live first in the hearts of the Democracy. . . . That this Convention expresses a nation's regret that this same . . . ability which cleansed and purified the city and State governments of the great Empire State cannot now be turned upon

[19] *Letters*, II, 655.   [20] *Ib.*, 677.   [21] *Herald*, July 10, 1884.
[22] Nevins, *Cleveland*, 154.

the Augean stable of national fraud and corruption." [23] A committee arrived at Yonkers on September 3 to present the resolutions. Tilden thanked the committee in a few words and said that the state of his health necessitated the delay of his formal reply.[24]

Tilden's farewell address to the Democratic Party was written on October 6, 1884. He expressed his belief that the reform of the Federal Government could come only through their party, because of its "freedom from the corrupt influences which grow up in the prolonged possession of power."

"For sixty years after Jefferson it mainly directed our national policy . . . and laid the foundations of all our national greatness. . . . On the other hand, the Republican Party has always been dominated by principles which favor legislation for the benefit of particular classes at the expense of . . . the people. It has become tainted with . . . abuses . . . and false finance. The patriotic and virtuous elements in it are now unable to emancipate it from the sway of selfish interests.

All history shows that reforms in government must not be expected from those who sit serenely on the social mountain tops enjoying the benefits of the existing order of things. Even the divine Author of our religion found His followers not among the self-complacent Pharisees, but among lowly-minded fishermen. The Republican Party is largely made up of those who . . . aspire in politics to advantages over the rest of mankind. . . . The Democratic Party consists largely of those who live by the work of their hands, and whose political action is governed by their sentiments or imagination. . . . It, more readily than the Republican Party, can be molded to support reform measures which involve a sacrifice of selfish interests." [25]

Cleveland, some of whose friends were among the Western supporters of the Canal Ring, was no admirer of Tilden in 1874 and opposed him for Governor.[26] Later, like so many Democrats, he came to admire Tilden's wise policies and regarded himself as one of his followers. As a student of Tilden's career, he asserted that one of the penalties of 1876 was the long time the country had to wait to see Tilden's sound ideas on money adopted.[27] Tilden in 1882 cordially supported Cleveland for Governor and from that time on Cleveland's closest friends in New York were Tilden men like Manning, Apgar and Lamont.

Tilden was much elated over Cleveland's election and expressed his

---

[23] *Life,* II, 286; *Letters,* II, 682; *Proceedings,* 134.
[24] *Life,* II, 287.   [25] *Letters,* II, 652, 658; *Life,* II, 278.
[26] Nevins, *Cleveland,* 75, 79, 96; Parker, *Recollections,* 282, 337, 388.
[27] Parker, 288.

admiration for him. When someone asked whether Cleveland had the backbone requisite for his exalted office Tilden replied: "Backbone? Why he has so much that it makes his stomach stick out in front." [28] On another occasion Cleveland was described as a man "who'd do something badly himself rather than have someone else do it well." Tilden regarded the party as lucky to have at the helm a man "who always knows what to do next and is never caught in a corner with no resources beyond." [29]

Tilden's relations with Cleveland, while never friendly, were cordial enough. Smith M. Weed informed Tilden on July 28, 1884, that Governor Cleveland wished to consult him about his letter of acceptance. D. S. Lamont wrote Tilden that Cleveland and he would call on August 5.[30] That conference did not materialize, but Lamont was sent with the letter to Tilden for his advice, but without liberty to change the substance. As Lamont read the letter to Tilden, A. H. Green kept grunting disapprovals. "Oh, shut up," exclaimed Tilden, who opposed both the "form and tone of the letter." [31] In the Presidential campaign Tilden took no active part, although repeatedly urged to do so.

After Cleveland's election, the Cabinet became the general theme of discussion. It was assumed, as a matter of course, that Tilden's opinion would be dominant in the selection and this was Tilden's own expectation. George Hoadley of Ohio, whom Tilden wished to see nominated as Vice President, rejoiced that a President who "has sat at your feet" was elected, and wrote, "I should like to be Attorney General. . . . You are the honored head of our party. . . . I take it for granted that your wishes will have great weight with the President-elect." Tilden replied that he did not know to what extent Cleveland would consult him about the Cabinet but he did "not intend to intrude upon him any advice unasked. . . . If consulted, I shall not act as a partisan of any of my numerous friends. . . . Do you mean to say that you have an invincible repugnance to every other post?" Hoadley in reply said he was willing "to take orders cheerfully," but was disturbed at Tilden's intimation that he might not be consulted about the Cabinet. "It will be a sad day for him and for his government if he ignores you and does not seek your counsels." [32] By no direct effort did Tilden

[28] Pyle, *Life of J. J. Hill*, I, 426.   [29] Parker, 341, 388.
[30] *Letters*, II, 657.
[31] Parker, *Recollections*, 338; Cleveland to Lamont, Aug. 14, 1884.
[32] *Letters*, II, 659, 660, 662.

seek to force his convictions on Cleveland. In a pathetic letter to Manning, he offered to give his best advice to the President-elect in case he wished it, and added that this would be in all probability the last important service he could hope to render his country.[33]

Randall, excited over a dispatch that Cleveland had offered Bayard any portfolio in the cabinet he might wish and that he had selected the Secretaryship of the Treasury, wrote "This means an end of our friends."

Would the President-elect or the Sage of Graystone fashion the fruits of victory? It would have been much better for the peace of mind of both Cleveland and Tilden had the latter completely withdrawn and left the problems to Cleveland and the younger party leaders. Temperamentally Tilden could not do that. The triumph, he felt, was his; so why should he not point out the course of action? In searching for a trustworthy man to serve as his mouthpiece without making it appear that he was doing so, he selected Smith M. Weed whose loyalty was unquestioned. Besides did not Tilden hold his notes for loans of $133,000? To Weed he wrote as a monarch might instruct a secret emissary: "To wise conduct two things are necessary —first that the proportion between things in their relative importance be observed; secondly, that their urgency in point of time be respected. . . . You must sacrifice the nonessential for the essential" until the crisis is passed and the "right direction" is given to events. "You should be a minute man for some weeks." Weed hurried down to Graystone to receive verbal instructions from his master, and for the next two months gave most of his time to the organization of Cleveland's Cabinet. Perhaps Cleveland suspected this relationship, because, while he seemed to welcome Weed's counsel, he did not heed it to any great degree.[34]

To such aspirants as A. H. Garland and Gross,[35] Tilden sent letters almost identical with that to Hoadley. Feeling the need of an understanding with Cleveland, Tilden, on January 2, 1885, invited him "to take a few days' repose at Graystone" with the Mannings. But acceptance of the invitation had to be postponed, so it was not until some weeks later that Manning informed Tilden that Cleveland was going to New York City about February 1 and would call. "No com-

[33] Cleveland Papers, Nov. 12, 1884.   [34] Tilden Papers, Dec. 4, 1884.
[35] *Life*, II, 289; *Letters*, II, 664.

mittals have been made," said Manning, "nor will any be made until after these visits. . . . Will you want to see me before we make our proposed call?" [36] Weed informed Tilden that Cleveland "will not give B(ayard) anything but Secretary of State . . . and thinks he better stay in the Senate. . . . He is very set on Whitney. . . . Let him alone for a couple of weeks." [37] Cleveland disliked Andrew H. Green and thought he reflected Tilden's views.[38]

On February 4 Cleveland went to New York City to confer with leaders over his Cabinet and other matters. His secretary, D. S. Lamont, informed Tilden that the President-elect "hopes soon to have the pleasure of making you a visit," at a time to be arranged by Manning. Meanwhile R. T. Merrick informed Tilden that Frank Jones and Horace White wanted Manning for Secretary of the Treasury and opposed Whitney's appointment to the Cabinet; and that Jones had told Cleveland that "You *regained, preserved* and have *transmitted* a political estate" to him; and that he should avail himself "of your wise counsel" and not "allow . . . your friends . . . to be pushed aside by the unscarred sycophants around him." From Washington came the news that the men who cheated him out of the Presidency—Bayard and Thurman—were making "insidious efforts" to get Cabinet positions.[39] Thus when the Cleveland-Tilden conference occurred at Graystone, Tilden was thoroughly posted. The formation of the Cabinet was discussed at length and Tilden urged the appointment of Manning as Secretary of the Treasury, to which Cleveland consented—reluctantly, Bigelow asserted.[40] Tilden also extended his advice on the silver question.

When Manning hesitated to accept, Tilden reminded him that if he refused the Cabinet would "have no true and reliable friend" in it. Further, that office should be filled by a New York man. If he declined absolutely, then Tilden wished to recommend Bigelow. "My career is completely ended," he said, but he wished to see a policy shaped that would "appeal overwhelmingly to the people" and not "impair the repose and comfort for which I have surrendered all public honor." Although Manning was ill at the "very thought" of the job and begged Tilden to release him, the latter was firm and Manning accepted. Weed sent Tilden a full account of the secret conference

[36] *Letters,* II, 665, 666.   [37] Jan. 25, 1885.   [38] *Letters,* II, 666.
[39] *Ib.,* 667, 669.   [40] *Life,* II, 291.

at Albany at which the Cabinet was completed.[41] Men like Hewitt and Godkin opposed Manning, but Randall supported Tilden's choice.[42] Through Weed, Tilden sought to have Frank Jones given the Navy portfolio, instead of W. C. Whitney, but failed. Hill asserted that Tilden wished Cleveland to accept Bigelow as Secretary of State,[43] but there is nothing in the documents to prove it. He did recommend Robert M. McLane as "highly qualified for a Cabinet place," but without effect.[44] Dr. George L. Miller, wished to become Postmaster General and thought "Tilden could decide it," [45] but the recommendation was waved aside, and Miller wrote, "I have been ashamed to see some of my friends since I went up like a rocket and came down like a stick." [46]

Tilden was disappointed in Cleveland's Cabinet but was too discreet to show his feeling to the public. He fully realized that "The formation of a Cabinet is a piece of mosaic in which each element may be affected by the size, texture, and color of the others entering into the combination; and it is impossible to foresee how much an individual element may be affected by the cast of the whole." [47] In the Cabinet Manning was the one member in whom Tilden could place implicit confidence. As a result he took more interest in the work of the Treasury Department than in any other. From Hugh McCulloch he obtained information upon which a sound financial policy might be constructed.[48] He induced C. N. Jordan to serve as Treasurer of the United States. He assisted Manning in the selection of trustworthy subordinates, and Manning, wisely enough, never arrived at any important decision without asking Tilden's advice. Indeed he seemed to be Tilden's rather than Cleveland's Secretary of the Treasury. Thus through Manning Tilden influenced the Cleveland administration for the first two years. In strictest confidence Tilden instructed him about the reorganization of his department and told him to consult Marble "about men." [49] The part of his *Annual Report* dealing with silver was written by Sidney Webster and Marble after consulting with Tilden.[50]

To a certain extent Tilden sought to control patronage through

[41] *Letters*, II, 677–678.   [42] Nevins, *Cleveland*, 195.   [43] *Times*, May 5, 1895.
[44] Tilden Papers, Apr. 6, 1885.   [45] *Ib.*, Miller to G. W. S., Jan. 2, 1885.
[46] *Ib.*, same to same, Nov. 26, 1885.   [47] *Letters*, II, 661, to Hoadley, Dec. 5, 1884.
[48] *Ib.*, 665, 672; *Life*, II, 291, 293.   [49] *Letters*, II, 680.
[50] Tilden Papers.

Manning to whom he wrote that H. J. Sibley, who transferred "support from me to Mr. Cleveland," should have a Federal position instead of J. M. Morton, whose father was "the principal concoctor and executor of the fraud of 1876." He sent Manning letters urging General Young as Minister to Bogota.[51] With W. P. Barnum he advised the appointment of F. E. Canda, a practical railroad man, as a director of the Union Pacific Railroad.[52] When grumblers like Watterson denounced Cleveland for neglecting Tilden's friends, Tilden explained that the President could not know men in all parts of the land and must deal with every class impartially, although he might act a bit more graciously. "I depended on ideas," Tilden said, "and less on party machinery." His policy was non-interference, and the newspaper gossip that his hand was seen in this or that policy was untrue. "If I were really to take an active part in appointments, it would impose on me a burden . . . I could not endure." To most applicants for positions he replied, "I am not in communication with Cleveland in respect to his appointments" and suggested that the President be reached through Manning.[53]

When a "Manning Club" was organized by employees of the Treasury Department, the President suppressed it. Manning was more amused than irritated by the incident, and immediately informed Tilden of it.[54] When in July, 1885, he had an apoplectic stroke, he turned pathetically to Tilden for advice, and went to see him.[55] Tilden urged him to take a long vacation and then, if well enough, to return to his post. Manning wrote on March 5, 1886, "No day passes that I do not wish I were near enough to you to get the benefit of your safe judgment." [56] Shortly thereafter he had a second stroke and hurried off to Hot Springs, Virginia, for treatment. To Fairchild, acting Secretary of the Treasury, Tilden offered his services, which were accepted.[57]

Manning was pathetically dependent on the aged Tilden's judgment for every step he took at Washington. En route to Albany from Hot Springs, Virginia, he called on Tilden,[58] and reported that the visit did him much good.[59] Tilden had his own physician make a thorough

---

[51] Manning Papers.   [52] Tilden Papers; *Letters,* II, 689.
[53] *Life,* II, 311, 316.   [54] *Letters,* II, 688, 690.   [55] Aug. 7, 1885.
[56] *Letters,* II, 704, 711.   [57] Tilden Papers, July 27, 1886.
[58] July 5, 1886.
[59] *Letters,* II, 727–728, July 11, 1886.

examination of Manning, who refused to accept the revenue cutter *Grant* for a cruise because he did not wish to be under any obligation to Cleveland. Determined to resign his office on October 1, 1886, he asked Tilden, "What shall I say?" Just a few days before he died, Tilden advised a short letter and said, "I will try my hand on a draft and send it to you." [60] The letter was prepared with the assistance of Weed and Marble and signed by Manning six months after Tilden's death.[61]

Few direct communications passed between Tilden and Cleveland because the former felt slighted and the latter wished to be free to carry out his own policies. At times, however, Tilden boldly asked the President for favors like the retention of D. A. McKnight "in the cause of public justice." [62] He sent on an office seeker's letter with the admonition, "Throw it in the waste basket." [63] When public policy seemed to demand it, he did not hesitate to wire Cleveland, "I think the country would greatly prefer you should not leave Washington till after the meeting of Congress." [64] Upon receiving an announcement of Cleveland's wedding, Tilden sent warm congratulations.

Anxious to stop the compulsory coinage of silver, Tilden discussed the problem with Cleveland personally [65] and, with Marble's help, wrote the President's "silver letter" issued on February 24, 1885. Later Cleveland declared that this was the first—and it would be the last—paper prepared by another hand for him. But Tilden, elated, wrote: "Your silver letter is absolutely perfect. It is the only silver thing I know that transmutes itself into gold." To Marble he sent the order, "Stick to Cleveland's silver letter—no novelties." [66] Six months before his death he was writing to George Bancroft about the danger of departing from the gold standard.[67] About the same time he prepared a brief on the "accountability of Corporations" in connection with a bill to repeal the Broadway Railroad Company's charter, and issued the warning that the "corruption of public officers, to obtain possession of valuable franchises at much less than their real worth, can only be stopped by making such schemes impossible to result in

[60] *Letters*, II, 729, July 21, 1886, 730.
[61] Typed copy of Weed's statement in Manning Papers, Lib. of Cong.
[62] Tilden Papers, Oct. 21, 1885. McKnight was the author of *The Electoral System; Letters*, II, 701.
[63] Tilden Papers, July 5, 1885.   [64] *Ib.*, Nov. 28, 1885.
[65] *Ib.*, Tilden to Randall, Feb. 14, 1885.   [66] *Ib.*, Feb. 28, 1885.
[67] *Letters*, II, 705, 706.

any profit." Hence he advocated a law for the public auction of such franchises and the criminal punishment of wrongdoers.[68]

The many years of friendship with Seymour may have been lukewarm but were never broken. When Tilden published his *Public Writings,* Seymour sent him a list of errors.[69] Tilden replied that he would let posterity "discredit or confute" Seymour's "misapprehensions." He would welcome a visit but understood that Seymour's hearing was impaired, so "social intercourse" would be difficult "between a dumb man and a deaf one." [70] The admiration of these two old political war horses for each other was impressive. Friendly rivals always and at times inclined to jealousy, they never had an open quarrel. Now Seymour was seventy-five, deaf, infirm of memory, suffering from "nervous attacks," and so fat that he looked better but felt worse; [71] Tilden was seventy-one, with sight, hearing and mind unimpaired, but no voice and his body wracked with aches. Seymour seldom read the papers, lived quietly in the country and had a man in constant attendance.

Tilden studied the political news daily, had a stream of callers at his rural retreat, and, through the devotion of younger Democrats, had a firm grip on the party. There was little question as to which was the abler statesman. Both were compared to Cleveland, and not always to his advantage. Hewitt described Cleveland as "the greatest master of platitudes since George Washington." [72]

Like his venerable friend Seymour, who died only a few months before Tilden,[73] the latter retained a deep interest in State politics as long as he lived. He took a fatherly interest in Governor D. B. Hill because he had watched him from the time he entered politics and it was he who suggested Hill for Governor in 1882. Colonel William Gorham Rice of Albany tells of an incident, both suggestive and amusing, of the relation of these two men. When Tilden was Governor, Hill was a rising young attorney in Elmira and deeply interested in party activities. Tilden, recognizing him as a man with excellent possibilities of leadership, had Apgar ask him to come to Albany. Hill, thinking that the call must be urgent, hurried up to the Capital. He arrived in the morning and made his way at once to the Executive Chamber. There

[68] *Ib.,* 708–711; H. J. Carman, *Railway Franchises of New York,* 1919.
[69] Clipping in the Rochester *Post Express,* in Tilden Papers.
[70] Tilden Papers, Sept. 22, 1885.   [71] *Letters,* II, 699, Sept. 25, 1885.
[72] Bishop, *Notes and Anecdotes,* 183.
[73] *Letters,* II, 707.

he waited all day, and it was not until evening that Tilden came out, shook his hand, and said, "Hill, you must remain until tomorrow." So he remained overnight and was in the Governor's outer office early the second day, hoping that the occasion for his summons would be explained so he could start home. But again he waited the whole day without being admitted to the inner office of the Governor, and was angry and impatient when the Governor at last appeared, shook his hand and whispered in his ear, "Hill, you must wait till tomorrow." Hill replied, "Governor, I have some important lawsuits and have to get back." Tilden put his hand on Hill's shoulder and said, "Hill, it's very important; come back tomorrow." The mystery and the insistence led Hill to believe that it must be a matter of much importance, so he remained the third day, and again cooled his heels all day, growing furious as the hours slipped by. Toward evening the Governor appeared, took Hill's arm and led him off to a corner of the room, put his hand on his shoulder, and whispered in his ear: "Hill, we must elevate the standard! We must elevate the standard! Thank you for coming. Good-bye." [74]

Governor Hill repeatedly asked Tilden for his opinion on important measures and his counsel was given generously. He wrote Hill at length about the bill to dissolve the Broadway Surface Railroad Company and advised its passage,[75] praised his messages, counseled him about vetoes, persuaded him to protect the Adirondacks and to save Niagara Falls, and instructed him about the State canals.[76] From the time Hill sat in the legislature with Tilden, onward, their "acquaintance ripened into a warm friendship which continued until Tilden's death." [77]

At the end of his career, Tilden considered the publication of his public papers and the preparation of his biography. He was urged to arrange his papers and include his own explanations.[78] Dana asked for the loan of his papers from 1837 to 1885 to write a history of politics, but never completed the project. He declared that in the previous history of fifty years only Bismarck, Disraeli and Tilden had the genius to rule men through their intellect.[79] Tilden turned over to Bigelow a mass of materials from which was prepared Tilden's *Writings and Public Papers*. Tilden took a deep interest in the compilation, insisted upon

[74] Personal conference, 1932.
[75] *Letters*, II, 684.
[76] *Life*, II, 295, 334, 338, 340.
[77] N.Y. *Times*, May, 1895.
[78] *Letters*, II, 615.
[79] *Ib.*, 656, 657.

including in the Preface "a full statement of his position," and corrected all the introductory explanations.[80] Autographed, complimentary copies were sent to his friends and brought forth many significant replies. "I look upon you," said W. G. Sumner, "as the best instance in our time of the . . . misapprehension and abuse which a man must endure if he tries to do any good to his fellow men. . . . In the end . . . your immense service to the people of New York City and the State, and to the whole country will meet with due recognition."

With a Democratic administration installed at Washington, Tilden believed the time had come to write the history of the fraud of 1876, because the Federal archives would be open. He purchased the large collection on the election of 1876 owned by W. M. Haden,[81] and employed A. M. Gibson to make the research and to write the book. Since 1870 Gibson had been exposing the corruptions of Republican administrations, such as the Crédit Mobilier, the Navy Ring and the Star Mail Routes. Being "embarrassed financially," he asked Tilden to employ him to prepare from the sources a book entitled *A Political Crime*,[82] and Manning was asked to give him "every facility for facts about the frauds of 1876." Although in working through the records of the various departments he found many important papers missing, yet he told Tilden, "The history of the Great Fraud has never been told, but it will be when I get through." An edition of 2,500 copies was printed, and the work had a "fine sale." Tilden not only paid him for his work but also loaned him $2,500 to pay for his home. After the publication of this work, Gibson, from Washington, sent Tilden information about railroads and the Cleveland administration, and pressed Tilden to secure his appointment as consul.[83]

Tilden devoted time in 1885 to a study of the defense of New York Harbor and other seaports. He paid for investigations, consulted engineers, conducted a heavy correspondence on the subject and wrote "Sea-Coast Defenses" for presentation to Congress. He asked Manning to persuade the President to incorporate it in his message to Congress or to include it in his own departmental report, but Manning feared that such action would seriously embroil his "personal relations" with the Chief Executive. Then Tilden, saying that he would "use the material in some other way," sent it to Randall and to Speaker Carlisle, who gave

[80] Tilden Papers, to Bigelow, March 28, 1885, and later dates.
[81] *Ib.*, Jan. 10, 1885. [82] *Letters*, II, 681.
[83] Tilden Papers, June 24, 1885, and later dates.

it to the press. The newspapers praised Tilden's recommendations, which made a deeper impression on the public mind than the President's message, and consequently they were "regarded with anything but satisfaction at the White House." [84] Tilden took pains to correct the impression that his voice carried much influence with Cleveland, who in fact felt competent to formulate and to execute his policies without advice from the Sage of Graystone.

Closely related in Tilden's mind with coast defenses was the responsibility implied in the Monroe Doctrine. Hence he prepared a concise history of that national policy after 1815 and asserted that Monroe had consulted Jefferson and Madison before issuing his famous message of 1823. He thought the germ of the doctrine was found in Jefferson's letters but gave Canning full credit for co-operation. English statesmen claimed too much credit, he thought, for the principle. [85] In like manner Tilden was in sympathy with Home Rule in Ireland and watched the movement with deep interest. A visit to the Emerald Isle had given him first-hand information and he placed great reliance on the wise statesmanship of Gladstone in solving the problem.

The Sage of Graystone had declared, "My career is completely ended" but it is obvious from the events narrated in this chapter that such was far from true—he was still a power to be reckoned with in State and national politics.

[84] *Life*, II, 297, 304, 306, 309.   [85] *Ib.*, 323–351.

IN 1884 Tilden told Bigelow that he believed he would live two more years and die at seventy-two. This was not a mere guess but the conclusion of a careful calculation based on all the factors involved—a trait characteristic of his whole life. Considering his frailty, these two years were crowded full of fruitful activities—a determination to make the most of his remaining days.

From childhood to death, real or imagined illness was an important factor in his existence. He was "troubled all his life with a delicate stomach." Dyspepsia and fits of vomiting ailed him to the end. If he ate things that did not agree with him, he paid the penalty with nausea and headache. If he went out to dine, and dinner was served a little later than usual, he suffered from it. Eventually he gave up tea, coffee and an occasional use of tobacco, because he thought they upset his stomach. Toward the end of his life he ate four times a day, and took a "great deal of mutton broth, meat, and bread, but not many vegetables." He was "inclined to be costive" and hence consumed stewed prunes regularly and, once a week, "took a cathartic of Carlsbad water, sprudel, or rhubarb and aloes." Walking and horseback riding aided his dyspepsia, and he used to ride in Albany in 1875 when the thermometer was fourteen degrees below zero. At seventy he lamented that he could no longer use a horse and had to take his exercise in a carriage or in walking. In the summer he made excursions on his steam yacht *Viking,* but only for "a few hours at a time." [1]

As a young man Tilden was severely afflicted with toothache and neuralgia, but skillful dentistry relieved him of this trouble as he grew older. As a result of a lifelong attention to diet, he developed positive convictions as to what he should not eat. In old age he abandoned his own judgment and followed the advice of his physicians in respect to food. He took pains to dress warmly, and to carry rubbers and an umbrella. Annoying colds, common in youth, almost disappeared during middle life, only to return during his last years as a cough and catarrh. As the foundation of his ailments he complained of a lack of "vital

[1] *Life,* II, 321–322.

nervous force"—whatever that might be. His associates noticed after 1875 a pronounced physical decline. An apoplectic stroke partially paralyzed one leg, one arm, and one eye. Shaking palsy affected his hands, and, after fatigue or excitement, his legs, and brought on "pulsations in the back of his head." Almost to his death he boasted of eyes and ears "more acute than those of most people" and of "strong and sound" vital organs, yet he complained of a mysterious malady of the "nerves of motion" and an impaired voice that deprived him of "the pleasures of conversation." [2]

A confirmed hypochondriac, Tilden was everlastingly diagnosing his condition and giving medical advice to his friends. Somewhere, he believed, there was a panacea for his ailments—hence his resort to non-narcotic drugs, to patent medicines, to mechanical manipulations and to electricity. Only late in life did he entrust his case to physicians and then spent a small fortune consulting specialists in America and Europe. He tried health resorts, the seashore and the mountains. For years he was a user of quinine to allay neuralgia and cure indigestion. His "regular habit" was to take four grains three times a day. Although Dr. Edward Bayard told him that this had broken down his constitution and that he must gradually reduce the dose,[3] he was of the opinion that the drug "gave him more strength." [4] For a long time he took hyoscyamus, a heart stimulant, four times daily as prescribed by Dr. Hamilton. "I think I am getting too much hyoscyamus into my system," he said to Dr. Simmons, who replied, "For God's sake don't stop it, for I wouldn't guarantee your existence twenty-four hours if you do." Tilden smiled and remarked, "Well, but I did stop it ten days ago."

For some years Dr. Austin Flint was Tilden's physician and in 1875 was paid $5,000 for his services. After 1881 he was constantly under the care of Dr. Charles E. Simmons, a brother-in-law of Dr. Flint, who had a summer home at Graystone rent-free, and lunched daily at Tilden's table. As compensation he received a check for $500 now and then. Angered because he was not provided for in Tilden's will, he presented the executors a bill for $143,350 and carried the case to court. Elihu Root acted as attorney for the executors, and seven years later an adjustment was made.[5] The report that a dental bill for

[2] *Life*, II, 320, 322.   [3] Tilden Papers, Mar. 27, 1884.
[4] *Life*, II, 322.   [5] Tilden Papers.

$150,000 was settled for half that sum was flatly denied by G. W. Smith.[6]

For twenty years G. W. Smith served Tilden faithfully as his private secretary. He always had a room in Tilden's home and was treated like a son. His wife, whom he married in 1875, was distantly related to Tilden and ably supplemented her husband's ministrations. Tilden's last words were "Where's Smith?"[7] Smith took delight in relating anecdotes of the eccentricities of his employer. "Take a quarter out of my pocket," he would say to Smith, "and get me some peppermint lozenges." Of inferior plants and animals at Graystone, he would remark with a grin, "Oh, those are Smith's." When Tilden was asked before the Potter Committee, "But Mr. Smith was your private secretary, wasn't he?" he snapped, "That is what he calls himself." Angered, Smith absented himself from the office next day. "Where's Smith?" Tilden asked and upon being told roared: "Send for him at once! Damn it, I can't get along with him and I can't get along without him!" When dictating, Tilden would munch crackers as he walked up and down the room; hence his words were indistinct. "I didn't get that," complained Smith. "You must be getting deaf," retorted Tilden. "No, but you seem to be losing your power of speech," answered Smith, "besides I don't see any sense in this." "Well, read it." Smith read, "The barbarous civilization of an uninhabitable wilderness." Tilden stopped walking and asked: "What's that? Read it again." That being done, he curtly ordered, "Cross it out." At Sea Girt for a rest with Smith, he remarked to a hotel waiter, "I can't cut this steak." "I'll get you a better knife," politely answered the waiter, "No, bring me a better steak," suggested Tilden. Amusingly, he often said his relatives did not know how to make money; and when they did make it, they didn't know how to keep it.[8] To his attendant, William H. Davis, he said, "Don't snore until I get to sleep; then I don't care how much you snore."[9]

As the summer of 1886 approached, Tilden's physical decline was marked. He slept two hours in the daytime and four stretches of an hour and a half each at night. Always an early riser, he was up at six. After a bath and a shave, he took a walk about the grounds and then had breakfast, being fed by his valet. Miss Gould usually fed him at

[6] *Sun*, Feb. 25, 1912. [7] Mrs. G. W. Smith, Ms. Notes.
[8] *Ib.* [9] *World*, Aug. 17, 1886.

other meals because of his unsteady hands. He took whiskey and soda at lunch and enjoyed champagne at dinner.[10] Edward Riley, a young Irishman, dressed in blue with a white hat,[11] drove him out, in a carriage built with sensitive springs and flexible cushions so as to give him an airing without jarring fatigue. He never knew how to use his hands with the simplest tools or to tie his cravat. He never carried a cane, except for a short time in Paris in 1877 by his doctor's orders, yet he had dozens of them presented to him, of which about fifty are preserved in the Tilden chemical plant in New Lebanon.[12] He was a wretched driver and made his friends nervous for his safety. Always careless about his attire, this habit was accentuated as he grew older. Henry Havemeyer was ashamed of his untidy appearance when he dined with him at Delmonico's but forgot all about it when Tilden began to talk. His clothes were expensive and clean but his coat and trousers did not seem to hang becomingly. His tastes were few, simple, and rural.

The nickname "Whispering Sammy" originated before he became Governor, but because of an ailment of the bronchial tubes, toward the end of his life he lost the full and natural use of his voice. The drooping eyelid resulted from an abscess above the eye about 1874. His eyes were blue and unusually expressive—twinkling with merriment, opening with amazement, half-closing with sternness, or flashing with anger. His nose was large for his round face and was frequently reddened with colds, his chin was prominent and indicative of a firm will. His face as a whole was pleasant and attractive.[13] Good stories "rested him," but he seldom told any himself except by way of reminiscence. He was both a good listener and a fluent talker. In his old age a few intimates felt free to call at anytime, but others had to make appointments. Old friends like Watterson and Marble continued to write him affectionate letters to the end of his days.[14]

Without wife or children, Tilden's affection for his animals was delightful. Indeed, one might say that he was fonder of animals than of humans. None of them was permitted to be killed. His saddle horse was kept till he died of old age. From his youth he had owned horses and when rich paid as much as $10,000 for a span and $1,500 for a

[10] W. H. Davis, *Sun*, Aug. 22, 1886.   [11] *Ib.*
[12] Interview with Harry J. Cox.   [13] Mrs. G. W. Smith, Ms. Notes.
[14] "You are the only shadow who has ceased with dignity from pursuing shadows," wrote Marble. Marble Papers.

saddle horse.[15] At Graystone he kept a stable of thirteen horses. He would have turned over in his grave had he known that his hostler suggested the sale of "Topic" for $30. He took the deepest pride in his fine poultry and livestock, winning prizes at county fairs. Companionship with his cats and dogs was one of his joys. In 1879 he paid $100 for a St. Bernard and bought a mate. These huge dogs were his constant companions in his walks about his farm. He soon added a mastiff, and these dogs were exhibited at kennel shows, while their master was a member of various dog clubs. Fond of flowers and plants, he took keen delight in his thirteen hothouses, his orchards, and his gardens. To him no present to a friend could surpass a bull calf, or a prize rooster, or a red-ribboned apple.[16]

Although at Graystone Tilden usually had a house full of relatives and a large staff of employees, he enjoyed getting away to one of his clubs in New York City with Dana, Bigelow, or some other friend. Among the clubs to which he belonged were the Free Trade, Union, Yacht, Century, St. Nicholas, Union League, American Jockey, and Manhattan.[17] When his sister Mrs. Pelton wished to go to live with her granddaughter, Mrs. Hazard, Tilden made her a generous allowance and bought her a home of her own in New York City. He was always a gracious host to political friends and particularly to visitors from Columbia County. One morning a farmer from New Lebanon called and exclaimed as he shook hands, "I am glad to see you, but Lord, how you have changed!" Without expression, Tilden asked for all the news and pressed his visitor to stay for luncheon. Another agriculturist, lunching with Tilden and some other guests, when asked by the butler whether he would have another cup of tea, said, "No, but I'll have this fired." Noting the butler's puzzled look, Tilden explained, "Henry, Mr. H*** would like some more hot tea in his cup." [18]

Tilden had the reputation of being parsimonious, but this seems to have been due to the fact that, not liking to be bothered drawing checks, he allowed his accounts with merchants to run over long periods of time. His secretary finally induced him to sign a number of blank checks at one time and filled them out as they were needed to pay current bills. He was never known to turn a beggar aside and would take from his pocket the first piece of money his fingers touched, large or

[15] W. H. Davis, *Sun*, Aug. 22, 1886.   [16] *Ib.*   [17] Tilden Papers.
[18] Mrs. G. W. Smith, Ms. Notes.

small, present it, and pass on. Smith said to his wife repeatedly: "What does Tilden do with his pocket money? I cash a check for $50 for him and in two days it is gone." He always gave more than he was asked to good causes, such as $25,000 to relieve the potato famine in Ireland, but he hated to be imposed on. When the Democratic Committee asked for a contribution, he inquired of Smith, "How much?" "Doesn't say," replied his secretary. "If they don't know what they want, send them nothing," added Tilden. When Hancock complained that no one was assisting his campaign financially, Tilden sent a check for $25,-000.[19] While Samuel J. Tilden II was visiting at Graystone, a caller arrived. Tilden sent his nephew into an adjoining room while he conferred with his visitor and handed him a check. After the caller departed, Tilden said, "Samuel, I've just saved forty thousand dollars." In astonishment the nephew exclaimed, "Why, I don't understand how you could do that, because I saw you hand him a check." "Aha," answered Tilden, "I was under deep obligation to that man. He asked me for a loan of fifty thousand, and I made him a present of ten thousand—and he was perfectly satisfied. Ha! Ha! So you see I saved forty thousand." [20]

Tilden took no interest in games such as cards, billiards, chess and checkers. He never learned how to play, and such diversions as horse racing and poker never appealed to him. He derived little enjoyment from either music or the theater. His box at the Opera, which he always took and occasionally occupied, was usually turned over to his secretary, with suggestions for guests. He subscribed regularly for tickets to the Charity Ball and other social functions, but gave them to friends, rarely attending himself. Nor did a beautiful painting, or a striking work of sculpture or a noble building kindle any appreciative enthusiasm, although he bought some fine canvases to adorn his home. He had no ear for music and never learned to dance. Indeed from childhood to old age his pleasures were all intellectual [21]—a gigantic mind driving a body too frail and weak for the power directing it. Deriving his happiness from within, he was dependent on neither friendly associations nor material amusements. He took pride in worldly possessions because they brought intellectual stimulus and gave him joy in increasing his own comforts and those of others.

[19] Mrs. G. W. Smith, Ms. Notes.   [20] Interview with J. Harry Cox, New Lebanon.
[21] *Life*, II, 375–376.

This man of large affairs devoured journals and books. Almost to the day of his death the newspapers were read to him at breakfast, and at other times during the day as they were delivered. He must know what was going on in the world. When he was so weak that he could neither hold a book nor turn its pages, books were read to him day and night.

The reading done by Tilden during the last few years of his life, mostly in biography and history, is almost unbelievable. In his active career he read the newspapers with careful reflection but the use of books was limited and spasmodic. Miss Anna T. Gould, his faithful attendant, kept a list of materials read to him from April, 1882, till August, 1886, which includes about 700 titles. In addition there were constant references to the encyclopedia, and all the magazines. Certain of Macaulay's essays were "read over and over again." He was fond of guidebooks, which recalled to mind his visits to European lands.[22] Much of Tilden's time during 1886 was devoted to the completion of the Tilden genealogy.[23] He cared little for poetry or fiction, and even less for metaphysics and the natural sciences.

His love of books was stimulated by his father. Carefully preserved among his papers is a small volume entitled *The Bucktail Bards,* which bore the inscription: "E. Tilden, New Lebanon, May 1, 1820." First he collected a library of schoolbooks, then a law library which was one of the best in New York City. As he became affluent, he branched out into history, biography and general literature, with excellent taste and little regard for expense, until he had assembled about twenty thousand volumes, many of them rare and costly publications. He had the spirit of a true collector, appreciated rare items, enjoyed beautiful bindings and fine printing, and took discernible pride in possession. Much reliance was placed on the recommendations of trusted dealers and bibliophiles. Less than a month before his death, Tilden asked Bigelow to arrange for the purchase of valuable manuscripts for his library.[24] He owned an original volume of Jefferson's personal accounts[25] and in 1885 he purchased the original diary of Jefferson.[26]

Not long after a visit by Bigelow, on July 17, 1886, Tilden was prostrated by a bad cold and bowel trouble while watching the erection of a railroad from his mansion down to his yacht. He enjoyed ob-

[22] *Life,* II, 348; Appendix C, 411, gives a list of books read.
[23] *Ib.,* 411.   [24] *Ib.,* 352.   [25] *Ib.,* 357.
[26] Tilden Papers.

serving the progress of the construction and conversing with the engineer. His English nurse, William H. Davis, a man of fifty, who had been with him since October 10, 1885, said he was "an easy patient, always cheerful . . . never peevish . . . like so many old men, but often nervous and annoyed." Though wakened at 4 A. M. to take his medicine, he never complained. During the later months, he was unable to close his lips, and used his left hand to move his lower jaw or to tilt his head. By sheer will power he utilized every atom of physical strength to keep alive.[27]

Tilden died at 8:45 A. M., August 4, 1886, at Graystone, in the presence of Dr. C. E. Simmons and Dr. Samuel Swift. When the news reached Yonkers, Hudson and the city, the flags on public buildings and some newspaper offices were floated at half-staff.[28] Governor Hill in a eulogistic proclamation ordered a similar display on all State buildings in memory of "One of the ablest statesmen and . . . a foremost citizen." [29] President Cleveland wired his "individual sorrow" at the loss of New York's "most distinguished son" and one of the nation's "wisest and most patriotic counselors." [30] Hill with his staff, Cleveland with his Cabinet, and a host of other distinguished men, journeyed to Yonkers for the simple funeral on August 7.[31]

The list of names as they appeared in the newspapers sound like a Democratic National Convention with a few Republicans, such as W. A. Butler and General Alexander Hamilton. Among those attending, were Mayor Grace, Bigelow, Barnum, Jordan, Murphy, Green, Beattie, Sullivan, Perrin, Fellows, Merriman, Hewitt, Flower, Dana, Randall, Campbell, Schofield, Purcell, Pulitzer, Canda, Fryer, Hutchins, Hughes, Bartlett, Fairfield, Pearsall and Whitney. Among the many organizations represented appeared the delegates of Tammany Hall, Irving Hall, the Manhattan Club, the Bar-Association, whose delegate was Wm. M. Evarts, and the County Democracy.

The body in full dress with a white tie was placed in a casket covered with violet velvet and lay in state in the Blue Room of Graystone.[32] Hundreds took a last look at the departed statesman—the greatest Democratic leader between Andrew Jackson and Grover

---

[27] *Sun*, Aug. 23, 1886.

[28] *Life*, II, 356. Age 72 years, 5 months and 26 days, in death certificate. His last words were: "Where is Smith?" alluding to his confidential secretary. Mrs. G. W. Smith, Ms. Notes.

[29] Newspapers, Aug. 5, 1886.   [30] *Life*, II, 358.   [31] *Argus*, Aug. 8, 1886.

[32] Nevins, *Cleveland*, 366.

Cleveland. Tilden's death left Cleveland the peerless leader of his party. Moved by a deep emotion, the President was the last to leave Graystone.[33] He had never liked Tilden, yet his own political ideals and principles had been molded to a greater degree than he himself realized by the voice stilled by death.

In the absence of Dr. Charles Parkhurst of the Madison Square Church, where Tilden had a pew, brief rites with simple music were conducted by Dr. William Jewett Tucker, President-emeritus of Dartmouth College, Tilden's former pastor.[34] The honorary pall-bearers were: Bigelow, Manning, Randall, Weed, G. L. Miller, Dana, Dr. Simmons, W. A. Butler, A. J. Vanderpoel, Magone, J. B. Trevor and C. F. Adams. The next day the remains, accompanied by eight of Tilden's employees, were conveyed in Chauncey M. Depew's private car along a route showing everywhere evidence of sorrow. At Hudson, where an extra car was added to the funeral train, the church bells tolled. At New Lebanon the funeral procession of 32 carriages proceeded to the Presbyterian Church. There, where Tilden and his family had worshiped and a chapel was being built as his gift, five thousand people bade farewell to him while the organ played solemn music. The inhabitants of the village and countryside for miles around were present. As the Episcopal burial service was read by Mr. Barsill, his mortal remains were placed in a steel box within a marble-lined tomb in the beautiful cemetery. Among those present were Tilden's boyhood friends, Hampton Bull and Nelson Tanner, Shakers.[35] Tilden's last visit to New Lebanon had been in September, 1876.

From the pen of John G. Whittier, Tilden's death called forth the following lines:

> Once more, O all-adjusting Death!
>   The Nation's Pantheon opens wide;
> Once more a common sorrow saith
>   A strong, wise man has died.
>
>   .   .   .   .   .
>
> Ambitious, cautious, yet the man
>   To strike down fraud with resolute hand;
> A patriot, if a partisan,
>   He loved his native land.
>
>   .   .   .   .   .

[33] *Ib.*, 75.   [34] Mrs. G. W. Smith, Ms. Notes.
[35] *Argus*, Aug. 9, 1886.

> Then let us vow above his bier
> To set our feet on party lies,
> And wound no more a living ear
> With words that Death denies.[36]

The newspapers commented on Tilden's passing as a national calamity. The Boston *Transcript* summed up his career as "a politician, a philosopher and a patriotic citizen." "The Great Democrat is Dead," announced the *Herald*. Reviewing his career, this paper said that he was a master of the art of politics, who for thirteen years as Chairman of the State Democratic Committee had managed his party. He invented the "still hunt" for votes, and had a list of 48,000 Democrats outside of the metropolis. After ceasing to be State Chairman his influence was well-nigh as great as before. The *World* characterized him as a "thoroughly equipped statesman." The *Sun* described him as "amiable, affectionate, unpretending and kindly"—qualities that became more marked in his old age than in the prime of his activity. The Albany *Journal* suggested that Hill, in traveling the path of thorns, would miss the steadying hand of Tilden.

Tilden's remains were buried in the Tilden lot in the cemetery at New Lebanon, where a special lot was purchased on which a beautiful memorial tomb was built. George F. Hull reported on December 28, 1895, that the body had been placed under the monument on Christmas morn. Next year the monument was completed and several summers were devoted to landscaping the plot.[37] And there in "the beautiful valley in which I was born," as Tilden was accustomed to refer to New Lebanon,[38] rest his ashes.

On the evening of May 23, 1887, the legislature's memorial exercises were held in honor of Tilden in the Assembly Chamber at Albany before a distinguished audience. Among the relatives present were Samuel J. Tilden II, Misses Susie and Ruby Tilden, and Mrs. Swan. Judge Rufus W. Peckham presided and the Honorable George Raines delivered the eulogistic address.[39]

On March 18, 1888, thirty-seven admirers and friends of Tilden presented to the State of New York, through Governor Hill, a portrait painted by Frank Fowler. Among the donors were: S. L. M. Barlow,

[36] *Letters*, II, 730. Five stanzas in poem. [37] Tilden Papers.
[38] *Letters*, II, 447.
[39] Albany and New York newspapers, May 24, 1887.

August Belmont, C. J. Canda, Bourke Cockran, Richard Croker, C. A. Dana, R. P. Flower, W. R. Grace, H. O. Havemeyer, George Hoadley, and Peter B. Olney.[40]

[40] Tilden Papers.

AFTER the Civil War, Tilden's shrewd investments made him wealthy, but that fact was not commonly known until advertised to the nation by the Republicans in 1876. In popular imagination thereafter he was a Croesus, and the report caused him considerable embarrassment. Perhaps he was the richest lawyer in the United States and might be ranked with opulent captains of industry, but a fortune of half a century ago was a trifle compared with the possessions of magnates today. Tilden was several times a millionaire; that was all.

From Tilden's papers prior to his death no one could gain more than a rough approximation of either his capital or his earnings, and it may be doubted whether even his private secretary knew the exact figures. After his demise his estate was appraised by experts at $5,229,-115.[1] About 10% was in houses and lands, 10% in iron mines in Michigan, and 80% in personal property, including stocks, bonds, and cash. The real estate consisted of Graystone, given a market value of $165,-000 [2] and finally sold at auction for $150,000; Gramercy Park, appraised at $310,000; a house and lot on Broadway, valued at $28,000; the Baldwin tract, estimated to be worth $25,000; building lots in Brooklyn; and some property in Bergen County, New Jersey. The appraised worth of his real estate was $473,753.[3]

Tilden's part in developing the mining of iron ore deserves more space than can be given to it here. The New York Iron Mine in Michigan was incorporated in March, 1863, on property leased, on a royalty of 27 cents a ton, for $500,000, with 20,000 shares, of which Tilden owned 14,667 shares and the Wetmores, local owners of the original land, 5,333 shares. On May 20 of that year Wetmore sold his twenty-year lease to Tilden for $6,000, but remained manager of the company until 1878. Meantime the New York & Boston Iron Mining Company was incorporated under a lease from A. H. Harlow, and 8,000 tons of ore were shipped in 1864. These two companies were amal-

---

[1] *Case on Appeal,* 148. Testimony of G. W. Smith.
[2] Tilden Papers, Dec. 27, 1886.
[3] *Ib.,* Report of executors, Jan. 24, 1887. When a real estate agent told him that he could sell Graystone at a profit of $100,000, Tilden replied, "How annoying! I have just set out 50 fine peach trees."

gamated on April 8, 1865, under the title of the New York Iron Mining Company, with a capital stock of $250,000, in 10,000 shares, of which Tilden owned 6,000 and J. P. Sinnott and John Rankin, Jr., 2,000 shares each. Royalties at 8 cents a ton paid to Harlow three and a half years amounted to $44,877.19. In 1883 the New York Iron Mining Company was reorganized as the New York Mining Company on a 35-cent-royalty basis, with a capital of $500,000, and 20,000 shares, of which Tilden owned 15,000, G. W. Smith, 4,985, and others, 15. These mining ventures brought Tilden a profit of $1,000,000 and also enriched some of his friends. He acted as president and treasurer and virtually owned the concern. Tilden's executors inherited the mine and with it considerable litigation.[4]

The Iron Cliffs Company in the same region was incorporated by Tilden, W. B. Ogden and J. W. Foster, on September 15, 1864, with a capital stock of $1,000,000 in 40,000 shares at $25 each. This company bought the St. Mary's Ship Canal, 38,000 acres owned by the Mineral Land Company in Marquette County, and 2,000 acres from the Pioneer Company. It also acquired and operated the Foster Mine, opened in 1865, and the Barnum Mine somewhat later and erected a furnace. The first shipment of ore was made in 1866, and charcoal pig iron became one of its products. Out of this investment Tilden made $500,000. After his death the mine was managed by his executors until 1890, when the stock was selling for $90 a share. It was merged as a subsidiary concern with the Cleveland-Cliffs Iron Company.[5] Tilden also owned, with W. L. Wetmore, 1,560 acres of land, about 30 miles south of Marquette, which in 1886 was estimated as worth $7,800.[6] Tilden, owning shares in 8 companies, was accustomed to visit these properties at least once a year and was frequently the guest of Peter White, who honored him with a display of flags in the harbor. To ship ore by water, an extensive ore dock was built at Escanaba, and Tilden and his friends acquired possession of the railroads in that area, together with 1,200,000 acres of land.[7]

The bulk of Tilden's estate consisted of personal property amounting to $4,713,648. There were bonds in 24 railroad companies; stocks in 16 railroad companies; $10,000 of Tammany Society first mortgage

---

[4] Tilden Papers.
[5] L. A. Chase to the author, Nov. 2, 1929; James E. Joppling to the author, Dec. 3, 1929. See *Geological Survey of Michigan,* 1869–73.
[6] Tilden Papers, Wetmore to G. W. Smith, Aug. 12, 1886.
[7] Letter from J. E. Joppling, Dec. 3, 1929.

bonds; and Michigan timber lands. A few worthless securities were found, such as Lebanon Springs Railroad bonds and a loan for $5,000 to A. M. Gilbert. Tilden & Company was indebted to him for about $300,000. Cash in New York banks amounted to $41,713 and there was a cash account of $647,475 in the Union Bank, London. Furniture was estimated at $20,000; books at $18,000; and wines and liquors at $5,703. There were 48 full bottles and 157 pint bottles of "Steinberger Cabinet Imperial 1868"; 64 bottles of "Château Lafitte 1864"; 70 bottles of "O. O. Maderie"; 17 cases of "White Bordeaux"; 74 bottles of champagnes; some Johannisberger Blue Seal of 1862 and 1865; a case of "Château Pope Clement 1871"; 16 gallons of bourbon and rye whiskey; 11 jugs of Schiedam gin; 7 bottles of cognac; 3 bottles of cider brandy; and 150 bottles of Apollinaris and seltzer.[8] Tilden was a connoisseur of wines and took delight in sending a bottle to a friend. When a caller drank a glass of fine wine in a gulp, Tilden said to his butler, "Give him a glass of beer next time."[9]

Included in the personal property were loans of $133,000 to Smith M. Weed; $45,000 to Dana; and certain sums to H. A. Richmond and others. A loan of $20,000 to Bigelow had been canceled, Tilden saying: "Draw a line through that. Bigelow is a litterateur—he will never be able to pay it." Weed tried to induce the executors to return his notes, on the ground that he had repaid Tilden in political services, but they refused and the notes were paid in full.[10] Cosby the artist owed $10,000 and the executors accepted the picture "Stoke Pogis" in payment for the debt.[11] The yacht was sold for $35,000.[12]

The property enumerated above was what Tilden had to dispose of by will. In 1873, while planning a trip to Europe, he instructed J. P. Sinnott to draft his first will, but it was destroyed when A. H. Green drew up the second will which still survives and presaged the third and final document. There was much speculation as to what he would do with his large fortune. Representatives of numerous causes sought to influence his decision and friends proffered advice. Tilden himself gave serious thought to the problem of his wealth and felt that "a rich

[8] Tilden Papers. See *World*, Apr. 18, 1888.　　　[9] Seitz, *The Also Rans*.
[10] Tilden Papers.
[11] Mrs. G. W. Smith, Ms. Notes.
[12] About $200,000 in stocks and bonds was found in Smith's name. He claimed that Tilden intended them for him. Bigelow and Green contended that these securities be turned over to the estate and Smith, after much deliberation, did so to save his reputation. Mrs. G. W. Smith, Ms. Notes.

man is primarily a trustee of society." [13] While working out the terms of his last testament, his secretary called attention to $74,000 placed in his hands for investment by Miss Catherine Pierson, between 1849 and 1868. So wisely had the money been handled that it amounted to $270,000, which was sent to her representative.[14] He promised Mrs. G. W. Smith that her husband would be so well cared for that he would never "work for anybody else." [15] The will of 10,000 words in 43 sections was executed on April 23, 1884. As a lawyer he concerned himself with wills now and then, the most notable instance being that of Martin Van Buren, but he did not profess to be an authority on the law in such matters.

Cautious as usual, he turned the long document over to Charles O'Conor for examination. After several conferences with Tilden and Bigelow, O'Conor approved the will as "wise and absolutely valid," but advised a few changes. He praised the provisions safeguarding female relatives against any masculine influence, for "if the money were left to them outright . . . some man . . . would either kiss it out of them or kick it out of them." [16] However, he suggested that it be submitted to James C. Carter, who gave it a hasty examination and returned it with assurance that it was good law.[17] Procrastination and illness prevented Tilden from having the points raised by O'Conor definitely settled, so the will stood as written with a few minor alterations.

On the Monday following the funeral, August 9, the will was read in the library at Graystone by James C. Carter, in the presence of the three executors; Mrs. Mary B. Pelton and her granddaughter, Laura A. Pelton; six children of Henry A. Tilden—two nephews and four nieces; and the adopted daughter of Moses Y. Tilden, Adelaide E. McGuire Buchanon. It made the following provisions:

1. That George W. Smith, Andrew H. Green, and John Bigelow be executors and trustees at an annual salary of $5,000 each in lieu of commissions and charges. In case of death the survivors were empowered to choose successors, thus making the board self-perpetuating. From Smith's salary was to be deducted his pay as private secretary and as an officer in two iron companies.

2. That Mrs. Mary B. Pelton during her life should have the use of

[13] Brooklyn *Union*, Aug. 12, 1886.
[14] *Life*, II, 380. Miss Pierson was his mother's sister.   [15] Mrs. G. W. Smith, Ms. Notes.
[16] Tilden Papers, G. W. Smith to *Times*, Sept. 19, 1916.
[17] Mrs. G. W. Smith, "The Tilden Will and Its Vicissitudes."

the house at 38 West Thirty-Eighth Street free and clear, and also the interest on three life trusts of $50,000 each. After her death the house and one of the life trusts should go to her granddaughter, Laura A. Pelton; the interest on a second life trust was to go to Caroline B. Whittlesey, a niece of Tilden; and the third life trust was to revert to the Tilden estate.

3. Two life trusts of $25,000 each were set aside for Lucy F. Tilden, widow of Moses; and after her death one of the life trusts to go to her adopted daughter, Adelaide E. Buchanon, if not otherwise disposed of. To Mrs. Buchanon [18] was conveyed $5,000 in loans to her husband and the interest for life on $20,000 in bonds of the Oregon Short Line Railroad.

4. The sum of $50,000 to go as a life trust to Susan G. Tilden, widow of Henry, and upon her death to her daughter Henrietta A. Swan.

5. The interest on 100 shares of the Cleveland & Pittsburgh Railroad to go to his niece, Caroline B. Whittlesey; and after her death to her heirs. To her was also assigned the stock in the Delphic Iron Company, the debts owed Tilden by her husband, and enough cash to make a life trust of $50,000.

6. A life trust of $50,000 and 100 shares of the Cleveland & Pittsburgh Railroad went to his niece, Henrietta A. Swan.

7. The heirs-at-law of Moses and Henry were requested to convey to their respective widows the Tilden properties for life so as to keep the Elam Tilden property at New Lebanon, N.Y. intact during the lifetime of George H. and Samuel J. Tilden, II.

8. His nephews George H. and Samuel J. Tilden, II, were released from a loan of $34,000 and a mortgage of $33,000, and from certain notes given to Catherine H. Pierson, which he endorsed to save his mother from doing so. For each of these two brothers a special trust of $75,000 was created, and on their written request loans to their father amounting to $300,000 were to be canceled.

9. Special trusts of $150,000 each were to be set up for his two unmarried nieces, Ruby S. and Susan G. Tilden.

10. A trust of $100,000 was created for Anna J. Gould, his attendant, who was given power to dispose of half of that sum; the sum of $500 a year for life was to be paid to Henrietta Jones of Monticello; the sum

[18] The daughter of Tilden's dentist, Dr. B. F. McGuire, at whose house Tilden had rooms for awhile. He settled Dr. McGuire's estate and after Mrs. McGuire's death persuaded his brother Moses to adopt the eight-year-old daughter.

of $5,000 was given to John J. Cahill, a secretary; not over $500 a year was to go to Mrs. James P. Sinnott for five years to educate her children; and ten employees were to receive from $500 to $1,000 each.

11. His "friend" Marie Celeste Stauffer, of New Orleans, was to have for life the income on $100,000 in railroad bonds free "from control of any husband;" and she had power to dispose of the principal by will.

12. The sum of $50,000 was given for a Library and Free Reading Room in Yonkers; $80,000 for a similar institution and a school for training girls in New Lebanon; and the residue of his estate was to be used to establish and maintain a like institution in New York City and for "such charitable, educational and scientific purposes" as the executors might judge best for "the interests of mankind." His books were to be given to libraries or disposed of. The sum of $10,000 was left to care for the New Lebanon Cemetery and a like amount was to be applied according to instructions. A suitable monument was to be erected to his memory; his public papers were to be published; and the executors were authorized to "burn and destroy any of my letters, papers or other documents, whether printed or in manuscript, which in their judgment will answer no useful purpose to preserve."

13. The executors were empowered to manage the trusts and funds as they "shall deem advisable" until all the terms of the will were met or until the death of his niece Ruby S. Tilden and his grand-niece Susie Whittlesey. And any heir who under any pretense opposed the probate of the will should lose all share in the estate.[19]

These bequests show that Tilden was generous with his relatives, giving them approximately $1,400,000, while outsiders were bequeathed only $225,000. George H. and Samuel J. Tilden, II, received the largest share—a total of $567,000—although all but $75,000 each was in canceled debts. Particular care was taken to safeguard the Tilden fortune from speedy disintegration by setting up life trusts and making provision for its inheritance by the second and third generations. The outstanding significance of the will is that through it Tilden intended to devote about two-thirds of his wealth for cultural and scientific purposes.

The Albany *Argus* on August 8 reported that George H. and Samuel J. Tilden, II, asserted that the will would not be broken,[20] but after

[19] Will printed in *Life*, II, Appendix D, 420; Hun., *Supreme Court Reports*, LXI, 231.
[20] August 9, 1886.

it was read the next day some members of the family "immediately manifested their bitter disappointment that larger sums were not left to them . . . and announced their intention to attack it." [21] They thought of engaging Judge Charles F. MacLean, but, upon learning of his large fee, they had Robert D. Buchanon, husband of the adopted daughter of Moses, obtain a loan of $50,000 from Robert G. Dun of the well-known mercantile agency. This sum was put in the hands of George H. Tilden for action. So distrustful were the seven heirs of one another that each engaged an attorney. Judge E. Countryman and Joseph H. Choate each received $150,000 for his services, the latter serving as the leading counsel of the contesting heirs and also representing the interests of Marie Celeste Stauffer. Lyman D. Brewster got $50,000; and no one seems to know how much Delos McCurdy, a close friend of Henry A. Tilden was paid. James M. Hunt appeared for the Yonkers Library; New York City had its own attorney, and the executors employed Carter and Ledyard. The situation was complicated by the fact that banks from Fishkill to Albany expected to have their loans to the tottering firm of Tilden & Company repaid out of the Tilden fortune. John Bigelow and G. W. Smith, executors, sought Governor Hill's advice about the will.[22]

On the day the will was probated at White Plains, October 10, 1886, George H. and Samuel J. Tilden, II, nephews, contested its validity in the Supreme Court of New York County, special term, through Vanderpoel, Green and Cuming, attorneys.[23] Bigelow states that these nephews were "largely in debt" and were pressed by their creditors to take that action.[24] Their counsel claimed that the provision for libraries at New Lebanon and Yonkers, and the 35th clause of the will were too indefinite, since they gave the executors authority to use the residue of the estate for "such charitable, educational and scientific purposes" as they might deem "beneficial to the interests of mankind." The case came up for trial in November, 1888, in a special term, with Joseph H. Choate, L. D. Brewster and Delos McCurdy counsel for the heirs; and James C. Carter, Lewis C. Ledyard, Daniel Rollins, George F. Comstock and Smith M. Weed representing the executors.[25] In January, 1889, Justice

21 Mrs. G. W. Smith, Ms. Notes.
22 Hill Papers. John Bigelow to D. B. Hill, Sept. 13, 1886.
23 Mrs. G. W. Smith, Ms. Notes; *Bulletin* of the New York Public Library. The will was also probated in England.
24 *Life*, II, 361.   25 Mrs. G. W. Smith, Ms. Notes.

Lawrence decided that the contested clause was valid.[26]

The case was then appealed to the general term of the Supreme Court—Smith M. Weed now joining the heirs as counsel—where the decision of Justice Lawrence was reversed on November 8, 1889, by a vote of two to one. The executors then carried the case to the second division of the Court of Appeals where on October 27, 1891, by a vote of four to three, it was decided that the 35th clause was invalid, thus reversing the lower court. Judge Brown wrote the major opinion that the "fatal defect" of the will was that "The will of the trustees is made controlling, and not the will of the testator." [27] The motion of the executors on November 30 for an opportunity to reargue the case was denied, also by a divided vote. Thus the Tilden will was broken. This division of the Court of Appeals was composed of judges of the Supreme Court temporarily designated by Governor Hill to assist in clearing its clogged calendar. Angling for votes for the United States Senatorship, Hill promised Samuel J. Tilden, II, who was on his military staff, that he would "fix it" so the family and creditors would "succeed in what they wanted." Hence he arranged to have the case brought before the second division, on which sat two judges "who would positively vote against the validity of the Tilden will and one other who, he thought, might." The last named judge was Alton B. Parker, whose vote turned the decision "against the validity of the will." Before this final settlement of the legality of the will, G. W. Smith suggested to Smith M. Weed that his client, Mrs. Laura P. Hazzard, might be persuaded to compromise with the executors, which she did before the final decision was rendered.[28]

The Tilden will contest, known as *Tilden vs. Green,* attracted wide attention in both legal and popular circles, first because the will had been drawn by a pre-eminent lawyer who presumably knew what would and what would not stand a test in the courts; and, secondly, because of the large fortune involved. By the breaking of the will New York City stood to lose most. It was generally said that in almost any other state of the Union the laws would have prevented such a decision based on an ancient Elizabethan statute. It was commonly reported that politics played no small rôle in the outcome of the contest. The

[26] *New York State Reports,* XVIII, 752.

[27] Judge Daniels upheld Justice Lawrence, but Judges Van Brunt and Brady voted against his decision.

[28] Mrs. G. W. Smith, Ms. Notes and "The Tilden Will and Its Vicissitudes."

rumor persisted that creditors, bankers and interested friends raised a pool of $100,000 to fight the will and that Lou Payn of Columbia County, who was behind the project, profited from the outcome.[29] However, the sources which would either prove or disprove these allegations have disappeared. It seems quite certain that the nephews were not able financially to conduct such expensive litigation without assistance from some quarter. And in 1896 Samuel J. Tilden, II, assigned to the National Hudson River Bank of Hudson his claims on the Tilden estate to meet his financial obligations.[30] The merits of the case were widely discussed in the newspapers and law reviews. One result was the passage of a law in 1893 to make impossible for the future such a denial of the right of a man to dispose of his wealth through trustees for noble purposes.[31]

Meanwhile during this litigation of five and a half years, so wisely was the estate managed that it had been increased to $6,110,859.[32] After the final decision the executors proceeded to settle with the heirs on March 30, 1892. Interest was paid on the special trusts until they were liquidated or the final accounting made on November 1, 1909. Mrs. Marie Celeste Stauffer Eastwick was still receiving interest in 1895. The Buchanon trust was finally settled in 1906; the Blatchford trust in 1913. Thus by degrees the estate was gradually distributed in accordance with the court decision and the will.[33] By March, 1892, over $5,500,000 of the personal estate was divided among the beneficiaries.[34] An inventory of the estate left in the hands of the executors in 1895 amounted to $1,967,020.[35] In 1914 there was about $600,000 still unexpended.[36]

The Tilden estate was in the hands of the executors for 44 years before it was finally settled on May 6, 1930, by the surviving appointee, Mrs. George W. Smith.[37] After the death of A. H. Green,[38] Bigelow and Smith appointed L. V. F. Randolph. When Bigelow died in 1911, Randolph refused to join Smith in naming a successor. The Tilden heirs then made an unsuccessful effort to remove Smith; and Randolph, losing a suit to oust his colleague, resigned in 1919. After Smith's demise Surrogate Slater of Westchester County appointed Al-

[29] Interview of the author with Major Albert Callan, of Chatham, N.Y. The Elizabethan statute was dug up by Delos McCurdy.
[30] Tilden Papers.   [31] Laws of New York, Chapter 701, 1893.
[32] Case on Appeal, 148. Testimony of G. W. Smith, May 26, 1890.
[33] Tilden Papers.   [34] Life, II, 367.   [35] Tilden Papers.
[36] Ib.   [37] Mrs. G. W. Smith, Ms. Notes.   [38] Nov. 13, 1903.

ton B. Parker as executor to wind up the business with Mrs. G. W. Smith. Upon the former's death, Judge Digney was named to take his place. In the end Mrs. Smith made the final accounting of the estate.[39]

Tilden's will contemplated the creation of a Tilden Trust with its own trustees to execute the provisions relative to the establishment of educational and scientific institutions. Upon the advice of Judge George F. Comstock,[40] the executors had the legislature incorporate the Tilden Trust on March 26, 1887.[41] The charter made the three executors "permanent trustees" and authorized them to associate with them two more trustees, Stephen A. Walker and Alexander E. Orr, and empowered them to fill vacancies, to elect officers, to build a library and reading room, and to invest such funds as the executors turned over to them. The heirs made a desperate effort to prevent the formation of the Tilden Trust.[42] The trustees first met April 26 and elected Bigelow president, Green vice president, Smith treasurer and Orr secretary. Bylaws were adopted and a seal approved. When the contest over the will was settled, the trustees turned their attention to the establishment of the library, for which purpose they had in hand $2,250,000—about a third of the sum provided by Tilden. This money came from Mrs. Pelton's granddaughter, who, in exchange for $975,000, relinquished to the Tilden Trust her interest in the Tilden estate.[43]

For some years the creation of a great library in the metropolis had been discussed, and on January 11, 1886, Adolph L. Sanger had asked Tilden to serve as one of the incorporators of the "New York Public Library."[44] Seth Low, president of Columbia, in 1894 invited the trustees of the Tilden Trust to co-operate in building up a great Columbia Library, but this request, together with many others to divert the fund for various scientific, charitable and educational purposes, was declined.[45] Eventually in 1901 the Tilden funds were amalgamated with the Astor and Lenox Libraries to form the New York Public Library, for which a splendid building was erected in 1911 on Fifth Avenue. To this imposing structure went Tilden's library of 20,000 volumes, manuscripts, and works of art.[46] Thus was realized, in part at least, the supreme ambition of one who as a poor young man in New

---

[39] Mrs. G. W. Smith, Ms. Notes.   [40] Tilden Papers, Dec. 31, 1886.
[41] *Laws of 1887*, Chapter 85.
[42] *Bulletin* of New York Public Library, Feb., 1917.   [43] *Ib.*
[44] Tilden Papers.   [45] *Ib.* Minutes of the Trustees of the Tilden Trust.
[46] *Bulletin* of the New York Public Library, Feb., 1917.

York City had gained so much of knowledge and inspiration from the inadequate libraries and reading rooms of an earlier day. He had become one of its pre-eminent citizens and public benefactors.

With characteristic caution Tilden's will provided that his executors should have his papers carefully sifted and that those which in their judgment the public should see should be printed. John Bigelow assumed responsibility for making the initial selection. John J. Cahill, a trusted clerk of Tilden, advised that Tilden's telegrams and letters to members of Congress about the "unconstitutional tribunal" should be included, because "he was opposed from the start to the creation of the Commission and certainly to the lottery plan." Tilden's bitter denunciation of the Florida verdict should be mentioned; also "O'Conor's tears at the spectacle of the judges of the Supreme Court . . . refusing to investigate a question of fraud." It should be shown, too, that Cleveland was hated more than Tilden by Kelly.[47]

Preparatory to the compilation an effort was made by Smith to obtain copies of letters which Tilden had written to business and political associates, but not many were secured. Marble wrote from England that he had examined "a bushel of letters from Tilden," but all were marked "private" or "confidential" and he did not feel like having them made public. "Tilden's letters were almost illegible," he commented. "One note said 'I now write you three legible lines . . . I would rather walk 11 miles than write one letter.'" Marble had gone through the files at Graystone and had abstracted a large number of his own letters to Tilden. In 1891 he asked for the return of his remaining letters, and they were sent him in batches while Tilden's papers were being combed over.[48] Senator Gorham, G. M. Miller and Hewitt said their letters from Tilden had been burned; Havemeyer, Thurman, Barnum, E. Cooper, McLean and Fairchild had none; Perry Belmont had a few; Edward Murphy refused to allow those in his possession to be published; A. C. Beach reported that all his were marked "private"; Magone had two boxes of Tilden letters but no time to sort them out; and Grover Cleveland refused to return his Tilden letters because of Bigelow's treatment of him in the *Life of Tilden*. The Seymour family and Spriggs complied with Smith's request, and Barlow promised to do so but never found it convenient.[49] Some letters written to Tilden were returned, and Bigelow thought "the immediate combustion of all of Weed's and Marble's correspondence" best.[50] As late as 1906 Randolph was searching for the "Stauffer letters" and could not find them.[51] A few of the Tilden letters were presented to public institutions and a canceled check for $130,000 in payment of Tilden's share of a joint interest in the Harlem Elevated Railroad was given to the Tilden High School of Brooklyn.[52]

Bigelow's compilation of Tilden letters for publication was the work of a vindicator, not a historian. About the materials he had assembled he wrote, "We are going to have new material . . . to make this nation realize what amount of reprobation it owes to Hewitt, Bayard and Thurman, the . . . accessories to the crime of 1876 without whose complicity it could never have been consummated." Copies were sent to the other trustees for criticism. Randolph wanted the letters to make Tilden appear in a more "favorable light," advised cutting out those that were "dead or tame," all "Copperhead" communications, and those to Henry and Moses, suggested the improvement of the English, and condemned everything that "would taint the name of Tilden." [53] When published in 1908 the Letters were widely distributed gratis.

Tilden's papers were examined carefully at least four times to eliminate everything derogatory to his reputation. Such action, however regrettable to a biographer, was distinctly authorized by Tilden in his will. Joseph L. Hance, secretary to Tilden when Governor, spent an entire year picking out letters and papers that might be destroyed—"only dunning letters and unimportant items." Then John J. Cahill helped to sort the papers but declared that "no important letters were destroyed." He kept no list of those destroyed and did not remember what they were. A third examination was supervised by Smith and Bigelow.[54] And the surviving executor, Mrs. G. W. Smith, made the final survey before turning the papers over to the New York Public Library. The contents of eighteen trunks were so condensed as to require only thirteen containers.[55] Seemingly the subtractions occurred in the papers relating to the last twenty-five years of Tilden's life, noticeably in the periods of the Civil War and the disputed election of 1876, and in connection with railroad and business transactions. Thus Tilden's wishes expressed in his last will and testament were carried out by a long line of faithful executors.

[50] *Ib.*, Randolph to Smith, Mar. 21, 1906.   [51] *Ib.*, Randolph to Bigelow, June 5, 1906.
[52] Mrs. G. W. Smith, Ms. Notes.   [53] Tilden Papers, June 1, 1904.
[54] Tilden Papers.   [55] Mrs. G. W. Smith, Ms. Notes.

In 1914 Tilden's younger admirers observed the centennial of his birth. The State voted $10,000, and the Governor appointed a Memorial Commission,[1] which arranged public exercises at New Lebanon, in Albany and in New York City.[2] Lieutenant Governor Wagner presided over the services in the Assembly Chamber, and called attention to Tilden's "keen sympathy with Democratic ideals and his complete absorption of self in the common weal." Speaker Sweet characterized him as the wise leader who once in a generation "overtops others of his time." Dr. Talcott Williams, reviewing his work as a reformer, said he had the capacity for finding the kernel in every problem, and that his tireless energy flamed "into ugly honesty at the sight of wrong." [3] In the metropolis Carnegie Hall was filled with 1,500 people who listened to addresses by Governor Baldwin of Connecticut, Mayor John Purroy Mitchel, Francis Lynde Stetson, Charles S. Fairchild and others, and to letters from prominent men of the nation.[4] Mitchel asserted that Tilden's remedy for the ills of his day was more, not less, democracy and that he was an inspiration to every man in public life. Stetson surveyed the election of 1876 and explained that the relation between Tilden and Cleveland was like that between Frémont and Lincoln, or Roosevelt and Taft.[5] Fairchild declared that no man "saw the present and future with such clear and prophetic vision" or had the power to move men with such high ideals. Had he been heeded there would have been no Civil War, no reconstruction atrocities, no currency evils, no centralization of government, fewer officials and less taxation.[6]

The Tilden Democratic Club of New York City held a meeting at which Samuel Untermyer vigorously assaulted Tammany rule and a telegram was read from Franklin Delano Roosevelt, Assistant Secretary of the Navy, declaring that there could be no alliance between the Democratic Party and grafters.[7] The New York Public Library opened an exhibition of Tildenana. For years Congressman William

---

[1] *Public Papers of Gov. Sulzer,* 507.   [2] Feb. 8, 9 and 10, 1914.
[3] *Argus* and *Times,* Feb. 9 and 10, 1914.
[4] Printed under title "Samuel J. Tilden, the Great Democrat."
[5] *Times,* Feb. 11, 1914.   [6] "Memorial Address."   [7] *Times,* Feb. 10, 1914.

Sulzer had attempted in vain to persuade Congress to appropriate $50,000 for a Tilden statue in the national Capitol; [8] now friends of Tilden joined his executors in erecting a statue on Riverside Drive at 114th Street, which was presented to the city after tributes by J. W. Gerard, G. A. Slater and Chancellor E. K. Brown.[9]

The life of the man thus honored covered the period from the War of 1812 to President Cleveland. "Completely at home in the Revolutionary Fathers," he referred to them continually in his public papers and from them learned statesmanship, "a deep and well-ordered political philosophy" to which he rigidly adhered.[10] With the enthusiasm of a young knight, he drew his sword first as the champion of Jackson and then of Van Buren, mentors who fixed both the form and content of his convictions. With their passing he became the "most authoritative expositor" of Democracy and the leader of his party. The influence of his thought was felt across the land. Nahum Capen compared him with young Pitt, who "became a statesman before his majority." [11]

At thirty-four he led the revolt within the Democracy of the Empire State against the creation of five new slave States, but did not, like others, desert the party. With Silas Wright he helped to persuade Van Buren to run on the Free-Soil ticket in 1848 and thus contributed to the defeat of Cass. Although favoring the Wilmot Proviso and opposing war, yet when war came he sought a successful conclusion without irreconcilably alienating the two sections. He stood with the North, was consulted by Lincoln's Cabinet, and, while his war record was criticized, it was vindicated by later events.

He became a successful lawyer—next to O'Conor, the shrewdest in New York. Hugh McCulloch pronounced him the "ablest corporation lawyer in America." [12] He was famous for settling cases out of court. His was the first master mind in consolidating independent railroads and other business concerns on a profitable basis. He was rarely successful in addressing a jury because he was not an easy, graceful and persuasive speaker; but he had no superior as a legal counselor. Most of his wealth was acquired by sagacity and courage in rescuing rundown transportation lines and mines from bankruptcy. Few men have had a more intelligent comprehension of the

---

[8] "Address before Committee on the Library," May 3, 1910.
[9] Oct. 5, 1926. New York papers.   [10] *World,* Aug. 20, 1886.
[11] Tilden Papers.   [12] *Men and Measures,* 413.

nature and power of wealth for good or evil.[13] Having amassed a fortune and freed himself from the necessity of earning a living, he assisted the Democratic Party in recovering its leadership by his determined fight aginst the Tweed Ring. That triumph made him Governor and enabled him to attack successfully the bipartisan Canal Ring. This reform work resulted in his nomination for President, but he was excluded from the office to which he was elected by a tribunal not recognized by the Constitution. Had his ethical standards been as low as those of some leaders in both parties in 1876, he might have been President; but he refused to purchase venal electors or to enter the White House by the back door.

For four years he comported himself as the true Chief Executive but excluded from office. Had he cared to renew the contest in 1880 or 1884, he might have been vindicated; but impaired vigor induced him, against vehement protests, to withdraw his name. His death removed a statesman about whom had rallied the best men in the nation —young men wishing to support constructive principles,[14] party men desiring reformed local and national government, Republicans distrusting their own leaders, and the common folk seeking an honest civic guide. On the other hand, he was assailed not only by bitter party opponents but also by those of his own political faith who fought progress, denounced reform as a sham, and selfishly wished to make politics pay rewards in graft and patronage. The political corruption so common after the Civil War was one of the results of American industrial growth. While Tilden's talent was devoted to the success of the economic order, he emerged with cleaner hands than the Goulds and Fisks. The prediction that with the subsidence of party hatreds he would be "classed among the eminent men of his era" has come true.[15]

The outstanding characteristic of Tilden as a lawyer, man of affairs, reformer, politician and publicist was his scientific mind. As a thinking machine he dealt with realities, facts, figures and positive evidence— not philosophical speculations nor hypothetical vagaries. Throughout life he believed that the moral world was as subject to fundamental laws as the physical world. Hence he proceeded under the conviction that government, finance, economics, and business must follow such

[13] J. C. Carter, *Atlantic Monthly*, Oct., 1892.
[14] Speech of Governor Hill at Tilden Dinner, Brooklyn, Feb. 9, 1888.
[15] Stanton, *Recollections*, 244.

laws or chaos would result. In every problem he studied—state economy, taxation, justice, internal improvements, and public administration—he sought the underlying principle. Nor was his inquiring mind satisfied until he had discovered it, in private as well as public affairs. A lawsuit, a bond issue, the reorganization of a crippled corporation, or the consolidation of several business concerns must all conform to this essential principle. An early example of this mental trait was the case of *Flagg vs. Giles*. This inexorable insistence on the underlying forces gained for him the epithet "Old Skinflint," but it won success in the investigation of the Rings. This mentality made him a farseeing, fearless and reliable party leader who was admired if not loved by his followers. He would have made a pre-eminent jurist. To reach his generalizations required infinite patience and a rare capacity to gather and sift facts. Tilden possessed both qualities and by practice gained proficiency and speed. "Extreme subtleness of intellect," said Joseph H. Choate, "was a predominating characteristic . . . that gave him fame and success. . . . In middle life he abandoned law and became a politician. . . . He was a master of the science of politics."

Tilden's powers of analysis and synthesis were remarkable. His mind was as accurate as a Swiss watch, as searching as an X-ray, and as merciless as a scalpel. He put everything under the microscope of his brain and trusted nothing to his heart. Impulse was one percent and intellect ninety-nine percent. Invincible in reason, his single-track mind always put the most important thing first. While his mental vision mastered details, at the same time it was prescient.[16] Despite his desultory education he learned the value of concentrating on a problem until completely mastered. Others vaporized, theorized; he crystallized. He cared naught for surmises, but was hypnotized by realities. Glittering generalities were abhorred, but hard facts and dry figures were a delight. "No man I have known," said D. B. Hill, "could better resolve a proposition into its constituent elements, and then reconstruct them for the true result." [17] As a real political scientist, he treated governmental issues like problems in algebra—found the value of all the factors and then with unerring logic worked out his solutions.

Things mathematical elicited his interest—statistical documents and Government reports were read with intense delight and carefully pre-

[16] Martin H. Glynn, *Sun* and *Herald,* June 20, 1920.　　[17] *Times,* May 5, 1895.

served. Framed charts and diagrams hung in his study—one showing the increase in the national debt for 1860–76, another indicating shrinkage in value of eighteen railroads from 1873 to 1877.[18] This talent for figures brought legal victories involving finance, made him an outstanding business lawyer, and pointed the way to wealth. All his life he enjoyed computing distances, population, taxes, national income and expenditures. Like Van Buren—who, to persuade B. F. Butler to enter his Cabinet, said he could travel from Washington to Albany in a day and night on the new railroad [19]—Tilden's thoughts before 1870 were on canals, iron mines, and transportation.

His mental power and knowledge of human affairs compelled other men to follow him, even though he possessed no personal popularity. He won his place at the head of his party not by the dash of a soldier, nor by spectacular deeds, but by his intellectual resource and fearlessness in battling for the right. He paid no attention to threats, whether from friend or foe. Disliking those who "took counsel in their apprehensions," he revealed boldness in design but caution in execution, never moving until he had provided against every contingency. At times this judicial temperament irritated his friends, but in the end they applauded his sagacity. He was "well-poised, evenly balanced in his understanding, industrious, had tenacity of purpose, and was self-reliant." Perhaps a retentive memory that "never forgot" was a factor in making him cautious and reticent. He employed history to explain the present, used the classics to embellish his style, and knew such poets as Dryden, Pope, Milton, and Scott, but seldom quoted them.[20]

Along with a mathematical mind went a judgment such as a few men in a generation possess. A methodical intelligence enabled him to reach conclusions that seemed to be intuitive, but were really the results of cold logic. Although not infallible, yet he seldom made a mistake and always felt safe to act on his conclusions. An irritating hesitancy to commit himself, his reiteration of the phrase "Not yet," and his insistence on deferring a decision arose from no evasion of responsibility but from the determination not to give a positive commitment until he could weigh all the factors involved and arrive at a conclusion on which he could stand without fear of dislodgment. Hence his legal, business, and political associates came to rely implicitly on

[18] Sent to the New York Public Library by executors.
[19] Butler Papers, Nov. 8, 1833.   [20] A. M. Gibson, *World*, Aug. 20 and 27, 1886.

his advice. The boast that he knew how "to limit theory by practice and to enlighten practice by theory" was not an idle one.[21] An illustration of the value placed on his financial judgment is afforded by the following example. A Western railroad, wishing to sell an issue of bonds, had a well-known judge draw up a form and then offered the bonds to J. P. Morgan and Company. Morgan said that he would buy the bonds if Tilden approved them, and could afford to pay a higher price. Tilden put in the clause that bondholders could not foreclose in case the payment of dividends was delayed by a strike. That was a new idea, for such an event had never occurred, but under Cleveland a strike took place on that very road, and the provision saved the road from receivership.[22] Tilden was a man to be consulted, and his counsel was always wise. Recognized as a profound student of finance and an authority on all its phases, he was acknowledged to be one of the ablest business men of his day, who supplemented his wide information with originality.[23]

With his intellectual acumen, his ability to comprehend a given situation, and his sound judgment based on the weighing of all the factors involved, Tilden had no difficulty in amassing a fortune. Possessing a "subtle, money-making faculty," [24] he not only accumulated wealth for himself but likewise advised his friends how to get rich. Not understanding conditions, his opponents accused him of making money as a wrecker of railroads and corporations, and as a Wall Street gambler. Dorsheimer apologized publicly for such a charge.[25] On the contrary, his fortune was made by rescuing, not ruining, these sick concerns. By applying intelligent common sense to enterprises in trouble, his remedies worked out to the advantage of the vast majority of the investors. With the skill of a great physician, he advised these patients how to recover. This almost uncanny discernment gained for him the reputation of being "the best financier in the United States." That he took an inordinate pride in his monetary accomplishments is quite evident. He had an abundance of personal vanity, which grew out of his consciousness of a superior intellectual endowment and an almost unrivaled judgment. The display of egotism, coupled with blunt-

[21] Carter, *Atlantic Monthly*, Oct., 1892.
[22] Interview with Harry J. Cox of New Lebanon.
[23] *Commercial Advertiser*, Aug., 1886. Statement of Dorsheimer.
[24] D. B. Hill, *Times*, May 5, 1895.   [25] *Life*, II, 382–384.

ness, secretiveness, and the habit of retorting "I told you so," made him unpopular with those who could not comprehend the worthy motives that lay behind his behavior. Chief Justice Waite accused Tilden of being miserly—perhaps because he refused to pay Waite $30,000 to get his consent to foreclose a railroad mortgage.[26] But Judge Martin Grover said, "That man has given away more money and made less fuss about it than any other man in the State of New York."

An annoying procrastination was one of Tilden's besetting sins. His father at times was wild with impatience because Samuel failed to answer questions or to perform commissions; and Bigelow asserted, "Tilden was one of the most difficult men to get an opinion out of that I ever knew." [27] He was tardy at committee meetings, failed to keep appointments, and no one knew when to find him in his office. He had a "repugnance for dangerous extremes." This indecision probably cost him the Presidency, for it was generally believed that, had he acted promptly and decisively, his opponents would have conceded the election. But he wavered, hesitated, was stubbornly over-confident, and cautioned delay—and lost the high honor. As a rule, however, in important matters he delayed action only long enough to reach a sound decision; and those who knew him well understood his unexpressed thought.[28] Thoroughness was the explanation of his success; he was seldom deceived and never a second time by the same man or problem. Asked to explain his success, he replied, "I have never taken anything for granted." That reveals his mental attitude toward every situation and every man. It was always easier to elicit from him a question than a positive statement.

Nothing brought Tilden a higher degree of satisfaction than to master obstacles. One who knew him well called him "the silent and thoughtful worker who always looked to the future" and "measured merit by consequences." [29] On a challenging problem he would work day and night until he had settled it to his complete satisfaction. The same exclusive application he exacted from his employees and associated party colleagues. On matters he weighed, his mind was made up; on others he was as inquisitive as a child.[30] No one could detect more quickly than he a fallacy in reasoning or in conduct. Never transgress-

---

[26] Hayes, *Diary and Letters*, III, 362. [27] *Retrospections*, V, 302.
[28] D. B. Hill, *Times*, May 5, 1895, said Tilden never procrastinated when it was unsafe to do so. This was not true in 1876. *Life*, II, 386.
[29] George F. Comstock's "Brief in Tilden Will Case." [30] *Tribune*, Sept. 16, 1886.

ing the rules of orderly thought, he treated opponents courteously, manifested no resentment, never imagined enmity and was slow to wrath. Those who knew him best testified that he was modest, unassuming, and retiring.

If in commonplace matters he seemed to be a negative personality, a grave issue could electrify him into aggressiveness. When Smith M. Weed took General Thomas Ewing to call, the latter remarked: "I'll not be bored by the old gent's views on finance. I have my own convictions." Tilden received the soft-money advocate graciously and lectured him on the greenback heresy until midnight. Ewing's comment was, "He is the most marvelous man I have ever met." Tilden's mind was at its best in a man-to-man conference rather than in addressing an audience. In a small group, he held the center of the stage with his fund of information and illustration. They asked questions, but none took the lead in the discussion. "In the two rather incompatible qualities of calm, studious, and philosophical statesmanship, and the capacity to gather, classify and apply the statistics of a political campaign, I do not remember to have met his equal," said a disciple, "but far above all else rose his genius for administrative reform." [31] He was inscrutable only to those who did not know him well. As a rule he was not a subtle schemer behind the scenes but a deliberate observer of passing events, who took the world as he found it, balanced men's good and bad qualities, and believed that human effort could improve civilization.[32] Hence the three great peaks in his life were, first, his overthrow of the Tweed Ring, secondly, his disruption of the Canal Ring as Governor, and, third, his frustrated plan to reform the Federal Government.

Tilden will live in American history as a pioneer political reformer who used legal processes to punish the guilty but at the same time did a good deal of preaching to arouse public opinion behind him. Were he alive today, his voice would be raised to secure the abolition of social and economic injustices. Indeed, over half a century ago he remarked, "I am appalled at the inequality of human justice." When he inspected the prisons of the State, he meditated on the offenses of the inmates and the circumstances surrounding them in comparison with "the crimes of great public delinquents who claim to stand among our best society" and yet went unpunished year after year. The problems of organized society should be "analyzed, studied and reduced to form-

[31] A. M. Gibson, *World*, Aug. 20 and 27, 1886.   [32] Watterson, *Century*, May, 1913.

ulas." He believed implicitly in the natural law of supply and demand in the economic field. He was a champion of individualism and did not believe that "three hundred wise men in . . . Washington should decide and specify what we shall sell and what we shall buy in order to save us from . . . calamity." Yet he did believe that in human society there was order, method, law and "an equilibrium of forces." He heartily commended a scientific investigation of pauperism, crime, and insanity where intelligent governmental interference was necessary. At the same time he thought that the "industrious millions who keep out of the poorhouses and penitentiaries are also entitled to the consideration and the care of the Government."[33] D. B. Hill maintained that Tilden was a friend of both labor and capital.[34]

If Tilden was personally ambitious, it was always to use official power to promote a cause or a principle. Tenacious and unchanging was his faith in the capacity of the people to solve their problems aright. Fond of appealing to American history to prove the operation of the law of progress, he was a foe of unscrupulous private monopoly, unjust taxation, dangerous centralism in government, organized greed in civic affairs, special legislation, and corruption in local and national rule. Inspired by the Founding Fathers and the Constitution, he was the chamipon of equal rights, justice in the courts, and liberty in the best sense of the word. He was a patriot who never shirked his civic responsibilities, who regarded himself as a living ancestor with a duty to the future, and who gained courage by looking backward. At the same time he was the friend of the latest immigrant and the humblest citizen. For these reasons no man after Lincoln had the confidence of the common people to a greater degree, and no publicist of his generation found his public papers and speeches more widely studied.

He was not deficient in moral standards; his emotions were under close control, and his attacks on fraud in public life reveal a remarkable sensitiveness to political right and wrong. His crusades were based on reason, not on feeling, and his appeals for popular assistance in his reform programs were gauged to the people's intelligence, not to their passions. Nevertheless his heart could be touched in cases of genuine distress. James C. Carter relates that, while he was working with Tilden late at night in Albany, a little girl called to see the Governor. Dropping everything, he spent half an hour with the ragged, miserable child,

[33] *Writings*, II, 377, 378.   [34] *Times*, May 5, 1895.

whose story of her home life aroused both his sympathy and indignation. Immediately he sent a secretary with a pardon for the imprisoned mother of the girl. When Carter asked whether he was not acting hastily, Tilden replied, "Don't I know that the little girl told me the truth?" [35] Sentiment he possessed—even affection as vouched for by D. B. Hill and Manton Marble—but he could be as "cold as a clam" and was never afflicted with sentimentality. His confidences were not too effusive; friendship was given to a few men generously but in return he made unlimited demands on their time and energy. Assistance was given to relatives, to acquaintances and to causes; and the provisions of his will for the public weal entitle him to rank with the nation's greatest benefactors.

In no sense was Tilden a religious enthusiast. At nineteen he and his sister Mary were admitted to the Presbyterian Church at New Lebanon. He held a pew in the Madison Square Presbyterian Church; as Governor he went to hear Dr. Upson pretty regularly; but after 1877 he seldom attended any church.[36] No conspicuous benefactions were made to any church work. When in the mood he attended St. Patrick's Cathedral and contributed to its work among the poor.[37] He had a high opinion of the honest Shaker, but took no interest in the religious fads of the day—not even the spiritualism of his old friends J. W. Edmunds and John L. O'Sullivan.[38]

Tilden's critics admitted his skill as an administrator and his ability as an organizer, but thought him "personally cold, subtle, selfish, and unscrupulous." [39] Dr. Charles E. Simmons, his physician for a decade, said that he cultivated mystery and pretended extraordinary confidence in his fellow men.[40] He was admired, respected, and applauded but not loved—a human iceberg who fired his party and the American people to high action. His closest friendships were not based so much on common likes and dislikes or on social equality as on common devotion to certain civic ideas or to some economic purpose. Enemies might question both his motives and his deeds, but those who knew him best vouched for his "stainless integrity" and his "pure and noble" conversation.[41] He assumed a protective attitude toward those who served him faithfully but was indifferent to others. When someone

[35] *Atlantic Monthly,* Oct., 1892. [36] *Life,* II, 393. [37] Statement of John J. Cahill.
[38] Tilden Papers, Apr. 27, 1881. [39] Foulke, *Life of O. P. Morton,* II, 403.
[40] *Times,* Aug. 5, 1886. [41] G. F. Comstock, "Brief in Tilden Will Case."

complained about Apgar's conduct, he replied, "Yes, Apgar may be irregular in his habits and get up late in the morning, but he has the best political judgment of anyone about me. He knows what ought to be done in an emergency." [42] With employees he was exacting. When a newly appointed clerk in the Executive Chamber at his first interview with Tilden asked, "How much vacation shall I have?" he received the curt reply from the Governor, "Your vacation will begin at once and continue indefinitely." When Colonel William Gorham Rice first met him, he was much confused by Tilden's question, "Can you write well?" Tilden wanted a staff who could express their ideas on paper and thus be of more than ordinary usefulness.[43] To a clerk who delayed the delivery of an important message he remarked caustically, "When you go anywhere for me, take the first, not the second train."

As an egotist Tilden was pleased with praise and interpreted it as an endorsement of his conduct and mental superiority. He was given to quotations of what friend and foe said about him. Self-exaltation characterized his letters and papers, which are full of "I" and "my." His conceit was justified by his accomplishments, and was part of his political leadership. It was earned commendation that he craved, not indiscriminate admiration, and he was not given to shallow boastfulness or empty pride. If he was as vain as Conkling, he was as sure of himself as Disraeli. He gave rather than sought advice. During the fifteen years prior to his death, he developed in manly stature and was admired by friend and foe alike.[44]

Once convinced of a truth or of a course of action, Tilden realized that there remained the difficult problem of convincing others. Hence he recognized the importance of the right word or phrase, of an effective paragraph, and of a logical and complete composition. To acquire this facility he greatly improved his natural gift for clear, effective language and even stressed the value of the art of rhetoric both in speaking and writing. He wrote and rewrote tirelessly, changed words and phrases until he got the shade of meaning desired, and rearranged sentences so that when a public paper left his hand it would convey to the reader what was in his own mind. His report on the Antirent disorders, his address to the Constitutional Convention in 1867 on a

[42] Interview with Col. William Gorham Rice, of Albany, N. Y.
[43] *Ib.*   [44] Henry Watterson, *Century*, May, 1913.

wise canal policy, and his second Annual Message to the Legislature in 1876 were models of convincing argumentation.

Bigelow, who helped Tilden prepare many of his letters and public papers, said that the first draft was corrected over and over until the logic was irresistible. He "neglects no fair advantage," must follow the order of his own mind, insists on "having every point in," never uses a "weak expression," is a good judge of the sequence of sentences, and always seizes the strong phrase with "unerring accuracy." [45] Tilden was a master of the art of understatement and of indirection in setting forth his legal, business and political ideas.[46] An examination of his private and public papers reveals an erudition both solid and versatile. Watterson, who enjoyed a "warm fellowship" with him for twenty-six years, found him a "genial and overflowing scholar" who lived an orderly life in a luxurious home, enjoyed good books, employed a celebrated chef and entertained with an unpretentious hospitality.[47] When busy with some absorbing task or vexed with an annoyance, he could be gruff to those he liked best, but those who knew him well enough to visit him familiarly in his home, or to entertain him as a guest in theirs, found him a witty and delightful conversationalist. Of Tilden's stay with him for a week, Peter White wrote, "I had a profound veneration for Mr. Tilden. . . . I never enjoyed such a delightful time in all my life." [48]

Once more, but finally, it must be explained that the supreme factor in Tilden's life was his health, which at times absorbed all his attention. Like Thomas H. Benton he talked about his ailments for hours, but unlike Benton he did not have his servant rub him down with a horsebrush every morning. As a substitute for the horsebrush he resorted to massage, but had he heard of Benton's alleviation he most certainly would have tried it, because he took every patent medicine he heard about and suffered all kinds of diseases except "housemaid's knee." [49] Tilden was one of those figures in history whose physical condition—nerves, aches and pains—played an important, perhaps a decisive, part in his career from childhood to the end of his life. His singularity, if not abnormality, showed itself in the maturity of his youth. Fortunately he was a younger man at 40 than at 16. Later in

[45] *Retrospections*, V, 291.   [46] *Saturday Evening Post*, May 3, 1919.
[47] *Ib.*, Aug. 25, 1886.   [48] Tilden Papers. Letter written in 1908.
[49] M. H. Glynn, N.Y. *Sun* and *Herald*, June 20, 1920.

life, as his physical infirmities grew more pronounced, the brilliance of his mentality became more accentuated—the vigor his body lacked seemed to be transferred to his intellect.

Next to his health the greatest concern to Tilden was the welfare of his party, which he always identified with his country. From boyhood to death the Democratic Party had his complete devotion, and in his life it took the place of wife, children and church. It was his faith, his inspiration, and his medium for advancing American civilization. Because of his notable contributions to its literature and accomplishments, Tilden takes rank with Jefferson, Madison, Jackson, Van Buren, Cleveland, and Wilson. Like Moses he lived to see his party enter the Promised Land although under the guidance of another political prophet.

His masterful political leadership was recognized by allies and opponents alike. Knowing how to make the most of both patronage and the party machine, he realized that ideas and not mechanics were of supreme value. Victories at the polls, to be lasting, must be won by a convinced electorate. If he could not reach a major goal, he was content with a minor one gained by compromise or concession, but there was a line beyond which he would not go. Obstinacy he possessed, but made it yield to wisdom. Guided by an intense "partyism," he found it difficult to understand the psychology of an independent, nonparty voter. His rise to party leadership was slow but certain, and as a manager he was "able, alert and incomparable" because he perfected party organization, chose dependable local leaders and looked after details. He knew how to stress the right issues. When old leaders deserted him, he recruited new ones.[50] Possessed of a political mind and soul, he threw himself into the welter of a campaign as a fanatic devotes himself to a cult. Knowing the science of government, economics, finance and taxation better than a college professor, he also understood practical politics like the alphabet. Mastery of these fundamentals, coupled with experimental knowledge of party mechanics, made him a forceful party leader for nearly half a century, despite the lack of personal magnetism and social amenities; but that leadership was intellectual and not that of a tribal chieftain or a dictator. His faith in democracy as a pattern of civil life was genuine; and if he trusted the people's judgment, they in turn put faith in the wisdom of

[50] D. B. Hill, *Times*, May 5, 1895.

his guidance. As the "inspirer of the new Democracy," he was regarded as the "ablest Democrat of his time." [51]

While prudent always, when conditions warranted it, he was a "cruel
breaker of slates and wrecker of plans." He gave the appearance of
abstention from office-seeking and let the office find him. Generous
contributions were made to political campaigns, but his "barrel" was
never used to "fix things." He owned no newspapers, but through
financial favors to owners he virtually subsidized several. To him politics was the greatest national game, which should be played according
to established rules, but contestants were justified in taking advantage
of every legitimate opportunity to win. Blaine called him "the most
striking figure in the Democratic Party since Andrew Jackson." He
took his sly ways from Van Buren and improved them.

"He moved forward to unchallenged personal supremacy with a vigor and
rapidity which in the political life of the United States has seldom been
equaled. . . . The scepter of power in the Democratic Party did not drop
into his hands; he seized it and wielded it at his own will. He molded the
conditions which suited his designs, and when the hour was right he assumed
command as of divine right. . . . He was adroit, ingenuous, and wary; skillful to plan and strong to execute; cautious in judgment and vigorous in action;
taciturn and mysterious as a rule and yet singularly frank on occasions; resting on old traditions yet leading in new pathways; surprising in the force of
his blows yet leaving a sense of reserve power—the greatest master of political
management our day has seen." [52]

Mrs. G. W. Smith who had an unusual opportunity to study Tilden
intimately for many years and under all conditions summarized his
outstanding characteristics as follows:

"Tolerance and forgiveness; justice and sympathy; sagacity and caution;
truthfulness and honesty; unsuspicious but relentless in seeking facts; resentful of injustices but held no prejudices except against deceit; and generosity to
family and friends in their personal needs." [53]

Tilden's idealism was rooted in realism. He worked for the advancement of a cause rather than for himself. His campaigns, from the Assembly in 1846 to the Presidency in 1876, were conducted on reform
programs that appealed to the people. Looking deeper and seeing further than others, he discerned desirable changes. Understanding the
social ills of his day, he "did not regard principles and politics as in-

[51] Springfield *Republican*, Aug. 5, 1886.
[52] *Twenty Years in Congress*, II, 573–577.   [53] Ms. Notes.

compatible." [54] As a liberal progressive and a practical reformer, he strove for the attainable. He was as truly a democratic philosopher and as good an essayist as Jefferson. Less aggressive than Jackson, he was more intellectual and level-headed. Quite as astute as Van Buren, with a broader knowledge and greater reasoning powers, he was an equally bad orator. Not a match for Webster in the forum, he was his superior with the pen. He was a master of compromise like Clay and as able an expounder of political science as Calhoun or Wilson. Like Theodore Roosevelt he was a popular idol of the masses and even the children, but never with his own party leaders. Not a hero on horseback like Taylor and Grant, nor endowed with audacity, like Blaine, he was a statesman with the sagacity of Madison, J. Q. Adams and Cleveland. In America's list of illustrious sons, as time submerges the lesser lights, Tilden will survive in public esteem as one of the great builders of civilization.

"Tilden will necessarily remain as a problem for the critics and historians, and as long as his name is mentioned there will be a division of opinion in regard to him." [55] "What happens to the memory of a great man when he dies?—first panegyrics of his friends and followers, the dispraise of the enemies he made; then the slow, final judgment of history." [56]

[54] Springfield *Republican*, Aug. 5, 1886.
[56] Abbott, *Conflicts with Oblivion*, xviii.

[55] Illinois *State Journal*, Aug. 5, 1886.

Bibliography

Manuscript Material

George Bancroft Papers. Library of Congress. A large number of papers but not many direct references to Tilden. Some Bancroft letters in the Tilden Papers.

John Bigelow Papers. New York Public Library. His Diary has not yet been opened to scholars but much of it has been printed in *Retrospections*.

Jeremiah S. Black Papers. Library of Congress. A few Tilden letters. A number of Black's letters in the Tilden Papers.

Francis Preston Blair, Francis Preston Blair, Jr., and Montgomery Blair Papers. In possession of Gist and Woodbury Blair, Washington, D. C. Many Blair letters among the Tilden Papers and of much value in the interpretation of Tilden's political life.

J. C. Breckenridge Papers. Library of Congress. Give information on the Democratic National Convention of 1860.

W. C. P. Breckenridge Papers. Library of Congress. Of value for the pre-Civil War period.

Benjamin Franklin Butler Papers. In possession of Miss Harriet Butler, Yonkers, N. Y. Contain some unused Tilden sources.

William Allen Butler papers. In possession of Miss Harriet Butler, Yonkers, N. Y.

William E. Chandler Papers. Library of Congress. A small collection.

Salmon P. Chase Papers. Library of Congress. Not many Tilden items but of importance for the Democratic National Convention of 1868.

Sanford E. Church Papers. In possession of the family but not yet accessible to students.

Grover Cleveland Papers. Library of Congress. Some Tilden material and many letters from Tilden's associates during the latter part of his life.

Charles A. Dana Papers. Library of Congress. A small collection of letters on the Civil War period. A number of Dana letters in the Tilden Papers.

James R. Doolittle Papers. Wisconsin Historical Society. Several Tilden items.

J. P. Doolittle Papers. Library of Congress. Little Tilden data but much of collateral importance.

William M. Evarts Papers. In possession of Mrs. Edward C. Perkins and Mr. Allen Evarts, Windsor, Vt. Many gaps in the collection.

Thomas Ewing Papers. Library of Congress. Of value.

Charles H. Fairchild Papers. New York Historical Society. Of much value.

Azariah C. Flagg Papers. New York Public Library. Contain letters of Silas Wright, Michael Hoffman and other contemporaries of Tilden.

Horace Greeley Papers. New York Public Library. Throw light on political issues.

Rutherford B. Hayes Papers. A large collection at Fremont, O. Photostat copies of many of them in Library of Congress. Important for the election of 1876 and subsequently.

Abram S. Hewitt Papers. In the hands of Allan Nevins. Indispensable for the election of 1876 and its interpretation.

David B. Hill Papers. In private hands. Valuable for the period from 1872 to 1886.

Andrew Johnson Papers. Library of Congress. Some Tilden letters. Of value for the period following the Civil War.

George W. Julian Diary, 1865–1877. In possession of Grace Julian Clarke, Indianapolis. A revealing source of information.

Francis Kernan Papers. In possession of the family at Utica, N. Y. Of importance.

Daniel S. Lamont Papers. Library of Congress. All after 1892, but references to Tilden and his contemporaries. Not so valuable as they might be.

Daniel Magone Papers. In private possession at Ogdensburg, N. Y. Magone was a close friend of Tilden.

Daniel Manning Papers. Library of Congress. One of Tilden's staunchest admirers. Earlier letters not included but valuable for 1885 and 1886.

Manton Marble Papers. Library of Congress. Indispensable but disappointing because of the destruction of so many letters and documents. A collection of his papers also left in London University, London, England.

William L. Marcy Papers. Library of Congress. Contain much information on New York politics in the 40s and 50s.

George B. McClellan Papers. Library of Congress. Recently enlarged.

Cyrus H. McCormick Papers. Library of McCormick Historical Association, Chicago. A few Tilden letters and considerable supplementary information.

Hugh McCulloch Papers. Library of Congress. An observing participant in national affairs from the Civil War to 1889.

Carl Schurz Papers. Library of Congress. A Liberal Republican who appreciated Tilden's work as a reformer.

John Sherman Papers. Library of Congress. Information on reorganized railroads and the disputed election of 1876.

Samuel J. Tilden Papers. New York Public Library. A large, indispensable collection of letters and documents. Carefully sifted four times by the executors to exclude everything derogatory to Tilden.

Allen G. Thurman Papers. In the Ohio Archeological and Historical Society, Columbus, O. An able interpreter of Democratic politics during the period of Tilden's activities.

Martin Van Buren Papers. Library of Congress. A number of letters from and to Elam Tilden, Moses Y. Tilden and Samuel J. Tilden prior to the

Civil War. See Calender, 1910, which does not include 150 pieces added in 1912.

Israel Washburn Papers. Library of Congress. A Maine man in touch with a number of New York statesmen and an astute political observer.

Henry Watterson Papers. Library of Congress. An ardent champion and apologist of Tilden. Disappointing in Tilden items.

Smith M. Weed Papers. In possession of the family but mostly destroyed. A trusted follower of Tilden. Many Weed letters in the Tilden Papers. A number of letters in the Daniel S. Lamont Papers after 1892.

Gideon Welles Papers. Library of Congress. Diary, letters and scrap books. Diary printed in 1911.

Printed Materials

Newspapers

Practically all of the newspapers of the nation, both weekly and daily, contained more or less information about Tilden. In the New York Public Library there are a number of volumes of clippings about Tilden taken from various newspapers. In the State Library at Albany there are sixteen volumes of clippings relating to Horatio Seymour. The New York newspapers contain most of the original material and were widely copied. Among these the following give the most information:

Albany: *Argus; Atlas; Argus and Atlas; Evening Journal; Freeholder; Rough Hewer; Times.*

Brooklyn: *Eagle; Times; Union.*

Buffalo: *Commercial Advertiser; Courier; Express.*

Hudson: *Columbia Republican; Columbia Centinel; Gazette; Register.*

New York City: *The Campaign* (1844); *Catholic World; Citizen; Commercial Advertiser; Democratic Review; Daily Morning News; Evening Post; Harper's Weekly; Herald; Independent; Legal Observer; Mail and Express; Nation; Star; Sun; Times; Tribune; World; Democratic Advance.*

Syracuse: *Courier; Herald; Journal; Standard.*

Rochester: *Democrat and Chronicle; Post Express; Union and Advertiser.*

Utica: *Herald; Observer; Press.*

Out of State Newspapers

Baltimore, Md.: *News; Sun.*

London, Eng.: *Review; Times.*

Pittsfield, Mass.: *Sun.*

Philadelphia, Pa.: *Evening Star; Evening Telegraph; Herald; Record; Press; Saturday Evening Post; Times.*

Springfield, Mass.: *Republican.*

Washington, D. C.: *Chronicle; Globe; National Intelligencer.*

ARTICLES AND PAMPHLETS

Of the large number of articles in papers and magazines, and of pamphlets, the following are of special significance:

Abbott, E. H., "Francis Channing Barlow." *Harvard Graduates Mag.*, June, 1896.

Abbott, J. G., "Protest of Minority of Electoral Commission." Bangor (Me.) *Commercial*. Oct. 29, 1891. Printed in Bigelow, *Life*, II, 397.

Adams, C. F., "An Episode in Municipal Government." *North American Review*, Oct., 1874, Jan., July and Oct., 1875. Over the name of C. F. Wingate.

Adams, H. B., "The Gold Conspiracy." *Westminster Review*. Oct. 1, 1870.

Bigelow, John, "Why Mr. Tilden did not seat himself." Nashville *Banner*, April 2, 1880—"Some Recollections of Charles O'Conor." *Century*, March, 1885—"The Supreme Court and the Electoral Commission." New York, 1903—"Who Counts the Electoral Vote?" New York, 1877.

Black, J. S., "The Electoral Conspiracy." *North American Review*, July-Aug., 1877—"Letter to Mr. Stoughton on the Great Fraud." N. Y. *Sun*, Nov. 11, 1877.

Bone, Fanny Z. Lovell, "Louisiana in the Disputed Election of 1876." Louisiana *Historical Quarterly*, July and Oct., 1931.

Brown, Irving, "Charles O'Conor." *Green Bag*, Jan.-Feb., 1895.

Brown, R. B., "How Tilden Lost the Presidency." *Harper's Weekly*, July 30, 1904.

Bryant, C. O'B., "Finance, Taxation and Reform by Samuel J. Tilden." *Sunny Side Tract No. 2*, 1876.

Butler, W. A., "Samuel J. Tilden: Memorial Read before the Bar of the City of New York." New York, 1886.

Carter, J. C., "Mr. Tilden." *Atlantic*, Oct., 1892.

"Catalogue of Books, Pamphlets, Periodicals, Prints, etc., of Mr. Tilden at Gramercy Park." No date.

"The Centenary of Samuel Jones Tilden." Albany, 1914.

"The Cipher Dispatches. Mr. Tilden's letter and testimony." New York, 1869.

Childs, R. S., "Who Defrauded Samuel J. Tilden?" Albany *Argus*, March 4, 1901.

Cochran, John, "The Charleston Convention." *Mag. of Am. Hist.* Vol. XIV. New York, 1885.

Cox, J. D., "The Hayes Administration." *Atlantic*, June, 1893.

Coyle, J. F., "Concerning Some Features in the Making of Our Laws, of Interest to the Average Citizen." New York, 1875. "Tilden and the Electoral Commission." N. Y. *Sun*, Aug. 8, 1886.

Creel, George, "Scandals of 1876." *Collier's*, Sept. 17, 1927.

Dodd, W. E., "Samuel J. Tilden—A Prophet Unheeded." N. Y. *Times*, Apr. 17, 1827.

Edmunds, G. F., "Another View of the Hayes-Tilden Contest." *Century*, June, 1913. Comment by Henry Watterson in the same issue, p. 285.

Edwards, E. J., "Tammany." *McClure's*, Vol. IV, 1894–95—"Chapters in the History of Tammany." Vol. V, 1896–97.

Fairchild, C. S., "Report to Hon. Lucius Robinson . . . Tweed Suits." Albany, 1877.

Flick, A. C., "Samuel Jones Tilden." *New York History*. Oct., 1931.

Field, D. D., The Vote that Made the President. New York, 1877—The Electoral Votes of 1876: Who Should Count Them? New York, 1877.

Fox, D. R., "The Economic Status of the New York Whigs." Reprint from *Political Science Quarterly*, Dec., 1918.

Gardiner, O. C., "For Governor of New York and Reform, Samuel J. Tilden." New York, 1874.—"The Great Issue." New York, 1848.

Genung, A. P., "The Frauds of the New York City Government Exposed." New York, 1871.

George, Henry, "The Question Before the People." San Francisco, Aug. 15, 1876—"Who Was Elected President?" San Francisco, 1876—"Who Shall Be President?" Jan. 8, 1877—"History of a Great Fraud," 1877.

Glentworth, J. B., "A Statement of the Frauds on the Elective Franchise in New York in 1838 and 1839." New York, 1839.

Godwin, Parke, The Real Issues of the Canvass, or the Need of New Men and New Measures. Doc. No. 17, New York, 1876.

Gould, Anna T., List of the Books Read to Mr. Tilden during the Last Four Years of His Life. 1893. Printed in Bigelow, *Life*, II, 411.

Greeley, Horace, "Letter to a Politician." Brooklyn, 1877 (Oct. 29, 1869).

Green, A. H., "A Year's Record of a Reformer as Comptroller of New York City." New York, 1872.

Gregory, H. E., "Charles O'Conor," in Great American Lawyers, Vol. V. Philadelphia, 1908.

Haynie, Henry, "How a Newspaper Man Elected Hayes in 1876." Boston *Herald*, Jan. 30, 1897.

Hewitt, A. S., "Speech of Feb. 24, 1879, in Defense of Mr. Tilden."—"Preservation of Constitutional Government." Jan. 25, 1877.

Hill, F. T., "Hayes-Tilden Contest—A Political Arbitration." *Harper's*, March, 1907.

Howly, W. L., "What New York Owes to Tweed." *Munsey*, Vol. 36, p. 616.

Home, Rufus, "The Story of Tammany." *Harper's*, 1872.

"How Tilden Lost the Presidency." *Harper's Weekly*, March 28, 1908.

"Inauguration Day." Albany *Argus*, Jan. 2, 1875.

"Interview with Tilden." *Independent*, May 23, 1901.

"Investigation of Alleged Electoral Frauds in the Late Presidential Election." H.R. 45th Cong. 3rd Sess., Report No. 140. Potter Report.

"Inventory of Effects of Samuel J. Tilden." New York, 1886–87.

Kasson, J. A., "Governmental Expenditures." Washington, 1876—"Who Is Samuel J. Tilden and What Is His Record?" Washington, 1876.

Lamb, C. R., "The Tilden Mansion—Home of the National Arts Club." No date.

Lamb, M. J., "Judge Amasa J. Parker." *Mag. Am. Hist.*, Sept., 1890.

"How New York Is Governed. Frauds of the Tammany Democrats." New York, 1871.

Lawrence, William, New York Election Frauds. Washington, 1869. U.S. Cong. Report. Feb. 23, 1869.

"The Louisville and Nashville Railroad 1861–1869." *Am. Hist. Rev.*, July, 1924.

McDowell, W. O., "The Tilden Picture—A Memory." *Home and Country*, 1892.

Manning, Daniel, "Interview—Tilden's Renomination in 1880." *Sun.* Vol. I, No. 275.—"David Davis Corrected."

"Mass Meeting of the Citizens of New York, Held in Cooper Institute, Feb. 22d, 1866, to Approve the Principles Announced in the Messages of Andrew Johnson." New York, 1866.

Marble, Manton, "A Secret Chapter of Political History." *Sun*, Aug. 3, 1878 (Reprinted in pamphlet form).—"What Mr. Marble Saw in Florida." *World*, Jan. 17, 1878.

"Memorial Services in Honor of S. J. Tilden." Cal. State Dem. Club, Oct. 20, 1886.

Newcomb, Simon, "Our Antiquated Method of Electing a President." *North Am. Rev.*, Jan., 1908.

"New York City Council of Political Reform." New York, 1871.

New York *Times*, "How New York Is Governed. Frauds of the Tammany Democrats." New York, 1871.

Northrop, M. H., "A Grave Crisis in American History." *Century*, Oct., 1901.

O'Conor, Charles, "Peculation Triumphant." New York, 1875—"Address to the Bar Association of New York City." New York, 1876—Origin of the Tweed Ring. Printed in Bigelow, *Life*, I, 402—"The Court of Appeals and Its Relation to the Methods by which Public Peculations Have Evaded Justice." New York, 1876.

"Opinions of the Press." Reprint from the *Tribune*, Oct. 21, 1874.

"Opinions of the Press." Reprint from the *Times*, 1871 and 1875.

"Papers from the Society for the Diffusion of Political Knowledge." New York, 1862. Twenty-two addresses and the constitution of the society representing the opinions of the War Democrats.

Parton, James, "Manual for the Instruction of Rings." New York, 1866. Reprinted, Chicago, 1876.

Peck, H. T., "Twenty Years of the Republic." *Bookman*, March, 1905.

Potter, C. N., "The Danger and Duty of the Democracy." A Letter to the Hon. Francis Kernan. June 17, 1876. New York.

"Proceedings of the Senate and Assembly . . . Relative to the Death of S. J. Tilden." Albany *Argus*, May 23, 1887.

Randall, S. J., The Results of a Democratic House of Representatives in Behalf of Retrenchment and Reform. Doc. No. 10. New York, Aug. 14, 1876.

Raymond, H. W., "Extracts from the Journal of Henry J. Raymond." *Scribner's,* Nov., 1879, Jan., March and June, 1880.

Remarks of Mr. Justice Clifford in the Consultations of the Electoral Commission respecting the Electoral Votes of the State of Florida. Washington, 1877.

Remarks of Mr. Justice Field in the Electoral Commission on the Florida Case. Washington, Feb. 7, 1877.

"Report of Tilden Commission." *Municipal Affairs,* III, 434.

"Review of Letters and Literary Memorials." *Dial,* Apr. 1, 1908; *Nation,* Apr. 9, 1908.

Rogers, J. M., "How Hayes Became President." *McClure's,* May, 1904.

Root, Elihu, "Duties and Responsibilities of Citizenship." Yale Lecture. *Sun,* May 21, 1907.

Rosewater, V., "Oregon Muddle: A Curious Phase of the Hayes-Tilden Controversy." *Century,* Sept., 1913. *South Atlantic Quarterly,* 1920.

Ross, E. D., "Samuel J. Tilden and the Revival of the Democratic Party."

Sellers, J. L., "James R. Doolittle." *Wisc. Mag. of Hist.,* Sept. and Dec., 1934.

Seymour, Horatio, "Judicial Corruption." New York, Oct. 27, 1874.

Shepard, E. M., "Abram S. Hewitt, a Great Citizen." *Rev. of Rev.,* Feb., 1903.

Stetson, F. L., "Samuel J. Tilden, the Great Democrat." New York, 1914.

Stevens, J. A., Jr., "Proceedings at the Mass Meeting of Loyal Citizens, on Union Square, New York, 15th of July, 1862." New York, 1862—"The Union Defense Committee of New York." New York, 1885.

"The Three Secession Movements in the United States. Samuel J. Tilden, the Democratic Candidate for the Presidency; the Adviser, Aider and Abettor of the Great Secession Movement of 1860; and One of the Authors of the Infamous Resolution of 1864." Boston, 1876.

Tilden and Hendricks Club of California, "Give Us the Old Ticket of 1876." 1884.

Tilden, S. J., "The Union. Its Dangers. And How They Can Be Averted." A Letter to Hon. William Kent. New York, 1860—"The Canal Bill and the Constitution: Pay as You Go." N. Y. *Evening Post,* 1851—"Speeches of Ex-Governor Horatio Seymour and Hon. Samuel J. Tilden at Albany, March 11, 1866."—"New York State Finances and Canals." 1867—"Argument: Delaware and Hudson Canal Co. versus Pennsylvania Coal Co. 1863, New York Supreme Court."—"New York City Ring: Its Origin, Maturity and Fall." New York, 1873—"Statement in re Public Lands in Answer to Questions Addressed to John Commerford by Samuel J. Tilden."—"Record of Four Years' Campaign against Official Malversation in the City of New York, 1871 to 1875." New York, 1875—"The Governor." Buffalo *Courier,* Aug. 10, 1875—"Republic or Empire." Letter, Feb. 21, 1880—"Bill of Discovery" in the Income Tax Case—Notes on the Origin of the Tilden Name and Family. Printed in Bigelow,

Life, I, 317—Last Will and Testament. *Ib.,* II, 420. New York State Finances and Canals. Speech of Hon. Samuel J. Tilden in the Constitutional Convention on the 11th of September, 1867. New York, 1874.

Tilden Pamphlets. A collection under this title in the New York Public Library.

"Tilden Memorial. Proceedings of the New York Legislature at the Capitol, May 23, 1887." Albany *Argus,* 1887.

Tweed Ring Pamphlets. Twenty in Columbia University.

Walsh, J. C., "Charles O'Conor." *Jour. Am. Irish Hist. Soc.,* 1928.

Watson, W. H., "Address in Memory of Hon. Francis Kernan, 1816–1892." 1893.

Watterson, Henry, "Hayes-Tilden Contest for the Presidency." May, 1913— "Comments on Hayes-Tilden Contest." *Century,* June, 1913.

Williams, Talcott, "Tammany Hall." New York, 1899. In *Historic New York* Series.

Wingate, C. F., "An Episode in Municipal Government." *North Am. Rev.,* Oct., 1874, Jan., July, 1875. Written by C. F. Adams.

"Tweed Ring" Investigation Committee. Report to the Board of Supervisors. Dec. 29, 1877.

BOOKS

(A partial list only.)

Adams, C. F. Life of Charles Francis Adams. Boston, 1900—An autobiography. Boston, 1916.

Adams, C. F., Jr., and Henry Adams. Chapters of Erie and other Essays. Boston, 1871.

Alexander, D. S. A political history of the State of New York. New York, 1923—Four famous New Yorkers. New York, 1923.

Alexander, Holmes. The American Talleyrand. New York, 1935.

Allen, W. A. Governor Chamberlain's administration (S. C.).

The American annual cyclopedia. New York, 1861–1886.

Ames, J. B. Lectures on legal history. Cambridge, 1913.

The *Argus* almanac, 1875 and 1876. Albany, 1875 and 1876.

Asbury, Herbert. The Gangs of New York, New York, 1928.

Auchampaugh, P. G. James Buchanan and his cabinet. Lancaster, Pa., 1926 —Robert Tyler, Southern Rights Champion. Duluth, Minn., 1934.

Association of the Bar of the City of New York, Annual reports. New York, 1901—Reports of proceedings. New York, 1870.

Bancroft, Frederick. Speeches, correspondence and political papers of Carl Schurz. New York, 1913—Life of Seward. New York, 1900.

Bancroft, Frederick and Dunning, W. A. The reminiscences of Carl Schurz. New York, 1908.

Bancroft, George, Martin Van Buren to the end of his public career, 1889.

Barnard, G. G. Charges against Justice George G. Barnard and testimony thereunder, before the judiciary committee of the Assembly. Albany, 1872—Proceedings of the Court of impeachment in the matter of George G. Barnard. Albany, 1874.

Barnes, D. M. Draft riots in New York. New York, 1863.

Barnes, J. A. John G. Carlisle: financial statesman. New York, 1931.

Barnes, T. W. Memoir of Thurlow Weed. Boston, 1884.

Beal, H. K. The critical year. New York, 1930.

Belmont, August. Letters, speeches and addresses. New York, 1890.

Benton, T. H. Thirty years' view . . . from 1820 to 1850. New York, 1854–56.

Bigelow, John. The writings and speeches of Samuel J. Tilden. New York, 1885—The life of Samuel J. Tilden. New York, 1895—Letters and literary memorials of Samuel J. Tilden. 1908—Retrospections of an active life. New York, 1909 (Vols. IV and V prepared by his son John).

Bigelow, John, et al. The presidential count. New York, 1877. Tilden contributed much to the preparation of this survey.

Biographical directory American Congress. Washington, 1928.

Bishop, J. B. Presidential nominations and elections. New York, 1916—Notes and anecdotes of many years. New York, 1925—A chronicle of one hundred and fifty years. The chamber of commerce of the state of New York, 1768–1918. New York, 1918—Our political drama. New York, 1904.

Black, C. E. Essays and speeches of Jeremiah S. Black. New York, 1885.

Black, C. F., Ed. Reminiscences; some account of the work of Stephen J. Field. Great American lawyers, Vol. VII. Philadelphia, 1909.

Blake, E. V. History of the Tammany Society from its organization to the present time. New York, 1901.

Blaine, J. G. Twenty years in Congress. Norwich, 1884.

Boutwell, G. S. Reminiscences of sixty years in public affairs. New York, 1902.

Bowers, C. G. The tragic era. Boston, 1929.

Brace, C. L. The dangerous classes of New York. New York, 1872.

Breen, M. P. Thirty years in New York Politics. New York, 1899.

Brevard, Caroline M. A history of Florida. Deland, Fla., 1924.

Brigance, W. N. Jeremiah Sullivan Black. Philadelphia, 1934.

Brinkerhoff, Roeliff. Recollections of a lifetime. Cincinnati, 1900.

Brockway, Breman. Autobiography. Watertown, N. Y., 1891—Fifty years in journalism. Watertown, N. Y., 1891.

Brooks, Noah. Men of achievement. New York, 1895 (No. 6 Chase; No. 9 Tilden).

Brown, H. C. Fifth Avenue, old and new, 1824–1924. New York, 1924—The story of old New York. New York, 1934.

Browning, O. H. Diary. Ill. State Lib. Colls. Springfield, 1933. J. G. Randall, Ed.

Brummer, S. D. Political history of New York State during the Civil War. New York, 1911.

Buckman, B. E. Samuel J. Tilden unmasked. New York, 1876.

Buchanan, James. The works of James Buchanan. Philadelphia, 1908–11.

Burgess, J. W. Reconstruction and the constitution. New York, 1911—The middle period. New York, 1897.

Burton, T. E. John Sherman. Boston, 1906.

Butler, W. A. A retrospect of forty years. New York, 1911—Martin Van Buren: lawyer, statesman and man. New York, 1862.

Butler, B. F. Autobiography and personal recollections. Boston, 1892.

Byrdsall, F. The history of the Loco-Foco or Equal Rights party. Its movements, conventions and proceedings. With short characteristic sketches of its prominent men. New York, 1842.

Calkins, Hiram, and Van Buren, D. W. Biographical sketches of John T. Hoffman and A. C. Beach. New York, 1868.

Campaign text book (Democratic). New York, 1876; 1880; and 1884.

Carroll, Howard. Twelve Americans. Life of Horatio Seymour. New York, 1883.

Cary, Edward. Life of G. W. Curtis. New York, 1894.

Cary, Mathew. The Democratic speakers' handbook. Cincinnati, 1874.

Casson, H. N. Cyrus Hall McCormick, his life and work. Chicago, 1909.

Catalogue of the officers and students of Yale College, 1836–1837.

Catterall, R. C. H. The second bank of the United States. Chicago, 1903.

Chandler, Zachariah. An outline sketch of his life and public services. Detroit, 1880.

Chase, S. P. Diary and correspondence. Annual report of the Am. Hist. Assn., II, 1902. Washington, 1903.

Chestnut, Mary B. A diary from Dixie. New York, 1905.

Chester, Alden. Courts and lawyers of New York. New York, 1925.

Child, Hamilton. Gazetteer and business directory of Columbia county. Syracuse, 1871.

Chidsey, D. B. The gentleman from New York: a life of Roscoe Conkling, New Haven, 1935.

Chittendon, L. E. Personal reminiscences 1840–1890. New York, 1904.

Clarke, Grace J. George W. Julian. Indianapolis, 1923.

Clews, Henry. Fifty years of Wall Street. New York, 1908.

Clifford, P. Q. Nathan Clifford, Democrat. New York, 1922.

Clinton, H. L. Celebrated trials. New York, 1897.

Cole, A. C. The Whig party in the South. Am. Hist. Assn., 1913.

Coleman, C. H. The election of 1868. New York, 1923.

Collier, E. A. History of old Kinderhook. New York, 1914.

Constitutional Convention, 1846, Journal of. Atlas edition. Albany, 1846.

Cook, T. M. and Knox, T. W. Horatio Seymour. Public Record. New York, 1863.

Cook, T. F. The biography and public services of Hon. Samuel J. Tilden. New York, 1876.

Conkling, A. R. Life and letters of Roscoe Conkling. New York, 1889

Cooper, Peter. Autobiography. Boston, 1904.

Cornell, W. M. Lives of Tilden and Hendricks. Boston, 1876.

Cortissoz, Royal. Life of Whitelaw Reid. New York, 1921.

Cowan, Frank. Andrew Johnson. Greensburgh, Pa., 1894.

Cowley, Charles. Memoir of Josiah Gardner Abbott. Boston, 1892.

Cox, S. S. Three decades of Federal legislation. Providence, 1888.

Cox, W. Van Z., and Northrup, M. H. Life of Samuel Sullivan Cox. Syracuse, 1899.

Crapsey, Edward. The nether side of New York. New York, 1872.

Croly, D. G. Seymour and Blair: their lives and services. New York, 1868.

Crook, W. H. Memoirs of the White House. Boston, 1811—Andrew Johnson in the White House. *Century,* Sept. and Oct., 1908—Through Five Administrations. New York, 1910.

Cullum, S. M. Fifty years of public service. Chicago, 1911.

Curtis, Francis. The Republican party: a history of its fifty years' experience and a record of its measures and leaders. New York, 1904.

Curtis, G. T. Constitutional history of the United States. New York, 1889.

Curtis, G. W. Orations and addresses. C. E. Norton, Ed. New York, 1893–94 —"An autobiographical sketch," *Cosmopolitan,* Oct., 1894.

Dana, C. A. Recollections of the Civil War. New York, 1899.

Davenport, J. I. Election and naturalization frauds in New York City, 1860–1870. New York, 1894—Population of New York. New York, 1884.

Davis, Elmer, History of the New York *Times.* New York, 1921.

Davis, W. W. The Civil War and Reconstruction in Florida. New York, 1913.

Dennett, Tyler. John Hay: from poetry to politics. New York, 1933.

Depew, C. M. My memories of eighty years. New York, 1922.

Dickinson, D. S. Life and Works. New York, 1867.

Detroit *Post* and *Tribune.* Zachariah Chandler. Detroit, 1880.

Dewitt, D. M. The impeachment and trial of Andrew Johnson. New York, 1903.

Dictionary of American biography. A. Johnson and D. Malone, eds. New York, 1928–37.

Dix, Morgan. Memoirs of John A. Dix. New York, 1883.

Documents of the Board of Aldermen of the City of New York. No. 8. 1877.

Donovan, H. D. A. The Barnburners. New York, 1925.

Dorsheimer, William. Life and public services of Grover Cleveland. Philadelphia, 1888.

Doughtery, J. H. Electoral system of the United States. New York, 1906; Constitutional history of the State of New York. New York, 1915.

Duer, W. A. Reminiscences of an old New Yorker. New York, 1867.

Dunning, W. A. Reconstruction political and economic. New York, 1907— Essays on the Civil War and reconstruction. New York, 1898.

Durand, E. D. The finances of New York City. New York, 1898.

Eckenrode, H. J. A political history of Virginia during reconstruction. Baltimore, 1904—Rutherford B. Hayes, statesman of reunion. New York, 1930.

546   BIBLIOGRAPHY

Elliott, Maude H. Uncle Sam Ward and his circle. New York, 1939.
Ellis, Franklin. History of Columbia County. Philadelphia, 1878.
Evarts, Sherman. Arguments and speeches of William M. Evarts. New York, 1919.
The *Evening Journal* almanac, 1875 and 1876. Albany, 1875 and 1876.
Ewing, E. W. R. History and law of the Hayes-Tilden contest. 1910.
Fessenden, Francis. Life and public services of William Pitt Fessenden. Boston, 1907.
Ficklen, J. R. History of reconstruction in Louisiana. Baltimore, 1910.
Field, D. D. The electoral votes of 1876. New York, 1877.
Field, H. M. Life of D. D. Field. New York, 1898.
Fitch, C. E. Encyclopedia of biography of New York. Boston, 1916.
Fiske, Stephen. Off-hand portraits of prominent New Yorkers. New York, 1884.
Flack, H. E. The adoption of the Fourteenth Amendment. Baltimore, 1908.
Fleming, W. F. Documentary history of reconstruction. Cleveland, 1906.
Flick, A. C. History of the state of New York. 10 vols. New York, 1933-37.
Flint, H. M., The railroads of the United States. Philadelphia, 1868.
Flower, F. A. Edward McMaster Stanton. Akron, O., 1905.
Foord, John, The life and public services of Andrew Haswell Green. New York, 1913—Life of Simon Sterne. New York, 1903.
Ford, H. J. The Cleveland era. New Haven, 1921.
Ford, W. C. The letters of Henry Adams, 1858-1891. Boston, 1930—A cycle of Adams letters 1861-1865. Boston, 1920.
Forney, J. W. Anecdotes of public men. New York, 1873.
Foulke, W. D. Life of Oliver P. Morton. Indianapolis, 1899—Fighting the spoilsmen. New York, 1919.
Fourtier, Alcée. A history of Louisiana. New York, 1904.
Fox, D. R. The decline of aristocracy in the politics of New York. New York, 1919.
Fuess, C. M. Carl Schurz reformer. New York, 1932.
Fuller, H. B. Speakers of the House of Representatives. New York, 1896.
Fulton, Chandar, History of the Democratic party—Jefferson to Cleveland. New York, 1892.
Genung, A. P. The frauds of the New York City government exposed. Sketches of the members of the Ring and their confederates. New York, 1871.
George, Henry, Jr. Life of Henry George. New York, 1900.
Gibson, A. M. A political crime. New York, 1885.
Gilder, R. W. Grover Cleveland, a record of friendship. New York, 1920.
Gillet, R. H. The life and times of Silas Wright. Albany, 1874—Democracy in the United States. New York, 1868.
Godkin, E. L. Reflections and comments. New York, 1895.
Goodnow, F. J. The Tweed Ring in New York City. New York, 1888.
Goodrich, F. E. Life and public services of Grover Cleveland. Boston, 1884.

Godwin, Parke. Life of William Cullen Bryant. New York, 1883.

Going, C. B. David Wilmot, free soiler. New York, 1924.

Gorham, G. C. Life and public services of Edwin M. Stanton. Boston, 1872.

Gover, W. C. The Tammany Hall democracy of the city of New York and the general committee for 1875. New York, 1875.

Grant, U. S. Personal memoirs. New York, 1885.

Greeley, Horace. The American conflict. Hartford, 1866—Proceedings of the first three Republican national conventions of 1856, 1860 and 1864. Minneapolis, 1893—Recollections of a busy life. New York, 1868.

Greer, F. H. Men of mark of the 19th century. New York, 1872.

Hall, C. R. Andrew Johnson, military governor of Tennessee. Princeton, 1916.

Hamilton, Gail. Biography of James G. Blaine. Norwich, 1895.

Hamilton, J. G. De R. Reconstruction in North Carolina. New York, 1914.

Hammond, J. B. Political History of the state of New York. Syracuse, 1849 —Life of Silas Wright. Syracuse, 1852.

Hancock, Mrs. W. S. Reminiscences of Winfield Scott Hancock. New York, 1887.

Harrison, Mrs. Burton. Recollections grave and gay. New York, 1911.

Harsha, D. A. Noted living Albanians and state officials. Albany, 1891.

Hart, A. B. Salmon Portland Chase. Boston, 1889.

Havemeyer, J. C. Letters and addresses. New York, 1914.

Hawkins, D. A. New York City Council of Political Reform. Five Reports. New York, 1873.

Haworth, P. L. Reconstruction and union 1865–1812. New York, 1912—The United States in our time. New York, 1920—The Hayes-Tilden election. Indianapolis, 1927.

Hay, John. Letters and diaries. Privately printed.

Hayes, R. B. Diary and letters. Columbus, O., 1922–1926.

Hibbin, Paxton. Henry Ward Beecher. New York, 1927.

Hill, F. T. Decisive battles of the law. New York, 1907.

Hinds, A. C. Precedents of the House of Representatives. Washington, 1907.

Hoar, G. F. Autobiography of seventy years. New York, 1903.

Holcombe, J. W., and Skinner, H. M. Life and public services of Thomas A. Hendricks. Indianapolis, 1886.

Hovey, Carl. The life of J. Pierrepont Morgan. New York, 1911.

Howard, O. O. Autobiography. New York, 1907—Life of Rutherford B. Hayes. Ohio Archeological Publications, No. 4.

Howe, M. A. DeW. The life and letters of George Bancroft. New York, 1908.

Hudson, W. C. Random recollections of an old political reporter. New York, 1911.

Hunt, C. H. Life of Edward Livingston. New York, 1864.

Hutchins, Stilson. Political manual for 1880. Washington *Post*, 1880.

Ingraham, A. A. A biography of Fernando Wood. New York, 1856.

Irelan, J. R. The Republic. Chicago, 1887.

Ivins, W. M. Machine politics and money in New York City. New York, 1887.

Jameson, J. A. The Constitutional Convention—History, powers, etc. New York, 1867.

Jenkins, J. S. History of political parties of New York, 1789–1849. Auburn, 1849—Life of Silas Wright. Auburn, 1847.

Johnson, W. F., and Smith, R. B. Political and governmental history of the state of New York. Syracuse, 1922.

Jones, T. F. New York University, 1832–1932. New York, 1933.

Jones, Willoughby. The life of James Fisk, Jr. Philadelphia, 1872.

Judson, Isabella F. C. W. Field, his life and work. New York, 1896.

Julian, G. W. Speeches on political questions. New York, 1872—Political recollections 1840–1872. Chicago, 1884—The life of Joshua R. Giddings. Chicago, 1892.

Junkin, D. X. and Norton, F. H. Life of Winfield Scott. New York, 1880.

Kent, F. R. The Democratic party: a history. New York, 1928.

Kinley, David. The independent treasury and its relations to the banks. Washington, 1910.

Kirkland, E. C. The peace makers of 1864. New York, 1927.

Krock, Arthur. The editorials of Henry Watterson. New York, 1923.

Lamb, Martha S. History of the city of New York. New York, 1897.

Laughlin, J. L. The history of bimetalism in the United States. New York, 1896.

Leech, W. L., Ed. Collection of papers of Pierce. Washington, 1917.

Lester, C. E. Lives of Tilden and Hendricks. New York, 1876—Life and character of Peter Cooper. New York, 1883.

Lewis, A. H. The Boss and how he came to rule New York City. New York, 1903.

Lieber, Francis. Changes in the present constitution of New York. New York, 1867.

Lincoln, C. Z. Constitutional history of New York. New York, 1906—Messages from the governors. Albany, 1909.

Livingston, John. Biographical sketches. New York, 1853.

Lloyd, H. D. Wealth against commonwealth. New York, 1894.

Logan, Mrs. J. A. Reminiscences of a soldier's wife. New York, 1913.

Lonn, Ella. Reconstruction in Louisiana after 1868. New York, 1918.

Lynch, D. T. Grover Cleveland: a man four square. New York, 1932—Boss Tweed, the story of a grim generation. New York, 1927—An epoch and a man: Martin Van Buren and his times. New York, 1929.

Mackenzie, W. L. Lives and opinions of B. F. Butler . . . and Jesse Hoyt . . . with anecdotes. Boston, 1845.

Martin, E. S. The life of Joseph Hodges Choate. New York, 1920.

Martin, E. W. The life and public services of Schuyler Colfax, New York, 1868—Behind the scenes in Washington. New York, 1873.

Martin, I. T. Recollections of Elizabeth Benton Fremont. New York, 1912.

Maverick, Augustus. Henry J. Raymond and the New York Press for thirty years. Hartford, 1870.

Mayes, Edward. Life of Lucius Q. C. Lamar. Nashville, 1896.

McCabe, J. D. The life and public services of Horatio Seymour, together with a complete and authentic life of Francis P. Blair. New York, 1868— Lights and shadows of New York life. Philadelphia, 1872.

McClellan, G. B. McClellan's own story. New York, 1887.

McClure, A. K. Recollections of half a century. Salem, 1902.

McCarmac, E. I. James K. Polk: a political biography. Berkeley, 1922.

McCormack, J. T., Ed. Memoirs of Gustave Koerner, 1809–1896. Cedar Rapids, Ia., 1909.

McCulloch, Hugh. Men and measures of half a century. New York, 1888.

McElroy, W. H., and McBride, Alexander A. Life sketches of executive officers and members of the legislature of the state of New York. Albany, 1873.

McGrane, R. C., Ed. The correspondence of Nicholas Biddle, dealing with national affairs. Boston, 1919—William Allen: a study in western democracy. Columbus, O., 1925.

McGuire, J. K. The Democratic party in the State of New York. New York, 1905.

McLaughlin, A. C. Lewis Cass. Boston, 1899.

McLaughlin, J. F. The life and times of John Kelly. New York, 1885—Tilden memorabilia: a series of historic letters. New York, 1880.

McLeod, Donald. Biography of Hon. Fernando Wood. New York, 1858.

McKnight, D. A. The electoral system of the United States. New York, 1877.

McPherson, Edward. Political manual, 1866–1869; handbook of politics. Washington, 1868–1894.

Merriman, G. S. The life and times of Samuel Bowles. New York, 1885.

Merritt, E. A. Recollections, 1828–1911. Albany, 1911.

Miller, M. M. Great debates in American history. New York, 1913.

Miller, P. F. A group of great lawyers of Columbia County, New York. Hudson, 1904.

Milton, G. F. The age of hate: Andrew Johnson and the radicals. New York, 1930—The era of conflict. New York, 1934.

Minor, Henry. Story of the Democratic party. New York, 1928.

Mitchell, E. P. Memoirs of an editor. New York, 1924.

Mitchell, Stewart. Horatio Seymour of New York. Cambridge, Mass., 1938.

Moore, J. B. The works of James Buchanan. Philadelphia, 1908–1911.

Morris, F. The American metropolis from Knickerbocker days to the present time. New York, 1897.

Morse, J. T., Jr., Ed. Diary of Gideon Welles. Boston, 1911.

Murphy, C. B. S. J. Tilden in the Civil War. *Ind. Hist. Bulletin*, Vol. 9, p. 192. Indianapolis, 1932.

Myers, Gustavus. The history of Tammany Hall. New York, 1895—History of public franchises in New York City. New York, 1900.

Myers, W. S. The Republican party, a history. New York, 1928—General George Brinton McClellan. New York, 1934.

Muzzey, D. S. James G. Blaine: a political idol of other days. New York, 1934.

Muzzy, H. R. Combination in the mining industry: a study of concentration in Lake Superior iron ore production. New York, 1905.

Nevins, Allan. The *Evening Post:* a century of journalism. New York, 1822 —Frémont, the West's great adventurer. New York, 1928—The emergence of modern America. New York, 1927—Henry White: thirty years of American diplomacy. New York, 1930—Grover Cleveland: a study in courage. New York, 1932—Abram S. Hewitt. New York, 1935.

New York Red Book. Albany, 1874–1886.

New York State. Assembly proceedings. Albany, 1845–1886—Assembly Documents. Albany, 1845–1886—Senate proceedings. Albany, 1845–1886—Senate documents. Albany, 1845–1886.

New York State, Courts. Court of Appeals: the Tilden will case, 1891. Vol. 77. Printed documents on the case bound in one volume—Supreme Court: J. Bigelow *et al vs*. G. K. Tilden *et al*. 1897. Various printed legal briefs bound in one volume—Supreme Court: the board of supervisors of the county of New York vs. William M. Tweed. New York, 1872.

New York State laws, 1842–1886.

Nicolay, J. G., and Hay, John. Abraham Lincoln. New York, 1890.

Nichols, R. F. The Democratic Machine, 1850–1854. New York, 1923— Franklin Pierce. Philadelphia, 1931.

Northrop, H. D. The life and achievements of Jay Gould. Philadelphia, 1892.

Noyes, A. D. Forty years of American finance. New York, 1907.

O'Brien, F. M. Story of the Sun. New ed. New York, 1918.

Oberholtzer, E. P. A history of the United States since the Civil War. New York, 1922.

Official proceedings of the Dem. Nat. Convention. New York, 1884.

Ogden, Rollo. Life and letters of Edwin Lawrence Godkin. New York, 1907.

Paine, A. B. Thomas Nast, his period and his pictures. New York, 1904.

Parker, G. F. Recollections of Grover Cleveland. New York, 1909.

Parton, James. Manual for the instruction of "Rings," railroad and political; with a history of the Grand Chicago & Northwestern "Ring" and the secret of its success. New York, 1866—James Jackson. New York, 1897.

Patton, J. H. The Democratic party: its political history and influence. New York, 1884.

Paxson, F. L. Recent history of the United States. New York, 1928.

Pearce, H. J. Benjamin H. Hill. Chicago, 1928.

Phelps, Mary M. Kate Chase, dominant daughter. New York, 1935.

Pierce, E. L. Memoirs and letters of Charles Sumner. Boston, 1894.

Political reformation of 1884. Democratic Campaign Book, New York, 1884.

Poore, B. P. Perley's reminiscences of sixty years in the national metropolis. Philadelphia, 1886.

Porcher, F. A. A last chapter in reconstruction in South Carolina. Southern Historical Society Papers. Vols. 12–13.

Potter, C. N. Investigation of electoral frauds. New York, 1878.

Powell, T. E. The Democratic party in the state of Ohio. Columbus, 1913.

Pray, I. C. Memoirs of James Gordon Bennett and his times. New York, 1855.

Proceedings of the electoral commission. *Congressional Record.* Part IV, vol. V, of the 44th Cong., 2d Sess. Washington, 1877.

Quaife, M. M. The diary of James K. Polk. Chicago, 1910.

Ralphdon, H. F. Age of Cleveland. New York, 1888.

Randall, J. G. Constitutional problems under Lincoln. New York, 1926.

Raymond, R. W. Peter Cooper. New York, 1901.

Raymond, William. Biographical sketches of the distinguished men of Columbia County. Albany, 1851.

Reid, T. W. Life of the Right Honorable William Edward Forster. London, 1888.

Rhodes, J. F. History of the United States from Hayes to McKinley. New ed. New York, 1919.

Roberts, E. R. New York—The planting and growth of the Empire State. Boston, 1887.

Robinson, W. A. Thomas B. Reed, parliamentarian. New York, 1930.

Rogers, W. P. The three secession movements in the United States. Boston, 1876.

Roosevelt, Theodore. Historic towns—New York. New York, 1910.

Ross, E. D. The liberal Republican movement. New York, 1910.

Russell, W. H. My diary North and South. London, 1863.

Sargent, Nathan. Public men and events. New York, 1875.

Schell, Francis. Memoir of the Hon. Augustus Schell. New York, 1885.

Schuckers, J. W. Life and public services of Salmon Portland Chase. New York, 1874.

Schurz, Carl. Speeches, correspondence and political papers. Frederick Bancroft, ed. New York, 1913—Reminiscences. New York, 1909—Intimate letters, 1841–1869. Wisconsin Historical Society, 1929.

Scrugham, Mary. The peaceable Americans of 1860–1861. New York, 1921.

Seitz, D. C. Joseph Pulitzer, his life and letters. New York, 1921—Horace Greeley. Indianapolis, 1926—The dreadful decade, New York, 1926—The James Gordan Bennetts. New York, 1928.

Seward, F. W. Reminiscences of a war-time statesman and diplomat, 1830–1915. New York, 1916.

Sheperd, E. M. Martin Van Buren. Boston, 1888.

Sherman, John. Recollections of forty years. New York, 1895.

Shores, Venila L. The Hayes-Conkling Controversy. Northampton, 1919.

Smith, W. E. The Francis Preston Blair family. New York, 1933.

Spencer, Edward. Life of Thomas F. Bayard. New York, 1880.

Sprague, A. P. Speeches, arguments and miscellaneous papers of David Dudley Field. New York, 1884.

Stanton, H. B. Random recollections. New York, 1886.

Stanwood, Edward. A history of presidential elections. Boston, 1884. New edition revised by C. K. Bolton, 1928, as A history of the presidency.

Starr, H. E. William Graham Sumner. New York, 1925.

Stebbins, H. A. Political history of New York, 1865–1869. New York, 1913.

Stevens, F. M. The beginnings of the New York Central Railroad. N. Y., 1926.

Stevens, J. A. Progress of New York in a century. New York, 1876.

Stevenson, A. E. Men I have known. Chicago, 1909.

Stokes, A. P. Memorials of eminent Yale men. New Haven, 1914.

Strong, T. G. Landmarks of a lawyer's lifetime. New York, 1914.

Stryker, L. P. Andrew Johnson. New York, 1929.

Sumner, Charles. Works. Boston, 1883.

Sumner, W. G. A history of banking in the United States. New York, 1926.

Sweeny, P. B. On the ring frauds and other public questions. New York, 1894.

Swinton, W. How the ring ran Pacific mail. New York, 1867.

Swisher, C. B. Stephen J. Field, craftsman of law. New York, 1930.

Tarbell, Ida M. The tariff in our times. New York, 1911.

Taussig, F. W. The tariff history of the United States. New York, 1914.

Terry, R. W., and Prentiss, J. W. Civil list of Columbia County and official handbook, 1786–1886. Hudson, 1888.

Thomas, H. C. The return of the Democratic party to power in 1884. New York, 1919.

The Tilden will case. New York, 1886–1897. 2 vols. of documents.

Tilden, S. J., and others. The presidential counts. New York, 1877.

Todd, C. B. Story of the city of New York, New York, 1902.

Townsend, G. A. Washington, outside and inside. Chicago, 1874.

Townsend, J. O. New York in bondage. New York, 1901.

Townsend, J. W. Kentuckians in history and literature. Neale, 1907.

Tweedy, John. A history of the Republican national conventions from 1856 to 1908. Danbury, Conn., 1910.

Tyler, M. C. In memoriam: Edgar Kelsey Apgar. Ithaca, N. Y., 1886.

United States, *Congressional Globe*. Washington, 1834–1873—*Congressional Record*. Washington, 1873–1886.

Vallandigham, J. L. Life of C. L. Vallandigham. Baltimore, 1872.

Van Buren, Martin. Inquiry into the origin and growth of political parties in the United States. New York, 1867—Autobiography. Edited by J. C. Fitzpatrick. Annual Report of the Am. Hist. Assn. Washington, 1920.

Van Wyck, Frederick. Recollections of old New York. New York, 1932.

Villard, Henry. Memoirs of Henry Villard, journalist and financier, 1835–1900. Boston, 1904.

Wall, A. J. A sketch of the life of Horatio Seymour, 1810–1888. New York, 1929.

Wallace, D. D., The history of South Carolina. New York, 1934.

Wallace, John. Carpetbag rule in Florida. Jacksonville, 1888.

Warden, R. B. An account of the private life and public services of Salmon Portland Chase. Cincinnati, 1874.

Warmouth, H. C. War, politics and reconstruction. New York, 1930.

Warren, Charles. The Supreme Court in United States history. Boston, 1922.

Watterson, Henry. History of the Manhattan Club. New York, 1915—Marse Henry Watterson: An autobiography. New York, 1919.

Weed, Harriet A. Life of Thurlow Weed. Boston, 1884.

Welles, Gideon. Diary. Boston, 1911.

Wells, D. A. The recent financial, industrial and commercial experiences of the United States. A curious chapter in politico-economical history. New York, 1872—Robinson Crusoe's money. New York, 1876.

Wells, E. L. Hampton and reconstruction. Columbus, S. C., 1907.

Werner, M. R. Public papers of John T. Hoffman. New York, 1872—Civil list. Albany, 1886—Tammany Hall. New York, 1928.

Wheeler, E. P. Sixty years of American life. New York, 1917.

White, A. D. Autobiography of Andrew D. White. New York, 1905.

White, Horace. Life of Lyman Trumbull. Boston, 1913.

White, Trumbull. The wizard of Wall Street and his wealth, or the life and deeds of Jay Gould. Chicago, 1902.

Whitford, N. E. History of the canal system of New York. Albany, 1905. Supplement to the Report of the State Engineer.

Whitlock, Brand. Forty years of it. New York, 1925.

Whittle, J. L. Grover Cleveland. London, 1896.

Williams, C. R. Diary and letters of R. B. Hayes. Columbus, O., 1924.

Williams, R. D. The honorable Peter White. Cleveland, 1907.

Wilson, J. G. The memorial history of the city of New York. New York, 1893.

Wilson, Henry. Rise and fall of the slave power. Boston, 1872–1877.

Wilson, J. H. Life of Charles A. Dana. New York, 1907.

Wilson, W. L. The national Democratic party. Baltimore, 1888.

Wilson, Woodrow. Congressional government: a study in American politics. Boston, 1885.

Winston, J. A. Andrew Johnson, plebeian and patriot. New York, 1928.

Woodburn, J. A. The life of Thaddeus Stevens. Indianapolis, 1913.

Wright, Mable O. My New York. New York, 1926.

Index

555

but in reality he managed it, 184-185; Tilden persuaded Seymour to go on a speaking tour to Middle West, 185; uproar over Democratic ticket by middle October, 185; demands that Seymour and Blair withdraw, 186-187; Tilden refused to let them do so, 187; results of the campaign, 188

Campaign of 1876, 300 ff.; major problems of the canvass, 300; Tilden directed his own campaign, 301; publicity, 301-302; funds, 304; an exciting campaign, 307; mud-slinging, 307-308; bloody shirt and villification of Tilden's character, 309-312; Republican speakers, 313-314; attacks on Hayes, 314; Democratic workers, 316; summary of the campaign, 318-321; election, 322 ff.; doubtful result, 328; force threatened, 331; a peaceful revolution, 333; four doubtful states, 334; all went to Hayes, 349; electoral commission to pass on doubtful returns, 387 ff.; Tilden's solution simple, 379; election of Hayes, 396; bargain with South, 399; Hewitt's resignation, 401-402

Campbell, J. A., attorney for Tilden, 388

Canal Board, must have power over bids for work, 266; Tilden recommended an inspector of Public Works and a paymaster independent of the Board, 266; guilty of misconduct but not suspended by Tilden on advice of Seymour, 272

Canal Ring, defeated Kernan as delegate in 1874, 242; tried to defeat Tilden's nomination for Governor, 243; worked against him after his nomination, 248; McGuire allied with, 257; broken 265 ff.; overthrow of Gov. Tilden's second major reform, 265; composition of and its operation, 265; tried in vain to delay Tilden's investigation, 272; revelations of corruptions, 273; Ring broken, 273; punishments, 273; voted against Tilden in 1876, 318; its overthrow made Tilden President, 522

Canals, discussed in Constitutional Convention of 1846, 77

Canda, F. E., Tilden advised his appointment as a director of the Union Pacific Railroad, 491

Capen, Nahum, compared Tilden to young Pitt, 521

Cardoza, Albert, a Tweed Ring judge, 196; resigned, hence not impeached in 1872, 237

Carroll, Chancellor, admitted Tilden to the bar, 52; how he collected a law library, 52

Carroll, J. L., visiting statesman in 1876, 338

Carter, James C., on commission to study city government, 261; working with Tilden on a lawsuit when he was nominated for President, 293-294; approved of Tilden's will, 511; gave illustration of Tilden's humanitarianism, 528

Carter and Ledyard, employed by the executors in the Tilden will contest, 514

Casanave, G., colored, on Louisiana Returning Board, 337

Cass, Lewis, beaten for President, 521

Cass, G. W., arbiter, 203

Cassatt, A. J., supplied Tilden with passes and private cars, 240

Casserly, Eugene, of California, wrote Tilden a confidential letter in 1866, 154; in 1868 said that Pendleton could not carry Pacific States and should be nominated for Vice President, 172; investigating abuses in New York Custom House, 225; nominated Tilden and Hendricks in 1874, 252; with Gwin reported California "Tilden all over," 282

Cassidy, Eugene, criticism of Constitutional Convention of 1846, 78; borrowed money from Tilden, 88

Cassidy, William, Tilden's source of political gossip, 114; in Constitutional Convention of 1867, 160; said Tammany had cut adrift from the State organization, 220-221

Caten, Judge J. D., on Tilden's war record, 138

Central New York Fair, address by Tilden in 1875, 270-271; a guest of Senator Kernan, 271

Champlain, Marshall B., of Allegany, presided over State Convention of 1868, 168; as Attorney General authorized O'Conor to set up a Bureau of Municipal Correction to oust the Tweed Ring, 215

Chandler, W. E., explanation of what was done in Louisiana in 1876, 342-343; in Florida, 344

Chandler, Zachariah, forcing officeholders to pay a party tax, 304; ordered Tilden's income tax investigated, 310; worried over election of 1876, 323; betting in Tilden's favor, 323; Tilden and Hayes on election day, 323; people went to bed feeling that Tilden was elected, 323-324; Hayes record in his *Diary*, 323; accused of plotting to take the doubtful States, 339; in Florida in 1876, 344; and Thomas Nast, 350; claimed election for Hayes, 352

Channing, W. E., 104

Chapin, Arthur L., president of Beloit College, a classmate of Tilden at Yale, 28

Chapman, B. B., thought Seymour the best candidate, 180

Charleston Democratic National Convention in 1860, 118; Tilden an alternate delegate, 118; Soft delegates of New York pledged to Douglas first and then Guthrie, 118; secession of seven States over slavery

ator Hager and James Beard of California to Oregon, and to telegraph Governor Grover and Senator Kelly, 348; opposed Tilden for President, 283

Coyle, J. F., carried Johnson's respects to Seymour and Tilden, 180; visiting statesman in Florida in 1876, 344

Credit Mobilier, associated with Dix, 248

Croker, Richard, made a marshal by John Kelly, 249

Cronin, E. A., certified as Oregon elector, 349

Crosby, Howard, Chancellor of New York University, criticized Gray Nuns act, 277

Croswell, Edwin, editor of the Albany *Argus*, 40; advised Polk about his Cabinet, 65

Crowley, R. R., nominated for Inspector of State Prisons in 1875, 270

Cumberland Coal and Iron case won by Tilden, 102

Curtis, Edward, Collector of the Port, and illegal voting, 53

Curtis, George T., address, 141

Curtis, G. S., volunteered to take the stump for Seymour in 1868, 182

Curtis, G. W., in Constitutional Convention of 1867, 160; as chairman of Republican State Convention promised to help Tilden in correction of abuses, 269

Daily Graphic claimed honor of having first nominated Tilden for President, 281

Daily New York Morning News, 62-65; suspended, 65

Dana, Charles A., wrote Tilden editorials in the *Sun*, 447; asked for a loan, 469; wanted Tilden's opinion in a railroad case, 469; sent a box of Steinberger wine by Tilden, 472

Davis, David, Judge, elected U.S. Senator and refused to serve on the Electoral Commission, 382-383; Hewitt's disappointment, 383; distrusted the Commission, 384; Justice N. N. Swayne advised him to resign at once, 384; Judge Bradley selected to take Davis' place on the Commission, 385; might have had a place in Tilden's Cabinet and might have been his successor, 415

Davis, G. S., of Massachusetts, 123

Davis, T. C., indicted for cheating, 273

Davis, William H., Tilden's English valet, 504

Dawson, Henry B., Tilden saved his home, 472

Day, J., President of Yale, letter, 32

Dayton & Union Road, 164

Delavan House, Albany, in 1868, 168

Delaware & Hudson Railroad, opened to Montreal, 275

Delmonico's, 140; reception to Tilden and

Wickham in 1874, 252; dinner to J. S. Morgan addressed by Tilden in 1877, 424-425; untidy appearance of Tilden at, 500

Delphic Iron Company stock mentioned in Tilden's will, 512

Democratic National Convention of 1848, 82; both Hunker and Barnburner delegations admitted to seats, 83; Barnburners incensed withdrew, 83; Lewis Cass nominated for President, 83

Democratic National Convention of 1868 at New York summoned by Belmont, 170; a list of candidates, 170; John Dash Van Buren Jr., his confidential agent, 171; deluged with rumors in May, 1868, 171; Tilden had thought of Johnson in 1867, 171; Frank P. Blair in touch with Tilden, 171-172; Tilden consulted R. J. Walker in Washington, 172; so far as Tilden had a choice it was Chase, 172; convened in Tammany Wigwam July 4, weather hot, 175; called to order by Belmont, 175; Tilden helped to write the platform, 176; first ballot, 176; nomination of Seymour, 177; second place given to F. P. Blair, 178; nobody pleased with the ticket, 178

Democratic National Convention at St. Louis in 1876, 287 ff.; called to order on June 27 by Augustus Schell, 287; oration by Watterson, temporary chairman, 288; McClernand named permanent chairman, 288; Dorsheimer read resolutions demanding reforms, 288; contents 288-289; Kelly asked for the floor, 289; nominations made by States in alphabetical order, 289-290; Kernan nominated Tilden, 289; first ballot, 290; Tilden nominated on second ballot, 290; Hendricks named for Vice President, 291; opposition papers made fun of the ticket, 291-292; delegates returned home feeling that the best man had won, 292

Democratic National Convention at Chicago in 1884 with Cleveland and Flower as candidates from New York, 484; Tilden's abnegation increased his popularity, 484

Democratic State Convention of 1847 controlled by the Hunkers, 81; named State ticket and reorganized State Committee, 81; Barnburners seceded, 81

Democratic-Republicans of New York in 1832, 17-18

Democratic Party, fathers of, lauded by Tilden, 153; not responsible for Tweed Ring, 216; recover its leadership under Tilden, 522

Democrats at Albany in 1865, promised Johnson cordial support, 151

Democrats, radical, or Barnburners, gave prominence to free-soil, 80

Democratic State Convention of 1875 at

New York Public Library celebrated the Tilden centennial with a collection of Tildenana, 520

New York Society Library, 52

New York *Star* announced in 1880 that at a conference it was decided that Tilden would not run, 350-351

New York State, appropriated $3,000,000 and raised 120,000 soldiers for the War, 131

New York State Convention in 1868, at Albany, 168-169; Seymour urged that no candidate should be designated, 168; delegates, 170; no candidate endorsed, 170

New York University, why founded, 30-31; Law School organized in 1838, 44

Nicholls, Gen. F. T., Democratic nominee for Governor of Louisiana, 336

Nilsson, Christine, a friend of Tilden, 477

Nordhoff, Charles, voted for Tilden in 1876, 320

Northern people not ready to put government in Copperhead hands, 159

Noyes, Governor, a visiting statesman in 1876, 338

O'Brien, C. L., taken into Tilden's office on the recommendation of Havemeyer, 240

O'Conor, Charles, helped Tilden draft incorporation papers, 88; helped Tilden win Flagg case, 97-98; gave Tilden comradeship, 104; a sincere friend, 110; helped Hards nominate Brady for Governor in 1860, 120; member of the Committee of Fifteen in 1860, 124; consoled Tilden over results of election of 1860, 126; presided over Pine Street Meeting, 128; sent by Tilden in 1868 to see Bennett about a presidential candidate, 167; contributed $10,000 to Seymour's campaign in 1868; consulted by Tilden about the Fourteenth Amendment, 189-190; an ally in the reform crusade, 212; consulted by Tilden about Tweed Ring, 214; advised Connolly to appoint Green deputy Comptroller, 217; skeptical, 217; warned against any compromise with the Ring, 218; Tilden tried to persuade him to run for the Assembly, 222; on Tilden's affidavit against Tweed, 225; insisted that Tilden continue investigations, 226; in charge of suits against the Ring, 226; believed there was a conspiracy to protect Tweed, 229; replaced Curtis and Porter with Peckham and Wickham, 229; still pressing Tweed suits when Tilden became Governor, assisted by Peckham, Barlow, and Carter, 259; when Tweed was freed, Tilden ordered him rearrested, 259; E. Delafield Smith said suits authorized by Barlow

were invalid, and dismissed Peckham, Barlow and Carter, 259; movement to drive Smith and Green from office, 259; encouraged by Mayor Wickham, 259-260; O'-Conor opposed dismissal of Green, 260; O'Conor had Tilden insist that he had right to approve dismissals, 260; Tilden removed Smith but kept Green, 260; a greater lawyer than Tilden, 521; disappointed at Tilden's timidity in Rochester, 268; said "Your speeches make the welkin ring," 226, 269; attorney for Tilden before the Electoral Commission, 388; would have been in Tilden's Cabinet, 415; consulted about his income tax suit, 439; his death a blow to Tilden, 474; approved of Tilden's will, 511

Ogden, Fleetwood Company, 117

Ogden, William B., consulted Tilden about railroad investments, 116; Tilden tried to influence Lincoln through Ogden, 128; associated with Tilden in railroads, 164; helped incorporate the Iron Cliffs Company, 509

Oil fields of Pennsylvania, investigated by Tilden, 118

Oregon, steamboat, sold, 164

Olney, P. B., greeted Tilden on his return from Europe in 1877, 423

Ontario & Western Railroad, 469

Oregon in election of 1876, 334; one elector disqualified because he was a deputy postmaster, 348; Oregon Democrats deluged with telegrams to have a Democratic elector chosen, 348; J. N. H. Patrick of Omaha sent to Oregon and wired for money to win over a Republican elector, 348; Gov. Grover certified a Democratic elector, but Elector Watts resigned his deputy postmastership and claimed to be the true elector, 249; hence the Oregon returns were doubtful, 349

Oregon Short Line, bonds mentioned in Tilden's will, 512

O'Rourke, Mathew J., his estimate of the thefts of the Tweed Ring, 230

Orr, Alexander E., a trustee of the Tilden Trust, and secretary, 517

Osborne House in Rochester, citizens greet Tilden at, 268

Oswego Douglas Club, 125

O'Sullivan, John L., romanticized Samuel J. Tilden, 5; quoted by Tilden, 60; joins Tilden in founding the *Morning News,* 63-64; keeps up his friendship with Tilden, 92; comradeship with Tilden, 104; visited Miss Easul with Tilden, 106; a sincere friend, 110; a friend of, George N. Sanders, at Niagara Falls to make peace in 1864, 146; refused a loan for his fiber factory, 470

fraud of 1876, 495; studied the defense of
New York Harbor in 1885, 495-496; wrote
the history of the Monroe Doctrine, 496;
Tilden expected to live to age of 72, 497;
illness a factor in his life, 497; a physical
decline after 1875, 498; a confirmed hypochondriac, 498; resort to drugs, 498; his
physicians, 498; his physical decline
marked in 1886, 499-500; origin of "Whispering Sammy," 500; affection for animals, 500-501; pride in his fruits and gardens, 501; his social clubs, 501; relatives
in his home, 501; not parsimonious, 501-
502; no interest in games, art or music,
502; a great reader and a lover of books,
503; his last illness, 503-504; died Aug. 4,
1886, 504; Governor Hill ordered all flags
at half-mast; names of attendants at his
funeral sounds like a Democratic Convention, 504; ceremony at Graystone attended by Governor Hill and President
Cleveland, 504; services at Graystone
conducted by D. William Jewett Tucker,
505; honorary pallbearers, 505; services
at New Lebanon, 505; Whittier's poem,
505-506; newspaper comments, 506; legislative memorial exercises, 506; Judge Rufus W. Peckham presided and Senator
George Raines delivered the oration, 506;
in 1888 friends presented a portrait to
the State, 506-507; Tilden's will broken,
508 ff.; his wealth, 508-509; iron mines,
508-509; personal property the bulk of
his fortune, 509-510; wines, 510; loans,
510; his first will in 1873, followed by one
drawn up by A. H. Green and a third
one, 510; third will approved by O'Conor,
and James C. Carter, 511; provisions of
the will, 511-513; powers of the executors,
513; validity of the will contested Oct.
10, 1886, on the ground of indefiniteness,
514; trial in November, 1888, and Justice
Lawrence decided that the contested clause
was valid, 514-515; Supreme Court on appeal reversed the decision by a two to one
decision, 515; second division of the Court
of Appeals pronounced the 35th clause of
the will invalid by a vote of four to
three, 515; Mrs. Laura Pelton Hazard
compromised with executors, 515; case
aroused wide interest, 515-516; a law of
1893 made such a contest impossible for
the future, 516; estate gradually distributed in accordance with the court decision,
516; estate after 44 years settled in 1930
by Mrs. G. W. Smith executor, 516; Tilden Trust created in 1887, 517; New York
Public Library created, 517; Bigelow issued a careful selection of Tilden's *Letters*,
518-519; Tilden's letters combed over
four times to exclude everything injurious

to Tilden's reputation, 519; effort made
to have Tilden's letters returned but without much success, Edward Murphy refusing to have those in his possession published and Cleveland refusing to return
his, 518; when the Tilden Papers were
finally turned over to the New York Public Library the eighteen containers had
been reduced to thirteen, 519; centennial
of Tilden's birth observed, 520 ff.; exercises at New Lebanon, Albany and New
York, 520; at Albany Lieut. Gov. Wag-
ner and Dr. Talcott Williams spoke; in
New York addresses by Gov. Baldwin of
Conn., Mayor Mitchel, F. L. Stetson and
C. S. Fairchild, 520; Tilden Democratic
Club in New York addressed by F. D.
Roosevelt and Samuel Untermeyer, 520;
Congressman Wm. Sulzer asked Congress
to erect a Tilden statue in the Capitol,
521; erected on Riverside Drive in New
York, 521; Tilden's career as a lawyer,
521-522; relations with Cleveland like
Fremont and Lincoln or Roosevelt and
Taft, 520; his life spanned the period from
the War of 1812 to Cleveland, 521; led revolt for free soil, 521; standing as a lawyer, 521-522; groups of his followers, 522;
a thinking machine with a scientific mind,
522; believed moral world subject to laws,
522; insisted on discovering the fundamental principle in every problem, 523;
"Old Skinflint," 523; master of the science
of politics, 523; had keen powers of analysis and synthesis, 523; a mathematical
bent, 523-524; won leadership by his intellectual resources, 524; judicial temperament, 524; marvelous judgment, 524;
bonds of a western railroad, 525; money-
making faculty, 525; cured sick business
concerns, 525; had personal vanity, 525;
Morgan, J. P., insisted on having Tilden's
approval of railroad bonds, 525; Chief
Justice Waite accused Tilden of being
miserly but Judge Martin Grover said he
was a spendthrift, 526; given to annoying
procrastination, 526; thoroughness explained his success, 526; never took anything for granted, 526; enjoyed mastering
obstacles, 526; could detect a defect in
reasoning and in conduct, 526; a negative
personality whom a grave issue could electrify, 527; best in a man-to-man conference, 527; three peaks in his life: Tweed
Ring, Canal Ring, and plan to reform the
Federal Government, 527; will live in
American History as a pioneer political
reformer, 527; believed in law of supply
and demand and was a champion of individualism, 528; a friend of capital and labor, 528; ambitious to use political power

Tilden's indifference to reforms, 75

Watson, James, City Auditor, accidental death, 210; had burned vouchers, 211

Watterson, Henry, wanted Tilden's States' rights utterances for use in Kentucky and the South, 282; urged Tilden to send committee to Louisiana, 337; a visiting statesman in 1876, 338; wired Tilden of plan to cheat, 339; suggested a compromise with Hayes, 338; spent Christmas with Tilden planning a mass meeting of 100,000, 359; said that Tilden refused to buy the Presidency, 407; three offers made, 407; comment on Tilden's Manhattan Club dinner in 1877, 412; found South against the Tilden ticket in 1880, 450; comment on Tilden's letter of 1880, 459; read platform in 1880, mention of Tilden in it, 462; asked Tilden for a loan, 469; report on Tilden for 1884, 480-481; wrote Tilden affectionate letters to end of his life, 500

Watts, J. W., an Oregon Republican elector was a Federal office holder, hence disqualified, 348; resigned his office and claimed to be a true elector, 249

Wealth, its power for good or evil, comprehended by Tilden, 521-522

Webber, D. A., and James Anderson make terms with John Sherman about vote of Louisiana in 1876, 340

Webster, Daniel, Tilden compared with, 534

Weed, Smith M., in Constitutional Convention of 1867 with Tilden, 160; after electors of South Carolina in 1876, 336; saw Tilden off for Europe in 1877, 418; revelations of cipher telegrams, 430; met Henry A. Tilden at Cincinnati in 1880, 457; letter to Tilden from Cincinnati, 464; in Tilden will contest, 514-515

Weed, Thurlow, worked with Democrats in 1865, 155; invited Tilden to dine with him in 1874; spread rumor about Tilden's health and bad habits, 273-274; believed Tilden more popular than Grant, 447

Welles, Gideon, Diary, 144; promoting Johnson for President in 1868, 154; distrusted Tilden, 159; accused Tilden of partyism, 166; thought he was using Chase as a smoke screen for Seymour in 1868, 166; said nominee would be either Chase or Seymour, 171; said 1868 was not a time to nominate a Copperhead, 186

Wells, David A., economist helped Tilden with his second message, 277-278; doubtful about Connecticut because of Barnum, 282; offered to write letters to support Tilden, 299; opened the Social Science Association at Saratoga, in 1876, 306; Tilden's conference there over governorship, 306; would have been in Tilden's Cabinet, 415

Wells, J. M., president of Louisiana Returning Board, 337; shopped around for a purchaser of the State's electoral vote, 340-341; his letter to Senator West, 340; sent Col. John T. Pickett to see Hewitt, 340-341; President Grant told that electoral vote of Louisiana was for sale, 341; Hewitt refused to buy, 341; promised to return Hayes electors, 341-342

West, DeWitt C., urged on Tilden for Governor, by Seymour, 306

West, Senator J. R., in touch with J. M. Wells, 341

Western House of Refuge for boys hear Tilden, 268

Western railroads took much of Tilden's time, 117

West Shore Railroad stock sold by Tilden, 470

Wetmore, W. L., owned Michigan land with Tilden, 509

Whigs in control of New York City in 1844, 59; nominated Gen. Zachery for President and Millard Fillmore for Vice President, 84; selected Fish and Patterson for Governor and Lieutenant Governor in 1848, 86; entire Whig ticket elected, 86; replaced by the Republican Party, 93

White, Andrew D., invited Tilden to Cornell commencement, 275; invitation accepted through G. W. Schuyler, 275

White House, Tilden had an open road to, 279

Whitney & Barnum paid G. R. Raum in Tilden income tax suit, $5,000; Garfield, $5,000 and Edwards Pierrepont, $10,000, 441

Whitney, W. C., introduced to Tilden, 146; consulted Tilden about railroads, 164; recommended by John Kelly to replace E. D. Smith, 262; hoped Tilden would force a modification of the arbitration bills, 367; attorney for Tilden in 1876, 388; greeted Tilden on return from Europe, 423; interested Elihu Root in Tilden's income tax suit, 440; quoted on the "muddled" situation in 1880, 454; thought Tilden had expressed a preference for Henry B. Payne, 455; wire to Henry A. Tilden, 457; reply, 457; Whitney's comment on 1880, 463; given Navy Portfolio against Tilden's wish, 490

Whittlesey, Caroline B., provided for in Tilden's will, 512

Wickham, William H., John Kelly's candidate for Mayor, a grafter, 249; reception at Delmonico's, 252; greeted Tilden on his return from Europe, 423

Wilkins, W. A., asked Tilden for a loan, 469